A
GEOGRAPHY
OF
WORLD
ECONOMY

A GEOGRAPHY OF WORLD ECONOMY

Anthony R. de Souza
National Geographic Society

Merrill Publishing Company
A Bell & Howell Information Company
Columbus Toronto London Melbourne

Cover Art: *A Manufacturing Town* (1922) by L. S. Lowry.
Oil on panel. 43.2 × 53.3 cm.
Reproduced courtesy of Ms. Carol Ann Danes.

Title Page Photo: Local market near Nikki in northern
Benin. (Source: WFP photo by J. Van Acker.)

Published by Merrill Publishing Company
A Bell & Howell Information Company
Columbus, Ohio 43216

This book was set in Zapf.

Administrative Editor: Stephanie Happer
Development and Copyediting: Ann Mirels
Production Coordinator: Carol S. Sykes
Art Coordinator: James H. Hubbard
Cover Designer: Russ Maselli
Text Designer: Cynthia Brunk

Library of Congress Catalog Card Number: 89-63841
International Standard Book Number: 0-675-20565-4
Printed in the United States of America
1 2 3 4 5 6 7 8 9—94 93 92 91 90

For Nadia, Jason, and Sam

PREFACE

A Geography of World Economy adopts an international perspective to examine how people earn a living and how the goods and services they produce are geographically organized. It emphasizes conflicting arguments and theories essential for understanding a world economy in rapid transition. Designed around the themes of distribution and economic growth, it explores the nature of the dynamic international environment and key international issues that arouse the concern and interest of geographers. Among the issues discussed are population growth, pollution and resource depletion, food and famine, patterns of production and land use, economic justice, social and economic development, and multinational and international commerce.

Although the text progresses logically from one topic to another, the book is designed to be used in geography courses of varying lengths. I recommend that chapters be read sequentially, but because I wrote each chapter to stand alone the book can serve as a reference or refresher. Prepared as an introduction to economic geography, the material can be read and understood without college-level prerequisites.

The text offers some specific pedagogical features, including chapter objectives, key terms, end-of-chapter summaries, suggested readings, and a glossary. It also contains many photographs, a wealth of maps and diagrams, as well as vivid examples and box essays which illustrate concepts. Most of all, it encourages students to think through problems. It provides the information and concepts to help students evaluate issues without necessarily subscribing or submitting to a particular set of values.

This book is an outgrowth of *World Space Economy* by de Souza and Foust, published by Merrill in 1979. That book concentrated heavily on the United States and on the national effects of international processes. *A Geography of World Economy* takes a wider view, enabling students to appreciate what is going on not only in the United States, but elsewhere as well. An insular view of the world is untenable in the 1990s; the world is too much with us.

Among colleagues who read the manuscript and offered useful comments, I am especially grateful to Nancy Ettlinger of the Ohio State University and James E. McConnell of the State University of New York at Buffalo. I am indebted to Gregory Chu, director of the University of Minnesota Geography Department's Cartographic Laboratory, and his assistants for their efficiency and skill in designing and drafting the maps; to Alice Thiede for rendering the noncartographic art; to Joyce Green, Kim Higel, and Bill Moore for word processing; and to Ann Mirels for editing. I am also indebted to the many people at Merrill, without whom the successful completion of the book would have been impossible. My thanks go to Carol Sykes, production coordinator; Cherie Marchio, product manager; and Jim Hubbard, art coordinator.

Finally, I wish to thank my wife, Nadia, for her support and immense understanding. She knows the debt I owe her.

A. R. de Souza
Bethesda, Maryland

CONTENTS

A
GEOGRAPHY
OF
WORLD
ECONOMY

1
PROBLEMS AND SOLUTIONS IN AN UNSETTLED WORLD

OBJECTIVES

☐ To explain the context in which economic geographers perceive world events

☐ To outline the development of the crises we now face

☐ To introduce the major problems of environmental constraints and disparities in economic development

☐ To indicate why economic geographers are interested in development problems and how geography can help to resolve these problems

☐ To acquaint you with the field of geography and, in particular, with the major paradigms and concepts of economic geography

New York Stock Exchange. (Source: N.Y. Convention and Visitors Bureau.)

In his novel *Cataclysm*, former Vice President of the World Bank William Clark presented the following scenario: One day in 1987 debt-ridden Mexico proposes a global debt conference, but it is rejected by the Western industrial democracies. The rejection angers Third World countries and, as a group, they default on their debts. The Western powers retaliate by expelling the delinquent nations from the Bretton Woods Agreement. A North-South cold war develops. Cut off from the North's resources, aid, and markets, the underdeveloped South soon buckles under rampant food shortages and political chaos, but not before sending out their secret agents to infiltrate the North's major financial institutions. Once inside, the agents wreak havoc by feeding false data into the North's economic computers. Wall Street breaks down.

Clark's dramatic prediction has failed to materialize, but his novel warns that the "poverty bomb" is as capable of destroying the world as a nuclear bomb. To avert catastrophe, we must become aware of what is known as the world crisis and take it seriously. The world crisis may be conceived of as a long-term issue of human survival in terms of population, food, energy, resources, and environment. It is marked by disparities in the distribution of wealth and the quality of life that we have come to call the problem of development.

World development implies progress toward desirable goals. It is a concept full of hope and enthusiasm, even though the consequences of the jolting and dislocating process can be horrendous for people when long-standing traditions and relationships break down. The purpose of development is to improve the quality of people's lives—to provide secure jobs, adequate nutrition and health services, clean water and air, cheap transportation, and education. Whether development takes place depends on the extent to which social and economic changes and a restructuring of geographical space help or hinder in meeting the basic needs of the majority of people.

Problems associated with the uncertainty and disorder of the development process occur at all scales, ranging from a villager's access to a modern clinic to the international scale of trade relations between rich and poor countries. Attempts to understand development problems at local, regional, and international levels must consider the principles of resource use as well as the principles surrounding the exchange and movement of goods, people, and ideas. This book, written from a geographer's perspective, discusses these principles within the context of world crises.

Why is the world in crisis? What are some of the major problems that need immediate attention? Why are geographers interested in these problems? What concepts help geographers illuminate issues of resource-use inequalities and problems of poverty? How can the geographer's skills be used to help resolve these problems? This opening chapter sets out to answer these questions. Its objective is to demonstrate to you that the world is in crisis, to focus your attention on some of the specific problem areas we will deal with later on in the text, and to help you understand the geographer's approach to the study of the world economy.

A WORLD IN CRISIS—A TIME OF OPPORTUNITY

A crisis is a decisive turning point filled with uncertainty and disorder, the outcome of which may be life or death. A crisis may give rise to a new beginning if people are able to survive through a period of wrenching and rapid changes to the capitalist economic system.

Capitalism, the economic system based on profit and private property, is by nature crisis-prone. From its earliest days, it has been as critically ill as it has been intensely alive. Crises have been as prominent features of capitalist development as its incredible productivity, technical advances, and global expansion. Periods of boom characterized by increasing prices, production, technological innovation, and profits are always punctuated by crashes characterized by deflation, low growth rates, cost-reducing inventions, and declining profits. What follows the present crisis in the ongoing accumulation process of the capitalist world is still a closed book. Will this period of instability be followed by a resumption of the steady and sustained growth of the 1950s and 1960s?

The decades of the 1950s and 1960s were remarkably stable and predictable for the rich industrial countries. They were years that witnessed unparalleled prosperity and growth in the United States, the recovery of Europe from World War II, and the emergence of Japan as a tower of economic strength. They were years when developed countries commanded an increasingly disproportionate share of the fruits of the world economic system, and when multinational corporations (MNCs), or transnationals as they are sometimes called, controlled a growing share of world production and trade. Although most poor countries failed to benefit from the postwar boom, their problems were regarded as temporary aberrations to be corrected by the free-market system based on the U.S. dollar.

After 1970, however, the economic system that had served developed countries so well began to go wrong. Nothing was certain anymore. A series of unfortunate events ended the postwar boom led by the United States. In 1971, the financial order collapsed with the devaluation of the U.S. dollar. But if there was a pivotal year, it was 1973. The year that began with the American withdrawal from Vietnam ended with the quadrupling of oil prices by the Organization of Petroleum Exporting Countries (OPEC). A year later, the economies of the West slipped into a deep recession accompanied by high levels of unemployment and inflation. They recovered slightly from 1975 to 1978 before plunging into recession again in 1979 and 1980. The economies of the poor countries followed those of the West. Even the socialist countries of Eastern Europe and the USSR suffered from the general economic downturn. For a while, the oil-exporting countries escaped the storm, but they, too, revealed their vulnerability when they were hit by declining oil prices in the mid-1980s.

Framework of the World Economy

The world in crisis is a subject that requires immediate and critical attention. Only by virtually boycotting front-page news is it possible to ignore the fact that we live in an age of crisis. We read of debt, unemployment, and limited food and energy resources. We read of demographic, ecological, environmental, industrial, and of rural and urban problems. These problems are rooted in the structure and development of the world economic system, and their manifestations are aggravated by economic and political policies.

An understanding of the reasons for the new economic crisis begins by recognizing the domination of the world economy by developed countries and the existence of an international economic order established as a framework for an international economic system. The term *world economy* refers to the capitalist world economy, a multistate economic system that was created in the late fifteenth and early sixteenth centuries. As this system expanded, it took on the configuration of a core of dominant countries and a periphery of dominated countries. The dominant countries are in the industrial capitalist West, or in the First World. The dominated countries, in the capitalist underdeveloped Third World in the South, are sometimes also called "developing" or a bit more accurately "less developed countries" (LDCs). Socialist countries

of the East, or countries of the Second World, have become increasingly linked to the capitalist world economy. Since 1953, East-West trade and East-South trade has increased. Beyond trade, the East-West/ South international division of labor has been extended through long-term agreements for cooperative production, distribution, and finance. Perhaps the most symbolic expression of the accelerating connections between the Second World and the capitalist world economy is the branch office of Rockefeller's Chase Manhattan Bank at Number One, Karl Marx Square, Moscow.

The term *international economic system* refers to the system of geographically expanding and evolving capitalism and, in the world today, such underlying processes as the internationalization of capital. By *internationalization of capital* is meant the export of capitalist production, banking, and services through direct investment by firms that create subsidiaries abroad. Multinational corporations are the principal actors of this export.

The term *international economic order* refers to institutions such as those established after World War II to reflect the style and interests of the United States. Among these institutions are the World Bank, the International Monetary Fund (IMF), and the General Agreement on Tariffs and Trade (GATT). As the hegemonic power, the United States created institutions that were required to establish a liberal international economic order. Consequently, these institutions had a mandate to dismantle trade and currency restrictions of the interwar years and to facilitate capital mobility.

At any given time, the core of the world economy is dominated by one or more core states. In the postwar period preceding the 1970s, the United States was the principal power. The relative decline of U.S. power that became evident after 1973 was triggered by intense competition from rivalrous core states such as Japan and the Federal Republic of Germany. By the late 1970s, the world order created by the United States after World War II came to an end. And out of the old order, the tentative birth of a new one.

The oil shock has been blamed for the worldwide crisis and the realignment of the world order, but capitalist competition was the cause of the trouble. A major reason for the breakdown of the postwar world was a decline in the rate of profit of many firms in the industrial West. Faced with intense global competition, firms had to "automate, emigrate, or evaporate" (Magirier 1983, p. 61). Some firms did go out of business, but others responded to the challenge to automate and especially to "go international." They

IBM corporate headquarters, Armonk, New York. Whether measured in terms of value of sales, value of assets, or number of employees, IBM is one of the largest multinational corporations in the world. The domestic activities of multinationals are only a part of their worldwide activities. They are the epitome of direct investors abroad. (Source: IBM.)

became more international thanks in large measure to the speed of travel and the technology of information handling.

Among the manifestations of the nascent world order are (1) increased mobility of capital, (2) growing interpenetration of banking and industrial activities, and (3) the extension of the industrial frontier into an increasingly heterogeneous Third World. In recent years, we have seen the movement not only of labor-intensive industries (e.g., textiles and certain kinds of electronics) but also capital-intensive industries (e.g., steel and automobiles), as well as some white-collar service industries (e.g., data processing) from high-cost areas of the First World to low-cost areas of the Third World. We have seen increased mobility and rationalization of capital as evidenced by mergers, acquisitions, and the use of new technologies and labor processes. We have also seen the state become an increasingly important force in organizing world production, especially in underdeveloped countries where governments often keep wages low through repressive political policies. Governments also compete among themselves in providing attractive incentives for companies to come to their countries to produce goods and services for the world market.

The worldwide crisis has changed the daily life of people in most countries. Economic and social relations have become increasingly global. The globalization of product and financial markets has made people more dependent and more vulnerable to

events that occur in far-away places. What happens in places from Bangkok to Buenos Aires may affect the salaries of municipal workers in Boston, the cost of a new home in Buffalo, or the solvency of pension funds in Bakersfield.

The new global integration has brought with it all sorts of tensions and disruptions—closed factories, empty offices, home mortgage and farm foreclosures, millions of unemployed and hungry, explosions of violence, political repression, fear. The result is a world of "international economic disorder" (Thrift 1986, p. 12). A shift to economic planning and a reform of the world economy hold out hope for alleviating the crisis, but change on this order can be slow in coming.

WORLD DEVELOPMENT PROBLEMS

We noted that a worldwide crisis followed the long postwar boom and that it was caused, like the depression of the 1930s, by economic expansion. We also noted that it is uncertain whether the world economic system will again experience the sustained growth of the 1950s and 1960s.

Two major elements in the current crisis require immediate attention. One element is the challenge to economic expansion posed by the environmental constraints of energy supplies, resources, and pollution. The other element is the enormous and explosive issue of disparities in the distribution of wealth between rich country and poor country, between city and rural area, between wealthy people and poor people, and between men and women. Extreme disparities of wealth and income between developed and underdeveloped countries have led to Third World demands for a New International Economic Order (NIEO). This program, which was initiated following the success of OPEC in raising oil prices, is an attempt to diminish existing disparities by distributing future economic growth more equitably.

Environmental Constraints

The world environment—the complex and interconnected links among the natural systems of air, water, and living things—is caught in a tightening vice. On the one hand, the environment is squeezed by the massive overconsumption and waste of consumer culture and its ethos of "trying to keep up with the Joneses." On the other hand, the environment is squeezed by the Third World's poor who destroy their resource base in order to stay alive. The constraints of diminishing energy supplies, resource limitations, and environmental degradation are three big obstacles that threaten the possibility of future economic growth and life itself.

Energy is the key to the long-run sustainability of human life. The oil shock brought to the attention of many Americans the possibility of a world drained of energy. In 1973, OPEC raised oil prices and these prices continued to rise until 1982 (Figure 1.1). This action dealt a blow, but not a fatal blow, to the world economy. The so-called energy crisis stemmed more from the concerted action of OPEC to slow down production for political reasons than from an actual shortage of world oil reserves. In the 1980s, oil prices fell as demand for energy dropped. Unlike the 1970s, oil prices were shaped as much by world economic trends and the traditional oil-pricing system as by a cartel agreement. But the day will come when the pressure of demand will force oil prices to rise steadily, with no help from OPEC at all, unless substitutes for gasoline and heating oil are discovered. Without substitutes, proven oil reserves at current rates of extraction are projected to be exhausted in the next thirty to forty years (Table 1.1).

There is already a significant poor-world energy problem. Oil is an unaffordable luxury for more than 50 percent of the world's population who cook and heat with fuelwood, charcoal, animal wastes, and crop residues. Even during the years of falling energy prices in the 1980s, Third World countries obtained more than 40 percent of their energy from noncommercial sources. In countries such as India, Haiti, Indonesia, Malaysia, Tanzania, and Brazil, fuelwood collection is a major cause of deforestation, one of the most severe environmental problems in the underdeveloped world.

In addition to the eventual increase in oil prices and the intensifying poor-world fuel crisis, the availability of other natural resources will also affect economic growth. The demand for resources in the coming years will require vast investments in mineral

FIGURE 1.1
Average U.S. price per barrel of oil, 1971–1986. (Source: International Institute for Environment and Development and World Resources Institute, 1987.)

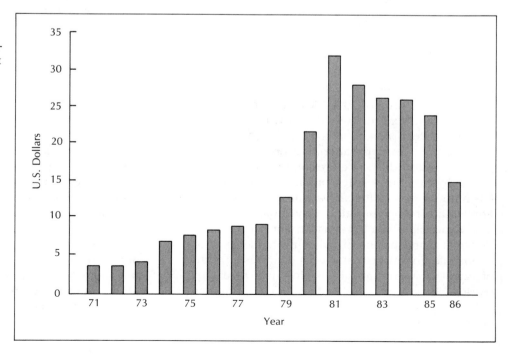

TABLE 1.1
Proven oil reserves at the end of 1984 in thousands of millions of tons and life of reserves in years at current rate of extraction.

	Proven Oil Reserves	Life of Reserves
Developing Countries		
Saudi Arabia	23.0	*
Kuwait	12.4	*
Mexico	6.8	45
Iran	6.6	61
Iraq	6.0	*
Abu Dhabi	4.0	*
Venezuela	3.7	38
Libya	2.8	52
China	2.6	23
Nigeria	2.3	33
Indonesia	1.2	17
Algeria	1.2	27
Developed Countries		
Soviet Union	8.6	14
United States	4.4	9
United Kingdom	1.8	14
Norway	1.1	32
Canada	1.1	15
World	96.1	34

*Over 100 years

SOURCE: Cole, 1987, p. 31.

extraction and food production. According to a study of global needs conducted for the United Nations by Wassily Leontief (1977), the consumption of common minerals must rise fivefold and food production fourfold if a moderate rate of world economic growth is to continue. Above all, Leontief's study indicates that because of energy, mineral, and food constraints we will have about another twenty-five years of growth followed by an almost certain curtailment.

The fragility of the environment poses the most formidable obstacle to the economic process. Are there limits to growth? Is the world overpopulated? Some of our present activities, in the absence of controls, may lead to a world that will be uninhabitable for future generations. Topsoil is being lost because of overcultivation, improper irrigation, plowed grassland, and deforestation. Water tables are falling. In the United States, parts of the Ogallala water basin under the Great Plains are at least half depleted. Forests are being torn down by lumber companies and by people trying to keep warm or cook their food. Water is being poisoned by domestic sewage, toxic chemicals, and industrial wastes. The waste products of industrial regions are also beginning to threaten the world's climate. Accumulated pollutants in the atmosphere—primarily carbon dioxide, methane, and chlorofluorocarbons—are said to be creating a

"greenhouse effect" that will cause world temperatures to rise. Chlorofluorocarbons, which are used as aerosol propellants and coolants, and in a variety of manufacturing processes, are blamed for damaging the earth's ozone layer. Ozone protects life from ultraviolet radiation given off from the sun. The U.S. Environmental Protection Agency estimates that a 2.5 percent reduction in the ozone layer could cause 15,000 human cancers a year as well as extensive damage to plants and animal life (Toronto *Globe and Mail* 1986). Yet another hazard to the environment is the fallout from nuclear bomb tests that took place in the 1950s and 1960s and from nuclear power reactor accidents such as those at Three Mile Island and Chernobyl.

These trends confirm the immediate need for monitoring, supervising, and controlling the economic process. Defenders of the market mechanism claim that some of these functions, particularly the allocation of scarce resources, can be performed by an efficient free-enterprise system. Critics of the market mechanism disagree. They argue that it results in an inequitable allocation of scarce resources. Moreover, they claim that a free-enterprise economy is unable to monitor safety, impose decisions about the rate of growth, or its sharing within and between countries. Proponents of either position would agree, however,

Emissions from smokestacks, such as these in the Saar industrial region of West Germany, increase acidic deposition and contribute to the buildup of carbon dioxide in the atmosphere. Until recently, carbon dioxide released from fuel combustion and deforestation was considered the chief contributor to the greenhouse effect. In the 1980s it was discovered that other trace gases—methane, ozone, chlorofluorocarbons, nitrous oxide—contribute to greenhouse warming on a scale comparable to that of carbon dioxide. (Source: United Nations.)

that the problems of the environment and its natural resources are now so great that planning the economic process is imperative.

Planned capitalism must include policies regulating energy and other natural resources and policies curtailing activities that threaten the health and well-being of people. The shift to planning, which is already underway, is essential to ameliorate the problems brought by the economic system. It is also essential if the extraordinarily resilient and persisting system is to survive the worldwide crisis.

Disparities in Wealth and Well-being

There is poverty that afflicts the few in predominantly rich countries—hunger and malnutrition among families in Appalachia, bankrupt farmers on the Minnesota prairie, unemployed factory workers in Detroit, and single mothers on welfare in New York. This kind of poverty, that of poor individuals and families, is an issue of considerable importance. But there is another kind of poverty that affects all but the few in poor countries. It is mass poverty, and it is the most important world development problem of our time. You cannot doubt this assertion when you see the halt and the maimed sidewalk people of Bombay, when you see insistent begging children in the streets of Mexico City, or when you see women and children carrying firewood on their backs in the countryside north of Nairobi. Mass poverty is intolerable and a crisis that we must grapple with and try to overcome.

Poverty afflicts the minority in predominantly affluent societies. Why are some people, such as this destitute woman in New York, excluded from the general well-being? (Source: U.S. Department of Housing and Urban Development.)

Who are the world's poor? They are the 15 million children in Africa, Asia, and Latin America who die of hunger every year. They are the 1.2 billion people, or 24 percent of the world's population, without access to safe drinking water. They are the 1.4 billion without sanitary waste disposal facilities. They are the 2.3 billion people—nearly 50 percent of the world's population—who live in thirty-five countries where the per capita income was less than $400 in 1983.

The poor of the world are overwhelmingly the people of Third World countries that have slipped behind the economic levels of the West since the beginning of the modern colonial period in the sixteenth century. During the boom that followed World War II, the gross national product (i.e., the total domestic and foreign output claimed by residents) of the developed countries rose from $1,250 billion to $3,070 billion. That increase was three and one-half times the gross product, $520 billion, of the underdeveloped countries in 1972. Although per capita real income rose from $175 in 1952 to $300 in 1972, the per capita real income in developed countries rose from $2,000 to $4,000. Developed countries enjoyed 66 percent of the world's increase, whereas half of the world's population in underdeveloped countries (excluding China) made do with an eighth of the world's income. By 1982, the national income of the United States (235 million people) was about equal to the total income of the Third World (over 3,000 million people). In that year, 43 percent of Third World countries had national incomes amounting to less than one-thousandth that of the United States. The natural incomes of 89 percent of Third World countries were not equal to one-hundredth that of the United States.

There is no absolute discontinuity between the national incomes of developed and underdeveloped countries, however (Figure 1.2). The largest Third World countries do have national incomes that are greater than those of the smallest developed countries. Even so, the degree of overlap is strikingly small (Figure 1.3).

The Third World is far from a homogeneous entity: there are enormous differences among underdeveloped countries. Mexico had a per capita gross national product of $2,240 in 1985; Bangladesh had $130. There are also huge differences in wealth within countries and among people. In India in 1983, 15.1 percent of the population of the Punjab was below the official poverty line of sixty-five rupees ($6.50) per person per month in rural areas or seventy-five rupees ($7.50) in urban areas. By contrast, more than half the population (57.5 percent) in the state of Bihar in northeast India fell below the poverty line. Household income is also uneven. In Bangladesh, the richest 20 percent of the population gets six times as much as the poorest 20 percent; in Brazil, the richest get more than thirty times as much as the poorest (Table 1.2). Land ownership is the ultimate indicator of economic inequality in the Third World. In Bangladesh, 22 percent of the population owns 75 percent of the land; in Brazil, 1 percent owns 40 percent.

Despite the large differences between and within regions of these countries, there is a commonality that binds the Third World together. It is an unfair economic system that fails to provide the poor with the basic human rights of adequate food, clothing, housing, and medical care. The misery of the Third World is now so intense that many countries must first benefit from a greater share of the world's wealth

FIGURE 1.2
Countries with the largest gross national products, 1982.
(Source: World Bank, 1985.)

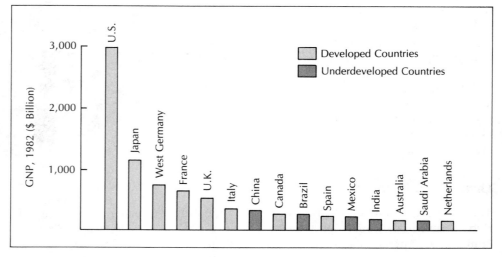

FIGURE 1.3
Distribution of Gross National Products, 1982. (Source: World Bank, 1985.)

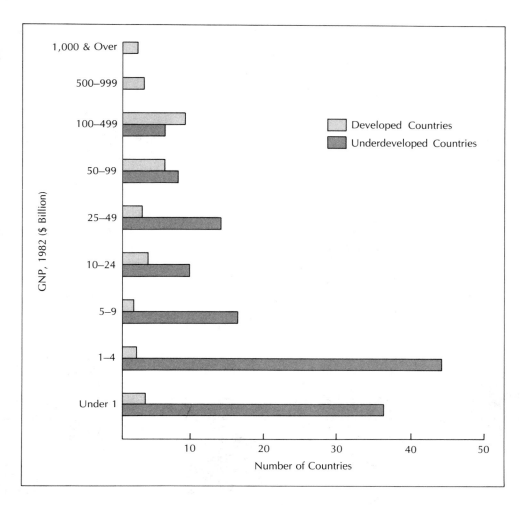

TABLE 1.2
Distribution of household income.

	Poorest 20 Percent	Wealthiest 20 Percent
Developed Countries		
Netherlands (1977)	8.1	37.0
United Kingdom (1979)	7.3	39.2
United States (1972)	4.5	42.8
France (1975)	5.3	45.8
Underdeveloped Countries		
Bangladesh (1973-74)	6.9	42.2
Hong Kong (1980)	5.4	47.0
Argentina (1970)	4.4	50.3
Venezuela (1970)	3.0	54.0
Malaysia (1973)	3.5	56.1
Kenya (1974)	2.6	60.4
Mexico (1977)	2.9	57.7
Brazil (1972)	2.0	66.6

SOURCE: World Bank, 1985, pp. 228–29.

before they can even begin to better themselves, in absolute or relative terms. Except possibly for China and India, most Third World countries are presently too weak and too enmeshed in the world's trading and financial system to withdraw and adopt relatively isolationist policies without considerable economic cost.

In response to glaring international disparities in income and wealth, political leaders of Third World countries have proposed a new world order with their New International Economic Order (NIEO) program. The program was introduced at the Sixth Special Session of the General Assembly of the United Nations in 1974 and approved as a resolution on "Development and International Economic Cooperation" in the Seventh Session one year later. The group of underdeveloped countries (the Group of 77) that submitted their demands for a NIEO call for a redistribution of income and wealth from the North to the South. They also want more control over the use of

The hardships of poverty are reflected in the faces of this Latin American woman and her child. An estimated 750 million people in the Third World (excluding China and other centrally planned economies) live in absolute poverty; that is, they have less than enough income to ensure a minimum daily diet of 2,150 calories per person. (Source: WHO/PAHO by J. Vizcarra.)

their own natural resources as well as over their interactions with developed countries.

NIEO is essentially trade-oriented. Underdeveloped countries want improved terms of trade and are seeking measures to ensure stable and equitable prices for their raw material exports. Moreover, they want improved access to developed markets, especially for processed commodities and manufactures. Underdeveloped countries also want a larger say in the transportation, marketing, and distribution of their products.

In addition to improved terms of trade, NIEO asks for more foreign aid and rescheduling of debts. It also asks for more control by underdeveloped countries of the international monetary system and of its institutions. NIEO wants an easier transfer of technology through new patent laws and commercial practice. NIEO calls for more regulation of transnational corporations in the interests of underdeveloped countries through the formulation, adoption, and implementation of an international code of conduct. NIEO also calls for a rapid increase in Third World food production, increased food aid from developed countries, seabed and ocean management, and the conservation of natural resources.

Although the NIEO proposals are a challenge to the existing liberal international order, the program cannot be considered revolutionary. For example, as far as improving world trade is concerned, NIEO only aims at terms of trade. There is little talk about changing the world division of labor. The NIEO program is really a charter for some kind of capitalism for everyone.

Social critic Michael Harrington (1977) referred to "the utter moderation of what is proposed" (p. 217). He gave the following rationale for U.S. acceptance of the program: "First the ideology of the demand for a New International Order is impeccably capitalist. Second, the poor countries have been extraordinarily patient and long suffering. . . . Third, American capitalism could make money from a modest increase in world social justice" (p. 232). Harrington emphasized that acceptance of NIEO would be a point of departure, not a solution, to outrageous world inequality.

What are the prospects for the NIEO program? First, there is a gap between Third World rhetoric and reality. When it comes to specific demands, Third World countries seldom present a unified front. For example, when something as meaningful as reducing the Third World's technological dependence on the MNCs is at stake, there is little common ground. In fact, many Third World countries are individually reducing or even eliminating the few restrictive provisions that they had imposed in the late 1960s and early 1970s. Malaysia, India, Zaire, Mexico, Argentina, and many other countries are all relaxing controls on foreign enterprises and are competing with each other to grant more concessions to the MNCs.

Second, there is little evidence to date that NIEO demands will be accepted by major developed countries any time soon. The tactic U.S. officials often use in North-South discussions about reconstructing the basis of international exchange is to batten down the hatches and let the Southern hurricane of demands blow itself out. Indeed, the United States has often told the Third World that its demands are unnecessary when the world economy is in such fine shape, and that there are more pressing priorities when it is not doing so well.

Scarcity and Inequality

So far, our discussion of world development problems has considered the concepts of scarcity and inequality separately. But, in fact, these two concepts are intimately related. Economic growth, which proceeds faster in some places than others, creates the structure of the world economy with its pattern of inequalities.

Under the market mechanism people must be prepared to trade off growth and equality; that is, to accept inequality as a mechanism for stimulating growth. In developed countries, during the long postwar boom, most people were satisfied with this arrangement. As a result, there were few complaints about disparities in income and employment opportunities. In underdeveloped countries, the benefits of economic expansion never reached the masses. Underdeveloped countries of the world were dissatisfied with the relationship between growth and equality. As a result, they submitted demands in the form of the NIEO program to achieve a more equitable distribution of economic growth.

Glaring inequality between the rich and the poor and between developed and underdeveloped countries is not conducive to world peace and stability. Unfettered economic growth stimulates inequality, creates new wants, and leads to increased competition for resources. Moreover, the distributional problems that growth creates have been responsible in greater measure for heated debates on limits to growth than has the fear of running out of scarce resources.

THE GEOGRAPHER'S PERSPECTIVE

World development problems are of immense interest to geographers. Many development problems have geographical solutions, or more accurately, partial solutions. They certainly raise the important geographical questions of location and accessibility, of relationships between settlements and land use, of changing transport and communication linkages, of efficient flows of commodities, and of the spread of ideas and innovations. They also raise questions about center-periphery relations at a hierarchy of scales ranging from a farmer's access to a market to connections between First and Third Worlds.

Before exploring the geographical character of the world in crisis, however, you should be acquainted with the geographer's perspective. What exactly is geography? What are the concerns of economic geography and how has this part of the discipline changed over the years? What are the fundamental concepts of the geographer's enterprise? What useful knowledge and advice do geographers provide to help resolve development problems? Answers to these questions will give you a framework for understanding how geographers go about the task of analyzing and interpreting problems of the world economy.

The Field of Geography

Geography is concerned with place. Geographers describe the changing pattern of places, explain how these patterns evolved, and attempt to unravel their meaning. Geography's continuing quest is to understand the physical and cultural features of places and their natural settings on the face of the earth.

Geography uses a distinctive language—the language of maps. A map reveals human excitement, wonder, and concern for spatial relations. The oldest recorded map was carved about fifteen thousand years ago on a piece of mammoth bone at an ice age camp on the bank of the River Dnieper in the southwestern USSR. Since then geographers have systematically recorded what is where on the face of the earth. Modern geographers also use the map as a research tool to ask and answer questions about spatial relations.

The spatial dimension is central to geography. It is also central to the internationally interdependent character of our lives. Events in one place have a direct and immediate impact on another place. An increase in the price of OPEC oil swells the coffers of countries such as Kuwait and Saudi Arabia, but impoverishes other countries such as Tanzania and Bangladesh that feel the pinch much more than the United States or Japan. To keep their trucks moving, poor countries must pay for oil in hard currencies that leaves less money left over for fertilizers, schools, hospitals, and new development projects.

In order to describe, sample, measure, and explain physical and human elements on earth, geographers refer to knowledge and insights derived from other disciplines. Thus, geography can be viewed as a synthesizing discipline. And some scholars—President Emeritus of the National Audubon Society, Russell Peterson, for one—argue that geography is in a unique position to demonstrate the relatedness of all knowledge.

So broad is the field of geography that no one scholar can hope to have expertise in more than a few areas of the discipline. For that reason, geographers specialize in one or two topics or regions. There are physical, urban, rural, social, political, and economic geographers. The study of each topic may embrace the whole world or may be confined to one or more areas. Some geographers bring all the topical specialties to bear in exploring a particular region. The scope of this book is the world, and it emphasizes economic geography.

The Nature of Economic Geography

Economic geography is concerned with the distribution of economic activity, the use of the world's resources, and the spatial organization and expansion of the world economy. In its infancy, economic geography was called *commercial geography*, which developed during the era of European exploration and discovery from the fifteenth century through the nineteenth century. All was excitement and adventure, then. Commercial geographers were on the voyages, and their reports brought masses of factual information about other lands to merchants and government officials.

Probably the best known commercial geography was written by British scholar G. G. Chisholm (1899). In his view, the purpose of commercial geography was to stimulate intellectual interest in geographical facts relating to trade; hence, virtually all of his book was an inventory of commodity and trade statistics. Such a treatment was not highly regarded by those who wanted to see an analytical rather than a descriptive approach to economic geography.

The term *economic geography* was coined in the United States in 1888. Twelve years later Ellen Stemple authored a book with that title. By the end of World War I, economic geography was a respected part of the discipline, and in 1925 a new journal, *Economic Geography*, began publication.

As a distinct field of study, economic geography was affected by three major themes of geography in general: human-environmental relations, areal differentiation, and spatial organization. Although all three thematic approaches have always been present, a human-environmental emphasis flourished largely by itself until the 1930s, areal differentiation was most influential from the late 1930s to the late 1950s, and spatial organization has since emerged as the dominant approach. To better understand the fundamental concepts of geography we will turn to later, it is useful first to take a brief look at these three approaches.

Human-Environmental Relations The economists hoped that economic geographers would apply the principles of classical economic theory in a geographical context. Events turned out otherwise. The geographers sought to explain variations in economic development in terms of *environmental determinism*. For example, Ellsworth Huntington (1924) argued that certain areas of the globe stimulated human efficiency more than others. The industrial countries, in Huntington's view, had the most "stimulating climates," whereas most Third World countries had "difficult climates."

The environmental dictum was ideologically acceptable during the years of twentieth-century colonial expansion. It helped to justify the view that economic "backwardness" in Africa, Asia, and Latin America was caused by "unfavorable" climates that induced low levels of productivity among indigenous peoples. Disease, climate, and the "colored races" were also seen as major obstacles to white settlement in the tropics. Many of the American Geographical Society's Special Publications from the 1920s to the early 1950s were devoted to environmental questions about human physiology and European residence in the tropics (Jefferson 1921; Price 1939; Pelzer 1945).

Few, if any, geographers who study human-environmental relations now claim that the physical environment is the sole determinant of people's economic behavior. Geographers now place emphasis on human adaptation and adjustment to potentialities in the environment. They attempt to discover how particular groups of people, especially in a local area, organize their thoughts about the environment and how to come to grips with it (Porter 1965).

Areal Differentiation Economic geographers were badly "burnt" with their encounter with environmentalism and its underlying preoccupation with race. The main reaction to the period of excessive environmental determinism was to adopt the view that all geographical phenomena were unique, and that theory building was of little value. Hence, for a period between the late 1930s and late 1950s, the primary focus of concern was *areal differentiation:* differences, rather than similarities, between places.

The "unique" approach resulted in detailed descriptions of production, exchange, and consumption. At the teaching level, textbooks were organized by regions or topics, and they contained voluminous factual data. In some respects these texts resembled nineteenth-century commercial geographies. At the research level, scholarly papers and monographs became increasingly specialized.

The areal differentiation concept, which led to some of the great regional writing on which much of the present academic status of geography was built, led geographers to overlook the need for comparative studies. Areal differentiation dominated geography at the expense of areal integration. In the 1950s and 1960s, geographers such as William Bunge (1966) scorned the "unique" approach. They argued that economic geography needed to become a theoretical subject, which it did.

Spatial Organization This theme in geography came to the fore in the decade of the 1960s. It has done a great deal to help geographers think in new ways about geographical distributions and spatial relations. *Spatial organization* is concerned with how space is organized by individuals and societies to suit their own designs. It provides a framework for analyzing and interpreting location decisions (e.g., market versus raw material location, accessibility versus transportation costs) and spatial structures (e.g., land-use patterns, industrial location, and settlement). The popularity of the organization-of-space theme was influenced by governments who were subsidizing geographical research, especially for planning and policy-oriented studies. It was also influenced by the "quantitative revolution," with its emphasis on quantification and experimentation with a wide range of statistical techniques. A more important emphasis, however, was on the formulation of hypotheses and the search for theory. Economic geographers found some of the theories they were looking for in the social and biological sciences, including location and general systems theory.

Location theory attempts to explain and predict geographical decisions that result from aggregates of individual decision making. The main aim of location theorists is to integrate the spatial dimension into classical economic theory. The origins of location theory stem from the work of Johann Heinrich von Thünen on agricultural location in the 1820s and subsequent contributions to industrial and settlement theory by Alfred Weber and Walter Christaller.

They developed normative (i.e., theory-building) models relating to business and industry in a world of pure competition that assumed entrepreneurs are completely rational and attempt to maximize profits with perfect knowledge of the cost characteristics of all locations (Figure 1.4). This image of an entrepreneur became known as "economic person"—an omniscient, rational individual who is driven by a single goal—to maximize profits.

Location theorists often use *general systems theory* as a framework for explaining the interrelatedness of places and activities. In particular, a *spatial system* is a set of interdependent and interactive parts: land uses, business firms, trade flows, regions. In more abstract terms, a spatial system consists of *movements* (e.g., people, goods) that result in channels along which the movements occur, a *network* (e.g., roads) structured around *nodes* (e.g., towns, villages) organized as a *hierarchy*, with the interstitial zones viewed as *surfaces* (Haggett 1965, p. 18) (Figure 1.5).

In the 1970s and 1980s there were at least three departures from location theory. First, behavioral geographers criticized location theory for its emphasis on abstract patterns of land use and maximization of profits. They questioned the relevance of location theory for understanding location decisions and spatial structures in the real world. They also noted that economists were replacing the image of "economic person" with the "satisficer." According to the satisficer concept, people rarely achieve, or even wish to achieve, maximum profits. They seek a variety of goals and often trade off some income to realize other goals. The "satisficer" idea led to a shift in economic geography from "economic person" to how people perceive risks and opportunities and how their perceptions affect decision making. The notion that we live in a world that is a probabilistic mixture of choice, calculation, and chance is evident in studies of resource management (Saarinen 1969).

Second, phenomenological geographers rejected "economic person" and the notion that we live in an "objective world." Life takes on meaning only through individual experiences and needs; for example, resources have no existence apart from human wants. The phenomenological approach in geography is based on a relationship between observer and observed. The scholar looks at a problem from the subject's viewpoint. An illustration of the phenomenological approach is work on "mental maps." A mental map compares personal views with the collective image. The map in Figure 1.6, for example, is a preference surface of where Pennsylvania State University students would most like to live if they had

FIGURE 1.4

A conceptual framework for locational analysis. (Source: Berry, Conkling, and Ray © 1987, p. 29. Reprinted by permission of Prentice-Hall, Inc. Englewood Cliffs, New Jersey.)

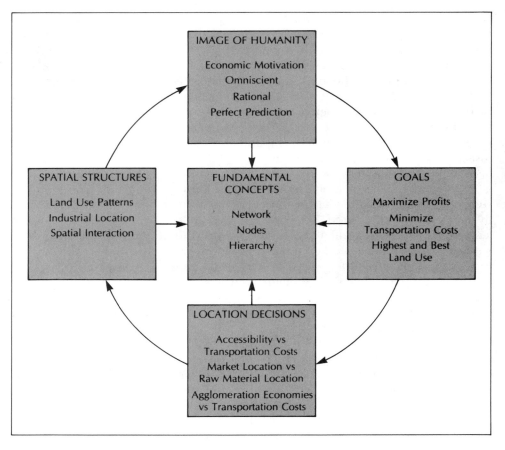

FIGURE 1.5

Elements of spatial system. (Source: Haggett, 1965, p. 18.)

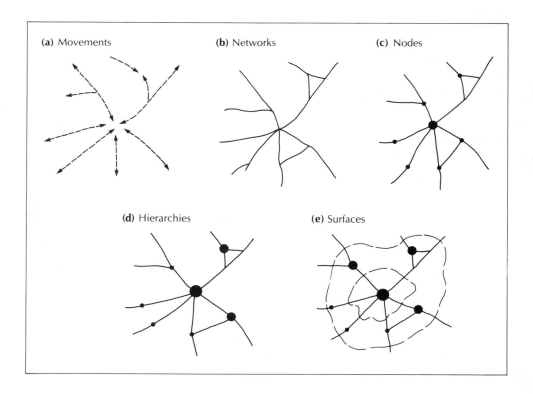

FIGURE 1.6

The preference surface, or "mental map," of students at Pennsylvania State University in 1982. (Source: Gould, 1983, p. 161.)

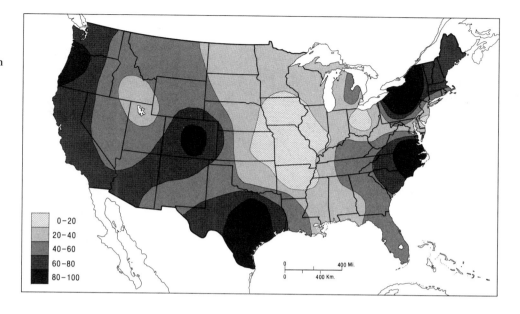

0–20
20–40
40–60
60–80
80–100

no financial worries or concern about finding a job after graduation. It uses a simple scaling with the most preferred state one hundred, and the least preferred zero.

Third, Marxist geographers charged that traditional theories of spatial organization obscure more than they reveal. In their view, location theories are narrowly conceived and blind to historical facts— designed primarily to serve the goals of those who wield power in the economic system. These geographers believe that a Marxist view can provide a more precise set of ideas about the world economy by recognizing and drawing attention to the power relations of societies. They see the relations of places in the context of the world's political economy. They recognize a contemporary reality—the disadvantageous situation of most people with respect to the control and use of resources—and expose the structure that preserves and intensifies that situation. Marxist geographers acknowledge and analyze prevailing value systems, a topic largely ignored by most economic geographers.

Economic geography has been characterized by major changes in thinking. These shifts reflect a need to deal with new realities of the world. However, to attempt to reduce the mosaic of views of the economic geographer's task to one or two general views would be misleading. Nonetheless, many geographers would agree that the theme of spatial organization is particularly valuable in helping us to understand world development problems. This theme receives more attention than others in this book.

Fundamental Concepts of Geography

When geographers study development issues, they ask questions about the world's space, as we have shaped, structured, and organized it. They answer these questions with the aid of concepts. The major concepts used in this book are grouped under three headings: properties of space, spatial process and structure, and spatial interaction.

Properties of Space Geographers examine space at multiple levels. There is a hierarchy of spatial perspectives from personal space to international space. *Personal space* is the familiar "close at hand" world of the individual. *International space* is the entire world—those vast areas controlled more by governments and institutions than by individuals.

Geographers also consider various dimensions of space. They sometimes consider three-dimensional space (a volume) or one-dimensional space (a line between two points), but most of the time they consider two-dimensional patterns that can be represented on a plane. Maps are examples of two-dimensional space.

Geographers divide space into abstract and concrete space. *Abstract space* is a conceptualization of one-, two-, or three-dimensional space independent of any point of reference on the earth's surface. It is homogeneous in all respects and movement is equally easy in all directions. On a plane, abstract space is called an *isotropic surface;* it allows geographers to develop normative models of idealized

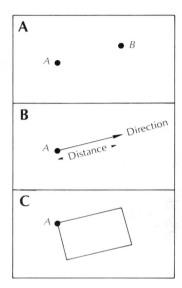

FIGURE 1.7
Point, line, and area defined by distance and direction.

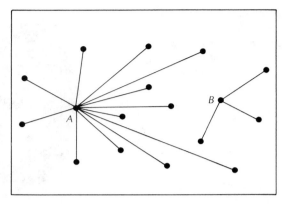

FIGURE 1.8
Connectivity.

landscapes. *Concrete space* is the actual surface of the earth, with all the variety and differentiation of the real world.

Only a few terms are required to describe, define, and measure space. Imagine a sheet of blank paper representing a two-dimensional abstract space. This featureless plane devoid of pattern is of no interest to geographers. But once some phenomena are mapped onto the paper, a pattern begins to emerge. *Point, line,* and *area* are the most elementary terms that can be used to describe this pattern. Points may represent cities or manufacturing plants, lines may represent transport arteries or boundaries between areas, and areas may represent agricultural or manufacturing regions.

The spatial elements of point, line, and area may be used to define the basic geographical concepts of *distance, direction,* and *connectivity.* If two points are placed on our blank piece of paper, Point *A* can be described in terms of its distance from Point *B* and vice versa (Figure 1.7a). If Point *A* is chosen as an arbitrary starting place, all other points can be defined in terms of their distance and direction from Point *A*. A line can be defined as a series of points or a given distance from a point in a specific direction (Figure 1.7b). A series of defined lines describe a bounded area (Figure 1.7c).

The concept of connectivity refers to how well points are linked to others (Figure 1.8). Point *A* is connected to many other points by lines, whereas *B* is connected to only a few points. The points may represent cities and the lines scheduled air-passenger

flights. Point *A* has a higher degree of connectivity than *B*.

Other measures of space are extensions of the concepts of distance, direction, and connectivity. An area may be defined by a series of distances and directions. Once defined, these terms can be used to describe and measure the area's *size* and *shape.* The size and shape of an area has economic implications. A farm that is too large or small may not be conducive to efficient operation. A large country is more likely than a small one to have the resources needed for economic development, but then again largeness may inhibit effective control and organization. Other things being equal, compact countries have an advantage over countries with less efficient shapes. For example, the long, narrow shape of Chile creates problems for communication and national unity.

Agglomeration and *accessibility* are extensions of the concept of distance. Consider two clusters of points (Figure 1.9). Points in Cluster *A* are closer together than points in Cluster *B*. Cluster *A* represents greater agglomeration or reduced aggregate distance. For example, a shopping center reduces the

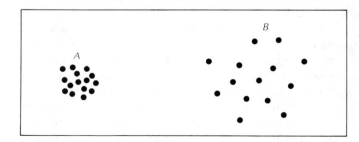

FIGURE 1.9
Agglomeration.

distance consumers must travel to purchase goods by clustering many stores at one point. A city itself is a clustering strategy reducing aggregate distance among residential, business, and recreational functions.

Accessibility is the concept of being close to things (Figure 1.10). Point X has a high degree of accessibility and Point Y, a low degree of accessibility. Accessibility is, therefore, another measure of aggregate nearness. Agglomeration refers to aggregate nearness of points in a cluster, whereas accessibility refers to the nearness of a given point to other points.

Basic geographical concepts and their extensions are absolute concepts when applied to an abstract space such as an isotropic surface. Absolute measures of space also apply to concrete spaces. A kilometer on the earth's surface is the same as any other kilometer. Yet, the use of relative measures of distance, direction, and connectivity often provide a more meaningful view of concrete space than the use of absolute measures.

For example, *relative location* is measured by the cost, in both money and time, required to overcome it. These costs are referred to as the *friction of distance.* The handicap of distance has declined historically because of transport improvements, but it may increase in the future with a rise in

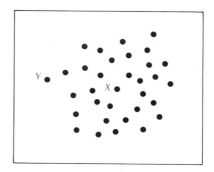

FIGURE 1.10
Accessibility.

the cost of oil. In general, the retarding effect of distance is less in developed countries with their modern and well-managed transport systems than it is in underdeveloped countries. At the same time, geographical space is much more "sticky" in traffic-clogged New York or Washington D.C. than it is in rural Wyoming.

Concrete qualities of space are referenced to specific points or areas on the earth's surface. Any *location* requires a fixed reference point. Geographers deal with two kinds of location: absolute and relative. *Absolute location* (site) is position in relation to a conventional grid system, such as latitude and

New York City's situation is a good one, allowing the city to serve as gateway between a rich hinterland and the rest of the world. (Source: N.Y. Convention and Visitors Bureau.)

longitude or street addresses. *Relative location* (situation) is position with respect to other locations. It is a measure of connectivity and accessibility, and it usually changes over time. The concept of relative location is of greater interest to economic geographers than absolute location.

To illustrate the importance of relative location, consider the position of New York City. The absolute location of New York (40° 45′ north latitude and 74° 00′ west longitude) tells us nothing about the city if we are interested in understanding why it became one of the world's great cities and ports. In 1820, there were four main ports on the northeastern seaboard competing for trade between the United States and Europe: Boston (pop. 61,000), Baltimore (pop. 63,000), Philadelphia (pop. 64,000) and New York (pop. 131,000). But New York's slight edge over its rivals became unassailable after 1825. Why? Geographers find the answer in the relative location of New York. The Appalachian Highlands represented a cost and time barrier (high friction and distance) between the resources of the American interior and the return flow of manufactured goods from Europe. New York is at the mouth of the Hudson River. The Hudson River is almost at sea level all the way to Albany where it is joined by the Mohawk River that cuts through the Appalachians (Figure 1.11). In 1825, the Erie Canal was completed linking the Hudson-Mohawk corridor with Lake Erie. An advantageous location relative to a primary traffic artery provided a major impetus for New York's explosive growth during the nineteenth century. By 1840, New York with a population of 349,000 was nearly three and one-half times the size of its closest rival, Baltimore.

The concept of relative location is vital to our understanding of the integration of the world economy. *Spatial integration*—the linking of points of production (absolute location)—was mandatory for the development of the economic system. It involved, through the construction of transport networks, the transformation of absolute space into relative space. Growth of the world economic system, proceeding at different rates in different regions, determines the relativity of geographical space.

Spatial Process and Spatial Structure A *spatial process* is a movement or location strategy. Geographers are interested in movements, such as the flow of raw materials to processing plants, the distribution of finished products from manufacturing plants, and the trade in commodities. Also of interest are location strategies, such as the decision of Chagga farmers on the slopes of Mount Kilimanjaro to grow coffee, the choice of the most accessible place for a new school

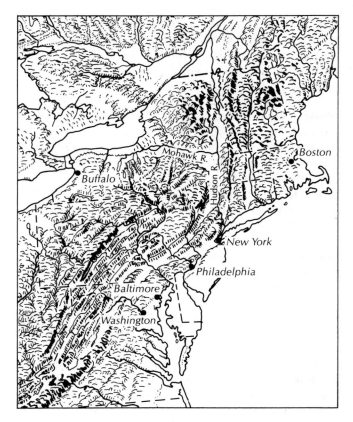

FIGURE 1.11
The Hudson-Mohawk corridor and the relative location (situation) of New York.

serving children in villages of a rural area in India, and the decision of Japanese companies to locate assembly plants near the U.S. market in cities along the U.S.-Mexican border.

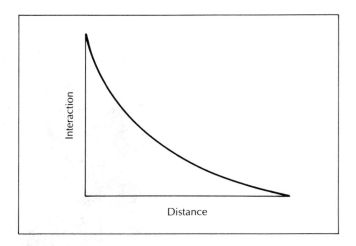

FIGURE 1.12
The "distance-decay effect": the greater the distance, the fewer the number of interactions.

The mud-constructed city of Kano in the savanna belt of northern Nigeria owed its early growth to a measure of complementarity between the people of the forests to the south and the people of the desert to the north. Ivory and spices from the south were exchanged for salt from the north in Kano's thriving market. (Source: British Airways.)

Spatial Structure is the internal organization of a distribution—the location of the elements of distribution with respect to each other. Spatial structures limit, channel, or control spatial processes. Since they are the result of huge amounts of cumulative investment over years and centuries, large alterations to the spatial structures of towns, regions, or countries are difficult to make.

Spatial structure and spatial process are circularly causal. Structure is a determinant of process and process is a determinant of structure. For example, the existing distribution of regional shopping centers in a city will influence the success of any new regional shopping center in the area.

Spatial Interaction Flows of goods, people, and information are collectively known as *spatial interac-tion*. The amount of spatial interaction tends to decline with distance (Figure 1.12). This rule, called the *distance-decay effect*, holds for all sorts of things and all sorts of geographical scales. Information people have about places declines with distance and, at larger geographical scales, air-passenger traffic is subject to the same effect.

The amount of interaction between places is also a function of their size. Big places generate more information, people, and goods than small places. New York and Chicago have more interaction than New Orleans and Cincinnati, even though both pairs of cities are about the same distance apart.

To explain the bases for spatial interaction, geographers make use of the concepts of *complementarity*, *intervening opportunity*, and *transferability*. Movement occurs between two places when there is a supply of goods or services in one place and a demand for them in another place. The oil fields of Saudi Arabia and Kuwait have complementary relations to the industrialized countries of North America, Europe, and Japan. Movement between places is modified or even eliminated because of the existence of intervening opportunities. Fewer goods and services move between Boston and Philadelphia because New York lies between them. Chicago attracts fewer immigrants from the Dakotas because of the intervening opportunities offered by Minneapolis-St. Paul. "In a sense, intervening opportunities are spatial sponges soaking up potential interaction between complementary places" (Abler, Adams, and Gould 1971, p. 194). The third condition for spatial interaction is transferability—the friction of distance. All movement increases costs and costs increase with distance. If the costs of traversing a distance are too great, movement will not take place despite complementarity and the absence of intervening opportunities.

Geographical Research in Aid of Development

A basic function of geographical research is to influence planning or organized action and the development of policy. An equally important function is to influence scholars, teachers, and students in the field and in the other social and environmental sciences.

The sort of knowledge and advice geographers provide their important constituencies fits under three headings: human-environment, spatial organization, and inventorying and monitoring research. In the human-environment area, geographers provide information about the best match between the environment and the "product" realized from the environment. They provide information about how the biophysical environment, ecosystem management, and systems of livelihood are linked. In the area of spatial organization, geographers provide information about the kinds of spatial structures that favor processes of development and the procedures that can bring these structures into being. Inventorying research involves the collection and analysis of information, especially for planning the use of human and natural resources. Monitoring research provides information about change—whether certain changes are harmful to people, the resource base, or both, and whether the goals of development are being achieved.

Geographers do not always solve development problems directly, but their skills and ways of thinking can help to resolve the world crisis. Our major responsibility as teachers and students is to try to

understand the world in crisis and to explore the causes of that reality. The world, developed and underdeveloped, poses challenges of immense importance and complexity. In this exciting and dangerous age of uncertainty, we can help to meet these challenges.

SUMMARY AND PLAN

The world is in crisis. To justify this assertion, we provided evidence of two challenges to the present world order: first, the challenge of constraints of energy supplies, resource availabilities, and pollution dangers; second, and equally formidable, the problem of the distribution of wealth. Will these problems exceed the capabilities of the capitalist system? Will capitalism, which has demonstrated a remarkable capacity for adaptability over the centuries, be able to push through this age of crisis?

The unsettled state of the world arouses the concern and the interest of the geographer. World development problems raise geographical questions, and development involves varying degrees of change over geographical space. In this chapter, we presented the geographer's perspective. We provided a definition of the field and introduced the main concepts and paradigms geographers use to interpret and explain world development problems at a variety of scales, ranging from small areas and regions to big "chunks" of the world.

This book describes how geographers study and analyze the world economy and how they attempt to resolve world development problems. Geographers approach such problems from a variety of perspectives. These alternative world views are the focus of discussion in Chapter 2. It is important to appreciate different perspectives and be aware of how various attitudes and views can influence approaches to foster development. Conflicting arguments and theories are interwoven in the chapters that follow.

These chapters, which progress in logical sequence, are organized around the themes of distribution and economic growth. Chapters 3 and 4 deal with population and resources, the prime variables in economic geography. To understand the effects people and resources exert on the world economy, we need to learn about the principles of location. Chapters 5 through 11 supply the foundation stones required to understand these principles: decision making, transportation, agricultural land use, urban land use, cities as service centers, and industrial location from the standpoint of firms and places.

The two chapters on industrial location provide a link between the development of businesses and the development of places—a link vital to the issues discussed in the remaining chapters. Chapter 12 deals with the expanding world of international business— its operations, environments, and its patterns. The final chapter examines the geography of development and underdevelopment. It illustrates how economic growth and resource use can combine to create a world of uneven and unequal development.

KEY TERMS

accessibility	international economic system
agglomeration	internationalization of capital
areal differentiation	intervening opportunity
complementarity	isotropic surface
connectivity	location (absolute and relative)
development	location theory
direction	space (abstract and concrete)
distance	spatial integration
distance-decay effect	spatial interaction
environmental determinism	spatial organization
friction of distance	spatial process
general systems theory	spatial structure
human-environmental relations	transferability
international economic order	world economy

SUGGESTED READINGS

Abler, R.; Adams, J. S.; and Gould, P. 1971. *Spatial Organization.* Englewood Cliffs, NJ: Prentice-Hall.

Bhagwati, J. N., ed. 1977. *The New International Economic Order: The North-South Debate.* Cambridge, MA: MIT Press.

Frank, A. G. 1980. *Crisis in the World Economy.* London: Heinemann.

———. 1981. *Crisis in the Third World.* London: Heinemann.

Gould, P. 1985. *The Geographer at Work.* London: Routledge and Kegan Paul.

International Institute for Environment and Development and World Resources Institute 1988. *World Resources 1988–89.* New York: Basic Books.

Johnston, R. J. 1979. *Geography and Geographers: Anglo-American Human Geography Since 1945.* London: Edward Arnold.

Johnston, R. J., and Taylor, P. G., eds. 1986. *A World in Crisis? Geographical Perspectives.* New York: Blackwell.

Laszlo, E; Baker, R., Jr.; Eisenburg, E; and Raman, V. 1978. *The Objectives of the New International Economic Order.* New York: Pergamon.

Lozoya, J.; Estevez, J.; and Green, R. 1979. *Alternative Views of the New International Economic Order.* New York: Pergamon.

2
WORLD VIEWS

OBJECTIVES

☐ To explain why it is useful to analyze and understand alternative world views

☐ To demonstrate that any presentation involves abstraction and is laden with theory

☐ To emphasize that there is no one indisputable reality

☐ To compare and contrast conservative, liberal, and radical mindsets

The United Nations' General Assembly: An international forum for discussion of diverse issues. (Source: UN photo 172.801/Yutaka Nagata.)

Almost every day we hear of development problems: overpopulation in the Sahel of Africa, hunger and malnutrition in Bangladesh, balance-of-payments difficulties in Central America, massive unemployment in northern England, and the farm credit crisis in the United States. Yet, there is little agreement on what causes these human tragedies or how they might be prevented.

The classic fable of five blind men touching an elephant recalls this dilemma. Each feels a different part of the elephant and thinks he knows what it is. The man who grabs the tail thinks he's holding a rope; the one who grabs the leg believes it's a tree trunk; the one who touches the elephant's side says it's a wall; the one who feels the ear is certain it's a big leaf; and the one who holds the trunk exclaims that it's a snake. For a concrete example to illustrate the dilemma, consider the world food problem. An American resource pessimist declares, "Soaring numbers of people are overrunning our food supplies. It seems to me that lifeboat ethics is not such a bad solution to the situation. Countries like Bangladesh are basket cases. If we continue to give them handouts, it will only serve to maintain high population growth rates. Compassion is a luxury we can no longer afford. We have to learn to let the starving die for the survival of the human race." A United Nations adviser pipes up, "I think that high population growth rates and consequent population pressure, land fragmentation, poor soils, and unreliable rainfall keep people from feeding themselves. The best way to stabilize overpopulation and food scarcity problems is to provide the poor with contraceptives. A World Bank official adds, "People are hungry because of inefficient food production. If we want to solve the world food supply situation, we have to transform traditional agricultural methods. The only way to do this is for rich industrial counties to supply progressive farmers with imported technology, new types of seeds, artificial fertilizers, pesticides, irrigation, and machinery." A Marxist from Niger breaks in, "The cause of hunger is not the tropical environment, not too many people, not scarcity of available land, not lack of technology, and not overconsumption by greedy Americans. The real problem is the unequal distribution of global wealth, which is the end result of capitalist countries gaining control of the global economy. The only guarantee of long-term food security is for us Third World people to take control of our own food resources."

Different perspectives on the causes of world hunger lead to different solutions that have different effects on people. If human suffering and misery are to be alleviated, we must appreciate alternative world views and understand how different ideologies influence efforts to resolve crisis situations. Here, an important question naturally arises: Does one perspective provide more meaningful insights into world development problems than another? To answer this question, we must be aware that scholars use different theoretical and analytical frameworks to argue their cases. And such awareness can only be achieved if we embrace a level of learning that permits us to think critically about the world.

These villagers are planting rice in Bangladesh. This nation, with some of the world's most fertile land, also is home to some of the world's hungriest people. Is there a world view that sheds more light on this paradox than others? (Source: World Bank.)

Hunger strikes hardest at the young. Is hunger in the Third World natural and inevitable? What human action can help end the hunger of millions of people? (Source: WHO/UNICEF/ W. Campbell.)

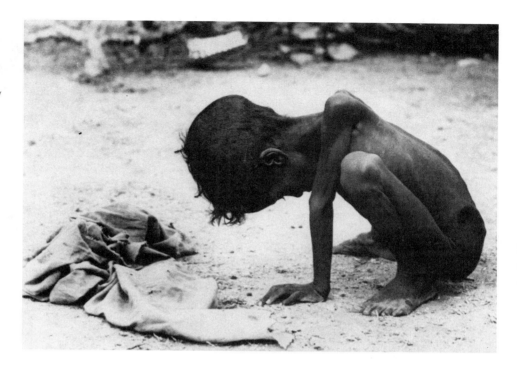

LEARNING IN AN IDEOLOGICAL WORLD

This chapter describes different levels of learning, explains why most of us find it difficult to alter the way we think and learn, and demonstrates that a world view is part of a particular theoretical perspective. We also introduce three general perspectives: conservative, liberal, and radical. A comparison of these competing mindsets will help you appreciate their crucial assumptions and the policies that follow from them.

Levels of Learning

People acquire knowledge on at least four recognizable levels. First-level learning involves simple perception of fact. For example, we are hungry and are conscious of that fact. In second-level learning, at least two facts are interrelated. During a drought we harvest less food per unit area and, therefore, we recognize the increased likelihood of hunger. When we attain a higher level of consciousness within an existing system, we are learning on the third level. Several options are possible: (1) if there is recurring drought, we can improve food yields either by planting drought-resistant crops or by irrigating traditional crops; or (2) if we choose not to change our traditional agricultural practices, there will be less food. When fourth-level learning is achieved, we can perceive the nature of existing systems, re-examine them, and

perhaps improve or change them to create new options. If we stay with the overpopulation/food scarcity issue, we can consider solutions beyond improved food yields when we evaluate the entire agricultural system. For example, we could consider expropriating prime agricultural lands that are now used to produce export crops such as coffee and cotton. This land could be given back to local farmers who could then produce food for their own needs instead of depending on purchased food and food from the industrialized countries.

Our understanding of the world comes mainly from third-level learning. At this level, learning is laced with a strong dose of ethnocentrism. It traps us into thinking that our way of seeing the world is the only way to see the world. Consequently, we tend to rely on strategies that optimize existing institutions rather than considering a wide range of alternative strategies.

In fourth-level learning, the goal is to move beyond present perceptions of reality. This point can be illustrated by a simple problem. Try to connect the following nine points with four continuous straight lines:

If you stay within the area delimited by the points, you will not find the solution. But if you move outside and self-imposed square, the following solution quickly comes to mind:

Similarly, if we are to understand different approaches to world problems, we must be willing to broaden the basis of our inquiry to include alternative ideologies outside the traditional norms that limit how we perceive problems and solutions.

Ideological Inertia

Most of us find it difficult to change the way we think and learn. Our perspectives on the world tend to persist. This ideological inertia is not surprising in that we are shaped by the culture, language, and habits of thought of the particular setting in which we were born and raised. The problem comes when our personal view of the world prevents us from seeing it in another way. A drawing by Henri de Toulouse-Lautrec, which is a perceptual illusion, illustrates this point (Figure 2.1). Those of us who see an old woman in the picture have difficulty seeing a young woman, and vice versa. To learn to see is to impose order on stimuli. The manner in which we impose order is determined by our expectations and is, therefore, value-laden.

Distortions and Abstractions of Reality

In an ideological world, *value-free* positions are impossible to maintain, even in science. Scholars use different paradigms or frameworks that guide the way questions are asked about observed reality. To a large extent, these frameworks govern the particular facts gathered and the manner in which they are analyzed; thus, they stipulate the form of the answers, if not the answers themselves. They lead us to see what we want to see, to explain what we want to explain.

Concepts, classifications, and "facts" are distortions and abstractions of reality and are laden with theory. They are predicated on different *theoretical perspectives*. Three examples clarify this argument.

FIGURE 2.1
A picture of ·. . . ?

Mercator and Peters Map Projections A Mercator projection world map gives a different view of the world from a Peters projection (Figure 2.2). The Mercator map, which is the world most Americans are accustomed to seeing, presents a fairly accurate picture of the shapes of the world's land masses, but grossly distorts their relative sizes. This distortion might be acceptable if it did not have ethnic implications. Countries that appear more important on the Mercator map are countries inhabited mainly by white people. North America appears in the Mercator map to be larger than Africa, although Africa is actually much larger. Greenland appears at least as large as South America, but South America is nine times larger. Area relationship is shown accurately in the Peters map. But as with any attempt to project the world on a two-dimensional piece of paper, the Peters map must also distort. In this case, the shapes of the continents are squeezed and elongated. Thus, both Mercator's and Peters' projections distort the world in attempting to abstract it on a two-dimensional plane.

The World in Statistics Similarly, any attempt to summarize the world statistically presupposes some model as a basis for selecting "facts" to represent "reality." What classification or grouping of countries do we choose? We could choose the World Bank country groupings shown in Table 2.1 and Figure 2.3. In this classification countries are grouped primarily according to whether they are "developing" or "developed." After this initial breakdown, they are grouped into six catagories: low-income economies, middle-

FIGURE 2.2
Perspectives on the world.

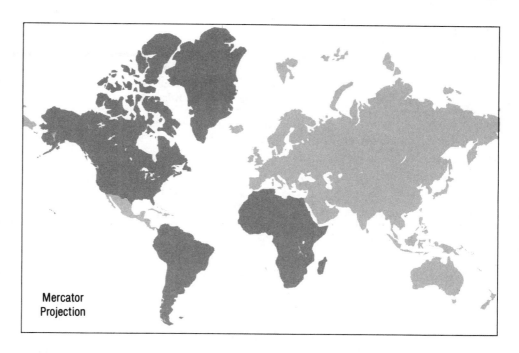

Mercator
Projection

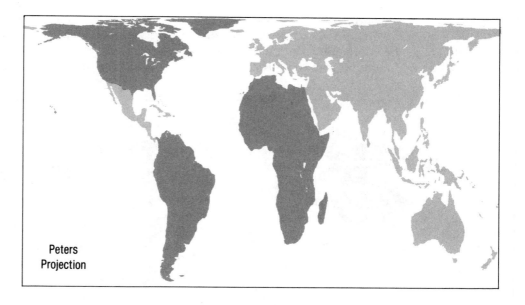

Peters
Projection

income oil importers, middle-income oil exporters, high-income or capital-surplus oil exporters, industrial market economies, and East European nonmarket economies. The emphasis of the classification is on relative income (gross national product per capita), the need for energy (oil), the type of technology used (industrialization), potential access to high technology (capital surplus), and the type of institutional structure (centrally planned or market economy). Using this mix of criteria, the world's land area, popula-

tion, and GNP per capita may be divided into groups.

This classification is neither objective nor value-free. Why are some countries called "developed" and others "developing"? Why are they sometimes also called "less developed" or "underdeveloped" in other classifications? Classifications are abstractions of reality and are not as innocuous as they appear at first glance. They follow from particular theories or underlying ideologies.

TABLE 2.1
The world in statistics, 1983.

Country Group	Land Area (Thousands of Square Kilometers)	Population (Millions)	GNP per Capita (U.S. Dollars)
Low-income economies	31,603	2,335	260
Middle-income oil importers	25,014	623	1,530
Middle-income oil exporters	15,511	543	1,060
High-income oil exporters	4,312	18	12,370
Industrial market economies	30,935	729	11,060
East European nonmarket economies	23,422	386	—

SOURCE: World Bank, 1985, pp. 174–75.

The World Bank classification is based on a Western conception of development. It stresses that a free market is the most effective path to economic growth and the improvement of human well-being. By contrast, another conception of development is used by Third World dependency theorists. By *dependence* is meant a conditioning situation in which the economies of one group of countries are underdeveloped by the development of others. Dependency theorists argue that developing countries suffer not from less development but from underdevelopment.

The Three Worlds The division of the world into First World, Second World, and Third World is also laden with theory. For Westerners, the First World includes the countries of Western Europe, North America, Israel, Australia, New Zealand, and Japan. Some would even include the Republic of South Africa and Argentina. The Second World is represented by the Soviet Union and Eastern Europe. The Third World consists of the remaining countries in Latin America, Africa, the Middle East, and Asia. Through the eyes of the "free world," the Second and Third

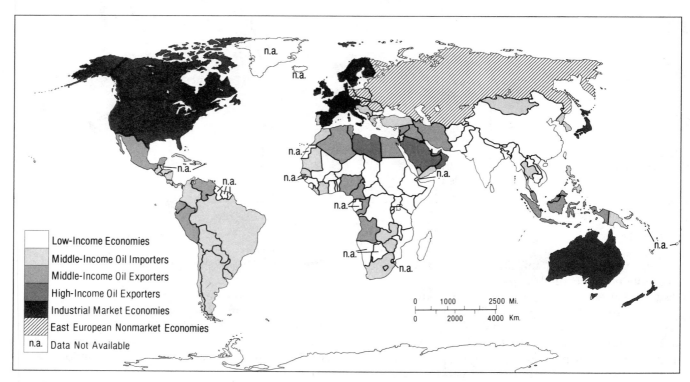

FIGURE 2.3
World Bank groups of economies. (Source: World Bank, 1985, pp. 170–71.)

Labeling/Libeling the Third World

The yawning chasm between prosperity and poverty in the world has created a language of its own. Or, is it in fact the rich person, not the yawning chasm, who has created this language? Author Goran Palm, writing for the Swedish International Development Authority (SIDA) journal *Rapport*, took a closer look at the vocabulary we use.

"The developed world" is contrasted to "the Third World." "Industrialized countries" are contrasted to "the poor in the South."

UN trade statistics commonly divide the world into three areas or "economic classes": industrialized countries or developed (Western) countries; developing countries or underdeveloped countries; socialist countries, Eastern bloc countries, or planned economies.

In addition to North America and Western Europe the "industrialized countries" include Japan, Australia, New Zealand, South Africa, and sometimes Israel. The "developing countries" are mainly the nearly one hundred nations of Asia, Africa, Latin America, and Oceania which within the framework of the UN, form the Group of 77 (sometimes identified with the non-aligned states). This latter includes several nations with certain ties to the Soviet Union or China such as Guinea, Yugoslavia, India, Tanzania, but also members of the "Eastern bloc." Lastly, the "socialist countries" include all nations of Eastern Europe except Yugoslavia, a handful of countries in Asia and a single country in Latin America—Cuba.

This may seem like a bold enough preliminary classification but on closer inspection we find that the first group of countries is the only one to be given an indisputably positive label. To be labeled "underdeveloped" or to represent a "developing country" is less gratifying. Such labels imply that one is somehow a little inferior or backward, that one, say, lives in tribes, worships holy cows, is afraid of contraceptives, doesn't know one's own best interests.

To be reckoned a member of the "Eastern bloc" or one of the "communist countries" is not much better. It amounts to being excluded or discriminated against on political grounds. Such countries are not a part of the "development" and "industrialization" so craved throughout the Southern Hemisphere.

Labels like "socialist countries" and "planned economies" are in that case more accurate, but here, too, a different norm is applied to these countries than to the other groups. They are identified not according to their level of development, but according to ideology and the nature of their economic system.

If we take industrialization as the criterion, any differences between the Eastern and Western countries evaporate. A similar lexicographical justice might be extended to all the countries outside the industrial world. Most of the countries of Latin America, Africa, and Asia depend on the production of foodstuffs and primary materials for industry for their livelihood. To sidestep the problem of ideology we may conveniently categorize the world into "industrialized countries" versus "raw materials-producing countries."

It is perfectly acceptable to say "industrialized countries" just as long as they are not contrasted to "developing countries" but to "agrarian" or "raw materials-producing countries." It is fine to say "socialist countries" as long as they are contrasted to "capitalistic countries." Fine to say "underdeveloped" just as long as it is contrasted to "overdeveloped." The old terminology is perfectly admissible; the problem lies in the misleading pairs of opposites so frequently used.

SOURCE: *Development Forum*, 1978, 6 (No. 10):6.

TABLE 2.2
Alternative explanations of reality under capitalism.

Alternative Paradigms	Human Nature	Work Incentives	Analysis Based on	Human Goals	Nature of Market Exchange Economy	Nature of Societal Problems	Role of State	Social Change
Conservative Focus on individuals: persons or companies	Humans are naturally unproductive and individualistic	Essentially material: (1) positive—raise in income (2) negative—unemployment	Classical and neo-classical economics: Competition and individuals maximizing profits	Maximum personal liberty and material well-being	Harmonious state of equilibrium created by supply and demand forces	(1) Individuals: lack of motivation, unrealistic demands, culture of poverty, racial inferiority (2) Government interference in the economy	Ideally, only police power to maintain law and order so that the market can work freely	Gradual change results from individual interactions in the market place
Liberal Focus on individuals and groups in society	Humans are naturally unproductive, but of goodwill	Essentially material: (1) positive—raise in income (2) negative—unemployment	Keynesian economics: competition and individuals maximizing profits with government assistance	Individual equality and social justice (equal opportunity)	State of equilibrium, achievable with government involvement in the economy	(1) Monopolistic tendencies in major economic sectors (2) Insufficient and inappropriate government programs	Police power and offsetting inadequacies in the economy whenever basic human needs and social justice are not achieved	Rapid change through government actions
Radical Focus on classes in society	Humans are naturally productive and cooperative	None really necessary; socially valuable rewards	Marxist economics: labor theory of value, theory of surplus value, theory of class struggle and revolution	Social equality: from each according to one's ability, to each according to one's need	Contradictions and crises of production and consumption; exploitation of workers; irrational allocation of natural and human resources	Private ownership of resources; production for profit rather than for human use; alienation; class conflict; unequal regional development	Police and economic power is used to maintain and enhance capitalism	Revolutionary change through mass movements to transform society's structure and values

SOURCE: Vogeler and de Souza, 1980, pp. 8–9.

Worlds are associated with negative and undesirable traits (lack of freedom and poverty) in contrast to the positive and desirable characteristics of First World countries.

Many Third World people disagree with this ethnocentric view. Mao Tse-tung's Three World theory categorizes the world's people in very different terms. The First World consists of the superpowers—the United States and the USSR—with their inordinate military and economic influence on the rest of the world. The Second World includes the allies of the two superpowers—the remaining industrialized countries. The Third World represents the underdeveloped countries and the hope for the whole world, not the despair that most Westerners see. This theory views Third World "problems" as assets that will serve to create a better future for the masses everywhere.

Because there is no one indisputable reality, it is desirable to be aware of different world views. For this reason, we have attempted to select and organize the material for this text from a broad base of inquiry. The focus is on a comparative approach in which different perspectives are explained and contrasted. Looking at the world through different ideological lenses better enables us to meet the challenge of world development problems.

COMPETING MINDSETS

Analytically, this book compares three general theoretical perspectives: conservative, liberal, and radical (Table 2.2). They rest on different assumptions about human nature, normative values, and social authority. They also employ different concepts to describe the nature and causes of world development problems.

The Conservative Perspective

The *conservative view* of the world economy is inherited from the ideas of Adam Smith (1723–1790), David Ricardo (1772–1823), and their latter-day followers. Conservatives assume that people need positive and negative material incentives to be productive. They are convinced that a capitalistic free-enterprise economy based on competition and maximizing profits allows egoistic and calculating individuals to achieve maximum personal worth and well-being. Individual decision-making units (individuals, households, firms) act freely and rationally to produce a harmonious and moving equilibrium by means of market forces. Consequently, the process of social and economic change is a gradual cumulative and unidirectional evolution. Faith in the efficiency and opti-

Adam Smith, the first economist, was born in the small town of Kirkaldy, Scotland in 1723. At the age of fourteen he was admitted to Glasgow University and won a scholarship to Oxford in 1740. After Oxford, Smith returned to Scotland where he lectured at Edinburgh from 1748 to 1751. His major work on economics, *An Inquiry into the Nature and Causes of the Wealth of Nations*, was published in 1776. The work became the foundation upon which classical economics was constructed. (Source: Scottish National Portrait Gallery.)

mality of private market mechanisms, especially those of *supply and demand*, allows conservatives to postulate a limited role for governments. They are likely to point to maintenance of social order as the single most important function of the state to ensure that capitalism can operate freely. Conservatives hold that government involvement in the economy usually causes more problems than it solves. They argue that many national and international problems trace to government interference and that the solutions to these problems lie in fewer government regulations and programs. Finally, conservatives believe that social change occurs gradually through the free actions of individuals in the marketplace.

The conservative approach to development problems rests on two points. First, more participation by poor countries in the world economy, not less as some socialists argue, will ensure faster and greater economic growth. The main theory conservatives use to assert that poor countries will benefit from more interaction in the world economy is Ricardo's theory of *comparative advantage.* Ricardo wrote, "It is quite important to the happiness of mankind that our enjoyments should be increased by a better division of labor, by each country producing those commodities for which by its situation, its climate and its other material or its artificial advantages, it is adapted, and by their exchanging them for the commodities of other countries. . . . Under a system of perfectly free commerce, each country naturally devotes its capital and labor to such employments as are most beneficial to each. This pursuit of individual advantage is admirably connected with the universal good of the whole" (cited in Harrington 1977, p. 36). Ricardo illustrated his trade theory by means of a two-country labor-cost model. The theory holds that it is in the best interest of poor countries to exchange more labor for less. According to conservatives, this unequal *division of labor* works to the advantage of all, allowing each country to make the best use of its natural resources, stock of skills, and infrastructures. Moreover, any deviation from free trade sacrifices efficiency and reduces world output and income. An example of a contemporary Ricardian is Henry Kissinger, former U.S. secretary of state. In 1975, at the Seventh Special Session of the United Nations General Assembly, he stated, "Comparative advantage and specialization, the exchange of technology and the movement of capital, the spur to productivity that competition provides—these are central elements of efficiency and progress. For developing nations, trade is perhaps the most important engine of development" (cited in Harrington 1977, p. 37).

Second, difficulties of economic growth in poor countries can be traced to internal obstacles in local environments and indigenous cultures. The tropical environment, in particular, is viewed as a major obstacle to progress. Soils are poor and fragile; rainfall is unreliable; and numerous endemic, debilitating diseases reinforce low levels of productivity. Above all, conservatives hold that the traits of individuals, rather than international market forces, prevent the advancement of people in poor countries. They account for the lack of development on the basis of backward cultures; traditional religious beliefs, values, and habits of life; insufficient incentives and entrepreneurship; and unstable political systems.

The Liberal Perspective

The *liberal view* of the world did not attract much attention until the depression of the 1930s and John Maynard Keynes's (1883–1946) analysis of the causes of unemployment. In *The General Theory of Employment, Interest, and Money*, Keynes (1936) discredited the conservative belief that the capitalist economic system is self-righting. He did not think that a modern capitalist economy would sustain a high enough level of investment to maintain full employment. While advocating government control of the level of economic activity in the national interest (state capitalism), he advised that the economy in general be left free to respond to the decisions of welfare-maximizing consumers and profit-maximizing producers.

Keynes presented an alternative to socialism. His theory, which permitted government to borrow and spend the proceeds to cure an economic depression, did not amend the conservative paradigm to any great degree. It was designed less to alter market-exchange economies than to preserve and revitalize them.

Like Keynes, liberals of the present day do not launch a thorough-going critique of either the conservative theory of human nature or the capitalist system. Indeed, liberals share with conservatives the view that people are naturally unproductive, and they share a faith in the capitalist system. Unlike conservatives, however, they place great emphasis on the goals of individual equality and social justice. To achieve these goals, they believe that government legislation and programs are necessary. Although liberals criticize inequality of opportunity based on wealth, position and power, they understand that certain inequalities are based on inherited characteristics such as family structure or ethnic culture (e.g., "culture of poverty"). The state redistributes wealth by taxing the rich to assist the poor and, therefore, societal changes can occur more rapidly than under the conservative laissez-faire model. They attribute problems at national and international levels to monopolistic tendencies in major economic sectors and insufficient and/or inappropriate government programs. In their view, the state must intervene on behalf of everyone whenever market mechanisms fail to satisfy consumer preferences or provide basic human needs (e.g., housing, health care, food, and adequate income). John Kenneth Galbraith's (1967, 1969) analyses of the industrial state and the affluent society reflect this perspective.

Liberals share with conservatives many of the same assumptions about barriers and bottlenecks to development in poor countries. They believe that traditional values and social institutions are the prime obstacles to development, and they are convinced that the town is the gateway for innovations. As centers of innovation, large towns can transmit modern values and social institutions to smaller centers and rural areas. Although liberals also employ the "blaming-of-victim" approach (Ryan 1972) to explain the causes of world problems, they, unlike conservatives, are willing to provide governmental assistance to the world's needy. Consequently, liberal governments provide unilateral and multilateral foreign aid (e.g., U.S. Agency for International Development, World Bank); food aid (e.g., U.S. Food for Peace Program); volunteers (e.g., Peace Corps); and military and technical assistance.

The Radical Perspective

Conservative and liberal perspectives are sometimes collectively known as traditional or orthodox approaches. According to radicals, their analyses do not go to the root of problems. Radicals argue that in capitalist societies the dynamics of socioeconomic organization (mode of production, in Marxist terms) produce certain kinds of class and institutional structures that result in a particular set of social problems. In their view, such problems cannot be solved without changing the form of socioeconomic organization at national and international levels.

Contrary to conservatives and liberals, radicals assume that people are naturally productive and cooperative and, therefore, that material rewards are not really necessary. They also assume that people are not inherently passive; rather, that passive, unproductive, or uncooperative behavior is in response to demands the economic system makes on them. Radicals reject the liberal's belief that people can enjoy equality of opportunity in a class society when the majority produces the wealth and when power is in the hands of the few. In such a society, the pursuit of profit by the dominant class shapes all aspects of life, including the quality of personal relations. Under capitalism, they argue, human needs are subordinated to the needs of the marketplace. Only commodities (goods and services) that have exchange value are produced, while other use values remain unmet. For example, the United States sells most of its food surplus to countries that can afford to buy it (exchange value) rather than distributing food to countries on the basis of need (use value).

Radicals claim that in a market economy the state predominately serves the interests of the ruling class, not the workers whose labor produces more wealth than is returned to them in the form of wages (Figure 2.4). Karl Marx (1818–1883) called this extra wealth "surplus value," or the product of exploitation.

Exploitation of workers can be intensified and surplus value increased when employers stretch the working day. If the work week were stabilized, employers could expand surplus value by substituting capital for labor. Marx argued that the process of introducing even more labor-saving equipment is inimical to workers. Displaced laborers form a reserve army of the unemployed, which keeps wages at minimal levels. Employed workers know that others are readily available to take their jobs if productivity falls.

The essence of the radical argument is that the engine that drives economic growth is *capital accumulation* for its own sake. The argument holds that economic growth is always unbalanced, since competitive production fails to achieve equilibrium. Short-run cyclical crises (unemployment and declining rates of profit) are corrected by increasing rates of accumulation through concentration (the trend toward larger, more efficient firms in each industry) and by geographical extension (imperialism). Periodic crises become more frequent over time. During each crisis, big capitalists devour little capitalists; individual capitalism becomes corporate capitalism. Capitalists seek larger outputs and bigger profits, and they deploy bigger machines that replace more and more laborers. Thus, the misery and alienation of workers intensifies in an increasing class struggle that charts the course of socioeconomic development.

From this sketch of Marxist theory, it is plain that radicals argue that inequality of wealth among classes originates in the capitalist system. Exploitation of one class by another is based on the private ownership of the means of production. From the radical perspective, irreconcilable conflict between classes is the key to understanding the need for revolutionary change through mass movements.

Uneven development pertains not only to the unequal distribution of wealth among classes, but also to the geographical dimension of development: underdevelopment and dependence. Radicals argue that Third World countries were underdeveloped first by the development and expansion of Europe; later, neo-European countries (the United States, Canada, Australia); and most recently, Japan. The capitalist world economy causes underdevelopment by generating and reinforcing an infrastructure of dependency that includes institutions, social classes, and processes such as urbanization, industrialization, and modernization. Dependency is, therefore, not an external matter. Foreign exploitation is possible only when it finds support among local elites who profit from it. To break out of dependency and to achieve development, radicals argue that underdeveloped countries must go beyond capitalism to a collectively owned and collectively governed economic system. To achieve the goals of socialism, political leaders have followed different paths: Fidel Castro took a

FIGURE 2.4
Exploitation of labor through
the extraction of surplus value.
Reprinted by permission of
Fred Wright, United Electrical,
Radio and Machine Workers of
America.

military approach in Cuba whereas Julius Nyerere favored an evolutionary approach in Tanzania.

SUMMARY

When geograpehrs or other experts examine problems of the world economy, they bring to the task a set of values that shapes the results of the inquiry. In this chapter, we illustrated how five experts with different ideologies offered five different explanations for the causes of world hunger. It is, therefore, important that we become aware of different theoretical frameworks experts use to argue their cases. And such awareness can only be achieved if we are willing to acknowledge that our own way of seeing the world is not the only way of seeing the world.

A presentation is laden with theory and presupposes some framework as a basis for selecting and organizing material. It involves abstraction and distortion as epitomized in our examples of presenting the world in map form, summarizing the world statistically, and dividing the world into First, Second, and Third worlds. We argued that our understanding of the world is enhanced when alternative theoretical perspectives are considered in a comparative framework.

The last section of the chapter looked at conservative, liberal, and radical perspectives. These perspectives are an integral part of the chapters that follow. Each viewpoint lumps many different theories and models together. The categorization of theories and models into three groups is an abstraction, but is most useful for providing alternative explanations of world development problems. The labels "conservative," "liberal," and "radical" are less important than the ideas behind them.

KEY TERMS

conservative view	radical view
liberal view	theoretical perspective
ideology	value-free

SUGGESTED READINGS

Benton, T. 1977. *Philosophical Foundations of the Three Sociologies.* London: Routledge and Kegan Paul.

Cole, K.; Cameron, J.; and Edwards, C. 1983. *Why Economists Disagree: The Political Economy of Economics.* London: Longman.

Galbraith, J. K. 1977. *The Age of Uncertainty.* Boston: Houghton Mifflin.

Gordon, D. 1971. *Problems in Political Economy.* Lexington, MA: D. C. Heath.

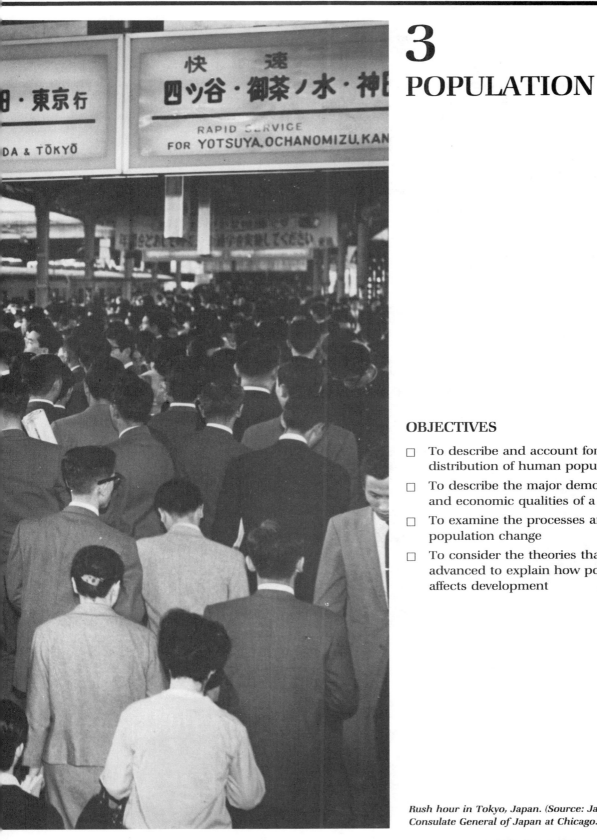

3
POPULATION

OBJECTIVES

☐ To describe and account for the variable distribution of human populations

☐ To describe the major demographic, cultural, and economic qualities of a population

☐ To examine the processes and consequences of population change

☐ To consider the theories that have been advanced to explain how population growth affects development

Rush hour in Tokyo, Japan. (Source: Japan Information Service, Consulate General of Japan at Chicago.)

uman beings are the most important element in the world economy. Not only are people the key productive factor, but their welfare is the primary objective of economic endeavor. As world population continues to grow by leaps and bounds, we face the critical question of whether there is a looming population crisis. Does overpopulation reduce the standard of living? Does it wipe out gains from economic growth? Does it lead to poverty, unemployment, and political instability?

To help answer these questions, this chapter examines the determinants and consequences of population change for developed and underdeveloped countries. It analyses population distributions, characteristics, and trends. It also reviews competing theories on the causes and consequences of population growth.

POPULATION DISTRIBUTION

In 1987 there were 5 billion people in the world—and very unevenly distributed. *Population distribution* refers to the arrangement, spread, and density of people. Contrasts in population distribution are stud-

ied on different scales of observation. On a macroscale, we examine broad geographical areas—continents, countries, regions. On a microscale, we look at small areas, such as population variations within cities. In this discussion, the emphasis is on population distributions across large geographical areas.

Population Size

A comparison of the world's population by continents shows that Asia's population is the largest. In 1987, Asia contained 2.9 billion people or 59 percent of the world's population. Europe (495 million) and the USSR (284 million) were home to about 16 percent, Africa (601 million) to 12 percent, Latin America (421 million) to 8 percent, North America (270 million) to 5 percent, and Oceania (25 million) to less than 1 percent. The populations of the underdeveloped continents—Africa, Asia (excluding Japan and the USSR), and Latin America—accounted for nearly 77 percent of all people in 1987. Of the 3.8 billion in the underdeveloped world, 73 percent lived in Asia, 16 percent lived in Africa, and 11 percent lived in Latin America.

Given such large variations among continents, it is not surprising that national population figures

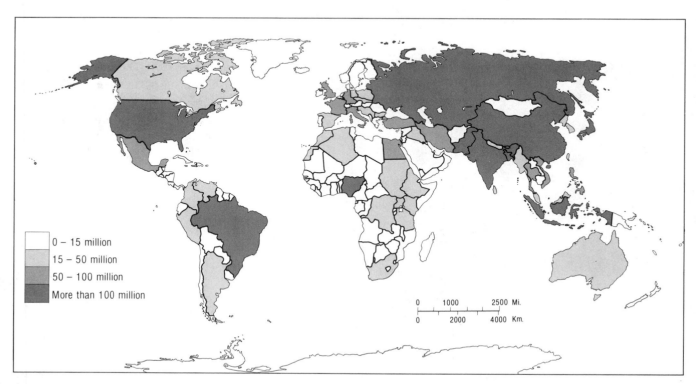

0 – 15 million
15 – 50 million
50 – 100 million
More than 100 million

0   1000   2500 Mi.
0   2000   4000 Km.

FIGURE 3.1
Population size. (Source: Population Reference Bureau, 1987.)

TABLE 3.1
Ten countries with the largest populations in 1987.

Country	Population (Millions)	Population as a Percentage of World Total	Area in Square Kilometers (Thousands)	Density (Population per Square Kilometer)
China	1,062	21	9,561	111
India	800	16	3,288	243
USSR	284	6	22,402	13
United States	244	5	9,363	26
Indonesia	175	3	1,919	91
Brazil	142	3	8,512	17
Japan	122	2	378	323
Nigeria	109	2	924	116
Bangladesh	107	2	144	743
Pakistan	105	2	796	132

SOURCE: Population Reference Bureau, 1987, and World Bank, 1987.

show even more variability (Figure 3.1). Ten out of two hundred countries accounted for 63 percent of the world's people in 1987 (Table 3.1). Four countries—China, India, the USSR, and the United States—contained 48 percent of the world's population. Approximately 21 percent of all people lived in China, 16 percent in India, 6 percent in the USSR, and 5 percent in the United States. Six of the top ten countries in population size—China, India, Indonesia, Japan, Bangladesh, and Pakistan—were in Asia. Seven of the countries with the largest populations were underdeveloped.

Population Density

Because countries vary so greatly in size, national population totals tell us nothing about crowding. Consequently, population is often related to land area. This ratio is called *population density*—the average number of people per unit area, usually a square kilometer.

Several countries with the largest populations have relatively low population densities (Table 3.1). For example, the United States is the fourth most populous country, but in 1987 it had a population

TABLE 3.2
Ten most densely populated countries in 1987.

Country	Population (Millions)	Area in Square Kilometers (Thousands)	Density (Population per Square Kilometer)
Bangladesh	107	144	743
South Korea	42	98	428
Netherlands	15	41	366
Lebanon	3	10	330
Japan	122	378	323
Belgium	10	31	323
Rwanda	7	26	269
West Germany	61	249	245
India	800	3,288	243
Sri Lanka	16	66	242

NOTE: Countries with areas of less than 10,000 square kilometers are not included.
SOURCE: Population Reference Bureau, 1987, and World Bank, 1987.

density of only 26 people per square kilometer. If the entire world population were placed inside the United States, its population density would be roughly equivalent to that of England. The United States is one of the sparsely populated areas of the world.

Many of the world's most crowded countries are small city-states or islands, such as Hong Kong (5,200 people per square kilometer) and Singapore (3,900 people per square kilometer). Excluding countries with an area of less than 10,000 square kilometers, Bangladesh is the world's most crowded nation (Table 3.2). In Bangladesh over 100 million people are crowded into an area the size of Iowa. Four of the top ten densely populated countries—the Netherlands, Japan, Belgium, and West Germany—are developed, and one, South Korea, is a newly industrializing country (NIC).

Contrary to popular opinion, not all crowded countries are poor. But what explains the fact that many people in the Netherlands or Singapore live well on so little land? What part of the explanation lies in their industrious people and their ability to adapt to change? What part of the explanation lies in their history of trade or their relative locations? Singapore is on one of the great ocean crossroads of the world. But being on a crossroad has worked no similar miracle for Panama. In 1985, Singapore had a per capita income ($7,420) that was more than three and one-half times that of Panama ($2,020).

Density figures can be more meaningful if they are expressed as the amount of arable land per person. This measure is called *physiological density*. In 1982, the Food and Agricultural Organization of the United Nations (FAO) estimated that for the world as a whole there was one-third of a hectare of cropland per person. The amount of arable hectares per person was 1.5 in Oceania, 0.9 in the USSR, 0.7 in North and Central America, 0.6 in Africa, 0.3 in South America, 0.3 in Europe, and 0.2 in Asia (excluding the USSR). Physiological density is a crude measure, however, because it fails to take into account the relative quality of arable land. The per capita supply of arable land in Africa is well above the world average, but its quality is generally inferior to that in Europe and North America.

Population density is a valuable abstraction, but it conceals much variation. Egypt had an estimated 49 people per square kilometer in 1984, but 96 percent of the population lived on irrigated, cultivated land along the Nile Valley where densities exceeded 1,500 people per square kilometer. Similarly, in the United States there are densely populated and sparsely populated areas. Large areas to the west of the Mississippi are essentially devoid of people, whereas the Northeast is densely settled. In 1985, the island of Manhattan had an estimated density of more than 25,000 people per square kilometer.

Most people are concentrated in but few parts of the world (Figure 3.2). Four major areas of dense

The trains are crowded in Bangladesh. Here, in one of the world's most fertile lands, the combination of high population density and the concentration of land into fewer and fewer hands contributes to continuing poverty and hunger. (Source: World Bank.)

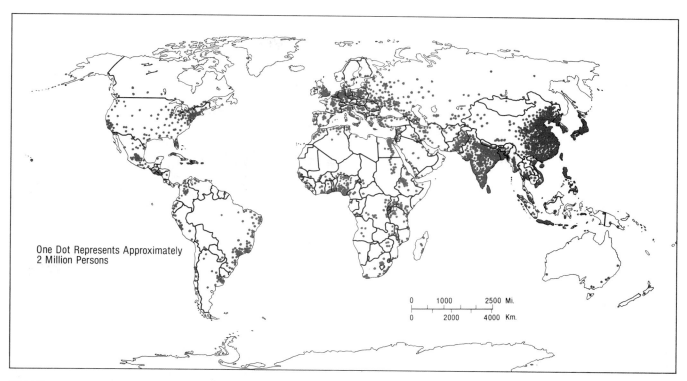

FIGURE 3.2
World population distribution.

settlement are East Asia, Europe, and the eastern United States and Canada. In addition, there are minor clusters in Southeast Asia, Africa, Latin America, and along the U.S. Pacific coast. More than 80 percent of the world's population lives in major and minor areas of dense settlement.

Factors Influencing Population Distribution

Is there a reason for the massing of people in some areas? One possible explanation is physical environment. People tend to concentrate along edges of continents, at low elevations, and in humid midlatitude and subtropical climates. Lands deficient in moisture, such as the Sahara Desert, are sparsely settled. Few people live in very cold regions, such as northern Canada, arctic Russia, and northern Scandinavia. Equatorial heat and moisture, as in the Congo and Amazon basins, appear to deter settlement. In addition, many mountainous areas—whether because of climate, thin stony soils, or steep slopes—are inhospitable habitats. There are, however, many anomalies relative to population distribution and physical environment correlations. For example, more people inhabit highland than lowland environments in many Latin American and East African locales.

Caution must be exercised in ascribing population distribution to natural elements alone. Furthermore, to hold that natural elements control population distribution is deterministic. Certainly climatic extremes such as insufficient rainfall present difficulties for human habitation and cultivation; but given the forces of technology, the deficiencies of nature can be overcome. Air-conditioning, heating, water storage, and irrigation are examples of the extensive measures that technology offers to residents of otherwise harsh environments.

If physical environments alone cannot explain population distribution, what other factors are involved? Human distributions are molded by the organization and development of economic systems. They are influenced by cultural traits, which also affect demographic components of fertility, mortality, and migration. Such social disasters as war may alter population distribution on any scale. Social and political decisions, such as tax policies or zoning and planning ordinances, are eventually reflected on the population map. None of these factors, however, can be considered without reference to historical circumstance. Present population distribution is explicable only in terms of the past. For example, the nineteenth-century industrial revolution made British coal sites major centers of population concentration and economic growth. Populous areas in Britain associated with coal include the Birmingham-Coventry district, Bradford-Leeds, Stoke-on-Trent, Manchester, South Wales, and Glasgow in Scotland. The influence of coal upon population distribution in Britain is still strong, yet its significance is waning as other sources of energy free industry and people from the coalfields.

Urbanism

The city is the most impressive and forceful expression of humankind's struggle with nature. It is a built environment—a giant resource system—that has little regard for the physical environment. As a center of commodity production and final consumption, it exerts a major influence on population distribution. Population concentrations reach their most extreme form in cities.

Modern urban growth is the result of agricultural, industrial, and transport revolutions of the late eighteenth and nineteenth centuries in Europe. The agricultural revolution allowed farmers to produce a surplus of food needed for growing nonagricultural populations. The industrial revolution spurred the mass movement of surplus population away from the countryside and into the emerging factories in cities. And the transport revolution permitted the cheap and fast distribution of the goods required by an expanding urban population. These three developments also increased the size of the trade areas that acted as markets for the goods and services of the growing towns.

The outcome of these revolutions was an increase in the size of urban areas and in the level urbanization. *Urban growth* is the increase in the size of city populations. Cities grow through natural increase—the excess of births over deaths—and through in-migration. *Urbanization* refers to the process through which the proportion of population living in cities increases. An *urban area* may be defined on the basis of numbers of residents. In the United States, any place with at least 2,500 residents is classified as urban. There are no universal standards, however. Countries have developed their own criteria for differentiating urban from rural places.

Urban growth and urbanization occur simultaneously in most countries, but their rates vary. Indian cities are growing by about 3.6 percent annually, but the percentage of total population in urban places is increasing slowly, from 20 percent in 1970 to 24 percent in 1985. Brazil, with a similar urban growth rate, is experiencing a much faster rate of urbaniza-

A stream of human-powered trishaws moves slowly along a crowded street in Dhaka, Bangladesh. The street is lined with small shops in row buildings two or three stories high. Because dwelling places also tend to be places of work, population densities are extremely high—over 40,000 people per square kilometer—in Dhaka's inner-city districts. (Source: World Bank.)

tion. The percentage of total population living in urban areas increased from 46 percent in 1970 to 71 percent in 1985.

World urbanization has increased dramatically since 1800. In 1800, some 50 million people—about 5 percent of the total population—lived in urban areas. By 1985, more than 2 billion people—about 41 percent of the total population lived in cities.

Levels of urbanization vary widely among regions and countries of the world (Table 3.3 and Figure 3.3). In 1985, developed countries were 72 percent urbanized, whereas underdeveloped countries were

TABLE 3.3
Proportion of the population living in urban areas, 1950–2000.

Region	1950	1970	1985	1990	2000
World	29	37	41	43	47
Developed countries	54	67	72	73	74
Underdeveloped countries	17	25	31	34	39
Africa	16	23	30	33	39
Latin America	41	57	69	72	77
East Asia	17	27	29	30	37
South Asia	16	21	28	30	37
North America	64	74	74	74	75
USSR	39	57	66	68	71
Europe	56	67	72	73	75
Oceania	61	71	71	71	71

SOURCE: International Institute for Environment and Development and World Resources Institute, 1987, p. 27.

only 31 percent urbanized. Latin America became a predominately urban continent between 1950 and 1985, but Asia and Africa are still overwhelmingly rural.

The degree of urbanization in a country usually corresponds to its level of economic development. In general, developed countries have the highest urbanization and income levels (Figure 3.4), but the relationship between town-dwelling population and the level of income per person does not imply that urbanization equals development. Third World urbanization is not being accompanied by a rapid increase in prosperity. High urban growth rates are diluting capital resources and reducing living standards. They are generating congestion, deteriorating services, slums, and employment problems.

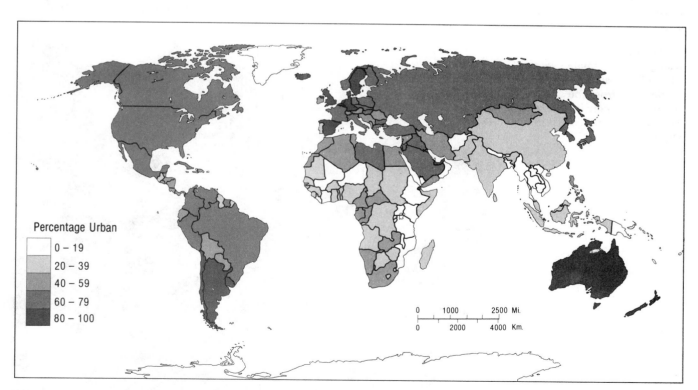

Percentage Urban

- 0 – 19
- 20 – 39
- 40 – 59
- 60 – 79
- 80 – 100

FIGURE 3.3
World urbanization. (Source: Data from Population Reference Bureau, 1987.)

FIGURE 3.4
Relationship between per capita
GNP and urbanization, 1987.
(Source: Compiled from Popula-
tion Reference Bureau.)

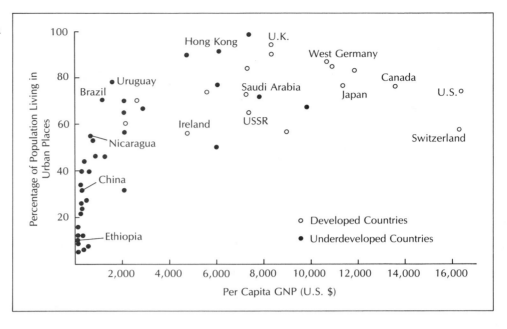

To understand the role of rapid population growth in urban problems, it is necessary to distinguish between the increasing proportion of urban to total population (urbanization) and the absolute growth of urban population (urban growth). Urbanization increased during the economic expansion of developed countries from 17 percent in 1875 to 26 percent in 1900. It also increased at about the same rate in the Third World between 1950 and 1975: the rise was from 17 to 27 percent. This comparison suggests that economic development rather than population growth is the main determinant of urban growth. But Third World urban population increased at an annual rate of 4.1 percent between 1950 and

Mexico City is a spectacular
example of a primate city. But
most of its residents dwell a
world apart from the glitter of
the high-rise corridor. (Source:
Mexican Government Tourism
Office.)

1975, far faster than the rate of 2.8 percent a year in developed countries between 1875 and 1900. Urban growth rates reflect national growth rates. In the Third World, urban growth is paralleled by high rates in rural areas. Natural increase accounts for 60 percent of the urban population growth. Rural-to-urban migration accounts for the remaining growth.

The most striking feature of Third World urbanization is the growth of large cities. In 1950, only three cities in underdeveloped countries ranked in the top ten in the world (Table 3.4). By 1980, the number had grown to five. Furthermore, it is projected that in 2000 all but two of the top ten cities will be in the Third World. Compared with developed countries, the projected rates of big-city growth are very rapid indeed (Table 3.5).

A large part of the population of many Third World countries is concentrated in a major center of growth called a *primate city*. In 1985, at least one in five people in Argentina, Iraq, Peru, Chile, Egypt, South Korea, Mexico, and Venezuela lived in a primate city. At the present time, cities such as Lima, Bangkok, Baghdad, and Buenos Aires account for over 40 percent of the total urban population of their respective countries.

POPULATION COMPOSITION

So far we have dealt with numbers and distributions of people, but not with population composition. By *population composition* we mean demographic, cultural, and economic characteristics. These characteristics vary from region to region. They differ markedly from rich nation to poor nation, from city to rural area, and from city to suburb.

Demographic Structure

Except for total size, the most important demographic characteristic of a population is its age-sex structure. The age-sex structure determines the needs of a population; therefore, it has significant policy implications. A fast-growing population implies a high proportion of young people under the working age. A small proportion of workers results in a smaller output per capita, all else being equal. A youthful population also puts a burden on the educational system. And when this cohort enters the working ages, a rapid increase in jobs is needed to accommodate them. By contrast, countries with a large proportion of older people must develop retirement systems and medical facilities to serve them. Therefore, as a population ages, its needs change from schools to jobs to medical care.

The age structure of a country is often examined through the use of *population pyramids*. They are built up in five-year age groups, the base representing the youngest group, the apex the oldest. Population pyramids are compared by expressing male and female age groups as percentages of total population. The shape of a pyramid reflects long-term trends in fertility and mortality and short-term effects of "baby booms," migrations, wars, and epidemics. It also reflects the potential for future population growth or decline.

TABLE 3.4
Ten largest cities in the world

City	Population (Millions)
1950	
New York/NE New Jersey	12.4
London	10.4
Rhein/Ruhr	6.9
Tokyo/Yokohama	6.7
Shanghai	5.8
Paris	5.5
Greater Buenos Aires	5.3
Chicago/NW Indiana	5.0
Moscow	4.8
Calcutta	4.7
1980	
Tokyo/Yokohama	20.0
New York/NE New Jersey	17.7
Mexico City	15.1
Shanghai	15.0
São Paulo	12.6
Beijing	12.0
Los Angeles/Long Beach	10.1
Greater Buenos Aires	10.1
London	10.0
Paris	9.7
2000	
Mexico City	27.6
Shanghai	25.9
Tokyo/Yokohama	23.8
Beijing	22.8
São Paulo	21.5
New York/NE New Jersey	19.5
Greater Bombay	16.3
Calcutta	15.9
Jakarta	14.3
Rio de Janeiro	14.2

SOURCE: United Nations, 1982, p. 61.

The Primate City: Mexico City

The primate city phenomenon is most obvious in Latin America. Mexico City is an outstanding example. Mexico City's population grew from 1 million in 1930 to 15 million in 1980, and is projected to be over 27 million in 2000. During the 1960–1970 decade alone nearly 1.8 million rural migrants settled in the city, representing 48 percent of the growth for that period.

Mexico City's credentials as a primate city are borne out by the following facts: it has 21 percent of the total Mexican population, 46 percent of the gross domestic product, 53 percent of manufacturing labor, 42 percent of higher education institutions, 52 percent of the theaters, 76 percent of the radio stations, and all five television stations. Much of the imbalance has been caused by favoring urban-based industrial development over rural development. Consequently, the inhabitants of the densely populated rural areas that surround the federal district view Mexico City as a place of opportunity for economic, cultural, and educational advancement.

SOURCE: Based on FAO, 1985, p. 81.

Three representative types of pyramid may be distinguished (Figure 3.5). One is the squat, triangular profile. It has a broad base, concave sides, and a narrow tip. It is characteristic of underdeveloped countries having high birth rates and declining death rates, exemplified by Mexico in 1980. What does Mexico's population future portend? The number of Mexicans working or looking for work will more than double between 1980 and 2000, from 20 million to 42 million. Will the Mexican economy be able to support such an increase, or will the potential for out-migration be enhanced?

On the other hand, the pyramid for the United States describes a slowly growing population. Its shape is the result of a history of declining fertility and mortality rates. By definition, the *fertility rate* is the number of births per thousand women of childbearing age (15–49 years) in a particular year, and the

TABLE 3.5
Projected populations, percentage of total urban populations, and number of cities larger than 4 million people.

Region	1980			2000		
	Population (Millions)	Percentage of Urban	Number of Cities	Population (Millions)	Percentage of Urban	Number of Cities
World	305	16.7	38	681	21.7	79
Developed countries	130	16.1	15	167	16.5	20
Underdeveloped countries	175	17.2	23	514	24.2	59
Africa	7	5.4	1	74	20.4	12
East Asia	75	19.5	7	154	23.0	14
South Asia	66	19.1	11	199	25.8	23
Latin America	57	23.5	6	123	28.6	12

SOURCE: FAO, 1985, p. 83.

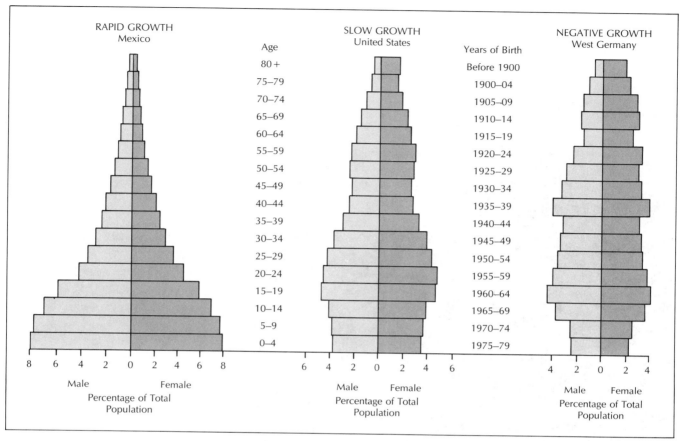

FIGURE 3.5
Population pyramids. (Source: Censuses of Mexico, the United States, and West Germany.)

mortality rate is the number of deaths per thousand people in a particular age group. With lower fertility fewer people have entered the base of the pyramid, and with lower mortality a greater percentage of the "births" have survived until old age. As a result, the U.S. population has been aging, meaning that the proportion of older persons has been growing. The pyramid's waist reflects the "baby dearth" of the depression years when total births dropped to about 2.5 million from an average of close to 3 million a year. At the time, the fertility rate dropped close to 2.1, which is the level that leads to a stable population if maintained indefinitely. The bulge above the base of the pyramid is a consequence of the "baby boom" that followed World War II. In the mid-1950s, the fertility rate increased to 3.8 and the number of births each year exceeded 4 million. After 1964 there was another "baby bust." By 1976, the fertility rate had fallen to 1.7, a level below replacement. Members of the baby-boom generation, however, were having children in the 1980s. Thus, even though the birth rate is lower than ever before, the U.S. population continues to grow.

A few developed countries have "negative population growth." They have low birth rates, low death rates and, in some case, net out-migration. West Germany is one of these countries. Because many West Germans are in the older age groups, the country is experiencing natural population decrease (annual deaths exceed annual births) and, with net out-migration, the result is a steady population decline. If the current fertility rate of 1.3 births per woman were to remain constant, the population would decline from 61 million in 1982 to 10 million in 2132—an 84 percent decline in 150 years. West Germany is an example of what may occur in other developed countries if low fertility levels are sustained. Drastic population declines are of great concern to many European countries. Who will run the nursing homes and fill the future labor force? Is the solution the immigration of guestworkers from Third World countries?

These elderly park-bench inhabitants in Moscow typify the aging populations common to many European countries, the western Soviet Union, and Japan. What are the implications of low-fertility, aging populations? What measures might slow or reverse fertility decline? (Source: United Nations.)

Cultural Traits

Culture—the customs and civilization of a particular people or group—is the result of learned behavior. People learn to eat only certain foods; dress in certain ways; speak in certain languages and dialects; assign various roles and status to men, women, children, and to different races; and hold certain concepts about life and death. Culture affects demographic characteristics, influences the structure of production and consumption, promotes or handicaps economic progress, and shapes views about other countries of the world.

Nationality Nationality affords people a sense of identity and promotes unity through commonality of purpose. However, dissention among different nationality groups leads to economic and social problems. These conflicts and tensions are prevalent in Europe; for example, the antagonism between the Flemings and French-speaking Walloons in Belgium. Ethnic conflict frequently occurs in Africa and has often thwarted development there. Before independence, Africans willingly united to support the fight against colonial rule; but the task of building a nation in the years following the granting of independence has not commanded such unity of purpose. Economic and political fragmentation is a major external problem of African and Asian countries.

Language Language also fosters group unity, but it reduces communication with outsiders. In Kenya, tribal linguistic diversity is considered a handicap to development; hence, the government is promoting Swahili as a national language. Linguistic differences can promote territorial segregation and spawn separatist movements, as in India and Canada. Yet in contrast, Switzerland is a cohesive nation, despite its German, French, Italian, and Romansch-speaking populations.

Race and Gender The belief that some racial groups are "superior" to others continues to create many problems. Subjugated races suffer psychological rejection as well as economic and social discrimination. Africans, long denied their status under apartheid policies in the Republic of South Africa, are severely repressed. A great part of Canada's native American population lives outside the mainstream of society on reservations. American blacks and hispanics also experience discrimination.

In addition to racial discrimination, there is also discrimination on the basis of gender. In many societies, women are considered inferior to men. For example, in highly populated areas of Asia and the Middle East, female infants and children die in greater numbers than their male counterparts, not because of natural causes, but because of social factors. Sons are more highly valued: they will carry on the family name, earn money for the family (often at a very young age), and eventually care for the parents. Hence, sons receive preferential treatment. Daughters are more likely to suffer from lack of adequate health care. In Bangladesh, more females than males under the age of five are malnourished, and females are 21 percent more likely than males to die in the first year of life.

Religion Religious differences also disrupt national economies. Examples are the effects of rivalries between Moslems and Christians in Beirut, Lebanon and between Catholics and Protestants in Belfast, Northern Ireland. In Belfast, the population is sharply divided into Protestant and Catholic residential areas. And Protestant employers frequently discriminate against Catholics.

Cultural characteristics of a population are frequently cited by social scientists to explain development. One example is Max Weber's (1930) concept of the Protestant work ethic to account for the rise of industrial capitalism in Western Europe. Another is the notion that Japan's economic miracle owes much to the servility of the Japanese worker. By contrast, social scientists sometimes use negative attributes of culture to explain Third World underdevelopment. The example of India's sacred cattle is often used to illustrate "backward" cultures. Contrary to the conventional wisdom, anthropologist Marvin Harris (1966) argued that the sacred cow concept in Hinduism protects small-scale farmers from starvation. The prohibition of slaughtering cows allows these farmers to use cattle as draught animals, as dung producers for fuel and fertilizer, as milk providers, and as sources of beef and hides for the untouchables and non-Hindus. Harris concluded that the "sacred cow complex" is a rational economic device.

We have only briefly touched on what are actually highly complex and emotionally charged issues and myths surrounding cultural traits. It is important, however, that economic geographers be aware of these issues and dispel any notions that have no basis in fact. For example, the popular idea that workers in Japan are naturally docile is fallacious. Japan has a very long history of bitter labor-management confrontation. The development of lifetime employment is but one attempt to integrate workers into the fabric of Japanese enterprise.

Economic Characteristics

Economic characteristics of a population include the working or active population, industrial composition, unemployment, and income.

Active Population The population of a country is conventionally divided into two parts: the economically active and the economically inactive. Economically active people are the productively employed and temporarily unemployed. They compose what is known as the income-earning *labor force*. Men are still dominant in the paid labor force but the proportion of men to women is changing slowly. In 1950, women accounted for 31 percent of the world's income-earning labor force; in 1985, the figure was 35 percent. But the absolute number of women engaged in wage and employment increased considerably. Between 1975 and 1985 over 100 million women joined the labor force and in 1985 an estimated 676 million women were gainfully employed.

Official labor-force statistics are deceiving, however. They exclude adults and children in the informal sector, whose work may involve begging, shoe-shining, selling handicrafts, prostitution, drug-dealing, or petty theft. They also ignore the invisible, unpaid work of men, women, and children.

FIGURE 3.6
Percentage of each type of work done by women and men in Africa. (Source: United Nations, 1975.)

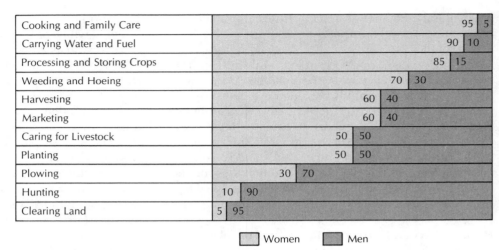

	Women	Men
Cooking and Family Care	95	5
Carrying Water and Fuel	90	10
Processing and Storing Crops	85	15
Weeding and Hoeing	70	30
Harvesting	60	40
Marketing	60	40
Caring for Livestock	50	50
Planting	50	50
Plowing	30	70
Hunting	10	90
Clearing Land	5	95

Women workers are especially invisible to official enumerators. In 1970, Egypt's census revealed that only 3.6 percent of women did agricultural work, but local surveys discovered up to 40 percent who were involved in planting, tilling, and harvesting. In Africa, women generally do the lion's share of the agricultural work (Figure 3.6). Women's agricultural work is also underestimated in the developed world.

Women are also engaged in other forms of unpaid work—cooking food, feeding infants, washing and mending clothes, collecting water and firewood. A woman in a Pakistani village spends approximately sixty hours a week on domestic work. And in the developed world, women who are "just housewives" work an average of fifty-six hours a week.

Industrial Composition The wage-earning labor force engages in thousands of different kinds of activities that may be classified into three sectors, as follows:

1 primary activities including agriculture, mining, quarrying, forestry, hunting, and fishing;
2 secondary activities including manufacturing and construction; and
3 tertiary activities including commerce, transportation, storage, and communications.

Economic development alters labor-force composition. As the U.S. economy grew, the proportion of the labor force in secondary and tertiary activities increased at the expense of primary activities, partic-

FIGURE 3.7
The changing composition of the U.S. labor force. (Source: World Bank, 1984, p. 259.)

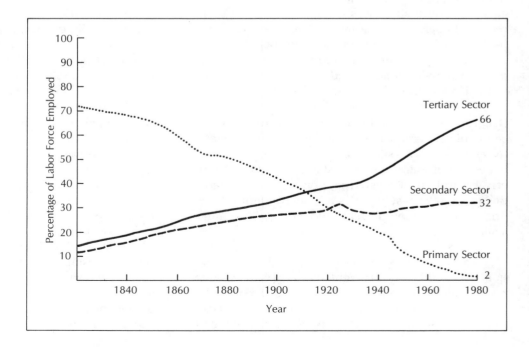

TABLE 3.6
Percentage of labor force by sectors, 1981.

Country	Primary	Secondary	Tertiary
Developed			
United Kingdom	2	42	56
United States	2	32	66
Australia	6	33	61
Underdeveloped			
Argentina	13	28	59
India	71	13	16
Tanzania	83	6	11

SOURCE: World Bank, 1985, pp. 214–15.

ularly agriculture (Figure 3.7). Compared with the United States, the share of the labor force in agriculture in the contemporary Third World is high (Table 3.6).

The ratio of industrial to agricultural workers provides a measure of a nation's economic advancement and power (Figure 3.8). As expected, underdeveloped countries have a low ratio of industrial to agricultural workers. Although manufacturing industries are moving to the Third World, most people have been barely touched by the iron embrace of the industrial age that is more than 200 years old. The majority of people continue to live their lives by rhythm of the seasons, not of machines.

Unemployment *Unemployment* means able and willing workers with no jobs. In the United States, the jobless rate was 3.4 percent in 1971, 9.0 percent during the recession of 1974–1975, and 7.1 percent in 1986. Levels of unemployment are much higher for women, blacks, and the young than for adult males. Unemployment of young people (twenty-four years of age and under) was 16 percent in 1981. Unemployment figures, however, underestimate the problem. People who have failed to find work and stop trying are excluded from the statistics. Moreover, the figures fail to account for adults, especially women, who want formal employment but who never obtain it because of domestic responsibilities or the lack of acceptable occupations.

In underdeveloped countries, official unemployment is a phenomenon of an urban sector composed of a minority of the population. Although unemployment rates are officially around 10 percent, an estimated 25 percent of those living in Third World cities survive outside the mainstream economy, and a

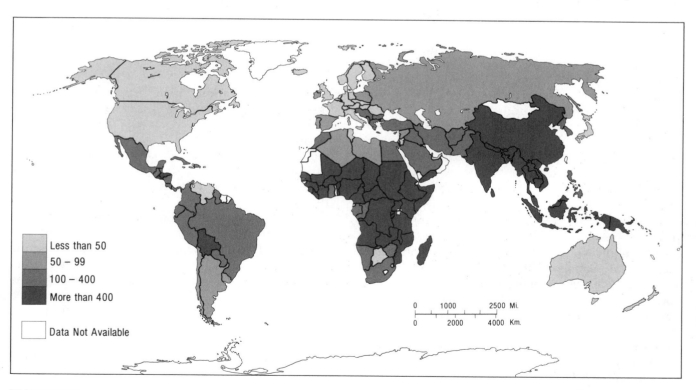

Less than 50
50 – 99
100 – 400
More than 400

Data Not Available

0   1000   2500 Mi.
0   2000   4000 Km.

FIGURE 3.8
Number of agricultural workers for every 100 industrial workers in the early 1980s.
(Source: Compiled from data in Kidron and Segal, 1984.)

further 750 million are unemployed or underemployed in the rural sector. People who work less than a specified number of hours are not underemployed. *Underemployment* is the gap between the amount of labor required for a decent living and the actual payment given for work; thus, underemployment is an index of poverty.

Income   Per capita income is the most familiar index to measure a population's relative development, its economic well-being and its capacity to consume. A cartogram, prepared by the World Bank, shows the distribution of total gross national product among selected countries in 1982 (Figure 3.9). The wealth produced by the United States and Canada alone was nearly five times greater than the combined gross national products of Africa and Latin America, which had about three and one-half times the population of North America. In 1982, North America had a per capita income of $13,910. The corresponding figures for Africa and Latin America were $740 and $1,900, respectively.

However well income per capita may seem to reflect international disparities, this measure should be viewed with caution. First, it fails to indicate ways in which incomes are distributed through the strata of societies. In most underdeveloped countries, wealth is concentrated in a small elite. Even within developed countries, major inequities in the internal distribution of income exist. A second problem stems from the fact that countries measure income per capita in a variety of ways. Finally, the per capita income indicator fails to take into account economic activities outside national monetized accounting systems in underdeveloped countries. Street vending, for example, which plays an important role in the lives of many people in the Third World, is not officially accounted for. For these reasons, per capita income has only limited utility, and often serves only to publicize the problem of poverty.

To delve more deeply into the problems of poverty, social scientists have constructed multidimensional measures of human well-being. An example is the Population Crisis Committee's (1987) Human Suffering Index constructed from ten variables: income per capita, average annual inflation rate, average annual growth of labor force, average annual growth of urban population, infant mortality rate, daily per capita calorie supply, percentage of population with access to clean drinking water, energy consumption per capita, adult literacy rate, and personal freedom/governance. Each of 130 countries was assigned a score of zero (high) to ten (low) for each variable, and these scores were added together to form an index.

Countries ranged from Mozambique (most human suffering) to Switzerland (least human suffering) (Figure 3.10). The Human Suffering Index is a useful descriptive measure of the differences in living conditions among countries.

MIGRATION

The population of any geographical area changes through the interaction of three demographic variables: births, deaths, and migration. The difference between births and deaths produces *natural increase* (or decrease) of a population. *Net migration* is the difference between immigrants and emigrants. Natural increase usually accounts for the greatest population growth, especially in the short run. But in the long run, migration contributes far more than the number of people moving into an area because the children of immigrants add to the population base.

The Migration Process

Migration is a purposeful movement involving a change of permanent residence. It is a complex phenomenon that raises a lot of questions. Why do people move? What factors influence the intensity of a migratory flow? What are the effects of migration? And what are the main patterns of migration?

Causes of Migration   Most people move for economic reasons. They move to take better-paying jobs or search for jobs in new areas. They also move to escape poverty or low living standards. Some people move because of cultural pressures or adverse political conditions. Others move to fulfill personal dreams. Whatever the motive, migrants seek generally to better themselves.

The causes of migration are sometimes divided into "push-and-pull" factors. *Push factors* might be widespread unemployment, population pressure, shortage of land, famine, or war. Hunger in Sweden in the 1860s is a good example of a push factor. In the half century between 1861 and 1910, more than a million Swedes moved to the United States. In the late 1970s and early 1980s, the various communist purges in Vietnam, Kampuchea, and Laos "pushed" out approximately a million refugees who resettled in the United States, Canada, Australia, China, Hongkong, and several countries in Western Europe.

Pull factors may be free agricultural land, the "bright lights" of a Third World primate city, or a

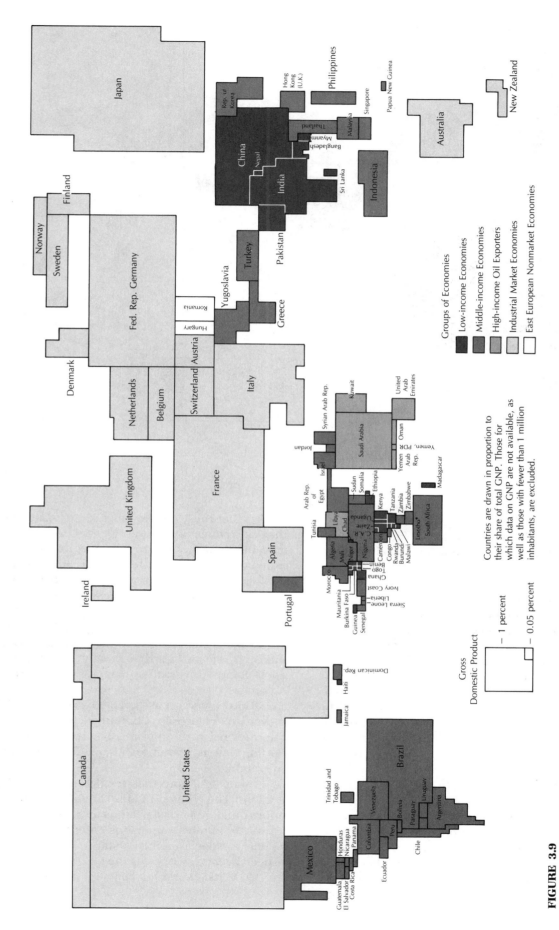

FIGURE 3.9

Distribution of gross national product among selected countries, 1982. (Source: World Bank, 1984, pp. 14–15.)

53

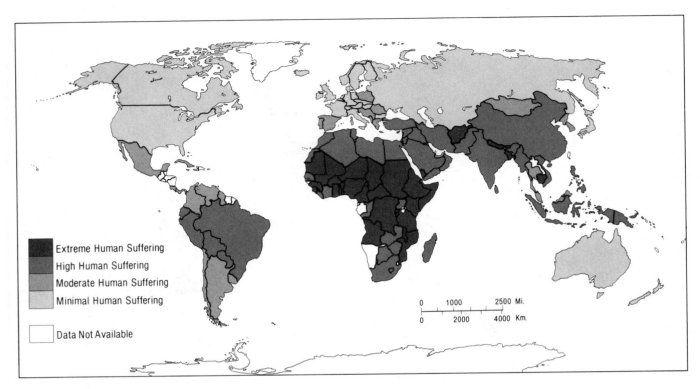

FIGURE 3.10
The Human Suffering Index map of the world. (Source: Based on Population Crisis
Committee data, 1987.)

booming economy. The rich oil-exporting countries in
the Middle East act as a pull factor for millions of
immigrants seeking employment. In Kuwait, 59 percent of the 1980 population was composed of foreigners, primarily working-age males.

Migrations can be *voluntary* or *involuntary*. Most
movements are voluntary, such as the westward
migration of pioneer farmers in the United States and
Canada. Involuntary movements may be forced or
impelled. In forced migration, people have no choice;
their transfer is compulsory. Examples include the
African slave trade and the deportation or "transportation" of British convicts to the United States in the
eighteenth century. In impelled migration, people
choose to move under duress. In the nineteenth
century, many Jewish victims of the Russian pogroms
elected to move to the United States and the United
Kingdom without the immediate lash of fear.

Barriers to Migration The intensity of a migration
flow is reduced by would-be migrant characteristics,
political restrictions, and distance. In the late nineteenth century, British sociologist E. G. Ravenstein
(1885, 1889) studied migration in England and con-

cluded that most people move short distances; also,
that the frequency of moves declines with distance. All
movement costs, but long-distance moves are more
expensive than short-distance ones. Subsequent studies have modified some of Ravenstein's generalizations on the migration process. The concept of
intervening opportunity, for example, holds that people's perception of a far-away place's comparative
advantage is changed when there are closer opportunities. In steamship days, many British emigrants
chose South Africa rather than cross another ocean to
Australia.

Governments have erected barriers to the free
movement of people. Communist countries control
interregional migration and restrict emigration. The
Berlin Wall is the most dramatic impediment to
migration.

Almost all countries regulate the flow of immigration. The United States limits immigration to
approximately 450,000 persons annually. Additionally,
a variable number of persons enter the United States
under a special refugee status. Some foreigners,
especially Mexicans, cross the U.S. border illegally and
live in a half-world of constant threat. Billions of

dollars are spent annually to police the borders of the United States, and much of this money is used to keep Mexicans out.

Where there are no political barriers to migration, people may stay where they are because of family or cultural ties. Even the grip of poverty is sometimes insufficient to break these links. Many of the rural poor of the southern Appalachians or the unemployed of industrial areas of northern England prefer to stay at home than to make their escape to growth areas where jobs are available. However, certain members of any society are more apt to break their kinship and cultural ties than others. Traditionally, young adult males are the most mobile.

Consequences of Migration Migration has demographic, social, and economic effects. Obviously, the movement of people from Region *A* to Region *B* causes the population of *A* to decrease and of *B* to increase. But because of migratory selection, the effects are more complicated. If the migrants are young adults, their departure increases the average age, raises the death rate, and lowers the birth rate in Region *A*. For the region of in-migration, *B*, the opposite is true. Thus, *A*'s loss and *B*'s gain is accentuated in the short run. If migrants to Region *B* are retirees, their effect is to increase the average age, raise the death rate, and lower the birth rate in the region of reception. Arizona, for example, has attracted a large number of retirees resulting in a higher-than-average death rate.

Conflict is an important social consequence of migration. It often follows the mass movement of people from poor countries to rich. There were tensions in Boston after the Irish arrived. And the same tensions have come with recent migrants—Cubans to Miami and Puerto Ricans to New York. Social unrest and instability also follows the movement of refugees from poor countries to other poor countries.

Generally, poor migrants have more difficulty adjusting to a new environment than the relatively well educated and socially aware. But migrants, on frequent occasion, do suffer from guilt. Many migrants to the United States feel they should go back to their home country to share in its tasks and problems.

The economic effects of migration are varied. With few exceptions, migrants contribute enormously to the economic well-being of places to which they come. For example, guestworkers are indispensible to the economy of West Germany. Without them, assembly lines would close down, and patients in hospitals and nursing homes would be unwashed and unfed. And without Mexican migrants, fruits and vegetables

in Texas and California would go unharvested and food prices would go up.

In the short run, the massive influx of people to a region can cause problems. The U.S. Sunbelt states have benefited from new business and industry but are hard-pressed to provide the physical infrastructure and services required by economic growth. In Mexico, migrants to Mexico City reduce the standard of living in their competition for scarce food, clothing, and shelter. Despite massive relief aid, growing numbers of refugees in the Third World impoverish the economies of host countries.

Emigration can relieve problems of poverty. Had the Irish and Italians remained at home in the nineteenth century, they would have added to the population pressure. External migration relaxed the problem of poverty and may have averted revolution in Jamaica and Puerto Rico in the 1950s and 1960s. However, emigration can also be costly. Some of the most skilled and educated members of the population of Third World countries migrate to developed countries. Each year, the income transferred through the "brain drain" to the United States amounts to billions of dollars.

Patterns of Migration

To examine patterns of migration, it is helpful to consider migration as either *external* (international) or *internal* (within a country). It is also convenient to subdivide external migration into *intercontinental* and *intracontinental*, and internal migration into *interregional*, *rural-urban*, and *intermetropolitan*. International migrations, so important in the past, are now far exceeded by internal population movements, especially to and from cities.

Intercontinental Migration The great transoceanic exodus of Europeans and the Atlantic slave trade are spectacular examples of intercontinental migration. In the five centuries before the economic depression of the 1930s, these population movements contributed strongly to a redistribution of the world's population.

It has been estimated that between 9 and 10 million slaves, mostly from Africa, were hauled by Europeans into the sparsely inhabited Americas. The importance of the "triangular trade" of Europe, Africa, and the Americas can hardly be exaggerated, especially for British economic development. Africans were purchased with British manufactured goods. They were transported to plantations where they undertook production of sugar, cotton, indigo, molasses, and other tropical products. The processing of these products created new British industries. Plantation owners and slaves provided a new market for British manufacturers whose profits helped further to finance Britain's industrial revolution.

The Atlantic slave trade was dwarfed by the voluntary intercontinental migration of Europeans. Mass emigration began slowly in the 1820s and peaked on the eve of World War I, when the annual flow reached 1.5 million. At first, migrants came from densely populated northwestern Europe. Later they came from poor and oppressed parts of southern and eastern Europe. Between 1840 and 1930, at least 50 million Europeans emigrated. Their main destination was North America, but the wave of migration spilled over into Australia and New Zealand, Latin America, Asia, and southern Africa. These new lands were important for Europe's economic development. They offered outlets for population pressure and provided new sources of foodstuffs and raw materials, markets for manufactured goods, and openings for capital investment.

Since World War II, the pattern of intercontinental migration has changed. Instead of heavy migratory flow from Europe to the New World, the tide of migrants is overwhelmingly from underdeveloped to developed countries. Migration into industrial Europe and continued migration to North America is spurred partly by widening technological and economic inequality and by rapid rates of population increase in the underdeveloped world.

Intracontinental Migration The era of heavy intercontinental migration is over. Mass external migrations still occur, but at the intracontinental scale. In Europe, forced and impelled movements of people in the aftermath of World War II have been succeeded by a system of migrant labor. The most prosperous industrial countries of Europe attract workers from the agrarian periphery. France and West Germany are the main receiving countries of European labor migration. France attracts workers especially from Spain, Italy, and North Africa (Figure 3.11). And West Germany draws workers from Italy, Greece, and Turkey.

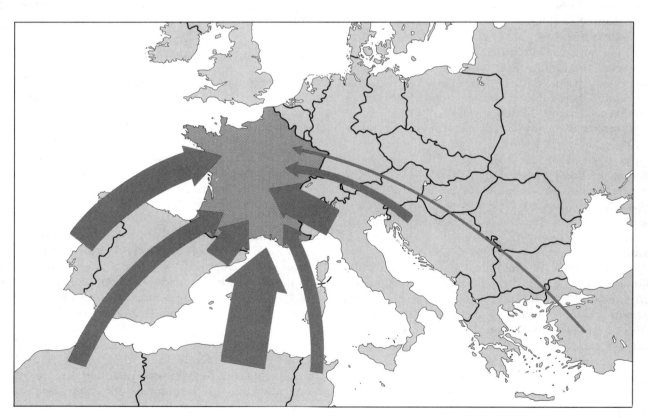

FIGURE 3.11
Origins of major foreign groups resident in France in 1982. (Source: Adapted from Ogden, 1984, p. 26.)

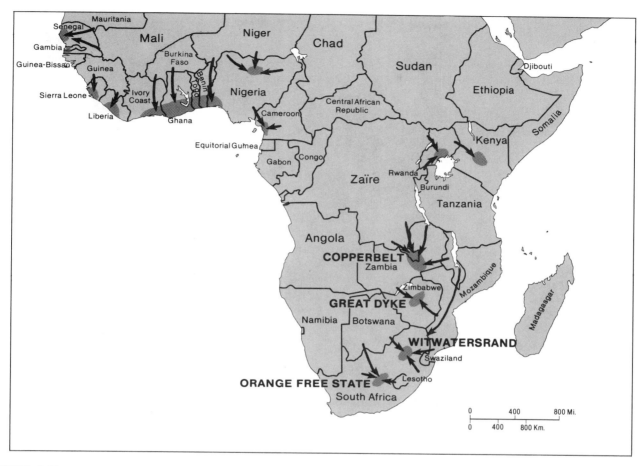

FIGURE 3.12
Major labor migrations in Africa.

Migrant workers from southern Europe usually have low skills and perform jobs unacceptable to indigenous workers. Similarly, thousands of Mexicans, many of whom are illegal aliens, find their way to the United States each year to work in the fields.

The system of extraterritorial migrant labor also exists in the underdeveloped world, most notably in Africa, where laborers move great distances to work in mines and on plantations (Figure 3.12). In West Africa, the direction of labor migration is from the interior to coastal cities and export agricultural areas. In East Africa, agricultural estates attract extraterritorial labor. In Southern Africa, migrants focus on the mining-urban-industrial zone that extends from southern Zaire in the north, through Zambia's Copper Belt and Zimbabwe's Great Dyke, to South Africa's Witwatersrand in the south.

In the modern era, the refugee problem has shifted from Europe to the Third World. Refugee

generating and receiving countries are concentrated in Africa (6 million people), Southeast Asia (4 million), and Latin America (2 million). The causes of refugee movement include wars or ideology (Vietnam, Cuba); racial persecution (South Africa); economic insufficiency increased by political intervention (Ethiopia, Chad); and natural and human-caused disasters (Belize hurricane of 1861, Bhopal chemical accident of 1984).

Interregional Migration *Colonizing migration* and *population drift* are two types of interregional migration. Examples of colonizing migration include the nineteenth-century spontaneous trek westward in the United States and the planned eastward movement in the USSR beginning in 1925. General drifts of population occur in almost every country, and they accentuate the unevenness of population distribution. Since World War I, there has been a drift of black Americans

Each year, during cotton-picking season, several hundred thousand migrant workers find employment on holdings in the Sudan's Gezira plains, between the White and Blue Nile rivers. (Source: World Bank.)

from the rural South to the cities of the nation's industrial heartland. Since the 1950s in the continental United States, there has been net out-migration from the center of the country to both coasts and a shift of population from the Frost- and Rust-Belt states to the Sunbelt (Figure 3.13).

Rural-Urban Migration   The most important type of internal migration is rural-urban migration, which is usually for economic motives. The relocation of farm workers to industrial urban centers was prevalent in developed countries during the nineteenth century. Since World War II, migration to large urban centers has been a striking phenomenon in nearly all underdeveloped countries. Burgeoning capital cities, in particular, have functioned as magnets

attracting migrants in search of "the good life" and employment.

Intermetropolitan Migration   In highly urbanized countries, intermetropolitan migration is increasingly important. Although many migrants to cities come from rural areas and small towns, they form a decreasing proportion. Job mobility is a major determinant of intercity migration. So, too, is ease of transportation—especially air transportation. For intermetropolitan migrants from New York, the two most popular destinations are Miami and Los Angeles.

POPULATION GROWTH

The chief force affecting world population distribution used to be migration. This was until European

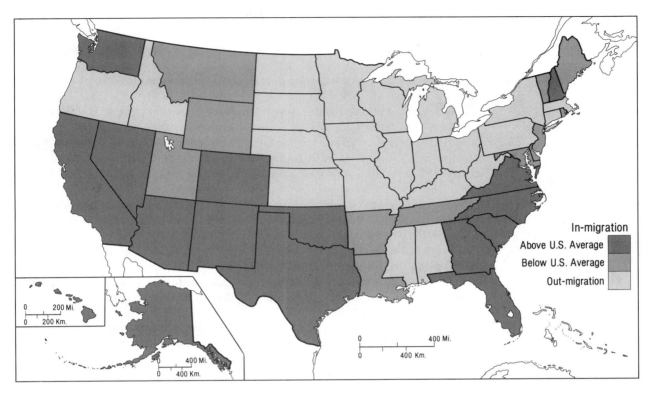

FIGURE 3.13
United States net migration, 1980–1985. (Source: Population Reference Bureau, 1986a.)

FIGURE 3.14
Population growth, 1750–2100.
(Source: Based on Merrick, 1986,
p. 4.)

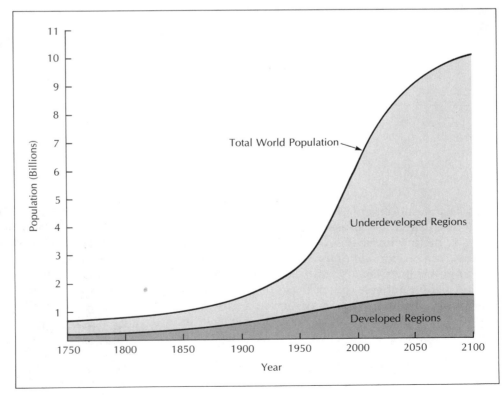

Central American Migrants and Refugees

Over 1.2 Salvadorans, Guatemalans, and Nicaraguans live outside their native countries, a figure unlikely to decline as the region's economic and political instability continues. Official refugee and unofficial migrant populations are active in various rebel insurgencies, contribute to strained bilateral relations and tensions in border areas, and are the subject of heated political debate in host countries. Although 800,000 migrants have gone to the United States, most refugees are in Honduras, Costa Rica, and Mexico.

The 470,000 Nicaraguans who have emigrated constitute a wide range of socioeconomic and ethnic groups. About 115,000 Nicaraguans, including Creoles from the Atlantic coastal states, live in Costa Rica; only 24,000 are registered by the United Nations High Commission for Refugees (UNHCR). Although Nicaraguans have for generations migrated to Costa Rica to work as field hands, their presence has increased since the Nicaraguan civil war. The government of Costa Rica accepts Nicaraguan refugees and does not repatriate illegal immigrants, but complains about the economic and political strains they impose on the country.

Roughly 90,000 Nicaraguans live in Honduras, including illiterate peasants near the border, draftdodgers in UNHCR camps, and Miskito Indians who are found along the Rio Cocos in the isolated eastern region. Domestic poverty and the arrival of more immigrants in Honduras ensures continued public debate over the rebel presence and continued conflict between Nicaraguan migrants and their reluctant hosts.

Half a million Salvadorans live abroad, including 21,000 in Honduran refugee camps. The Salvadoran emigration flow has slowed down from the peak years of 1979–1984, and some refugees have returned; but the continued fighting and a population of over 450,000 displaced persons in El Salvador makes the repatriation of many more migrants improbable.

Over 282,000 Guatemalans have emigrated; 43,000 are in Mexican refugee border camps, but at least twice that number illegally work as agricultural laborers. Many refugees have lived in Mexican camps for over four years and may stay permanently. Since 1983, only 1,100 have been repatriated.

---

transoceanic movements were disrupted during the economic depression of the 1930s. Today, the main cause is natural increase—the excess of births over deaths. Human population is increasing, and threatens to go on increasing. Each year an additional 83 million people inhabit the earth—the equivalent of the U.S. population every thirty-six months. The major impetus to world population growth comes from underdeveloped countries, in which more than three-fourths of humankind dwell. With 3.8 billion people already, and another billion expected by the year 2000, how will the Third World manage? How will the vast population increase affect efforts to improve living standards? Will the Third World become a permanent underclass at the bottom of the world economy? Or will the reaction to an imbalance between population and resources be waves of immigration and other spillovers to the developed countries?

Rates of Growth

The current rapid growth rate of the world population is a recent phenomenon. It took from the emergence of humankind until 1850 for the world population to

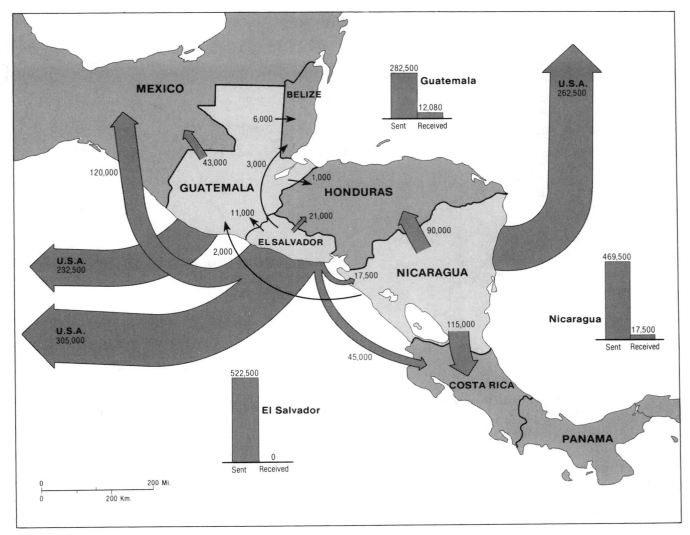

SOURCE: Demko and Wood, 1987, p. 227.

reach the billion mark. The second billion was added in eighty years (1850–1930), the third billion was added in thirty years (1931–1960), the fourth in sixteen years (1960–1976), and the fifth in only eleven years (1977–1987). Although the overall rate of population growth is slowing down, a sixth billion will be added by about 2000 (Figure 3.14).

The immediate cause for the surge in the growth of the world population is the difference between the crude birth rate and the crude death rate. The *crude birth rate* is the number of babies born per thousand people per year, and the *crude death rate* is the number of deaths per thousand per year. For example, the U.S. birth rate in 1987 was sixteen and the death rate was nine. During that year, the growth rate was sixteen minus nine, or seven per thousand, which is a percentage rate of natural increase of 0.7.

Population grows exponentially (1,2,4,8) rather than arithmetically (1,2,3,4), which is why population can increase so rapidly. At an annual increase of 0.7, the doubling time for the U.S. population is one hundred years. As growth rates increase, doubling times decrease sharply. At 1.7 percent—the rate of world increase in 1987—the doubling time is forty-

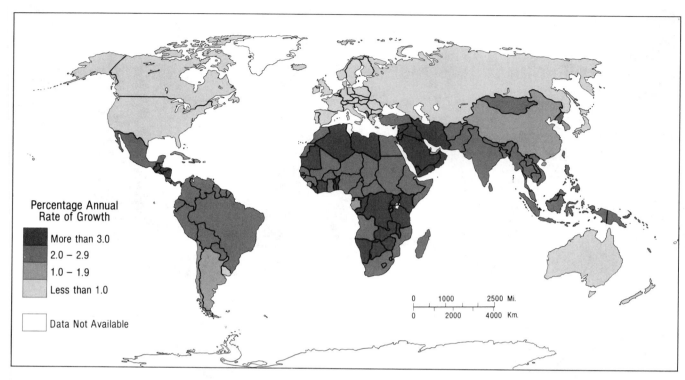

FIGURE 3.15
Population growth, 1987. (Source: Compiled from Population Reference Bureau.)

one years. The rate of growth in the Ivory Coast is 3.0 percent and the doubling time is twenty-three years. The doubling time for a population can be determined by using the number "seventy" as a dividend for the growth rate. Therefore, seventy divided by three equals twenty-three years.

Most of the world's population growth is occurring in the underdeveloped world (Figure 3.15 and Table 3.7). Of all the continents, Africa has the fastest rate of growth. In 1987, the population of Africa was growing by 2.8 percent per year. For Kenya, with a fertility rate of eight births per woman, the rate was 3.9 percent. At that rate of increase, Kenya's 1987 population of 22.4 million will double in eighteen years.

Rapidly declining death rates and continued high birth rates are the cause of this explosion. Death rates have been falling to about ten deaths per thousand people each year in Asia and Latin America, but to only sixteen per thousand in Africa (Figure 3.16). Birth rates are changing less spectacularly (Figure 3.17). They are highest in Africa (forty-four births per thousand people annually), Latin America (thirty per thousand), and Asia (twenty-eight per thousand). These figures compare with thirteen per thousand in Europe and fifteen per thousand in North America.

After accelerating for two centuries, the overall rate of world population growth is slowing down. In

TABLE 3.7
Population growth rates, 1987.

Region	Birth Rate (per Thousand)	Death Rate (per Thousand)	Annual Percentage Rate of Growth	Population Doubling Time (Years)
World	28	10	1.7	41
Developed countries	15	10	0.5	128
Underdeveloped countries	32	11	2.1	33

SOURCE: Based on Population Reference Bureau, 1987.

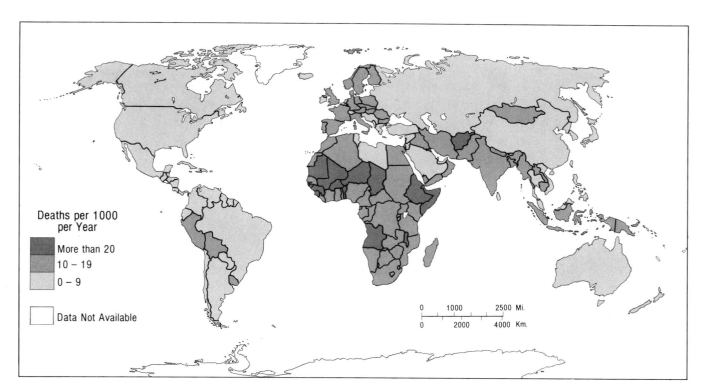

FIGURE 3.16
Death rates, 1987. (Source: Compiled from Population Reference Bureau.)

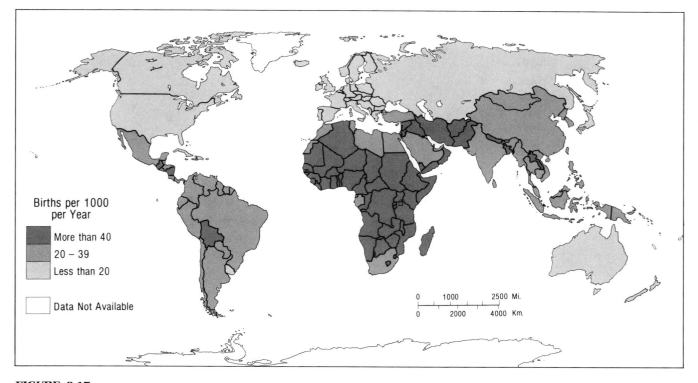

FIGURE 3.17
Birth rates, 1987. (Source: Compiled from Population Reference Bureau.)

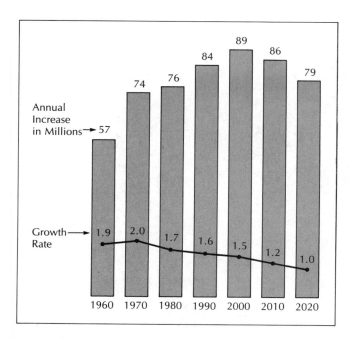

FIGURE 3.18
World population growth: Annual increase in numbers and growth rates. (Source: Population Reference Bureau, 1987.)

1987, population was growing at 1.7 percent a year, down from a peak of 2.04 percent in the late 1960s. The rate of growth is expected to continue to decline to about 1.5 percent in 2000 and 1.0 percent in 2020. However, the absolute size of population will continue to increase because the size of the base population to which the growth rate applies is so large (Figure 3.18).

The United Nations projects world population at 6.1 billion in 2000 and 8.2 billion in 2025. Between 1985 and 2025, world population is expected to increase by 3.4 billion (Table 3.8). Africa, Asia, and Latin America will account for 93 percent of this increase. The largest absolute increase, 1.7 billion, is projected for Asia, reflecting its huge population base. Africa is projected to add 1.1 billion, and Latin America 374 million. Population growth between 1985 and 2025 will further accentuate the uneven distribution of the world's population. In 1985, 76 percent of the world's population lived in the underdeveloped world, but by the year 2025, the proportion will increase to 83 percent.

Theories on Population Growth and Development

Malthus's Theory of Population In Western social science, the most frequently discussed theory is that of Thomas Malthus, an English clergyman, historian, and political economist, born in 1766. In his *Essay on the Principle of Population* published in 1798, Malthus (1970) pointed out that while population increases geometrically, production of foodstuffs and raw materials increases only arithmetically. From this observation, he concluded that for a population living in a given area and drawing its food supplies from that area, the *law of diminishing returns* eventually reduces productivity per head. This law states that additional applications of labor and capital to a given area of land will, in general, increase production, but not in proportion to the application of labor and capital. Diminishing per capita production continues until a new equilibrium is established. Excess population is removed by what Malthus termed the "positive" checks of disease, famine, and war. Later, he admitted there was an escape from the deadly equilibrium:

TABLE 3.8
Population growth, 1950–2025.

Region	Total Population (Millions)							
	1950		1985		2000		2025	
	Number	%	Number	%	Number	%	Number	%
World	2,516	100.0	4,837	100.0	6,122	100.0	8,206	100.0
Developed countries	835	33.2	1,181	24.4	1,284	21.0	1,407	17.1
Underdeveloped countries	1,618	66.8	3,657	75.6	4,837	79.0	6,799	82.9
Africa	224	8.9	555	11.5	872	14.2	1,617	19.7
Asia	1,292	51.4	2,697	55.8	3,419	55.8	4,403	53.7
Latin America	165	6.6	405	8.4	546	8.9	779	9.5

SOURCE: Based on Merrick, 1986, pp. 12–13.

prudent sexual habits—moral restraint before and moderation during marriage. A deeply religious man, Malthus considered artificial birth control theologically unacceptable.

History proved Malthus's static theory of population and income wrong for the developed countries. Europe's nineteenth-century population growth was accompanied by increased prosperity. This increased prosperity occurred because of technical change. The newly invented steam engine used energy more efficiently. New agricultural and industrial techniques increased labor productivity. National and international trade supplied raw materials for industries and food for urban workers. Growing populations provided labor for industries and markets for their products. Moreover, emigration reduced population pressure at home and helped expand Europe's trade networks. By the end of the nineteenth century, Malthus's argument that population growth must reduce the standard of living was all but forgotten.

Neo-Malthusianism Malthus's concerns about a gloomy future of "vice and misery" became more immediate in the 1950s. The developed countries held most of the world's income, but the underdeveloped countries were home to most of the world's population. Food supplies in underdeveloped countries were thought to be in jeopardy due to the relentless population growth. To neo-Malthusians, underdeveloped countries seemed caught in a trap caused by surging population growth and low levels of economic development.

The neo-Malthusian view of the population problem was mapped out by Ansely Coale and Edgar Hoover (1958) who predicted that continued high fertility in India would reduce economic growth by lowering the average production per worker. Following Coale and Hoover, the first Club of Rome report (Meadows et al. 1972) developed a limits-to-growth model that produced dire results when projected increases in population were matched against a fixed stock of resources and a fixed absorptive capacity of the environment. The model indicated that limits to population growth and economic growth were very near, and that world-wide death rates would soar if we permitted ourselves to approach the limits to growth too closely. Fifteen years later, the Population Crisis Committee (1987) found a positive correlation between high population growth rates and human suffering (Figure 3.19).

According to the neo-Malthusian formulation, underdevelopment and poverty are direct products of the population problem. Furthermore, poverty will not diminish without intervention to reduce birth

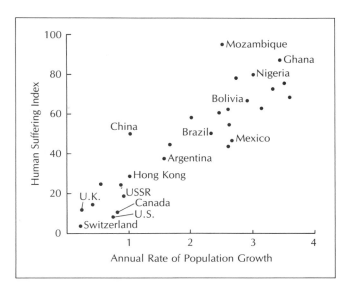

FIGURE 3.19
The relationship between population growth and human suffering. (Source: Compiled from Population Crisis Committee, 1987.)

rates. The neo-Malthusian view advocates efforts to educate Third World families in birth control techniques and to supply the contraceptive means for family planning. In this approach to poverty, overpopulation is primarily a numerical problem to be solved through the regulation of births.

The "Cornucopian" Thesis "Cornucopians" challenge neo-Malthusian ideas. According to Julian Simon (1981, 1986), humans have omnipotent power to extract resources, and the earth is infinite in its capacity to supply resources. While Simon does acknowledge that Malthusian theory is logically unassailable—the more people using a stock of resources, the lower the income—he adds that the theory is also incomplete. The left-out element is the advance of technical knowledge, which more than compensates for a reduction in resources caused by additional people. "Cornucopians" believe that history provides their best evidence. They cite Europe's experience during the industrial revolution and improvements in agricultural productivity that followed increased demand for food generated by population growth.

But can modern technology and its benefits offset the effect of additional people on the general standard of living in the Third World countries of today? Modern technologies are oriented to capital-intensive industries and generate few new jobs. Moreover, few new technologies have been created in

In a New Delhi birth control clinic, a doctor explains how to use an IUD. Who benefits from birth control clinics—individual women, families, local communities, national economies, and/or the world? Which classes benefit from family-planning programs? (Source: P. Pittet for the FAO.)

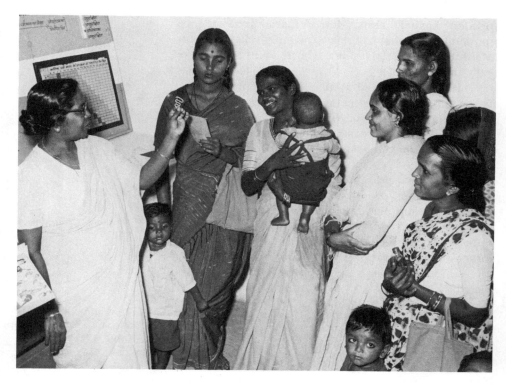

Third World countries. To acquire them, underdeveloped countries must borrow money, which exacerbates their debt problem.

The Marxist View Marxists also reject the neo-Malthusian formulation of the population issue as it applies to the Third World. They do not think so much in quantitative terms—sheer numbers of people—but in terms of poverty and exploitation, which they attribute to the growth of capitalism. In the Marxist view, overpopulation exists when people lack the basic means of subsistence or when there is massive and permanent unemployment. Poverty breeds overpopulation. Being impoverished, the poor must maintain large families in order to survive. Children play an important role in housework, rearing younger siblings, gathering firewood, fetching water, shining shoes, and begging. The Marxist solution to the problem of overpopulation is to eliminate poverty and exploitation so that the Third World poor will opt for small families rather than large ones. With economic strengthening in a Third World country, the labor-value of children to their parents will decrease, and the economic costs of children to their parents will increase.

Marxists believe that the Malthusian concept of overpopulation is a dangerous political idea. If part of 5 billion people is surplus, then as geographer David Harvey (1974) pointed out:

The meaning can all too quickly be established. Somebody, somewhere, is redundant, and there is not enough to go around. Am I redundant? Of course not. So who is redundant? Of course, it must be them. And if there is not enough to go around, then it is only right and proper that they, who contribute so little to society, ought to bear the brunt of the burden. (p. 237)

For Marxists, then, the neo-Malthusian concept of overpopulation has little value as a policy measure unless those in power are willing to face the moral dilemma of deciding which human groups constitute the surplus. Their argument does not imply, however, that there should be no physical constraints to population and economic growth. The world has finite resources; thus, population growth cannot follow an exponential course indefinitely.

The Demographic Transition

Most Western social scientists do not accept the idea of a population crisis as a permanent state for an impoverished group. Instead, they hold out hope that Third World countries will reduce their fertility rates. This hope is expressed in the theory of the *demographic transition*—a certain sequence of changes that took place in many European countries beginning in the eighteenth century. According to transi-

In Mali, women often have to travel several miles from their villages to gather firewood. Their heavy workloads are one of the factors that contribute to high fertility. The children are needed to help with house chores and farmwork. (Source: F. Mattioli for WFP/ FAO.)

tion theory, countries pass through the following four distinct phases as they undergo economic development (Figure 3.20):

1 **High Stationary Phase** Population grows slowly if at all. It is kept stable by a combination of high birth rates and high fluctuating death rates. Variable death rates reflect epidemics and variations in food supplies. This phase, characteristic of Europe before the industrial revolution, describes some contemporary ethnic groups who inhabit rain forests in Africa, Asia, and Latin America.

2 **Early Expanding Phase** Death rates fall and birth rates remain high causing a "population explosion." Causes for a decline in mortality are improvements in nutrition, sanitation, public health, and medicine. This phase began in Europe and North America late in the eighteenth century and early in the nineteenth century. At present, most underdeveloped countries are in Stage 2 of the demographic transition.

3 **Late Expanding Phase** Birth rates decline. Popula-

tion expansion slows down. In urban-industrial society, the altered status of women, delayed marriages, the economic disadvantages of children, the growing awareness and acceptance of birth control techniques, and rising expectations depress the birth rate. After 1900, countries of the industrial West registered big reductions in their birth rates. In many underdeveloped countries, declining mortality rates are not yet accompanied by falling birth rates.

4 **Low Stationary Phase** Population increases slowly or is stable (zero population growth). Mortality and fertility rates are low. Death rates are relatively constant, but birth rates may vary. The demographic transition from high to low fertility is complete. Countries of Western Europe have entered the terminal phase of the demographic transition.

The demographic transition in underdeveloped countries is following a course that is different from that of Europe. Present population increases are

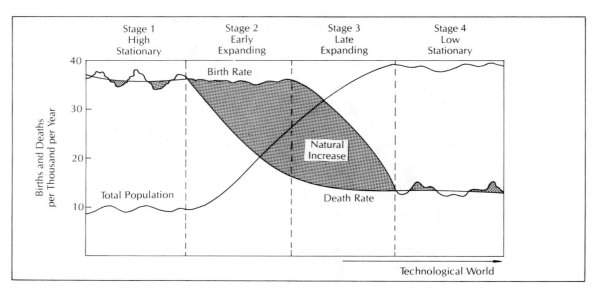

FIGURE 3.20
The demographic transition in idealized form.

much faster than they were in Europe. Prior to World War II, underdeveloped countries had high birth rates, but their population increases were checked by comparable death rates. Since then, birth rates have continued to be high—twice as high as in developed countries—but death rates have plunged toward the low levels of developed countries. Falling death rates, caused by the spread of up-to-date health measures, are expected to continue in the years ahead.

Transition theory is not a theory in the strict sense of the word. It describes demographic, social, and economic events that took place in Europe, but does not contain a specifiable and measurable mechanism of "causation" or a definite time scale. It does not pinpoint threshold levels of economic development necessary to establish preconditions for a decline in fertility within marriage. It fails to predict precisely the onset and pace of fertility decline. Moreover, it is unable to explain how fertility decline occurred in areas of slight economic development, such as the highlands of Scotland or the Central Massif of France (Teitelbaum 1975, p. 422).

Population and Development: An Integrated View

Criticism of the neo-Malthusian view especially by Marxists in the 1970s and 1980s created considerable interest in the question of whether and how additional numbers of people affect the standard of living.

In 1983, the National Research Council of the U.S. National Academy of Sciences convened a panel of experts to review evidence on this question. The conclusion was that "slower population growth would be beneficial to economic development for most of the developing world"; yet, the panel added that "a rigorous quantitative assessment of these benefits is context-dependent and difficult" (National Research Council 1986, p. 90).

The National Research Council experts advocated a cautious approach to the complex issue of population and development. Rapid population growth and large numbers of people are *among* the problems, but not *the* problem contributing to underdevelopment. This more integrated view of population-development linkages sees demographic variables as playing an "accomplice" role in many development problems. Rather than being the root cause of the problem, they magnify the effects of unequal distribution of wealth and political power, poor management and organization, and scarcity or misallocation of resources. On the other side of the coin, slower population growth, in itself, does not guarantee solutions to the problem, but it does make it easier to achieve those solutions. The integrated view stresses that efforts to slow population growth and other development efforts to improve people's health, nutrition, and education; upgrade the status of women; increase productivity; and introduce better management of agriculture are complementary and often mutually reinforcing (Merrick 1986, p. 48).

Competing Views of the Population Problem

The problem of rapid population growth, often regarded as a major stumbling block to economic progress in underdeveloped countries, has brought into sharp focus a number of competing views. The conservative view is epitomized by biologist Garrett Hardin (1974), who proposed what he termed "lifeboat ethics." Metaphorically, each rich country is a lifeboat full of rich people. In the ocean outside each lifeboat float the poor of the world who would like to climb aboard. What should the lifeboat passengers do? In Hardin's view—absolutely nothing. The rich will be materially ruined if they help the poor; complete justice is complete catastrophe.

Barry Commoner (1975), a radical, found Hardin's position intolerable. He argued that in the distant future population numbers may outrun food and other necessary resources. In the short run, poverty, not overpopulation, is the problem. In his view, the demographic transition that allowed European societies in the last two hundred years to go from high birth and high death rates to low birth and low death rates holds the solution to population growth in the Third World. He explained that the demographic transition has not come about in underdeveloped countries because of the poverty imposed by colonialism. Colonialism brought death control in the form of improved medicine and sanitary conditions, but robbed the Third World of the means to achieve industrialization. The affluence produced by industrialization could lead to lower birth rates as it did in Europe. However, being impoverished, the poor have to maintain large families in order to survive.

Lord Ritchie-Calder (1974), a former United Nations advisor, also considered the deliberate discrimination against the poor morally abhorrent. His liberal formulation argues that the population problem arises from lack of birth control knowledge. For Western policymakers and private elites who support family programs for the poor of the world, family planning is considered an essential substitute for structural and institutional change in the world's economy. They believe that population control is essential because rapid population growth increases the potential for social unrest, economic and political instability, mass migration, and possible international conflicts over control of land and resources.

David Harvey (1974), a Marxist geographer, exposed the ideological nature of the population-resources debate. His radical analysis reveals that there are numerous ways of dealing with the population-resources question: (1) we can change our societal goals, (2) we can change our technology and appraisals of natural resources, (3) we can change our material demands, and (4) we can change population growth. Harvey argued that, under capitalism, the least threatening and easiest way to attack the population-resources question is to deal with only one option—reduce population growth—and to ignore the other three possibilities.

SUMMARY

Because people are the most important element in the world economy, it is essential to learn about population distribution, qualities, and dynamics. After considering the variable distribution of populations and their demographic, cultural, and economic characteristics, we examined the processes of population change. The components of population change are migration and natural increase. The principal force affecting world population distribution used to be migration, now it is natural increase.

Although the population growth rate is falling, the world's population is projected to increase for decades to come due to the large momentum built into the vast and youthful population of the Third World. As a result, there is considerable interest in the question of whether and how population growth affects economic growth. We compared and contrasted a number of viewpoints, including conservative and progressive. Some were optimistic; others, pessimistic. Most population experts believe that overpopulation deters growth, depletes natural resources, and destroys the environment. Hence, efforts must be made to slow population growth. Organized fertility-reduction programs, however, must be combined with development strategies that give poor people more control over the processes of social change that affect their lives.

KEY TERMS

birth rate

death rate

demographic transition

labor force

law of diminishing returns

migration

natural increase

neo-Malthusianism

physiological density

population composition

population distribution

population pyramid

"push-and-pull" factors

urban growth

urbanization

unemployment

SUGGESTED READINGS

Birdsall, N. 1980. *Population Growth and Poverty in the Developing World.* Population Bulletin, Vol. 35, No. 5. Washington, DC: Population Reference Bureau.

Jones, H. R. 1981. *Population Geography.* New York: Harper and Row.

Mamdani, M. 1973. *The Myth of Population Control.* New York: Monthly Review Press.

Merrick, T. W. 1986. *World Population in Transition.* Population Bulletin, Vol. 41, No. 1. Washington, DC: Population Reference Bureau.

National Research Council. 1986. *Population Growth: Consequences and Policy Implications.* Washington, DC: National Academy Press.

Newman, J. L., and Matzke, G. E. 1984. *Population: Patterns, Dynamics, and Prospects.* Englewood Cliffs, NJ: Prentice-Hall.

Ogden, P. 1984. *Migration and Geographical Change.* Cambridge, England: Cambridge University Press.

Sauvey, A. 1961. *Fertility and Survival: Population from Malthus to Mao Tse Tung.* New York: Chatto.

Simon, J. L. 1986. *Theory of Population and Economic Growth.* Oxford, England: Basil Blackwell.

Thomas, I. 1980. *Population Growth.* London: Macmillan Education.

4
RESOURCES

OBJECTIVES

☐ To describe the nature, distribution, and limits of the world's resources

☐ To examine the nature and extent of world food problems and to make you aware of the difficulties of solving them

☐ To describe the distribution of strategic minerals and the time spans for their depletion

☐ To consider the causes and consequences of the "energy crisis"

☐ To compare and contrast "growth-oriented" and "balance-oriented" lifestyles

Mining coal: The world's most abundant fossil fuel. (Source: International Labour Office.)

Our prosperity depends on the availability of natural resources and the quality of the environment. Yet economic activities in developed countries, and increasingly in underdeveloped countries, are depleting resources and degrading the environment. How did we get into this situation? What can be done to effectively manage resources and protect the environment?

According to Marxists, the world got into trouble under the capitalist law of accumulation. They argue that mindless exploitation of nature pushes society to the limits of its resource base. Although technological change may roll back resource limitations, capitalist accumulation soon reaches these new limits. But is capitalist resource use bound to be wasteful, polluting, and socially irresponsible? And is the situation any better in socialist economies? In the USSR, there is widespread evidence of oil spills, extinction of fishing grounds, high levels of air pollution, and considerable loss of topsoil. There is also evidence that the battle is being lost to conserve water, soil, and forest resources in socialist Mozambique, Vietnam, and Nicaragua. Marxists counter this evidence by saying that, ideally, socialism has the capacity to make a less wasteful and more socially acceptable resource use possible.

Those who do not endorse a Marxist view may be divided into two broad groups: resource optimists and pessimists. The resource optimists believe that economic growth in a capitalist society can continue indefinitely; they see "no substantial limits . . . either in raw materials or in energy that the price structure, product substitution, anticipated gains in technology and pollution control cannot be expected to solve" (Notestein 1970, p. 20). On the other hand, pessimists assert that there are limits to growth imposed by the finiteness of the earth—by the fact that air, water, minerals, space, and usable energy sources can be exhausted or overloaded. They believe these limits are near and, as evidence, point to existing food, mineral, and energy shortages and to areas now beset by deforestation and erosion. To pessimists, a world with a projected population of 10 billion in the year 2100 is unthinkable. Population and economic growth *ought* to stop.

Some scholars think that academic debate on resources and the environment is counterproductive, evading practical issues that demand our immediate attention. Geographer Thomas Vale (1985) argued that resource and environmental problems do not yield to ideological theories and solutions. For example, the purpose of Marxists in Central America is to create more egalitarian societies, but the achievement of that goal will not save the tropical forests. Continued population growth will require, for food production, the forest land "freed" from destruction by the ouster of foreign interests. Improvements in the diets of people in Central America will also hasten the need for cleared forest land. Saving the forest environment is only possible if population growth ceases.

Vale recommends that we keep our purposes in mind and try to understand how to achieve our ends. If our purpose is to create a habitable world for generations to follow, how can we redirect present and future output to serve that end? One solution is to transform our present "growth-oriented" lifestyle, which is based on a goal of ever-increasing growth, to a "balance-oriented" lifestyle designed for harmony and endurance. A balance-oriented lifestyle would include an equitable and modest use of resources, a production system compatible with the environment, and small-scale technology. The aim of a balance-oriented world economy is maximum human well-being with a minimum of material consumption. Growth occurs, but only growth that truly benefits people. But what societies, rich or poor, are willing to dismantle their existing systems of production to accept a lifestyle that seeks satisfaction more in quality and equality than in quantity and inequality? Are people who are programmed for maximum consumption by a value system constantly reinforced through advertising willing to change their ways of thinking and behaving.

This chapter, which discusses growth-oriented versus balance-oriented philosophies of resource use, deals with the complex components of the population-resources issue. Have population and economic growth rates been outstripping supplies of food, minerals, and energy? What is likely to happen to the rate of demand of food, minerals, and energy? What is likely to happen to the rate of demand for resources in the future? Could a stable population of 10 billion be sustained indefinitely at a reasonable standard of living utilizing currently known technology? These are the salient questions with which this chapter is concerned.

RESOURCES AND POPULATION

Popular perception appreciates the need to reduce population growth, but overlooks the need to limit economic growth which massively exploits resources. A maximum-growth economy assumes a world that can tolerate rampant waste, unlimited pollution, and indestructible ecosystems.

The developed world has suffered from a view of limitless resources; yet, its affluent way of life is threatened in a world economy under great stress.

The earth is our only suitable habitat. (Source: NASA/U.S. Geological Survey EROS Data Center, Sioux Falls, South Dakota.)

The industrial West is liquidating the resources on which it was built. Underdeveloped countries are aggravating the situation. Their growing populations put increasing pressures on resources and the environment. And their governments aspire to affluence through Western-style urban industrialization. But the production technology and patterns of consumption in the developed countries depend on the intensive use of energy resources. Poor countries do not have the means for running the high-energy systems that are manifest in the West.

Even by conservative estimates, a middle-class basket of goods requires six times as much in resources as a basket of essential or basic goods. The expansion of gross national product through the production of middle-class baskets means that only a small minority of people in poor countries would enjoy the benefits of economic growth. There are resource constraints that prevent the large-scale production of middle-class goods for swelling numbers of people in underdeveloped countries.

However, measures of material well-being (e.g., per capita incomes, calories consumed, shelter and clothing, life expectancy) show that people in many countries are better off today than their parents or grandparents. Consider per capita income growth rates between 1960 and 1982 (Figure 4.1). Virtually every country recorded some improvement in per capita income. The lowest growth rates occurred among the poorest Third World countries. The highest growth rates occurred not in First World countries, but among the wealthiest Third World countries. The largest increases in per capita income occurred in Brazil and in newly industrializing countries on the western margins of the Pacific.

But there are problems with this optimistic assessment. These improvements are *averages;* they say nothing about the *distribution* of material well-being. In addition, the gap between rich and poor countries widened during the period. In 1960, per capita income in Pakistan was $104, whereas that in the United States was $5,484. By 1982, even though Pakistan's per capita income had grown more rapidly than that of the United States in the interim (2.8 versus 2.2 percent), the levels were $380 and $13,160—a gap between the two countries over $7,000 greater than in 1960. The growing gap in per capita income between developed and underdeveloped countries is due in part to the more rapid population growth in underdeveloped countries, which reduces the benefits of economic growth.

Another difficulty is that the world may be achieving improvements in material well-being at the expense of future generations. This would be the case if economic growth were using up the world's re-

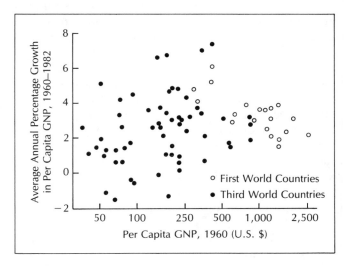

FIGURE 4.1

Relationship between per capita GNP, 1960 and average annual percentage growth in per capita GNP, 1960–1982. (Source: Compiled from World Bank, 1971, 1984.)

source base or environmental carrying capacity faster than new discoveries and technology could expand them.

Carrying Capacity and Overpopulation

Population growth and increasing use of resources in traditional ways cannot continue indefinitely. If present trends of population growth and resource depletion continue, the world could eventually be brought into a stationary state known as carrying capacity. *Carrying capacity* refers to the population that can be supported by available resources. A population decline occurs when population outstrips resources available for sustaining life. Decline may result from overpopulation relative to the food supply or to the rate of consumption of energy and resources.

The immediacy of the population-resources problem is much debated. Pessimists believe that the world will enter a stationary state. They point to the food crisis and famine in parts of Ethiopia and adjacent countries in 1984 as a result of overpopulation. On the other hand, optimists believe in the saving grace of modern technology. Technological advances have increased agricultural yields; they have enabled us to produce more electric power. In the last two hundred years, the world's carrying capacity has been raised, and future technical innovations hold the promise of raising carrying capacity still further. Modern technologies use fewer resources and allow fewer wastes per unit of product than old ones, and they will even solve pollution problems.

Economist Ernest Schumacher (1973) sounds a note of caution. In his view, a completely technical solution to the population-resources problem may never be realized. Technologies may be unable to cope with the critical matter of supplying growing populations with raw materials for existence in light of the *second law of thermodynamics*. This law holds that the amount of energy in the universe is fixed, but the amount of work that can be derived from that energy is irreversibly diminished. For example, once gasoline is burned in the engine of an automobile, its value as a source of useful energy is gone forever.

The answer to the population-resources problem also depends on the standard of living deemed acceptable. To give people an essential basket of goods instead of a middle-class basket of goods would roll back resource limitations. The establishment of a basic-goods economy depends on our capacity to develop alternatives to the high-energy, material-intensive production technologies characteristic of the industrial West. Already there are outlines of a new theory of productive resources based on the conservation of energy, materials, and capital that is suited to the needs of a basic-goods economy. Some of the main ideas are (1) the adoption of a sun-based organic agriculture to replace energy-intensive chemical agriculture; (2) the conservation of energy through the harvesting of renewable sources of energy; (3) the use of appropriate or small-scale technology, labor-intensive methods of production, and local raw materials; and (4) the decentralization of production in order to increase local self-reliance and minimize the transport of materials. These productive forces would minimize the disruption of ecosystems and engage the unemployed in useful, productive work. Current trends indicate that economies engaging people in useful labor that produces essential goods for human consumption face neither unemployment nor overpopulation. The availability of secure supplies of basic goods will also provide the best motivation for reducing family size. Most elites in Third World countries appear unwilling, however, to place top priority on the production and distribution of goods to satisfy basic human needs.

Optimum Population and the Quality of Life

The best possible world would be one with an optimum population that permits progressive improvements in human well-being. But what is "optimum" for one country may not be for another. Furthermore, governments of rich industrial countries set the terms for what is optimal or suboptimal in relation to resources. And yet it is only through the operation of the world economy that wealthy countries can appropriate the resources necessary to support the large numbers of people who enjoy middle-class lifestyles.

In simple terms, human well-being is a function of the relationship between population and the ability to make efficient use of resources. If we assume fixed resources and population growth in a country, then average well-being diminishes as resources are consumed. In reality, the situation is much more complex. Other factors are involved: some make the situation better; others make it worse. For example, improved extraction techniques, recycling, and finding substitutes for resources decrease the rate of resource depletion, but increasing the per capita rate of consumption and misuse of technology can accelerate resource depletion and increase pollution.

TYPES OF RESOURCES AND THEIR LIMITS

All economic development comes about through human labor and skills. But in order to produce goods and services we need to obtain natural resources. What are natural resources and what are their limits?

Resources and Reserves

Resources have meaning only in terms of technical and cultural appraisals of nature and must be defined with reference to a particular level of development. *Resources*, designated by the entire box in Figure 4.2, include all the materials of the environment that may some day be used under specified technological and socioeconomic conditions. Because these conditions are always subject to change, we can expect our determinations of what is useful to change also. For example, oil bubbling to the surface in ancient Persia was a nuisance, but it is a vital source of energy and export earnings to modern Iranians. Although it is hard to imagine, iron ore may eventually cease to be useful when replaced by some other material.

At the other end of the extreme are reserves, designated by the upper left-hand box in Figure 4.2. *Reserves* are quantities of resources that are known and available for economic exploitation with current technologies and at current prices. A financial analogy clarifies the distinction between reserves and resources. Reserves are liquid assets, like money in a checking account, and resources are frozen assets or

future income that cannot be used for this month's car payments.

When current reserves begin to be depleted, the search for additional reserves is intensified. Estimates of reserves are also affected by changes in prices and technology. If prices increase or costs of mining decrease, it becomes feasible to mine lower grade ores; consequently, the quantities available for current exploitation must be reassessed. *Prospective reserves* represent estimates of the quantities likely to be added to reserves because of the discoveries and changes in prices and technologies projected to occur within a specified period—say fifty years.

Renewable and Nonrenewable Resources

Natural resources may be classified in various ways, but the primary distinction made is between nonrenewable and renewable resources. *Nonrenewable resources* consist of finite masses of material, such as fossil fuels and metals, which cannot be used without depletion. They are, for all practical purposes, fixed in amount. This is because they form very slowly over time. Consequently, their rate of use is very important. Large populations with high per capita consumption of goods deplete these resources fastest.

Some nonrenewable resources are completely altered or destroyed by use. Petroleum is an example. Others, such as iron, are available for recycling. Recycling possibilities expand the limits on the sustainable use of a nonrenewable resource. At present, these limits are very low in relation to current mineral extraction.

Renewable resources are those resources capable of yielding output indefinitely without impairing their productivity. They include soil, vegetation, air, and water. Renewal is not automatic, however. Renewable resources can be depleted; they can be permanently reduced by misuse. Productive fishing grounds can be destroyed by exploitation. Fertile top soil, destroyed by erosion, can be difficult to restore and impossible to replace. The future of agricultural land is guaranteed only when production does not exceed its maximum sustainable yield. The term *maximum sustainable yield* means maximum production consistent with maintaining future productivity of a renewable resource.

The misuse of resources is often described in terms of the "tragedy of the commons" (Hardin 1968). This metaphor refers to the way public resources are ruined by the isolated actions of individuals. We appear to be unwilling to use a minimum share of a resource. People who fish, when there is no rule of

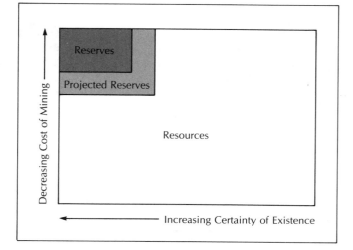

FIGURE 4.2
Classification of resources.

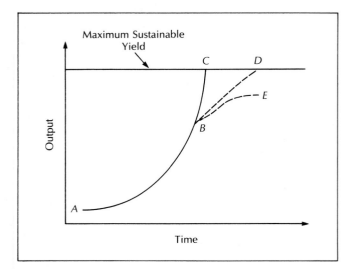

FIGURE 4.3
Limits to growth of a renewable resource. (Source: Based on Lecomber, 1975, p. 38.)

Limits of Natural Resources

The limitations natural resources place on growth can be illustrated with two simple models: one, for a renewable resource; the other for a nonrenewable resource.

Renewable Resource Let us assume that (1) a renewable resource such as soil produces a single consumer good, food; (2) maximum sustainable yield per hectare is fixed; and (3) cultivated land and food production grow exponentially. Eventually no more arable land can be freed for cultivation without destroying all of the surrounding forest environment, so that the economy reaches point C (Figure 4.3). The best strategy would be to stop growth at C and maintain maximum sustainable yield thereafter, but this is difficult to accomplish in practice. The physical limits are often reached quickly. For example, when production increases at an annual rate of 4 percent per annum, the doubling time is only about eighteen years. Arable land soon becomes a scarce factor of production. Furthermore, farmers at C, accustomed to increasingly high outputs, will take whatever steps they feel necessary to maintain the improvement. So they clear additional forest land and overcrop existing arable land, ruining the precious soil. To avoid this outcome, a better strategy would be to slow growth at say, B, and follow path *ABD* or, more cautiously, path *ABE*.

capture law, are likely to try to catch as many fish as they can, reasoning that if they don't, others will. Similarly, dumping waste and pollutants on public waters and land or into the air is the cheapest way to dispose of worthless products. There is an apparent unwillingness to dispose of these materials by more expensive means unless mandated by law.

FIGURE 4.4
Limits to growth of a nonrenewable resource. (Source: Based on Lecomber, 1975, p. 39.)

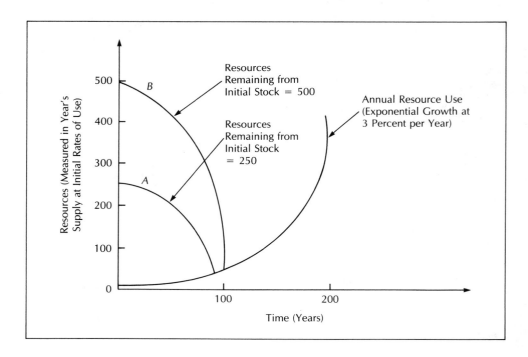

Nonrenewable Resource Let us assume that our nonrenewable resource is coal, and that population and resource productivity are fixed. Coal supplies are soon exhausted (Figure 4.4). At 3 percent annual growth in mining activity, the depletion time for a 250 years' supply of coal is eighty years (curve *A*). Even if coal supplies are doubled, the depletion time is postponed only twenty-five years (curve *B*).

These two models demonstrate that resources, both renewable and nonrenewable, are exhaustible. However, the models project resource depletion on the assumption that resource productivity is fixed. We know, however, that resource productivity can be expanded by technical progress or by substitution of other resources.

FOOD RESOURCES

People need access to enough food at all times for an active and healthy life. Food security is also important because good nutrition is an investment in the productivity of a country's population. Although there are enough food resources to provide for all, there is

no food security for hundreds of millions of people. Somewhere between 340 and 730 million people (excluding China whose government refuses to release much demographic information) suffer from chronic *malnutrition* (lack of protein, vitamins, and essential nutrients), and an even larger number suffer from *undernutrition* (lack of calories). These people are concentrated in the underdeveloped world (Figure 4.5), but they are increasingly apparent in the West.

Nutritional Quality of Life

The gulf between the well fed and the hungry is vast. Average daily calorie consumption is 3,300 in developed countries and 2,100 in underdeveloped countries. The largest number of calories available is in Ireland and the lowest number available is in Ghana (Table 4.1). A similar pattern emerges in considering "calorie requirement satisfaction." This measure is defined as the calories needed per day to sustain a person at normal levels of activity and health. People in Ghana eat only 68 percent of what they need compared to Ireland's 162 percent. But these are average figures. There are people on the breadline in

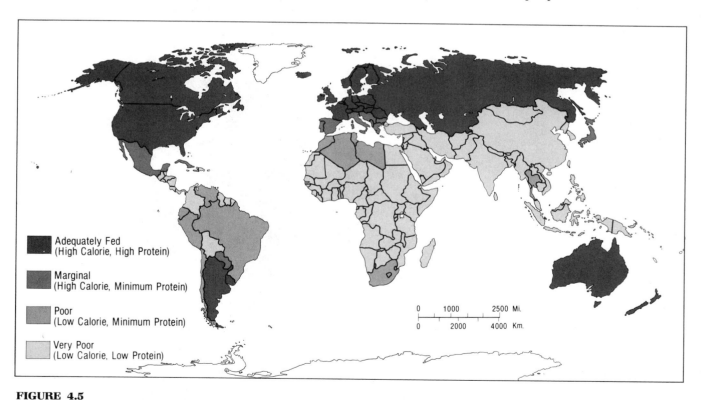

FIGURE 4.5
Comparative nutritional quality of life. (Source: U.N. Food and Agriculture Organization, 1983.)

TABLE 4.1
Calorie intake and calorie requirement satisfaction, 1983.

	Highest Calorie Intake			Lowest Calorie Intake	
Country	Calorie Intake per Person per Day	Percentage of Requirements	Country	Calorie Intake per Person per Day	Percentage of Requirements
Ireland	4,054	162	Ghana	1,573	68
Denmark	4,023	150	Chad	1,620	68
East Germany	3,787	145	Mali	1,731	74
Belgium	3,743	142	Kampuchea	1,792	81
Bulgaria	3,711	148	Uganda	1,807	78
Yugoslavia	3,642	143	Mozambique	1,844	79
United States	3,616	137	Burkina Faso	1,879	79
Czechoslovakia	3,613	146	Haiti	1,903	84
UA Emirates	3,591	N.A.	Bangladesh	1,922	83
Libya	3,581	152	Guinea	1,987	86

SOURCE: World Bank, 1985.

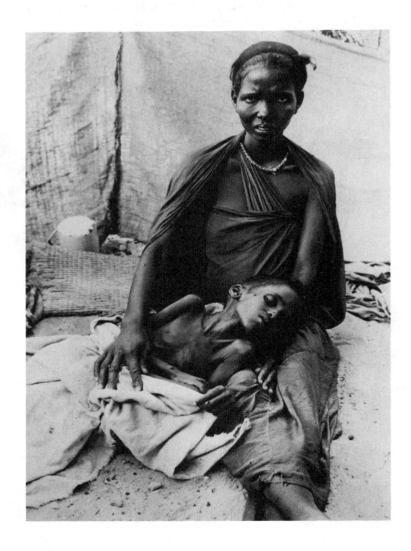

This African mother can do little to save her child's life. He is suffering the complications of undernutrition and malnutrition. (Source: UNICEF/WHO photo by B. Campbell.)

Ireland and there are those who have enough to eat in Ghana. Averages mask extremes of undernourishment and overconsumption.

Even with a high calorie satisfaction, people may not have an adequate intake of protein, fat, vitamins, and other essential nutrients. The most important measure in assessing nutritional standards is the daily per capita availability of calories, protein, fat, calcium, and other nutrients. In Latin America, the best-fed populations live in Argentina and Uruguay; the worst-fed live in Haiti and Bolivia (Table 4.2)

Data for assessing the nutritional quality of life based on national averages conceal wide regional differences in the quality and content of the diet.

TABLE 4.2
Latin America: Comparative nutritional quality of life. (national averages).

Country	Rating
Argentina	10.00
Uruguay	8.80
Barbados	8.50
Paraguay	7.80
Cuba	7.20
Mexico	7.20
Trinidad-Tobago	7.20
Venezuela	6.60
Chile	6.20
Costa Rica	6.20
Jamaica	6.20
Brazil	5.00
Nicaragua	4.80
Guyana	4.60
Colombia	4.20
Panama	4.20
Dominican Republic	3.80
Ecuador	3.60
El Salvador	3.20
Peru	3.20
Honduras	3.00
Guatemala	2.80
Bolivia	2.60
Haiti	1.20

NOTE: The scale is based on selected criteria, including available daily per capita calories, grams of protein and fat, milligrams of calcium, and calories as a percentage of minimum requirements. Using the same criteria, the rating is 12.09 for the United States and 3.67 for the entire world.

SOURCE: Augelli, 1985, p. 276.

Third World farmers, such as these in Indonesia, depend on high rice yields. Rice is the staple food for more than half of the world's population. While rice and other grains supply energy and some protein, people must supplement grains with fruits, nuts, vegetables, dairy products, fish, and meat in order to remain healthy. (Source: World Bank.)

People of the Pampas in Argentina have a better diet that those who live in southern Patagonia. In Brazil, people in the northeast have a far less nutritious diet than those who live in the states of São Paulo and Rio de Janeiro.

The sharpest nutritional differences, however, are not from country to country, or from one region to another within countries. They are between the rich and the poor. The wretched of the earth carry the major burden of hunger.

Causes of the Food Problem

Hunger in the Third World is often attributed to the low productivity of the tropical soils, the frequency of droughts, and the impact of storms such as hurricanes. Although the environment does have a bearing on the food problem, it has limited significance compared to the role of socioeconomic conditions. Hunger is overwhelmingly a problem attributable to human endeavor.

Population and Urbanization   Population growth is among the causes of the food problem. But at the global level, there is no food shortage. Food production is increasing faster than population growth. Even by the end of the twentieth century, there should be enough food to feed the projected 6 billion people if productivity continues to increase at current rates. Beyond the year 2000, the situation is more uncertain. Much will depend on dietary standards, but also on the possibilities for unfavorable climatic change and loss of agricultural capacity through such factors as soil erosion. Breakthroughs in food production technology may be able to compensate for these types of adverse conditions, should they occur.

The promising global food situation is not reflected at the scale of continents and countries. Between 1960 and 1980, food production increased at similar rates in developed and underdeveloped countries. Yet the increase was cancelled in the underdeveloped world where rapid population growth reduced food production per capita (Table 4.3). Since that time, the ability of the Third World to feed itself has declined.

The food and hunger problem is most severe in sub-Saharan Africa. Food production is not keeping pace with population growth (Figure 4.6). During the 1970s, the annual gain in food production fell to about 1.3 percent, less than one-half the population growth rate of 2.7 percent. And between 1981 and 1983, per capita food production plunged 14 percent.

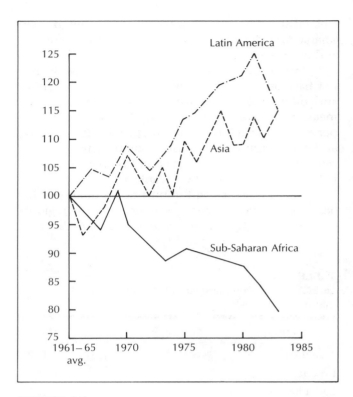

FIGURE 4.6
Index of food production per capita (percentage of 1961–1965 average). (Source: Based on World Bank, 1984.)

Sub-Saharan Africa went from near food self-sufficiency in 1970 to heavy food dependence by the mid-1980s. In 1984, imports provided 20 percent of the region's cereal requirement. Despite food imports, a high proportion of the population is chronically malnourished. Declining per capita food production combined with chronic malnutrition means that when drought strikes, as it did in the early 1970s and

TABLE 4.3
Indices of food production per capita, 1960–1984.

Region	1960	1970	1980	1984
World	92	97	99	103
Developed countries	91	94	103	107
Centrally planned countries	81	95	98	108
Underdeveloped countries	91	97	100	102
East Asia	83	89	102	112
South Asia	95	101	96	103
Latin America	83	94	105	103
Middle East	88	92	95	94
Africa	113	106	99	93

NOTE: 1976–1978 = 100.

SOURCE: U.S. Department of Agriculture, 1985, p. 54.

again in the 1980s, the result can be severe physical and mental damage—even starvation. In the mid-1980s Chad, Ethiopia, Mali, Mauritania, Mozambique, and Niger confronted famine. Food supplies were also inadequate in Angola, Botswana, Burkina Faso, Burundi, Kenya, Lesotho, Rwanda, Senegal, Somalia, Sudan, Tanzania, Zambia, and Zimbabwe.

The pace of Third World urbanization has also contributed to the food problem. In recent decades, millions and millions of people who previously lived in rural areas and produced some food have relocated in the urban areas where they must buy food. As a result of urbanization there is a higher demand for food in the face of a lower supply. This problem has contributed to rising food costs, inflation, and indebtedness.

Maldistribution The problem of food distribution has three components. First, there is the problem of moving food from one area or region to another. Although transport systems in underdeveloped countries lack the speed and efficiency of those in developed countries, they are not serious impediments to the movement of commodities under normal circumstances. Food can reach stores in the most isolated regions just as easily as batteries and matches. The problem arises either when massive quantities of emergency food aid must be transported quickly or when the distribution of food is disrupted by political and military conflict. For example, food shortages in southern Africa, which trace to the 1981–1983 drought, have been exacerbated by the military activities of the guerrillas of the Mozambican National Resistance movement. The guerrillas destroyed key transport systems, preventing supplies of seeds and fertilizers from reaching local farmers and making it impossible for food-surplus countries such as Zimbabwe and Malawi to ship food to deficit regions.

Second, serious disruptions in food supply in the Third World are traceable to problems of marketing and storage. Food is sometimes hoarded by merchants until prices rise and then sold for a larger profit. Also, much food in the tropics is lost due to poor storage facilities. In the 1970s, up to 30 percent of Tanzania's harvested crops were destroyed in storage by vermin. Improvements in storage facilities would provide people, especially in the villages, with security against disasters, including a breakdown of communications.

A third aspect of the distribution problem is the inequitable allocation of food. Only a few regions have large grain surpluses. They are Australia, Western Europe, and North America. The grain belt of North America is the global breadbasket. With about 6 percent of the world's population—and approaching zero population growth—Canada and the United States account for 25 percent of all grain output. But food grain is not always given when it is most needed. Food aid shipments and fluctuating grain prices are intimately related. Thus, U.S. food aid was low around 1973, a time of major famine in the Sahel region of Africa, because cereal prices were at a peak. To remedy the grain gluts of previous years, the U.S. government paid farmers $3 billion to take 50 million hectares out of production. The induced grain shortage was made even greater by sales of wheat to the USSR. Food, unavailable to feed the hungry of Africa, was used to feed cattle to increase the supply of meat in the USSR.

Cooperation between the "haves" and "have nots" is possible, however, and has been demonstrated. During the Ethiopian famine of 1986, a privately organized group of socially conscious Westerners rallied support to provide relief to the starving of the Sahel. In this instance, grain surpluses were successfully converted to life-saving relief supplies.

Poverty The inequitable allocation of food is related to poverty, the major cause of the hunger problem. Food goes to markets that can afford it, not to where it is needed most. Where food is produced is immaterial as long as costs are minimized and a profitable sale can be made. As one U.S. rancher commented on the costs of production, "Here's what it boils down to—$95 per cow per year in Montana, $25 in Costa Rica" (Lappé and Collins 1977, p. 203). Thus, in the midst of hunger, beef is exported for profit. If Americans are prepared to pay more for meat than many Costa Ricans, then it is not surprising that the market fails to include the poor.

Agriculture Closely associated with poverty as a cause of hunger in the Third World is the structure of agriculture, including land ownership. Land is frequently concentrated in a few hands. In Bangladesh, less than 10 percent of rural households own over one-half of the country's cultivable land. Sixty percent of Bangladesh's rural families own less than 2 percent. In fact, many of them own no land at all. They are landless laborers who depend upon wages for their livelihoods. But without land, there is often no food.

Most food for domestic consumption is produced by small farmers who often have yields equal to, or higher than, those of large farmers. Large landowners underutilize land, labor, and water. Small farmers till the soil with their hands and know their work determines what they will eat. The incentive for large landowners is not as great, and the incentive for their wage laborers is often minimal.

Third World agriculture has expanded in recent decades. The expansion is in the export sector, not in the domestic food-producing sector, and it is often the result of deliberate policy. Governments and private elites have opted for modernization through the promotion of export-oriented agriculture. The assumption is that capital-intensive agriculture based on modern technology, management, and know-how spurs development. The result is the growth of an agricultural economy based on profitable export products and the neglect of those aspects of farming that have to do with producing food for local populations.

Increasing Food Production

Hunger is a problem that affects only the poor—those who lack the opportunity to participate in the econ-

omy in a way that allows them to support themselves. Yet hunger is usually considered a problem of inadequate food production. According to this view, growing more food will end hunger. Food supplies can be increased (1) by expanding the amount of land under cultivation, and (2) by increasing yields per unit of land.

Expanding the Cultivated Area   The world's potential available land for cultivation is estimated to be twice the present cultivated area. Vast reserves are theoretically available in Africa, South America, and Australia, and smaller reserves in North America and in the USSR (Figure 4.7). But estimates of unused cultivable land are misleading. Unused cultivable land is unevenly distributed and rarely occurs where the need for it is greatest. Land suitable for cultivation at a reasonable cost and with present technology is easier to find in temperate areas than in the tropics, where fragile soils and aridity are limiting factors.

FIGURE 4.7
Continents sized in proportion to the area of their potentially arable land. The silhouette map within each outline shows how much of that potentially arable land is cultivated.

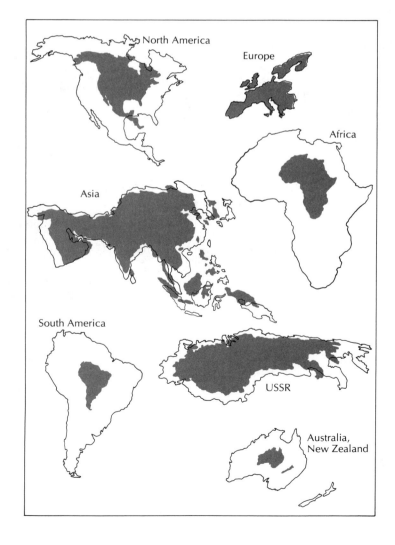

TABLE 4.4

Population-supporting capacity of sub-Saharan Africa countries with all cultivable land under food groups, 1975 and 2000.

1975 Subsistence Level Farming			2000 Subsistence Level Farming			2000 Intermediate Level Farming		
Unable to support even 1975 population on a sustained basis	Able to support 1–5 times 1975 population	Able to support more than 5 times 1975 population	Unable to support 2000 population on a sustained basis	Able to support 1–5 times 2000 population	Able to support more than 5 times 2000 population	Unable to support 2000 population on a sustained basis	Able to support 1–5 times 2000 population	Able to support more than 5 times 2000 population
Botswana	Benin	Angola	Benin	Angola	Cameroon	Burundi	Benin	Angola
Burundi	Burkina Faso	Cameroon	Botswana	Chad	Central African Republic	Kenya	Botswana	Cameroon
Ethiopia	Chad	Central African Republic	Burkina Faso	Gambia	Congo	Lesotho	Burkina Faso	Central African Republic
Kenya	Gambia	Congo	Burundi	Guinea	Equatorial Guinea	Mauritania	Ethiopia	Chad
Lesotho	Ghana	Equatorial Guinea	Ethiopia	Guinea-Bissau	Gabon	Niger	Gambia	Congo
Malawi	Guinea	Gabon	Ghana	Ivory Coast	Zambia	Rwanda	Ghana	Equatorial Guinea
Mauritania	Guinea-Bissau	Ivory Coast	Kenya	Liberia		Somalia	Malawi	Gabon
Namibia	Mali	Liberia	Lesotho	Madagascar			Mali	Guinea
Niger	Mozambique	Madagascar	Malawi	Mozambique			Namibia	Guinea-Bissau
Nigeria	Sierra Leone	Zaire	Mali	Sudan			Nigeria	Ivory Coast
Rwanda	Sudan	Zambia	Mauritania	Tanzania			Senegal	Liberia
Senegal	Swaziland		Namibia	Zaire			Sierra Leone	Madagascar
Somalia	Tanzania		Niger	Zimbabwe			Swaziland	Mozambique
Uganda	Togo		Nigeria				Tanzania	Sudan
	Zimbabwe		Rwanda				Togo	Zaire
			Senegal				Uganda	Zambia
			Sierra Leone					Zimbabwe
			Somalia					
			Swaziland					
			Togo					
			Uganda					

SOURCE: Goliber, 1985, p. 18.

The uneven distribution of cultivable land is most evident in sub-Saharan Africa. Although the region has plenty of land to feed the current population and many more people, there exist large areas that are insufficiently fertile to feed the people living on them (U.N. Food and Agriculture Organization 1983). Fourteen countries had 1975 populations that were too large in relation to their cultivable land to achieve and maintain food self-sufficiency, assuming subsistence farming methods (Table 4.4). These countries account for one-third of sub-Saharan Africa's land area and about one-half of its population. Twenty-one countries will be unable to support their populations by the year 2000 if technology remains unchanged. Seven of these countries—Burundi, Kenya, Lesotho, Mauritania, Niger, Rwanda, and Somalia—will be unable to achieve food self-sufficiency by the year 2000 with the continuing rapid growth of their populations, even if farming methods were to advance to the "intermediate levels" now existing on commercial farms in Asia and Latin America, where fertilizers and pesticides, improved seed varieties, and simple conservation techniques are being used. On the other hand, eleven countries have plenty of underused land and could support populations at

least five times their 1975 size, even at subsistence farming levels.

About half of the world's potentially arable land lies within the tropics, especially in the rain forests of the Congo and Amazon basins. Growing crops on cleared forest land has not proved very successful, however. Once the trees are chopped down, the thin soils are vulnerable to rain and soon lose their nutrients. Farmers have only a few seasons to reap light yields before the soil is gone. They are left with rock, clay, or hardpan (acidic subsoil that is difficult to work).

Most of the remaining land reserves exist in areas of excessive dryness. This land must be irrigated if it is to become productive, but irrigation schemes are expensive to construct and administer. Moreover, irrigated agriculture is possible only in a small proportion of the world's dry lands. It is restricted to areas near rivers, such as the Nile, that flow through deserts and to areas where abundant ground water is available.

The expansion of agriculture into rain forest and desert environments contributes to *deforestation* and *desertification*. Since World War II, about one-half of the world's rain forests in Africa, Asia, and Latin

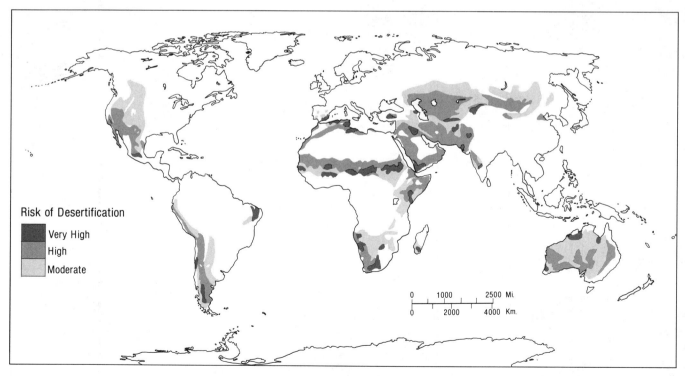

FIGURE 4.8
Areas at risk of desertification. (Source: Based on International Institute for Environment and Development and World Resources Institute, 1987, p. 71.)

America have disappeared. If destruction continues at the current pace, one-half of what is left will have gone by the end of the twentieth century. Desertification—the growth of human-made deserts—threatens about one-third of the world's land surface and the livelihood of nearly a billion people. Many of the world's major rangelands are at risk (Figure 4.8). The main factor responsible for desertification is overgrazing, but deforestation (particularly the cutting of fuelwood), overcultivation of marginal soils, and salinization caused by poorly managed irrigation systems are also important influences. Deforestation and desertification are destroying the land resources on which the development of many Third World countries depend.

Raising the Productivity of Existing Cropland   The quickest way to increase food supply is to raise the productivity of land under cultivation. Remarkable

increases in agricultural yields have been achieved in developed countries through the widespread adoption of new technologies. Corn yields in the United States are a good illustration. Yields expanded rapidly with the introduction of hybrid varieties, herbicides, and fertilizers. Much of the increase in yields came through successive improvements in hybrids. Just how long these yields will go on increasing will depend on the future development of hybrids.

The Western approach for increasing land productivity in developed countries has been proposed for underdeveloped countries. This technology-package approach to farming in the underdeveloped world is known as the *Green Revolution*, in which new high-yielding varieties of wheat, rice, and corn are developed through modern plant genetics.

The Green Revolution began in 1943 when four American scientists, financed by the Rockefeller Foundation, introduced new wheat and maize seeds on

The Kenyan rangelands on which these herders' cattle graze are in jeopardy. With growing grazing pressures, more than 60 percent of the world's rangelands and at least 80 percent of African, Asian, and Middle Eastern rangelands are now moderately to severely desertified. About sixty-five million hectares of once productive land in Africa have become desert over the last fifty years. (Source: World Bank.)

mainly large farms in the Sonora District of Mexico. It was not very long before crop yields began to increase. Following this triumph, the Rockefeller Foundation teamed up with the Ford Foundation to introduce "miracle" rice to selected parts of Asia, such as the Philippines.

The Green Revolution is a major scientific achievement, but it is not a panacea. It depends on new seeds, fertilizers, pesticides, and herbicides produced and controlled by multinationals such as Fisons, Imperial Chemical Industries, and Standard Oil. It depends on large-scale, one-crop farming which is ecologically unstable because of its susceptibility to pestilence. It depends on controlled water supplies, which have increased the incidence of malaria, schistosomiasis, and other human diseases. It is restricted primarily to wheat, rice, and corn hybrids that are strictly low-grade protein foods. It is confined mainly to a group of eighteen heavily populated countries that extend across the subtropical part of the world from Korea in the east to Mexico in the West (Figure 4.9). It is also benefiting countries that include 18 percent of the world's land surface and that are home to 56 percent of the world's population.

Politically, the Green Revolution promises more than it can deliver. Its sociopolitical application has been largely unsatisfactory. Even in areas where the Green Revolution has been technologically successful, it has not always benefited large numbers of hungry people without the means to buy the newly produced food. In the Punjab, India, for example, it has benefited mainly the farmers who were already wealthy enough to adopt a complex integrated package of technical inputs and management practices. Farmers make bigger profits from the Green Revolution when they purchase additional land and mechanize their operations. Some effects of labor-displacing machinery and the purchase of additional land by rich farmers include agricultural unemployment, increased landlessness, rural-to-urban migration, and increased malnutrition for the unemployed who are unable to purchase the food produced by the technology of the Green Revolution.

Where does the food produced by the new technology go? In Pakistan, much hybrid maize is processed into corn sweetener for soft drinks purchased by urban middle- and upper-income groups. In Colombia, large quantities of rice go to feedlots and breweries. In Mexico, more basic grains are consumed by animals than by 20 million peasants. In Central America, export fruits and vegetables that have been turned back from the United States are fed

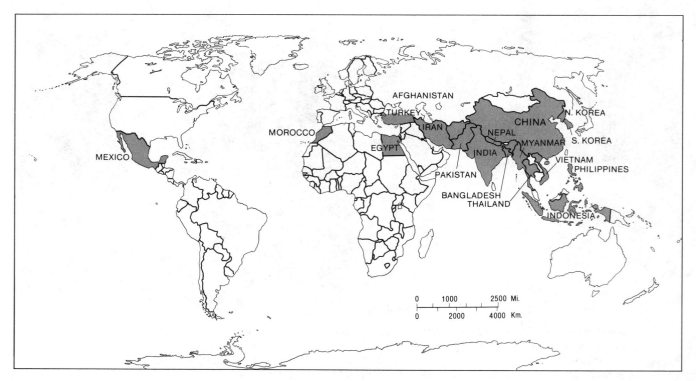

FIGURE 4.9
The chief benefiting countries of the Green Revolution. (Source: Huke, 1985, p. 248.)

to livestock or dumped instead of being given to local people too poor to buy anything (Lappé and Collins 1976, p. 2).

The Green Revolution is not winning its battle against hunger because it focuses on food production. The world food problem is not so much one of food production, but of food demand in the economic sense. Unfortunately, the Green Revolution does nothing to increase the ability of the poor to buy food.

We have portrayed the Green Revolution as a poisoned gift. It has helped to create a world of more and larger commercial farms alongside fewer and smaller peasant plots. But given a different structure of landholdings and the use of appropriately intermediate technology, the Green Revolution could help underdeveloped countries along the road toward agricultural self-sufficiency and the elimination of hunger. *Intermediate technology* is a term that means low-cost, small-scale technologies "intermediate" between primitive stick-farming methods and complex agroindustrial technical packages.

A Solution to the World Food Supply Situation

What is to be done about the world food problem? As we have emphasized, there is a widely shared belief that people are hungry because of insufficient food production. Thus, we are often treated to the "new release" approach to hunger. We learn of breakthroughs—protein from petroleum, harvests of kelp, extracts from alfalfa—to expand food supply. We are told that strains on the food-producing capacity of the world would be lessened if the affluent one-third of humankind did not consume two-thirds of the world's total food supply. We are even reminded that the food crisis would be lessened if Americans consumed one less hamburger a week.

But the fact is that food production is increasing faster than population, and still there are more hungry people than ever before. Why should this be so? It could be that the production focus is correct, but soaring numbers of people simply overrun even these dramatic production gains. Or it could be that the diagnosis is incorrect—scarcity is not the cause of hunger, and production increases, no matter how great, can never solve the problem.

The simple facts of world grain production make it clear that the overpopulation/scarcity diagnosis is actually incorrect. Present world grain production could more than adequately feed every person on earth. Even during the "scarcity" years, 1972 to 1973, there was 9 percent more grain per person than in "ample" 1960. Inadequate production is clearly not the problem.

Ironically, the focus on increased production has actually compounded the problem of hunger by transforming agricultural progress into a narrow technical pursuit instead of the sweeping social task of releasing vast, untapped human resources (Lappé and Collins 1976, p. 2). We need to look to the policies of governments in underdeveloped countries to understand why people are hungry even when there is enough food produced to adequately feed everyone. These policies influence the access to knowledge and the availability of credit to small farmers, the profitability of growing enough to sell a surplus, and the efficiency of marketing and distributing food on a broad scale.

The fact is that small, carefully farmed plots are more productive per unit area than large estates. They use fewer costly inputs (Figure. 4.10). Yet, despite considerable evidence from around the world, Third World government production programs pass over small farmers. They rationalize that working with bigger production units is a faster road to increased productivity.

FIGURE 4.10
Small farm efficiency: India and Taiwan.

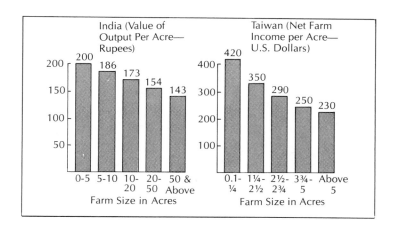

Alternatives for Solving the World Food Problem

Many proposals have been advanced for dealing with world hunger and malnutrition. The two alternatives that follow are based on sharply contrasting views of what lies at the heart of the problem.

TRIAGE

William and Paul Paddock's book, *Time of Famines*, argues for triage as an inevitable and acceptable solution to the world food problem. Triage is a variant of "lifeboat ethics," the notion popularized by Garrett Hardin.

> "Triage" is a term used in military medicine. It is defined as the assigning of priority of treatment to the wounded brought to a battlefield hospital in a time of mass casualties and limited medical facilities. The wounded are divided on the basis of three classifications: (1) Those so seriously wounded they cannot survive regardless of the treatment given them; call these the "can't-be-saved." (2) Those who can survive without treatment regardless of the pain they may be suffering; call these the "walking wounded." (3) Those who can be saved by immediate medical care. (Paddock and Paddock, 1976:206)

Applying this system to the food problem, Paddock and Paddock argued that limited stocks of American foods should not be made available to nations that form the "can't-be-saved" group. Food aid also should not go to the "walking wounded" nations because they have the necessary agricultural resources or foreign exchange to obtain the food they require. Only nations that can be saved should be recipients of American food. According to Paddock and Paddock, compassion is a luxury no longer affordable in this era of scarcity. We must learn to let people die for the survival of the human race.

TRANSFORMING THE WORLD ECONOMIC SYSTEM

Francis Lappé and Joseph Collins in *Food First* explained that the cause of hunger is not too many people, not scarcity of arable land, not lack of technology, and not overconsumption by the wealthy. For Lappé and Collins no country, not even a Bangladesh, is a "basket case." Every country has the capacity to feed itself. The real food problem is the inequality generated by the world's political economy. Social justice must become a priority.

> There is no other road to food security—for others or for us. Americans are made to believe that if justice becomes a priority, production will be sacrificed. We have found the opposite to be true. It is the land monopolizers, both the traditional bounded elites and corporate agribusiness, that have proved themselves to be the most inefficient, unreliable, and destructive users of food resources. The only guarantee of long-term productivity and food security is for people to take control of food resources here and in other countries. (Lappé and Collins 1977, pp. 8–9)

NONRENEWABLE MINERAL RESOURCES

Although we can increase world food output, we cannot increase the supply of minerals. A mineral deposit, once used, is gone forever. The term *mineral* refers to a naturally occurring inorganic substance in the earth's crust. Thus, silicon is a mineral whereas petroleum is not, since the latter is of organic origin. Although minerals abound in nature, many of them are insufficiently concentrated to be economically recoverable. Moreover, the richest deposits are unevenly distributed and are being depleted.

Except for iron, nonmetallic elements are consumed at much greater rates than elements used for their metallic properties. Industrial societies do not worry about the supply of most nonmetallic minerals, which are plentiful and often widespread. There is no foreseeable world shortage of nitrogen, phosphorus, potash, and sulfur for chemical fertilizer, or of sand, gravel, clay, and dimension stone for building purposes. Those commodities the industrial and industrializing societies do worry about are the metals—the raw materials of economic power.

On a per capita basis, Americans use more minerals than any other people. They consume almost one-third of the world's minerals to supply less than 6 percent of the world's population. If the entire world population were to use metals at the same rate as the United States did in 1970, world production of iron would have to increase 75 times, that of copper 100 times, and that of tin 250 times.

Depletion Curves and Depletion Rate Estimates

By *depletion* is meant that time it takes to consume a proportion of a resource—typically 80 percent. It is not meaningful to speak about completely running out of a resource. Ultimately, it is uneconomic to exploit marginal deposits because of either low quality or inaccessibility.

To project the lifetime of a nonrenewable resource we construct *depletion curves* (Figure 4.11). Curve A assumes the prevalent practice of mining,

using, and discarding a resource. Curve B assumes improved mining techniques and recycling. Curve C assumes not only improved mining techniques and recycling, but also reduced demand. Obviously, a substitute resource would negate curves A, B, and C. In many cases projections based on depletion curves have been revised in light of more advanced resource location methods.

Location and Projected Reserves of Key Minerals

Only five countries—Australia, Canada, South Africa, the United States, and the USSR—are significant producers of at least six strategic minerals vital to defense and modern technology (Figure 4.12). A larger number of mainly Third World countries are major producers of between one and six minerals required by modern industry. Of the major mineral-producing countries only a few—notably the United States and the USSR—are also major processors and consumers. The other major processing and consuming centers—Japan and West European countries—are deficient in strategic minerals. Compared to the USSR, the United States lacks several important metallic ores. Examples include chromium and manganese.

How good is the world supply of strategic minerals? Our knowledge of world mineral reserves is summarized by the U.S. Bureau of Mines (Table 4.5). The table indicates the number of years sixteen strategic minerals will last under two assumptions: (1)

FIGURE 4.11
Depletion curves for a nonrenewable resource. (Source: Based on Hubbert, 1962.)

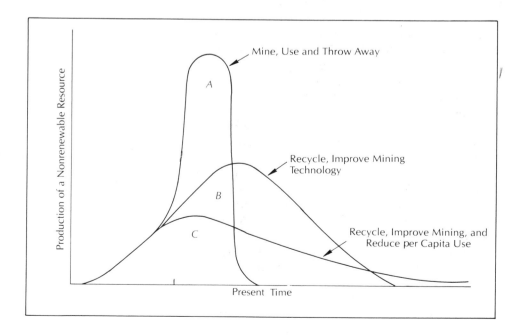

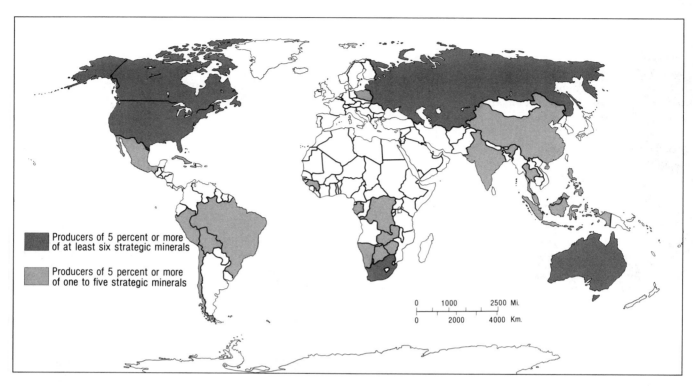

FIGURE 4.12

Major producers of strategic minerals. (Source: Based on data in U.S. Bureau of Mines, 1986.)

the number of years reserves will last with consumption growing at current rates (Column 2) and (2) the number of years reserves will last with consumption continuing to grow exponentially (Column 3). Data in Column 3 are more realistic than those in Column 2; they indicate that most of the key minerals will be exhausted within one hundred years and some will be depleted within a couple of decades. Column 4 shows "U.S. Consumption as a Percentage of World Total." Except for molybdenum, an alloying element, domestic production is insufficient to cover production (Column 5).

The United States is running short of domestic sources of strategic minerals (Table 4.6). Its dependency on imports has grown rapidly since 1950; prior to that year, the country was dependent on imports for only four designated strategic minerals. If measured in terms of the percentage imported, U.S. dependency increased from an average of 54 percent in 1960 to 78 percent in 1986.

The United States is not only dependent on imports for over 50 percent of the minerals it consumes, but depends heavily on certain countries for particular minerals (Table 4.6). The United States imports most minerals from "friendly" countries such

as Canada, Brazil, and South Africa. In 1985, the United States imported 33 percent of its manganese, 45 percent of its platinum, and 56 percent of its chromium from South Africa. Dependency on South Africa for these three critical substances helps to explain U.S. foreign policy toward that nation.

Minerals projected as future needs by the United States are unevenly distributed around the world. Many are concentrated in the USSR and Canada and in the underdeveloped countries of Africa, Asia, and Latin America (Table 4.6). Whether these critical substances will be available for U.S. consumption may depend less on economic scarcity and more on international tensions and foreign policy objectives.

Is the U.S. technological society gravely threatened by the degree to which domestic supplies must be supplemented by importing them from other countries? The need for a country to import a particular material does not mean that the material is unavailable at home. We have merely scratched the solid crust of the earth for the materials we need. Given an economical source of ultraterrestrial energy (solar radiation) and even more ingenious methods of extraction, who can say how much of our mineral needs could eventually be obtained domestically? The

TABLE 4.5
Projected reserves of selected strategic minerals.

Resource	Static Index (Years)*	Exponential Index (Years)†	U.S. Consumption as a Percentage World Total	Percentage of U.S. Consumption Imported	Sources of Major Reserves
Aluminum	100	31	42	97	Guinea, Australia, Brazil, Jamaica
Chromium	420	95	19	73	South Africa, Zimbabwe, Finland
Cobalt	110	60	32	95	Zaire, Zambia, Canada
Copper	36	21	33	27	Chile, United States, Zambia, Canada, USSR
Gold	11	9	26	31	South Africa, USSR, United States
Iron	240	93	28	22	USSR, Brazil, Australia, India
Lead	26	21	25	16	United States, Australia, Canada
Manganese	97	46	14	100	USSR, South Africa, Australia
Mercury	13	13	24	57	Spain, USSR, Algeria
Molybdenum	79	34	40	0	United States, Chile, Canada
Nickel	150	53	38	68	New Caledonia, Canada, Cuba
Platinum	130	47	31	92	South Africa, USSR, Zimbabwe
Silver	16	13	26	64	United States, Canada, Mexico
Tin	17	15	24	72	Malaysia, Indonesia, Thailand, China
Tungsten	40	28	22	68	China, Canada, United States, South Korea
Zinc	23	18	26	69	Canada, United States, Australia

NOTES: *Static Index refers to the number of years reserves will last to 80 percent depletion with consumption growing at current rates.
†Exponential Index refers to the number of years reserves will last to 80 percent depletion with consumption growing at 2.5 percent per annum.
SOURCE: U.S. Bureau of Mines, 1986, pp. 5–6.

environmental cost of "moving mountains" to win these commodities would be another matter, however.

Ocean Mineral Resources and Recycling

Affluent countries are unlikely to be easily defeated by a looming mineral shortage. They will devote more attention to programs for discovering new deposits, developing substitutes, and improving mining technology. Certainly, they will emphasize recycling and reusing minerals, and they may be forced to win more resources from the sea. Are the oceans and recycling the answer to our mineral problems?

Minerals from the Sea Vast mineral resources exist in sea water and on the ocean floor. With existing technology, however, only a few minerals (magnesium, table salt) are abundant enough to be extracted from sea water profitably. The deep-ocean floor is unlikely to solve mineral shortages. The only known minerals on ocean floors are manganese oxide nodules that contain about 24 percent magnesium, 14 percent iron, and small amounts of copper, nickel, and cobalt. Although manganese mining is feasible, political considerations are postponing actual mining operations. Developed countries are fighting among themselves over who should be allowed to exploit seabed wealth. Leaders of underdeveloped countries are opposed to exploitation of these resources by developed countries. They maintain that deep-ocean resources belong to all people and should be divided equally.

Recycling Resources Every year in the United States huge quantities of household and industrial waste are disposed of at sanitary landfills and open dumps. These materials are sometimes called "urban ores," because they can be recovered and used again. For years, the United States has been recycling scarce and highly valuable metals such as iron, lead, copper, antimony, silver, gold, and platinum. But large

TABLE 4.6
United States imports of selected strategic minerals.

Resource	Percentage Imported	Primary Source and Percentage of Imported Minerals		Major Source of Imported Minerals
Columbium	100	Brazil	74	Brazil, Canada, Thailand
Manganese	100	South Africa	33	South Africa, France, Brazil, Gabon
Mica	100	India	75	India, Belgium, France
Strontium	100	Mexico	96	Mexico, Spain
Aluminum	97	Guinea	27	Guinea, Australia, Jamaica
Cobalt	95	Zaire	40	Zaire, Zambia, Canada, Norway
Platinum	92	South Africa	45	South Africa, United Kingdom, USSR
Tantalum	92	Thailand	25	Australia, Thailand, Brazil, Malaysia
Chromium	73	South Africa	56	South Africa, Zimbabwe, Yugoslavia, Turkey
Tin	72	Thailand	25	Malaysia, Thailand, Bolivia, Indonesia
Asbestos	71	Canada	94	Canada, South Africa
Zinc	69	Canada	51	Canada, Peru, Mexico, Australia
Nickel	68	Canada	38	Cuba, Canada, Norway, Botswana, Australia
Tungsten	68	Canada	18	China, Canada, Bolivia, Portugal
Silver	64	Canada	28	United States, Canada, United Kingdom, Mexico, Peru
Mercury	57	Spain	36	Spain, Japan, Turkey, Algeria
Cadmium	55	Canada	32	United States, Canada, Peru, Mexico, Australia
Gold	31	Canada	56	South Africa, Canada, Uruguay, Switzerland

SOURCE: U.S. Bureau of Mines, 1986, p. 6.

amounts of scrap metals are still being wasted. Although we could recover a much greater proportion of scrap with improved technology and economic incentives, recycling will not solve our environmental problems. Reclaiming and recycling depends on one resource that for the most part cannot be recycled—energy.

Environmental Impact of Mineral Extraction

Mineral extraction has a varied impact on the environment, depending on mining procedures, local hydrological conditions, and the size of the operation. Environmental impact also depends on the stage of development of the mineral: exploration activities usually have less of an impact than mining and processing mineral resources.

Minimizing the environmental impact of mineral extraction is in everyone's best interest, but the task is difficult because demand for minerals continues to grow, and ever-poorer grades of ore are mined. For example, in 1900 the average grade of copper ore mined was 4 percent copper. By 1973 ores containing

as little as 0.53 percent copper were mined. Each year more and more rock has to be excavated, crushed, and processed to extract copper. The immense copper-mining pits in Montana, Utah, and Arizona are no longer in use, however, because foreign sources, mostly in underdeveloped countries, are less expensive.

Open-pit mines and quarries amount to a small fraction of the total area of a country. In general, their impact on the environment is local. But so long as the future remains technological and materialistic, the demand for minerals is going to increase. Lower and lower quality minerals will have to be used, and even with good engineering, environmental degradation will extend far beyond excavation and surface-plant areas.

ENERGY

Commercial energy, which accounts for more than 80 percent of all human energy use, is the lifeblood of modern economies. Indeed, it is the biggest single item in international trade. Oil alone accounts for about one-quarter of the volume of world trade.

Until the energy shocks of the 1970s, commercial energy demands were widely thought to be related to population growth and rising affluence. Suddenly, higher prices in the international oil market brought energy demands in the industrial countries to a virtual standstill. The increase in oil prices even surprised energy analysts. It signalled a change of the control of the oil market from the international oil companies headquartered in the United States to the capitals of the producing countries.

There have been many attempts to account for the transition of power within the international oil market. Was it the international oil companies' scramble for higher profits? Was it a result of the U.S. government's effort to preserve American leadership in the international oil market? Or was it greed on the part of the sheiks? Whatever the answer, Americans came face- to-face with the "energy crisis," especially during the winter of 1976–1977. A combination of below-normal temperatures and a shortage of fuel was devastating. Thousands of factories were cut back to "plant protection" levels and had to shut down, and over 3 million workers were laid off. Americans appreciated that this was not "just another 'crisis'." They learned first-hand that when energy fails, everything fails in an urban-industrial economy.

During the 1980s energy demand forecasts were consistently excessive, resulting in excess capacity in energy industries. Oil prices fell from a high of more than $30 in 1981 to $15 in 1987, shaking predictions made in 1980 that costs would soar to more than $40 per barrel. OPEC, once considered an invincible cartel, lost oil sales between 1980 and 1987. Its share of world oil output dropped from 57 percent in 1975 to 30 percent in 1985 as non-OPEC countries expanded production. Many Third World countries, strapped by heavy energy debts, were relieved to see prices falling. Only oil-exporting underdeveloped countries, such as Mexico, Venezuela, and Nigeria, which came to depend on oil revenues for an important source of income, were hurt.

The events of the 1980s led many to think that those who had cried "energy crisis" in the 1970s resembled the boy who cried wolf. True, there appears to be no world oil crisis now, but what of the next twenty to forty years? Will there be ways to keep the oil wolf from the door a generation from now— around the year 2015?

Energy Production and Consumption

Most commercial energy produced is from nonrenewable resources; and most renewable energy sources, particularly wood and charcoal, are used directly by producers—mainly poor rural people in underdeveloped countries. Although there is increasing interest in renewable energy development because of the growing scarcity of easily accessible fossil fuels, commercial energy is the core of energy use at the present time.

Only a handful of countries produce several times more commercial energy than they consume (Figure 4.13). The top ten energy-surplus countries, ranked by size of surplus, are the USSR, Saudi Arabia, Mexico, Iran, Venezuela, Indonesia, Algeria, Kuwait, Nigeria, and the United Arab Emirates. Nearly one-half of all African countries are energy paupers. And several of the world's leading industrial powers— notably Japan, many West European countries, and the United States—consume more energy than they produce.

Energy Consumption The United States leads the world in total energy consumption, but Canada and Norway are the highest per capita users. With only 5 percent of the world's population, the United States consumes about one-quarter of the world's energy. By contrast, underdeveloped countries also consume about one-quarter of the world's energy but they contain 77 percent of the population. Thus, there exists a striking relation between energy consumption and income per capita (Figure 4.14). Maps of the consumption of electric power and of major oil and coal flows also reinforce the image of the developed world as the all-consuming energy sink (Figures 4.15, 4.16, and 4.17). Most of the poorer underdeveloped countries receive a meager energy ration, well below levels consistent even with moderate levels of economic development. They do not have the money to buy a better energy ration.

Oil Dependency Because Americans were seriously affected by the 1973 Arab oil embargo, and because imported oil as a proportion of total demand increased from 11 percent in the late 1960s to 50 percent in the mid-1970s, political leaders called for a national policy of oil self-sufficiency to end U.S. dependency on uncertain suppliers of petroleum. President Richard Nixon implemented such a policy in 1973 and, four years later, President Jimmy Carter reaffirmed the policy and its purposes. In 1985, President Ronald Reagan also endorsed this policy, but called for minimum government intervention and greater reliance on market forces to supply current and future energy requirements. The Reagan administration proposed the development of energy sources on most federal land and off-shore sites, filled a 500-million gallon strategic oil reserve, and encouraged the devel-

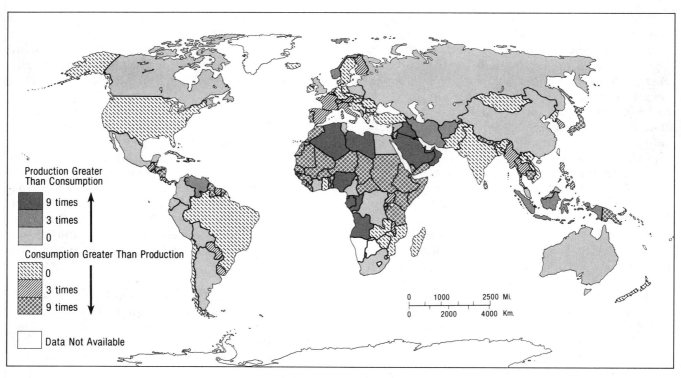

FIGURE 4.13
Production and consumption of commercial energy, 1984. (Source: International Institute for Environment and Development and World Resources Institute, 1987, pp. 300–301.)

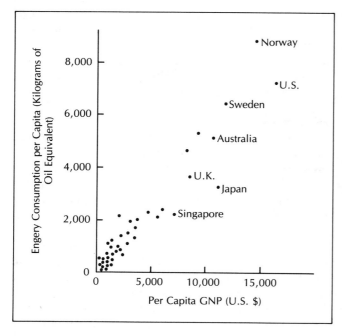

FIGURE 4.14
Relationship between per capita GNP, 1985 and commercial energy consumption, 1985. (Source: World Bank, 1987.)

opment of nuclear power. At the same time, air and water pollution regulations were relaxed, tax credits for home energy conservation expenditures were ended, a bill to compel firms to build energy-efficient appliances was vetoed, and fuel-economy standards for new cars were delayed (Darst 1987; Shabecoff 1987).

These conflicting policies did not help to end U.S. dependency on imported oil and downgraded federal efforts to encourage American households and companies to conserve fossil fuels. High-priced oil from OPEC temporarily reduced U.S. consumption of oil (by 39 percent between 1973 and 1986), but in the mid-1980s dependence on cheap imported oil began to rise again in response to lower prices.

Although the United States is dependent on imported oil, most of it does not come from the Middle East. The United States imports 37 percent of the oil it consumes, but only 6 percent from the Persian Gulf (Table 4.7). Japan, Italy, and France are much more dependent on Persian Gulf oil.

Production of Fossil Fuels   The Arab oil embargo stimulated fossil fuel production in the United States

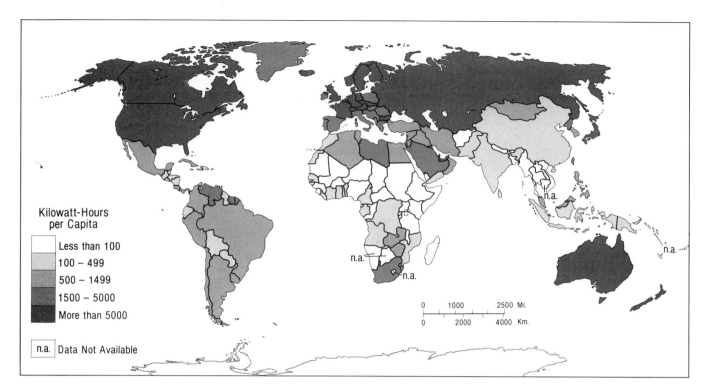

FIGURE 4.15
Annual consumption of electric power per capita, 1984. (Source: Based on data in Encylopaedia Britannica, 1987.)

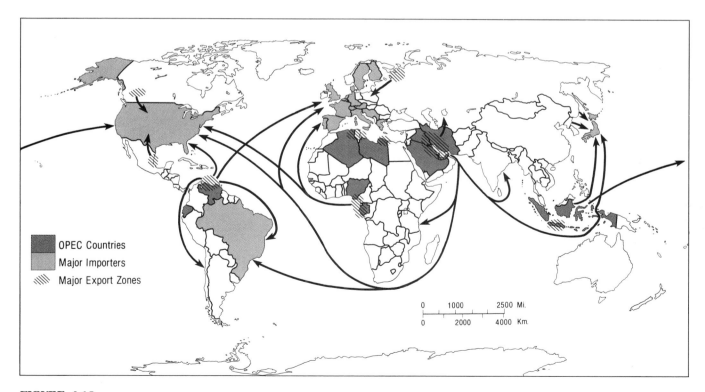

FIGURE 4.16
Major world oil flows. (Source: Based on data in United Nations, 1987.)

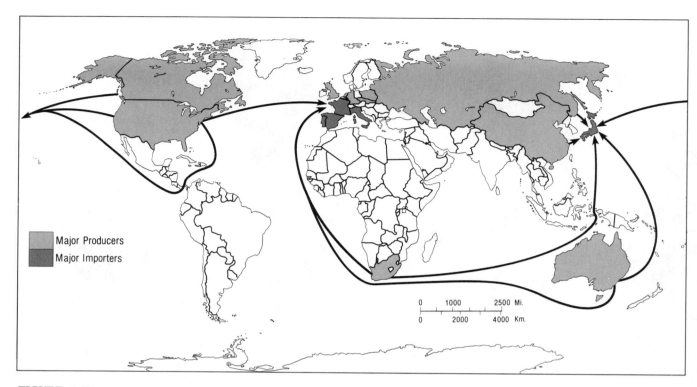

FIGURE 4.17
Major world coal flows. (Source: Based on data in U.S. Bureau of Mines, 1985.)

and throughout the world. In the United States, coal production increased in the mid- and late-1970s in response to the increase in the price and decrease in the supply of OPEC oil. But in the 1980s the apparent decline of the OPEC cartel and the entry of important new producers—notably Mexico, Britain, and Norway—led to a drop in oil prices. The willingness of new producers and others, such as Saudi Arabia, to put oil on the world market forced a reduction in U.S. oil production. Had it not been for the long war

TABLE 4.7
Oil consumers and their dependence on Persian Gulf oil, 1986

	United States	Japan	West Germany	France	Italy	United Kingdom
Total oil consumption (millions of barrels per day)	16.1	4.3	2.4	1.8	1.6	1.5
Percentage of total oil consumption imported	37	100	100	94	100	
Percentage of total oil consumption imported from the Persian Gulf by tanker or pipeline	6	60	10	33	51	

	United States	Japan	Western Europe
Percentage of total oil consumption passing through the Strait of Hormuz by tanker	4	60	11

NOTE: Britain is a net exporter of oil.

SOURCE: Shipler, 1987, p. 1.

between Iran and Iraq, the drop in oil prices might well have had more drastic consequences on U.S. production and on the economies of the oil-patch states of Texas, Oklahoma, and Louisiana.

The embargo made Americans and other industrial societies aware of their dependency on imported oil and on the world distribution of fossil fuel reserves. The United States is richly endowed with coal but has only modest reserves of oil and natural gas. Over 50 percent of the world's known reserves of oil are located in the Middle East compared with 19 percent in the Americas. Sub-Saharan Africa and China are critically short of oil. Natural gas, often a substitute for oil, is also unevenly distributed with nearly 40 percent of supplies located in the USSR and about 26 percent in the Middle East.

Energy Policy According to some experts, the "energy crisis" of the 1970s occurred in the United States because a national energy policy was not a high priority. In Western Europe, on the other hand, effective energy policies already existed. Following the Arab oil embargo, the United States began to form a national energy policy and enacted a major piece of legislation, the Energy Policy and Conservation Act of 1975. An important goal of this law is to reduce energy demand through conservation. Because of investments made in efficient technologies during the 1970s and early 1980s, energy conservation promises to continue despite lower oil prices.

To ensure that an "energy crisis" does not reoccur, the United States must embrace a firm energy policy advocating the conservation of remaining oil and coal while renewable forms of energy are being developed; the elimination of industrial and home energy inefficiency; and the betterment of environmental quality. In addition, recurrent "crises" can only be prevented if the United States takes full account of world energy considerations. Energy is a worldwide problem that cannot be solved by confrontation among groups of countries. Sharing energy is essential to protect the interests of all producers and consumers.

Who was to blame for the "energy crisis" of the 1970s? The big oil and electric companies were at least in part responsible in their maneuvers to restrict production and imports in the manner of monopolies, oligopolies, and global cartels. The large, often excessive, profits enjoyed by the oil companies were obtained at high cost to Americans, who saw no appreciable improvement in national energy self-sufficiency.

Who suffered from the "energy crisis"? Certainly most people in developed countries (especially those on fixed incomes), many small firms, and even independent oil companies. Non-oil-producing underdeveloped countries such as Jamaica, Guyana, Mali, and Zambia were hurt much more. They could ill-afford to spend foreign exchange on expensive oil imports.

Adequacy of Fossil Fuels

In the next few decades energy demands are expected to increase much faster than population increase. The question people are asking these days is, How long can fossil fuel reserves last given our increasing energy requirements?

A Shell/Esso production platform in Britain's North Sea gas field. British oil exploration was stimulated by a dramatic increase in the price of oil in the mid-1970s and early 1980s, as well as by a recovery of oil prices in the late 1980s. Britain's North Sea oil and gas investment may keep the country self-sufficient in oil to the end of the twentieth century. (Source: Shell.)

Oil Current world oil reserves of 700 billion barrels are approximately thirty times the annual world oil production. United States oil reserves, however, are less than nine times U.S. annual production. Probably some 500 billion barrels of new proved reserves will be added to the world reservoir in the next forty years. But the distribution pattern around the world indicates a shift of leverage that will become apparent in the next two generations. If nothing is done to change present trends, the global oil market will be in grave trouble about the year 2015. Exports from Africa and Latin America will peak by about the year 2000, and both continents will cease to be exporters before 2025. The Middle East will then be the only major exporter of oil. Import dependencies of North America, Western Europe, and Japan/Far East will range from 92 to 98 percent. By 2015 demand will exceed production capacity. We could change this grim scenario through increased conservation, use of alternative fuels, and improved oil recovery techniques.

Coal   Coal is the most abundant fossil fuel and, at current production levels, world reserves will last about 500 years. Use of this resource, however, has been limited due to inefficient management by the international coal industry, the inconvenience of storing and shipping the fuel, and the environmental consequences of large-scale coal burning.

With the exception of the USSR, the United States has the largest coal reserves. Coal constitutes 67 percent of America's fossil fuel resources, yet it accounts for only about one-fifth of its energy consumption. If this share does not increase, the projected life of coal is 200 to 400 years. If this share increases, and more than one-half of the net energy is lost in mining, shipping, or by converting to more convenient forms of energy such as electricity, gas, and synthetic oil, the projected life is sharply reduced. Scientists say coal gasification and liquefaction could deplete U.S. supplies within fifty years.

Energy Options

The age of cheap fossil fuels is coming to an end. Americans are told by corporations and the government that they must conserve energy and find alternatives to fossil fuels, especially alternatives that will not rape the environment. How viable are the options?

Conservation   According to utility companies and the government, the way to reduce the gap between domestic production and consumption in the short run is for consumers to restrict consumption. Energy conservation stretches finite fuel resources and reduces environmental stress. Conservation can substitute for expensive, environmentally less desirable supply options, and help to buy time for the development of other more acceptable sources of energy.

Many people believe that energy conservation means a slow-growth economy; however, data indicate that energy growth and economic growth are not inextricably linked. In the United States, from the early 1870s to 1950, gross national product per capita increased sixfold, whereas energy use per capita only slightly more than doubled. Energy efficiency, the ratio of useful energy output to total energy input, increased substantially between 1921 and 1975.

At least two approaches to energy conservation have been suggested by the government and energy companies. One approach is to increase energy efficiency. Consumers can add insulation and storm windows to their homes; they can drive more slowly, use smaller automobiles, and ride buses. Power plants can transmit "waste heat" to nearby plants. At best, utilities convert 27 percent of fuel energy into electricity. The rest escapes as heat in the form of warm air and gases. Consumers can lower thermostats, switch to lower wattage light bulbs, and take showers instead of baths. Industry could rely on less energy and more labor. The other approach is less attractive to most Americans: compulsory allocation and rationing. If consumers are unwilling to alter their styles of life voluntarily in order to save energy, then compulsory methods could be introduced to make sure that everyone shares the burden equally.

Alternative Energy Options   One alternative is *nuclear energy*. Atomic energy, however, can result in radioactive fallout to the environment—a major concern, especially since the nuclear accidents at the Three Mile Island plant in the United States in 1979 and at the Chernobyl station in the USSR in 1986. The wisdom of a commitment to nuclear energy depends ultimately on the ability of human beings—their technology and institutions—to manage a very hazardous enterprise. There has been heated debate as to whether human societies are capable of managing nuclear energy wisely. But so long as industrial countries are locked into increased energy consumption, it seems inevitable that nuclear power will be required to help meet the demands.

The development of *geothermal power* holds promise for the future in several countries that have hot springs, geysers, and other underground supplies of hot water that can easily be tapped. The occurrence of this renewable resource is highly localized, however. New Zealand obtains about 10 percent of its electricity from this source, and smaller quantities are utilized by Italy, Japan, Iceland, the USSR, and the United States.

Another source of electric power, and one that is virtually inexhaustible, is *hydropower*—energy from

The large hyperbolic cooling tower and reactor containment dome of the Trojan nuclear power plant in Ranier, Oregon, add to the tranquility of this night scene. Safety issues surrounding the use of nuclear energy are fraught with turmoil. (Source: U.S. Department of Energy.)

rivers. Developed countries have exploited about 50 percent of their usable opportunities, the USSR and Eastern Europe about 20 percent, and the Third World only 7 percent. In developed countries further exploitation of hydropower is limited mainly by environmental and social concerns. In the Third World, a lack of money and markets for the power is the main obstacle.

Like river power, tidal, wind, and solar energy are inexhaustible. In the 1970s and early 1980s, *solar energy* caught the public eye through publicity of the relatively few solar homes and buildings constructed

The Wairakei geothermal facility in New Zealand produces electricity by drawing steam from a natural underground reservoir. Although the earth's interior heat is enormous, it is difficult to harness with present technologies. In general, geothermal resources can be economically exploited only when molten rock lies within three thousand meters of the earth's surface. Although geothermal's environmental impacts are minor compared to those of many other energy sources, they do include possible pollution of surface waters and ground water. (Source: United Nations—New Zealand Information Services.)

in the United States. Large-scale utilization of solar energy, however, still poses technical difficulties, particularly that of low concentration of the energy. It has been estimated that the energy of the direct rays of the sun at sea-level is slightly more than one horsepower per square meter. So far technology has been able to convert only slightly more than 30 percent of solar energy into electricity; however, depending on the success of ongoing research programs, it could provide a large proportion of power needs in the twenty-first century.

Still another form of renewable energy is *biomass*—wood and organic wastes. In 1980 biomass accounted for about 14 percent of global energy use. For Nepal, Ethiopia, and Tanzania, more than 90 percent of total energy comes from biomass. The use of wood for cooking—the largest use of biomass fuel—presents enormous environmental and social problems because it is being consumed faster than it is being replenished. Fuelwood scarcities—the poor world's energy crisis—now affects 1.3 billion people and could affect about 3 billion people by the year 2000 unless immediate corrective actions are taken.

With good management practices, biomass is a resource that can be produced renewably. It can be converted to alcohol and efficient, clean-burning fuel for cooking or transportation. Its production and conversion are labor-intensive, an attractive feature for

underdeveloped countries that face unemployment problems. But the low efficiency of photosynthesis requires huge land areas for energy crops if significant quantities of biomass fuels are to be produced.

Many countries have expanded their use of biomass for fuel since the 1973 oil embargo. The United States is using more wood-fired boilers for industrial and domestic purposes and is producing gasohol from corn. In 1985, twenty Third World countries formed the Biomass Users Network (BUN) that proposes, among other things, to convert unprofitable export crops such as sugar cane into biomass fuel for local consumption.

From a Growth-oriented to a Balance-oriented Lifestyle

It appears unlikely that energy availability will place a limit on economic growth on "Spaceship Earth"; however, drastic changes in the use of energy resources seem certain. The ultimate limits to the use of energy will be determined by the ability of the ecosystem to dissipate the heat and waste produced as more and more energy flows through the system.

In countless ways, energy improves the quality of our lives—but it also pollutes. As the rate of energy consumption increases, so too does water and air contamination. Sources of water pollution are numer-

Waste products of all kinds are discharged into rivers, endangering aquatic life and people. The thick white foam on the River Seine, Paris, in this 1966 photo is clear indication of detergents, among the most common of pollutants. (Source: F. Bibal for UNESCO.)

TABLE 4.8
Comparison of growth-oriented and balance-oriented lifestyles.

Growth-oriented Lifestyle	Balance-oriented Lifestyle
Essentially infinite resources and energy.	Finite resources and infinite energy (if fusion or solar energy can be developed).
Linear flow of matter and energy.	Linear flow of energy but recycling of matter.
Increase flow rates of matter and energy and output (maximize throughput).	Stabilize flow rates of matter and energy by deliberately reducing throughput—a steady-state system with balanced inputs and outputs well below the limits of the system.
Goals of efficiency, quantity, simplification, and cultural and physical homogeneity to attain short-term stability.	Goals of quality and deliberate preservation of cultural and physical diversity to attain long-term stability at the expense of some efficiency.
Output control of pollution (consequences of second law of thermodynamics can be avoided or minimized by cleaning up output).	Input and output control (consequences of the second law of thermodynamics can be decreased in the long run by decreasing input and flow rates along with controlling output).
Continued growth provides capital for output control and redistribution of wealth (trickle-down theory).	If growth continues, capital must be increasingly devoted to maintenance and repairs, thus decreasing life quality and preventing redistribution of wealth.
Free enterprise, a competitive market system, or a centralized control economy that can respond to undesirable side effects.	Market responds only if we find ways to include quality of life indicators into the price of goods and services.
Short-term view and planning.	Long-term view and planning.
Local and national outlook.	Global outlook.

NOTE: The table suggests that we can transform our growth-oriented lifestyle into a balance-oriented lifestyle without restructuring our economic system. In striving to attain "balance," can we, at the same time, maintain our existing market system?

SOURCE: Adapted from Miller, 1975.

ous: industrial wastes, sewage, and detergents; fertilizers, herbicides, and pesticides from agriculture; and coastal oil spills from tankers. Air pollution reduces visibility; damages buildings, clothes and crops; and endangers human health. It is especially serious in urban-industrial areas, but it occurs wherever waste gases and solid particles are discharged into the atmosphere.

Pollution is the price paid by an economic system emphasizing ever-increasing growth as a primary goal. Despite attempts to do something about pollution problems, the growth-oriented lifestyle characteristic of Western urban-industrial society continues to widen the gap between people and nature. "Growthmania" is a road to nowhere. It is easy to see why. If the U.S. economy grew at a 5 percent annual growth rate, by about the year 2110 it would reach a level 50,000 percent higher than the present level. Problems of acquiring, processing, and disposing of materials defy imagination.

There are many who argue that we must transform our present linear or growth-oriented economic system into a balance-oriented system (Table 4.8). A balance-oriented economy explicitly recognizes natural systems. It recognizes that resources are exhaustible, that they must be recycled, and that input rates must be reduced to levels that do not permanently damage the environment. A balance-oriented economy does not mean an end to growth, but a new social system in which only desirable low-energy, high-labor growth is encouraged. It requires a de-emphasis on the materialistic values we have come to hold in such high esteem. If current resource and environmental constraints lead us to place a higher premium on saving and conserving than on spending and discarding, then they may be viewed as blessings in disguise.

SUMMARY

We introduced this chapter by restating the resources-population problem. It is possible to solve resource problems by (1) changing societal goals, (2) changing consumption patterns, (3) changing technology, and (4) altering population numbers. In the Western world much of the emphasis is on technological advancement and population control.

Following a review of renewable and nonrenewable resources, we explored the question of food resources. The food "crisis" is essentially a conse-

quence of societal goals. Food production is increasing faster than population growth, yet more people are hungry. Socioeconomic conditions offer a more cogent explanation of why this is so than either population growth or environmental factors. In the course of transforming agriculture into a profit base for the wealthy, the Third World poor are being forced out of the production process.

Unlike food, which is replenished by the seasons, nonrenewable minerals and fossil fuels, once used, are gone forever. We discussed some of the alternatives to fossil fuels, and pointed to energy conservation as a potent alternative with potential that remains to be fully exploited. In conclusion, the comparison between growth-oriented and balance-oriented lifestyles underscored the importance of quality concerns as they relate to economic growth.

KEY TERMS

balance-oriented lifestyle	maximum sustainable yield
biomass	minerals
carrying capacity	nonrenewable resource
conservation	overpopulation
deforestation	pollution
depletion curves	recycle
desertification	renewable resource
energy	reserve
Green Revolution	resource
growth-oriented lifestyle	second law of thermodynamics
intermediate technology	stationary state
malnutrition	undernutrition

SUGGESTED READINGS

Anderson, J. 1984. *Oil: The Real Story Behind the Energy Crisis.* London: Sidgwick and Jackson.

Bartelmus, P. 1986. *Environment and Development.* Boston: Allen and Unwin.

Darmstadter, J., and Landsberg, H. 1983. *Energy Today and Tomorrow: Living with Uncertainty.* Englewood Cliffs, NJ: Prentice-Hall.

Frank, R. W., and Chasin, B. H. 1981. *Seeds of Famine: Ecological Destruction and the Development Dilemma in the West African Sahel.* Montclair, NJ: Allenheld, Osmun.

International Institute for Environment and Development and World Resources Institute 1988. *World Resources 1988–89.* New York: Basic Books.

Lappé, F. M., and Collins, J. 1980. *Food First.* London: Abacus.

Rees, J. 1985. *Natural Resources: Allocation, Economics, and Policy.* New York: Methuen.

Repetto, R., ed. 1985. *The Global Possible: Resources, Development, and the New Century.* New Haven: Yale University Press.

Repetto, R. 1987. *Population, Resources, Environment: An Uncertain Future.* Population Bulletin, Vol. 42, No. 2. Washington, DC: Population Reference Bureau.

Schumacher, E. F. 1973. *Small is Beautiful.* London: Blond and Briggs.

Simon. J. L., and Kahn H., eds. 1984. *The Resourceful Earth: A Response to Global 2000.* Oxford, England: Blackwell.

U.S. Council on Environmental Quality. 1982. *The Global 2000 Report to the President.* New York: Penguin.

Warnock, J. W. 1987. *The Politics of Hunger.* New York: Methuen

5
DECISION MAKING

OBJECTIVES

☐ To describe how predictable geographical patterns are produced by omniscient, single-minded, rational decision-makers

☐ To consider ideas of bounded rationality and satisficing behavior

☐ To emphasize the importance of capital-labor conflict in locational decision making

☐ To explain how locational decision making occurs on a global scale and involves the interrelations of multiple actors

Nigerian small farmers decide to purchase fertilizer, hoping that it will increase yields. (Source: World Bank.)

The physical environment in all of its variety is the raw material for human activity. For thousands upon thousands of years, people have used their culture and tools to gain control over their environment and to shape their tangible landscape. Today there is not a square inch of the world that has not been modified by human action.

Our impact on the environment began when prehistoric nomadic groups modified substantial areas of the land by setting fires in the course of hunting for food. Centuries later, farmers altered the environment much more drastically than hunters. They cleared forests, eliminated "weeds," and grew more food than they required for themselves. With food concerns taken care of, some people used their new-found leisure time to produce a variety of goods, including shoes, clothes, farm implements, weapons, and household objects. The growth of urban settlements provided further opportunities for specialization. Eventually networks developed for the extraction and movement of raw materials and for the distribution of finished products. By the twentieth century, a technological culture occupied the entire globe.

This chapter, "Decision Making," and the next, "Transportation," are cornerstones to an understanding of the world created by technological culture. They are fundamental to an appreciation of the forces that underlie geographical patterns. They are also basic to a comprehensive analysis of specific patterns discussed in succeeding chapters.

Patterns of economic activity are a reflection of human decisions. Bulldozers clear tropical rain forest for cattle ranching in Costa Rica. Farmers in Kenya build terraces to fight soil erosion on sloping cropland. Heavy engineering plants close in the older industrial regions and cities in the United States. High-technology firms spring up along the M4 Corridor west of London and in Silicon Glen near Glasgow, Scotland. Semiconductor production moves to the newly industrializing countries of Taiwan, Malaysia, and the Philippines and to the automated production facilities in Japan. Offices flee San Francisco for the suburbs and beyond. Blocks of apartments and townhouse communities locate close to the Metro in suburban Washington, D.C. These decisions affect the appearance of the landscape and influence human well-being.

What are the goals of spatial human behavior, and what are the restraints? Who are the significant actors in locational decision making, and what factors play a part in their decisions? What are the economic consequences of decision-making processes? This chapter answers these questions by examining different approaches to locational decision making. In the

IBM's manufacturing plant in Silicon Glen near Glasgow, Scotland, produces display systems, finance industry systems, and keyboards for customers in Europe, the Middle East, and Africa. IBM chose this Silicon Glen location to take advantage of the area's skilled labor, universities, and environmental attractions. (Source: IBM.)

1960s and 1970s, classical and behavioral models of individual behavior flourished, and geographers invariably treated location issues as intrastate decisions. Since then two developments have gained prominence: one is theoretical; the other, a matter of empirical focus. The first involves the adoption and adaptation of Marxist theory of industrial capital and uneven development. Most Marxists stress capital-labor conflicts in locational decision making. The second development involves a change from the study of individual locational decisions to a consideration of such decisions in the context of multiple actors and factors, and in the context of the wider economy. Geographers have come to recognize that governments, multinational corporations, international service and trading companies, national and international labor groups, intergovernmental organizations, and special interest groups all play a part in economic decision making in an interactive mode. Geographers also recognize that it is essential to adopt a global perspective in the analysis of decision making because of dramatic shifts since the mid-1950s in the distribution and organization of economic activities around the world.

THE CLASSICAL LOCATION-THEORY APPROACH

In the late 1950s and 1960s, a small band of self-proclaimed "new" geographers decried exceptionalist traditions in geography (Schaefer 1953)—attempts to understand the areal differences on the earth's surface by studying specific regions and their cultures—and pronounced geography as the science of spatial relations (Bunge 1966). This science is based on a well-established body of classical location theory built on the formulations of Johann Heinrich von Thünen (1826), Alfred Weber (1929), and Walter Christaller (1966), and synthesized by Walter Isard (1956, 1960). Within a few years, the methods of spatial analysis had diffused into college textbooks (Abler, Adams, and Gould 1974; Lloyd and Dicken 1972).

The aim of spatial analysis is to explain the location of phenomena in geographical space in terms of spatial variables (Sack 1974, p. 1). Instead of focusing on absolute location (e.g., describing the industries found in Tokyo or the agricultural activities undertaken on the Canadian Prairies), spatial analysts study geographical distributions in terms of relative location. They search for recurrent patterns such as the distribution of agricultural land uses with increasing distance from a large city.

Spatial theorists identify the friction of distance—the cost of moving commodities, people, or information between places—as the key variable for explaining recurrent geographical patterns and, therefore, underscore the role of transport costs in locational decision making. In order to isolate the effects of the distance variable and to construct models undisturbed by the distortions of the "real" world, location theory is often elaborated in an "isotropic environment"—an imaginary plain or surface with uniform environmental conditions, equal transport costs in all directions, and an equal distribution of population having identical capacities and preferences. All inhabitants on this plain are called *optimizers* or *economic persons*. They have perfect knowledge of all possible outcomes of a given action and act solely to maximize utility. Their objectives are to organize space efficiently—to locate activities and use land in the "best" way.

The Goals of Spatial Behavior

Richard Morrill (1970, pp. 175–76) summarized the goals of spatial behavior as two principals: (1) to use every piece of land to the greatest profit and utility and (2) to achieve the highest possible interaction at the least possible cost. Pursuit of these goals involves the following four types of locational decision:

1 Land costs can be substituted for transport costs when seeking accessibility. Expensive sites close to the core of a settlement can be selected and used intensively, or less expensive sites, further away, can be selected and used less intensively with the same total costs.

2 Production costs at sites can be substituted for transport costs when seeking markets. The cost benefits of larger production volume must be balanced against increased transport costs of moving raw materials to the point of fabrication and distributing resulting products to markets.

3 Agglomeration benefits can be substituted for transport costs. The savings achieved by proximity to related businesses must be balanced against the risk of competition from rival producers who can bite into potential revenues.

4 Self-sufficiency (higher production costs) can be substituted for trade (higher transport costs). Importing higher quality resources or goods from outside the region, involving higher transport costs, must be balanced against using lower quality local resources or producing goods locally at a higher cost.

The fresh sweet corn this farmer is loading on his truck will be sold directly to consumers at the nearest central place—the farmers' market in Jackson, Mississippi. (Source: USDA photo by David Warren.)

The spatial structures resulting from these decisions include *land-use gradients* and a *hierarchy of market areas*.

Land-Use Gradients

Land-use gradients are the result of differing rates of return of activities in the limited areas of space near a point of maximum accessibility. In any area, a point exists that is central to all other points. This central point, which geographers call a central place, is the market. As distance from the market increases, producers incur higher and higher transport costs and lower and lower net revenues per unit area until they cannot survive unless they sell their labor power. At that critical distance, net revenues equal transport costs. Because productivity and transferability vary for different activities, a spatial gradient of land use results. Activities involving higher transport costs are concentrated near the market; those with lower

transport costs are displaced to more distant locations.

To illustrate, imagine a region with a single market—a city. Demand for locally produced foodstuffs is concentrated in the city, where goods are manufactured to be exchanged for agricultural commodities. Farmers in areas surrounding the city grow vegetables, potatoes, and wheat.

In order to isolate the effect of distance on location relative to the city and land-use patterns, assume that the land surface is homogeneous in every respect. There are no barriers to movement, physical resources are evenly distributed, and soils are equally fertile. The farmers are equally distributed. They have identical incomes, demands, and tastes. Their production capacities are equal, and they all have perfect knowledge and act to maximize cash income. Prices for each commodity are stable and fixed in the city. With these assumptions, the only variable affecting the pattern of agricultural production is transport costs. These costs are a simple, linear function of distance. Costs are the same per kilometer regardless of distance traveled. Only one form of transportation exists.

Each crop brings a different market price per hectare. The market price for vegetables is higher than the market price for potatoes, which in turn is higher than the market price for wheat. Market-price inequalities may be a function of demand (willingness of people to pay a higher price for vegetables), or the intensity of production (larger yield from a hectare of vegetables than from a hectare of wheat), or both.

The transport rate for each crop is also different. It is highest for vegetables and lowest for wheat. Vegetables are more perishable, more easily damaged, and bulkier than wheat. Tomatoes dropped into a boxcar by conveyor will not bring a high market price. Wheat will keep for a long time under proper conditions and can be easily loaded for transporting. Potatoes are intermediate; they are less perishable and fragile than vegetables but more so than wheat.

Using hypothetical figures, the net returns of different crops in different locations can be illustrated (Figure 5.1). The origin of each curve on the graph is the market price of the commodity, and the slope is the transport rate. The steeper the curve, the greater the transport rate per kilometer. Vegetables are the most profitable crop within twenty-four kilometers of the city because throughout this distance net income exceeds the net income from potatoes and wheat. At a distance of twenty-four kilometers, however, the net income from vegetables equals the net income from potatoes. Between twenty-four and forty-eight kilometers, potatoes are the most profitable crop. From forty-eight kilometers to one hundred kilometers, the margin of cultivation, wheat is the most profitable crop. Beyond one hundred kilometers, it is unprofitable to grow any crops for market.

In our imaginary region, farmers at a given location have one option; they must grow the most profitable crop. They either perceive this as their best option, which any optimizer would do, or are forced to by the competitive bidding process. A farmer ten kilometers from the city who wants to grow potatoes would be outbid by a potential grower of vegetables.

Hierarchy of Market Areas

A spatial hierarchy involves not just one point but a whole system of central points. Each point attracts sellers and customers within its market area, but seeks to put as much distance as possible between itself and other centers. This behavior creates an efficient division of space into regional markets.

Many central-place activities require little space in which to operate and depend for support on final consumers who, on an isotropic plain, have constant purchasing power and are evenly spread over the landscape. These activities are mutually attracted to each other. Different activities with the same *thresh-*

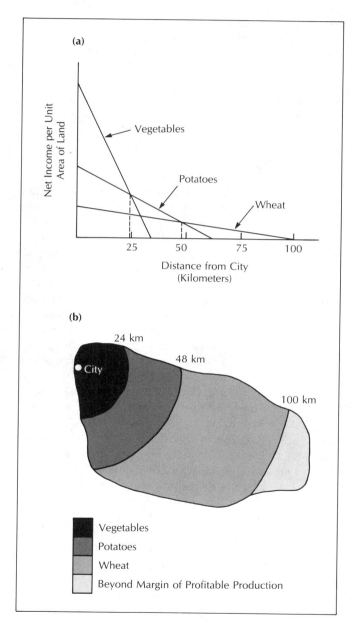

FIGURE 5.1
Land use in a hypothetical region: (a) net income from different crops at different distances from the capital city; (b) the geographical patterns of agricultural production. (Source: Pred, 1967, p. 25.)

olds (i.e., the minimum sales or population needed to sustain the activity) and *ranges* (i.e., the maximum distance customers are willing to travel to obtain a good or service) find it profitable to cluster, since rational customers act to minimize their efforts in obtaining goods and services they require with equal frequency. By allowing customers to obtain several goods and services on a single trip, the agglomeration of central-place activities results in large economies.

Sellers of the same good or service, however, repel each other. They push each other apart in order to grab as many customers as possible from their surrounding market areas. This process results in a triangular arrangement of sellers, each one equidistant from the other. Together, these triangular patterns form a hexagonal lattice, which is the geometrical figure that most resembles a triangular arrangement of circles but packs space tightly without any bits left over (Figure 5.2a,b).

A hierarchical structure of central places emerges if some points succeed in adding more specialized activities requiring larger market areas. An optimal arrangement occurs when new activities require support from the markets of six surrounding

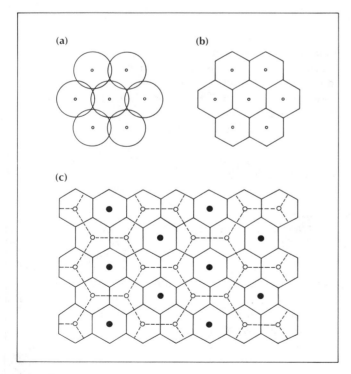

FIGURE 5.2

Development of central-place patterns: (a) triangular arrangement of circular market areas; (b) collapse of circular market areas into hexagons; (c) two-level hierarchy of central places. (Source: Pred, 1967, p. 92.)

places in order to reach threshold levels (Figure 5.2c). Similarly, if one of these second-level places adds additional activities requiring even larger market areas, a third level of market areas is created. In this way, a region is divided into a hexagonal structure of markets having as many hierarchical levels as the economy can support.

Central places arranged in a triangular pattern with a separate hexagonal field about each center represent the "best" spatial division on a homogeneous land surface. This pattern becomes more complex when some central places offer more specialized activities than others. The resulting hierarchy of centers is a result of grouping as many activities as possible in as few places as possible to obtain the greatest economies of agglomeration and of minimizing the number of trips and the total distance traveled.

Gradient-Hierarchies

The economic landscape has a joint gradient and hierarchical structure if a homogeneous environment and the existence of only agricultural and central-place activities are assumed. A land-use gradient results from activities competing for geographical space on the basis of their productivity. The competition forces a dispersal of population and activities. A hierarchy of market areas emerges if the area surrounding a regional central place is large enough to permit the development of smaller competing central places and market areas. In a large (national) space-economy, the hierarchical structure is much more elaborate; the gradient around the major market is modified by local gradients and regional markets.

A combined gradient and hierarchical structure also exists within cities. In small cities, all the distributional facilities are located in the central business district (CBD), and there is a simple gradient of land uses outward from the center. But in large cities, the pattern is disturbed because thresholds for the establishment of competing (suburban) service centers are reached. The simple gradient is punctuated by centers of greater intensity around district service centers (Figure 5.3). In very large cities, a complex hierarchy of central-place nodes dot the urban landscape.

Environmental Variations and Factory Location

Nowhere is space homogeneous in all respects. Optimal patterns of agricultural land use and central places are modified by *environmental variations*. Agricultural gradients and the spacing of central places

FIGURE 5.3
The gradient-hierarchical landscape in an urban setting.

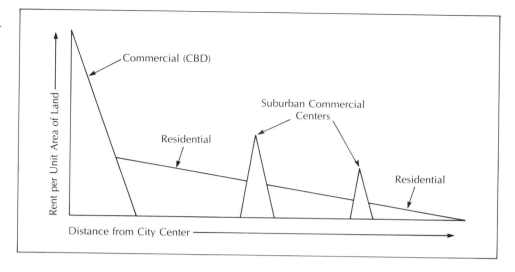

are distorted by topographical variations. They are also distorted by variations in land productivity.

A major response to environmental variation is factory location. Almost all industrial resources are unevenly distributed across space. Manufacturing involves collecting raw materials from a limited number of places, reworking and combining raw materials to produce finished products, and distributing the finished products, often to other industries at specific locations. Compared to the gradient-hierarchy landscape, the industrial landscape shows greater concentration of activities at large markets and material sources.

What is the "best" location for a factory? For simplicity, let us assume that a firm manufactures one commodity. It uses two inputs available at two points, and sells the product at one market located at another point. Finally let us say that movement is equally easy in all directions. On the basis of these assumed conditions, a factory locates where total or aggregate transport costs are minimized. The total transport bill per unit of marketed output consists of assembly costs plus marketing costs.

One simple way to illustrate the least-transport-cost location is Alfred Weber's *weight triangle* (Figure 5.4). Each corner of the triangle exerts a pull on the least-cost location (P) as indicated by the arrows. The manufacturer of one unit of production requires X tons of raw material M_1 and Y tons of raw material M_2 and sells the finished product at the market, C. The factory locates somewhere inside the triangle as determined by the relative weight of the factors. An initial location, thus determined, is subsequently affected by the growth of agglomeration economies—clustering of firms to effect cost savings—that help to develop a locational inertia for interrelated industries.

The effect of industrial location on the landscape is to concentrate population and production in fewer, larger places than is the case of the gradient-hierarchy landscape serving an agricultural population.

Distorting Factors

In addition to the differential quality of the environment, two other elements distort theoretical patterns:

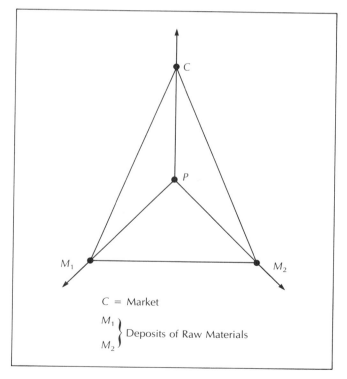

FIGURE 5.4
Weberian weight triangle.

spatial error and the *evolution of the spatial structure as conditions change.* First, efficient location is a short-run condition. The economic environment in which decisions are made is never static. Technology, transport quality, productivity, kind and volume of demands, and manufacturing processes all change. The effect of these changes is to invalidate once-valid decisions and to force individuals, firms, industries, and governments to alter their behavior.

Efficient location is also constrained by spatial error or nonoptimal decision making. People make decisions on the basis of information, expectations, and predictions. Typically, they make decisions without knowing all the facts. Facts about the future are unknown, and other facts are only partly known or poorly understood. People also accommodate tradition (e.g., cultural attitudes, beliefs, and practices), personal whim, as well as economic requirements when they make decisions. When a location decision must be made and implemented, they adapt to the world as they see it. To confound the situation still more, many events operate out of the realm of individual decision-makers. Nature and the economic and political environment may be hostile, benign, or generous in the affairs of decision-makers.

THE BEHAVIORAL APPROACH

The classic *normative models* of human behavior, which describe how people should behave and make decisions if they wish to achieve certain well-defined objectives, assume that the economic landscape is the work of optimizers under conditions of perfect competition. Optimizers know all the answers and act rationally to maximize utility. They know what crops to grow, where to locate central-place activities, and where to produce industrial goods. The landscape created by optimizers does not go through any intermediate adjustment stages; rather it goes from undifferentiated to optimal instantly.

In the late 1950s, H. A. Simon (1957) drew attention to the insufficiency of classical models of human behavior. Subsequently, geographer Julian Wolpert (1964) demonstrated that the optimizer model is not completely satisfactory. For a large farming region in Sweden, Wolpert determined the potential assumptions (Figure 5.5a). The potential productivity surface reflects the monetary return for an hour of labor if farmers decided to use all farm resources optimally and if the environment held to average values of temperature and precipitation. Us-

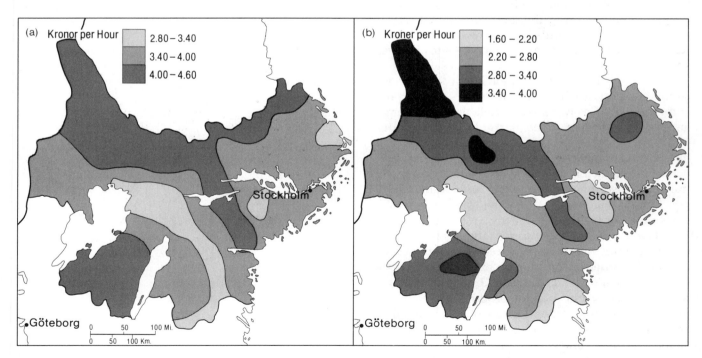

FIGURE 5.5
Contrast between (a) the potential productivity of farm labor (optimizer) and (b) the actual productivity of farm labor (satisficer) in middle Sweden. (Source: Wolpert, 1964, pp. 540-41.)

ing data from a Swedish government survey, Wolpert then plotted actual labor-productivity values (Figure 5.5b). The whole surface is lower than the potential surface, because no farmers organized their farm activities to reach the values derived under normative conditions. Large farms and those near agricultural experiment stations (the source of much information on improved farming practices) came closer to the optimal productivity than their smaller and more distant counterparts. Therefore, the pattern of departures from potential yield could be explained in terms of personal and geographical factors. Interviews indicated that the farmers were generally content with their lot in life and felt they were doing the best job they could. The farmers were not rationalizing their suboptimal behavior; rather, they were unaware of the full economic potential of their land parcels.

Demonstration of the inadequacy of normative models of human behavior led to the emergence of *stochastic models* based on the uncertainty principle. These models recognize that human decisions are a probabilistic amalgam of choice, calculation, and chance.

Intrinsic to behavioral models based on uncertainty are two major assumptions. First, economic landscapes are created by fallible and unequal human beings. People cannot foresee the outcomes of all possible actions; their knowledge is imperfect. People also cannot synthesize large amounts of information instantly. Economic landscapes are the result of a trial-and-error process. They are strongly structured by existing patterns of production, exchange, and consumption. Second, decision-makers are not optimizers. They are *satisficers* who make decisions that are "good enough," or satisfactory. A "good enough" decision is one that results in profits or, at least, zero loss. Such decisions may be optimal, but only if decision-makers are lucky enough to choose an optimal location. Satisficers more often choose suboptimal locations, even when more profitable locations are known, if they are sufficiently motivated by noneconomic factors. This concept is termed "psychic income." *Psychic income* is the noneconomic satisfaction derived from operating in a specific physical environment—perhaps one's home town, or away from other environments such as high-crime areas.

The Behavioral Matrix

A conceptual approach to nonoptimal decision making involves the use of a behavioral matrix (Pred 1967) (Figure 5.6). The origin of the matrix is the top,

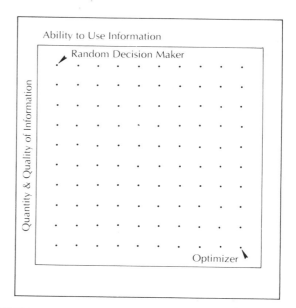

FIGURE 5.6
A behavioral matrix.

left-hand corner. The reliability and quantity of information increases to the right, and the ability and speed with which that knowledge is applied increases downward. A perfect optimizer locates in the extreme lower right-hand corner. A purely "random" decision-maker locates at the origin. In a small, one-plant firm, a single individual may make the locational decision. In the real world, the information and synthesizing ability of individual firms is limited and unequal. The personnel and data-gathering ability possessed by large multiplant corporations, on the other hand, allows them to make more precise locational decisions. In large corporations, such decisions are made not by an individual, but by a collective of middle-level managers each of whom brings specialized knowledge and skills to the decision-making process. This group of specialists constitutes the *technostructure* of an organization (Galbraith 1967). The specialized knowledge and skills of the technostructure may allow corporations to locate close to the optimum position on the behavioral matrix if they have largely eliminated the competition.

A diagram illustrates an elementary application of the behavioral matrix (Figure 5.7). The isolines below the matrix represent *spatial margins to profitability*. These margins delimit the geographical space beyond which a product can no longer generate a viable economic return on the entrepreneur's investment. Any chosen location that falls within those margins is a viable location. Decision-makers from the

FIGURE 5.7
A behavioral matrix and locational choice.

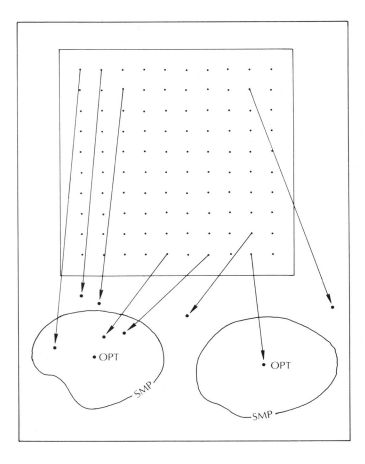

lower right quadrant of the behavioral matrix are most likely to choose viable locations, but they may also select nonviable sites and disappear penniless from the landscape. Decision-makers from the upper left quadrant are more likely to choose unprofitable locations, but they may be fortunate enough to select viable, or even optimal sites.

Agriculture

The behavioral matrix can also be applied to agricultural land use. Choosing the optimum crop in a given location is a trial-and-error process. The normative model helps us to understand the prevailing form of agriculture over large areas, especially when environmental aspects are added. Within the prevailing pattern of agriculture, however, there may be individual farms or larger subregions, where other forms of agriculture predominate. This situation may result from suboptimal decision making (Figure 5.8). Better decision-makers, with few exceptions, have chosen the more profitable form of agriculture for a given location. Others have chosen a less profitable, but still viable, form of agriculture. Most of the less profitable

decisions occur near the boundary of the two prevailing crops, where the decision is less clear-cut and information is often conflicting.

Many types of agriculture and farming practices result from cultural values that differ from the norm, and often exist even in a dominant market economy. In the United States, the horsepowered agriculture of Amish farms in the midst of tractor-based farming, the persistence of wheat farming in the margins of dry lands during the 1930s, and the continuation of tobacco as a secondary crop in parts of the South are examples. Residual farms surrounded by suburban housing at the margins of cities are another example. How can they persist in the face of more profitable forms of land use? Residual farms cannot persist in the long-run, but for a short period of years they can hold out, even considering the much higher income that would result from selling the land for housing purposes. Owners reap psychic income from remaining in farming, and increased real income when they do decide to sell. A farmer who owns the land controls the means of production and can persist against more competitive forms of land use. No beginning farmer, however, could afford to buy a residual farm for agricultural purposes.

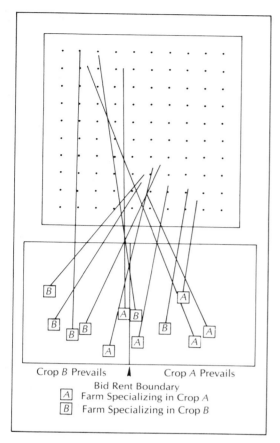

FIGURE 5.8
A behavioral matrix and agricultural regions.

Game Theory Environmental conditions provide a partial explanation for broad patterns of agriculture. In the United States and Argentina, for example, the boundary between wheat farming and livestock ranching is basically a function of precipitation. Some areas are too dry for wheat; others always have enough moisture. In the middle zone between wet and dry, some years will support wheat and others will bring losses to farmers attempting to grow wheat. Farmers in the middle zone have three options: (1) practice only ranching, (2) risk everything on wheat with its potentially high rewards or losses, or (3) mix the two types of agriculture as a hedge against the uncertainty of the environment.

Environmental decision making has been approached in a *game-theoretic* framework. We can fashion a model in which nature is "out to get" farmers, and it therefore plays the role of an enemy. Game theory is the study of situations in which more than one decision-maker is involved—a farmer and the environment, for example—with each trying to maximize utility or minimize disutility. The name "game theory" derives from the similar situations that occur in such games as chess, checkers, bridge, tic-tac-toe, or backgammon.

We can represent the underlying idea of game theory in the form of a payoff matrix (Figure 5.9). There are two players: a farmer and the environment. Each player has two strategies from which to choose, and the payoff to the farmer is shown in each cell of the matrix. We assume that the farmer always wins, and tries to win as much as possible, and that the environment always loses, but tries to minimize losses. For example, if the farmer chooses ranching and the environment chooses wet, the farmer reaps a "payoff" of $20 at the expense of the environment. If they both choose the second strategy—wheat and dry, respectively—the farmer only wins $2 at the environment's expense. This type of game is called a *zero-sum game*, because the "payoff" to the farmer is exactly the value "lost" by the environment.

What is the best strategy the farmer can adopt to maximize winnings? It is ranching. The farmer is certain of winning $10, but could win $20. From the standpoint of the environment, the best strategy is dry. Thus, the farmer should always choose the first strategy, whereas the environment should always choose the second. In this case, the farmer will always win $10. Notice that the value of $10 is a minimum value of a row and a maximum value in a column. This is called the *saddlepoint* or *minimax point* in game theory. The minimax point indicates that each player has the best strategy. Any deviation from the saddlepoint by one player results in the other seizing the advantage.

In a second, more complicated, example of game theory, consider a humid area in which four strategies are possible: (1) livestock ranching based on natural vegetation; (2) wheat farming; (3) corn, with all income

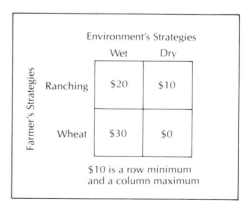

FIGURE 5.9
Payoff matrix: wheat and ranching.

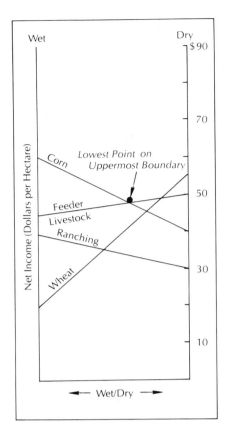

FIGURE 5.10
Locating a critical pair of strategies.

you have looked in vain. You will not find a saddlepoint, because there is no single best strategy for either the farmer or the environment. The farmer must mix the two available strategies to maximize the payoff for the game. How can we determine how much time the farmer should devote to each strategy? If we take the absolute differences (regardless of sign) between each pair of values, and assign the proportion derived from each strategy to the alternate one, the result will be the amount of time the farmer should spend on each. If we total the difference, we have twenty plus five, or twenty-five. Clearly, then, corn should be the primary cash crop 20 percent of the time and feeder cattle should account for sales 80 percent of the time. The type of agriculture that will result in the primary sale item must be planned ahead. Feeder cattle must be purchased early in the year for fattening, and the farmer cannot switch from feeder-cattle sales to sell corn for grain without first dumping livestock on the market or losing the total investment in the cattle by not feeding them at all.

How can farmers use the solution derived from the corn and feeder livestock payoff matrix? Should corn be the sole source of income 20 percent of the year and feeder cattle the remainder? Should total income be based on these proportions every year? In game-theory terms, and over the long run, it makes no difference.

Assume that dry years occur 50 percent of the time and farmers use 20 percent of their land to raise corn for grain and 80 percent for feeder cattle each year (Figure 5.12). Income per hectare will be the same ($48) whether the year is wet or dry. The same average will result if land is used exclusively for corn 20 percent of the year and for feeder livestock for the remainder. Farmers, however, must be concerned with short-run results. In a dry year, a below-average income will result if corn is the sole source of income; a wet year will yield a below-average income if total income is derived from feeder livestock. However, we assume that farmers desire at least an "average" income each year, and will, therefore, obtain the best

based on the sale of corn as grain; and (4) feeder livestock, with all income derived from animals fattened on corn. Which strategy (or combination of strategies) will yield the highest net income per hectare over the long run with the least risk? In a graphical solution to this question, the lowest point on the uppermost boundary indicates the two crops on which farmers should concentrate (Figure 5.10). These crops are corn-for-grain and feeder livestock. The two crops are then put in a payoff matrix (Figure 5.11). Look for the saddlepoint. Remember this value is a row minimum and a column maximum. In this case

FIGURE 5.11
Payoff matrix: corn and feeder livestock.

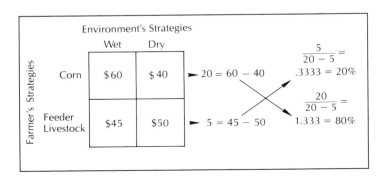

FIGURE 5.12
Determination of long-run average income per hectare.

ASSUME: Dry years occur 50% of the time
          20% of land used for corn for grain
          80% of land used for feeder livestock

WET YEAR: Corn = $12.00 = ($60.00 • 20%)
          Livestock = $36.00 = ($45.00 • 80%)
          Total (per hectare) = $48.00

DRY YEAR: Corn = $8.00 = ($40.00 • 20%)
          Livestock = $40.00 = ($50.00 • 80%)
          Total (per hectare) = $48.00

AVERAGE: $48.00 = $48.00 + $48.00 ÷ 2
          (dry years occur 50% of the time)

results if specific proportions of each type of agriculture are adopted each year.

Game theory provides only a framework to approach the problem of uncertainty. We must assume that patterns of production are the result of a trial-and-error process that has been modified over time. Agriculture is always a gamble because of random shocks caused by environmental extremes.

Innovation-Diffusion The margins of a particular kind of agriculture can shift because of changes in demand. They can also shift because of changes in technology. Hybrid corn exemplifies a technological innovation that shifted the margins of corn-based agriculture in the United States. Less than one-third of the corn planted in the United States in 1940 was hybrid, but by 1954 almost 90 percent was hybrid. And in the north central states, which constitute the heart of the Corn Belt, hybrid corn accounted for over 97 percent of the total crop. The use of hybrids increased the yield per hectare by as much as 20 percent and made the use of mechanical harvesters much more efficient. But the greatest benefit was the increase in the speed of maturation. Rapid maturation made corn a viable crop in formerly marginal areas, and a marginal crop in areas where it could not be grown for grain before the introduction of hybrids. In other words, the environmental margins of the crop were shifted northward in the United States (Roepke 1959).

Because changes in technology induce changes in agricultural patterns, geographers are interested in the forces that control the spread and adoption of technological innovations. Innovations are not adopted instantly by all potential users because of the presence of barriers. These obstacles may be environmental, cultural, economic, or psychological in nature. Nonetheless, the rate of adoption does follow a rather constant and predictable sequence. At the start, there are just a few innovators who adopt an innovation. These are followed successively by groups that may be termed the early majority, late majority, and the laggards (Figure 5.13). Very often, the distribution of people adopting an innovation describes a fairly symmetrical or bell-shaped curve. If we accumulate the distribution of acceptors, we get an *S*-shaped curve, which describes the proportion of adopters over time (Figure 5.14).

Geographers use simulation to analyze the adoption of technological innovations. They assume that an innovation *diffuses* outward from an initial core. The core is a given distribution of people who have already accepted the innovation. The problem then becomes one of determining the key variable(s) that control(s) the diffusion or spread of the innovation. As with all models, numerous factors are not

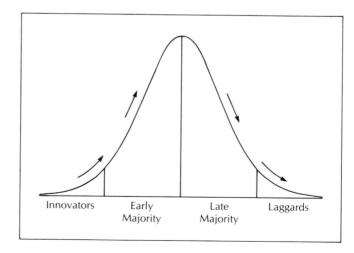

FIGURE 5.13
Distribution of innovation acceptors.

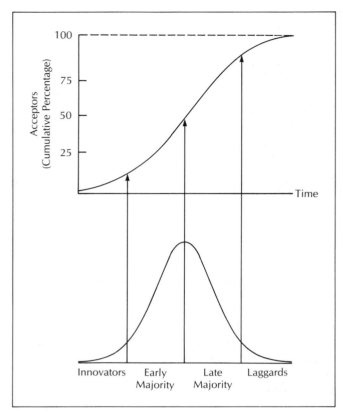

FIGURE 5.14
Accumulating the proportion of adopters.

In his studies on the diffusion of innovations, Torsten Hägerstrand, a geographer at the University of Lund, Sweden, observed a strong tendency for people to adopt new ideas when the ideas had already gained acceptance by others close by. The problem was to discover the rules of the game that produced the regularities in his detailed sequences.

included among the variables selected for controls. These other factors that might influence the spread of an innovation are considered to interact *randomly* in the diffusion model.

Some geographers argue that the technique of simulation illustrates the *speed* of diffusion rather than decision making. And others who have studied decision making in the Third World suggest that some of the assumptions on which innovation-diffusion research is based may be incorrect. Data from East Africa and Thailand, for example, show that ideas, plans, and innovations sent down from the core to the local level and to the villagers are often ignored (de Souza and Porter 1974). Ideas are accepted more readily at the village level if they are first introduced by local change agents.

The initial work on the diffusion of innovations was done by Torsten Hägerstrand, a geographer at the University of Lund in Sweden. His simulation model assumes that innovations spread through personal contacts, and that the frequency of personal contact is an inverse function of distance. The problem, therefore, is to determine the exact form of the relationship

between distance and the frequency of personal contact.

Hägerstrand first applied the technique of simulation to the diffusion of a government farm subsidy program in Sweden. The program was designed to encourage farmers to improve pastureland and to discourage grazing in open woodland. Personal contact was especially important in promoting the acceptance of the program in the 1930s, before the widespread use of radios, telephones, and automobiles in rural areas. Hägerstrand used the distances over which people migrated as an estimate of the distance/personal contact relationship (Figure 5.15). Most migrants settled rather close to home, and, as distance increased, the number of migrants tailed off. The curved line in the graph describes a *distant-decay effect*—in brief, how personal interaction decreases with distance.

The migration/distance curve (Figure 5.15) is one-dimensional. However, since geographical space is two-dimensional, Hägerstrand developed a "mean information field" map (Figure 5.16a) that indicates the probability of personal contact from a given point

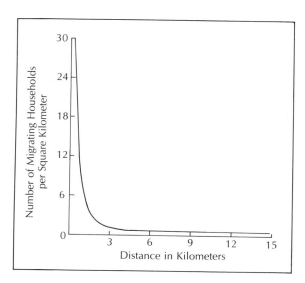

FIGURE 5.15
Migration as a function of distance.

(the center) to all others. The mean information field was calculated by rotating the migration/distance curve 360 degrees. The size of Hägerstrand's mean information field was 25 by 25 kilometers, with the value of each cell determined by the migration/distance curve. For example, a cell ten kilometers from the center square was assigned a value of .167. These values were then translated into migrant households per cell by multiplying by 25. For example, .167 times 25 equals 4.17 (Figure 5.16b), which is an estimate of the number of households migrating from the center cell to cells ten kilometers from the center. Because the distance-decay function for migration overestimated the number of migrants at very short distances, the value of the center cell was determined by using the actual number of migrants over this distance. Next, the values in the map in Figure 5.16b were converted into probabilities by dividing each value by the sum of all values (Figure 5.16c). The probabilities illustrated in the map in Figure 5.16c total 1.00. Finally, the probabilities were accumulated from .0000 to .9999 with the interval assigned each cell determined by its respective probability (Figure 5.16d). Each of the corner cells in this map, for example, has a probability of .0096 (from Figure 5.16c), and, therefore, an interval of 96.

Hägerstrand's simulation model proceeds by centering the mean information field over an acceptor

FIGURE 5.16
Calculation of a mean information field.

	(a)			
.095	.139	.167	.139	.095
.139	.299	.543	.299	.139
.167	.543		.543	.167
.139	.299	.543	.299	.139
.095	.139	.167	.139	.095

	(b)			
2.38	3.48	4.17	3.48	2.38
3.48	7.48	13.57	7.48	3.48
4.17	13.57	110.00	13.57	4.17
3.48	7.48	13.57	7.48	3.48
2.38	3.38	4.17	3.48	2.38

	(c)			
.0096	.0140	.0168	.0140	.0096
.0140	.0301	.0547	.0301	.0140
.0168	.0547	.4431	.0547	.0168
.0140	.0301	.0547	.0301	.0140
.0096	.0140	.0168	.0140	.0096

	(d)			
.0000 .0096	.0097 .0236	.0237 .0404	.0405 .0544	.0545 .0640
.0641 .0780	.0781 .1081	.1082 .1628	.1629 .1929	.1930 .2069
.2070 .2237	.2238 .2784	.2785 .7215	.7216 .7762	.7763 .7930
.7931 .8070	.8071 .8371	.8372 .8918	.8919 .9219	.9220 .9359
.9630 .9455	.9456 .9595	.9596 .9763	.9764 .9903	.9904 .9999

FIGURE 5.17
The simulation process.

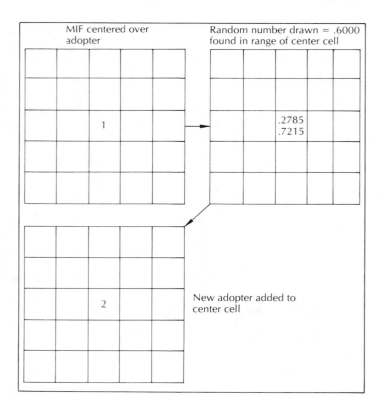

and drawing a random number from a table of four-digit random numbers. Suppose the first random number drawn is .6000. We then assume that information on the farm subsidy is passed from an initial acceptor to someone living in the center cell (Figure 5.17). This process is repeated for each initial acceptor. Given the probabilities, most information will be passed to people living a very short distance from someone already using the innovation, but the possibility of drawing any random number from .0000 to .9999 allows the innovation to diffuse to more distant farmers.

The process is continued for a series of rounds, with the mean information field centered on all acceptors from the preceding round. There will be differences, of course, between the simulated pattern and the actual pattern of diffusion, but the simulation does predict the actual pattern quite well (Figure 5.18). Furthermore, the model can be altered to account for the relative speed of acceptance of new ideas. We may decide that a given cell must be hit two or three times before the innovation is accepted. A cell's probability can be changed to accurately reflect its population density, and movements in certain directions can be limited to simulate inadequate transportation routes.

New technology is one of the prime forces operating to change agricultural patterns. Innovations may allow the farmer to increase the gross income per

hectare, lower the cost per hectare, or both. New technology can lower the risk the farmer must face in terms of weather or soil conditions. Irrigation systems lower risk; herbicides, pesticides, and fertilizers increase yields per hectare. The diffusion model enhances our understanding of how innovations spread; hence, we can better understand how agricultural patterns change. The diffusion model also allows us to simulate nonoptimal human decision making and portrays the landscape as evolutionary rather than instantaneous, which is typical of descriptive as opposed to normative models.

Agricultural patterns also shift in response to changes in demand. For example, the growing importance of meat in the American diet over the past hundred years has resulted in increased emphasis on feeder livestock in the Midwest. And in Europe, a growing demand for fresh fruit and early vegetables in Britain, France, Benelux, West Germany, and Scandinavia has led to increased specialization and commercialization of agriculture in the Mediterranean polyculture region.

Most agricultural pattern changes take years to occur. They reflect slowly changing demand and geographical restraints on the diffusion of information. They also reflect the unwillingness of farmers to accept risks they cannot afford. Today industrial agriculture requires a large capital investment. Ma-

ACTUAL

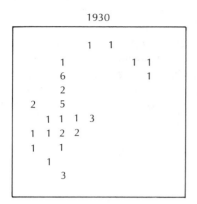

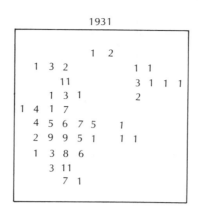

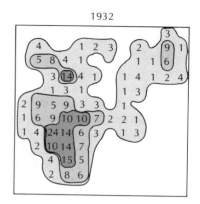

SIMULATED

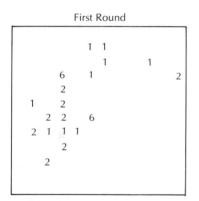

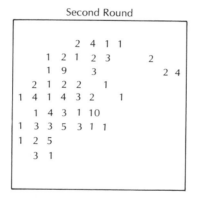

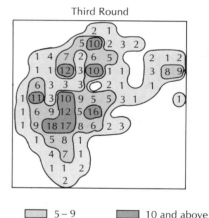

☐ 1–4   ☐ 5–9   ▨ 10 and above

FIGURE 5.18
Actual and simulated patterns. (Source: Adapted from Hägerstrand, 1965.)

chinery may be so specialized that it can be used for only one particular kind of agriculture. Thus, a given type of agriculture may persist in an area when farmers are limited by the investments of the past.

The Size and Spacing of Cities

The classical model provides a partial explanation of the distribution of central places. Its normative assumptions include an even distribution of population and resources and instantaneous adjustment of the hierarchy of market areas to produce a stable system. These two assumptions result in a static and precise geometric arrangement of cities in terms of size and

spacing. Actually, the size and spacing of cities is the result of many complex forces. An understanding of the arrangement of urban places must take the following factors into account:

1   the economic and social conditions that allow and/or encourage the concentration of all economic activities in settlements;

2   the geographical conditions that influence the spacing and size of settlements;

3   the fact that the development of the urban pattern is an evolutionary process in which the past exerts a powerful influence on the present; and

4   the fact that the urban system is the result of human decisions based on imperfect knowledge.

All of these factors distort the ideal pattern of urban places.

An example illustrates this distortion (Figure 5.19). Point *I* is the ideal location for the highest level central place. The shaded area represents a localized power resource, such as coal. The isoline is a spatial margin to profitability for the highest level central place. Because of the spacing geometry, we must assume that places outside that isoline can never attain the highest level. The first settlement in the area is at *A*, to exploit the resource base. The city prospers, increases in population through migration, and adds more and more service activities. A subsequent settlement develops at *I*, but is a pure central place. Because of its early growth and subsequent size, *A* assumes the major central-place role in the region. The final pattern is the result of both the unpredictability of human decision making and the evolutionary nature of the urban system. We are assuming that the localized resource can only support one large manufacturing city. The initial site chosen for development could have been at *I*, which would have optimized the spacing arrangement of the highest level central places, or at point *B*. Point *B*, however, is outside the spatial margins and could have never developed to that level. Its population would be supported by manufacturing and resource exploitation and a lower level central-place role.

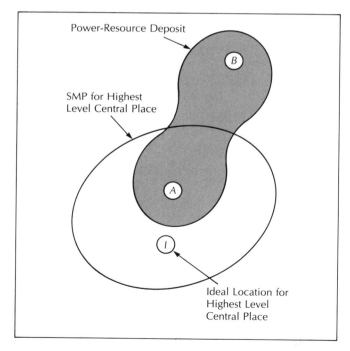

FIGURE 5.19
Actual and ideal locations: distortion by localized power-resource deposit.

Richard Morrill (1963), an American geographer, developed a stochastic model incorporating all aspects of a growing urban system, including the randomness of human decision making. Morrill's model takes the same approach as Hägerstrand's model of diffusion, an approach called *Monte Carlo simulation.* "Monte Carlo" evokes an image of gambling casinos, and it is used for good reason. It signifies a probabilistic model—a model that generates somewhat different results each time it is employed.

Morrill's model was employed in a study of the growth of towns in an area consisting of 155 local parishes in southern Sweden. The model runs in a series of twenty-year cycles from 1860 to 1980. Each simulation consists of five phases:

1 the benchmark distribution of population, routes, central places, manufacturing, and so on;
2 the assignment of non-central-place activities, such as manufacturing, the demand for which is determined by population, income, and resources;
3 the assignment of central-place activities, which is dependent on the population of the place;
4 the assignment of migrants between areas; and
5 the end of the first cycle, which becomes the starting point for the next simulation cycle.

The built-in flexibility and evolutionary (feedback) elements of Morrill's model constitute an important departure from the static and geometric normative model of central places. If the required data for a given area are collected, the model can be run to determine whether or not it adequately results in an urban system corresponding to reality. Of greatest importance, the model accounts for nonoptimal and indeterminate human decision making.

Morrill's model also assumes a "free economy" in which the development of the urban system is the result of the decisions of many individual entrepreneurs. Each decision-maker operates within the structure imposed by the past and within the confines of the existing market economy. Within these limits, however, there is enough "slack" to allow for random decision making. In a controlled economy, the state acts as a decision-maker and regulates the economy to achieve a variety of goals. Central economic planners may decide, for example, to spur the development of a depressed or underdeveloped area. This could be achieved by building transport lines or developing a heavy industrial complex to serve the area. The likelihood of such actions may be remote in a capitalist economy, however, because the depressed area could not bring the profits required by private development. This is not to say that controlled economies are unconcerned with the economies of development, but rather that the value they place on long-run social goals may outweigh the short-run losses that such a policy may bring. In the long run, the development of the depressed area may be "profitable" in both an economic and welfare sense. In an economy completely dependent upon many private decision-makers, each entrepreneur must wait for the development process to begin before acting; thus, development may never proceed. Actually, capitalist economies are subject to government intervention. A government may adopt a regional policy consisting of a set of "carrots and sticks" to change the geography that an entrepreneur faces when making a location decision.

Manufacturing

Manufacturing requires a decision to operate at a particular scale with a particular input combination at a given location. This decision is made without perfect knowledge. The reliability of an individual decision depends on the location of the decision-maker within the behavioral matrix. The behavioral matrix assumes that the store of knowledge (and ability) is information about the economic structures that determine the viability of a given location or many possible locations.

Let us assume that all industrial location decisions are made by individuals who fall in the extreme upper left-hand corner of the behavioral matrix (Figure 5.6). In other words, people have no relevant information (or ability) concerning the spatial structure of economic viability. The actions of such decision-makers can be characterized as completely random. This assumption raises the question about the difference between the industrial landscape created by perfect knowledge and one created by random decision-makers, or the difference between random decision-makers and those possessing some information (and ability) concerning the spatial structure of viability.

In exploring this question in detail, economist A. Alchian (1950) developed the following three major points:

1 If there are a large number of individuals making random decisions, some of them will choose viable, or even optimal, locations.
2 The pattern that results from random location-choosing will not necessarily differ from one chosen by rational foresight.
3 Even if decisions are random, the conditions that determine viability can still be specified. With a knowledge of the viability structure, we can state

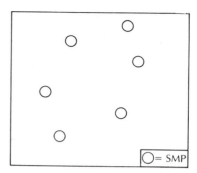

FIGURE 5.20
Spatial margins to profitability for industry X.

the types of location that will be more viable relative to other types, even if the decision-makers themselves do not know the locational conditions of success or try to achieve them by changing locations.

The congruency between the economic landscape produced by optimizers and one produced by satisficers can be amplified by a simple model. A diagram illustrates the spatial margins to profitability for a particular industry (Figure 5.20). These margins are very small, and the exact center of each viable area represents the optimum location for a manufacturing plant in the industry. The spatial margins to profitability and the optimum locations are determined by economic conditions that are independent of locational decisions. In other words, we are ignoring possible changes in profitability that might result from locational interdependence. *Locational interdependence* is the principle that says competition from rival producers can dramatically lower potential revenues at a given point in space.

A sheet of plywood is used to cover the map. Holes have been cut in this sheet to line up exactly with the spatial margins to profitability on the map

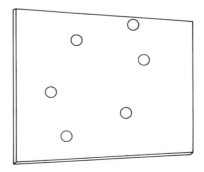

FIGURE 5.21
Map covered by a sheet of plywood (holes correspond to spatial margins to profitability).

underneath (Figure 5.21). With only six possible viable locations, we are assuming that only six manufacturing plants (one in each area) are required to serve total demand. The decision-making process is simulated by throwing darts at the plywood sheet. After all darts have been thrown, the sheet is removed and the resultant pattern observed.

The action of optimizers is simulated by the darts champion of an English pub, who is given only six darts to throw (Figure 5.22). The action of random decision-makers is simulated by someone with little experience at darts, who is given one hundred darts to throw (Figure 5.23). Comparing the two patterns after the sheets are removed, we see that the one produced by random decision-makers is exactly the same as the one produced by optimizers. In reality, the process is much more complicated, of course, because of the locational-interdependence factor. The structure of viable locations is constantly altered each time a new producer establishes a production site, but, if demand is stable, the final outcome is much the same. We can

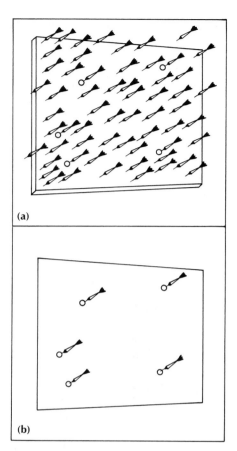

(a)

(b)

FIGURE 5.23
(a) Simulation by a satisficer and (b) the resultant pattern.

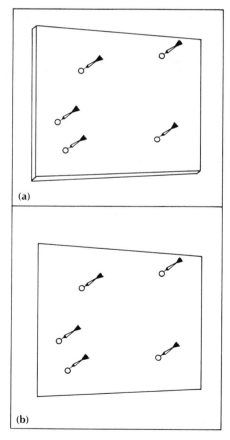

(a)

(b)

FIGURE 5.22
(a) Simulation by an optimizer and (b) the resultant pattern.

never be sure that current producers are in optimal sites, however; only that they are in viable sites during the current period.

Even decision-makers who pay careful attention to the spatial structure of economic conditions can never be sure they have selected an optimal site, although they may be certain of its viability. Shortages of time and money preclude the examination of all possible sites. A decision-maker may identify one set of spatial margins to profitability and the optimum location within these limits, but this is a local solution to the location problem. From a global standpoint, there could be other locations that would yield higher profits. This concept is illustrated by the graph (Figure 5.24). Decision-makers examine only the area to the right of the vertical line. Within that area, they determine the spatial margins to profitability and select optimum locations. In a global sense, however, more-profitable locations are possible. Total demand may be met by an aggregate of locations that are merely viable rather than optimal.

FIGURE 5.24
Local and global solutions to
the location problem.

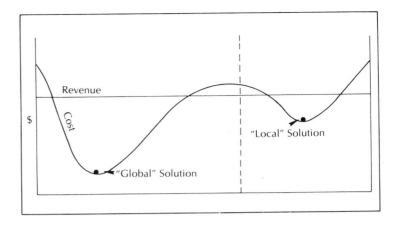

THE MARXIST APPROACH

Marxists criticize classical and behavioral approaches to locational decision making on the grounds that they are too inflexible to respond to the transformation that began to sweep the world economy after the mid-1950s. In developed capitalist countries, this transformation involved the decline of the old basic industries—coalmining, steelmaking, shipbuilding. It also involved a dispersal of industrial and service activities from major cities to smaller towns and suburbs, and from core regions to more peripheral ones. Much of these changing patterns occurred as a result of the increasing importance of large, multi-plant companies. The variety of behavior exhibited by various multilocational companies is not easily accounted for in a classical or behavioral location-theory approach.

Marxists charge that classical location theory, derived from the classical economics, is myopic in its focus on individual firms in absolute competition and responding blindly and perfectly to market forces. Moreover, traditional location theory is deterministic. It uses geographical factors to explain that geographical patterns are the result of geographical causes. For example, the distance variable causes predictable patterns of land use, and the geographical characteristics of inner cities cause their decline. Marxist geographers scorn those who segregate the spatial from the social for indulging in *spatial fetishism;* that is, attributing the cause of an event to locational factors. Moreover, Marxists find fault with the static nature of traditional theory; it cannot cope with the dynamic, unstable quality of the capitalist system.

Marxists also criticize the behavioral approach, itself a response to the inadequacy of classical location theory. Although behavioral geographers do acknowledge a variety of factors contributing to locational choices, they abdicate responsibility for "explaining" spatial forms and patterns of organization. Stochastic models, based on the concepts of uncertainty and probability, describe and predict rather than explain. Like classical theories, behavioral ones are a-historical. They isolate human decision making from the events of the past.

For Marxists, the sorts of characteristics that influence an entrepreneur's choice of where to build a factory, expand, or close hinge on the *nature* and *demands of production.* In turn, changes in production, and consequently in locational factors, are not the result of some autonomous choice by decision-makers, but of wider economic and political forces, relations with labor within firms, and of firms' reactions to both. Thus, the decisions of firms to decentralize, to leave old manufacturing areas for new ones, and to abandon central cities for suburbs and beyond are a reflection of attempts to contend with changes in the broader economic environment.

Marxists disagree among themselves about how to explain the social organization of production. It can be argued that some versions of Marxism foster a rigid and oversimplified mindset. There is a danger of viewing economic decisions as predetermined responses to a set of forces called the "demands of accumulation" and the "law of value." The Marxist approach is just as deterministic as traditional location theory. It normalizes particular decisions, which is particularly unfortunate in geography, a subject devoted to understanding unevenness, difference, place, and locality. It ignores geography, just as traditional location theory ignores social relations.

An alternate version of Marxism recognizes underlying causal processes, but recognizes, too, that such processes never operate in isolation. "The particular nature of capitalism in specific countries, the very different ways in which different parts of the economy respond to the general situation of economic recessions, the very different impact which the entry of particular forms of economic activity can have on different regions and local areas: all are products of many determinations" (Massey 1984, pp. 6–7). Instead of viewing differences as deviations from a norm, this approach recognizes their significance as causal factors and appreciates their effects.

Geographers who accept this perspective argue that changes in the spatial organization of production are a response to changes in class relations—economic and political, national and international. The geography of economic activity involves a struggle between capital and labor. To understand the causes of locational decisions, it is necessary to investigate relations between capital and labor and to examine their empirical form that varies among countries and over time.

The most interesting work in this version of Marxism so far concerns the locational behavior of companies (Massey and Meegan 1982; Scott and Storper 1986). What are the building blocks for understanding the locational strategies of firms? They include the nature of the labor process and the organization of capital, the social structure of capitalist production, and the relationship between the social and the spatial. These building blocks also help geographers appreciate the impact of locational decisions on particular places at different times.

Characteristics of Industry

Industry, as revealed in the Standard Industrial Classification (SIC), is a collection of hundreds of different types of firms. Locational decisions reflect a firm's particular type. For example, market-seeking firms—banks, hotels, and locally oriented manufacturers—locate within the market to serve it. Although it is vital to know about the locational strategies of different types of firms, it is equally vital to know how the labor process and the organization of capital affect the geographical distribution of firms.

The Labor Process   There are four phases in the development of the labor process (Aglietta 1979). Each phase represents an increasing division of labor functionally and geographically. The geographical manifestation of each phase depends on the interaction between the requirements of the labor process and the inherited spatial structure.

The first phase, *manufacture*, consists of the gathering of workers into a factory system with firms widely dispersed throughout the countryside. Dispersal was a characteristic of British firms before the industrial revolution. It enabled entrepreneurs to

avoid guild restrictions and high-cost labor in towns and to obtain access to water power (Perrons 1981).

In the second phase, *machinofacture*, mechanization occurs and the division of labor within production develops. The use of mechanical principles and steam power frees industry from rural locations. Production is increasingly concentrated in towns. This phase was characteristic of industrial capitalist countries during the industrial revolution.

The third phase, *Fordism* (integrated production and assembly), together with *Taylorism* (application of scientific management principles to production), results in further job fragmentation, especially the separation of conception from execution. Fordism results in the geographical separation of control and production. It leads to the growth of office-based activities that often replace industry in central cities. Industrial activities move to the suburbs and subsequently, in search of cheaper and less-organized labor, move beyond the suburbs to peripheral regions in the home country and the world.

The latest or fourth phase, *neo-Fordism*, results in further fragmentation of the labor force and the distilling of the traditional blue-collar class through the introduction of electronic information systems. Neo-Fordism reinforces the geographical pattern introduced by Fordism by increasing the physical separation of different production functions and by extending the possibility of decentralization of production to small-batch processes as well as large assembly runs.

These four phases represent different ways of combining capital and labor in the production process. They lead decision-makers to make different locational choices. The introduction of each new stage, however, does not imply a complete reshaping of all locational patterns. At any one place at any one time there are likely to exist a number of different production configurations.

The Organization of Capital   The adoption of a particular labor process is linked to the organizational structure of capital, especially the size of a company. Size distinguishes single-plant firms from multiplant firms or numerous small firms (small capital) from large firms (monopoly capital). It is also related to the development of the capitalist economy. Over time the organization of the economy into larger units of capital, through merger and takeover (centralization) and through internal expansion (concentration), represents an increase of control by individual companies.

The spatial structures of capital are diverse. Three simple examples are concentrated, cloning, and

FIGURE 5.25
Examples of spatial structures:
(a) concentrated; (b) cloning;
(c) part-process. (Source: Based
on Massey, 1984, p. 77.)

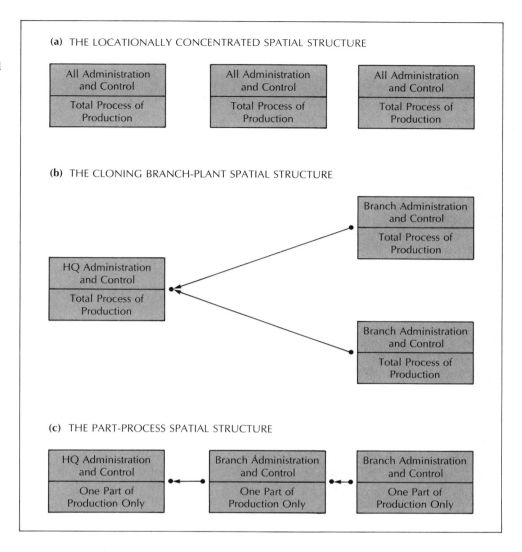

(a) THE LOCATIONALLY CONCENTRATED SPATIAL STRUCTURE

(b) THE CLONING BRANCH-PLANT SPATIAL STRUCTURE

(c) THE PART-PROCESS SPATIAL STRUCTURE

part-process (Figure 5.25). The *locally concentrated structure* is characteristic of small firms. The *cloning branch-plant structure* is characteristic of multilocational companies manufacturing final consumer goods (e.g., bottled and canned soft drinks). The *part-process structure* is also characteristic of multilocational companies and is exemplified by Ford's world car with its world-wide part-process organization. Other structures include *conglomerate ownership*, in which the production of a wide range of different commodities is under the same financial control, and *product-cycle*, in which the degree of financial and technological control is relaxed as commodities produced by different plants mature.

Social Structure of Capitalist Production

The labor process and the organization of capital attempt to link the day-to-day events in locational decision making to the longer term development of capitalism. But without a framework for understanding the social structure of capitalist production, they only provide guidance as to the locational strategies of firms. The defining classes of capitalist society are *capital* (bourgeoisie) and *labor* (proletariat) (Figure 5.26). Capitalists control the accumulation process through decisions about investment, the means of production, and the authority structure within the labor process. The working class does not exert this type of control.

No capitalist society is so simple, however. For example, within the working class, divisions between skilled and unskilled workers figure prominently in locational decisions. An industry may be rooted in a particular place because of the long experience of the area's workers. Changes in the labor process, however, may eventually free the industry from the labor market, and so also from its geographical ties. The

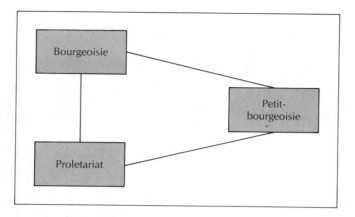

FIGURE 5.26
The internal social structure of capitalist production.

release of an industry from its traditional labor source is an impetus to move production from core regions to peripheral ones and from industrialized countries to industrializing ones.

In addition to capital and labor, there are other classes in the capitalist social structure; for example, there are landowners and the self-employed. The *self-employed* (petit-bourgeoisie) (Figure 5.26) have economic ownership and possession of the means of production, but exert no control over the labor of others. Self-employment is a precapitalistic inheritance, but it continues to grow and flourish. Like labor and capital, it is also differentiated. The classic example of the self-employed is the shopkeeper who

retains a foothold in those parts of an economy where capitalist firms have yet to fully take over. In many industrialized capitalist societies, shopkeepers are on the decline—corner shops are under threat from supermarkets. But there are also sectors of the economy in which self-employment is expanding. Examples include the new professional and business-service sectors.

This basic framework of the internal social structure of capitalist production is dynamic. It represents a set of social processes in which there is constant tension and conflict. It provides a basis for understanding locational decision making.

The Social and the Spatial

Geography involves distance and closeness, variations between areas, and the character and meaning of particular places or regions. These ingredients are essential to the operation of social processes. The development of the social structure of capitalist production takes place in a geographical world—the social and the spatial are inseparable. Take an example that illustrates the decision-making conundrum. Production change and locational change are alternative ways by which decision-makers can achieve the same ends. Geographical differences in the labor force may give management greater flexibility in decisions about production. If production is potentially mobile, it may be easier to move to low-wage areas than to introduce a change in the labor process. Either

Production change or location change can reduce a firm's labor costs. The European Component Corporation opted for locational change when it decided to open a branch plant on a trading estate on the outskirts of Belfast, Northern Ireland. The facility, which manufactures automobile seatbelts, employs many older, married women—an abundant source of low-wage labor. Many manufacturing firms in the United Kingdom decentralized their activities in the 1970s and 1980s by opening plants in peripheral regions. Service firms adopted a similar strategy. They decentralized the more routine elements of clerical work out of London, to regions where wage rates and office rents were lower. (Source: Industrial Development Board of Northern Ireland.)

strategy, production change or location change, can achieve the same result—a lowering of labor costs. The choice presents itself at a particular time; it generally serves to hasten a decision in a particular direction rather than to effect a departure from an existing trend. Nonetheless, results may be significant. What might have happened to the labor process in the clothing, textile, and electronic-assembly industries since the 1960s had multinational corporations not sought cheap labor reserves in the Third World?

DECISION MAKING ON A GLOBAL SCALE

Old and new industries located phases of their production process in low-wage countries in the 1970s and 1980s as a response to the new realities of capitalism. The new realities had their origin in the end of the post-World War II boom in the late 1960s and early 1970s. A crisis of profitability in production in developed countries created a deepening internationalization of capital on a scale never before known. Through the interaction of production and money capital, internationalization emerged as a major force in the organization of production, work, and space in all countries (Scott and Storper 1986).

Geographers, accustomed to viewing locational issues as local or national decisions, were slow to recognize the new realities of capitalism. Now, however, an international perspective cannot be ignored. "Global competition is the battlefield; competitiveness and excellence are the battle cries" (O'Loughlin 1988, p. 83).

The complexity and sophistication of the new economic geography calls into question the mechanistic conceptions of classical economic theory and Marxist crisis theory. Under classical criteria, factor endowments—land, labor, and capital—determine the location of economic activities in each country and among countries. Markets are left free to respond to supply and demand for products so as to allocate resources efficiently. But the relations of production defy this deterministic conception of economic behavior.

The new realities of capitalism also call into question Marxist crisis theory. In Marx's formulation, crisis, like the time of troubles in the 1970s, direct the long-term development of capitalism toward socialism (Figure 5.27). The crisis of the 1970s, however, did not result in a revolutionary "awakening"; instead, it led to yet another cumulative change in capitalism. During the 1980s, capitalism proved once again to be more technically dynamic and socially creative than predicted by Marx. For example, some Third World countries went beyond their initial role as cheap labor reserves and developed more complex patterns of industrialization, as the cases of Brazil, Hong Kong, and Singapore make clear.

In their reassessment of the new capitalism, a growing number of geographers accept the view that capital-labor struggles are the key for understanding locational decision making. However, they largely

FIGURE 5.27
Model of Marx's crisis theory. (Source: From *The Age of the Economist*, 5th ed. by Daniel R. Fusfeld. Copyright © 1986, 1982 by Scott, Foresman and Company. Reprinted by permission.)

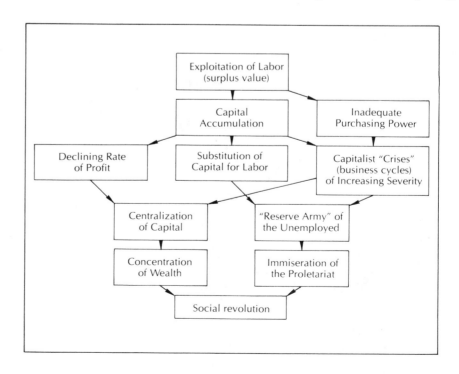

ignore the role played by other actors and factors—an essential aspect in the development of a comprehensive theory of locational decision making. The increasing complexity and sophistication of the new economic geography can be appreciated, however, with recourse to a descriptive model of industrial decision making. Richard Robinson (1981), a professor of international management at the Massachusetts Institute of Technology, recognized that since 1945, international business has moved through three general episodes and has started on a fourth. These episodes are defined by the number of actors relevant to locational decision making.

The Two-Actor Era

The postwar years up to about 1955 were characterized by European and Japanese reconstruction. Technology, machines, and consumer goods that the U.S. dollar could buy were highly demanded. Markets for U.S. exports exploded. Managers understood that to sell in volume to these markets required producing within those markets. They selected significant markets they were in danger of losing if they depended solely on exports, and markets they could not penetrate because of trade barriers, as was the case of Japan. During this postwar decade, the actors influencing industrial location were firms and their oversees commercial associates.

The Three-Actor Era

During the boom years, 1955 to 1970, some government officials recognized that business was an important international actor. Increasingly, the political impact of corporate behavior entered the decision-making methodology.

In this era reconstruction was complete in Japan and Western Europe, and their firms vigorously sought global markets. The Korean War ended, and the Japanese economy became a tower of economic strength. Colonialism collapsed like a house of cards, and the newly independent countries attempted to gain control over their development processes. An era of neonationalism gripped the world. Toward the end of the period, the United States expended enormous resources in Vietnam and accumulated massive balance-of-payment deficits as the goods and services priced in dollars became more expensive. Meanwhile, U.S.-based multinational firms created globally integrated production and marketing systems under headquarters administration and control. Increased international expertise at the headquarters and im-

proved international communications systems made this headquarters/branch-plant structure feasible.

The appearance of giant enterprises first in the United States, then in Western Europe, and last in Japan intensified the sensitivities of host governments. And by then, the dominance of U.S. power, technology, and capital were challenged. Alternative sources for needed capital, skills, machines, and technology could be found in Western Europe, Japan, and possibly in Eastern Europe. Host governments became key actors whose policies directly affected the decisions of the multinationals.

The Four-Actor Era

The 1970s was a time of crisis. Industrial overcapacity was pervasive. The profitability of capital decreased first in Britain in the mid-1960s and then in the United States. France, Italy, and West Germany experienced stress between 1974 and 1978. Even Japan's economy began to falter in the early 1980s. Persistent U.S. balance-of-payments problems ended the fixed exchange-rate system, and the value of the dollar dropped, especially in relation to the yen and deutschmark. The developing countries initiated efforts to restructure the world's economy and redistribute the world's wealth through the New International Economic Order. One of the main targets of the "Group of 77" was the large multinational firm, the chief allocator of goods and services internationally. The notion of a finite earth was dramatized by limits-to-growth rhetoric and by OPEC. An increasingly interdependent world economy became evident to all. As a consequence, parent governments acknowledged the economic, and hence, the political impact of international business. The conduct of international business was too important to be left to the technostructure, the market, and Third World politicians. So began the four-actor era of the 1970s with the discovery of multinationals as political actors.

The Multiactor Era

International industrial location is no longer solely the province of multinationals, host and parent governments, and markets. A number of other actors are indirectly influential: national and international labor groups, intergovernmental organizations, and various special interest groups. Labor makes its desires felt through governments or multinationals. Intergovernmental organizations exert their influence on national governments. Special interest groups—consumers, conservationists, political ideologists—act on governments or corporations to alter policies on safety, environmental protection, and products offered in different markets. These additional actors attempt to create a new international order in their own image.

The multiactor era of the late twentieth century introduces a new degree of uncertainty to corporate decision making. As the number and power of actors increase, so the cost of corporate decision making mounts, making it difficult for old-style multinationals to compete without more flexible methods of transacting international business. It appears that the multinational—a special form of international business that appeared in the 1950s and 1960s—is giving way to international service and trading companies. These organizations are engaged essentially in turnkey projects; they build and start up plants under contract, with an expanded training function (Robinson 1981, p. 18). Preeminent business organizations of the future may well be "those devoted to improving international markets in terms of special inputs— services, skills, knowledge, capital—and specific outputs—largely goods. The guts of such firms will be international information networks and data banks" (Robinson 1981, pp. 18–19).

Managerial Response

Managerial expertise in "reading" the environment and responding appropriately is vital in the location of economic activities. How do decision-makers perceive and respond to the complex and sophisticated international environment of the late twentieth century? "The perception of risk and uncertainty by decision-makers is a direct function of their perception as to the accuracy and adequacy of the relevant data and of their familiarity with the environment within which they act. The greater the faith one has in the data, the lower the perceived uncertainty in relation to the environment" (Robinson 1981, p. 19). This explains why U.S.-based firms invested first in Canada and England, countries culturally close to the United States. It also explains why decision-makers are reluctant to build plants in culturally remote countries until they become familiar with the market, often via exports.

Perceived risk and uncertainty are affected not only by the extent to which managers are geographically informed, but also by how much they know about the product and how to produce it. Managers with little or no knowledge about Brazil, production technology, or product X will likely assign higher risk and uncertainty to producing product X in Brazil than managers who are relatively well informed about Brazil, production, and product X. People exaggerate perceived risk and uncertainty as soon as they move

beyond their field of perceived competence. Hence, export-dominated firms investing in oversees production invariably require the introduction of new expertise and different rewards (Robinson 1981, pp. 20–21).

SUMMARY

In examining different approaches to locational decision making, we first considered traditional location theories. Classical location models assume the existence of *optimizers* who produce rigid geographical patterns based on perfect knowledge. Such *normative models* are deterministic—a given set of data always yields a specific pattern. They are also static; they do not deal adequately with the dynamics of the capitalist system.

Behavioral models are a response to the inadequacy of classical ones. Human decisions are merely satisfactory choices, often motivated by noneconomic factors. This forces a reliance on *stochastic models* that specify only the probability of a certain set of actions producing a particular pattern. Monte Carlo simulation is an example of a stochastic model. We saw how patterns produced by *satisficers* may not be appreciably different from those produced by optimizers, especially if the limits of choice are small and the number of individual decision-makers is large. The problem is complicated by the actions of other producers and by history.

We then turned out attention to Marxist theory, which points out that behavioral approaches describe or predict rather than explain. Behavioralism merely replaces the optimizer with the satisficer. Like classical theories, behavioral ones have failed to relate geographical changes to wider social relations.

Much Marxist work ignores geography and proceeds as if the world existed on the head of a pin. A growing number of geographers acknowledge that locational decision making is deeply structured by the capital-labor relation. Geographical variety is the outcome of capital-labor struggles, which means that a diversity of capitalist relations of production exist that must be recognized and explained.

In the last section of the chapter, we introduced the international dimension of locational decision making. Until recently, geographers treated location issues on a local or national scale rather than on a global scale. However, with the unprecedented internationalization of capital and associated shifts in the geographical distribution of economic activity that followed the end of the postwar boom, it has now become imperative for geographers to adopt a global perspective.

KEY TERMS

behavioral matrix

capital-labor conflict

Fordism

game theory

innovation-diffusion

labor process

land-use gradient

mean information field

Monte Carlo simulation

normative model

optimizer

organization of capital

psychic income

satisficer

social-spatial relations

spatial margins to profitability

spatial error

spatial fetishism

stochastic model

Taylorism

SUGGESTED READINGS

Alchian, A. A. 1950. Uncertainty, evolution, and economic theory. *Journal of Political Economy* 58: 211–21.

Behrman, J. N. 1984. *Industrial Policies: International Restructuring and Transnationals.* Lexington, MA: D. C. Heath.

Gore, C. 1984. *Regions in Question: Space, Development Theory and Regional Policy.* New York: Methuen.

Gould, P. 1963. Man against his environment: A game theoretic framework. *Annals, Association of American Geographers* 53: 290–97.

———. 1969. *Spatial Diffusion* Resource Paper No. 4. Washington, DC: Association of American Geographers.

Hägerstrand, T. 1967. *Innovation Diffusion as a Spatial Process.* Chicago: University of Chicago Press.

Massey, D. 1984. *Spatial Divisions of Labor: Spatial Structures and the Geography of Production.* New York: Methuen.

Morrill, R. L. 1965. Migration and the spread and growth of urban settlement. *Lund Studies in Geography*, Series B. 26.

Pred A. 1967. Behavior and location: Foundations for a geographic and dynamic location theory, Part 1. *Lund Studies in Geography*, Series B. 27.

———. 1969. Behavior and location: Foundations for a geographic and dynamic location theory, Part 2. *Lund Studies in Geography*, Series B. 28.

Scott, A. J., and Storper M., eds. 1986. *Production, Work, Territory: The Geographical Anatomy of Industrial Capitalism.* Boston: Allen and Unwin.

Simon, H. A. 1957. *Models of Man.* New York: John Wiley.

Smith, D. M. 1981. *Industrial Location: An Economic Geographical Analysis.* New York: John Wiley.

Wolpert, J. 1964. The decision process in a spatial context. *Annals, Association of American Geographers* 54: 537–38.

6
TRANSPORTATION

OBJECTIVES

☐ To develop an understanding of transportation systems

☐ To demonstrate the relationship between transport and economic development

☐ To trace the evolution of transport improvements and to consider their effects on "the tyranny of distance"

☐ To examine the structure of transport costs

☐ To consider the impact of transport costs on locational patterns

Traffic in Calcutta, India. (Source: World Bank.)

For most of human existence, economic development was tied to natural conditions. People occupied narrowly circumscribed areas, for the most part isolated from other groups of people. Gradually, improvements in the efficiency and flexibility of growing transportation systems changed patterns of human life. Control and exchange became possible over wider and wider areas and facilitated the development of more elaborate social structures.

The course of human history was changed when European capitalism and its overseas progeny laid the foundations for technological culture. From the sixteenth century onward, there were great revolutions in science and trade, great voyages of discovery, and a consequent increase in productive, commodity, and financial capital. Capitalism required a world market for its goods; hence, it broke the isolation of the natural economy and of feudal society. The engine that drove this economic expansion was accumulation for accumulation's sake. In an effort to increase the rate of accumulation, all forms of capital had to be moved as quickly and cheaply as possible between places of production and consumption. To annihilate space by time, some of the resulting profits of commerce were devoted to developing the means of transportation and communication. "Annihilation of space by time" does not simply imply that better transportation and communication systems diminish the importance of geographical space. Instead, the concept poses the question of how and by what means space can be used, organized, created, and dominated to facilitate the circulation of capital (Harvey 1985, p. 37).

The transformation in transportation technology, together with capitalist development, served to integrate isolated producers. The *integration* of points of production into a national or international economy does not change their absolute location (site), but it does alter their relative location (situation). Transport improvements increase the importance of relative space. The progressive integration of absolute spaces into relative space means that economic development becomes less dependent on relations with nature and more dependent on relations across space.

Most people no longer live in spatially restricted societies. Whether they live on farms or in cities, they can travel from place to place, communicate with each other over long distances, and depend on goods and information that come from beyond their immediate environment. Geographers refer to movements of goods, people, and ideas by means ranging from walking to digital telephone networks as *spatial interaction*.

The *Concorde* travels at supersonic speeds between London and Washington, D.C. But this status symbol does not fly cheaply; for example, it uses about four times as much fuel per passenger as wide-bodied jets. In this era of increasing fuel costs, there appear to be limits to the economical annihilation of space by time. (Source: British Airways.)

Improvements in transportation promote spatial interaction; consequently, they spur *specialization of location*. By stimulating specialization, better transportation leads to increased land and labor productivity as well as to more efficient use of capital. As societies abandon self-sufficiency for dependency on trade, wealth and income rise rapidly.

Trade occurs when time and money required to move goods over geographical space are within limits to permit local specialization. The amount of trade is related to the location of specialized production, the cost and time it takes to overcome the friction of distance, and the demand for goods. Production costs set the savings or additional wealth derived from local specialization and scale economies and influence the distance separating related activities. Specialization and trade may increase as long as production-cost savings exceed transport costs. For some activities, diseconomies occur at low levels of specialization; hence, production takes place at many locations. For

Transport networks are complex spatial systems as illustrated by the Santa Monica Freeway in Los Angeles. (Source: State of California, Department of Transportation.)

transport networks shape and structure space? How do they modify location? What is the impact of transport costs and transit time on the location of facilities? This chapter provides answers to these questions in a discussion of routes and networks, transport development, and transport costs.

ROUTES AND NETWORKS

Movements of goods, people, and information are highly channeled. But routeways do not exist all by themselves; rather, they are organized into networks. Individual networks—shipping lanes, railroads, highways, pipelines—service transport demand and bind regions together.

Networks as Graphs

A network is a highly complex system, and each different type has its own special characteristics. Networks differ in terms of density, shape, type of commodity or information carried, and type of flow (either continuous or intermittent). These widely varying characteristics make networks difficult to describe, evaluate, and compare. In order to uncover the basic spatial structure of networks, geographers reduce them to the level of graphs.

A network idealized as a graph consists of two elements of geographical structure: (1) a set of *vertices* (V) or nodes that may represent towns, railroad stations, or airports; and (2) a set of *edges (E)*, lines, or links that may represent highways, railroads, or air routes. The reduction of a network to a system of vertices and edges illustrates topological position only (Figure 6.1). The location of vertices is considered in terms of their relative position on the graph regardless of their absolute location. Distance between vertices is determined in terms of intervals, not route length.

A familiar example of a network reduced to a graph is a subway or transit map (Figure 6.2). For the user of the Metrorail system in Washington, D.C., a topological representation of the network is all that is required. On departing Dupont Circle, a passenger

other activities, concentration of production at a few locations is generally more profitable.

Transportation determines the utility or worth of goods. In today's world almost nothing is consumed where it is produced; therefore, without transport services, most goods would be worthless. Part of their value derives from transport to market. *Transport costs*, then, are not a constraint on productivity; rather, transport increases the productivity of an economy because it promotes specialization of location.

Transportation is a key for understanding geographical patterns. How does the geographical allocation of transport routes affect development? How do

FIGURE 6.1
Reduction of a network (a) to a graph (b). (Source: After Haggett and Chorley, 1969, p. 5.)

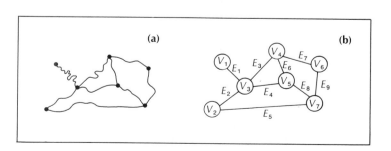

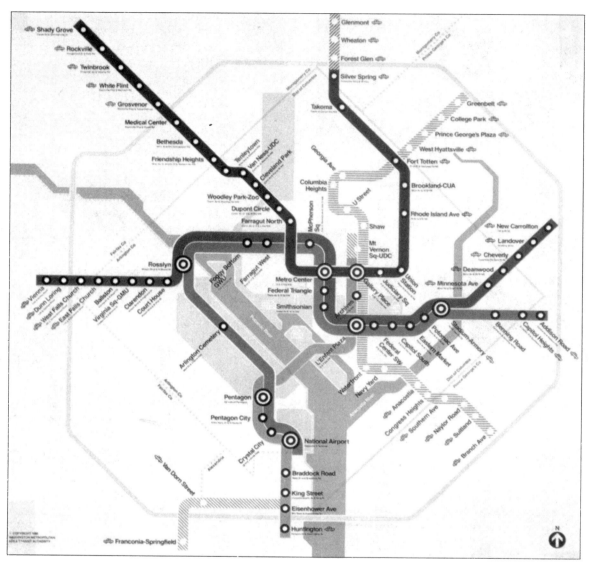

FIGURE 6.2
Metrorail, Washington, D.C.'s subway system. (Source: Washington Metropolitan Area
Transit Authority.)

needs to know only whether the stop for Medical
Center is before or after Bethesda. Neither Euclidean
distance nor the shape of the route is important to the
passenger. For this reason, all edges on the map can
be represented as straight lines.

Network Connectivity   We can evaluate the connectivity of a network simply by considering the system of
edges and vertices. By *connectivity* is meant the ease
of moving from one place to another within a network.
Some networks are more successful in achieving ease
of movement than others. The degree of success is
known as the efficiency of the network, a property that

we must be able to measure in order to compare
networks.

The *beta index* is one of the simplest measures of
network connectivity. It expresses the ratio between
the number of edges in a system and the number of
vertices in that system:

$$\beta = \frac{E}{V}$$

When the number of edges to vertices is large, the beta
value is large, indicating a well-connected network.
Conversely, more vertices than edges signifies a poorly

FIGURE 6.3
Beta values for seven 4-point graphs.

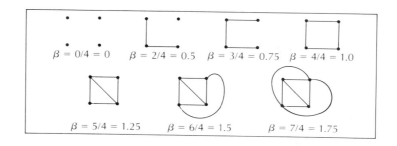

$\beta = 0/4 = 0$ $\beta = 2/4 = 0.5$ $\beta = 3/4 = 0.75$ $\beta = 4/4 = 1.0$

$\beta = 5/4 = 1.25$ $\beta = 6/4 = 1.5$ $\beta = 7/4 = 1.75$

connected network. A sequence of seven 4-point graphs illustrates how we can measure differences in connectivity (Figure 6.3). In the simplest case, there are four unconnected vertices; therefore, the beta value is zero. The index reaches unity when all vertices are connected by the same number of edges. It exceeds unity when there are more edges than vertices. Although the maximum value in Figure 6.3 is 1.75, larger graphs would yield higher beta values. High beta values imply that an economy is advanced and can afford bypass links around intervening places.

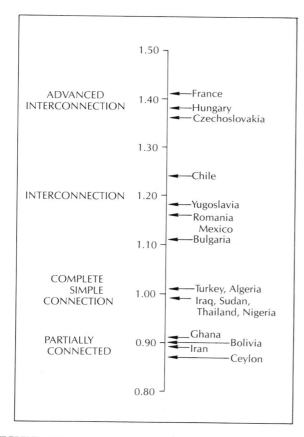

FIGURE 6.4
Beta values for the railroad networks of eighteen countries. (Source: After Kansky, 1963, p. 99.)

The beta index may be used to compare the structure of networks. For example, a nomogram portraying beta values for the railroad networks of several countries indicates that the index is high in developed countries, such as France, and low in underdeveloped countries, such as Ghana (Figure 6.4). In addition to comparing several different networks at the same time, the beta index may also be used to compare a single network as it changes over time. Maps of Ghana's evolving road system show that many roads were constructed between 1910 and 1959 (Figure 6.5). Beta values indicate a steady improvement in the quality of connections between places in Ghana during that period (Figure 6.6).

Measures of network connectivity, however, have low discriminating power. For example, with a ratio like the beta index, the same value may be obtained for two networks having patterns that are not at all alike.

Network Accessibility The search for indices of higher discriminatory power led to the development of graph-theoretical measures of accessibility. These include the *accessibility index* and the *Shimble* or *dispersion index*. The accessibility index measures the shortest paths from each vertex to every other vertex; the dispersion index computes the accessibility of a network as a whole.

The accessibility of a vertex is

$$Ai = \sum_{i=1}^{n} dij$$

where *dij* is the shortest path from vertex *i* to vertex *j*. For a hypothetical 4-point network, the accessibility index for $V_1 = 3$, $V_2 = 4$, $V_3 = 4$, and $V_4 = 5$ (Figure 6.7). These values correspond to our intuitive notions about vertex accessibility. The most accessible place is V_1, the least accessible is V_4, and V_2 and V_3 have intermediate accessibility. If the index were applied to the railroad system of the United States, we would find that Chicago has a low accessibility index compared to New York or Los Angeles, both of which are peripheral. When we deal with graphs much larger

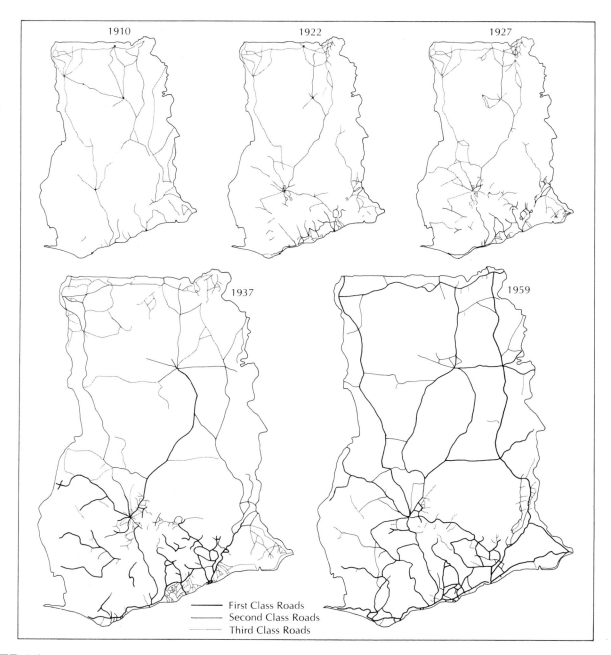

FIGURE 6.5
Evolution of Ghana's road system, 1910–1959. (Source: Based on Gould, 1960, frontispiece and pp. 39, 41, 67, 69.)

than a 4-point network, the accessibility value for a
vertex cannot be obtained by visual inspection. Computers are employed for large graphs, but for medium-
size graphs we can use a shortest-path matrix. A
matrix is an array of numbers ordered in rows and
columns. The shortest-path matrix for the 4-point
network in Figure 6.7 is illustrated in Table 6.1.

The Shimble or dispersion index is defined as

$$D = \sum_{i=1}^{n} \sum_{j=1}^{n} dij$$

For the 4-point network in Figure 6.7, the value of the
dispersion index is sixteen (Table 6.2). This value

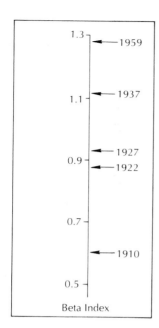

FIGURE 6.6
Increasing road connectivity in Ghana, 1910–1959.
(Source: Based on Gould, 1960, frontispiece and pp. 39, 41, 67, 69.)

defines the graph's compactness in terms of all the paths within it, and can be used to compare one network with another. For example, when the dispersion value is known, it can be used as a standard against which to measure the impact of new links on total accessibility.

Dispersion values are only an initial step in evaluating a transport network. Routes must be considered in terms of numerous criteria: characteristics of modes of transportation (carrier capacity, cost,

TABLE 6.1
A shortest-path matrix.

TO:	V_1	V_2	V_3	V_4	Row Sum
FROM:					
V_1	0	1	1	1	3
V_2	1	0	1	2	4
V_3	1	1	0	2	4
V_4	1	2	2	0	5

frequency of service, speed); vehicular capacity; technical quality (surface, curvature, gradient); and stress (overuse of certain links). The cost of building, improving, or maintaining links must also be taken into account, as well as the route's effectiveness in meeting given objectives. For example, the cost of improving a road to meet the capacity for peak demand must be balanced against the cost of congestion, time loss, and deterioration of the route from overuse.

Density and Shape of Networks

Graph theory is particularly useful in measuring accessibility, but it neglects important aspects of network structure. For example, graph theory fails to consider network density or shape.

Network Density By *network density* is meant the total number of route miles or kilometers per unit area. This measure may be considered in several dimensions of space.

Examination of topographic maps reveals strong differences in road density at the local level. Villages have a denser pattern that the surrounding countryside, and downtown areas of cities have denser street patterns than suburbs. In the central area of Detroit about 50 percent of the land is devoted to roads, but three kilometers from the central business district this

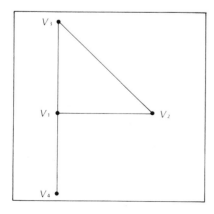

FIGURE 6.7
A 4-point network.

TABLE 6.2
Connectivity matrix and dispersion value.

TO:	V_1	V_2	V_3	V_4	Row Sum
FROM:					
V_1	0	1	1	1	3
V_2	1	0	1	2	4
V_3	1	1	0	2	4
V_4	1	2	2	0	5
				Total	16

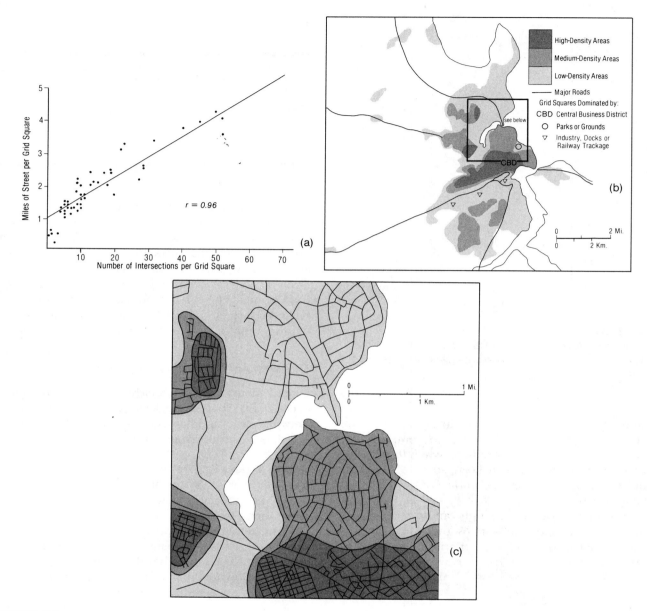

FIGURE 6.8

Density of the street network in Dar es Salaam, Tanzania in 1966: (a) relationship of the number of intersections per grid square to miles of street per grid square; (b) density pattern of street network; (c) sample area of the street network.

figure drops to 34 percent. Distance-decay gradients, however, vary directly with city size. As city size increases, the need for interaction increases, and the proportion of land devoted to transport needs increases in linear fashion.

A study of the road pattern in Minneapolis-St. Paul by John Borchert (1961) provides much information on distance-density gradients for urban transportation networks. Because there was a high correlation between number of road junctions and road length,

Borchert counted the number of road junctions on the map. Counting the number of junctions per unit area was much less tedious than measuring the number of miles of street per unit area. Borchert found a strong association between population density, as measured by the number of single-family dwellings, and the network density, as measured by the number of intersections. In replicating Borchert's study in Dar es Salaam, Tanzania in 1969, this author obtained similar findings (Figure 6.8).

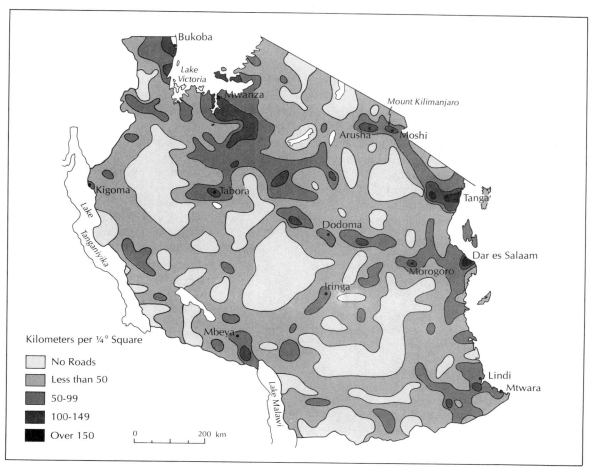

FIGURE 6.9
Road density in Tanzania in 1970.

At the regional level, variations in network density are closely related to patterns of uneven development. A map of the road density in Tanzania in 1970 provides an example (Figure 6.9). Densities for main and secondary roads were calculated by measuring the length of these roads in grid squares of approximately 740 square kilometers. The appropriate length was then assigned to the center of each square, and isolines were drawn to join places of equal density. Road density is positively associated with areas of high population density and of intense commercial activity. For example, high road densities occur around the primate city of Dar es Salaam and provincial towns such as Tanga and Iringa. They also occur in zones of export agriculture such as the cotton-growing area to the south of Lake Victoria and the coffee-growing area on the well-watered slopes of Mount Kilimanjaro.

At the world level, the distribution of network density is highly skewed (Table 6.3). Norton Ginsberg

(1961) calculated that a few countries have very dense networks and many countries have sparse networks. Nearly two-thirds of the countries have distributions below the world mean. The distribution of countries

TABLE 6.3
Distribution of route density.

Route Media	Roads	Railroads
Number of countries compared	126	134
World mean density, km/100 km^2	10.3	0.95
Maximum density, km/100 km^2	302.0	17.90
Minimum density, km/100 km^2	0.0	0.00
Percentage of countries below world mean	64	67

NOTE: Although these data are for the late 1950s, they are still an effective representation of world-scale network patterns.

SOURCE: Ginsburg, 1961, pp. 60, 70.

with high and low densities is related to levels of economic development.

The greatest concentration of surface transportation facilities appears in Western Europe, the United States and southern Canada, Japan, and in western parts of the USSR. In these regions, road and rail densities are so high that virtually no place is inaccessible. Somewhat less dense networks are found in parts of Uruguay, Argentina, eastern Brazil, eastern Australia, India and Pakistan, and in parts of the Mediterranean Middle East. Most underdeveloped countries are poorly served by roads and railways; for example, the vast tropical heartlands of South America and Africa and the interior of China are not easily accessed.

Network Shape   There is a striking contrast between developed and underdeveloped countries with regard to the *shape* and *orientation* of transport networks. In underdeveloped countries, these features are a reflection of their colonial history. Resulting networks often have a strong directional focus; they resemble drainage systems that converge on coastal ports. For example, railroad development in Brazil linked the port of Rio de Janeiro with São Paulo and the export-producing areas inland. In Argentina, railroad development centered on Buenos Aires (Figure 6.10a) and in Uruguay, on Montevideo. Port cities served as transshipment points for the export of primary products and the distribution of imported finished goods. Therefore, the networks of underdeveloped countries are typically fan-shaped. They distort and sharpen geographical and social inequalities because of an inadequate number of interlinkages.

In developed countries, the shape of transport networks is a fuller lattice, which allows a more even

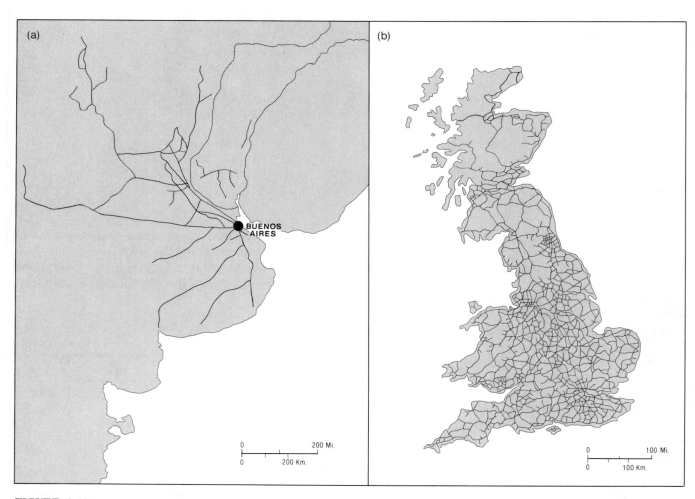

FIGURE 6.10
(a) The shape of the Argentinian railroad system in 1890; (b) the shape of the British railroad system in 1900. (Source: Based on Scobie, 1964, and Freeman, 1986.)

distribution of places by offering a degree of internal interchange. For example, Britain was crisscrossed with a dense network of main and branch railroads as early as 1900 (Figure 6.10b). The map does not reveal, however, that major routes converge on London. This tendency strengthened after World War II when the government nationalized and modernized the rail network.

Location of Routes and Networks

Spatial interaction depends on the existence of a demand-supply relationship. If a demand-supply relationship exists between two unconnected places and is profitable, then it is probable that a transport route will be constructed. Choosing the actual location for a new route is a political task, but the information used to aid decision making is based on economic principles. Of critical importance in deciding where to construct a new route is the balance between fixed and variable transport costs. Fixed costs are construction costs. Variable costs are operating costs that depend on the length of the routeway and the volume of traffic flowing along it.

A demand-supply relationship explains many, but not all, transport patterns. It does not, for example, account for the geographical pattern of Roman roads in Britain. Roman roads were built across the island to meet the government's need for fast communication between centers of civil administration in the south and east and defense lines and fortresses in the north and west. Postroads were constructed with little regard for construction costs and local economic needs.

Minimum-Distance Networks As an example of how costs influence the geographical pattern of routes in a network, consider two extreme minimum-distance solutions to a problem in which a demand-supply relationship exists between five towns (Figure 6.11). In Figure 6.11a operating costs are low, but fixed costs are high. The resulting network gives maximum benefit to users because each of the five towns is directly linked to every other town. In Figure 6.11b fixed costs are dominant. The resulting network minimizes construction costs. This network has a lower degree of connectivity and is less convenient to users (Table 6.4).

The railroad pattern of the United States can be understood partly in terms of *least-cost-to-use* and *least-cost-to-build* motives (Figure 6.12). The least-cost-to-user network is characteristic of the eastern half of the country where cities are clustered and transport demands are high. In the West, where

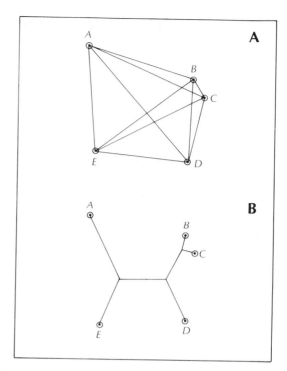

FIGURE 6.11

Alternative ways to connect five urban centers by a transportation network: (a) least-cost-to-use solution; (b) least-cost-to-build solution. (Source: After Bunge, 1962, p. 183.)

railroads preceded settlement and where cities are scattered, the least-cost-to-builder solution dominates.

Deviations from Straight-Line Paths Most transportation routes deviate from a direct straight-line connection. There are two main types of distortion from the straight-line connection; they are positive and negative deviations.

Positive deviations occur when routes are made longer in order to increase traffic. They are constructed to pick up as many settlements as possible. At one time, this type of deviation was common in

TABLE 6.4

Difference in connectivity between user-optimal and builder-optimal networks.

Network	Number of Edges	Number of Vertices	E/V	B
User optimal	10	5	10/5	2.0
Builder optimal	7	8	7/8	0.87

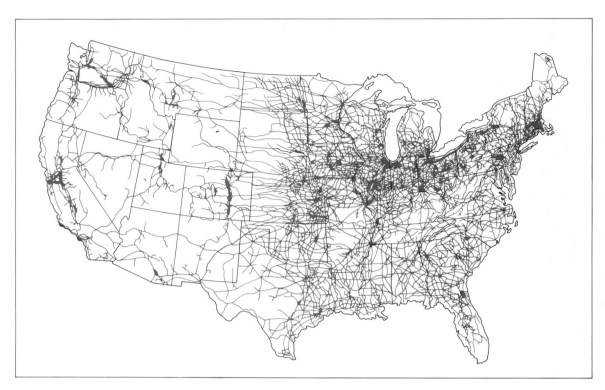

FIGURE 6.12
The railroad pattern of the United States. (Source: Courtesy of the Association of American Railroads.)

developed countries. Adherence to on-line settlement, however, declined in importance with economic development. An extreme example is the U.S. Interstate Highway System. When it was built, many small towns, villages, and hamlets were bypassed in favor of larger settlements that generated the bulk of the traffic. In underdeveloped countries, linking as many settlements as possible played hardly any part in the construction of routes during the colonial period. The length of the routes was geared to a pattern of economic growth based on export production. Areas where export production was insignificant or where there was little demand for imports were bypassed by road and rail. As a result, these places stagnated and lost ground.

Negative deviations arise from the need to reduce the distance traveled through high-cost areas. A transport route is often distorted from a reasonably straight line because different areas have different building-cost characteristics. For example, differential building costs may be the result of terrain difficulties, such as the presence of a mountain barrier. But economic development necessitates tearing down physical barriers to exchange. In the nineteenth century, a great deal of trade between the east and

west coasts of the United States was diverted via the Cape route—a diversion that added some 15,000 kilometers to the overland distance. When the time factor came to be more highly valued, the degree of distortion was reduced with the construction of the Panama Canal. Today, east-west surface transportation across the United States is hardly distorted at all by overland barriers.

Routes and Political Boundaries Political factors distort route patterns. An example is the Canadian transcontinental railroad, a project that was completed in 1885. The natural railroad route between southern Ontario and the western provinces of Canada is via Detroit, Chicago, and Minneapolis-St. Paul. But the Canadian government was unwilling to undertake a national railroad project that had to cross U.S. territory and be subject to possible interruption in times of conflicting policies. So at great expense, the government and then a private company, the Canadian Pacific Railway, constructed the railroad over the sterile Canadian Shield to the northern shores of Lake Superior, around it to Thunder Bay, and then north of Lake of the Woods to reach the Red River at Winnipeg.

Routes are also truncated by political boundaries. The U.S.-Canadian border distorts the pattern of railroad routes. In the approximately 1,120-kilometer stretch between International Falls, Minnesota, and Great Falls, Montana, only eight railroads cross the border, whereas more than twenty approach the border. The "aligning effect" of the U.S.-Canadian border on railroads is paralleled by the "blocking effect" of the provincial boundary between Ontario and Quebec on roads.

International transportation and communication links are particularly weak between neighboring underdeveloped countries. When European powers divided Africa into "artificial" political units, they established a circulation and communication system in each territory that facilitated external contact with the colonizing power, rather than with neighboring colonies. Thus, a telling colonial legacy is the scarcity of transport and communication lines crossing international boundaries, especially between adjacent territories that were colonized by different European powers. To illustrate, a long-distance telephone call from Kabale (southern Uganda) to Bukavu (eastern Zaire), a distance of 195 kilometers, had to be routed through operators in London and Brussels even in the 1970s.

Tanzania provides an excellent example of how the colonial mind organized space and movement to serve its own imperatives. The British treated transport in the three territories of Kenya, Uganda, and Tanganyika in a regional context. The railways were the backbone of the system, and the connecting road and boat services linked areas with the rail system. The consequences of an integrated policy for Tanzania have been great, as maps of the status of road and rail transport for 1932, 1952, 1962, and 1971 make clear (Figure 6.13). These maps show that in 1962, after independence, Tanzania's transport network was not yet unified. Historically, Tanzania has had seven separate circulation subsystems: (1) the northwest, Bukoba, and Mwanza areas, with exports and imports moving mainly through Kisumu and Mombasa; (2) the Arusha-Moshi area, with exports and imports moving mainly through Mombasa, a saving of 86 kilometers over the line to Tanga; (3) the Tanga-Lushoto area; (4) the Central Line, Dar es Salaam to Kigoma; (5) the Southern Highlands, with no rail links, but road services connecting with Dar es Salaam and with Arusha and Nairobi along the Great North Road; (6) the Southern Province, an area isolated from Dar es Salaam and the rest of the country during the rainy season by high water on the Rufiji River; and (7) southwestern Tanzania, isolated from the rest of the country by a lack of roads. Only in the early 1960s was

northwest Tanzania linked with the rest of the country by an all-weather road, when the Nzega-Singida section was built. By 1971, a hard-surface road finally linked the Tanga-Dar es Salaam systems by a shorter route than those formerly made through Morogoro and Handeni, reducing the journey from 574 kilometers in 1952 to 470 kilometers by 1962, to 272 kilometers by 1971. By 1973, the Mbeya-Dar es Salaam road was completely surfaced, and the Tanzam Railway line was completed in Tanzania. Following a war with Uganda in the late 1970s, which created an extremely difficult financial situation, Tanzania was hard-pressed to maintain its existing transport system, let alone improve it, during the 1980s.

One consequence of the political disruption of transport networks is a reduction in the intensity of movement and interaction. Ross Mackay (1958) studied telephone traffic between Montreal and Quebec cities, other Canadian cities, and U.S. cities (Figure 6.14). He found that telephone traffic between Montreal and other cities in Quebec was from five to ten times greater than traffic between Montreal and Ontario cities. American cities interacted with Montreal as if they were fifty times as distant.

Development of Transport Networks

Historically, the development of transport networks has reflected and induced settlement, industrialization, and urbanization. The impact of transport networks on regional economic development is demonstrated in the 1963 stage model of network change in underdeveloped countries created by Edward Taaffe, Richard Morrill, and Peter Gould. Studies in Nigeria, East Africa, Brazil, and Malaya provided the basis for their model. They defined the extension of transport in underdeveloped countries explicitly in terms of penetration from the coast. "[Transport links reflect] (1) the desire to connect an administrative center on the sea coast with an interior area of political and military control; (2) the desire to reach areas of mineral exploitation; [and] (3) the desire to reach areas of potential agricultural export production" (Taaffe, Morrill, and Gould 1963, p. 506).

The Taaffe, Morrill, and Gould model illustrates how the interplay between the evolution of a transport network and urban growth is self-reinforcing (Figure 6.15). The ideal-typical sequence begins the first stage when early colonial conquest creates a system of settlements and berthing points along the seacoast. Gradually, a second stage evolves with the construction of penetration routes that link the best located ports to the inland mining, agricultural, and population centers. Export-based development stim-

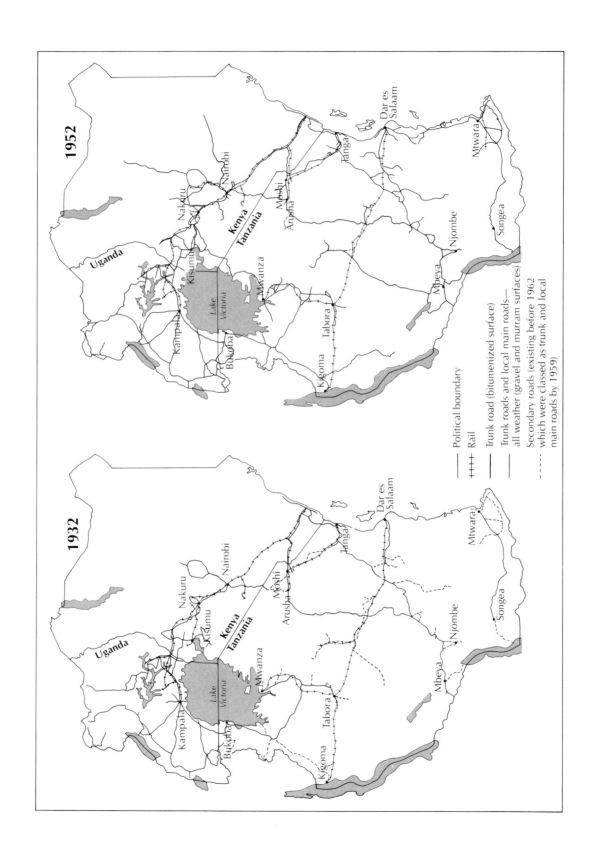

1952

Uganda

Kampala

Bukoba

Lake
Victoria

Mwanza

Nakuru

Kisumu

Nairobi

Kenya
Tanzania

Moshi
Arusha

Tanga

Dar es
Salaam

Kigoma

Tabora

Mbeya

Njombe

Mtwara

Songea

Political boundary
Rail
Trunk road (bitumenized surface)
Trunk roads and local main roads—
all weather (gravel and murram surfaces)
Secondary roads (existing before 1962
which were classed as trunk and local
main roads by 1959)

1932

Uganda

Kampala

Bukoba

Lake
Victoria

Mwanza

Nakuru

Kisumu

Nairobi

Kenya
Tanzania

Moshi
Arusha

Tanga

Dar es
Salaam

Kigoma

Tabora

Mbeya

Njombe

Mtwara

Songea

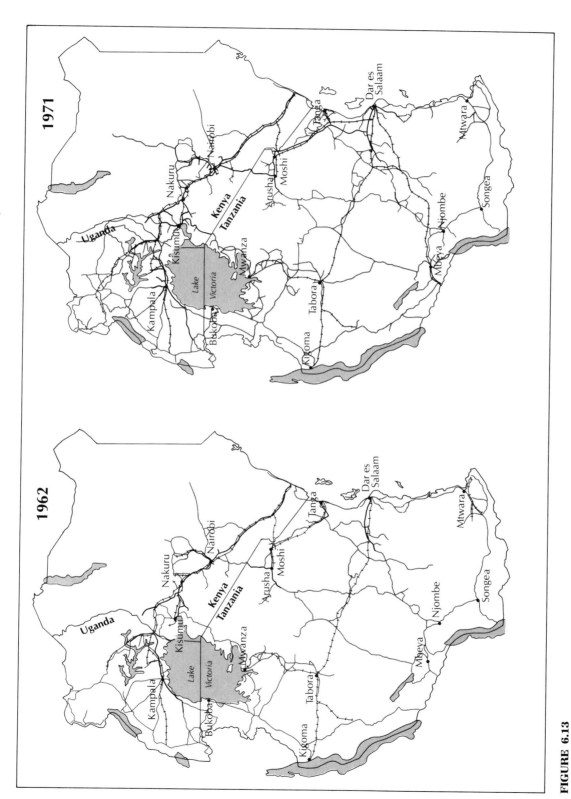

FIGURE 6.13

Evolution of the East African transportation system. (Source: de Souza and Porter, 1974, p. 45.)

The Effect of a Political Boundary on Flows of Telephone Calls

When telephone calls are plotted against distance, the intensity of interaction declines with increasing distance (diagram [a]). If a political barrier is placed across the area, then the intensity of interaction falls way below what could be expected from the distance-decay effect (diagram [b]). The effect of a political boundary upon flows of telephone calls can be measured by aligning the two pieces of the graph. This involves displacing the lower segment to the right (diagram [c]). The barrier effect then can be measured in distance terms; thus, we could conclude that a political barrier has the same retarding influence on interaction as, say, thirty kilometers of distance.

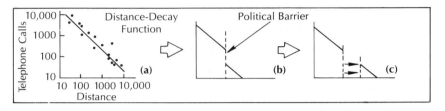

SOURCE: Based on Gould, 1975, p. 18.

ulates growth in the interior, and a number of intermediate centers spring up along the principal access routes. This process results in the third stage of transport evolution—the growth of feeder routes and links from the inland centers. By the fourth stage,

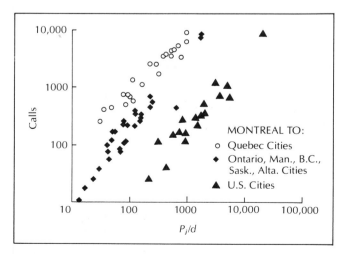

FIGURE 6.14
Telephone calls from Montreal to three sets of cities in a ten-day period. (Source: Mackay, 1958, p. 4.)

lateral route development enhances the competitive position of the major ports and inland centers. A few nodes along the original lines of inland penetration (for example, N_1 and N_2) become focal points for feeder networks of their own, and they begin to capture the hinterlands of smaller centers on each side. The fifth stage evolves when a transport network interconnects all the major centers. In the sixth and last stage, the development of high-priority linkages reinforces the advantages of urban centers that have come to dominate the economy.

According to Taaffe, Morrill, and Gould, high-priority linkages in underdeveloped countries are likely to emerge not along export-trunk routes, but along routes connecting two centers concerned with internal exchange activities. Nigerian geographer Akin Mabogunje (1980, p. 289) questioned the logic of this assumption in that the sixth stage arises from earlier phases in which export-trunk routes receive the greatest attention. He argued that this contradiction can only be explained by the fact that the model is grounded in the history of transport development in developed countries. Thus, stage six of the model emphasizes the difficulty of transforming a colonial network into one suitable for more self-centered development (McCall 1977, p. 102).

TRANSPORT DEVELOPMENT

The evolution of transport systems is linked to the process of development. For thousands of years, most people walked and carried the goods they consumed. This time-consuming mode of transportation greatly limited the movement of commodities until after 1500 when major improvements in transportation began to take place.

At the time of Columbus, a mercantile revolution occurred in which nation-states replaced the chained economies of feudal society. The ideology of merchant capital, *mercantilism*, points to foreign trade as the source of a country's enrichment. To mercantilists, there existed a finite amount of trade in the world; consequently, the goal was to obtain the largest share. Mercantilism, therefore, was rooted in commercial expansion, for which improved transport was vital. Commercial expansion first arose in Portugal and Spain; then, early in the sixteenth century, it became a characteristic of Western Europe. From many rival harbors—especially, Antwerp, Amsterdam, and London—a commercial network spread out to embrace parts of sub-Saharan Africa and its adjacent Atlantic islands, the Americas, and parts of Asia.

Opposition to mercantilism increased in the late eighteenth century, gradually giving rise to a climate of *economic liberalism*. This new climate was especially evident in Britain where economic life was being transformed by improvements in farming techniques and by the industrial revolution. From 1800 to the present, capitalism promoted the development of cheap and rapid forms of transport in an evolutionary process spurred by competition among the various transport modes. As described by James Vance (1986),

> The basic technology of each [transport medium] was initiated when it stood as technically the most advanced for its time. When the deficiencies of a specific medium became obvious, efforts were made to overcome these, normally leading both to the change in the original form and to the creation of distinctly new forms of transport that avoided the previous failings. Railroads, for example, could greatly ramify the networks of movement possible with canals. In turn, however, the suburbanization of population and industry showed up sharply the failings of the steam railroad, leading to the rapid expansion of the use of automobile transportation. (p. 618)

Improved Transport Facilities

Prior to the development of railroads, overland transportation of heavy goods was slow and costly. Movement of heavy raw materials by water was much

A passenger train pulls into the Terminus at Lagos, Nigeria. The Nigerian railway network is a colonial legacy. It serves the mines and the specialized crop-producing areas, carrying most of their products to the port of Lagos for export. (Source: World Bank.)

The idealized model of network change describes one typical sequence of development. It shows that a transport network has the short-run purpose of facilitating movement, but that its fundamental effect is to influence the subsequent development and structure of the space economy through the operation of geographical inertia and cumulative causation. The term *geographical inertia* refers to the tendency of a place to maintain its size and importance even after the conditions originally influencing its development have changed, have ceased to be relevant, or have disappeared. The term *cumulative causation* refers to the process by which economic activity tends to concentrate in an area with an initial advantage. The stage model, therefore, illustrates how a space economy roots itself ever more firmly as initial locational decisions that shaped the system are subsequently reinforced by other decisions. The result is a concentrated and polarized pattern of development.

FIGURE 6.15
An ideal-typical sequence of
transport development. (Source:
Based on Taaffe, Morrill, and
Gould, 1963, p. 504.)

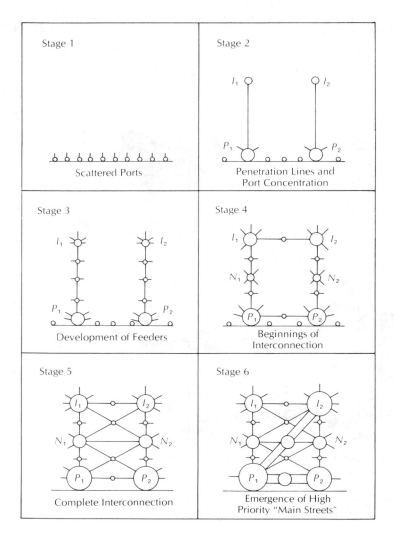

cheaper than by land. For this reason, most of the
world's commerce was carried by water transportation, and the important cities were maritime or
riverine cities.

To bring stretches of water into locations that
needed them, canals were constructed in Europe
beginning in the sixteenth century, with the height of
technology represented by the pound lock developed
in the Low Countries and northern Italy. Until the
nineteenth century, canals were the most advanced
form of transportation and were built wherever capital
was available. Road building was the cheap alternative
where the canal was physically or financially imprac-
tical.

The most active period of canal building coincided with the early industrial revolution. The vast
increase in manufacturing and trade fostered by the
canals paved the way for the industrial revolution
(Mantoux 1961). The canals were financed by central

governments on the Continent and by business
interests in England, where a complex network was
built during the last forty years of the eighteenth
century and the first quarter of the nineteenth
century. Somewhat later, artificial waterways were
constructed in North America. They supplemented
the rivers and Great Lakes, the principal arteries for
moving the staples of timber, grain, preserved meat,
tobacco, cotton, coal, and ores.

At sea, efforts before the industrial revolution
concentrated on expanding the known seas and on
improving ships (e.g., better hulls and sails) to allow
for practical transport over increasing distances. By
1800, or a few decades later in the case of the
technology of sail, the traditional technology of transport reached its ultimate refinement. Subsequently,
the rapid expansion of commerce and industry over-
taxed existing facilities. The canals were crowded and
ran short of water in dry periods, and the roads were

When the Grand Trunk Canal opened in Derbyshire in 1777, Britain's canal era began in earnest. The era was short-lived, however. Private investment in British canals virtually ceased with the coming of the railway in the nineteenth century. Appealing relics of the early industrial revolution, the canals are now being used increasingly for recreational purposes. (Source: British Tourist Authority.)

clogged when traffic in wet periods destroyed the surface on which it moved. The result was an effort to utilize mechanical energy as the motive power.

The invention of the steam engine by James Watt in 1769 paved the way for technical advances in transportation. Its application to water in 1807 and to land in 1829, through the development of the locomotive, heralded the era of cheap transportation. The steamship reduced the cost of transportation by water, but the locomotive had a revolutionary effect on land transportation. In England, the railway served existing markets and provided urban populations with an excellent system of freight and passenger transportation. In the United States, the railroad was an instrument of national development; it preceded virtually all settlement west of the Mississippi, helped to establish centers such as Kansas City and Atlanta, and integrated regional markets. In Third World countries, railroads linked export centers more firmly to the economies of Europe and North America.

Eventually, mechanical power was used for localized urban transportation. Until the late nineteenth century, cities were mainly pedestrian centers requiring business establishments to agglomerate in close proximity to one another. This usually meant about a thirty-minute walk from the center of town to any given urban point; hence, cities were extremely compact. The transformation of the compact city into the modern metropolis depended on the invention of the electric traction motor by Frank Sprague. The first electrified trolley system opened in Richmond, Virginia in 1888. The innovation, which increased the average speed of intraurban transport from about five to over fifteen miles per hour, diffused rapidly to other North American and European cities, as well as to cities in Australia, Latin America, and Asia.

The nineteenth century was a time when the road was reduced to a feeder for the railroad. Road improvements awaited the arrival of the automobile—"European by birth, American by adoption" (Rae 1965, p. 1). In the United States, heavy reliance on the automobile is a cross between a love affair with the passenger car and a lack of alternatives. In cities such as Denver and Los Angeles, roughly 90 percent of the working population travels to and from work by car; in the less auto-dependent cities like New York, cars still account for two-thirds of all work-related trips. By comparison, in Europe, where communities are less extensively suburbanized and average commuting distances are half those of North America, only about 40 percent of urban residents use their cars. In Tokyo, a mere 15 percent of the population drives to work.

In the Third World, technical developments in transportation have created a crisis—the result of a mismatch between transportation infrastructure, services, and technologies and the need for mobility of the majority of the population (Replogle 1988). Governments that favor private car ownership by a small but affluent elite distort development priorities. Importing fuels, car components, or already assembled cars stretches import budgets thin. Similarly, building and maintaining an elaborate highway system de-

At the close of World War I, the thirty thousand miles of street railways and trolleys in U.S. cities carried 14 billion passengers a year. Pictured here is Broadway and 14th Street, New York City in 1911. (Source: Library of Congress.)

vours enormous resources. The 1960s and 1970s saw a road-building boom in many Third World countries to the detriment of railroads and other forms of transport. With insufficient resources for maintenance, many Third World roads are in disrepair. In cities, bus systems and other means of public transportation are also in a poor state, meeting only a small proportion of transportation needs. And often the poor cannot afford public transportation at all. Walking still accounts for two-thirds of all trips in large African cities like Kinshasa, and for almost one-half the trips in Bangalore, India. Pedestrians and traditional modes of transportation are increasingly being marginalized in the Third World.

Transport changes in the last 175 years have not been confined to railroads and roads. At sea, ships equipped first with steam turbines and then diesel engines facilitated the rapid expansion of international trade. In addition, the opening of the Suez Canal in 1869 and the Panama Canal in 1914 dramatically reduced the distance of many routes. The trend in ocean shipping today is not so much increased size and speed of vessels as it is increased specialization. Bulk carriers of oil, grain, and ores are replacing break-bulk vessels. Containerships, which tie trucks and ships together, have become the basic transoceanic carrier (Figure 6.16). Planes have ousted passenger liners and trains as the standard travel mode for long-distance passengers. The shipment of cargo by air, however, is still in its infancy. Only perishable, high-value, or urgently needed shipments are sent by air freight.

Communication Improvements   Modernization of transportation has integrated the economic world, but equally important are technical developments in communication. Traditional forms of communication such as the letter post have been joined by telecommunications and computer-based methods of information transfer. In many ways, communication is the invisible layer of transport supplementing the physical transport links between cities, regions, and countries (Daniels 1985, p. 268).

In the nineteenth century, a major development in communication was that of the telegraph, which made possible the world-wide transmission of information concerning commodity needs, supplies, prices, and shipments—information that was essen-

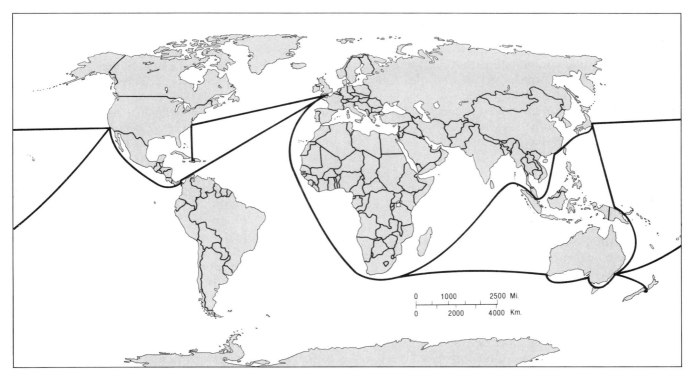

FIGURE 6.16
Major shipping lanes for containers. (Source: Based on Ewart and Fullard, 1973, p. 60.)

tial if international commerce was to be conducted on an efficient basis. By 1886, a basic skeleton of international telegraph links was completed when a cable along the west coast of Africa was laid. Today, an international telecommunications network based on optical fibers and digital technology has replaced the telegraph. Breakthroughs in information technology not only increase the productivity of business, but

Containerships at the Maher Terminal in Port Elizabeth, New Jersey. (Source: Photo courtesy of The Port Authority of New York and New Jersey.

also make it feasible to perform service tasks at a much wider range of locations than in the past. The "wired home" can now become the workplace as well as the base for many interactions that do not require travel (Azimov 1978; Toffler 1981). And the "global office" is becoming a reality. For example, Texas Instruments in 1989 opened a software development facility in Bangalore, India, that is linked by satellite to its headquarters in Dallas.

Cost-Space and Time-Space Convergence

Transport improvements have resulted in what geographers call *cost-space* and *time-space convergence*— that is, the progressive reduction in cost of travel and travel time between places.

Cost-Space Convergence Transport improvements have brought significant cost reductions to shippers. For example, the opening of the Erie Canal in 1825 reduced the cost of transport between Buffalo and Albany from $100 to $10 and ultimately to $3 per ton. Railroad freight rates in the United States dropped 41 percent between 1882 and 1900. Between the 1870s

and 1950s, improvements in the efficiency of ships reduced the real cost of ocean transport by about 60 percent.

Cheaper, more efficient modes of transport widened the range over which goods could be shipped economically. For example, the international trade in iron ore was negligible in the nineteenth century, but by 1950 exports of iron ore accounted for just under 20 percent of world production, and by 1967 for 36 percent (Manners 1971, pp. 348–49). Much of the trade is accounted for by long-haul traffic, from Venezuela to the United States or from Australia to Japan (Figure 6.17). Similarly, steam coal, exported from Alaska, Colombia, South Africa, Australia, and China is shipped, on average, 6,400 kilometers to its destination (Chisholm 1982, p. 122).

Cheap transportation also contributed to the growth of cities. It enabled cities to obtain food products from distant places and facilitated urban concentration by stimulating large-scale production and geographical division of labor. Furthermore, transportation improvements changed patterns of urban accessibility. North American cities have grown from walking- and horsecar-scale cities (pre-1800–1890), to electric streetcar cities (1890–1920), and,

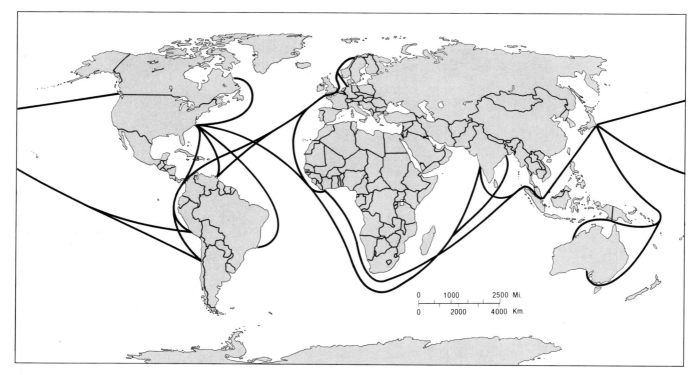

FIGURE 6.17
Major shipping lanes for iron ore. (Source: Based on Ewart and Fullard, 1973, p. 61.)

FIGURE 6.18
Stages of intraurban growth in a North American city.

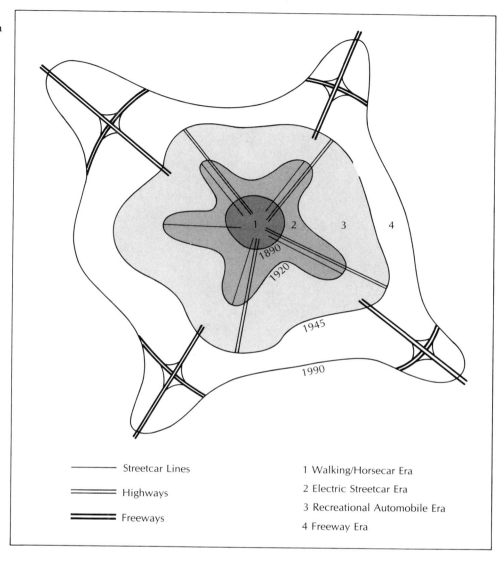

1 Walking/Horsecar Era
2 Electric Streetcar Era
3 Recreational Automobile Era
4 Freeway Era

————— Streetcar Lines

════ Highways

▬▬▬ Freeways

finally, to dispersed automobile cities in the recreational automobile era (1920–1945) and the freeway era (1945–present) (Figure 6.18).

Time-Space Convergence Developments in transportation have also cut travel time extensively—to where relative distances between places melt away. The travel time between Edinburgh and London—a distance of 640 kilometers—decreased from 20,000 minutes by stagecoach in 1658 to under 60 minutes by airplane today (Figure 6.19). Time-space convergence was marked during the period of rapid transport development; for example, in the 1840s travel time between Edinburgh and London was over 2,000 minutes by stagecoach, but by the 1850s, with the

arrival of the steam locomotive, the travel time had been reduced by two-thirds, to 800 minutes. By 1988, the rail journey between Edinburgh and London took 275 minutes, and when the line is electrified in 1995, travel time will be reduced to under 180 minutes.

Air transportation provides spectacular examples of time-space convergence. In the late 1930s, it took a DC-3 between fifteen and seventeen hours to fly the United States from coast to coast. Modern jets now cross the continent in about five hours. In 1934 QUANTAS/Empire Airways planes took twelve days to fly between London and Brisbane. Today the Boeing 747 SP is capable of flying any commercially practicable route nonstop. The result is that any place on earth is within less than twenty-four hours of any other place, using the most direct route.

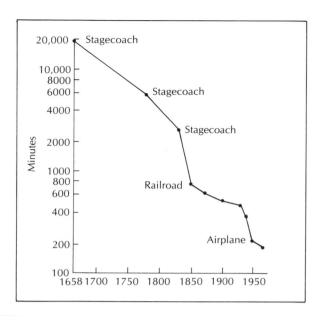

FIGURE 6.19
Time-space convergence between London and Edinburgh.
(Source: Adapted from Janelle, 1968, p. 6.)

TRANSPORT COSTS

One of the major forces structuring the spatial organization of production is "the tyranny of distance": the fact that all movement costs. Societies have made a tremendous investment in both human and natural resources to overcome the friction of distance.

Although transport innovations have reduced circulation costs, locational costs still exert a powerful influence on patterns of production—and for that reason we need to consider the following questions: What is the true form of transport costs? What determines specific transport rates? What effects do international regimes for shipping and aviation have on transport costs? What is the impact of transport costs on location? For what industries is transit time more crucial than cost?

General Properties of Transport Costs

Alfred Weber's industrial location theory emphasizes the cost of moving materials and finished products from place to place. Initially, it makes two normative assumptions about transport costs in order to concentrate on the idealized effects of distance. These assumptions are (1) that transport costs are a linear function of distance and (2) that transport costs are exclusively a function of distance (zero distance equals zero cost) (Table 6.5 and Figure 6.20). In reality, transport costs are much more complex.

Terminal and Line-Haul Costs Actual transportation costs can be categorized as either *terminal costs* or *line-haul costs* (Figure 6.21). Terminal costs must be paid regardless of the distance involved. They include the cost of preparation for movement, loading and unloading, capital investment, line maintenance, and

Boeing 747s line up at Terminal 4 of London's Heathrow Airport. (Source: British Airways.)

TABLE 6.5
Linear transport costs.

Kilometers	Cost $
0	0
100	1
200	2
300	3
400	4
500	5
600	6
700	7
800	8
900	9
1,000	10

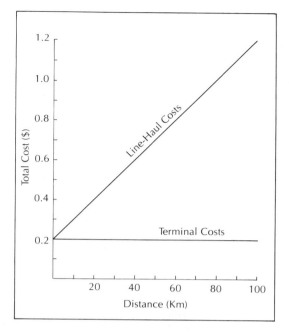

FIGURE 6.21
Terminal and line-haul costs.

other kinds of costs that are not a function of distance. Line-haul costs, on the other hand, are strictly a function of distance. For example, fuel costs are proportional to the distance a load must be moved.

Terminal costs are fixed in the short-run, but are altered by technological changes. International shipping provides an example. In 1960 most merchant ships were general cargo vessels and high loading and unloading costs as well as long turnaround times were involved in their operation. Since that time more and more ships have been built to handle specialized cargoes. The first of the new ships were oil tankers followed by vessels designed to carry ores, grain, and containers. The reduction in handling costs in ports and the rapid turnaround of the ships more than offset the cost of building specialized handling facilities (e.g., gantry cranes costing more than $2 million).

Recent developments in cargo handling have changed the location and appearance of ports. In the Netherlands, for example, old, enclosed dock systems of ports such as Rotterdam have been joined by new, deep-water terminals such as Europoort. In the 1960s,

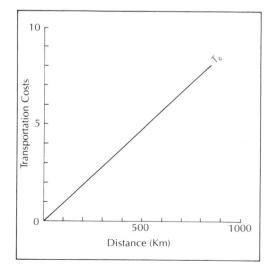

FIGURE 6.20
Linear transport costs.

Container cargo handling at the Maersk Line Terminal, Port Newark, New Jersey. (Source: Photo courtesy of The Port Authority of New York and New Jersey.)

oil terminals capable of handling tankers over 250,000 tons were constructed at Europoort. Subsequently, additional deep-water facilities have been developed to handle trade in grain, coal, and ores. The most recent development has been the provision of container-handling facilities and roll-on/roll-off terminals.

The world's first containerized service tied trucks and ships together in 1956. McLean, a U.S. trucking firm, organized this operation at Sea-Land and used converted tankers on trips from the port of Newark, New Jersey to Houston. Florida was added to this route in 1957 and Puerto Rico in 1958. By the mid-1960s, Sea-Land initiated service by new cellularized containerships from New York to Europoort, Bremen, and to Grangemouth in Great Britain. Three years later trans-Pacific service was established from Oakland to Hong Kong, Taiwan, and Singapore. By the early 1970s, numerous carriers entered into the containership business.

At first, the greatest appeal of the containership was its speed and economy in port. Moreover, it facilitated the multimodal transport of goods. For example, commodities from Japan and other Pacific Rim countries could be transported economically to Europe via North America. Later, container operations sought to speed up the ocean voyage as well. Top usable speeds increased from fifteen knots in the 1950s to thirty-three knots in the 1970s. But the oil crises of the 1970s also led to efforts to make more economical use of fuel to stabilize line-haul costs.

With the emergence of a new international division of labor, ports continue to modernize their methods of handling cargo as they compete with each other for shares of global commodity traffic. In developed countries served by many ports, competition has decreased the relevance of the traditional concept of the port hinterland (i.e., the area served by the port). On the West Coast of the United States, for example, ports in California, Oregon, and Washington compete fiercely for the mounting trade with the Pacific Rim. In underdeveloped countries, and in marginal zones within developed countries, limited port systems still serve particular hinterlands.

Carrier Competition Competitive differences in transport media account for variations in terminal and line-haul costs (Figure 6.22). Trucks have low terminal costs partly because they do not have to provide and maintain their own highways, and partly because of their flexibility. If provisions for parking are adequate, they can load and unload almost anywhere. However, trucks are not as efficient in moving freight on a ton-kilometer basis as are railroad and water carriers. Of the three competing forms of transport,

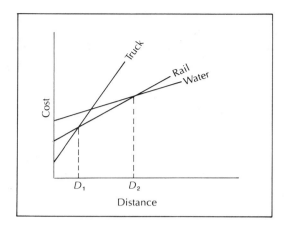

FIGURE 6.22
Variations in terminal and line-haul costs.

trucks involve the least cost only out to distance D_1. Railroad carriers have higher terminal costs than truck carriers, but lower than water carriers, and a competitive advantage through the distance D_1–D_2. Water carriers, such as barges, have the highest terminal costs, but they achieve the lowest line-haul costs, giving them an advantage over longer distances.

Curvilinear Line-Haul Costs Thus far, line-haul costs have been portrayed as a *linear* function of distance. Actual line-haul costs, however, are *curvilinear* (Figure 6.23). As the graph illustrates, line-haul costs increase with distance, but at a decreasing rate. The distance from O to D_2 is twice the distance from D_1 to D_2, but does not involve twice the cost (C_1 to C_2). As the distance increases, the average cost per kilometer constantly decreases. This characteristic of actual transportation costs is often called "economies of the long-haul," which occurs for at least three reasons. First, terminal costs are the same regardless of the length of the trip. As line-haul costs increase, terminal costs become proportionally less of the total. Second, line-haul rates are lower for longer hauls. Short hauls by rail, for example, are moved by "local trains"; longer hauls are moved by "through" freight trains, which stop less frequently and operate more efficiently. Third, tapered line-haul costs prevent rates from restricting long-distance hauls. Rates would soon become high enough to prevent traffic if they increased in direct proportion to distance.

Stepped Freight Rates Theoretically, every station along a line from a given origin should pay a different rate based on its actual distance from the origin. But computing large numbers of rates is both time-consuming and expensive to administer. Conse-

FIGURE 6.23
Curvilinear line-haul costs.

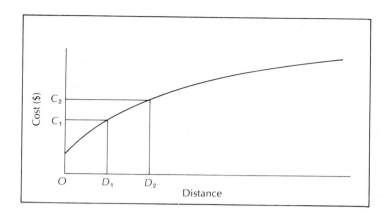

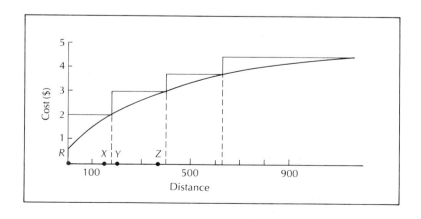

quently, zonal-rate systems are a common feature of transport companies. For example, railroads group stations into areas and charge a single rate for all stations within the same zone. In general, group rates are set in relation to control points, often the largest centers in each zone, thus reinforcing the urban dominance of these centers.

Railroad rate zones are step functions that retain the tapering principle and favor long-haul movements (Figure 6.24). The total transport bill per unit of delivered material from station R to Y should be only slightly more than to X, but because of the nature of the rate zones, Y pays a much higher price than X. Station Z pays the same price as Y because it is in the same rate zone. Station X has a competitive advantage over Y, but Y does not have a cost advantage over Z despite the greater distance of Z from R. Historically, cities such as Chicago, St. Louis, and some Missouri and Ohio River crossings have occupied and benefited from strategic positions in railroad rate groupings.

Commodity Variations in Transport Rates

The transportation cost curve varies according to differences in transport modes—but what deter-

mines specific rates? One set of factors pertains to the nature of the commodity. Factors that enter into any determination of commodity rates include (1) loading and packaging costs, (2) susceptibility to loss or damage, (3) shipment size, (4) regularity of movement, (5) special equipment and services, and (6) elasticity of demand.

Loading and Packaging Costs Of particular importance in determining the reasonableness of rates is the weight density of a commodity. Light, bulky commodities usually incur higher freight charges per carload or shipload than heavy, compact articles. This explains why rates generally favor "knocked-down" or "set-up" commodities. For example, parts for an automobile are shipped for a much lower rate than for a finished car.

A low weight-density factor is not the only reason why some commodities load cheaply. Ability to load commodities compactly must also be considered. Articles of odd shape such as furniture may not load efficiently. Sometimes containers cannot be filled without damage to commodities. Melons, for example, cannot be loaded more than a few layers deep without crushing those on the bottom. Furthermore, some

FIGURE 6.24
Stepped freight rates.

articles cost more to load. Rubber latex can be piped to ship rapidly and cheaply, whereas television sets must be handled with care to avoid damage. Coal requires little advance preparation for shipment, but furniture requires special crating and packing that add to terminal costs (Figure 6.25).

Damage and Risk Variations   Commodity rates reflect susceptibility to loss or damage. Except in the case of ocean carriers, most transport companies are liable for loss and damage during transit and must assume a greater risk for some commodities than for others. Sand, gravel, brick, and iron ore are not easily damaged, but fresh fruit and vegetables, television sets, and china run a high risk of damage because of perishability and/or fragility.

Shipment Size   Some commodities are shipped in bulk, whereas others must be carried in small quantities. Railroads charge higher rates for less-than-carload lots than for carload shipments. Rates are lower for commodities transported in volume over a period because carriers can better organize operation and handling methods and reduce costs. A high volume of a single commodity lowers line-haul costs per ton. Striking examples are fully loaded trains carrying only coal or iron ore.

Regularity of Movement   If traffic moves regularly, carriers can operate at lower costs, and should charge lower rates. Schedules are worked out more easily, and vehicle and labor needs can be planned. Irregularity of movement increases rates. This is often true of seasonal movements of fruits, vegetables, and wheat. Many railroad cars must be supplied over a short

period. These either have to stand idle much of the time or be diverted from other routes, disrupting regular service.

Special Equipment and Services   The type of equipment required for a commodity affects freight rates. Commodities that require refrigerator cars are more expensive to transport than articles that can be carried by ordinary boxcars. Some commodities require special services. For example, refrigerator cars may have to be precooled before being loaded with shipments of fresh fruits and vegetables, and carriers may charge extra for the costs incurred.

Elasticity of Demand   Previous factors related to the relative cost of transporting different commodities, but the *elasticity of demand* for transportation must also be considered. Defined in general terms, the elasticity of demand is the degree of responsiveness of a good or service to changes in its price.

Carriers generally charge what the market will bear. Very often goods with a very high value per unit of weight, such as television sets, are able to bear a higher transportation rate than goods with a very low value per unit of weight, such as coal (Figure 6.26). Thus, the left-hand graph illustrates transportation price inelasticity for television sets. An increase in the rate from P_1 to P_2 produces only a slight change in the quantity of shipments. Coal, however, (in the right-hand graph) exhibits a great change in the quantity of shipments, with only a slight change in the transportation rate (P_1 to P_2).

The value of an article does not completely determine a commodity's ability to bear a higher freight rate. Transportation services are not purchased simply for the sake of consuming ton-kilometers. Transportation is a means of distributing localized commodities. The most localized commodities can usually bear higher rates within the framework of loading, shipment size, and damage and risk characteristics.

Freight Rate Variations and Traffic Characteristics

The characteristics of carriers and routes form a second set of factors determining specific transportation rates. Important factors include (1) carrier competition, (2) route demand, and (3) backhauling.

Carrier Competition   An absence of competition between transport modes means a carrier can set rates between points to cover costs, and in the absence of government control, a carrier may set

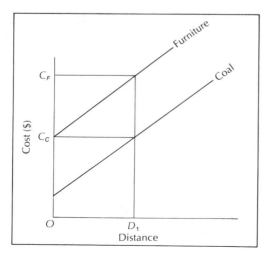

FIGURE 6.25
Variations in loading and packaging costs.

FIGURE 6.26
Demand elasticity for transportation.

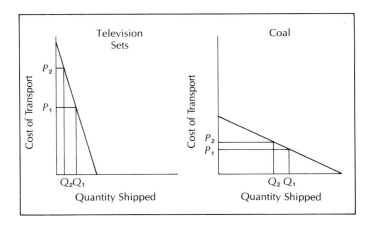

unjustifiably high rates. Intermodal competition and/or government regulation reduce the likelihood of such practices. The effect of competition between carriers is to reduce rate differences between competitors. For example, the opening of the St. Lawrence Seaway in 1959 resulted in lower rail freight rates on commodities affected by low water-transport rates.

Route Demand An important factor influencing the cost of haul is traffic density. High demand for transportation over a particular route can lower transportation rates. High demand lowers both line-haul and terminal costs per unit. The air-shuttle between New York and Washington, D.C. is an example. Demand for this trip is so high that rates per passenger can be much lower than rates for trips over routes of similar distance where demand is low. High volume lowers the terminal costs per passenger. Fully loaded aircraft mean lower line-haul costs per passenger.

Backhauling Many carriers face heavy demand only in a specific direction. Consider the large volume of produce shipped from Florida to New York. Trucks must often return empty for the next load. The cost of the total trip, however, is used to determine the transportation rate. Because carriers must make return trips anyway, they are willing to charge very low rates on the backhaul. Any revenue on backhaul is preferred to returning empty. Rates are higher where there is little or no possibility of backhauling; most such runs occur in the transportation of raw materials from resource points to production points. An example is the railroad that carries iron ore pellets from Labrador to the port of Sept Illes, Quebec. This railroad may be likened to a huge conveyor belt that operates in one direction only. By contrast, the distribution of finished products generally involves

traffic between many cities, creating a reciprocal flow and lower rates.

Regimes for International Transportation

In the international arena, transport rates and costs are affected by the nature of the regime governing the transport mode. To illustrate, let us consider the contrasting regimes of civil aviation and shipping. The international regime for aviation is dominated by the authoritative allocation of resources by states. By contrast, the international regime for shipping has been shaped by market-oriented principles. These different regimes were established by the industrialized countries. The regime for civil aviation developed in the early twentieth century and reflects a concern for national security. The regime for shipping evolved over more than five hundred years and has been more concerned with facilitating commerce than with security.

Civil Aviation The fundamental principle governing aviation is that states have sovereign control over their own air space. From this principle, rules and procedures have developed that permit countries to regulate their routes, fares, and schedules. As a result, many countries, developed and underdeveloped, have secured a market share that is more or less proportional to their share of world airline traffic. Third World countries have been able to compete with companies based in the industrialized world on an equal footing. Air India, Avianca, and Korean Air Lines can challenge Pan Am, Air France, and British Airways.

Shipping The international regime for shipping has left underdeveloped countries in a weak position with regard to establishing and nurturing their own merchant fleets. In a world of markets, few underdeveloped countries have much influence when it comes to setting commodity rate structures. Lack of control over international shipping is an important area of concern in the Third World's quest for a New International Economic Order.

Although the regime for shipping is characterized by the market, the market is inherently unfair: it favors developed countries over underdeveloped countries. Hence, Third World countries are faced with rate structures that work against them, inadequate service, a perpetuation of center-periphery trade routes, and a lack of access to decision-making bodies. Those Third World countries generating cargoes such as petroleum, iron ore, phosphates, bauxite/alumina, and grains cannot penetrate the bulk-shipping market, which is dominated by the vertically integrated multinational corporations based in developed countries. Cartels of shipowners, known as *liner conferences*, set the rates and schedules for liners (freighters that ply regularly scheduled routes).

Third world countries have attempted to change the international rules of shipping. They want to generate fleets of a size proportional to the goods generated by their ports. Their accomplishments have been limited, however. The UNCTAD Code of Conduct for Liner Conferences, which was adopted in 1974, was rejected by the United States. The Liner Code gives Third World-country carriers a presumptive right to a share of the market; however proposals to eliminate *flags of convenience* have not been accepted. Flags of convenience assume little or no real economic link between the country of registration and the ship that flies its flag. They inhibit the development of national fleets but for shipowners they offer a number of advantages, including low taxation and lower operating costs. Liberia and Panama are the most important open-registry, or flags-of-convenience countries. Flags of convenience are used mainly by oil tankers and bulk-ore carriers controlled by multinational corporations.

Transport and Location

Transport Costs and Location Theory With a knowledge of actual transport costs, it is possible to examine their implications on modifications of Weber's industrial location theory. Consider Weber's solution for one pure raw material (i.e., a raw material that loses no weight in processing) localized at M and sold as a finished product at MKT (Figure 6.27a). Terminal costs are zero and line-haul costs are linear. What happens to the Weberian solution when terminal costs are added? The solution is given in Figure

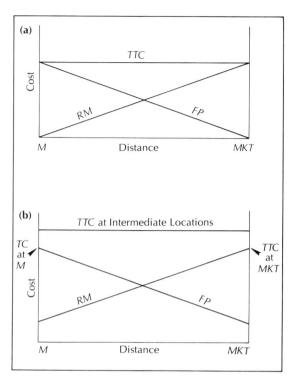

FIGURE 6.27
Weber's model: the effects of terminal costs.

6.27b. We must always pay at least one set of terminal costs, because either the raw material or the finished product must be moved. At either the mine or the market, one set of terminal costs is paid, but at any intermediate location, two sets of terminal costs must be paid. This raises total transportation costs by an amount equal to one set of terminal costs. Thus, mine or market locations have a clear advantage over intermediate points in terms of terminal costs.

Curvilinear line-haul costs also favor mine or market locations (Figure 6.28). For simplicity, the

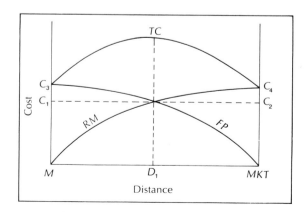

FIGURE 6.28
Weber's model: the effects of curvilinear line-haul costs.

diagram eliminates terminal costs. It shows that curvilinear line-haul costs favor the long haul. Shipping the raw materials from M to D_1 costs C_1; shipping the finished product from D_1 to MKT costs C_2. Shipping the raw material all the way to MKT, however, only involves a cost of C_4. Total transport costs are minimized at either mine or market.

Commodity rates influence the location of economic activities. As a very general rule, transport rates are lower for raw materials than for finished products favoring market locations (Figure 6.29). The graph retains linear transport costs for simplicity and shows that the lower raw material transport rate minimizes total transport costs (TTC) at the market.

Although tapering freight rates usually disfavor processing at intermediate locations because of additional terminal costs, these must be paid anyway at necessary transshipment or *break-of-bulk* points where a change in carrier must occur. This fact helps to explain why processing often takes place in port cities. Oil and sugar refineries, for example, often lie at tidewater. Iron and steel plants, the biggest and most visually impressive of all industrial establishments, are also attracted to coastal locations. The Ijmuiden works of Hoogovens in the Netherlands and the Mizushima works of Kawasaki steel on the north shore of the Japanese Inland Sea have deepwater access to ore and coal from international sources and can dispatch finished products to distant markets.

What is the effect of tapering freight rates on supply and market areas? They extend them. Consider for example, the market areas of producers. Suppose there are two producers of the same good (Figure 6.30). Firms A and B have the same terminal and line-haul costs, but A has lower production costs. With linear transport costs, the market boundary between the two occurs at D_1 (Figure 6.30a). The

The Mizushima works of Kawasaki Steel on the north shore of the Japanese Inland Sea has deepwater access for coking coal and iron ore from international sources. Major coking coal supply sources are Australia and Canada; major iron ore supply sources are the Philippines and Australia. Export shipments go mainly to Asia, the Communist Bloc, and North America. (Source: Kawasaki Steel Corporation.)

situation changes, however, when curvilinear line-haul costs are introduced. Because of long-haul economies, A is able to capture some of B's market area (Figure 6.30b).

Thus far we have examined the effects of transport rates on location in terms of *freight-on-board* or *FOB pricing*. Consumers pay the plant price plus the cost of transportation; those close to the plant pay less than more distant consumers (Figure 6.31). However, many producers adopt a pricing policy known as *cost-insurance-freight* or *CIF pricing*. In this pricing strategy, each consumer pays production costs plus a flat markup to cover transportation charges (Figure 6.32). Each consumer is charged a CIF price at C_1. Consumers from A to B are charged more than the actual cost of transportation. Consumers from X to A and B to Y are charged less than the actual cost.

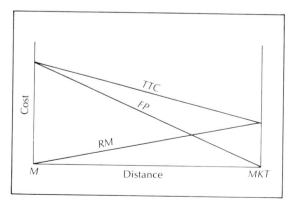

FIGURE 6.29
Weber's model: variations in commodity rates.

FIGURE 6.30
Market areas: (a) with linear
line-haul costs; (b) with curvilinear line-haul costs.

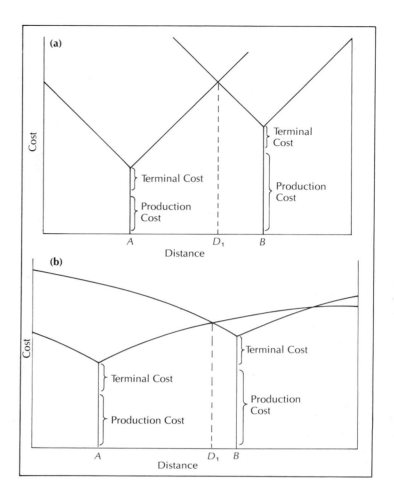

Close-to-plant consumers pay the distribution costs of more distant consumers.

What effect does CIF pricing have on the market area of producers? The FOB prices of producers A and B are shown in Figure 6.33. The market-area boundary is at X_1 with FOB pricing. If B adopts a CIF pricing strategy, the market-area boundary shifts to X_2. Pro-

ducer A can, of course, counter by also adopting CIF pricing. Thus, each consumer would pay the same price to each producer and price competition would disappear. Producers would then be forced to compete through advertising or other means. For finished products, such as clothing, CIF pricing tends to be the rule rather than the exception in the United States.

Transit Time and Location   Weber's industrial location theory and its modifications emphasize the cost of moving materials to the plant and finished products to consumers. Transport costs are of crucial importance for industries that are raw-material-seekers and market-seekers, but they are of little importance for industries dealing in materials and final products that are of very high value in relation to their weight. This is especially so for high-technology firms.

High-technology firms rely on input materials from a variety of domestic and foreign sources; thus, the advantages of locating a plant near any one supplier are often neutralized by the distance separating them from other suppliers. Their markets also

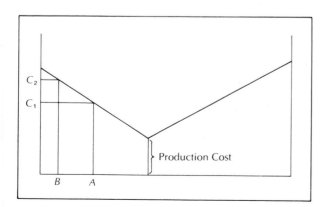

FIGURE 6.31
Freight-on-board pricing.

FIGURE 6.32
Freight-on-board and cost-insurance-freight pricing.

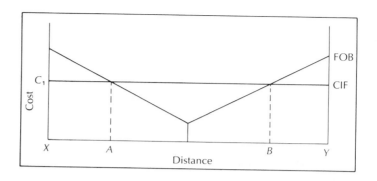

tend to be scattered. Transport is a factor of some locational significance for these firms, but *transit time* is more crucial than cost. High-technology firms require access to high-level rapid-transport facilities to move components and final products, as well as specialized and skilled personnel. For this reason, they are often attracted to sites near major airports with good national and international passenger and air-cargo facilities. Concentrations of high-technology firms and research and development facilities are located in Silicon Valley near San Francisco, along the M4 motorway from Slough to Swindon to the west of London's Heathrow Airport, and in Tsukuba Science City situated some sixty kilometers northeast of the center of Tokyo and forty kilometers northeast of the Narita International Airport.

Transport Improvements and Location Transport innovations have reduced circulation costs and fostered the new international division of labor. They have encouraged the decentralization of manufacturing processes in industrialized countries, both from major cities toward suburbs and smaller towns, and from central regions to those more peripheral. They have also encouraged the decentralization of manufacturing processes to those Third World countries with a free-market ideology and an abundance of weakly unionized, low-wage labor.

The "container revolution" and bulk-air cargo carriers have enabled multinationals based in the United States, Japan, and Western Europe to locate low-value-added manufacturing and high-pollution manufacturing processes "offshore" in more than eighty Third World free-trade zones. Almost one-half of these zones are in Asia and include Hong Kong, Malaysia, and South Korea. *Free-trade zones* are areas where goods may be imported free of duties for packaging, assembling, or manufacturing and then exported. These global workshops are geared to export markets, often with few links to the national economy or the needs of local consumers. They tend to be located near ports (e.g., La Romana, Dominican Republic), international airports (e.g., San Bartola, El Salvador), and in areas virtually integrated into global centers of business (e.g., Mexico's northern border or *maquila* zone).

SUMMARY

Movements of goods, people, and information take place over and through transport networks. We began this chapter by discussing how geographers analyze these networks by means of graph theory, reducing them to a set of vertices and a set of edges. Graph theoretic measures may be used to determine nodal accessibility and network connectivity. Geographers also examine other properties of networks—their shape and density. Using models of network change, they further demonstrate how the growth of transport media is inextricably tied to the process of economic growth.

In a discussion of transport development, we explained how improvements over the centuries have resulted in time-space and cost-space convergence.

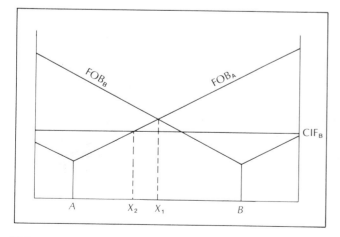

FIGURE 6.33
The effect of cost-insurance-freight on market-area boundaries.

They integrated isolated points of production into a national or a world economy. Although the friction of distance has diminished over time, transport remains an important locational factor. Only if transportation were instantaneous and free would economic activities respond solely to aspatial forces such as economies of scale.

For simplicity, industrial location theory assumes that transport costs are proportional to distance; however, in the real world, transport costs are much more complex. In our review, we considered some of the factors other than distance that play a role in determining transport costs—the nature of commodities, carrier and route variations, and the regimes governing transportation. Transport costs remain critical for material-oriented and market-oriented firms, but they are of less importance for firms that produce items for which transport costs are but a small proportion of total costs. For these firms, transit time is more crucial than cost. Modernized means of transport and reduced costs of shipping commodities have also made it possible for economic activities to decentralize. Multinationals have taken full advantage of transport developments to establish "offshore" branch-plant operations, especially in Asia's economic "tigers"—Taiwan, South Korea, Hong Kong, Singapore, and Thailand.

KEY TERMS

accessibility index	least-cost-to-build network
backhauling	least-cost-to-use network
beta index	line-haul costs
break-of-bulk point	Shimble index
communication	terminal costs
cost-insurance-freight (CIF) pricing	time-space convergence
cost-space convergence	transit time
freight-on-board (FOB) pricing	transport costs

SUGGESTED READINGS

Bird, J. H. 1971. *Seaports and Seaport Terminals.* London: Hutchinson.

Haggett, P., and Chorley, R. J. 1969. *Network Analysis in Human Geography.* London: Edward Arnold.

Hoyle, B. S., and Hilling, D., eds. 1984. *Seaport Systems and Spatial Change: Technology, Industry and Development Strategies.* New York: John Wiley.

Janelle, D. G. 1969. Spatial reorganization: A model and concept. *Annals,* Association of American Geographers 59:348–64.

Leinbach, T. R. 1975. Transportation and the development of Malaya. *Annals,* Association of American Geographers 65:270–82.

Lowe, J. C., and Moryadas, S. 1975. *The Geography of Movement.* Boston: Houghton Mifflin.

McCall, M. K. 1977. Political economy and rural transport: An appraisal of Western misconceptions. *Antipode* 53:503–29.

Schaeffer, K. H., and Sclar, E. 1975. *Access for All: Transportation and Urban Growth.* Baltimore, MD: Penguin Books.

Smith, D. M. 1981. *Industrial Location.* 2d ed. New York: John Wiley.

Taaffe, E. J.; Morrill, R.; and Gould, P. R. 1963. Transport expansion in underdeveloped countries: A comparative analysis. *Geographical Review* 53:503–29.

7

AGRICULTURE AND RURAL LAND USE

OBJECTIVES

☐ To discuss the origin and diffusion of agriculture

☐ To help you appreciate the effects of agricultural practices on the land

☐ To describe the variables that determine land use

☐ To explain the concepts of diminishing returns and rent

☐ To examine von Thünen's deductive model of agricultural land use

☐ To apply Thünian principles of spatial organization in several dimensions of space

Peasants plowing rice fields prior to planting in Central Luzon, Philippines. (Source: World Bank.)

Agriculture, the world's most space-consuming activity and humanity's leading occupation, is the science and art of cultivating crops and rearing livestock in order to produce food (and fiber) for sustenance or for economic gain. It is the basis for development and betterment. Throughout most of our existence as a species, we were hunters and gatherers, subsisting on what nature chanced to provide. Agriculture made possible a nonnomadic existence; it paved the way for the rise of cities and fostered the development of new technologies. Until the nineteenth century, however, agriculture produced very little food per worker, so that most of the population worked full or part time on the land. The small surplus released few people for other pursuits. It was not until the agrarian revolution that occurred in European settlement areas in the last two hundred years that large-scale employment in manufacturing and service activities became possible. The shift of labor from the agricultural sector to other sectors constitutes one of the most remarkable changes in the world economy in modern times. In the United States and the United Kingdom, only 2 percent of the economically active population now works directly in agriculture. By contrast, there are a number of countries in Africa and Asia where about 90 percent of the population is engaged in the agricultural sector.

Economic geographers are concerned with problems of agricultural development and change as well as with patterns of rural land use. Where was agriculture discovered? How did it diffuse? Why do farmers so often fail to prevent environmental problems? What are the characteristics of the main agricultural systems around the world, and what are their goals? What is the impact of industrialized agriculture on farmers and the traditional rural countryside? What principles can help us understand the spatial organization of rural land use? In this chapter, we will seek answers to these questions.

Of critical importance to many of the issues addressed in this chapter is the decision-making environment of land-users and managers. Who makes decisions to manage land, how are they made, and what are their consequences? Frequently, individual farmers make direct land-use decisions, but they often have to choose from a predetermined range of options. Farmers may be denied access to common property resources, such as water or grazing land. They may be forced to grow certain crops by landlords, multinationals, the state, or by social or market demand. They may be faced with fluctuations in prices for export commodities. It is incumbent on land managers to devise strategies to cope with such pressures and apply them to their land which, itself, is subject to changes in nature. To appreciate the response of land managers to changes in their circumstances, it is vital to recognize the significance of different scales. Patterns of production and land use are the outcome of a whole series of forces operating at a whole series of scales.

TRANSFORMING ENVIRONMENTS THROUGH AGRICULTURE

The course toward a technological culture was marked by the rise of farms at the expense of the wilderness, and by the rise of cities at the expense of the countryside. Agriculture was the first instance of human land use that significantly altered the natural environment. Before agriculture, landscapes evolved according to the laws of nature.

Revolutions in Agriculture

It was most likely through a series of accidents and deliberate experiments that people eventually learned how to produce food and fiber plants by using the components of soil, moisture, and the atmosphere. They also learned how to herd animals and control their breeding. Domestication of plants and animals probably emerged as an extension of food-gathering activities of preagricultural hunters and gatherers and as a response to a slow, sustained increase in population pressure.

Although scholars have been unable to say exactly where and when the earliest experiments in food production took place, they suspect that the first agricultural revolution began in the Fertile Crescent of the Middle East nearly ten thousand years ago (Figures 7.1 and 7.2). This was a well-watered area, extending from the highlands of the eastern Mediterranean through the foothills of the Taurus and Zagros mountains. Archaeological finds also indicate that domestication began early in parts of Central America and Southeast Asia.

A reliable food supply liberated people from food gathering. Increased security and leisure, resulting from the new way of life, allowed time for arts and crafts. Communities became involved in the spinning, weaving, and dyeing of cloth from vegetable fibers, cotton, silk, and wood and in the manufacture of pottery and containers. Adequate food supplies also allowed for the exchange of specialized goods in markets. In addition, plant cultivation weakened the forces that scattered populations and strengthened the forces that concentrated them. The new way of life allowed people to live in villages and towns, which

FIGURE 7.1
The Fertile Crescent.

FIGURE 7.1
The Fertile Crescent.

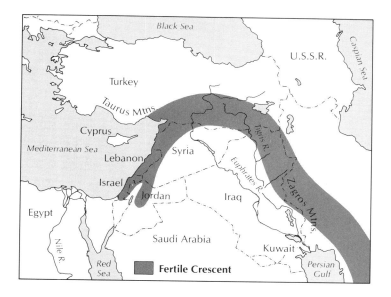

reached population densities far higher than those of preagricultural communities.

Farming practices that emerged during the Neolithic period changed little until the creation of a feudal hierarchy in medieval Europe. In this hierarchy, secular or religious overlords protected the serfs who farmed fields and paid taxes in kind or money according to the custom of the manor. English religious manors extracted the tithe—the tenth of a farmer's annual production. Bishops and abbots were bedfellows who put nothing into the farming business and took none of the risks, but harassed farmers at harvest time.

The most important innovations associated with farming in medieval Europe were the heavy plow, the replacement of oxen by horses for plowing, and the development of the open-field system, consisting of two or three large fields on each side of a village. These advances increased agricultural production, intensified human concentration in villages and towns, generated commerce, and changed patterns of environmental exploitation. The forested lowlands of Western Europe, for example, were gradually cleared when the heavy plow was invented. Clayey lowland soils could not be cultivated with the old Mediterranean scratch plow, which was suitable only for light limestone soils.

Medieval farming methods prevailed in Western Europe until capitalism invaded the rural manor. This resulted from a vast population increase in the new trading cities that depended on the countryside for food and raw materials. Another force that brought the market into the countryside was the alienation of the manorial holdings. Lords, who needed cash to exchange for manufactured goods and luxuries, began

to rent their lands to peasants rather than having them farmed directly through labor-service obligations. Thus, they became landlords in the modern sense of the term. The breakup of the manorial system, however, stemmed more directly from the Hundred Years' War (1337–1453) and the Black Death (1348–1349). The depopulation that resulted from these devastating events meant a shortage of labor. Wages rose, and land, relatively more plentiful, began to rent for less. Lords wanted to re-establish the labor-service obligation, but they were unable to turn back the clock. With the extension of the market into the countryside, peasants enjoyed greater independence and prosperity. Efforts to reinstate the old obligations were resisted in a series of peasant revolts that broke out all across Europe from the late fourteenth to early sixteenth centuries.

A second agricultural revolution that began with the demise of the manorial system replaced subsistence with market-oriented agriculture (Figure 7.2). Open fields were enclosed by fences, hedges, and walls. Crop rotation replaced the medieval practice of fallowing fields. Seeds and breeding stock improved. New agricultural areas opened up in the Americas. Farm machines replaced or supplemented human or animal power. The family farm came to represent the core model of commercial agriculture.

Since the late 1920s, there has been a third agricultural revolution (Figure 7.2). This revolution, which some observers believe is the logical extension of the second agricultural revolution, points to the resolution or rationalization of the distinction between family and corporate models of agriculture (Vogeler 1981). In other words, it signifies the elimination of distinct agrarian economies and communities.

	Beginnings and Spread	Subsistence to Market	Industrialization
Time	Pre-10,000 BP to twentieth century	c. 1650 AD to present	1928 to present
Key Periods	Neolithic Medieval Europe	Eighteenth-century England Nineteenth-twentieth century in "European" settlement areas	Present-day
Key Areas	Europe South and East Asia	Western Europe and North America	USSR and Eastern Europe North America and Western Europe
Major Goal	Domestic food supply and survival	Surplus production and financial return	Lower unit cost of production
Characteristics	Initial selection and domestication of key species Farming replaces hunting and gathering as way-of-life and basis of rural settlement and society Agrarian societies proliferate and support population growth Subsistence agriculture: labor intensive, low technology, communal tenure	Critical improvements, mercantilistic outlook, and food demands of industrial revolution replace subsistence with market orientation Agriculture part of sectoral division of labor: individual farm family becomes "ideal" for way-of-life and for getting a living Commercial agriculture develops growing reliance on technological inputs and infrastructure	Collective (socialist) and corporate (capitalist) ideologies and common agrotechnology favor integration of agriculture production into total food-industry system Emphasis on productivity and production for profit, replace agrarian structure and farm way-of-life Collective/corporate production utilizes economies of scale, capital intensity, labor substitution and specialized production on fewer, larger units

FIGURE 7.2
Three agricultural revolutions. (Source: Troughton, 1985, p. 256.)

Although the third agricultural revolution is incomplete, industrial agriculture has become the dominant form in most developed countries, capitalist and socialist, and is being applied to export enclaves of Third World countries. Key elements of industrial agriculture are capital intensity, technological inputs, high energy use, concentration of economic power, and a quest for lower unit costs of production. While industrial agriculture has increased output per unit of input, it has also depleted water and soil resources, polluted the environment, and destroyed a way of life for millions of farm families. During the 1960s and 1970s, many American family farmers who could avail themselves of the new technologies and expand their acreages were able to survive. But in the 1980s, foreclosures and bankruptcies became common, especially in the farm-dependent counties of the U.S.

Midwest. Indebted farmers were unable to remain solvent in a period of reduced export demand.

Industrial agriculture has drastically reduced the number of farmers in North America. In the United States, the number of farmers declined from 7 million in 1935 to around 2 million in 1990. In Canada, there were 600,000 farm operators in 1951 but only half that number in the late 1970s. Europe has witnessed similar trends. In Britain, for example, there was an annual 1.5 percent decline in the number of farm workers during the 1980s.

The Diffusion of Agriculture

The Fertile Crescent was one of several locales for plant and animal domestication (Table 7.1 and Figure 7.3). The spread of agriculture from these centers was

TABLE 7.1
Probable areas of origin of selected crops and domesticated animals.

Area	Crops	Animals
Fertile Crescent	barley, cabbage, date, fig, grapes, oats, olive, onion, pea, rye, turnip, rutabaga, wheat	camel, cattle, dog, goat, pig, pigeon
Central Asia	almond, apple, carrot, cherry, flax, hemp, lentil, melon, pea, pear, turnip, walnut	camel, cattle, chicken, dog, horse?, reindeer, sheep, yak
North China	apricot, cabbage, millet, mulberry, peach, plum, radish, rice, sorghum, soybean, tea	chicken?, dog, horse, pig?, silkworm
Southeast Asia	bamboo, banana, black pepper, citrus, egg plant, mango, sugar cane, taro, tea, yam	cat?, cattle, chicken, dog, duck, goose, pig, water buffalo
Ethiopia	coffee	
Nile Valley	cotton, cucumber, lentil, millet, melon, pea, sesame, sorghum	cat, dog, donkey
West Africa	kola, rice, watermelon	
Central America	avocado, beans, cocoa, corn, cotton, potato, pumpkin, red pepper, squash, sunflower, tobacco, tomato	dog, turkey
Northern Andes	beans, potato, pumpkin, squash, strawberry	alpaca, guanaco, guinea pig, llama, vicuna
Eastern South America	beans, cassava, cocoa, peanut, pineapple, potato, sunflower, squash, sweet potato	dog, duck

NOTE: Question marks indicate uncertainty as to area or areas of origin. Occurrence of crops and animals in more than one area points to the likelihood of independent invention.
SOURCE: Based on Mikesell, 1969, p. xxx.

a slow process. For example, archaeologists have calculated that it took from 6000 B.C. to 3000 B.C. for a form of shifting cultivation to spread along the Danube and Rhine corridors. Another thousand years elapsed before agriculture reached southern England. Shifting cultivation is a type of agriculture in which clearings are used for several years, then abandoned and replaced by new ones.

By 1500 A.D., on the eve of European overseas expansion, agriculture had spread widely throughout the Old World and much of the New World (Figure 7.4). In Europe, the Middle East and North Africa, central Asia, and in China and India, cereal farming and horticulture were common features of the rural economy. Nonagricultural areas of the Old World were restricted to the Arctic fringes of Europe and

Asia and to parts of southern and central Africa. Agriculture had not spread beyond the eastern Indian islands into Australia.

By the time of the first European voyages across the Atlantic, the cultivation of maize, beans, and squash in the New World had spread throughout Central America and the humid environment of the eastern half of North America as far north as the Great Lakes. In South America, only parts of the Amazon Basin, the uplands of northeastern Brazil, and the dry temperate south did not have an agricultural economy.

These patterns of agriculture persisted until the era of European overseas settlements. From the Age of Discovery to the mid-seventeenth century, Europeans did not attempt to establish large overseas settle-

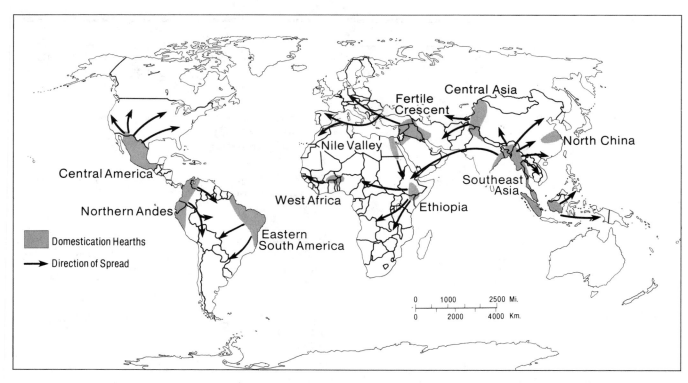

FIGURE 7.3
Origins of plant and animal domestication.

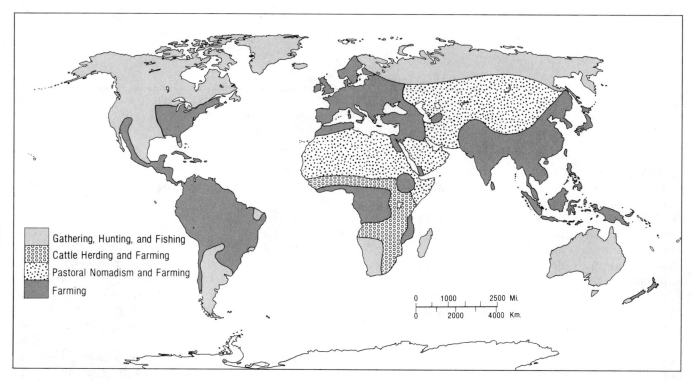

FIGURE 7.4
Patterns of land use, A.D. 1500.

ments. Eventually, European settlement assumed two forms: (1) "farm-family" colonies in the middle latitudes of North America, Australia, New Zealand, and South Africa and (2) "plantation" colonies in the tropical regions of Africa, Asia, and Latin America. These two types of agricultural settlements differed considerably.

Farm colonization in North America, for example, depended on a large influx of European settlers whose agricultural products were initially for a local rather than an export market. Europeans introduced the farm techniques, field patterns, and types of housing characteristic of their homelands; yet, they often modified their customs to meet the challenge of organizing the new territory. For example, the checkerboard pattern of farms and fields that characterizes much of the country west of the Ohio River resulted from a federal system of land allocation. It involved surveying a baseline and a principal meridian, the intersection of which served as a point of origin for dividing the land into six-by-six-mile townships, then into square-mile sections, and, still further, into quarter sections a half-mile long. Such an orderly system of land allocation prevented many boundary disputes as settlement moved into the interior of the United States.

In tropical areas, Europeans, and later Americans and Japanese, imposed a plantation agricultural system that did not require substantial settlement by expatriates. *Plantations* are large-scale agricultural enterprises devoted to the specialized production of one tropical product raised for market. It is believed that they first were developed in the 1400s by the Portuguese on islands off the tropical West African coast. Plantations produced luxury foodstuffs, such as spices, tea, cocoa, coffee, and sugar cane, and industrial raw materials, such as cotton, sisal, jute, and hemp. These crops were selected for their market value in international trade, and they were grown near the seacoast to facilitate shipping to Europe. The creation of plantations sometimes involved expropriating land used for local food crops. Sometimes, by irrigation or by clearing of forest, new lands were brought into cultivation. Europeans managed plantations; they did no manual labor. The plantation system relied on forced or poorly paid indigenous labor. Very little machinery was used. Instead of substituting machinery for laborers when local labor supplies were exhausted, plantation managers went farther afield to bring in additional laborers. This practice was especially convenient because world demand fluctuated. During periods of increased demand, production could be stepped up by importing additional laborers. This obviated the need for installing machinery during booms, and minimized the financial problems of idle capital during slumps.

The effect of centuries of European overseas expansion was to reorganize agricultural land use

On the world's largest rubber plantation at Harbel, Liberia, more than 36,000 hectares, or 30 percent of the total land area of Liberia, are cultivated by Firestone. The company also has established plantations in Brazil, Ghana, Guatemala, and the Philippines. How do plantations benefit host societies? (Source: Firestone Tire and Rubber Company.)

A tapper on the Firestone plantation in Liberia makes an incision in a rubber tree. The latex will flow down the incision through a spout and into a cup attached to the tree. Some of the latex is carried in pails by women to collecting stations. What would this tapper do if he were not working for Firestone? (Source: Firestone Tire and Rubber Company.)

worldwide. Commercial agriculture systems have become a feature of much of the habitable world. Hunting and gathering, the oldest means of survival, has virtually disappeared, although it still sustains groups such as the Bushmen of the Kalahari and the Pygmies of Zaire. Pastoralists, such as the Masai of Kenya and Tanzania who drive cattle in a never-ending search for pasture and water, have declined in numbers. Subsistence farming still exists, but only in areas where impoverished farmers, especially in underdeveloped countries, barely make a living from tiny plots of land. Few completely self-sufficient farms exist; most farmers, even in remote areas of Africa and Asia, trade with their neighbors at local markets.

Human Impact on the Land

The emergence of agriculture and its subsequent spread over the earth has meant that little if any land still can be considered natural or untouched. Vegetation has been most noticeably changed. Virtually all vegetation zones show signs of clearing, burning, and the browsing of domestic animals. The impoverishment of vegetation has led to the creation of successful agricultural and pastoral landscapes, but it has also led to land degradation or a reduction of land capability. Land degradation is a social problem of major significance—the "quiet crisis" that erodes the basis of civilization (Brown 1981).

Hunters and gatherers hardly disturb vegetation, but farmers must displace vegetation to grow their crops and to tend their livestock. Farmers are land managers; they upset an "equilibrium" established by nature and substitute one of their own. If they apply their agrotechnology with care, the agricultural system may last indefinitely and remain productive. If they apply their agrotechnology carelessly, the environmental base may deteriorate rapidly. How farmers actually manage land depends on their knowledge and perception of the environment, but also on their relations with groups in the wider society—in the state and the world economy.

As agriculture intensifies, environmental alteration increases. Ester Boserup (1965) proposed a simple five-stage model of agriculture systems based on frequency of land use (Table 7.2). Stage 1, forest-fallow cultivation, involves cultivation for one to three years followed by twenty to twenty-five years fallow. In Stage 2, bush-fallow cultivation, the land is cultivated for two to eight years, followed by six to ten years fallow. In Stage 3, short-fallow cultivation, the land is fallow for only one to two years. In Stages 4 and 5, annual cropping and multicropping, fallow periods

are either very short—a few months—or nonexistent. Boserup noted that the transition from one form of agriculture to another was accompanied by increasing population density, improved tools, increasing integration of livestock, improved transportation, more complex social infrastructure, more permanent settlement and land tenure, and greater labor specialization.

Forest-fallow or shifting cultivation survives in areas of the humid tropics that have low potential environmental productivity and low population pressure. Under ideal conditions, this form of agriculture leaves a good deal of original vegetation intact. Farmers make small discontinuous clearings in forests. They girdle some trees and cut down others, burn the debris, and prepare the soil by digging holes in a pattern of points for a variety of crops—groundnuts, rice, taro, sweet potato. Since no fertilizer is used, soil nutrients are quickly exhausted. Thus, farmers abandon their plots and establish new gardens every few years, but rarely move their residences. Except on steep slopes, where soil erosion can be serious, shifting cultivation can be a sustainable system of agriculture (Clarke 1977; Grandstaff 1978). It allows previous plots to regenerate natural growth. In Papua New Guinea, for example, about one-quarter of the country's forested area is well-developed secondary forest created and maintained by shifting cultivation.

Shifting cultivation can lead to degradation, however, when increasing population demands too much of the land or when new forces intrude into the farming system. In one sequence, common in Latin America, shifting cultivation follows loggers and oil prospectors into an area. After cropping is finished, the land is seeded with grass and sold to commercial ranchers who produce beef for the North American and European markets. Heavily grazed, the land quickly declines in carrying capacity and is then abandoned as the ranchers move to new areas (Nations and Komer 1983).

By contrast, permanent agriculture (annual cropping and multicropping) usually occurs in areas of high potential environmental productivity and of high population pressure. Under permanent cultivation, the land becomes totally transformed. Yet the beauty, fertility, and endurance of the land may not be impaired. Soils of the Paris Basin have been intensively cultivated for hundreds of years, and still they remain highly productive. In many parts of the Orient, carefully terraced hillsides have maintained the productivity of valuable soil resources after thousands of years. These agricultural landscapes are in harmony with nature.

TABLE 7.2
Agricultural intensification.

Dimensions of Change	Stages				
	Forest Fallow	Bush Fallow	Short Fallow	Annual Cropping	Multicropping
Population Density	Very low	Low	Moderate	High	Very high
Fallow: Cropland Ratio	10+	4–10	2–3	Annual	2–3 Year
Tools	Fire, ax, digging stick, hoe	Fire, ax, hoe	Hoe, plow, fire, draft animals	→ Plow draft animals, hoe; irrigation, tractors, chemicals may occur	
Livestock	Incidental	Possible manuring on some fields	Stock for plow and manure	→ Increasing provision of fodder; increasing conflict between grazing and cultivation rights	
Settlements	Unstable, dispersed	Stable, larger	Permanent settlement	→ Permanent settlements; increasing link to urban system	
Transportation	Paths, trails	→ Evolution of road network			Urban-focused road network
Social Infrastructure	Little formalization	→ Increasing complexity		Social organizations, health, water, other services	Greater elaboration
Land Tenure	General use right without permanent interest	→ Increasing tenacity of tenure; Persistent rights to cultivation land		→ Individual tenure	Permanent ownership possible, fragmental, landlord/tenant
Labor Specialization (Except by Sex, Age)	Little division of labor	Some division of labor crafts	Some non-agricultural fulltime craftsmen	→ Greater specialization; increasing labor inputs; emergence of wage labor	
Output to Labor	Very high	Moderate	Low	→ Moderate to high (industrial economies)	Low (traditional, Oriental economies)
Output to All Land	Very low	Low	Moderate	High	Very high

SOURCE: Knight and Newman, 1976, pp. 206–7. Copyright © 1965 by George Allen & Unwin, Ltd. Adapted with permission from Ester Boserup's *The Conditions of Agricultural Growth* (New York: Aldine).

Boserup's Model of Agricultural Intensification

Ester Boserup (1965, 1981) challenged the Malthusian view that unchecked population increases geometrically while food production increases only arithmetically. Her thesis was that food production is highly responsive to human innovation and effort; and she believed that the slow, sustained pressure of population on resources teaches people the virtue of labor and stimulates them to effect agricultural improvements, thereby increasing productivity.

Her model of agriculture presents a continuum of stages based on land-use frequency. For each stage, she described the relevant tools and techniques, relationships with livestock and grazing land, labor input, capital input, marginal return, land tenure, and social/political characteristics.

A point central to Boserup's thesis is that the vegetation that characteristically follows the end of a fallow cycle is best managed by a particular set of tools. For example, the digging stick, ax, and fire are the best (i.e., labor-minimizing) tools to use in preparing a regrowth forest for cultivation. As the fallow cycle is shortened, forest is replaced by bush, shrubs, and grass, and a hoe replaces the digging stick as the best tool. A still shorter fallow leaves a grass turf to be prepared in reopening a field, and the plow becomes a more effective tool than the digging stick, ax, or hoe—although the hoe and various mounding techniques still may be found in areas that lack draft animals.

The essence of Boserup's model is that the engine that drives agricultural growth is population pressure, and the fuel the engine runs on is human labor. A small, nongrowing population is unlikely to go beyond the stage of primitive agriculture to a higher level of technique and cultural development, whereas a growing population will be faced with the need to improve the land and invest in agriculture to a greater degree.

The model was designed explicitly as a development strategy for Third World countries (Boserup 1970). It was largely disregarded, however. In the 1960s and 1970s, the prevailing view among development scientists was that

---

In general, modern farming practices pose the main danger to land. Clean tillage on large fields, monoculture, and the breaking down of soil structure by huge machines are a few factors that may destroy the topsoil. Droughts and duststorms of the 1930s, 1970s, and 1980s in the Great Plains of the United States gave testimony of how nature and industrial agriculture can combine to destroy the health of a steppe landscape, transforming it into a desert.

Whether farmers achieve a harmonious relationship with nature does not depend necessarily on either their technologies or their political philosophies. Farmers with simple tools and technologies may destroy the long-run food-producing capacity of the land. Mechanical agriculture in both capitalist and socialist countries alike can degrade the land.

Agriculture threatens ecological balances when people come to believe that they have freed themselves from dependence on land resources. In capitalist countries, there is an inherent tendency to exploit the land as a result of pressure to reproduce economic conditions of production or to maximize profits. Household and corporate producers want to make land use more efficient and land more productive; thus, farming is often viewed as just another industry. But we must remember that land is more than a means to an end; it is finite, spatially fixed, and ecologically fragile. If we desecrate the land, human life cannot continue. As Ernest Schumacher (1973) pointed out in his book *Small is Beautiful*, there are three important goals of agricultural land use: health, beauty, and permanence. If these are not the objec-

the application of the modern biogenetic, chemical, and organizational agricultural revolution to the Third World, rather than labor intensification, would solve food problems.

Boserup's model has some validity in the broad sweep of history, but it is inadequate in several respects (Cassen 1976, p. 807). First, in setting up a continuum from forest to continuously cropped land, it pays insufficient attention to other vegetational forms, particularly to tropical savannas and grasslands. Second, the model does not completely account for spatial aspects, marketing, cash attributes of economies, and the process of underdevelopment in Third World countries. Boserup considers the development of a cash economy and market exchange, just as she regards the evolution of social differentiation and political institutions, always as *consequences* of changes in agricultural systems and never as *determinants* of the changes themselves (Datoo 1976, p. 8). In other words, a colonial government's requirement that farmers grow an export crop (cotton, coffee, groundnuts) may have caused increased population pressure. There is an inherent difficulty in sorting out cause from effect—of knowing whether increased population pressure is cause or consequence of agricultural development.

Third, the model is ambiguous about the innovation process. It may be likened to a toothpaste tube—population growth applies pressure on the tube and somehow squeezes out agricultural innovation at the other end. However, there are many counterexamples. "What appears at the other end of the tube is often not innovation but degradation" (Blaikie and Brookfield 1987, p. 30).

Fourth, the model comes close to the Malthusian idea that there are ultimate limits to the capacity of the land to support population without famine, damage, or both. "Boserup merely converts these limits into launching pads without successfully demonstrating that this conversion can always be made in all environments, or can continue indefinitely. . . . At least within the domain of preindustrial and early industrial agriculture which is her preferred ground, Boserup emerges more as a corrector of Malthus than as his refutor" (Blaikie and Brookfield 1987, p. 31).

tives of agriculture, it is hard to see how we can produce the foodstuffs that sustain us on any long-term basis.

FACTORS AFFECTING RURAL LAND USE

Rural land-use patterns, which are arrangements of fields and larger land-use areas at the farm, regional, or global level are difficult to understand. Worldwide, there are hundreds and hundreds of farm types. When faced with such diversity, geographers frequently divide the world into parts or regions to simplify the problem of description. A map of nine agricultural regions ranging from labor-intensive rice-paddy farming to nomadic herding is one of many that geographers have proposed to break down varied farm types into a few generalized patterns (Figure 7.5).

The most interesting aspect of the world's agricultural regions is not their number or extent, but the uniformity of land-use decisions farmers make within them. Given any farming region, why do farmers make similar land-use decisions? For example, why does one farmer on the slopes of Mount Kilimanjaro decide to mix coffee bushes with banana stands and likewise all other neighbors? The land-use pattern on Kilimanjaro, as elsewhere, reflects a host of factors. Geographers identify at least four groups of variables that determine land use. These are site characteristics, cultural preference and perception, systems of production, and relative location.

Dust storm over Lubbock, Texas, in the 1930s. (Source: Library of Congress.)

Site Characteristics

Variations in rural land use depend partly on site characteristics, such as soil type and fertility, slope, drainage, exposure to sun and wind, and the amount of rainfall and average annual temperature. As an example, consider the climate milieux in which crops grow. Plants require particular combinations of temperature and moisture. An optima-and-limits schema shows the range for a hypothetical crop (Figure 7.6). Increasing rainfall is plotted on the horizontal axis and increasing temperature on the vertical. Absolute physical limits of the crop are "too wet," "too dry," "too cold," and "too hot." A series of isopleths, which connect points of equal dollar yield per hectare, mark optimum conditions. The diagram emphasizes that a particular combination of temperature and moisture

conditions characterize each and every site. Absolute climatic limits are wide for some crops such as maize and wheat, but narrow for others such as pineapples, cocoa, bananas, and certain wine grapes.

Cultural Preference and Perception

Food preferences and prejudices are one of the most important variables that play a part in determining the type of agricultural activity at a given site. Some cultural groups would rather starve than eat edible but taboo food (Simoons 1961). Many Africans avoid protein-rich chickens and their eggs. Certain Hindus abstain from eating all meat, but particularly beef. Muslims do not eat pork; hence, pig raising is absent from the Muslim world which stretches from Mauri-

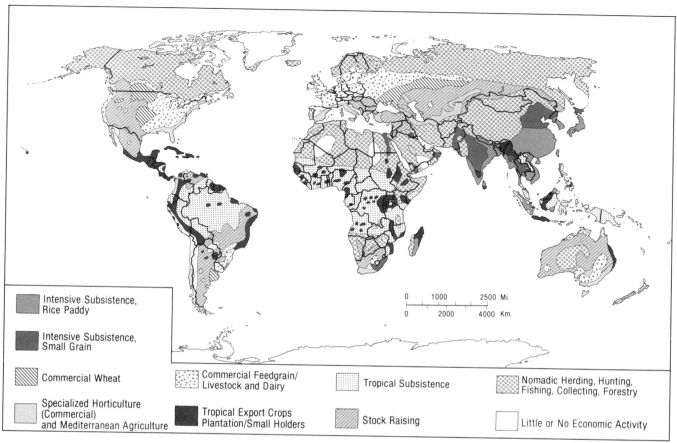

FIGURE 7.5
World agricultural regions.

Legend:
- Intensive Subsistence, Rice Paddy
- Intensive Subsistence, Small Grain
- Commercial Wheat
- Specialized Horticulture (Commercial) and Mediterranean Agriculture
- Commercial Feedgrain/ Livestock and Dairy
- Tropical Export Crops Plantation/Small Holders
- Tropical Subsistence
- Stock Raising
- Nomadic Herding, Hunting, Fishing, Collecting, Forestry
- Little or No Economic Activity

tania and Morocco to Pakistan and Bangladesh and to parts of Indonesia (Figure 7.7). The Chinese and some other people of East and Southeast Asia abstain from drinking milk or eating milk products. In the United States, a consumer preference for meat leads American farmers to put a greater proportion of their land in forage crops than do European farmers, who grow more food crops.

People interpret the environment through different cultural lenses. Their agricultural experiences in one area influence their perceptions of environmental conditions in other areas. Consider the settlement of North America. The first European settlers were Anglo-Saxons accustomed to moist conditions and a tree-covered landscape. They equated trees with fertility. If land was was to be suitable for farming, it should, in its natural state, have a cover of trees. Thus, the settlers of New England and the East Coast realized their expectations of a fertile farming region.

When Anglo-Saxons edged onto the prairies and high plains west of the Mississippi River, they encountered a treeless, grass-covered area. They underestimated the richness of the prairie soils, in particular, and the area became known as the "great American desert." In the late nineteenth century, a new wave of migrants from the steppe grasslands of Eastern Europe appraised the fertility of the grass-covered area more accurately than did the Anglo-Saxons who preceded them. The settlers from Eastern Europe, together with technological inventions such as barbed-wire fencing and the mold-board plow, helped to change the perception of the prairies from the "great American desert" to the "great American breadbasket."

In areas of new settlement, a succession of good farming years often engenders a false optimism about the environment. Until the disasters of the 1930s, farmers of the American Great Plains did not realize that the land they worked was highly sensitive. In fact,

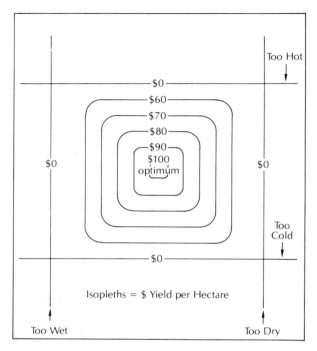

FIGURE 7.6
Optimal and marginal fertility ranges. (Source: Based on McCarty and Lindberg, 1966, p. 61.)

there was a belief that occupation of the Great Plains increased rainfall and could ban the specter of drought (Webb 1931). In Australia, the hazards of farming the semiarid regions were first ignored, then harshly recognized, and later only partly accepted (Meinig 1962; Williams 1979).

Ignorance of land degradation and its perception are a function of the rate and accumulated degree of degradation as well as the intelligence of land managers. In the mountains of Ethiopia, where cultivation has been going on for two thousand years with a fairly low rate of soil loss, the cumulative erosion of good soil has resulted in a serious decline in the capability of land. By comparison, in the hills of northern Thailand, where rates of soil loss are much higher, the local land-management system has "compensated" for soil erosion and the capability of the land has been maintained. (Hurni 1983).

However, land is sometimes devastated by land managers not because of ignorance or stupidity, but because of calculated human agency. A strong market imperative, a need to occupy new land for cropping, or a belief that "man" can and must "master nature" can ruin land in sensitive environments. Much land in the USSR has been degraded as a result of attempts by the state to "transform nature" (Komarov 1981). One of the most disastrous efforts to revive agriculture's lagging production was President Nikita Khrushchev's hasty, grandiose Virgin and Idle Lands Program (Jackson 1962). It involved massive plowing of dry steppe east of the Volga that resulted in increased corn and wheat production. Elimination of fallowing in the steppe reduced soil moisture reserves, encouraged weed and insect infestations, and depressed

FIGURE 7.7
Pork avoidance area. (Source: Based on Simoons, 1961, p. 14.)

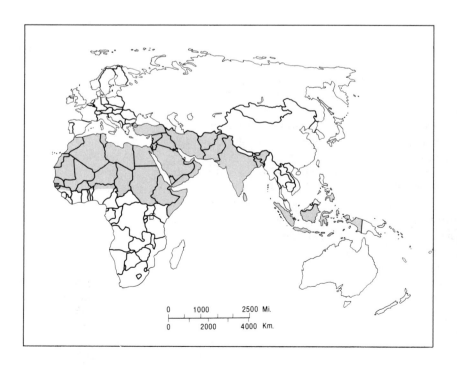

Settlers pose in front of their sod home in Nebraska in 1887. (Source: U.S. Department of Agriculture.)

yields, while frequent mold-board plowing pulverized the soils and led to enormous dust storms (Stebelsky 1983).

Systems of Production

Systems of agricultural production set their imprint on rural land use. Like manufacturing, agricultural endeavor is carried out according to three systems of production: peasant, capitalist, and socialist (Table 7.3). The major distinction among these systems is the labor commitment of the enterprise. In the peasant system, production comes from small units worked entirely, or almost entirely, by family labor. In the capitalist system, family farming is still widespread; but, as in the socialist system, labor is a commodity to be hired and dismissed by the enterprise according to

changes in the scale of organization, degree of mechanization, and the level of market demand for products.

In any geographic region, one system of production dominates the others. For example, capitalist agriculture dominates parts of South America, while peasant agriculture dominates other parts of the continent. Capitalist agriculture finds expression in a vast cattle-ranching zone extending southwest from northeastern Brazil to Patagonia; Argentina's wheat-raising Pampa, which is similar to the U.S. Great Plains; a mixed livestock and crop zone in Uruguay, southern Brazil, and south central Chile, which is comparable to the U.S. Corn Belt; a Mediterranean agriculture zone in middle Chile; and a number of seaboard tropical plantations in Brazil, the Guianas, Venezuela, Colombia, and Peru. Peasant agriculture

TABLE 7.3
Systems of production.

The Enterprise	Peasant	Capitalist	Socialist
Labor Commitment of the Enterprise	Total	Partial	Partial
Institutional Basis	Family	Family	Combine
		Joint Stock	
Control and Direction	Family	Family-Managerial	Managerial
Means of Distribution	Barter-Market	Market	Prescription-Market
Media of Distribution	Kind-Money	Money	Money
Mechanization	Possible	Usual	Usual
Regulator	Labor Supply	Market	State

SOURCE: Adapted from Franklin, 1965, p. 149.

dominates the rest of the continent. There is shifting cultivation in the rainforested Amazon Basin, rudimental sedentary cultivation in the Andean plateau country from Colombia in the north to the Bolivian Altiplano in the south, and a wide strip of crop and livestock farming in eastern Brazil between the coastal plantations and livestock ranching zones.

Peasant Mode of Production   Peasant agriculture is associated with underdeveloped countries, and it is *labor-intensive* (labor-centered). Farmers are small-scale producers who invest little in mechanical equipment or chemicals. They are interested mainly in using what they produce rather than exchanging it to buy things they need. Of course, food and fiber are exchanged, particularly through interaction with capitalist agriculture at global, national, and local scales. But farm families consume much of what they produce. Karl Polanyi (1971) called this *use value* rather than *exchange value*. To obtain the outputs required to be self-supporting, peasant farmers are frequently willing to raise inputs of labor to very high levels, especially in crowded areas where land is short. Highly intensive peasant agriculture occurs in the rice fields of South, East, and Southeast Asia. Most of the paddies are prepared by ox-drawn plow, and the rice is planted and harvested by hand—millions and millions of hands. Clifford Geertz (1963) coined the term *agriculture involution* to refer to the ability of the agricultural system in the densely populated parts of Asia, including Japan, to absorb increasing numbers of people and still provide minimal subsistence levels for all in rural communities.

An example of the peasant mode of production comes from the semiarid zone of East Africa. This zone includes the interior of Tanzania, northeast Uganda, and the area surrounding the moist high-potential heartland of Kenya. As in most parts of the Third World, peasant agriculture in this region has been complicated by the colonial and postcolonial experience.

According to Philip Porter (1979, pp. 31–43), people in the semiarid area of East Africa earn a living by combining several activities. They eat their crops and livestock and sell or exchange agricultural sur-

In Indonesia, harvesting rice is an example of labor-intensive peasant agriculture. (Source: World Bank.)

pluses at markets. They grow cash or export crops such as cotton. They maintain beehives in the bush and sell part of the honey and wax. They brew and sell beer. They hunt, fish, and collect wild fruits. They earn income by cutting firewood, making charcoal, delivering water, and by carrying sand for use in construction. Some of them have small shops or are tailors. Most important, people sell their labor, both short- and long-term, nearby and far away (Figure 7.8).

To farm and herd successfully in the semiarid zone, land managers must meet certain requirements set by the environment and the nature of crops and animals. Livestock require water, graze, salt, and protection from disease and predators. To meet these needs day after day, year after year, land managers must have considerable skill and knowledge. They must know a great deal about the ability of animals to withstand physiological stress, but also about environmental management—which grass to save for late grazing, where and when to establish dry-season

wells to enable the stock to withstand the rigor of the daily journey between water and graze. With respect to crops, land managers must know about plant-moisture and nutrient needs. They must also be sensitive to the variability of rainfall.

Most of the time, this system of agriculture in East Africa provides peasants with an adequate and varied food supply. In bad times, there are mechanisms for sharing out hardship and loss so that farmers hardest hit can usually rebuild their livelihood after bad times end. The peasant mode of production, however, has been forced to adjust to pressures from governments during colonial and postcolonial periods.

For a long time it was fashionable to decry the conservatism of peasant farmers. But conservatism does not mean an unwillingness to change. Peasant farmers who live in environments of high risk and uncertainty, such as those in the semiarid zone of East Africa, do adopt risk-aversion behavior; in fact,

FIGURE 7.8
The structure of the semiarid peasant agricultural system in East Africa. (Source: Porter, 1979, p. 33.)

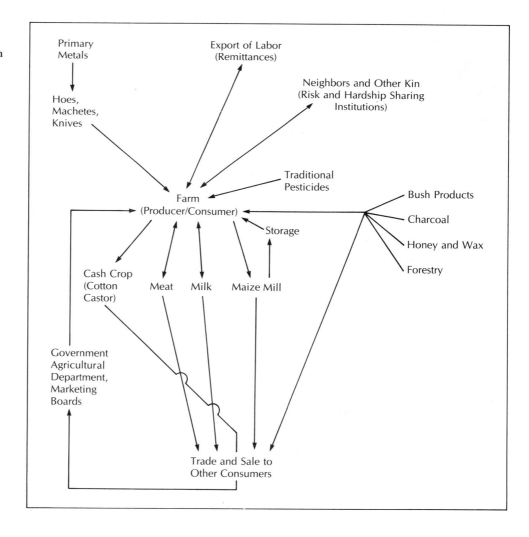

The development of the center-pivot irrigation system in the 1950s enabled large-farm operators to transform huge tracts of land in sandy and/or dry regions of the United States into profitable cropland. Here, alfalfa is being irrigated in Montana. (Source: USDA-SCS photo by Tim McCabe.)

they are more likely to behave in a risk-averting manner than wealthy, large-scale commercial farmers who have the resources to better withstand failure. Given proposals for change that will work in the environments in which they live, peasant farmers are just as willing to adopt new ideas and technologies as are their American or European counterparts.

Capitalist Mode of Production Agriculture in the United States epitomizes the capitalist system. Modern American farming is quick to respond to new developments, such as new production techniques. Consequently, farmers with sizeable investments of money, materials, and energy can bring about drastic changes in patterns of land use. For example, farmers in the low rainfall areas of the western United States have converted large areas of grazing land to forage and grass production with the use of center-pivot irrigation systems. Other farmers grow sugar beets and potatoes in western oases through federally subsidized water projects.

American farmers are more vulnerable to catastrophic events than their peasant counterparts. For the most part, peasant farmers can provide their families with food, clothing, and shelter. Most American farmers are completely tied to an elaborate marketing system. If their communication lines with the wider space economy were cut, they would quickly run out of the essentials: fuel, spare parts, fertilizer and seeds, and store-bought food and clothing (Figure 7.9).

At the frontier of American farming is *agribusiness,* which is associated with the trend on the part of such giant food companies as Ralston Purina, General

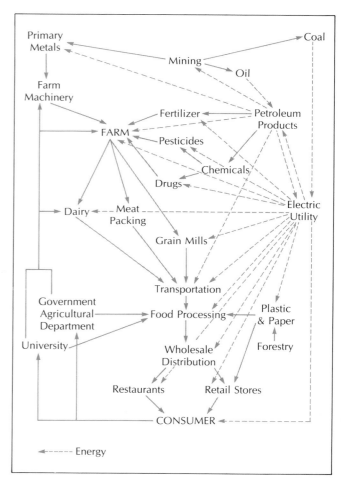

FIGURE 7.9
The structure of the U.S. agricultural system (Source: Knight and Wilcox, 1976, p. 23.)

Mills, General Foods, Hunt Foods, and United Brands to control the whole food chain from "seedling to supermarket." The concept to describe the control by food companies of production, processing, and marketing is *vertical integration*. The promise of high profits and a favorable tax structure has also attracted nonfood companies to move into food production. These include tractor firms, fertilizer and pesticide manufacturers, oil companies, and aircraft companies.

At the farm level, agribusiness is *capital intensive* and energy intensive. The very high per capita productivity results in rural depopulation. Although the family farm remains the basic unit in the American agricultural system, the direct role of agribusiness is increasing. The importance of corporate farming is growing in market gardening, which is sometimes called truck farming. Modern food-production truck farms specialize in intensively cultivated fruits, vegetables, and vines, and they depend on migratory seasonal farm laborers to harvest their crops. Other examples of modern food production include poultry ranches and egg factories. Agribusiness has also extended livestock farming in a big way. At one time, livestock farming (for example, in western Iowa) was associated with a combination of crop and animal raising on the same farm. In recent years, livestock farming has become highly specialized. An important aspect of this specialization has been the growth of factory-like feedlots, where companies raise thousands of cattle and hogs on purchased feed. Feedlots are common in western and southern states, in part because winters are mild. They raise more than 60 percent of the beef cattle in the United States.

American corporate farming is also extending overseas to become a worldwide food-system model. Family farming is still dominant in Western Europe, but beef feedlots are found in the Italian Piedmont. Poultry-raising operations in Argentina, Pakistan, Thailand, and Taiwan are like those in Alabama or Maryland. Enterprises such as United Brands, Del Monte, Unilever, and Brooke Bond Oxo are diverting more and more food production in underdeveloped countries toward consumers in developed countries.

Agribusiness means different things to different people. To corporate farmers, agribusiness means a profitable return to stockholders. To critics, it means gains to profit-conscious executives headquartered in large cities, but losses to most people in both developed and underdeveloped countries. In developed countries, for example, megafarming operations hurt small farmers who are driven out of business (Vogeler 1981). They also hurt consumers, since the free market does not exist in industries controlled by large firms. Workers sometimes find themselves without jobs when they "get in the way of corporate 'rationalization of production' or the 'free flow of capital'" (George 1977, p. 141). In the 1970s, for example, Del Monte and Dole found it "irrational" to produce pineapple in Hawaii because of hefty wage demands by cannery workers. The corporate strategy was to shift part of their pineapple-growing operation to the Philippines and Thailand where cheaper labor was available.

Socialist Mode of Production The USSR provides one example of a country with a socialist system of agriculture. This mode of production is based on the labor theory of value, in which the state, representing

Harvesting wheat by combine in the United States exemplifies capital- and energy-intensive agriculture. (Source: USDA photo by Doug Wilson.)

Corporate farming in the United States. (Top) One of the 120 employees watches a television monitor to see when a truck is in position to receive its load of computer-calculated feed ingredients at the Montfort feedlot in Greeley, Colorado. She will then release the ingredients into the truck and tell the operator by radio which pen gets the feed. (Bottom) Trucks mix the feed on the way to 265 separate feeding pens. The pens hold about one hundred thousand head of cattle at any one time, a number four hundred times greater than that required for efficient energy and resource use. (Source: USDA photos by Michael Lawton.)

peasants and workers, distributes wealth according to need, rather than ownership of land, factories, or stores.

Before the Bolshevik Revolution, agricultural land consisted of a mixture of small peasant holdings and estates of the rich. The Communists subsequently organized the land into Kolkhozes and Sovkhozes in response to the poorly organized peasant holdings they inherited from the Bolsheviks. *Kolkhozes* are collective farms resulting from the merger of land, livestock, and implements by peasants, who delegate management to elected officials and derive their income from the proceeds of the operation. *Sovkhozes* are state-owned enterprises whose managers, workers, and employees are paid wages and salaries from a state budget on the basis of the type of work they do. Sovkhozes are generally larger and better equiped than Kolkhozes and tend more to specialize. In 1980 the average size of a Sovkhoz was 17,000 hectares compared with 6,500 hectares for a Kolkhoz. In the 1970s cultivated land was fairly evenly divided between Kolkhozes and Sovkhozes. However, by 1980 Sovkhozes represented nearly 70 percent of the total agricultural area. The government intends eventually to convert the remaining Kolkhozes into state farms that will not be cultivated by peasants, but by workers who will receive the same regard as their industrial counterparts.

Tiny private plots or, in official Soviet parlance, personal subsidiary holdings exist alongside the giant socialized farms. These consist of small gardens where a typical collective farmer or state farm worker may keep a cow, a few pigs, and some chickens. The private plot helps make up for the deficiencies of socialized farming in the labor-intensive operations of animal husbandry and fruit and vegetable production.

Compared with the transformation of the Chinese earth, the organization of socialist agriculture in the USSR has not been strikingly successful. Soviet agricultural achievements also have been less impressive than their accomplishments in industry. Between 1930 and 1970 agricultural production increased by only 70 to 80 percent, whereas industrial output increased more than tenfold. According to Rhoads Murphy (1978), "[a major reason] agriculture has failed to match the gains of manufacturing and faced recurrent crises over food production has been the difficulty of changing archaic systems of land use in an immense country of nearly [285] million people. It has been much easier to change industrial techniques because there was less resistance to change, and fewer individuals, groups, or traditional regional structures were involved" (p. 172).

The USSR has attempted to increase agricultural production in three ways: first, by opening up new, but mainly marginal, lands on the cold and dry fringes; second, by improving farming methods (e.g., irrigation) and crops (e.g., drought-resistant varieties); and third, by mechanizing, especially its wheat and other grain lands. None of these methods has been totally successful. Aside from recurring weather problems, the food-production fiasco may be attributed to a low level of past agricultural investments, to poor management, and to a lack of incentives for farm workers to increase their output.

In the last few years, the Soviet government has increased levels of investment in agriculture and has provided more incentives for farm workers, including additional benefits for higher output. Recent reorganization at all levels may improve horizontal linkages (i.e., links with agricultural producers at the same stage of the production process) and vertical integration (i.e., agroindustrial integration). Vertical integration involves farms with forward linkages (processing, distribution) and/or backward linkages (supply of manufactured inputs and services for agriculture). But can agroindustrial integration succeed in the USSR without flexibility for decentralized decision making and incentives for industries to serve the farms? These conditions are best achieved under the American agribusiness model, which is unacceptable to the Communist doctrine. Without a more flexible and decentralized approach to land management, it is hard to see how investments in capital- and energy-demanding specialized farms will solve the agricultural crisis and end dependence on imports of much of the country's annual grain supply.

We can make some general observations about peasant, capitalist, and socialist agriculture. The peasant system of production is the most efficient from the standpoint of value of output per hectare. Capitalist agriculture, epitomized by American agribusiness, is the most productive—but it uses costly inputs. Finally, socialist agriculture, as in the USSR, is less efficient than peasant agriculture, and less productive than capitalist agriculture.

Relative Location

Despite the growing importance of public companies and corporations, farming is still, for the most part, a family business. An important factor that shapes individual farmers' land-use decisions is relative location or situation of a place in terms of its access to other places. Worldwide, the importance of situational components in agriculture increased as market exchange economies grew and developed. At one time, before commercial agriculture, a farmer's site relations—links with soil, sun, rain, and crops—were overwhelmingly important considerations in earning a living. Today, site relations have not ceased to be important; farmers still depend on the weather. But site relations have weakened as farmers have been drawn increasingly into situational relationships, with transport lines between farm and market linking them ever more strongly to a wider spatial economy.

VON THÜNEN'S MODEL

Relative location determines agricultural land use in several dimensions of space. The importance of relative location in rural land use was first discussed by Johann Heinrich von Thünen, a north German estate owner interested in economic theory and local agricultural conditions. From his experiences as an estate manager, he observed that identical plots of land (sites) would be used for different purposes depending on their accessibility to market (situation). The meticulous records he kept served as a framework for his book, *The Isolated State*, which was published in 1826. Von Thünen's aim was to uncover laws that govern the interaction of agricultural prices, distance, and land uses as landlords seek to maximize their income. His methods in many ways constitute the first economic model of spatial organization; his conclusions, even now, continue to be discussed and debated by economic geographers.

The Law of Diminishing Returns and the Concept of Rent

Von Thünen's principles of agricultural land use are based on traditional economic theory. In order to understand his main ideas, it is important to first review two classical concepts: the law of diminishing returns and the concept of economic rent.

The Law of Diminishing Returns The law of diminishing returns relates to the situation that confronts farmers in the short run. It considers existing possibilities of managing land, labor, and capital inputs. It considers the state of technical knowledge as given, and assumes no fundamental cost-reducing production changes. This law states: As successive units of a variable input (say, labor) are applied to a fixed input (say, land), total product (output) passes through three stages. First, total product increases at an increasing rate; second, it increases at a declining rate; and, third, it declines.

FIGURE 7.10
The stages of production.

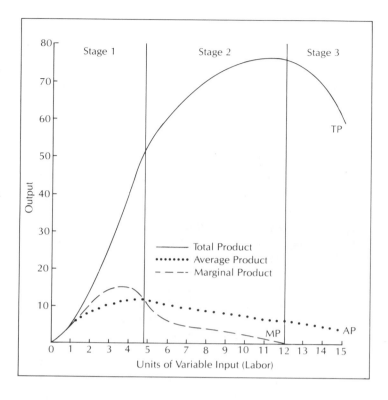

A standard example illustrates how the principle of diminishing returns works (Figure 7.10 and Table 7.4). Assume one fixed input (land) and one variable input (labor). *Average productivity* (AP) of labor is the total product (TP) divided by the number of labor units. *Marginal productivity* (MP) of labor is the addition to total output attributable to the last labor input employed. Throughout Stage 1, marginal product exceeds average product. The intersection of the marginal-product curve with the average-product curve marks the end of Stage 1 and the beginning of Stage 2. During Stage 2, the marginal-product curve

TABLE 7.4
An illustration of the law of diminishing returns.

Variable Input	Total Product	Average Product	Marginal Product	Stages of Production
0	0	0.00	0	
1	5	5.00	5	
2	16	8.00	11	1
3	30	10.00	14	
4	45	11.25	15	
5	55	11.00	10	
6	61	10.16	6	
7	66	9.42	5	
8	70	8.75	4	2
9	73	8.11	3	
10	75	7.50	2	
11	76	6.91	1	
12	76	6.33	0	
13	73	5.61	−3	
14	69	4.93	−4	3
15	60	4.00	−9	

declines, until it finally becomes zero. This marks the end of Stage 2 and the beginning of Stage 3.

Knowledge of total, average, and marginal productivity establishes some general boundaries for rational zones of agricultural production. If farmers are trying to obtain a maximum return for their investments, they will never operate in Stage 1. The level of intensity is too low; that is, the amount of variable inputs (labor) per unit land area is too small. Land is used too extensively. Farmers would want to take advantage of increasing returns to scale and add more variable inputs to intensify their operations. The boundary between Stage 1 and Stage 2 is termed the *extensive margin of cultivation*.

Farmers who are trying to maximize their returns also will never operate in Stage 3. Obviously, no rational farmer will operate in the range in which additional units of labor decrease total production, causing negative marginal-product values. The boundary between Stage 3 and Stage 2 is regarded as the *intensive margin of cultivation*. This leaves Stage 2 as the zone of rational production. In the real world, however, many enterprises—particularly large ones—do operate successfully in Stage 3 because of government regulations, subsidies, and lack of true economic competition.

Radicals find fault with the law of diminishing returns. Given the law's assumption of profit maximization, they claim it to be tautological in that the conclusions are concealed in the definitions. Farmers, for example, hire workers as long as they produce a surplus above their wages. When the additional profit falls to zero (i.e., when the marginal product from the last unit of labor added equals zero), then farmers stop adding workers. Radicals admit that the law does show farmers how to manipulate labor and capital to maximize profits, but argue that in a capitalist society it operates to the disadvantage of workers.

Economic Rent The concept of *economic rent* is central to von Thünen's discussion of agricultural land use. Economic rent is a relative measure of the advantage of one parcel of land over another. More precisely, it is the difference in net profits between two units of land. Net profit per unit area of land is equal to the total value of production minus the total costs involved in bringing forth the product. Differential rents may be due to variances in productivity of different parcels of land and/or variances in the distance from market.

At the beginning of the nineteenth century, British economist David Ricardo (1912) presented the idea of rent variations due to the impact of physical factors on productivity. We can illustrate Ricardo's ideas of rent variations attributable to fertility conditions in a productivity schema for a spatially restricted area (Figure 7.11). As we move away from a crop's optimum physical conditions, costs per hectare increase and rents decrease. A cross section is drawn through the line $A–A^1$. The side view is a space-cost curve, which graphs changes in cost across distance. Assume that the market price of a crop is $80 for one hectare of production. In this imaginary case, limits of production are determined by the intersection of the market-price line and the space-cost curve. No production occurs outside the $80 isoline, but rent increases toward the optimum.

What happens if the market price for a crop rises to $100 because of increasing demand (Figure 7.12)? Spatial margins to profitability spread out. Previously submarginal land is brought into production, and higher rent land is used more intensively. On the other hand, if the market price falls to $60, spatial margins to profitability draw back. Lower quality land is abandoned, and superior quality land is used less intensively.

An alternative view of economic rent was provided by von Thünen. Holding land quality constant, he demonstrated that rent is the price of accessibility to market. In other words, rents decline with distance from a market center. Geographers often use the term "location rent" as opposed to "economic rent" to express this concept of decline in rents with increase in distance from market.

The Isolated State

Features of the Isolated State In order to explain agricultural land use, von Thünen described an idealized agricultural region about which he made certain assumptions. He envisioned an isolated state with a large central city serving as the only market place. A uniform plain surrounded the city. A single mode of transport—the horse and cart—was used by the farmer to supply the market with produce. The farmers were price-takers, who attempted to maximize their profits. There were no extraneous disturbances in this ideal landscape; social classes and government intervention were absent. In addition to these constraints, von Thünen introduced one variable: transport to the central town—its costs increasing at a rate proportional to distance.

FIGURE 7.11
Optimal and marginal limits:
the space-cost curve.

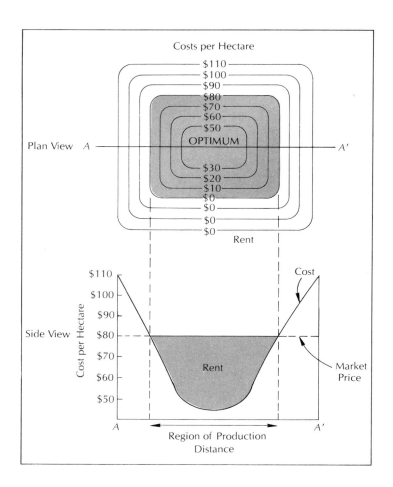

FIGURE 7.12
Spatial margins to profitability.

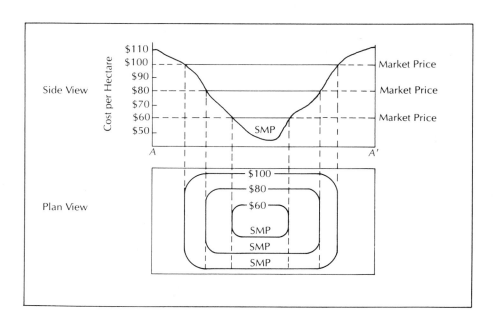

Location Rent

Location rent for any crop may be calculated by the following formula:

$$R = E(p - a) - Efk$$

where

R = location rent per unit of land
E = output per unit of land
k = distance to market
p = market price per unit of output
a = production cost per unit of land (including labor)
f = transport rate per unit of distance per unit of output

Thus, if we assume a wheat farmer located twenty kilometers from market obtains a yield of 1000 metric tons/km^2, has production expenses of $50/ton/km^2 to transport grain to market, and receives a market price of $100/ton at the central market, then the location rent accruing to a km^2 of the farmer's land can be calculated as follows:

$$
\begin{aligned}
R &= 1000\ (\$100 - \$50) - 1000\ (\$1 \times 20) \\
&= \$50,000 - 20,000 \\
&= \$30,000
\end{aligned}
$$

At fifty kilometers from the market, the location rent per km^2 of land in wheat is $0. Obviously, beyond fifty kilometers from the market no rational farmer in a competitive market economy would grow wheat.

Von Thünen's conditions are not representative of actual conditions in the early nineteenth century or in this century. Indeed, von Thünen regarded the Isolated State as an Ideal State—the ultimate stage in the development of "bourgeois" society. In his view, this Ideal State represented a goal humankind should strive toward. When it is attained, no further change is necessary. People live in a harmonious society free of exploitation.

The Problem After stating his assumptions in *The Isolated State*, von Thünen posed the problem that he wanted to investigate:

> The problem we want to solve is this: what pattern of cultivation will take shape in these conditions?; and how will the farming system of the various districts be affected by their distance from the Town? We assume throughout that farming is conducted absolutely rationally.

It is on the whole obvious that near the Town will be grown those products which are heavy or bulky in relation to their value and which are consequently so expensive to transport that the remoter districts are unable to supply them. Here also we find the highly perishable products, which must be used very quickly. With increasing distance from the town, the land will progressively be given up to products cheap to transport in relation to their value. For this reason alone, fairly sharply differentiated concentric rings or belts will form around the Town, each with its own particular staple product.

> From ring to ring the staple product, and with it the entire farming system, will change; and in the various rings we shall find completely different farming systems. (Hall 1966, p. 7)

Thus, von Thünen suggested that in a landscape free from all complicating factors, locational differences were sufficient to produce a varied pattern of land use. After he observed the role of transport costs, von Thünen relaxed his rigid assumptions, and introduced other variables to see how they modified his ideal pattern of land use.

Location Rent for a Single Crop Grown at the Same Intensity   To illustrate von Thünen's concept of differential rent, let us assume an isolated state producing one commodity (say, wheat) grown at a single intensity. Let us further assume that the market price of wheat is $100 per hectare per year, that it costs every farmer in the state $40 to produce a hectare of wheat, and that transport costs are five cents for each hectare of wheat (Figure 7.13). Under these conditions, what would be the net profit per hectare for farmers located zero, one, six, and twelve kilometers from the market? Farmers adjacent to the market pay no transport costs; therefore, their net profits would be simply market price ($100) minus production costs ($40)—or $60. Farmers one kilometer from the market pay five cents in transport charges; thus, their net profits would be $55. At six kilometers from the market, farmers would earn a net profit of $30, and at twelve kilometers, net profits would be zero. Beyond twelve kilometers, then, it would be unprofitable to grow a crop for market. In this outer area, only subsistence cultivation could be pursued, and cash would have to be earned by migrant labor.

Our example has shown that farmers near the central market pay lower transport costs than farmers at the margin of production. Clearly, net profits of the

closer farmers are greater, and the difference is known as *economic rent.* Farmers recognize this condition, and they know that it is in their best interest to bid up the amount they will pay for agricultural land closer to the market. Bidding continues until bid rent equals location rent. At that price, farmers recover production and transport costs, and land owners receive location rents as payments for their land. Competitive bidding for desirable locations cancels income differentials attributable to accessibility. The *bid rent*, or the trade-off of rent levels with transport costs, produces a spatial-equilibrium situation. It declines just far enough from the market to cover additional transport costs; hence, farmers are indifferent as to their distances from the market.

We can simplify Figure 7.13 by including production costs in a single expression with market price. This is illustrated in Figure 7.14a, which shows a rent gradient sloping downward with increasing distance from the central market. When the *rent gradient* is located around the market town it becomes a rent cone, the base of which indicates the extensive margin of cultivation for a single crop grown at a single intensity (Figure 7.14b).

Location Rent for a Single Crop Grown at Different Intensity Levels   Now let us suppose that wheat is grown at two intensity levels, reflecting two farming systems (Figure 7.15). The more intensive farming system has a steeper rent curve, and is profitable up to thirty-six kilometers from the market. The less intensive system occurs from thirty-six kilometers to the

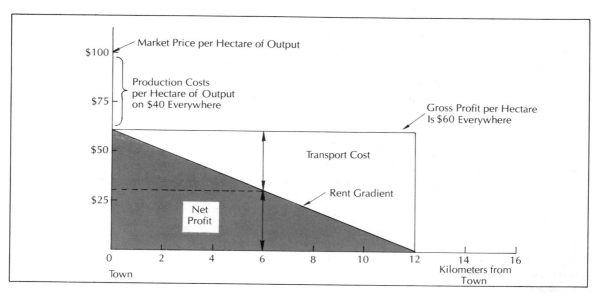

FIGURE 7.13
Net income from wheat production.

FIGURE 7.14
From a rent gradient to a rent cone.

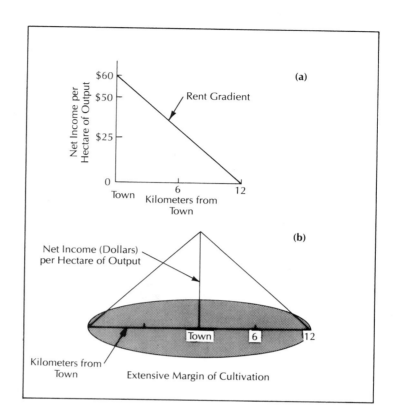

(a) Rent Gradient

Net Income per Hectare of Output — $60, $50, $25, 0 — Town — 6 — 12 — Kilometers from Town

(b) Net Income (Dollars) per Hectare of Output — Town — 6 — 12 — Kilometers from Town — Extensive Margin of Cultivation

limits of wheat farming, at seventy kilometers. At the margin of transference, the location rent for the two farming systems is the same. Separation between more intensive and less intensive systems illustrates the principle of *highest and best use*. According to this principle, land is used for the purpose that earns the highest location rent for its owner, but not necessarily for the workers.

Location-Rent Gradients for Competing Crops In von Thünen's analysis, patterns of agricultural land use form according to the principles of highest and best use as measured by the location rent at each distance from the market. To illustrate, consider location-rent gradients for an isolated state in which farmers have three land-use choices: vegetable production, dairying, and beef production (Figure 7.16). A

FIGURE 7.15
Rent gradient for a single crop grown at different intensities.

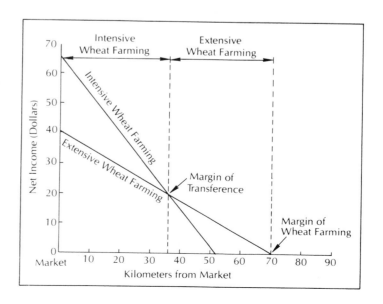

Net Income (Dollars) — 70, 60, 50, 40, 30, 20, 10, 0 — Intensive Wheat Farming — Extensive Wheat Farming — Intensive Wheat Farming — Extensive Wheat Farming — Margin of Transference — Margin of Wheat Farming — Market — 10, 20, 30, 40, 50, 60, 70, 80, 90 — Kilometers from Market

FIGURE 7.16
Location rent gradients for competing crops.

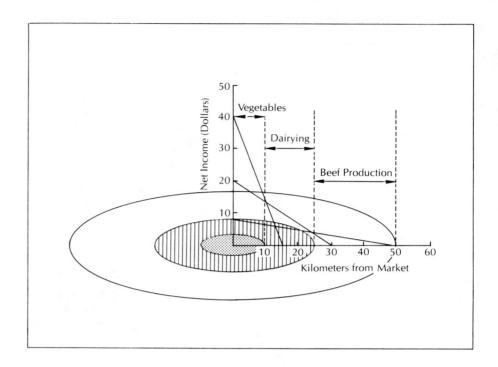

farmer close to the market could profitably carry on any one of the three activities. But which activity would maximize that farmer's income? Vegetable production has the highest rent-paying capability. All farmers seeking to maximize their incomes make the same decision: they grow vegetables between zero and ten kilometers from market. Dairying is the choice between ten and twenty-five kilometers, and beef production is the choice between twenty-five and fifty kilometers from market. Beyond fifty kilometers, no commercial land use is feasible.

Von Thünen's Original Crop System   In his theoretical Isolated State, von Thünen described six farming systems arranged in a series of concentric circles around the central city (Figure 7.17). The innermost zones produced perishable products (fluid milk and fresh vegetables) and heavy, bulky commodities in proportion to their value (wood fuel and lumber). On land most distant from the market, where transport costs were highest, land was used only for animal husbandry requiring little investment but large amounts of space (livestock ranching). Between these

FIGURE 7.17
Land-use zones in von Thünen's Isolated State.

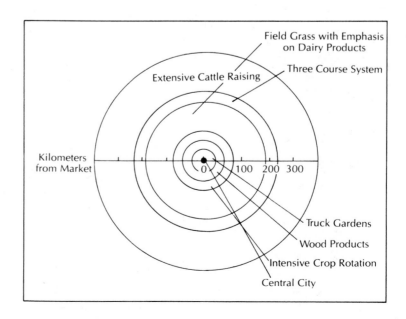

inner and outer rings, agriculture consisted of intensive and extensive arable farming.

At first, it seems rather odd that von Thünen would have put a forestry zone close to the market. This arrangement does not quite fit with our image of reality. But timber and fuel were in great demand in early nineteenth-century Germany. Consumers were not willing to pay high prices for items that were expensive to haul over long distances. The fact that patterns of agricultural land use in developed parts of the world in the late twentieth century differ from those of the early nineteenth century does not undermine von Thünen's methodology.

Modified Patterns of Agricultural Land Use Von Thünen was acutely aware that many conflicting factors—physical, technical, cultural, historical, and political—would modify the concentric patterns of agricultural land use. He modified some of his initial assumptions—the transportation assumption, for example—to approximate actual conditions more closely. Although he retracted the condition of a single-market town (Figure 7.18), he did not elaborate on the effects of several competing markets and a system of radiating highways. We can presume, however, that the tributary areas of competing markets would have had a variety of crop zones enveloped by those of the principal market town, and that a radiating highway system would have produced a "starfish" pattern (Figure 7.19). Von Thünen retracted other conditions as well, such as uniform physical characteristics, and considered other complicating factors such as the effects of foreign trade, taxes, and subsidies. He also emphasized the impact of distance on agricultural land use at all scales.

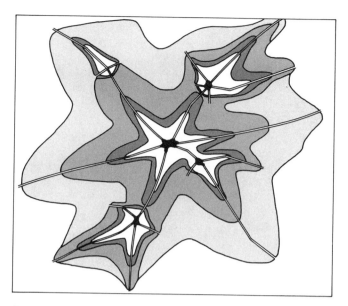

FIGURE 7.19
Distorting effects of several competing centers and arterial road systems.

Evaluation of von Thünen's Model

Among the conclusions to be derived from von Thünen's normative model of agricultural land use are the following:

1 that there is an inverse relationship between location rent and transport costs;
2 that there is a limit to commercial farming on a homogeneous plain with an isolated market town at its center;
3 that land values and intensity of land use increase toward the market; and
4 that crop types compete with one another and are ordered according to the principle of the highest and best use.

Von Thünen's most important contributions to studies of spatial organization were the concept of *location rent* and the principle of *highest and best use*. These two notions encompass three major aspects of land-use patterns: (1) circular bands or circles of land use around points of greatest accessibility, (2) axes of land-use development along major transport arteries, and (3) multiple nuclei with the emergence of additional satellite centers.

Von Thünen's pioneer model laid the groundwork for the study of land-use patterns; however, it has been criticized on several counts:

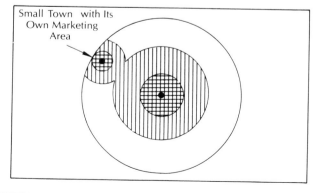

FIGURE 7.18
Distorting effects of a subsidiary market.

1 The model does not succeed in describing the spatial structure of an economic system. It oversimplifies the relationship between town and country. Although he later introduced multiple markets, von Thünen's analysis concentrated on various types of agriculture within a single market area with a large town at its center. He ignored the fact that agriculture tends to stimulate the growth of small *weight-losing* processing centers (e.g., sugar mills and distilleries), and that these industrial centers are connected to other larger centers. The products of "weight-losing" industries have large weight losses in processing.

2 The model assumes that differences in land rents have their origin solely in differences in costs of production. It disregards the existence of monopoly and absolute rents. Landowners receive monopoly rents (rents from excess profits due to monopoly prices), and they exact absolute rents, positive returns on all land in use including that at the margin of cultivation.

3 The model is static and deterministic. It represents a land-use system at a given time; therefore, it cannot predict changing patterns of land use. Furthermore, it assumes that from any change in technology, demand, or transport cost, instantaneous adjustments in land-use patterns follow.

4 The model does not consider the impact of economies of scale on production costs. Economies of scale around a large market may substantially lower production costs relative to a small market.

5 The model assumes constant, not variable, transport costs. This assumption, however, was appropriate given the transport conditions in early nineteenth-century Germany.

6 The model assumes that a farmer is *homo economicus*, who has perfect information and who uses it in a completely rational manner to maximize profits. Clearly, it is unrealistic to assume that farmers are *optimizers*; they make suboptimal decisions based on less than perfect information; and they depend on uncertain weather, economic, and political conditions.

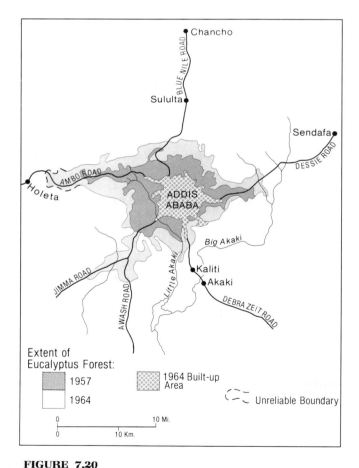

FIGURE 7.20
The forest zone surrounding Addis Ababa, Ethiopia. (Source: Based on Horvath, 1969.)

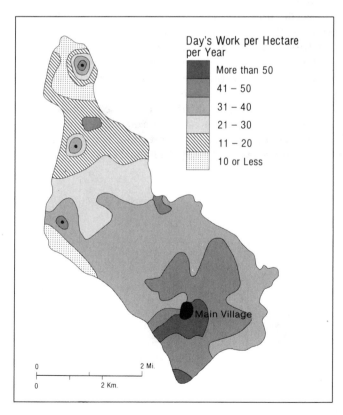

FIGURE 7.21
Intensity of farming around a village near Jodphur in Rajasthan, India. (Source: Based on Blaikie, 1971.)

7 The model assumes competitive agricultural markets. But over the past few decades the agricultural industry, especially in developed countries, has become controlled increasingly by giant corporations. "Superfarmers" are as profit-oriented as small farmers, but they are price-makers not price-takers, and can, therefore, operate successfully beyond the zone of "feasible" production.

Despite these limitations, von Thünen's model remains valuable. It provides insights into patterns of land use, and it can be used as a norm against which actual land-use patterns can be compared.

VON THÜNEN'S MODEL AND REALITY

Does the intensity of agricultural land use and the price of land increase toward the market as von Thünen's model suggests? We can answer this question by examining agricultural locations at local, regional, national, and international scales.

Local Scale

Thünian effects at the local scale can be observed in the Third World where there are localized circulation systems that resemble those of early nineteenth-century Europe. Ronald Horvath (1969) found such a pattern of land-use banding around Addis Ababa, Ethiopia. Thünen's original farming system placed

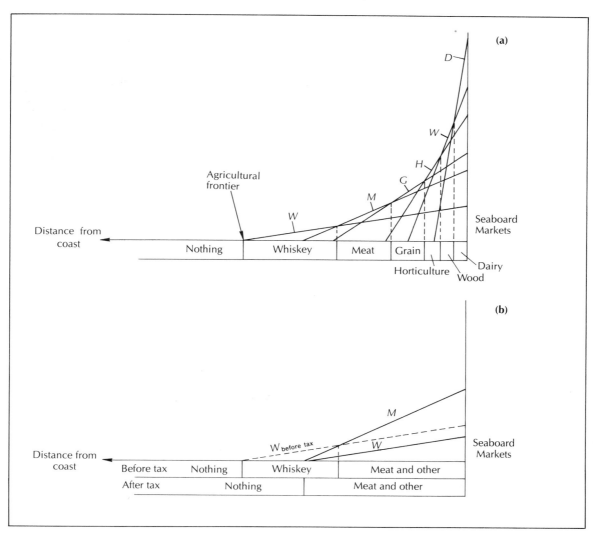

FIGURE 7.22
Circumstances leading to the Whiskey Rebellion in 1794. (Source: Abler, Adams, and Gould, 1971, p. 352.)

forestry in the second land-use ring, from which the city drew wood for building and fuel. Horvath described an inner wood-producing zone of eucalyptus forest that surrounded the Ethiopian capital (Figure 7.20). The zone was wedge-shaped rather than a ring, reflecting the greater accessibility to the city along major roads. Horvath also showed the expansion of the eucalyptus zone between 1957 and 1964, indicating transport improvements in the Addis Ababa area. The improvements permitted wood to be shipped to the city over increasingly greater distances and released more land near the city to be used for vegetable

production. Horticulture was a major activity of the innermost ring in von Thünen's ideal schema.

Additional studies have indicated distance-related adjustments in land use in the Third World. Piers Blaikie (1971) observed that small farmers in north India adjust land use to distance from their villages in order to reduce the total amount of work to be completed. Farmers living in these villages have to walk to the land that is under cultivation; therefore, the greatest effort is applied to land near the village and farming becomes less intensive in the outlying fields (Figure 7.21).

FIGURE 7.23
Theoretical land-use rings in the United States. (Source: Kolars and Nystuen, 1974, p. 258.)

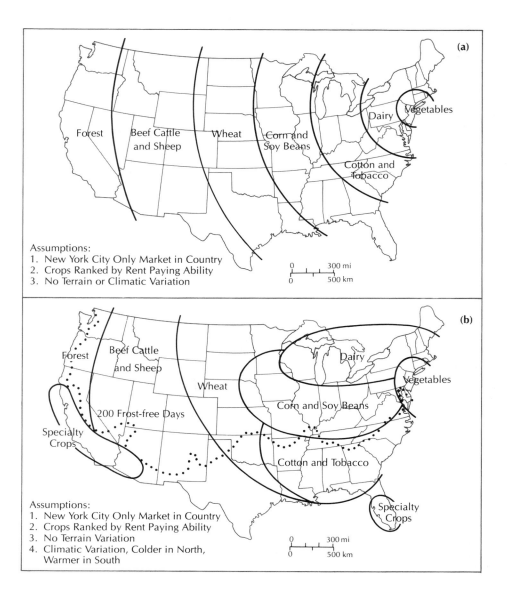

Regional Scale

We have seen that Thünian production patterns exist at the local scale. But does von Thünen's model work at other scales? Let's move up the scale from the local to the regional level, and take as our example the Whiskey Rebellion of western Pennsylvania farmers in 1794.

In the late eighteenth century, Eastern Seaboard cities—New York, Philadelphia, and Baltimore—were supplied with agricultural commodities by inland farmers. Close to the national market were dairy farms, market gardens, and woodlots. Beyond the woodlots were grain- and meat-producing areas. Still farther from the Eastern Seaboard, frontier farmers could profit only by raising grain and converting it to whiskey. Whiskey, which has a high value per unit of weight, was easy to transport. A few kegs were lashed onto the backs of mules and moved to market at low kilometer costs (Figure 7.22a).

Everything went smoothly for western Pennsylvania whiskey producers until 1794, when the U.S. government levied a special tax on inland whiskey. This tax effectively reduced the net profit for whiskey, so that the zone of profitable farm production shrank eastward (Figure 7.22b).

Frontier farmers having lost their source of income, rose up in rebellion. Federal troops were called in to restore order. As you know, the discriminatory tax was not permanent; it was repealed during Jefferson's administration.

National Scale

Agricultural land use at the national level represents another change of scale. Suppose we consider U.S. agricultural production going from the hypothetical to the real. Figure 7.23a is a map of hypothetical land-use rings. It assumes that the United States is a homogeneous plain, that New York is the only national market, that transport costs are uniform in all directions from New York, and that crops are ranked by rent-paying ability. These land-use zones, of course, are not consistent with reality. Other assumptions, such as a north-south temperature gradient, result in a more complex and realistic pattern (Figure 7.23b).

Now consider the map depicting the actual regionalization of U.S. agricultural production (Figure 7.24). The major agricultural regions, established for more than a century, developed largely within the

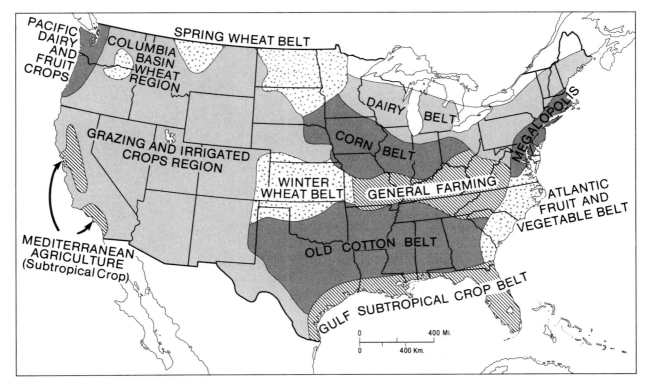

FIGURE 7.24
Major agricultural regions of the United States. (Source: Based on Wheeler and Muller, 1981, p. 315.)

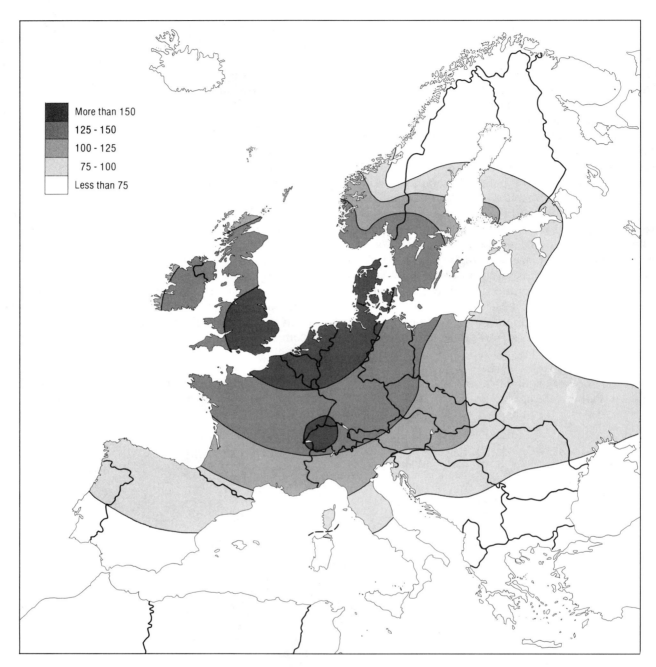

FIGURE 7.25
Intensity of agricultural production in Europe. The index of 100 is the average European yield per acre of eight main crops—wheat, rye, barley, oats, corn, potatoes, sugar beets, and hay. (Source: Van Valkenburg and Held, 1952, p. 102.)

framework of von Thünen's model. By 1900, early nineteenth-century crop zones had expanded with improving transport technology from local "isolated states" to the entire country. As the agricultural structure changed, the enlarged original Thünian zones were modified: (1) the first ring developed a distinct horticultural zone and a surrounding dairy-ing belt, (2) the forestry ring was displaced to the marginal areas of the system because the railroad could haul wood quite cheaply, (3) the crop ring subdivided into an inner mixed-crop/livestock belt that produced meat (the Corn Belt) and an outer cereal-producing area, and (4) the ranching area remained a peripheral grazing zone that supplied

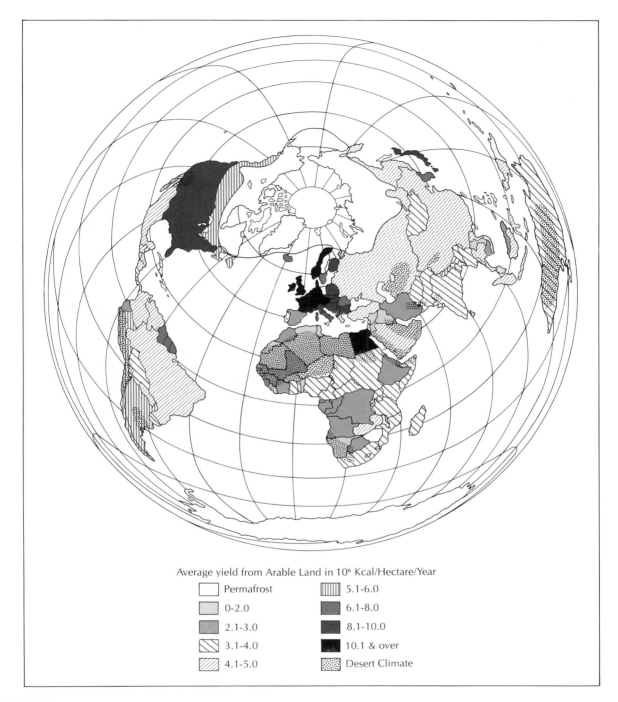

FIGURE 7.26
Average calorie yield from arable land as measured by yields from small grains and potatoes. (Source: Kolars and Nystuen, 1974, p. 266.)

young animals to be fattened in the Corn Belt. This super-Thünian regional system was anchored by a supercity—the northeastern Megalopolis.

Although the map of U.S. agricultural regions does not exhibit the classic rings, certain regularities are apparent. Of most importance, the intensity of

farming declines with distance from the national market. Thus, the Atlantic Fruit and Vegetable Belt, Dairy Belt, Corn Belt, Wheat Belts, and Grazing Belt conform to the model's structure. Deviations from the schema are the result of environmental variations and special circumstances. Central Appalachia supports only isolated valley farming (General Farming). Areas of the dry western mountains that have been reclaimed through huge federal investments in irrigation projects support "oasis" farming. California and the Gulf Coast-Florida region have mild winters and, with the help of irrigation and refrigerated transport, produce large crops of fruits and vegetables. The farms of the Pacific Northwest serve the local population—the nation—with potatoes, apples, and other specialty crops and Pacific Basin countries with wheat. The Old Cotton Belt, once poorly integrated into the national economy, specializes in the production of beef, poultry, soybeans, and timber (de Blij and Muller 1985, pp. 210–11).

International Scale

Finally, we can increase our scale of observation to the international level. In Europe, the intensive cash-cropping areas that extended only a few miles from the market have expanded far beyond von Thünen's estate at Tellow, southeast of Rostock, in Mecklenbury, Germany. We can now visualize Europe as a set of von Thünen rings. Production is most intense in the area centered on the Low Countries, Denmark, north Germany, northern France, and southeastern England (Figure 7.25).

The world, itself, may also be viewed as a set of von Thünen rings. At this scale, the world is the Isolated State and Europe-North America is the Thünian "Town." Figure 7.26 is a map projection centered on Europe showing the average calorie yield for small grains (wheat, rice, barley, rye, oats, maize) and potatoes. The general pattern is one of low average calorie yields in the underdeveloped world and intensive agricultural production in the urban-industrial complexes of Europe, North America, and Japan.

SUMMARY

Over many thousands of years a complex relationship has evolved between people and the natural environment. All people depend on agriculture for their well-being, but in our agricultural pursuits, we necessarily modify the land. Good land managers give back to

nature what they take; poor land managers degrade the environment.

Collections of plants and animals define fields that are organized around farms. And collections of farms make up farming regions. When geographers speak of agricultural regions, they are referring to the artificial division of the world into homogeneous farming types.

The most intriguing aspect of farming regions is not their number or extent, but the similarity of land-use decisions farmers make within them. After reviewing agricultural origins and dispersals and the impact of food production on the land, we identified four basic factors that influence agricultural land-use patterns. These are site characteristics, cultural preference and perception, systems of production, and relative location.

One theory that helps us to understand the distribution and location of agriculture was formalized by Johann von Thünen in the early nineteenth century. We described the normative model von Thünen developed to explain patterns of land use around the town in north Germany where he lived. We then presented some of the conclusions that can be drawn from this model: (1) there is an inverse relationship between location rent and transport costs; (2) there is a limit to commercial farming on a homogeneous plain with an isolated market town at its center; (3) land values and intensity of land use increase toward the market; and (4) crop types compete with one another, and are ordered according to the principle of the highest economic rent.

In the last section of the chapter, we saw how the basic Thünian principles can be applied to agricultural land-use patterns at scales ranging from the village to the world. Contemporary Thünian effects at the microscale are best observed in the Third World, where localized circulation systems provide a transport setting similar to that of early nineteenth-century Europe. Improvements in transport technology and the development of refrigeration have permitted the Isolated State to expand from the micro- to the macroscale. Thus, in the United States and Europe the model is no longer centered on a single city, but on a vast urbanized region. And at the global level, core nations are the market around which production zones develop (Schlebecker 1960; Chisholm 1979).

KEY TERMS

agribusiness

average product

capital intensive

cultural preference

environmental perception

extensive margin

highest and best use

intensive margin

isolated state

labor-intensive

marginal product

relative location

rent

site characteristics

space-cost curve

stages of production

systems of production

total product

use value

SUGGESTED READINGS

Blaikie, P., and Brookfield, H. 1987. *Land Degradation and Society*. New York: Methuen.

Boserup, E. 1981. *Population and Technology*. New York: Blackwell.

Chisholm, M. 1979. *Rural Settlement and Land Use: An Essay in Location*. 3d ed. London: Hutchinson.

Found, W.C. 1971. *A Theoretical Approach to Rural Land-Use Patterns*. London: Edward Arnold.

Gregor, H.F. 1982. *Industrialization of U.S. Agriculture: An Interpretive Atlas*. Boulder, CO: Westview.

Grigg, D.B. 1984. *An Introduction to Agricultural Geography*. London: Hutchinson.

Hall, P.G., ed. 1966. *Von Thünen's Isolated State*. Translated by C.M. Wartenberg. Oxford, England: Pergamon.

Hedlund, S. 1984. *Crisis in Soviet Agriculture*. London: Croom Helm.

Porter, P.W. 1979. *Food and Development in the Semi-Arid Zone of East Africa*. Syracuse, NY: Maxwell School of Citizenship and Public Affairs, Syracuse University.

Simoons, F.J. 1961. *Eat Not This Flesh*. Madison, WI: University of Wisconsin Press.

Troughton, M.J. 1982. *Canadian Agriculture*. Geography of World Agriculture 10. Budapest: Akadémiai Kiadó.

Vogeler, I. 1981. *The Myth of the Family Farm: Agribusiness Dominance of U.S. Agriculture*. Boulder, CO: Westview.

8
CITIES AND URBAN LAND USE

OBJECTIVES

☐ To explore the relationship between urban growth and capitalist development

☐ To explain how the process of city growth operates under free-market conditions

☐ To extend von Thünen's model to urban land use

☐ To introduce land-use models that describe the spatial dispersion of activities in cities

☐ To help you see how the free market for space in the metropolis has produced a pattern of sprawl and social problems

The heart of Amsterdam, Netherlands. (Source: KLM Aerocarta.)

A city is a built environment—a tangible expression of religious, political, economic, and social forces that houses a host of activities in close proximity to one another. Cities, the foundation of modern life, represent humanity's largest and most durable artifact (Vance 1977). They are living systems—made, transformed, and experienced by people.

Although the world pattern of cities is primarily the result of events triggered by the nineteenth-century industrial revolution, the city had its origins thousands of years ago. The first cities emerged in the Mesopotamian area of the Middle East about seven thousand years ago. Cities also developed early in the Nile Valley (about 3000 B.C.), in the Indus Valley (by 2500 B.C.), in the Yellow River Valley of China (by 2000 B.C.), and in Mexico and Peru (by A.D. 500). The raison d'être of cities from the start was to exchange goods and services with surrounding communities. As urbanization spread out from its ancient hearths, it was incorporated into the cultures of various regions.

The manifestations of the urban process display dazzling diversity. Because the historical antecedents of modern patterns of daily living differ from one part of the world to another, the structure of the city differs from region to region. For example, North American cities contrast strongly with those of Europe or Asia. North American cities are largely the creation of the last two hundred years, a period of free-market capitalist activity politically based on the concepts of democracy and a relatively egalitarian spirit. To be sure, most European cities have grown since the start of the nineteenth century, but the tradition of privatism has not been the only structural influence on their urban growth. For the majority of European cities, other socioeconomic structures (e.g., feudalism, absolutism, mercantilism), never significantly present in North America, have also played a role.

In Europe, urban life began more than two thousand years ago. Few European cities were created on virgin territory; most evolved from rural settlements. Some European cities existed before the growth of the Roman Empire. Apart from their own city-states, the Ancient Greeks were responsible for the foundation of other Mediterranean cities such as Naples, Marseilles, and Seville. By the end of the Roman Empire, a large proportion of Europe's largest present-day cities had been established.

From the fall of the Roman Empire to the early modern period, cities in Europe grew slowly or not at all. They ceased to be important during the period loosely referred to as the Dark Ages, a time when long-distance trade and rural-urban interaction drastically declined. Cities revived from the sixteenth century onward with the pursuit of profit in a period of incipient and later burgeoning capitalist economic activity. In commerce, a new middle class developed, and the revolution in the countryside squeezed out the peasant class and helped established the working class. The accumulation of capital, the growth of new social classes, the use of inexpensive labor in the colonies, as well as scientific and technological breakthroughs, destroyed the feudal fetter on production and created a new function for the city—industrialization. The *industrial city*, a product of capitalism, served to lower transport and communication costs for entrepreneurs who needed to interact with one another; hence, most commercial and industrial enterprises concentrated in and around the most accessible part of the city—the central business district (CBD). During the twentieth century, increasing affluence and the technologies of mass transportation and modern communications led to urban decentralization.

During the period of urban decline and rebirth in Europe, the urban process of the rest of the world exhibited different patterns. Before 1500, Europe was a mere upstart in a "world system" that included major interlocking subsystems of central places stretching from the Mediterranean to China. These subsystems were dominated by cities such as Constantinople, Baghdad, Samarkand, Calicut, and Hangchow that had greater continuity and played a more permanent role in the "world economy" than their European counterparts (Abu-Lughod 1987–88). Not until the commencement of European colonization were the urban civilizations of Asia, Africa, and the Americas threatened. Centuries of European penetration and occupation resulted in the growth of many cities that owe their origins to colonial foundations or to trading requirements.

Eventually, *colonial cities* dominated the urban patterns of Africa, Asia, and Latin America. Political independence and the development of the new international division of labor allowed underdeveloped countries to experience a transformation of the urban process as profound as that in nineteenth-century Europe and North America. Indeed, urban growth is now occurring more rapidly in the underdeveloped world than it had in Europe during its period of fastest growth in the late nineteenth century.

Waves of change have washed through cities, remodeling and redefining their shapes and details, but rarely have the traces of their historical legacies been completely obliterated. The legacy of history is of immense importance to economic geographers who study cities and attempt to find solutions to urban problems and crises. Questions of interest to the economic geographer include the following: What types of society and associated modes of economic exchange give rise to cities? What economic factors account for cities? What are the most vital influences on urban structure? What are the issues at the core of the urban process? Answers to these questions are the concern of this chapter.

CITIES AND SOCIETIES

Basic Forms of Society

Cities require the existence of a particular type of society in order to grow and develop. In the context of our discussion, a *society* refers to a group of people organized around a self-sufficient operating system that outlives any individual member. To maintain conditions of self-sufficiency, human groups must have forms of social organization capable of producing and distributing goods and services.

We can identify three main types of society with associated forms of economic exchange (Fried 1967). First, there are *egalitarian societies*, established through voluntary cooperative behavior. The economies of these societies are dominated by *reciprocity*, of which market barter is an example. Reciprocity involves trading without the use of money in a mutually beneficial exchange of goods.

Second, there are *rank societies*, examples of which are tribal and feudal societies. The economy of a rank society is dominated by *redistribution*. For example, African chiefs used to exact gifts in kind and/or money from their tribes according to custom. And under feudalism in Europe, serfs, who were bound to the land of some estate, owed the overlord (by tradition, or by force if necessary) food, labor, or military allegiance.

Third, there are *stratified societies*, in which members do not have equal access to the resources that sustain life. Their economies are dominated by *market exchange*. A market-exchange society adapts to scarcity by selling goods and services at a price. Pricing is the mechanism that connects the economic activity of large numbers of individuals and controls many decentralized decisions. Market exchange facilitates division of labor, specialization of production, and technological and organizational advances. It produces wealth for society out of scarcity, but often at the cost of even greater scarcity for the already poor. Socially created scarcities cannot be eliminated in market-exchange economies.

Cities do not evolve in egalitarian societies dominated by reciprocity. However, reciprocal forms of interaction, such as the mutually beneficial exchange of goods and services, do occur in cities. Everyday examples of reciprocity in an urban setting are exchanges among neighbors: lending a snowblower, gossiping, helping out when life crises occur.

Cities evolve in societies that can organize the exploitation of a surplus product. Rank and stratified societies have an especially suitable hierarchical structure to extract, appropriate, and redistribute a socially derived surplus product. A *social surplus product* is that part of the annual product of any society that is neither consumed by the direct producers nor used for the reproduction of the stock or the means of production. In rank and stratified societies, the social surplus product is appropriated by the ruling group. Surpluses are extracted from outside the confines of a city, as in the case of agriculture, and from inside a city, as in the case of manufacturing.

Stratified societies provide the most favorable conditions for the growth of cities. These conditions include unequal access to resources that sustain life, socially created resource scarcities, and institutions of market exchange. Except in countries that claim to have socialist economies (e.g., the USSR, China, and Cuba), contemporary cities exist in stratified societies.

Transformation of Market Exchange

Prior to the industrial revolution, market exchange was an appendage to the redistributive economy of the rank society. Under feudalism, cities of Europe were usually extensions of the personalities of those who governed them. For example, Venice, Italy, was the city of the Doges. Located at the seaward margins of the marshy Po Delta, Venice became one of Europe's most important centers of manufacturing and long-distance trade during the Middle Ages and early modern period. The dominant economic institutions of Venice and other European towns were the guilds—craft, professional, and trade associations. In Europe, before the industrial revolution, it was necessary for anyone who wanted to produce or sell any good or service to join a guild, which regulated members' conduct in all their personal and business activities. With the industrial revolution came a steady penetration of market exchange through the fabric of society. Cities ceased to be reflections of individual rule; they came to be instruments of industrial growth.

Individual capitalism was the hallmark of the early stages of the industrial revolution. Indeed, the period from the mid-1840s to 1873 has been called the

A canal in the merchant city of Bruges, Belgium. This Hanse town was the north European counterpart to Venice during the mercantile period. (Source: Belgian Tourist Office.)

A coal-cleaning plant in the industrial city of Pittsburgh, Pennsylvania. (Source: Library of Congress.)

golden age of individual or competitive capitalism. Under competitive capitalism, cities registered high rates of industrial innovation and prodigious increases in productive power. Their standards of achievement were based on industry and technology. If these prospered, then the city was considered to be good. The "best" city was the busiest one—the one that was growing most quickly and recording the largest increases in bank clearings. These producer cities, however, were ugly creations, and horrifying environments for the laboring poor. The British coined the term "Black Country" to refer to the grimy industrial cities of the English Midlands. Interestingly, the industrial city, which functioned as a "workshop" for purposes of production and capital accumulation, does not attract twentieth-century tourists in search of urban beauty. Tourists avoid rich industrial cities such as Toledo, Ohio, and overrun poor preindustrial cities such as Toledo, Spain.

In the late nineteenth century, capitalism took on a different form. There was a drift from competitive capitalism to monopoly, or corporate, capitalism. Through the elimination or absorption of small competitors, large industrial and financial corporations emerged, diminishing the community of competition. In today's developed countries, and in many underdeveloped ones, important areas of manufacturing

and strategic industries are dominated by a relatively small number of multinational corporations.

Large corporations have had a major influence on the twentieth-century Western city. Corporate administrative buildings and home plants dominate skylines and extensive land areas. For example, the organizational headquarters of such corporations as Standard Oil of Indiana and Sears Roebuck have helped to shape the image of Chicago.

The geography of contemporary Western cities has also been affected by the need of corporate enterprises to find ways to absorb their surpluses. An American example is the corporate penchant for disposing of their surpluses through urban renewal projects. Funds are sometimes used in projects sponsored by local governments to replace run-down, low-income housing with luxury office and residential buildings. Corporations and the federal government have poured resources into urban renewal projects in cities including Atlanta, Boston, Dallas, Houston, Minneapolis, New York, and Philadelphia.

In addition, American cities have been affected by the need for corporate enterprises to increase demand for their products and services. "Need-creation," a process whereby luxuries are marketed to be perceived as necessities, is exploited by corporations through daily appeal to potential customers.

Need-creation also operates as a consequence of urban spatial organization, itself. For example, low-density metropoli, such as Kansas City, Dallas, Houston, and Los Angeles, make a car, or two cars, a necessity. Residents are literally forced to drive the cars the auto industry produces.

Relative Importance of Different Modes of Exchange

All three modes of economic exchange (reciprocity, redistribution, and market exchange) operate in most cities, but the emphases have varied over time. Cities of medieval Europe reflected the dominant influence of redistribution, but market exchange also operated. In general, cities in the zone between the North Sea and Italy were more supportive of the market than those on the margin of this region. In the commercial area, as the old feudal ordering of society declined, the social and political influence of merchants grew. When commerce was permitted to operate freely, as in Venice and Florence, the market became a notable feature of city structure. Yet, the disposal of wealth through the construction of massive cathedrals, public buildings, and universities emphasized the pre-eminence of cultural values over worldly economic concerns. The imprint of cultural values is also unmistakable in other places with a long history of urbanization. For example, Lahore, the cultural focus of Islamic Pakistan, founded in the first or second century A.D., is adorned with palaces and mosques.

From the late medieval period onward, the importance of market exchange increased. Large commercial cities such as London, Amsterdam, and Antwerp boasted the triumph of the market over redistribution. By the nineteenth century, market exchange dominated life in Western Europe and in its overseas progeny.

In North America, where the medieval order did not exist, the nineteenth-century city was an expression of economic influence. The power of the American city did not rest in the nominal government; rather, it was based in the dominant economic institutions, which were usually industrial establishments. Nonetheless, city government did play a redistribution role that grew more important as the industrial revolution progressed. Urban bureaucracies collected taxes and provided a range of public services. Although much less prominent than the other modes of integration, reciprocity existed at every level of society, especially in working-class neighborhoods, where it provided residents with a degree of social solidarity and security.

In the modern Western city, the role of reciproc-ity is abridged. Market exchange prevails, but it is challenged by redistribution. Because of the growth of big business and government, redistribution is more important now than it was in the nineteenth century. The hierarchical status of employees in modern institutions is reminiscent of the structure of rank societies. Corporate and government bureaucracies have become major agents of redistribution in urban areas. Governments, for example, appropriate resources and return them to the populace at large in the form of various public services, welfare programs, public projects, and subsidies. The provision of funds for elementary and high schools is a good example of government redistribution at the local level. Most of the money for schools, which usually represent the biggest expense for local government, comes from property taxes.

THE PROCESS OF CITY BUILDING

What general forces operate to attract business and industry to cities? In a purely competitive market situation, we can account for the attraction of firms to cities in terms of two opposing forces. These forces are *scale economies* and *transport costs*. The influence they exert on city building will become apparent as we survey the classical economic principles that relate to the production and cost behavior of the single firm.

Production and Cost Behavior of the Single Firm

Although the capitalist world economy is oriented along monopolistic lines, a *pure competition model* provides one explanation for spatially concentrated production. It is also a reasonably correct model for the nineteenth century, an extremely important period in the growth of the world pattern of cities. The model of pure competition assumes that decision-makers operate in a completely rational manner to maximize total revenues and minimize total costs. A graph illustrates the output level for a hypothetical firm (Figure 8.1). The management of this firm will choose to produce OQ_1. To produce more or less than quantity OQ_1 will result in increased costs and reduced revenues.

Firms have short-run and long-run planning periods relative to the production function. The *production function* is a statement of the relationships between input (land, labor, and capital) used by a firm and the flow of output (goods and services) that results. By definition, *long run* is a period long enough to permit a firm to vary the quantity of all the inputs in

FIGURE 8.1
Output level for a profit-
maximizing firm.

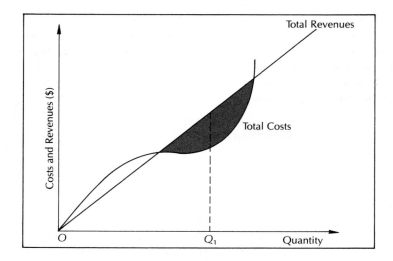

its production function; *short run* is a period short enough for at least one input to be fixed in amount and invariable. The firm's important long-run decision is on its future size—whether it should grow or contract. The firm's important short-run decision is on the most profitable rate at which to operate given the present plant size.

Suppose we have a simplified production function consisting of two inputs—a fixed supply of capital and a variable supply of labor. How would we determine the relevant short-run costs of production? Firms incur two types of costs: *fixed costs*, such as capital, and *variable costs*, such as labor. Fixed costs or overhead costs are expenditures firms must make in order to obtain the use of variable inputs. Fixed costs such as land and buildings do not vary with output. By contrast, variable costs rise as output rises; as output falls, these costs fall.

Managements of profit-maximizing firms are interested in total costs; that is, total fixed costs plus total variable costs. They are interested in a profit-maximizing rate of output at a given market price. One way to determine what firms should supply at each relevant price is to apply the law of diminishing

returns. Cost implications of this law are illustrated in Table 8.1. The price for a given amount of a variable input (column 2) and a fixed input (column 3) is $1. Total costs for different levels of output (column 1) are given in column 4. At four units of output, for example, total costs are $33; that is, $17 for the variable input plus $16 for the fixed input. Average total costs (column 5) are calculated by dividing total costs (column 4) by total output (column 1).

The average total-cost curve is important to a firm because it fixes the most profitable rate of operation. It is usually U-shaped, indicating a level of output that is optimum in the sense of yielding least-cost output. In our example, this is at point X (Figure 8.2). The cost per unit of output is $8 and five units of output are produced. Beyond five units, diminishing returns raise average costs.

Scale Economies and Diseconomies of the Single Firm

Scale economies are a key for understanding why economic activities concentrate in cities. The concept refers to a set of conditions in which average costs of

TABLE 8.1
Cost implications of the law of diminishing returns.

Output (1)	Variable Input (2)	Fixed Input (3)	Total Costs (4)	Average Total Costs (5)
1	6	16	$22	$22.00
2	10	16	26	13.00
3	13	16	29	9.67
4	17	16	33	8.25
5	24	16	40	8.00
6	36	16	52	8.67
7	55	16	71	10.14

FIGURE 8.2
Average cost curve.

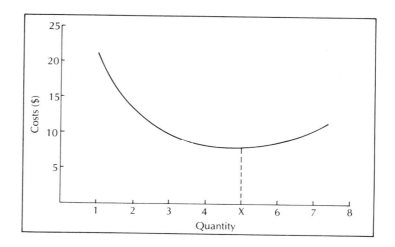

a firm decrease as the scale of production increases. Changing the scale of production means altering proportionately all inputs used in production. Costs of production under these conditions are called long-run costs. Dividing long-run costs by output yields the long-run average costs of a firm.

Two sets of forces influence a firm's long-run costs: internal scale economies and external economies. *Internal scale economies* are subject to direct management control. Managers may be able to take advantage of labor economies (more efficient labor specialization), technical economies (larger, more efficient machines), market economies, and managerial economies. Internal economies come into play because many factors of production (inputs) are indivisible and can be used more efficiently at larger scales of output. Thus, the concept of internal scale economies refers to cost-reducing changes that tend to lower average costs of firms as they grow in size (Figure 8.3a).

External economies represent two forms of agglomeration. These forms are called localization or industry economies and urbanization economies. Localization economies refer to declining average costs for firms as the output of the industries of which they are a part increases (Figure 8.3b). These economies stem from benefits industries derive within restricted geographical areas, such as the development of a large labor pool with skills needed by the industry.

Urbanization economies refer to declining average costs for firms as cities increase their scales of activity (Figure 8.3c). Cost reductions, which tend to be greater in large cities, stem largely from technologies that stimulate production on a scale that can be achieved only with firm specialization; that is, when plants perform only one or a few functions in the overall production process. As a result of transport

costs, firm specialization leads to geographical clustering which, in turn, promotes more geographical specialization and concentration. The garment industry of New York and London and the metal trades of Ohio and the English Midlands are outstanding examples of geographical clustering of specialized firms.

Internal and external economies only accrue up to a point. Consider internal diseconomies. At first, firms experience cost-reducing internal economies, but after a certain scale of production is attained, it becomes impossible to vary proportionately all inputs used in the production process (Figure 8.3d). Management, for example, does not grow proportionately as firms expand. Managers are forced to spread themselves ever more thinly over wider and wider areas of decision making. Decreasing returns set in, with an eventual decrease in efficiency.

External diseconomies also must be accounted for. For example, urbanization diseconomies—rising average costs accompanying an increasing scale of activity within a city—may arise for at least three reasons. First, firms may experience higher costs due to scarcity of land. Second, competition for labor and high living costs may force firms to pay workers higher wages. Third, firms may encounter transport congestion, parking problems, pollution, crime, and financial difficulties.

Transport Costs of the Single Firm

There would be no need to worry about transport costs if resources were ubiquitous, if production technology were the same everywhere, and, of course, if movement were instantaneous and free. But resources are rarely ubiquitous, technical aspects of production are highly variable, and movement over

FIGURE 8.3
Scale economies and diseconomies: (a) internal economies; (b) localization economies; (c) urbanization economies; (d) internal economies and diseconomies.

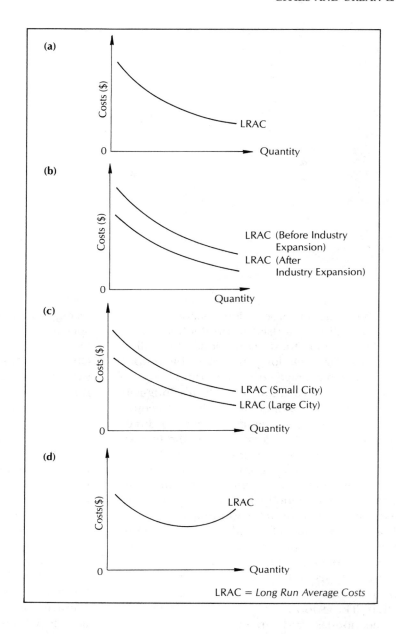

geographical space always encounters resistance. Transport costs represent the alternative output we give up when we commit inputs to the movement of people, goods, information, and ideas over geographical space. They are the swimming pools and libraries that must be surrendered for roads and railways.

What effect does the cost of overcoming the friction of distance have on the location of economic activities? As transport costs are directly correlated with distance, profit-maximizing firms select sites close to their inputs, to other firms, or to consumers who buy their products. Workers decide to live near their places of employment. Accessibility pays off in

the form of transport-cost savings that concentrate firms and workers. Moreover, incentives to concentrate activities are intensified by existing transport systems, which provide a high degree of access to only a limited number of geographical areas.

Economic Costs and City Building

Having explored the meaning of scale economies and transport costs, we are now in a position to see how these forces influence city building. First, let us consider an area in which people are dispersed geographically and a production technology in which economies of scale are absent. As the size of firms increases, they experience only constant returns to scale; that is, their output increases proportionately as the amount of all inputs increases. Firms could choose to locate in close proximity to one another, but such a choice would result in falling profits and rising costs. Geographically concentrated production would increase the distance and, hence, the cost of getting goods and services from producers to consumers. With scale economies absent, there would be no incentive for profit-maximizing firms to concentrate production.

Now let us alter the situation. Suppose a new technology were to generate increasing returns to scale. If consumers remained dispersed geographically, concentrating production would again increase transport costs. But this time transport-cost increases would be more than offset by cost-reducing economies of scale. Profit-maximizing firms would choose city sites, and their employees would live in or very near cities. Suppliers of goods and services to these firms and households would also move into cities. In this way, city building is cumulative; concentration demands more concentration because of the impact of transport costs.

Cities grow when they gain firms and population. To illustrate this process, geographers sometimes use the principle of *cumulative causation*. The principle states that increases in urban economic activity bring about an increase in population. In the case of urban decline, the reverse holds true. Cities decline when they lose firms and population, conditions that create negative cumulative causation.

INTRAURBAN SPATIAL ORGANIZATION

We have seen that activities locate in cities for sound economic reasons. But what factors influence where in a city the various activities will locate? Why are some parts of a city zoned for commercial land use, others for industrial, and still others for mixed single- and multifamily housing? Classical urban location theory provides one answer. This theory concerns the private land-use decision process; it is based on von Thünen's concept of location rent. Assumptions embodied in urban location rent are first, that the central business district (CBD) is the most economically productive location because of its concentration of transportation facilities; second, that rent falls to zero at the fringe of the city; third, that firms are competitive price-takers, not price-makers; and finally, that cities exist in competitive market-exchange econo-

mies without government and social classes. Although the concept of differential rent is a useful arranger of land uses, a word of warning is in order. In capitalist societies, the pursuit of the most profitable use of urban land is inhibited, to varying degrees, by monopoly, class divisions of society, racial discrimination, and public authority. Despite its deviations from real-world conditions, however, many economic geographers still use urban location theory to indicate and interpret problems of land use in cities.

The Competitive-Bidding Process

Classical location theory states that activities locate in cities according to the outcome of the *competitive-bidding process*. People willing and able to pay the highest price for a particular site win the competition and put the land to the economically highest and best use. Highest and best use, of course, can change as external market forces change. These forces include effective demand, public tastes and standards, and land-use regulations.

To illustrate the competitive-bidding process, imagine a city on a featureless plain in which there are just two demanders of land, Jason and Sam, who bid for sites that stretch from the CBD to the perimeter of the city (Figure 8.4). Each is willing to pay more for some sites than others. At site D_1, Jason is willing to pay \$25 and Sam only \$20. On the other hand, Jason has no interest in land at D_3, but Sam is willing to pay \$15 for D_3. If the bid-rent curves for Jason and Sam represented their actual behavior in the urban-land market, then the outcome of the competitive-bidding process would have Jason located between the CBD and D_2, and Sam beyond site D_2.

Our hypothetical example raises a fundamental question: Why do users bid for particular parcels of land? In some instances, a user may value the inherent characteristics of a site. For a residential user it may be a scenic vista; for a commercial user it may be nearness to potential customers. In other instances, site attributes such as natural hazards may detract from the value of a tract to all potential developers or bidders.

Although part of every tract's value depends on site characteristics, relative location is usually more important. For particular activities, some land parcels may be more desirably located than others because they are more accessible; that is, they reduce users' transport costs. For example, if accessibility to work is important to residential users, bid-rent curves will reflect higher bids near places of employment.

FIGURE 8.4
The bidding process.

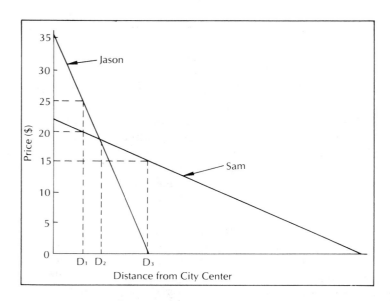

Ceiling Rents

According to classical economic theory, the competition for the use of available locations results in the occupation of each site by the user able to derive the greatest utility or profit from it, and therefore able to pay the highest rent. The maximum rental that a particular user pays for a site is called the *ceiling rent*.

Consider a hilly tract of land, commanding excellent views, on the outskirts of a city. Ceiling rents for this parcel of land might be $9,000 for residential, $6,000 for retailing, and $5,000 for manufacturing. Clearly this tract of land is likely to be sold or leased for residential land use. But if the tract owner thinks the site is worth more than $9,000, the land will remain vacant.

Another tract is for sale a few kilometers away from the parcel put to residential use. It is relatively flat and located adjacent to a major highway. Ceiling rents might be $3,000 for residential, $10,000 for retailing, and $7,000 for manufacturing. In this case, the tract is sold or leased for retailing—say a shopping center.

The Residential Location Decision

An important criterion for most people in selecting a home is accessibility to where they work in the city. The choice of a residential location depends, in part, on how much money a family can afford to spend on overcoming relative distance. For purposes of our discussion, we will assume a single-centered city; that

is, a city with only one center of employment—the CBD.

First let's consider patterns of residential land use and the cost of commuting to work. A family's budget must account for living costs, housing costs, and transport costs. Assume that people are either rich or poor. Poor families, who have little money to spend on commuting after living and housing expenses are deducted from income, have sharply negative bid-rent curves (Figure 8.5a). They attach great importance to living close to where they work. The only way the inner-city poor can afford to live on high-rent land is to consume less space. On the other hand, rich families have plenty of money to spend on transportation. Very often, proximity of residential sites to places of employment is of little consequence to them. They can trade access for agreeable lots away from the center of the city.

But now let's consider the impact of time costs on the residential decision. Time spent commuting is time that could be devoted to earning income. From this standpoint, distance is more critical for the rich, whose time is more valuable than that of the poor. Rich households have steep bid-rent curves, and they are located near the city center (Figure 8.5b). Meanwhile the poor with shallow bid-rent curves live farther away. This land-use pattern is characteristic of many Third World cities; the poor often live in peripheral squatter settlements, while the rich occupy high-rent city housing.

Up to now a single mode of travel to work has been assumed. A more realistic situation would involve two modes of travel—walking and driving

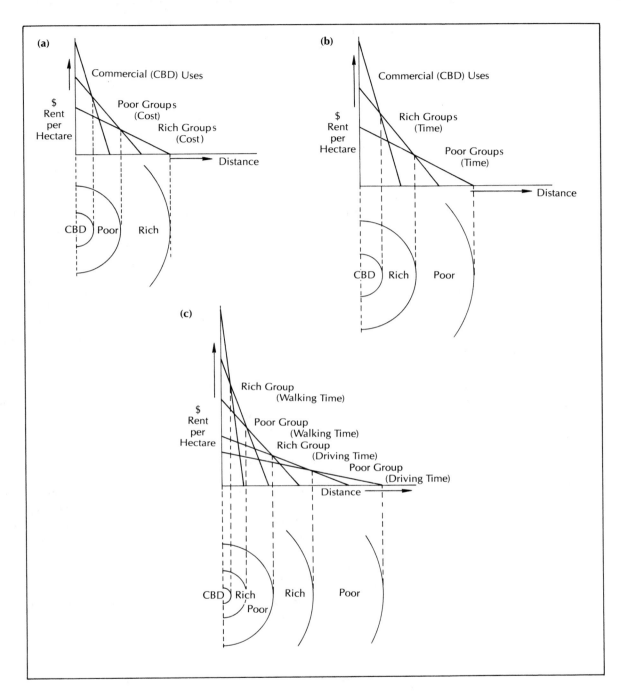

FIGURE 8.5
Land-use patterns: (a) cost criterion; (b) time criterion; (c) travelling-time criterion.
(Source: Harvey, 1972, pp. 17, 18.)

(Figure 8.5c). The steepest bid-rent curve is for the rich walking to work, followed by the poor walking, the rich driving, and the poor driving.

Although cost, time, and mode of travel to work have important implications for residential location, other dimensions to accessibility, such as nearness to services, must be considered. These and other factors influence bid prices. In every situation, however, the rich can always outbid the poor. The results of the competitive-bidding process in market societies are always relatively advantageous to the rich and relatively disadvantageous to the poor.

Profits from the Slums

What are the causes of the progressive rings of slum and suburb around the city centers? Why are slums located in the centers of cities? Why are not the poor and rich integrated in random patterns? Basically the answer is that the land nearest the city center can earn the highest rent per unit of land; this fact determines land use.

Technically, the explanation is known as the von Thünen rent model. In 1826, von Thünen, a German land owner, explained the rings of agricultural land use around settlements. The land closer to the settlement shows greater agricultural profitability and therefore earns higher rents. As the settlement grows, the rings grow in proportion. The shifts of farm economies in Fitzgerald, [Michigan,] from forestry through berry farming, were caused by the expansion of these successive rings through the neighborhood. Urbanization merely shifts the "crop" from agricultural to human. Rather than the agricultural products being more valuable as they are nearer the city, the human residents must be more valuable, must pay more rent per unit of land.

Transport costs per unit of land are an important factor in the location of slums. A bus fare hike represents an added cost for the individual, and limits how far he can live from his work. Slow transportation systems, requiring long waits for buses, represents a real cost. If a man with an automobile can go from one point to another in a city in half an hour, while another who waits for one bus and then a transfer bus makes the same trip in an hour and a half, the bus rider has paid the price of an extra hour's worth of time. Even a dollar-an-hour worker is paying a bus fare of one dollar and thirty-five cents, not just the thirty-five cent fare. The effect of high transport costs is to lock the slum dweller in the slum, and tends to keep him from work: a "hidden" structural unemployment.

Tragically, people fail to see the expansion of rings to be economically determined, not willfully caused by groups. The horror of this misconception is doubled: first, it causes wave after wave of "Founding Fathers" to hate wave after wave of "Invaders"; second, it diverts people from their only effective action, attack on the rent structures.

To measure the flows of Detroit's rent money, we simply make a mathematical application of von Thünen's discoveries. The total rent per unit of land (e.g., square mile or neighborhood) equals the number of individual renters in a neighborhood, times the difference between the average rent charged for an individual dwelling unit and the average cost of owning an individual unit (a cost that includes maintenance and taxes). In addition, it is necessary to subtract from the total rent the product of the number of renters per neighborhood times the round-trip transportation costs per month; because the more a neighborhood pays out for the inconvenience of the location, the less the neighborhood has available to pay out in rents. The daily transportation cost must be multiplied by thirty in order to convert this daily expense of commuting to a monthly cost comparable to monthly rental payments. The average geographic point of urban travel is downtown, though many trips do not originate or terminate there. "Downtown" is similar, as an average location of trip destination for householders, to "mass point" as an average location of mass in physics.

In functional form:

$$R = A(P - C) - 30\ ATD$$

where:

R = total rent per neighborhood

A = number of renters per neighborhood

P = per household unit rent

C = per household unit ownership cost

T = round-trip transport cost per unit of distance

D = distance to downtown

Graphing the formula shows that the rent commanded is always highest downtown, where transportation costs approach zero. Naturally, the residential use commanding the highest rent per unit of land at a particular distance from downtown is the residential use that prevails at that distance. The distance from downtown where a dominant rent changes, say from upper middle class to rich, is the change-of-class distance from downtown. By swinging a radius of this distance about the center of a city, residential class rings roughly corresponding to rent rings can be mapped around the center of a city.

Paradoxically, slums command the highest rents per land unit. The wealthy cannot afford to live in the slums. They cannot afford the rent, for although as individuals they pay much higher rent, per acre of land they pay much lower. Similarly, though the affluent may travel by expensive chauffeur, they cannot afford the collective transportation costs that slum dwellers pay per unit of impacted slum land. The rent per individual and transportation costs per individual is lower in the slums than elsewhere in the city. Slum dwellers, with their low incomes, are compelled to live there. Because of the number of people crammed into the hovels, the rent *per acre* is highest while *per individual* the rent is the lowest.

The irony of the slums is acrid. Considering the rent structure, sophisticated property owners welcome the slums since the slums are a financial "blessing" to those who own them. Homeowners detest slums because slums ruin the homes. Thus, home ownership and property ownership are at war. It is a bitter, bitter truth that the monetarily most profitable land is humanly the most bankrupt. "High profits" mean "low Life." This contradiction has produced a multi-billion dollar racket in America called "income property investment." Contrary to incessant propaganda that the slums suck money from the rest of the city, the truth is precisely the opposite! Living elsewhere and paying taxes elsewhere, slum-owners earn their incomes from the slums.

The equation of the von Thünen rent model yields some interesting "guesstimates" as to the magnitude of the economics involved. Assuming that a posh suburban square mile contains one hundred family units (a high estimate), charges an average rent per family of five hundred dollars per month with an overhead of three hundred dollars per month, demands a round-trip travel cost of twenty cents per mile, and lies fifteen miles from the city's center, what would be the per square mile rent in a thirty day month in this suburb?

$$R = 100 \ (500 - 300) - 100 \ (.20) \ 15 \ (30)$$
$$R = 20,000 - 9,000$$
$$R = 11,000$$

If the homes are fully paid for, this one square mile of affluent suburb yields $11,000 of paper rent per month or $132,000 per year. More likely the homeowners have whopping mortgages but the owners of the mortgages, the bank executives and so forth, all live in such neighborhoods so the money stays in the community though it might shift from one household to another within the community.

Turning to the slums, assume that a square mile contains 5,000 family units (a low estimate), with an average rent per family of eighty dollars per month, an overhead of thirty dollars per month, and a round-trip travel cost of twenty cents per mile. What would then be the rent in this slum in a thirty day month, if it were two miles from the city's center?

$$R = 5,000 \ (80 - 30) - 5,000 \ (.20) \ 2 \ (30)$$
$$R = 250,000 - 60,000$$
$$R = 190,000$$

That is, a square mile of slum at a two mile distance from downtown yields $190,000 per month. The money being pumped out from the slums to the slum lords of the suburbs is $2,311,345 per square mile a year.

The slumowner's deal is fattened still further through the American tax system. Since property taxes are based on the attractiveness of the property rather than profitability per unit of land, taxes drop as slum blight increases. Contrary to popular thought, the shrunken tax base of the slum is a very agreeable fact to the rich slumowner (who, as we said, lives in the suburbs). Essentially, the lower the taxes, the more money for slum profits. The shrinking of the taxes on slums deprives the city, not the suburbs, of tax money. Costs of maintaining and cleaning the buildings and controlling the rats are also notoriously low in slums.

Site Demands of Firms

Firms also compete for urban space, but because of the nature of their activities, the criteria they use in making locational decisions are not the same as for households. Given a rational market-exchange economy, firms want to maximize profits and households want to maximize satisfactions. If intraurban accessibility is important to sales, then firms should be willing to make higher bids for locations that are central to all potential customers. Increasing distance from the more productive locations in the urban area should increase costs to customers and therefore reduce sales. This would mean decreasing revenues, and, hence, lower profits. For *nonbasic* firms this is the case, but for *basic* firms it is not. Basic firms export what they produce to surrounding areas; nonbasic firms sell goods or provide services to city residents and businesses.

Revenues of nonbasic firms decline as they move away from downtowns or from other central loca-
tions. Department stores, for example, have high revenue requirements for profitable scales of operation. Traditionally, these firms required access to all parts of a city. They were willing to pay high rents for downtown sites where intraurban transport lines converge. Many nonbasic firms, such as grocery stores and beauty parlors, have much lower revenue requirements. Their revenue conditions allow smaller geographical scales of operation in the city.

Location within the city has little impact on the revenues of basic firms, but more impact on some of their costs. Firms requiring a lot of space might purchase sites at marginal locations where land costs are lower. Those drawing labor from residential areas throughout the city might be willing to pay high rents for central locations. Movement away from central locations could result in higher wage bills. To attract necessary labor, firms might be forced to increase wages to compensate for higher journey-to-work costs.

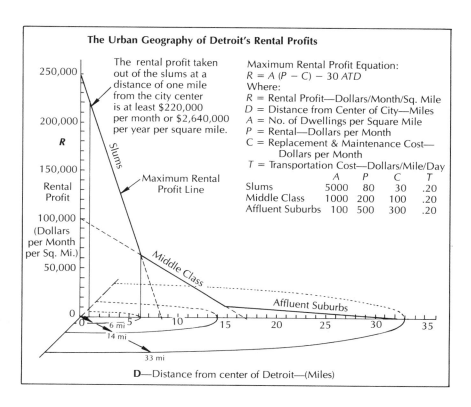

The Urban Geography of Detroit's Rental Profits

The rental profit taken out of the slums at a distance of one mile from the city center is at least $220,000 per month or $2,640,000 per year per square mile.

Maximum Rental Profit Equation:
$$R = A(P - C) - 30\ ATD$$
Where:
R = Rental Profit—Dollars/Month/Sq. Mile
D = Distance from Center of City—Miles
A = No. of Dwellings per Square Mile
P = Rental—Dollars per Month
C = Replacement & Maintenance Cost—Dollars per Month
T = Transportation Cost—Dollars/Mile/Day

	A	P	C	T
Slums	5000	80	30	.20
Middle Class	1000	200	100	.20
Affluent Suburbs	100	500	300	.20

SOURCE: Bunge, 1971, pp. 132–33.

Market Outcomes

We have looked separately at locational decisions of households and firms as they deal with distance frictions. Now let us fashion a model, analogous to von Thünen's crop model, that shows how a multitude of individual decisions combine to produce a pattern of urban land use in which rents are maximized and all activities are optimally located.

Consider three land-use categories: manufacturing, commercial, and residential. Figure 8.6a shows distinctive bid-rent curves for the three types of land use in our hypothetical single-centered city. Commercial activities that require the most productive central sites have steeply sloping rent gradients. Manufacturing firms have shallower bid-rent curves. They cannot afford to pay the high costs of a central location. Residences have gently angled bid-rent curves and are relegated to the outer ring where land prices are lower. We can complicate matters by considering a land-rent profile in a multicentered city (Figure 8.6b).

Apart from secondary peaks, perhaps at intersections of main traffic routes, the rent gradient still shows price bids declining outward from the CBD.

CLASSICAL MODELS OF URBAN LAND USE

So far our study of urban structure has been static. Now let us turn to three widely accepted urban land-use models that help explain city-building processes in North America. The first is the concentric-zone model of Ernest Burgess (1925), a sociologist; the second is the sector model of Homer Hoyt (1939), a land economist; and the third is the multiple-nuclei model of Chauncy Harris and Edward Ullman (1945), both geographers. All three concepts of urban structure are historical generalizations about the layout of the city; therefore, no particular city fits any of these types exactly.

FIGURE 8.6
Multiple land-use patterns: (a) single-centered city; (b) multi-centered city.

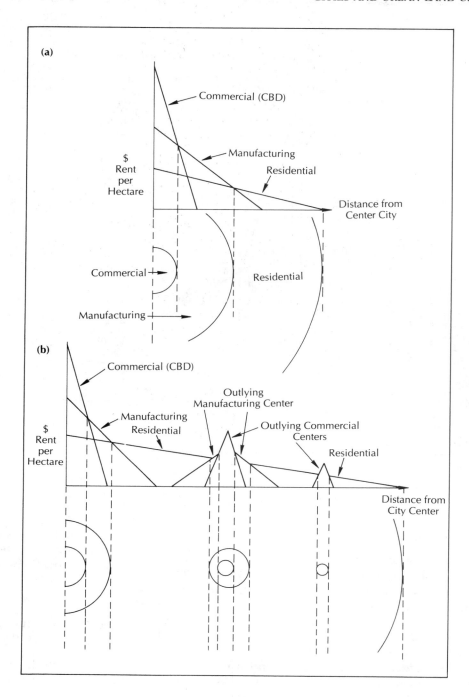

The Concentric-Zone Model

Burgess's *concentric-zone model* emphasizes centripetal forces that focus economic activity on the central business district, which was the dominant center of urban spatial organization in the industrial city. For simplicity, the model assumes conditions of a uniform land surface, universal accessibility, and free competition for space. Given these assumptions, cities expand symmetrically in all directions. Burgess sug-

gested a sequence of five zones from center to periphery (Figure 8.7):

1 **The Central Business District** This zone is the focus of commerce, transportation, and social and civic activity. It encompasses department stores, specialty shops, office buildings, banks, headquarters of organizations, law courts, hotels, theaters, and museums. Encircling the downtown retail district is a mixture of wholesaling and light-

manufacturing operations and truck and retail depots.

2 **The Zone of Transition** This area reflects residential deterioration. Older private homes have been subdivided into rooming houses. Mansions have been taken over for offices and light manufacturing (functional change). Abandoned dwellings have been torn down to provide space for urban renewal (morphological change). According to Burgess, this is the zone of "slums," with their attendant disease, poverty, illiteracy, unemployment, and underworld vice. In many American cities, the zone of transition is inhabited by recent immigrants; it is said to be home to unstable social groups.

3 **The Zone of Working-Class Homes** This ring is characterized by decreasing residential density and increasing quality and cost of homes. It is inhabited by blue-collar workers who have "escaped" the zone of residential deterioration, but who need to live close to work. It is regarded as an area of second-generation immigrants who have had enough time to save the money to buy homes of their own.

4 **The Zone of Better Residences** Still farther from the central business district, working-class residences give way to newer, more spacious single-family dwellings and high-rise apartment buildings occupied by middle-class families.

5 **The Commuter Suburbs** Beyond the zone of better residences is a broad commuter area. It is an incompletely built-up area of small satellite towns and middle- and upper-class residences along rail lines and major highways.

The Burgess model suggests that, as cities grow, resistances are encountered. Characteristic land uses of one zone exert pressure on future land uses of the next outer zone. This process is called *invasion and succession*. Residents of one zone try to improve their situation by moving outward into a zone of better housing units. New housing constructed at the edge of the city triggers a complex chain of moves. Dwellings vacated by the outmigration of middle- and high-income families are filled by lower income families moving from the next inner zone. At the end of the chain, the working poor move out of the zone of transition, leaving behind the least fortunate families and abandoned housing units. The result is an inner-city slum. This *filtering process*, which exerts downward pressure on rents and prices of existing housing, enables lower income families to obtain better housing. The major reason the filter-down process occurs is that the poor, with the strongest

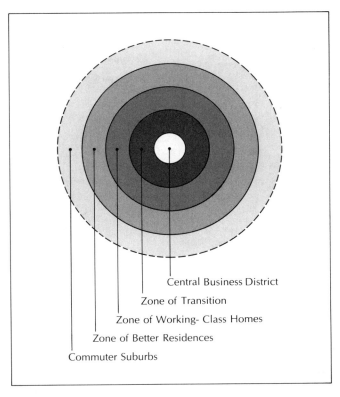

FIGURE 8.7
Burgess's concentric-zone model of urban structure.

Central Business District
Zone of Transition
Zone of Working- Class Homes
Zone of Better Residences
Commuter Suburbs

latent demand for housing, are the least able to afford new housing. By contrast, the rich can most easily afford to move into new housing and leave their old homes to others. The demand for high-income housing is generally elastic—a new demand generates a quick response from the private housing industry.

The Sector Model

The *sector model* takes into account differences in accessibility and, therefore, in land values along transport lines radiating outward from the city center. According to Hoyt's model, a city grows largely in wedges that radiate from the central business district (Figure 8.8). One wedge may contain high-rent residential; another, low-rent residential; and still another, industrial. Hoyt believed the contrasts in activity along various sectors usually became apparent early in the city's history, and continued to be marked as the city grew.

The Multiple-Nuclei Model

The concentric and sector models describe single-centered cities. However, most modern cities have *multiple nuclei*: a downtown with satellite centers on

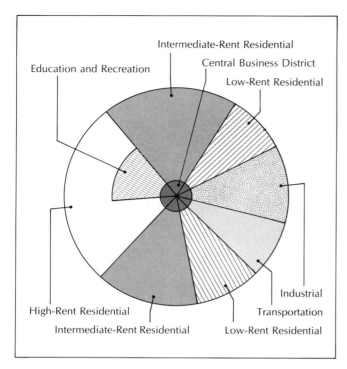

FIGURE 8.8
Hoyt's sector model of urban structure.

the periphery. In 1945, Harris and Ullman described a model city that develops zones of land use around discrete centers. Their model of urban structure encompasses five areas: (1) the central business district, (2) a wholesaling and light-manufacturing area near interurban transport facilities, (3) a heavy industrial district near the present or past edge of the city, (4) residential districts, and (5) outlying dormitory suburbs (Figure 8.9).

Harris and Ullman recognized that the number and location of differentiated districts depends on the size of the city and its overall structure and peculiarities of historical evolution. They also gave reasons for the development of separate land-use cells. The pattern of multiple cells might result from specialized requirements of particular activities, repulsion of some activities by others, differential rent-paying ability of activities, and the tendency of certain activities to group together to increase profit from cohesion.

Evaluation of the Classical Land-Use Models

Three observations on the classical land-use models can help put them in context. First, the models are not mutually exclusive. Elements of all three can be recognized in many urban areas. For example, Chicago has a semicircular structure that has been

especially fascinating for geographers interested in urban land use. It is characterized by wedge-shaped income sectors that fan outward from the Loop, ring-shaped zones relative to age and family size centered on the Loop, and a large number of nuclei or cells, such as Centex's industrial park at the edge of O'Hare International Airport.

Second, the classical models are historical statements depicting change through a process of invasion and succession. They describe change that is mechanistic; for example, the aging of structures, called *morphological change*, and succeeding occupance, called *functional change*, but ignore the importance of behavioral factors influencing urban structure. They emphasize methodical processes of urban growth, whereas real-world dynamics are not nearly so orderly. The private land-development process, for example, tends to skip over marginal tracts of land during the initial wave of building.

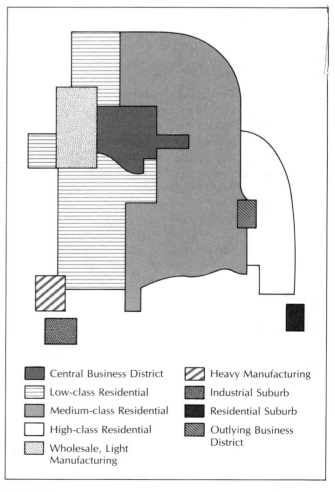

FIGURE 8.9
Harris and Ullman's model of urban structure.

Third, the classical models describe land-use configurations, but fail to explain that they are products of a particular form of economic organization. Burgess, for example, gave no indication that urban spatial organization has a lot to do with the need to produce and appropriate a surplus product. Interestingly, Friedrich Engels (1958, pp. 46–48), writing in the mid-nineteenth century, noted the same phenomenon of concentric banding in Manchester, England, but interpreted the pattern in class-stratification terms. He explained that the working class, who inhabit the dirty row houses that girdle the commercial district of Manchester, form the complement of the wealthy bourgeoisie, who live in suburban villas with gardens.

MODELS OF THIRD WORLD CITY STRUCTURE

The classical models are based on North American experience and are not universally applicable. They are tied to a particular culture. Although the forces of urban change may eventually result in greater similarity of city structure in the non-Communist world, attitudes toward density, land-use arrangements, open spaces, and architectural preferences will vary. In addition, institutional factors—zoning laws, building codes, the role of government in the housing market—will vary with culture and level of technology. Models of the structural elements of cities in Latin America and Southeast Asia exemplify different patterns of land use in different regions.

Latin American City Structure

Ernst Griffin and Larry Ford (1980) proposed a model of the Latin American city that may be applicable to cities in other parts of the Third World (Figure 8.10). Blending traditional elements of Latin American culture with modernizing processes, the framework of the idealized city is a composite of sectors and rings. The heart of the city consists of a vibrant and thriving central business district. A reliance on public transport and nearby concentrations of the affluent ensure the dominance of the inner city, with a landscape that increasingly exhibits skyscraper office and condominium towers.

Outward from the inner city is a *commercial/industrial spine* surrounded by a widening *elite residential sector*. The spine/sector is an extension of the central business district, characterized by offices, shops, high-quality housing, restaurants, theaters, parks, zoos, and golf courses, which eventually gives

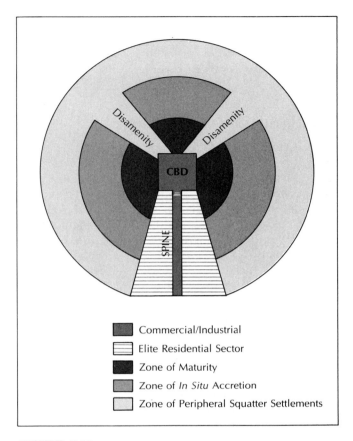

Legend:
- ▨ Commercial/Industrial
- ▤ Elite Residential Sector
- ■ Zone of Maturity
- ▦ Zone of *In Situ* Accretion
- ☐ Zone of Peripheral Squatter Settlements

FIGURE 8.10
A model of land-use areas in the Latin American city. (Source: Adapted from Griffin and Ford, 1980.)

way to wealthy suburbs. Within the spine/sector, the centrifugal forces are similar to those operating in North American cities.

Three zones, which reflect traditional Latin American characteristics, are home to the less fortunate who account for the majority of city residents. The *zone of maturity*, attractive to the middle classes, features the best housing beyond the spine/sector. Filtered-down colonial homes and improved self-built dwellings are common. In the *zone of in situ accretion*, the housing is much more modest, interspersed with hovels and unkempt areas. It is a transition zone between inner-ring affluence and outer-ring poverty. The outermost *zone of peripheral squatter settlements* houses the impoverished. Although this teeming, high-density ring looks wretched to a middle-class North American, the residents perceive that neighborhood improvement is possible; they hope, in time, to transform their communities.

The final structural element of the Latin American city is the *disamenity sector*. Here we find slums, known as *favelas* in Brazil. Open sewers line streets;

residents live in tiny huts built illegally and lacking sanitation. The worst of these poverty-stricken areas include people so poor that they live on the streets, often in doorways or in cardboard boxes they carry with them.

Southeast Asian City Structure

If the Griffin-Ford model provides a good interpretation of the organization of a Third World city, then Terry McGee's (1967) generalization about the Southeast Asian city provides a departure that occurs in colonial port cities that have continued to grow rapidly in the postindependence era (Figure 8.11). McGee's land-use diagram illustrates the old port zone, which is the city's focus, together with a surrounding commercial district. A formal central business district is absent, but its elements occur as separate clusters. There is a sector of government buildings; a European commercial area; a crowded alien commercial zone, where the bulk of the Chinese merchants live and work; and a mixed land-use strip of land along a railway line for various economic activities, including light industry. Other nonresidential zones include a peripheral market-gardening ring and, still farther from the city, a new industrial park. The residential zones in McGee's model are reminiscent of those in the Griffin-Ford model. There is a new high-class suburban residential area, an inner-city zone of comfortable middle-class housing, and peripheral areas of low-income squatter settlements with substandard sanitation and inadequate water supplies.

SPRAWLING METROPOLI: PATTERNS AND PROBLEMS

The Spread City

The classical models of land use fitted earlier patterns of North American city growth better than present-day patterns. The concentric-zone model, developed in the 1920s, placed emphasis on centripetal forces that concentrated economic activity in the downtown of the inner city. Subsequently, the sector and then, even more so, the multiple-nuclei model stressed centrifugal forces that have decentralizing influences. In the second half of the twentieth century, centrifugal forces have gained the ascendancy. As a result of automobile-based intraurban dispersal, the city has evolved into a restructured form variously called the *spread, suburban,* or *multicentered metropolis.* The classical models are unable to accommodate this new urban reality.

James Wheeler and Peter Muller (1981) have diagrammed the general characteristics of the contemporary multinodal North American metropolis, which may be regarded as an updating and extension of the classical models of intraurban structure (Figure 8.12). Their "pepperoni pizza" model consists of a traditional central business district and a set of coequal suburban minicities, serving a discrete and self-sufficient area. James Vance (1977, pp. 411–16) called these new tributary areas *urban realms,* in that each maintains a separate and distinct economic, social, and political significance and strength.

The rapid outward spread of urban North America owes much to the completion of the radial and

FIGURE 8.11
A model of land-use areas in the large Southeast Asian city. (Source: Adapted from McGee, 1967, p. 128.)

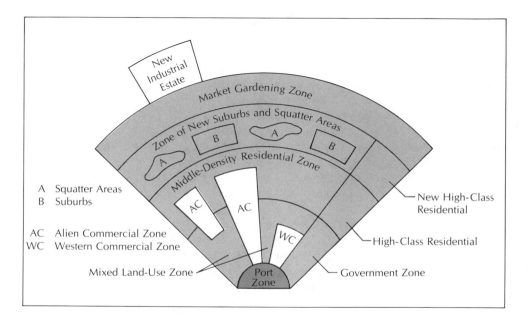

Cut off from the city's mainstream and many of its services, the urban poor live in makeshift shelters. In many Third World cities, more than half of the residents live in slums, such as this squatter settlement on the urban fringe of Jakarta, Indonesia. (Source: World Bank.)

circumferential freeway network, which resulted in near-equal levels of time convergence across the metropolitan area. In effect, the freeway system destroyed the regionwide advantage of the central business district, making most places along the expressway network just as accessible to the metropolis as the downtown was before 1970. No longer on the cutting edge, the downtown gave way in the 1970s and 1980s to an ever-widening suburban city that was being transformed—new neighborhoods, new business centers, and new shopping malls. Huge numbers of Americans now live, work, play, shop, and dine within the confines of this freeway culture.

The spreading out of the American city has captured the imagination of geographers. In the early 1960s an extreme form of a spread city was described by Jean Gottmann (1964), who coined the term *megalopolis* to describe the coalesced metropolitan areas on the northeastern seaboard. This superurban region stretches from Boston to Washington; hence, it is sometimes referred to as *BoWash*. It includes a whole network of cities fused together by expressways, tunnels, bridges, and shuttle jets. Another supercity in the process of evolving is the loosely knit lower Great Lakes Urban Region, also known as *ChiPitts*, centered on Chicago, Detroit, Cleveland, and Pittsburgh.

By the year 2000, trend projections indicate that the United States will consist of four superurban regions:

1 *BoWash*, extending along the Atlantic Seaboard;
2 *ChiPitts*, stretching from Chicago to Pittsburgh, and merging with *BoWash* via the "Mohawk Bridge" to form the Metropolitan Belt;
3 *SanSan*, a belt from San Francisco to San Diego; and
4 *JaMi*, a strip from Jacksonville to Miami.

These megalopolitan networks will be supplemented with about twenty-two other major urban regions, each containing at least a million people (Figure 8.13). According to Jerome Pickard (1972), five-sixths of the

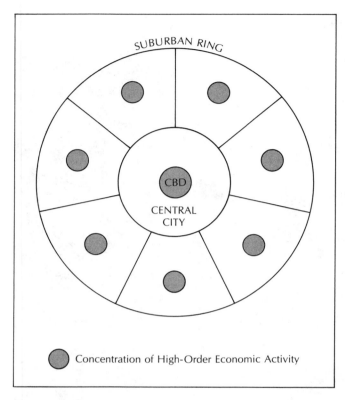

FIGURE 8.12

The general characteristics of the contemporary multi-nodal North American metropolis. (Source: Wheeler and Muller, 1981, p. 169.)

population will be concentrated on one-sixth of the country's land area.

Outside of the United States, *conurbations*, or "systems of cities," are also evident. In Canada, there is the Windsor-Quebec city axis, which geographer Maurice Yeates (1975) called Main Street (Figure 8.14). More than half of all Canadians live in this multicultural megalopolis, many of whom make their homes in Toronto and Montreal. In Britain, there is megalopolitan England that developed as an axial belt from London through Birmingham to Liverpool, Manchester, and Leeds (Figure 8.15). The five conurbations of megalopolitan England—Greater London, West Midlands, Southeast Lancashire, West Yorkshire, and Merseyside—as well as those of Tyneside and Central Clydeside, are home to one-third of the British population of 57 million. In the western Netherlands, there is the Randstad (or Ring City), running in a horseshoe-shaped line approximately 170 kilometers long (Figure 8.16). It centers on three major conurbations grouped around the cities of Rotterdam, The Hague, Amsterdam, and Utrecht. From this complex,

the E36 motorway joins the Netherlands to the heart of Europe, linking the Randstad with another vast urban agglomeration of continental Europe—the Rhine-Ruhr. The Dutch Randstad and the cities of the Rhine-Ruhr coalesced in the 1980s into a gigantic urban region: a European megalopolis stretching down the river Rhine from Bonn to the Hook of Holland. In Japan, too, there is an enormous, high-density megalopolis. Half of Japan's population of more than 120 million are crowded into three areas—the conurbations around Tokyo, Osaka, and Nagoya. One-third of all Japanese live within 150 kilometers of their emperor's palace in central Tokyo.

The formation of regional and urban systems also characterizes Third World urban processes. The rapid increase in the number, population, and expansion of urban agglomerations in some underdeveloped countries is leading to the growth of megalopoli. Such systems are developing in Brazil, where the major nodes are Rio de Janeiro–Belo Horizonte–São Paulo; in Mexico, where Mexico City–Puebla–Vera Cruz form the major centers; and in Egypt, where Alexandria and Cairo are the major cities. Elsewhere, urban growth is concentrated around one or two cities, as in Lagos and Ibadan, Nigeria; in Jakarta and Surabaja, Indonesia; and in Seoul, South Korea. Nearly 40 percent of South Korea's population of 42 million live in or near Seoul, the nerve center of the nation.

The geographer Peirce Lewis (1983) provided a provocative description of the outward spread of cities. For the United States, he coined the term "galactic metropolis" to refer to a vast continuum of urbanization stretching from coast to coast. In his national vision, huge urban concentrations are interspersed with small towns and cities, as well as with loosely separated clusters of houses and businesses around freeway interchanges. Lewis's vision can be extended to the global level where improved transport systems and modes of communication are leading to the ultimate form of human settlement—the *ecumenopolis*. According to the late Greek planner, Constantine Doxiadis (1970), an ecumenopolis, consisting of most of the world's population, will be highly integrated into a global urban network in the twenty-first century.

Causes of Urban Spread

What is at the heart of this spreading out of the American city? A number of economic and noneconomic factors are involved. Let us now look at one or two of them with reference to the locational decisions of households and firms.

FIGURE 8.13
Projected growth of U.S. urban regions with a population of 1 million or more by the year 2000. The four superurban regions are shown in a darker shade. (Source: Pickard, 1972, p. 143.)

1. Metropolitan Belt
   A. Atlantic Seaboard (BoWash)
   B. Lower Great Lakes (ChiPitts)
2. California Region (SanSan)
3. Florida Peninsula (JaMi)
4. Gulf Coast
5. East Central Texas–Red River
6. Southern Piedmont
7. North Georgia–Southeast Tennessee
8. Puget Sound
9. Twin Cities Region
10. Colorado Piedmont
11. Saint Louis
12. Metropolitan Arizona
13. Willamette Valley
14. Central Oklahoma–Arkansas Valley
15. Missouri–Kaw Valley
16. North Alabama
17. Blue Grass
18. Southern Coastal Plain
19. Salt Lake Valley
20. Central Illinois
21. Nashville Region
22. East Tennessee
23. Oahu Island
24. Memphis
25. El Paso–Ciudad Juarez

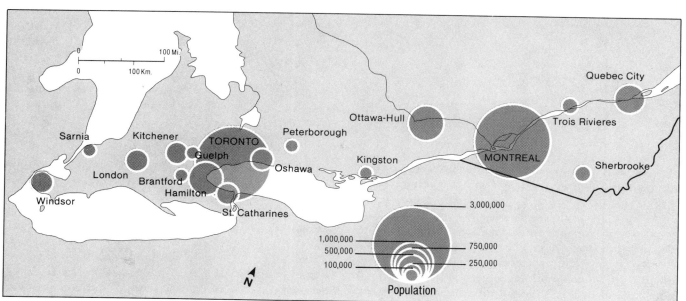

FIGURE 8.14
Canada's Main Street. (Source: Yeates, 1984, p. 242.)

233

FIGURE 8.15
Megalopolitan Britain. (Source:
Based on Herbert, 1982, p. 234.)

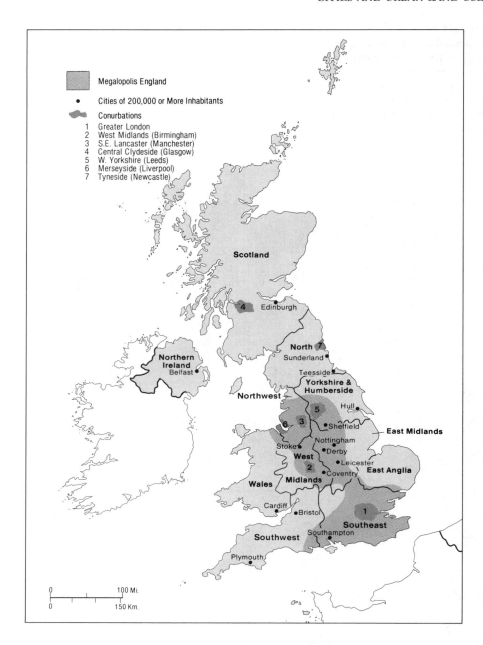

Suburbanization of households is closely associated with intraurban transport improvements (Figure 8.17). With each revolution in transportation travel costs were lowered, and families became less willing to pay high rents for central locations. Since 1945, the desire for a single-family home in the suburbs has resulted in rapid suburban expansion. Low-mortgage interest rates, loan guarantees provided under federal housing and veteran's benefit programs, property tax reductions for owner-occupied homes, cheap transportation, as well as massive highway subsidies, have reinforced this trend. The freeway-dominated auto

era has removed virtually all restrictions on intraurban population mobility so that residential land use is feasible just about anywhere in a metropolitan area, especially with auto companies buying up and closing down intraurban streetcar lines across the country.

The flight of households to the suburbs, the inhabitants of which outnumbered those of the central city by 1970, is also a consequence of rising real incomes, population growth, and the postwar movement of rural blacks to central cities. Between 1940 and 1970 large numbers of southern blacks were displaced from mechanized farms and moved to

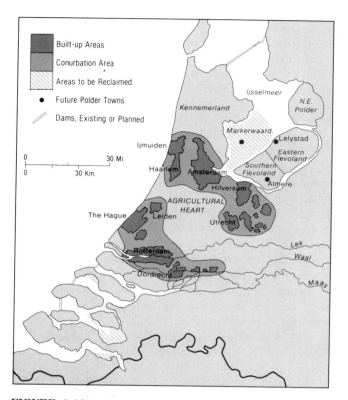

FIGURE 8.16
Randstad Holland: a horseshoe-shaped ring of cities, each performing specialized functions—government in the Hague, commerce in Rotterdam, shopping and culture in Amsterdam—with a central agricultural or "green" heart. (Source: Based on Hall, 1982, p. 236.)

ing of property by high-income settlers—which frequently results in the displacement of lower income residents.

Suburbanization of retailing was a response to the residential flight to the suburbs, new merchandising techniques, and technical obsolescence of older retailing areas. The automobile provided customers with a convenient mode of transport to shopping places, but downtown parking facilities were scarce and expensive. A need to improve the parking situation and a need to increase profits impelled retailers to the suburbs.

The decentralization trend began in the 1920s as stores began spreading out from the downtown along main thoroughfares. Yet, it was not until the postwar years that retailers moved to the suburbs in large numbers. First came the strip center, or neighborhood shopping center, consisting of a string of ten to thirty

Tokyo's Murunouchi business district with its row upon row of modern office buildings. Tokyo and its neighbors are home to over 20 million people. By contrast, the 2 million residents of Phoenix, Arizona, live in a metropolis that sprawls over two thousand square miles. (Source: Japan Information Service, Consulate General of Japan at Chicago.)

northern cities. Black migration from the rural south to the urban north peaked in the late 1950s. As blacks "invaded" city neighborhoods, white middle-class families experienced devaluation of their properties, often spurred by "block busting" by real estate brokers. Meanwhile, valuations of suburban locations increased. The number of whites who moved to the suburbs in order to maintain social distance from the immigrant blacks of the inner city has not been documented, however.

During the 1970s and 1980s there was reverse migration; middle-class families moving from suburbs to central cities. The number of families involved was relatively small, however. For every family that moved back to the inner city, eight moved out to the suburbs. Residential revitalization in and around the central business district clearly did not spawn a "return-to-the-city" movement by suburbanites. In fact, most reinvestment was undertaken by those already living in the central city. Such inner-city neighborhood redevelopment involves *gentrification*—the upgrad-

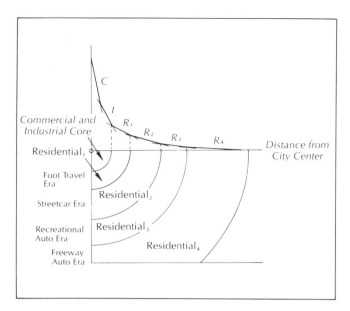

FIGURE 8.17
Passenger transportation improvements and housing density. (Source: Abler, Adams, and Gould, 1971, p. 358.)

shops, anchored usually by a supermarket. Then came the larger community center with a small department store or variety store as the principal tenant. The success of these early centers, which catered to a limited trade area, depended on a main-road location, free parking, and the persuasiveness of "super" everything, "drive-in" everything, self-service stores, and discount outlets.

Neighborhood and, later, larger community shopping centers became vulnerable to more attractive regional shopping centers that appeared after 1955. The newest and biggest of these centers in distant suburbs have several floors, three or more department stores and scores of specialty shops. Surrounded by huge parking lots, these shopping complexes are usually enclosed, enabling customers to shop in climate-controlled comfort. Unlike early suburban shopping centers, the giant regional shopping centers are catalysts attracting a variety of activities to locate nearby.

Decentralization of manufacturing began before the turn of the century. Technical advances, such as

Southdale Center, which opened in 1956 as the first enclosed, climate-controlled shopping center in the United States, is in the Minneapolis suburb of Edina, Minnesota. (Source: TCC The Center Companies.)

the development of continuous-material flow systems, induced many manufacturers, especially those engaged in large-scale production of industrial goods, to spread out along suburban rail corridors where land was relatively cheap and abundant. Nonetheless, most manufacturers, in spite of truck transportation, decided to remain in or near the central city until the 1960s when two technological breakthroughs were achieved. As described by Peter Muller (1976),

> these post-1960 breakthroughs involved the completion of the intraurban expressway system and the long-delayed attainment of scale economies in local trucking operations. Completing the freeway network made it possible to assemble goods at any number of points equally accessible to the rest of the metropolis, and newly economical short distance trucking helped to neutralize the transportation cost differential between inner city and suburb. With the near equalization of these costs across much of the metropolis, intraurban goods movement via truck became as efficient as interregional freight transport. And by eliminating the locational pull of central city water and rail terminals, most of the remaining urbanization economies of downtown were quickly nullified. (p. 33)

In the freeway metropolis, the economic advantages of a central-city location have disappeared. Consequently, the spatial organization of the manufacturing industry is responding increasingly to non-cost factors. Manufacturers are relatively free to select the most prestigious sites they can find in the outer city.

Expansion of offices into the suburbs began in the early postwar years, when large corporations began looking for new office headquarters. For example, General Foods, IBM, Reader's Digest, Union Carbide, and ESSO-Standard Oil left New York for the suburban countryside. This trend of the large corporations prompted an avalanche of similar moves by a host of small office firms. In that they were not able to create their own environments in the manner of the large corporations, the small firms began to rent or lease space in office parks. Tenants of these office buildings were attracted by the convenience, amenity, and prestige of an office-in-a-park address. The major factor in office site selection has been accessibility to an expressway.

Initially, suburban business and commerce located at any convenient highway intersection or at a site near a freeway. Today, suburban economic activities have a growing locational affinity for each other. Without doubt, the focal point of the outer city is the huge regional shopping center. Super shopping malls are catalysts for other commercial, industrial, recre-

ational, and cultural facilities. The result is the emergence of miniature downtowns called *minicities* (Figure 8.18). In many metropolitan areas, minicities are unplanned, loosely organized, multifunctional nodes, and they are strongly shaping the geography of suburbia.

Somewhat later than in North America, European cities expanded outward from the inner-city center to the suburbs and beyond. For the first time, in the 1950s, the population of major British cities started to fall. Often inner-city depopulation was a result of an official policy to relieve overcrowding. And in the 1960s, major cities also began to lose business. Old industries around which the cities had grown up, and which supported the economy of the inner cities, were in decline, and the newer growth industries could not make up the job losses. They were, in any case, often developed on greenfield sites well away from the central cities where building and land were less expensive. Although large European cities are beginning to resemble expanding doughnuts as they decentralize, their central business districts remain more vibrant than many in North America.

Urban sprawl is also a feature of Japanese cities. Tokyoites, who want to purchase their own homes, have been pushed farther and farther from the middle of the city by high land prices (Figure 8.19). Of Tokyo's 5 million or more daily commuters, 2.75 million live outside the city, itself an area larger than Luxembourg. Even though land prices in central Tokyo are astonishingly high by New York and London standards, Japanese companies still feel compelled to have their headquarters near the ministries and banks of the capital. Eventually, Tokyo—a megalopolis with the profile of a pancake—may become so big that it decentralizes itself. According to Kozo Amano, a specialist in land and transport economies, technology is the key to decentralization. Telecommunications and high-speed, magnetically levitated trains would make Japan's second city, Osaka, a sixty-minute ride from Tokyo against today's three-and-a-half hour ride in a "bullet train." The line would pass via Nagoya creating an urban corridor along central Japan's Pacific coast. Away from this spine would lie suburban centers linked by advanced telecommunication networks. Tokyo would become a vast, wired megalopolis of more than 60 million people stretched over 500 kilometers. This vision is less odd to Japanese than to Europeans. Japanese cities do not have centers like a Paris or a London, but a series of subcenters, more like a grand-scale, high-density Phoenix or Tucson.

By European or American standards, Japanese cities are overcrowded to Dickensian proportions, but

In the late 1970s, a decision was made to move Union Carbide's headquarters from New York City (at right) to Danbury, Connecticut (below). (Source: Union Carbide Corporation.)

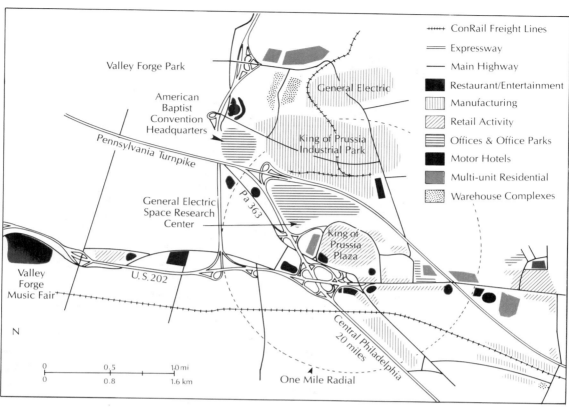

FIGURE 8.18
Internal economic geography of the suburban minicity: King of Prussia, Pennsylvania.
(Source: Based on Muller, 1976, p. 41.)

so too are the large Third World cities. In many a Third World country, the largest city is growing uncontrollably. Rapid growth is linked to what economic geographers call the *economies of agglomeration.* Firms locate in the large city because of the existence of modern infrastructure. When a plant locates in the city, it brings with it new jobs. And industry is not the only source of work in the metropolis. The growing bureaucracy needed to administer public investment in schools, transportation, communications, water, and sanitation provides many jobs, as does the semilicit service economy. Work in the industrial plant, bureaucratic office, or in the black market offers a higher standard of living than is available in the provincial town or village. The superior standard of living has a powerful attraction for the people of peripheral regions, who flock to the crowded, large cities.

Problems of the City

The free market for space in the metropolis has produced a pattern of suburban sprawl in advanced capitalist societies. From a rare social entity at the beginning of the twentieth century, suburbs have evolved into major growth centers for industrial and commercial investment. And a suburban way of life has become the way for millions of people. The decentralized metropolis fostered large-scale consumption and prosperity in the past, but it is causing real problems now. In some instances, the urban fringe has pushed out farther than workers are willing or able to commute. Urban sprawl has generated externalities such as uneven development, pollution, and the irrational use of space, which increasingly impinge on the life of urban residents. Furthermore, recurrent fiscal crises threaten to bankrupt central cities.

In the United States, the rationalization of the metropolis for the purpose of planned development is blocked by the political independence of the suburbs. The suburbs have resulted from the differential ability of various groups to organize and protect their advantages. They are not willing to abdicate clear-cut, short-run benefits for less certain long-run gains. Thus, metropoliswide planning in the face of a bewildering multitude of rigid and outdated municipal boundaries—1,200 of them in New York—is

Oxford Street is a major shopping district in London's West End. (Source: The British Tourist Authority.)

extremely difficult, if not impossible, to implement. Yet without planning, without redrawing areas of municipal authority, the continued profitability and stability of the metropolis and capitalist society is threatened.

Most cities in North America and Western Europe are now faced with a roughly similar situation—they are dying in the middle. Jobs are moving out with modern technology and communications, and so is shopping and entertainment. Violence is moving in. The need for the city, as far as the middle class is concerned, has diminished.

To be sure, there have been attempts to revitalize inner cities. For example, in England there are tax-incentive plans for the rebirth of blighted areas. The intent is to create jobs out of urban wastelands and transform old warehousing and waterfront districts. In London, dockland revival involves some light manufacturing, but it is dominated by office and commercial development as well as the construction or refurbishment of housing units (gentrification). The residential units are for the rich up-and-comers; they cost too much for the majority of the original East-enders. Small schemes aimed at revitalizing inner-city areas are narrow technical solutions to a broad problem created by capitalist development.

Most governments of Western Europe and North America have concentrated, often for decades, on relieving congestion and welfare pressures by demolishing block upon block of old housing, factories, and other buildings. A major problem for local governments has been where to rehouse the people affected

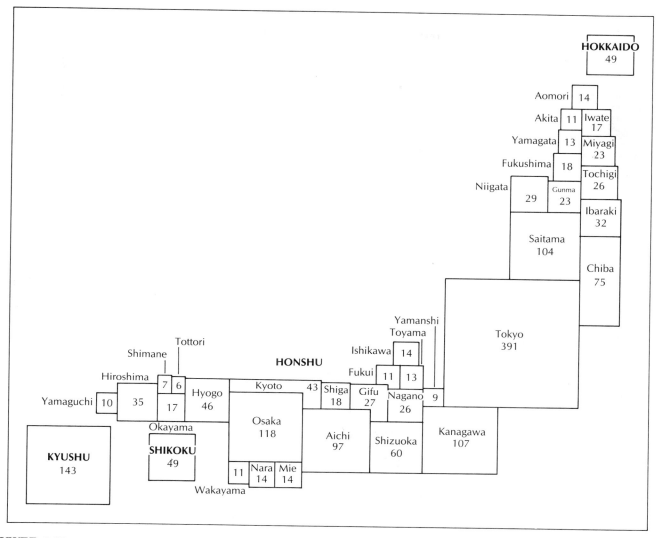

FIGURE 8.19
The price of Japan: the value of land assets in trillions of yen. (Source: *The Economist*,
1987b, p. 25.)

by clearance. One solution has been to replace crowded terraced streets with blocks of tall apartments. But besides being more expensive to build than houses, high-rise housing developments are generally regarded as dehumanizing environments.

Most redevelopment schemes can only rehouse about half of the population. The so-called overspill has to move out. Governments have tried a variety of methods to relieve the overspill problem. For London, in the 1940s, it was proposed that a green belt of open space be preserved around the build-up area, and that a number of new towns to house people from central London be developed beyond the Green Belt. The eight new towns that were built in the 1950s and 1960s were fashioned after the Garden City model, advo-

cated in Ebenezer Howard's (1946) book, *Garden Cities of Tomorrow*, first published in 1902. This model called for self-contained medium-sized cities with large areas of public open space separating urban functions.

New towns have been built in other parts of Britain as well, especially northern industrial areas (Figure 8.20). The British new-town model has also been adopted in the United States, Japan, and in other countries of Europe. In the United States, examples include Columbia, Maryland; Reston, Virginia; and Irvine, California.

New towns and other population redistribution schemes, such as planned public-housing estates, have not solved big-city problems. For example, there

In Liverpool, England, high-rise housing estates replace nineteenth-century row houses
in an attempt at urban renewal. (Source: WHO photo by E. Spooner.)

remains a deep-seated polarization between inner and outer city. Increasingly, the central city is home to the metropolitan disadvantaged and includes a few specialized services, while suburb and satellite cities house the affluent and support a wide range of activities that used to be city-bound. This pattern of spatial organization favors rich people who collect a disproportionate share of the surplus product with respect to the location of services and job opportunities. Examples of how the rich tend to be favored in U.S. metropolitan areas follow.

Retail Stores Shop location is a reflection of the economic behavior of entrepreneurs. Their decisions, however, are usually subject to some public control through zoning. Decision-makers select locations with a high demand potential. And since demand is income-related, it is natural for entrepreneurs to choose affluent suburban areas first. Many large

supermarkets, for example, locate in the suburbs, and sell their produce at lower prices than do inner-city neighborhood stores. Differential prices and accessibility to retail outlets contributed to the urban riots of the 1960s and 1970s.

Medical Care Health-care services provided by general practitioners, internists, and pediatricians are located mainly by private action. Since they, too, are sensitive to demand potential, they tend to locate in affluent areas even though the need for medical care is likely to be higher in low-income neighborhoods. In the inner city, the needy sick are taken care of in public hospitals, often poorly equipped and understaffed.

Public Utilities Provision of water, electricity, sewage and sanitation, and transport services provides additional examples of the inequitable appropriation of

FIGURE 8.20
New towns in Great Britain, 1946–1980. (Source: Based on Hall, 1982, p. 167.)

the surplus. Take water as an example. In some metropolitan areas, water prices are not seasonally adjusted, yet the peak demand for water in summer comes mainly from suburban families, who use a great deal to sprinkle lawns and fill swimming pools. Inner-city residents have neither yards to sprinkle nor pools to fill. When pricing systems for water fail to reflect seasonal demands, they effectively subsidize the already wealthy.

Noxious Attributes The value of a dwelling unit varies according to proximity to noxious attributes such as smoke, dust, noise and water pollution, and traffic congestion. The affluent who wield political

clout usually manage to exclude noxious facilities from their neighborhoods. But these facilities must go somewhere. Traditionally, facilities such as power stations have been located in inner-city communities and in rural areas.

Employment Opportunities Private and public discrimination (e.g., "redlining" by lending institutions, actions of realtors, screening devices adopted by subdivision developers) and exclusionary zoning practices give the poor, especially blacks, little recourse but to locate in inner-city areas. Meanwhile, most new employment opportunities matched to the work skills of these people are created in the suburbs.

Thus, the poor are faced with the problem of either finding work in stagnating industrial areas of the inner city or commuting longer distances to keep up with the dispersing job market. Although "reverse" commuting has increased, barriers abound. These include transportation constraints, such as increased time and cost of the daily journey to work and inadequate public transportation for those without cars, and communication constraints, such as difficulty in obtaining timely information concerning new job opportunities. Other serious obstacles to suburban employment of the inner-city poor include low work skills and biased hiring practices. In the face of these problems, many otherwise employable persons give up job hunting altogether, and contribute instead to the growing number of unemployed in inner-city neighborhoods.

Any serious effort to eliminate the polarized or dualistic metropolis must involve capitalist planning on a metropoliswide basis. Whether or not such an effort can succeed remains an open question; certainly, it is bound to be made more difficult by governments reactive to the needs of dominant economic interests.

If the dynamics of capitalist development have created urban problems in developed countries, they have created even more severe urban problems in non-Communist countries of the underdeveloped world. The rapid growth of Third World cities not only creates social divisions and tensions within them, but also a polarization of metropolis and periphery. For Third World countries, this polarization can lead to political and environmental disaster.

Policies to curb the expansion of major cities, which is largely a product of economic growth, are not easy to come by. It is more efficient from an economic standpoint to invest in the large city than to invest in the periphery. Thus, public and private capital tend to concentrate in the major city. The cost of providing public services—schools, roads, transportation, and systems for communications, water, and sanitation—is high in the metropolis, but there is considerable pressure on the government of an undeveloped country to invest its capital there. Part of the pressure is political. The stability of the country often depends on preventing unrest in the major city. To keep things running smoothly, public services are often provided in the metropolis before they are provided in the periphery.

The relatively high standard of living in the major city is the force that drives the concentration of population. To reduce the flow of people toward major cities, the differential in living standard between city and countryside must be reduced. This can be accomplished by slowing the pace of national economic growth and/or raising the standard of living in the countryside.

Migration toward major urban areas has been limited by economic depression, as in the case of Peru and Chile. It has also been curbed in socialist countries: stringent policies have reduced the growth of Havana, Cuba and Ho Chi Minh City, Vietnam. More interesting to policymakers are countries in which population flow to the bright city lights has been checked by improving the quality of life of those who live in the periphery. Examples include Argentina and Venezuela, countries that have achieved a high level of economic development. The case of Sri Lanka illustrates that even a poor country can upgrade living conditions in the countryside; however, in this case at the cost of sacrificing national economic growth and social cohesion.

In the foreseeable future, most public investment will take place in the major cities of underdeveloped countries. Without this investment, the stability of many of these countries may be threatened. However, some of the adverse effects of rapid concentration can be countered by governments who also give notice to areas beyond the traffic-choked, smog-wrapped cities.

SUMMARY

Cities exist in societies that create the conditions necessary for the appropriation of the *surplus product*. These conditions are met in *stratified market-exchange* societies. In the nineteenth century, stratified societies of Europe and North America experienced an urban transformation. During this period of widespread innovation, cities, especially large manufacturing ones, were ugly creations and horrifying environments for the poor. Denied access to the fruits of rapid economic growth, the worker bore the social costs of urban industrialization. The early nineteenth-century industrial city was characterized by a large number of small, relatively powerless enterprises. Toward the end of the nineteenth century, however, the market mode of economic integration took on a different appearance. There was a drift from individual to monopoly capitalism. As a result, control of the most important industries became more and more concentrated. Today, large corporations have a pervasive influence on cities throughout the capitalist world.

To explain how certain general forces tend to concentrate activities in cities, we considered the model of *pure competition*. This model, which approximates nineteenth-century capitalism, shows that profit-maximizing decisions lead to concentrated clusters of firms at nodes where production and assembly costs are minimized. In addition, the location of many firms in close proximity to one another helps to reduce the transport costs of shifting secondary inputs and outputs among them. Workers locate close to their places of employment, in dense residential districts scattered around the industrial and commercial heart of the city.

In a capitalist society, urban land-use arrangements are structured by a *rent-maximizing land market*. We used classical urban location theory to illustrate how land-using activities come to be located where they are. Although the private appropriation, exchange, and utilization of urban land are being steadily eroded by the progressive socialization of space via planning, urban land use in contemporary North America and Western Europe is governed primarily by a process of market exchange.

From the operation of the private land market emerge characteristic patterns of land use: a commercial core, a scattering of industry, and socially segregated neighborhoods. We described three widely accepted models that capture the essence of the urban land-use system in North America before the advent of suburbia: the *concentric-zone, sector,* and *multiple-nuclei models*. Departures from these patterns appear in cities in different culture realms, as exemplified by the models of Latin American and Southeast Asian cities.

The focus of the last part of the chapter was on the patterns and problems of urban sprawl in developed and underdeveloped countries. The growth of cities, which is the inevitable concomitant of economic growth, has witnessed a host of deleterious breakdowns and conflicts. In developed and underdeveloped countries, the predicament-laden course of urban expansion and land-use development highlights the need for social control and management.

KEY TERMS

average total costs

ceiling rent

central business district

central city

colonial city

competitive-bidding process

conurbation

egalitarian societies

filtering process

fixed costs

industrial city

invasion and succession

market exchange

megalopolis

minicity

new-town model

pure competition

rank societies

reciprocity

redistribution

scale economies

social surplus

spread city

squatter settlement

stratified societies

suburb

transport costs

urban land-use models

urban realm

variable costs

SUGGESTED READINGS

Armstrong, W., and McGee, T. G. 1985. *Theatres of Accumulation: Studies in Asian and Latin American Urbanization.* New York: Methuen.

Brunn, S., and Williams, J., eds. 1983. *Cities of the World: World Regional Urban Development.* New York: Harper & Row.

Castells, M. 1977. *The Urban Question: A Marxist Approach.* London: Edward Arnold.

Dear, M., and Scott, A. J., eds. 1981. *Urbanization and Urban Planning in Capitalist Society.* New York: Methuen.

Drakakis-Smith, D. 1987. *The Third World City.* New York: Methuen.

Gottmann, J. 1964. *Megalopolis.* Cambridge, MA: The MIT Press.

Harvey, D. 1973. *Social Justice and the City*. London: Edward Arnold.

Muller, P. O. 1981. *Contemporary Suburban America*. Englewood Cliffs, NJ: Prentice-Hall.

Palm, R. 1981. *The Geography of American Cities*. New York: Oxford University Press.

Tabb, W. K., and Sawers, L., eds. 1978. *Marxism and the Metropolis: New Perspectives in Urban Political Economy*. New York: Oxford University Press.

Vance, J. E. 1977. *This Scene of Man: The Role and Structure of the City in the Geography of Western Civilization*. New York: Harper and Row.

White, P. 1984. *The West European City: A Social Geography*. New York: Longman.

Yeates, M. 1980. *North American Urban Patterns*. New York: Halsted Press/V. H. Winston.

9
CITIES AS SERVICE CENTERS

OBJECTIVES

☐ To explain the concepts of threshold, range, and hierarchy

☐ To introduce central-place theory and the mercantile model of settlement

☐ To help you appreciate empirical regularities of the central-place concept

☐ To explore the market arrangements of different cultures

☐ To acquaint you with some practical applications of the theory of central places

☐ To examine the world urban hierarchy

Main Street, Schenectady, New York, in the 1940s. (Source: Library of Congress.)

In Chapter 8 we concentrated on individual cities and their patterns of urban land use. Urban society, however, reveals itself not as one but as many cities linked together in the form of an integrated *hierarchy of centers* of different functions and sizes. Why should there be urban hierarchies? What mechanisms control the size and spacing of cities? This chapter answers these questions by developing the concept of an urban hierarchy and by exploring patterns of service centers that have emerged to satisfy economic demands at local, regional, and international levels.

Although many factors determine locational patterns of cities, one classical location theory, *central-place theory*, provides insights into the urban hierarchy. Central-place theory considers the locational pattern of market-oriented retail and service firms and the hierarchy of urban places insofar as they are market centers. It deals with relationships between market centers and consumers *within* regions. There are also other types of relationships that link regions one to the other. Wholesale trade, for example, is conducted primarily *between* large regional centers; consequently, the locational pattern of these metropoli is determined by external trade linkages.

The "metropolis-and-region" network of retail and wholesale centers is a fairly accurate reflection of a domestic urban hierarchy. However, industrial restructuring throughout the world has led to the emergence of a global urban hierarchy. Today, a few international cities serve as centers of business decision making and corporate strategy formulation. To understand the urban hierarchy, these new business and corporate functions also must be considered.

CENTRAL PLACES AND THEIR HINTERLANDS

Locational Patterns of Cities

The concentration of population in cities is essentially the result of the spatial organization of secondary and tertiary activities. These activities can be conducted more profitably when they are clustered together rather than dispersed. Locational patterns of cities typically consist of three elements, often working in concert (Harris and Ullman 1945) (Figure 9.1):

1 A lined pattern of *transportation centers* that perform break-of-bulk and related services organized in relation to communication routes. These centers grow along transport routes and at the junction of different types of transport, such as road and railway junctions and the head of sea,

lake, or river navigation. Most of the largest U.S. cities originated along the seacoast, major rivers, and the Great Lakes, where there was a necessary break in transportation.

2 A pattern of *specialized-function centers*, which develop, either singly or in clusters, around some localized physical resource. They are usually dominated by one activity, such as mining, manufacturing, or recreation. Examples are steel-making and metal-finishing cities of Pennsylvania, in proximity to the coal resources of the Allegheny Plateau, and resort towns along the coasts of California and Florida.

3 A uniform pattern of centers that exchange goods and services with their hinterlands. Centers for the local exchange of goods and services are referred to as *central places*. Every settlement—large or small—is a central place, even though most cities do not depend exclusively on central-place functions. Central places provide retailing and wholesaling services; banking, insurance, and real estate services; governmental and administrative services; and recreational, medical, educational, religious, and cultural facilities.

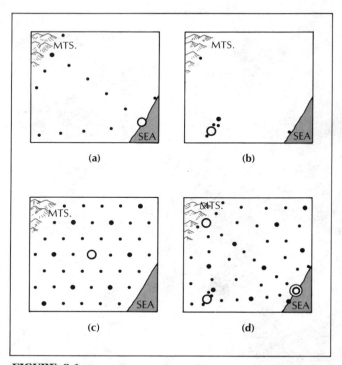

FIGURE 9.1
Different patterns of urban location: (a) transport centers, aligned along railroads or at coast; (b) specialized-function centers; (c) theoretical distribution of central places; (d) a theoretical composite grouping of different types of centers. (Source: Harris and Ullman 1945, pp. 7–17.)

Miami Beach, Florida, is a specialized-function center. Its warm, sunny climate and miles of sandy beach are primary localizing factors. (Source: U.S. Army Corps of Engineers.)

Cities and Trade

No single locational theory applies to all three components of a settlement pattern, but a great deal of research has been devoted to the arrangement and distribution of central places. The theory of central places emphasizes that cities perform extensive services for their hinterlands. Business conducted totally within the hinterland is called *settlement-forming trade*. A true central place is based exclusively on these activities and can never support a population that transcends its hinterland. The number of jobs and, therefore, population size is a direct function of the demand generated in the hinterland. Most settlements have other functions that are not dependent upon hinterland size. For example, a manufacturing plant that sells to a national or international market does not directly depend on the local retail and service hinterland. Such activity is called *settlement-building trade*. Each settlement also does some internal business—sales of goods and services to the residents of the center. This business is called *settlement-serving trade*.

Hinterlands

Central places serve areas larger than themselves. These areas are called hinterlands, tributary areas, trade or market areas, or urban fields. A *trade area* may be theoretically continuous. Take, for example, the circulation of a city's newspaper. Most papers are

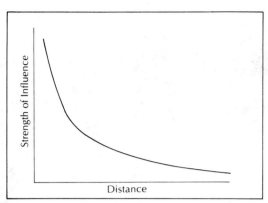

FIGURE 9.2
Cross Section of an idealized trade area.

purchased by people who live in or near the city, but some may be purchased by people living thousands of kilometers away. In a graph describing this theoretical relationship, the curve approaches the distance axis infinitely closely, but never reaches zero (Figure 9.2). For practical purposes, however, a city's trade area ends much closer to the origin. Geographers have often used a "median" or "line-of-indifference" boundary to delimit trade areas. The median boundary in newspaper circulation, for example, is the line between two cities along which 50 percent of the newspapers purchased are from one city. To illustrate, consider the "line-of-indifference" boundary for six goods and services provided by Mobile, Alabama (Figure 9.3). The outermost lines—the isopleths for business in wholesale meat, wholesale produce, and wholesale drugs—mark the approximate boundary of Mobile's influence. From this map we could delimit

the territory over which the city exerts more-or-less total dominance.

The map of areas influenced by Mobile is the result of fieldwork. To adopt the same method for a number of cities would be a very tedious task. A short-cut means of determining a city's trade area is to measure one activity that is particularly expressive of this characteristic. In the United States, for example, metropolitan trade areas may be determined by the extent and intensity of long-distance telephone calls, journey to work, or newspaper circulation. Newspapers are a conceptually good indicator of the social, economic, and cultural ties between a city and its tributary region (Figure 9.4). This is especially evident in large metropolitan areas. People in the tributary area look to the regional newspaper for information on sales and social events.

Areas that focus on central places through circulation networks are known as functional or nodal regions. Every city has its nodal region. The size and shape of this region depends on the size of the city, the influence or competition of neighboring dominant centers, and the ease of travel.

The Law of Retail Gravitation

When satisfactory data cannot be obtained to determine urban trade areas, a modification of W.J. Reilly's (1931) *law of retail gravitation* may be used to provide estimates. This model, analogous to Newton's law of physics, is designed to identify the exact point between competing centers at which consumers will choose to travel to one center rather than the other. Typically, it takes the form

FIGURE 9.3
Areas served and influenced by Mobile, Alabama. (Source: Ullman, 1943, p. 58.)

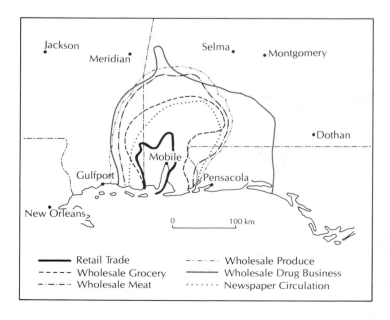

FIGURE 9.4
Metropolitan trade areas of the United States based on newspaper circulation. (Source: Based on Park and Newcomb, 1933, p. 107.)

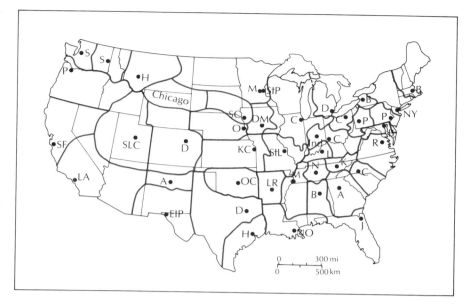

$$D_j = \frac{d_{ij}}{1 + \sqrt{P_i/P_j}}$$

where

D_j = the distance from city j to the breaking point

d_{ij} = the distance between the cities i and j

P_i = the population of the ith city

P_j = the population of the jth city

The identified breaking point is assumed to apply to all services located in each center.

Let us illustrate the *breakpoint model* with a simple example. City A and City B have populations of 20,000 and 80,000, respectively, and are sixty kilometers apart. According to the formula, the limit of the trading area of A in the direction of B is

$$\frac{60}{1 + \sqrt{\dfrac{80,000}{20,000}}} = \frac{60}{1 + 2} = 20 \text{ kilometers}$$

Therefore, according to the formula, the trading area of A would extend twenty kilometers toward B. This same analysis can be made in every direction from a particular city, resulting in a highly generalized trade area (Figures 9.5 and 9.6).

Although the breakpoint model provides a short-cut technique for determining trade-area boundaries,

FIGURE 9.5
Hypothetical trade area based on the breakpoint model.

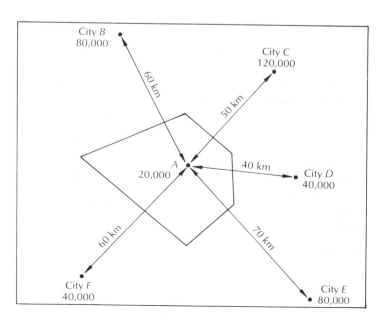

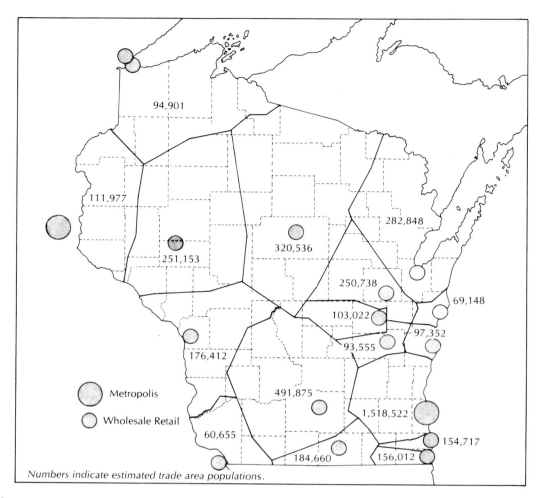

FIGURE 9.6
Wholesale trade areas in Wisconsin based on the breakpoint model.

it has its problems. City populations are assumed to be homogeneous masses; that is, the formula does not take into account cultural, economic, and other differences between people. Multipurpose trips and ease-of-transportation variables are not considered. The model also ignores the fact that each service has its own threshold and range characteristics.

The breakpoint model is therefore too rigid, a difficulty partially overcome in the probability model suggested by geographer David Huff (1963). The model still uses gravity-model principles, but assuming that consumers have several centers to choose from, it specifies the probabilities of choosing each of the centers. This can be mapped to produce probability surfaces for consumers choosing to shop in each center. Probability models have been used by applied economic geographers to assess the likely impact of adding to existing shopping centers or, more impor-

tantly, the consequences of introducing a new center into an existing system of centers (Clarke and Bolwell 1968; Batty and Saether 1972).

Gravity models are not as useful for understanding processes underlying retail and social behavior as they are for providing descriptions of the behavior of large populations. Moreover, they do not help us to understand the process underlying the formation of trade areas. Central-place theory does, however, provide a good basis for understanding the formation of trade areas.

AN ELEMENTARY CENTRAL-PLACE MODEL

In order to create a general theory of central places, it is common for geographers to begin with a normative model that assumes (1) an isotropic surface, (2) a given level and uniform distribution of demand and population, (3) equal ease of transportation in all directions, (4) settlements depending totally on hinterland trade, (5) optimizing producers and consumers, and (6) a steady-state economy free of government or social classes. The model also assumes a *linear market*, with consumers evenly spaced along a road that extends across the isolated plain (Figure 9.7). Given these seven constraints, we will now investigate the number of central places required to meet consumer demand, the size of trade areas, and the most efficient spacing of central places.

Threshold and Range

Threshold and range are key concepts in central-place theory. For a firm to offer a good—a *central function*—at a point along the road, it must sell enough to meet operating costs. The minimum level of effective demand that will allow a firm to stay in business is called the *threshold of a good.* But given the assumption of evenly distributed population and purchasing power, we can also speak of the minimum number of people necessary to support a central function.

The *range of a good* is the distance people are willing to travel to obtain the good at market price (Figure 9.8a). A consumer who lives next door to the shop pays the store price for a loaf of bread. A consumer who lives at some distance from the shop, however, must pay the store price plus the cost of travel to the central place. If travel costs are twenty cents per kilometer, then a consumer who lives five kilometers from the shop pays $1.50 for the bread. (Figure 9.8a). Clearly, the price a consumer pays is a direct function of distance. If price increases with distance from a central place or distribution point, then demand should decline with distance. We can

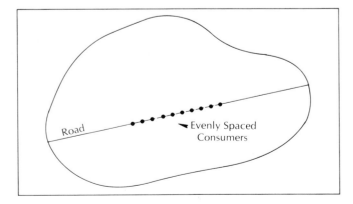

FIGURE 9.7
A linear market.

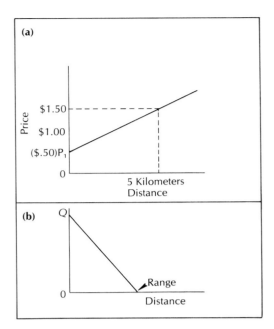

FIGURE 9.8
(a) Price and (b) range of a good.

find a distance from the central place at which demand is zero. That point is the range of a good (Figure 9.8b). To continue with our assumption of a linear market, the range of a good is the distance, R, in both directions from a distribution point on a linear market (Figure 9.9).

Order of a Good and a Center

Different goods have different thresholds. Inexpensive, frequently purchased everyday necessities have low thresholds. Goods that are costly and purchased infrequently have higher thresholds. Items with low thresholds, such as eggs purchased at a supermarket, are called low-order goods. Goods with higher thresholds, such as furniture, are called higher order goods. Thus, central functions can be ordered on the basis of their threshold size. The highest order good has the highest threshold, and the lowest order good has the lowest threshold.

Just as we can order goods, so we can order centers. The order of a center is determined by the highest order good offered by the center. Low-order centers offer only low-order goods; high-order centers offer high-order goods.

Emergence of a Central-Place Hierarchy

We are now in a position to derive a *hierarchy* of central places. Assume highest order places, or *A*-level

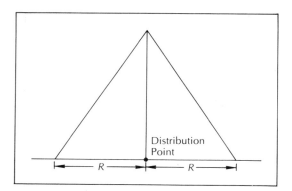

FIGURE 9.9
Range as distance.

places, offer all goods from 1,000 to 1 (Table 9.1). The market area of each *A*-level place must include at least 1,000 people. If there are 10,000 consumers along our imaginary linear market, ten *A*-level centers can be established. Two *A*-level centers and their market areas are shown in Figure 9.10. We assume a population density of ten people per kilometer, so that the minimum market area of each *A*-level center is 100 kilometers long, or fifty kilometers on either side of each *A*-level center. We also assume that competition forces market areas to be as small as possible—that is, 100 kilometers equals 1,000 consumers. This minimizes the travel cost the most distant consumer must pay. A consumer on the dividing line between two *A*-level centers will purchase goods from both of the centers in equal measure.

The good that defines the *A*-level of the hierarchy has a threshold of 1,000, but there is also a good with a threshold of *A* divided by two, or 500. The threshold market area for that good is fifty kilometers long, or twenty-five kilometers on either side of a distribution point. A market area of 500 centered on A_1 and A_2 allows an additional 500-person market area centered on the midpoint between the two *A*-level centers. A central place locating there is at the *B*-level; it can offer all goods with a threshold of 500 or less. The good that defines the *B*-level has a threshold of 500, and is called a *hierarchical marginal good*. A

hierarchical marginal good is the highest order good offered by a given level of the central-place hierarchy. What threshold size will define *C*-level centers? Their threshold size is *B* divided by two, or 250. They locate midway between higher order centers; thus, they occur every twenty-five kilometers along our imaginary road.

Our linear hierarchy follows the "rule of twos": each successive level is defined by a function with a threshold one-half the size of the next highest hierarchical marginal good. The rule of twos also applies to market-area sizes and the spacing of centers. In central-place theory this type of hierarchy is known as a *K*-equals-two hierarchy, since two is the constant parameter of the system. The letter *K* stands for the German word, Konstant.

So far in our discussion we have constructed a hierarchy of central places based on the concepts of threshold and range. We have seen that the number of required centers is minimized, the number of consumers served is maximized, and the distance consumers must travel for a given set of central functions is minimized. We have seen that higher order centers, which offer more functions and, therefore, employ more people, have larger populations than lower order centers. Higher order centers are also more widely spaced, serve larger market areas, and occur less frequently. In sum, our central-place hierarchy may be regarded as a multiple system of nested centers and market areas. Lower order centers and their market areas nest under the market areas of higher order centers. Now let us turn to the more complex two-dimensional hierarchies developed by Walter Christaller and others.

CHRISTALLER'S CENTRAL-PLACE THEORY

The foundations of central-place theory were established by the German geographer Walter Christaller (1966) in the early 1930s. On the basis of the simplifying assumptions we introduced earlier and the concept of a range of a good, Christaller constructed a deductive theory to explain the size, number, and

TABLE 9.1
Goods and threshold size.

		1,000,	999,	998,	...,	502,	501,	500,	...,	252,	251,	250,	...,	3,	2,	1
Centers	A	X	X	X	X	X	X	X	X	X	X	X	X	X	X	X
	B							X	X	X	X	X	X	X	X	X
	C											X	X	X	X	X

FIGURE 9.10
A $K = 2$ hierarchy.

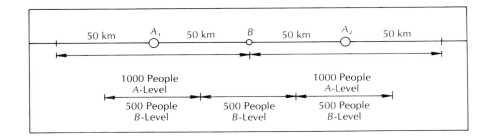

distribution of clusters of urban trade and institutions. To demonstrate hierarchical interrelations between places in a competitive market society, he built three geometric models. His central places are arranged according to marketing, transport, and administrative principles. According to Christaller, these three principles underlie the most efficient system of central places.

The Marketing Principle

The *marketing principle* assume the largest provision of central-place goods and services from the minimum number of central places (Figure 9.11). Each B-level central place is midway between three neighboring centers of the next highest order. Midway points are corners of hexagonal market areas of the next highest order. Each higher order place is surrounded by six places of the next lowest order.

Figure 9.12 illustrates the progression of central places and market areas for a three-level hierarchy. The market area of each A-level center passes through six lower order B-level central places. A-level market areas are three times larger than B-level market areas. Each A-level market area includes all of the B-level market areas centered on an A-level center, plus one-third of the six surrounding B-level market areas (⅓ of 6 = 2 + 1 = 3). Distances separating places at the same level of the hierarchy are the same. If lower order places are one unit apart, then rival higher order

places, dominating three times the area and three times the population, are $\sqrt{3}$ units apart, or 1.732 units apart. This arrangement of central places is a K-equals-three network in which the number of trade areas with successively less specialized levels progresses by a "rule of threes"; that is, central places increase geometrically—one, three, nine, twenty-seven.

Christaller argued that the system of central places developed on the basis of the range of a good is rational and efficient from an economic point of view. He did note, however, that real-world conditions produce deviations from this system. Actual conditions include historical circumstance, government interference, social stratification, income differences, and topographical variations not accounted for in the normative model.

The Traffic Principle

If an optimum road network is superimposed on a marketing hierarchy, B-level centers do not lie on the A-level road network (Figure 9.13a). More roads must be constructed if B-level centers are to be connected. Christaller rejected traffic routes in the marketing system, and asked: How can connectivity between places be maximized and network length minimized? By shifting B-level centers to a point midway between each pair of A- level centers, he found the answer. This arrangement maximizes connectivity and minimizes network length (Figure 9.13b). The pattern of centers arranged according to the *traffic principle* results in a K-equals-four hierarchy. The B-level market areas are one-fourth the size of the A-level market areas. Each A-level market area dominates all of the B-level areas centered on it plus one-half of the surrounding six (equals three), for a total of four. The number of market areas at successively less specialized levels of the hierarchy progresses by the "rule of fours"; that is, central places increase geometrically—one, four, sixteen, sixty-four. Compared with the marketing principle, more centers at each level of the hierarchy are necessary if the entire hexagonal landscape is to be adequately provided with central places for the dis-

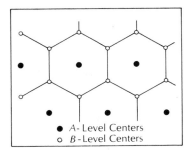

FIGURE 9.11
Location of centers: a $K = 3$ hierarchy.

FIGURE 9.12
Market areas: a K = 3 hierarchy.

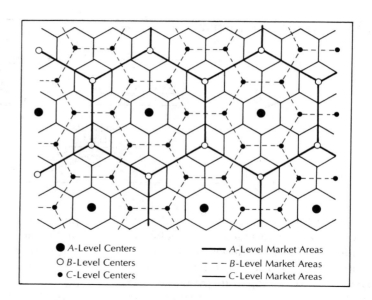

FIGURE 9.12
Market areas: a K = 3 hierarchy.

- ● A-Level Centers — A-Level Market Areas
- ○ B-Level Centers --- B-Level Market Areas
- • C-Level Centers — C-Level Market Areas

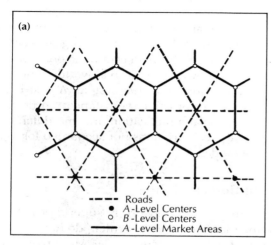

(a)

- --- Roads
- • A-Level Centers
- ○ B-Level Centers
- — A-Level Market Areas

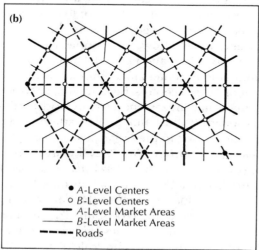

(b)

- • A-Level Centers
- ○ B-Level Centers
- — A-Level Market Areas
- — B-Level Market Areas
- --- Roads

FIGURE 9.13
The traffic principle: (a) optimum transportation net: maximum connectivity for A-level centers (K = 3); (b) a K = 4 hierarchy.

tribution of goods and services. The advantage of a more efficient transport system for moving goods cheaply is counterbalanced by the additional distance consumers must travel to reach a center at a given level of the hierarchy.

The Administrative Principle

The *administrative principle* requires sociopolitical separation of market areas. This is achieved when each central place controls six dependent centers (Figure 9.14). Hinterlands nest according to the "rule of sevens" (K-equals-seven). They are larger than in either K-equals-three or K-equals-four systems, which means that consumers must travel farther to reach a center of a given level in the system.

Southern Germany

Christaller tested his central-place model in southern Germany and bordering areas of France, Switzerland, and Austria (Table 9.2). He recognized a seven-level hierarchy ranging from market hamlets to regional capital cities in which centers at each level dominate three times the area (column 4) and three times the population (column 5). The distance between similar centers increases by three over the preceding smaller category (column 2). The smallest centers are about seven kilometers apart, since four or five kilometers, roughly a one-hour walking distance, corresponded to the market area for the smallest centers. Centers of the next order of specialization, township centers, are twelve kilometers apart.

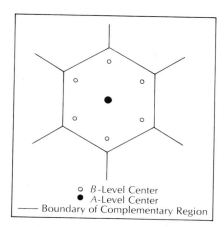

○ B-Level Center
● A-Level Center
—— Boundary of Complementary Region

FIGURE 9.14
Two-level hierarchy of central places under the administrative principle.

The actual distribution of cities, towns, and villages in southern Germany is shown in Figure 9.15. Networks of central places nest within the market areas of regional capital cities. The cities are Munich, Frankfurt, Stuttgart, and Nuremburg, together with the border cities of Strasbourg in France and Zurich in Switzerland.

Christaller found that the expected pattern was approached most closely in poor, thinly settled farm districts that were virtually self-contained. Thus, deviations from the rational pattern were uncommon in many parts of southern Germany. On the other hand, the theoretical ideal was not evident in the highly industrialized Rhine-Ruhr.

EXTENSIONS OF THE CHRISTALLER MODEL

Lösch's Ideal Economic Region

There have been several modifications of Christaller's original ideas. One of the most interesting is the ideal economic region proposed by fellow German August Lösch (1954). His work, based on classical economic theory of the firm, attempted to determine what a general equilibrium system of production centers and market areas would look like in abstract geographical space. He was interested in "best" or "rational" location patterns rather than actual location patterns. In his words "The real duty of the economist is not to explain our sorry reality, but to improve it. The question of the best location is far more dignified than determination of the actual one" (p. 4).

To simplify the determination of the economic landscape at equilibrium, Lösch assumed that "economic raw materials are evenly and adequately distributed over a wide plain which is homogeneous in every other respect and contains nothing but self-sufficient farms that are regularly distributed" (p.105). He then asked what would happen if the inhabitants on the plain decided to produce manufactured goods over and above their subsistence needs. How many producers would there be? How would they locate? How much would they produce?

Lösch began his analysis by considering one low-order good—beer. Assuming a given demand curve for beer (Figure 9.16a) and a given transport rate, it is possible to calculate the amount of beer demanded at various distances from the producer (Figure 9.16b). Whether it is worthwhile for someone

TABLE 9.2
The urban hierarchy in southern Germany.

Central Place (1)	Towns		Tributary Areas	
	Distance Apart (2)	Population (3)	Size (Sq Km) (4)	Population (5)
Market hamlet (Marktort)	7	800	45	2,700
Township center (Amtsort)	12	1,500	135	8,100
County seat (Kreisstadt)	21	3,500	400	24,000
District city (Bezirksstadt)	36	9,000	1,200	75,000
Small state capital (Gaustadt)	62	27,000	3,600	225,000
Provincial head city (Provinzhaupstadt)	108	90,000	10,800	675,000
Regional capital city (Landeshaupstadt)	186	300,000	32,400	2,025,000

SOURCE: Ullman, 1940–1941, p. 857.

FIGURE 9.15
The distribution of central places in southern Germany. (Source: Dickinson, 1964, p. 75.)

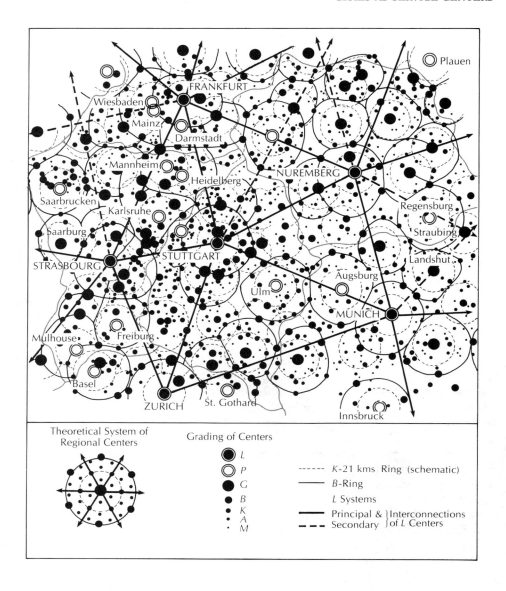

to begin beer production depends on production costs at different scales of activity and the revenues earned at different prices. From the area under the spatial demand cone (Figure 9.16c), it is possible to calculate the total revenue realized at a given price and the average revenue per unit of production. The average revenue a beer producer earns at various prices can then be estimated. If prices increase, the demand cone contracts; if prices decrease, the demand cone expands. As a result, the average revenue curve slopes down to the right (Figure 9.17a). Beer production is profitable as long as average revenues exceed average costs (Figure 9.17b). Profits lure more people into beer production. At first market areas surrounding each selling point are circular. But as additional producers crowd onto the plain, the areas

overlap and assume a hexagonal shape. Gradually, a producer's market area shrinks, so the area under the demand cone at a given price decreases and the average revenue curve slopes more steeply. Eventually, the whole system reaches equilibrium. When average costs equal average revenue (Figure 9.17c), a hexagonal network of market areas fills the plain.

If additional commodities are produced for the consumers on the plain, a series of market-area networks emerge, all with a different hexagonal mesh determined by production costs, transport costs, and elasticity of demand. To create the composite central-place network, Lösch coordinated the nests of hexagons so that all had at least one center in common— the regional metropolis. He then rotated them around the center until the greatest number of production

In Walter Christaller's system of central places, Munich, West Germany, represents a regional capital city (Landeshaupstadt). (Source: German Information Center.)

locations coincided. This operation resulted in what Lösch called the "ideal" economic region (Figure 9.18).

In Lösch's economic landscape, there is a hierarchy of central places providing goods and services to the surrounding population. Many of these places provide a narrow range of local services, while a few provide a wide range. And even though Lösch elaborated his analysis on a uniform plain devoid of resource differences, the equilibrium state is characterized by spatial disparities. For example, some parts of the plain—"city-rich" zones—have more central places producing more goods than other parts—"city-poor" zones (Figure 9.18). Thus, one of the most important conclusions of Lösch's work is that even when resource differences are eliminated, there still will be disparities in the spatial arrangement of productive units at equilibrium. For Lösch, these regional economic disparities or regional inequalities did not necessarily signal a state of disequilibrium.

Christaller and Lösch Compared

Christaller and Lösch agreed that the triangular pattern of settlement distribution with hexagonal market areas represents the optimal spatial organization for a single good under the constraint of uniform population density on an unbounded plain with equal access in all directions. They agreed on three major concepts of central-place theory: range, threshold, and hierarchy. However, they developed their economic landscapes from different starting points. Christaller built his hierarchy from the highest order good downward, and Lösch built his from the ubiquitous good upward. Christaller's framework allows for the analysis of an economic landscape founded in an area of sparse settlement, while Lösch's framework is better suited for the analysis of a landscape in a region of dense, long-established settlement undergoing rapid change. Furthermore, while Christaller's

FIGURE 9.16
The demand for beer: (a) price to consumer at different distances from the producer; (b) the demand curve for beer; (c) the spatial demand cone indicating the amount of beer demanded at different distances from the producer. (Source: Based on Berry, 1968.)

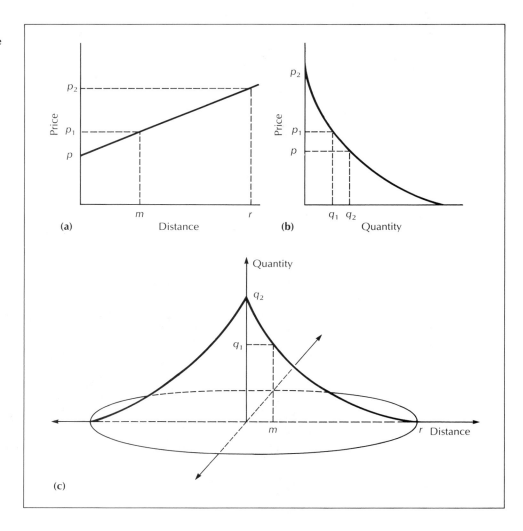

system sheds light on the distribution of retailing and service activities, especially for agricultural regions, Lösch's system appears more relevant to an understanding of the distribution of market-oriented manufacturing activities.

Isard's Modifications

Walter Isard (1956), an American regional scientist, found fault with the equal-area pattern of hexagons used by both Christaller and Lösch. Regular hexagons, he argued, are unlikely to occur in practice because of variations in population densities. In Isard's modification of Lösch's system, hexagons vary in size according to the underlying population patterns (Figure 9.19). Hexagonal market areas become larger with increasing distance from the metropolis due to the relatively lower population density. Unlike Lösch, Isard located his main traffic arteries through the

center of sectors, not along their boundaries. This arrangement of traffic lines is appealing in that it acknowledges the importance of urbanization economies and the effects of modern modes of transportation. Isard pointed out the difficulty in working with hexagons. He stated that a framework free of hexagonal geometry would provide a more realistic basis for understanding the forces controlling the location of tertiary or service economic activities.

Wholesaling and the Mercantile Model of Settlement

The argument that central-place theory is too parochial, sufficing as an explanation only for the trading-settlement structure of an area, was introduced by geographer James Vance (1970). Central-place theory deals with relationships between customers and sellers of goods *within* regions. It does not account for

FIGURE 9.17
The equilibrium pattern of beer production: (a) the aggregate demand curve assuming a single producer and no spatial competition for consumers; (b) average production costs and revenues, assuming no spatial competition for consumers; (c) long-run equilibrium with many producers and hexagonal market areas just large enough to ensure that $AC = AR'$. (Source: Based on Berry, 1968.)

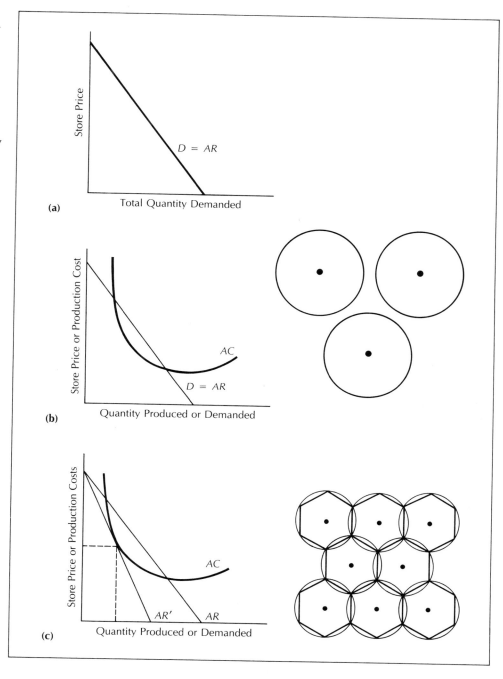

the wholesale trade that links regions. Wholesaling, which involves the sale of goods from one entrepreneur to another, is conducted primarily *between* higher order centers; and these external linkages influence their locational patterns. In addition, local settlement hierarchies are influenced by long-distance external ties.

Wholesalers subject regions to external change and stimulate growth of wholesaling centers. Vance

thought of these centers as "unraveling points" in the geography of trade. They link production areas, mediate trade flows, and determine the metropolitan centers from which central-place patterns develop to meet demands of consumers.

Vance doubted whether any region in North America was economically isolated enough to have begun in a closed local region. He preferred to view the history of settlement patterns not only in terms of

FIGURE 9.18
Lösch's equilibrium spatial arrangement of market areas and production centers with three different commodities. (Source: Based on Isard, 1956, p. 270.)

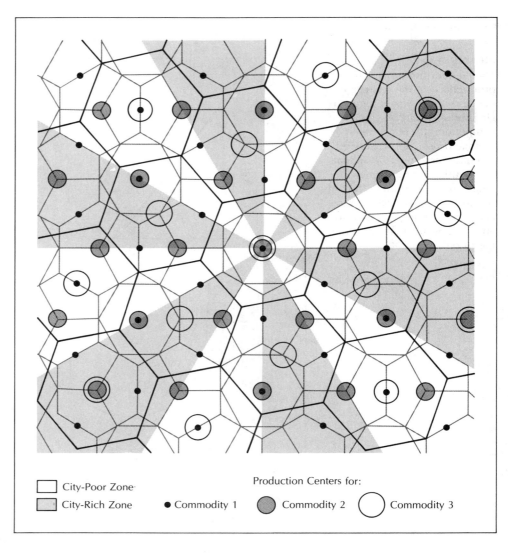

City-Poor Zone
City-Rich Zone

Production Centers for:

• Commodity 1   Commodity 2   Commodity 3

FIGURE 9.19
Isard's landscape modification. (Source: Isard, 1956, p. 272.)

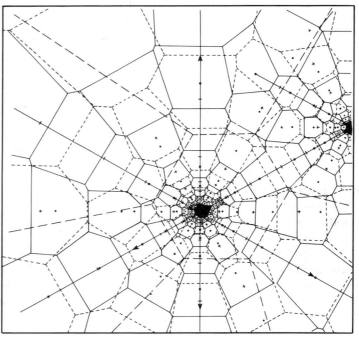

local trading patterns (central-place model) but also in terms of long-distance trading connections. He argued that broad-scale settlement of North America must be considered in the context of long-distance trade. Colonial towns—Boston, New York, Philadelphia, Baltimore, and Charleston—were traders' towns. Created before their hinterlands expanded, they served as unraveling points for the distribution and collection of goods. Subsequently, interior mercantile cities developed to serve as primary collecting points for resources shipped back to the East Coast. Such cities as Chicago, Cincinnati, Memphis, Minneapolis, St. Louis, Kansas City, and Omaha owe much of their early growth to their wholesaling function. Although Vance regarded only cities of more than 50,000 people as true distribution centers, many small towns also developed on the basis of long-distance trading connections. Eau Claire, Wisconsin, for example, was a workplace town of about 10,000 people in the 1880s; however, the products of its many lumber companies were shipped to places as far away as St. Louis.

Vance described the development of distant trade between Europe and North America and the subsequent evolution of the American urban hierarchy (Figure 9.20). After ascertaining that an area had sufficient economic potential, Europeans established mercantile centers within it. These centers linked European countries and their sources of raw materials, and they grew as the size of the trading system increased. Eventually, the central-place model began to characterize American settlement, with a subsequent parallel growth of settlement in accordance with both central-place and mercantile models.

Vance suggested that central-place dynamics may have sketched the European settlement pattern (Figure 9.20). For example, in areas like Christaller's southern Germany economies were fairly isolated from each other in the feudal middle ages. By the early modern period, however, the feudal economy was giving way to mercantilism, and central places with developing external ties grew rapidly. Long-distance trade accentuated the importance of Bristol, St. Malo, Seville, Cadiz, and Lübeck, to name only a few merchant cities.

Evaluation of Central-Place Models

We have previously alluded to the shortcomings of the classical models. They are static, descriptive equilibrium models that ignore nonoptimal consumer behavior. They also lack historical perspective; that is, they do not consider the historical process of developing capitalism as the framework within which

settlements become centers of dominance. Furthermore, they deal with closed local economic systems. Thus, central-place theory can provide a basis for understanding only those relationships between producers and consumers within a region. It cannot deal with settlement patterns that have grown out of long-distance trading connections between regions.

An assumption implicit in central-place theory is that "space is uniform and objects and activities can be manipulated and freely located within it; differentiation by significance is of little importance and places are reduced to simple locations with their greatest quality being development potential" (Relph 1976, p. 87). The existential significance of places is not acknowledged, nor their qualities of appearance considered. Low-order places in Nebraska, for instance, are equated with low-order places in Nepal. In other words, central place theory lacks humanism and involves no sense of *place* at all.

Finally, geographers have noted that theoretical hexagonal networks of central places do not resemble real economic landscapes. But it would be a perfunctory dismissal of central-place theory if solely on the grounds that pleasing hexagonal forms are not apparent in the real world. Richard Morrill (1970) asserted that the usefulness of central-place theory depends on its applicability of the following questions:

1 Does the spatial organization of retailing and services reflect the level and distribution of purchasing power?
2 Do central-place activities tend to be regularly spaced in areas with similar physical, cultural, and economic environments?
3 Do consumers try to reduce distances traveled to purchase goods and services?
4 Do consumers shop at a hierarchy of centers for different types of goods and services?

Many studies have dealt with questions such as these, which apply to tertiary activities within cities and to systems of cities. Our task now is to explore whether the location of service activities has been confirmed by the empirical evidence.

EVIDENCE IN SUPPORT OF CENTRAL-PLACE THEORY

Trade Centers of the Upper Midwest

We begin our examination by looking at the trade centers of America's northern heartland (Borchert 1987), or the Upper Midwest. The region coincides with the Ninth Federal Reserve District, which extends some 2,500 kilometers along the Canadian

FIGURE 9.20
Urban evolution in the mercantile and central-place models. (Source: Vance, 1970, p. 151.)

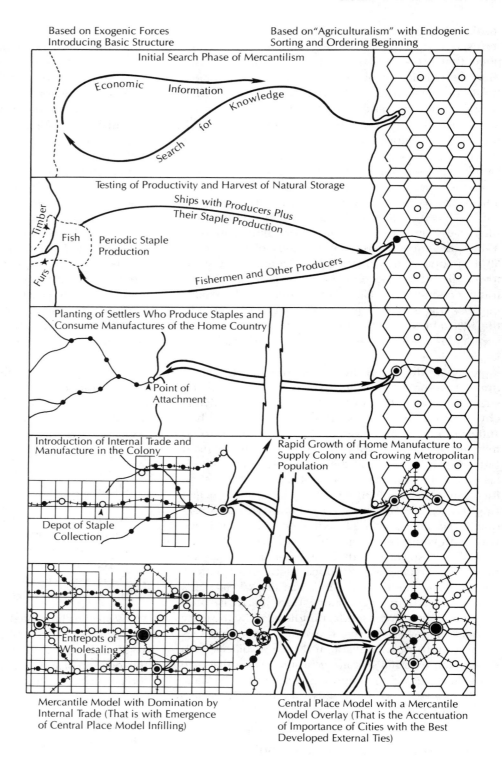

border, from Montana in the west to the Upper Peninsula of Michigan in the east. In this rather homogeneous region, we might anticipate the regular pattern of hexagonal market areas suggested by Christaller. But the underlying density of farm population varies considerably (Figure 9.21). Rural population densities are greatest in southern and eastern Minnesota, which represents the northern and western margins of the Midwest agricultural heartland. They decline towards the west and north. In the west,

FIGURE 9.21
Distribution of farms in the Upper Midwest. (Source: Kolars and Nystuen, 1974, p. 100.)

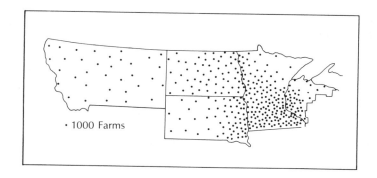

aridity reduces the carrying capacity of the land. In the north, infertile soils and short growing seasons bring lower yields per unit of farmland. Compared with southern parts of the region, the amount of land in farms is very small. The land in southern Minnesota is more than 90 percent in farms, but this figure falls off to less than 10 percent in northern Minnesota, where forests dominate. A hexagonal lattice that conforms to the distribution of the farm population shows that cells are smaller in areas of high population density and larger in areas of sparse settlement (Figure 9.22).

Hierarchy of Business Centers

John Borchert (1963), a geographer at the University of Minnesota, demonstrated that a hierarchy of central-place functions exists in the Upper Midwest. He selected forty-six functions, and determined those functions typical of various orders in the hierarchy of business types. He grouped central functions into convenience, specialty, and wholesale categories for eight types of trade centers (Figure 9.23).

Hamlets, the lowest order central place recognized by Borchert, have only gasoline service stations and eating and drinking establishments. The next two levels, *minimum convenience* and *full convenience centers,* provide everyday necessities. Minimum con-

venience centers have hamlet-level functions plus a hardware store, drugstore, bank, and two other convenience functions, such as a variety store. Full convenience centers have all hamlet-level and minimum convenience functions, as well as stores dealing in laundry or dry-cleaning, jewelry, appliances or furniture, clothing, lumber, building materials, shoes, and garden supplies. In addition to shops, most full convenience centers have a hotel or motel. Still higher in the hierarchy of business types are *partial shopping* and *complete shopping centers,* offering specialty goods and services. *Secondary wholesale-retail, primary wholesale-retail,* and *metropolitan retail centers* are the highest order places. With regard to the frequency of trade-center types, as the hierarchical level increases, the number of trade centers decreases. There is also a strong relationship between trade-center types and population size (Table 9.3).

Minneapolis-St. Paul is the largest and only metropolitan wholesale-retail center in the Upper Midwest. Besides convenience, specialty, and wholesale functions, the Twin Cities provides other services for its massive trade area, such as regional head offices of insurance companies, and specialized medical, educational, and administrative facilities. People living up to 1,600 kilometers away may never visit the Twin Cities. They obtain goods and services from lower order trade centers. The highest level centers that many people living beyond the Twin Cities need to

FIGURE 9.22
Hexagonal lattice conforming to the underlying rural population pattern in the Upper Midwest. (Source: Kolars and Nystuen, 1974, p. 101.)

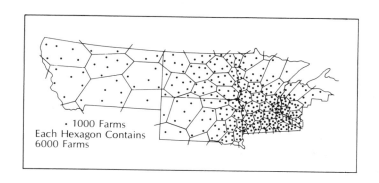

FIGURE 9.23
Trade center types in the Upper Midwest. (Source: Borchert, 1963, p. 12.)

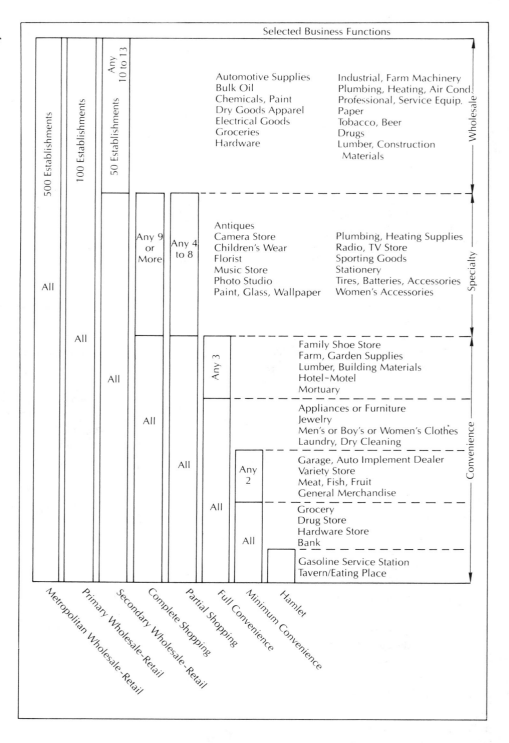

Selected Business Functions

500 Establishments | 100 Establishments | 50 Establishments | Any 10 to 13

Automotive Supplies
Bulk Oil
Chemicals, Paint
Dry Goods Apparel
Electrical Goods
Groceries
Hardware

Industrial, Farm Machinery
Plumbing, Heating, Air Cond.
Professional, Service Equip.
Paper
Tobacco, Beer
Drugs
Lumber, Construction
  Materials

Wholesale

Any 9 or More | Any 4 to 8

Antiques
Camera Store
Children's Wear
Florist
Music Store
Photo Studio
Paint, Glass, Wallpaper

Plumbing, Heating Supplies
Radio, TV Store
Sporting Goods
Stationery
Tires, Batteries, Accessories
Women's Accessories

Specialty

Any 3

Family Shoe Store
Farm, Garden Supplies
Lumber, Building Materials
Hotel–Motel
Mortuary

Appliances or Furniture
Jewelry
Men's or Boy's or Women's Clothes
Laundry, Dry Cleaning

Any 2

Garage, Auto Implement Dealer
Variety Store
Meat, Fish, Fruit
General Merchandise

Grocery
Drug Store
Hardware Store
Bank

Gasoline Service Station
Tavern/Eating Place

Convenience

All / All / All / All / All / All / All / All

Metropolitan Wholesale–Retail
Primary Wholesale–Retail
Secondary Wholesale–Retail
Complete Shopping
Partial Shopping
Full Convenience
Minimum Convenience
Hamlet

reach are primary and secondary wholesale-retail centers such as Eau Claire, Fargo-Moorhead, and Duluth. Nonetheless, the Twin Cities is the controlling center of the economy of the Upper Midwest. Trade-area residents feel the influence of the metropolis through communications, banking, agricultural marketing, and retail-wholesale relationships.

Central-Place Pattern The geographical distribution of trade centers in the Upper Midwest conforms roughly to central-place theory (Figure 9.24). Wholesale-retail centers are widely spaced and hamlets are the most numerous centers. Greater spacing of trade centers of all classes to the north and west is a striking feature of the map.

TABLE 9.3

Frequency and median size of trade center types in the Upper Midwest.

Type of Center	Number of Centers	Median Population (Thousands)
Wholesale-Retail Centers		
Metropolitan	1	1,440.0
Primary	7	55.4
Secondary	10	32.2
Shopping Centers		
Complete	78	9.5
Partial	127	2.5
Convenience Centers		
Full	111	1.5
Minimum	379	0.8
Hamlets	1,539	0.2

SOURCE: Borchert, 1963, p. 11.

It is generally agreed that there are too many trade centers in the Upper Midwest. Most of the 2,500 settlements that dot the Upper Midwest map were established under conditions quite different from those of today. After the railroads opened up the region in the late nineteenth century, immigrants established small farms. To meet the needs of farm families, low-order central places developed. These places were closely spaced in response to slow, difficult travel conditions. In recent decades, two changes have produced stress within the original framework of settlements: migration and transportation.

Migration has had the greatest influence on the structure of trade centers. In the past sixty years, farm population has declined sharply as farms increased in size and farmland was abandoned. In addition to a declining farm population, the region has experienced net out-migration. Within the region itself, population has shifted progressively from farms and small trade centers into larger urban areas, and from

The downtown Minneapolis skyline. Minneapolis-St. Paul represents the highest order central place in the hierarchy of Upper Midwest trade centers. (Source: Greater Minneapolis Convention and Visitors Association.)

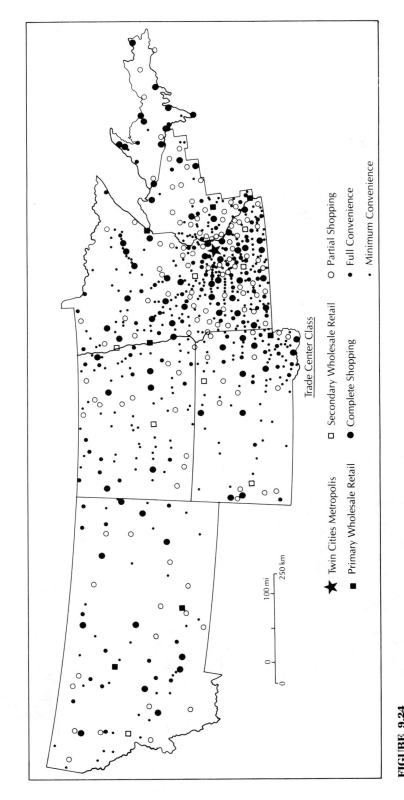

FIGURE 9.24

Distribution of trade centers in the Upper Midwest. (Source: Borchert, 1963, pp. 13–14.)

The central business district of
Shakopee, Minnesota, in 1875.
(Source: Minnesota Historical
Society.)

central cities into suburbs and countryside. Examples of trade centers that have grown rapidly are the Twin Cities, Rochester, and Fargo-Moorhead.

Modern highways crisscrossing the region illustrate a second influence on the structure of trade centers. Improvements in transportation after 1914, such as the widespread use of automobiles and paving of roads, enabled consumers to bypass smaller centers and patronize larger ones. Greater consumer mobility meant that small trade centers could not compete with larger towns that offered a greater variety of services in larger quantity.

Dispersed Cities   In the years to come, most of the population of the Upper Midwest will be concentrated in Minneapolis-St. Paul (metro cluster) and other low-density metropoli (urban clusters). These urban clusters or dispersed cities are products of modern transportation and communication networks and are formed by linkages of complete and wholesale-retail centers (Figure 9.25). They all share the following features:

1   The length of any link or corridor can be traveled in under sixty minutes or thirty minutes, respectively.
2   In each cluster there are multiple shopping and service centers, which are more complementary than competitive.
3   In each cluster there are many low-order retail and service centers.
4   Each cluster has industrial and wholesale zones, public higher education facilities, public hospital facilities, and newspapers and broadcasting stations.
5   Each city within a cluster functions independently to a large extent. However, there is also considerable interdependence—travel in every direction for business, shopping, education, health care, and social and recreational purposes.

High-Order Central Places   Minneapolis-St. Paul is one of twenty-four high-order central places in the United States (Figure 9.26). Borchert (1967) divided these important trade centers into three orders based

FIGURE 9.25
Dispersed cities. (Source:
Borchert and Carroll, 1971,
p. 14.)

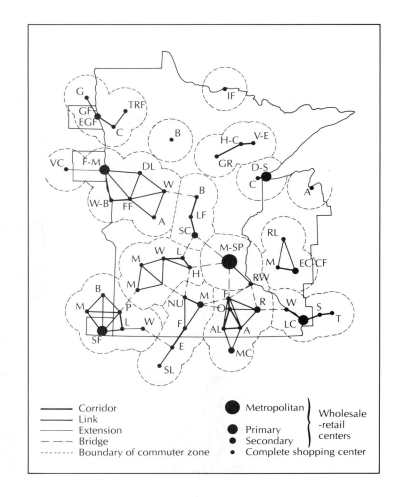

FIGURE 9.26
Higher order trade centers and
trade areas in the United States.
(Source: Based on Borchert,
1967.)

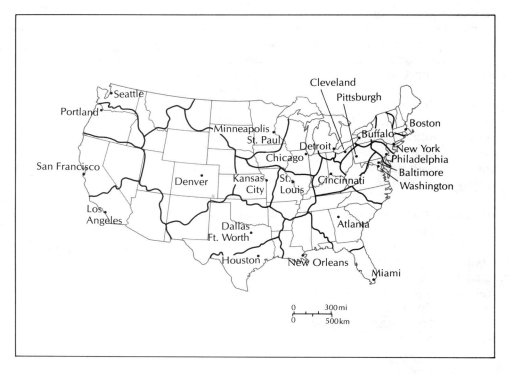

on their size and functional complexity. The first-order center is New York City, the national metropolis providing the widest range of specialized activities. There are six second-order centers in addition to New York (which is a second-order as well as a first-order center). These cities are Chicago, Boston, Philadelphia, Detroit, San Francisco, and Los Angeles. The second-order centers are regional metropoli for much of the U.S. market. Added to the seven second-order centers are seventeen metropolitan centers, for a total of twenty-four high-order central places. These cities are Baltimore, Washington, Atlanta, Miami, Buffalo, Cleveland, Cincinnati, Pittsburgh, New Orleans, St. Louis, Kansas City, Minneapolis-St. Paul, Dallas-Fort Worth, Houston, Denver, Seattle, and Portland.

Rank-Size Rule

In his study of the Upper Midwest, Borchert noted that the hierarchical structure of trade centers is reflected not only in their functional complexity, but also in their relative size, We can obtain an urban-size hierarchy by ranking centers according to their population size. The most well-known representation of this hierarchy is the *rank-size rule*, an empirical finding popularized by G. K. Zipf (1949). The rank-size rule states that if all settlements in an area are ranked in descending order of population size, then the population of the *r*th city is $1/r$ the size of the largest city's population. When plotted on double logarithmic graph paper, the relationship produces a straight, downward-sloping line with a gradient of forty-five degrees (Figure 9.27). The hypothetical rank-size distribution describes an urban system containing a few large metopoli, a large number of medium-sized cities, and a still larger number of smaller towns.

The urban-size hierarchy of the United States conforms closely to the rank-size rule (Figure 9.28). For example, New York, the first-ranking city, is nearly twice as large as Los Angeles, the second-ranking city, and nearly three times larger than Chicago, the third-ranking city. There are many countries, however, in which the population of the first or largest city is much greater than would be expected from the rank-size distribution, so that a condition of *primacy* exists.

Brian Berry (1961), an urban geographer, interpreted city-size distributions through a comparative study of thirty-seven countries (Table 9.4). Berry said that as countries become politically, economically, and socially more complex, they tend to develop straight-line rank-size distributions (Figure 9.29). In the early stages of national development, a simple primate pattern prevails. It is gradually transformed

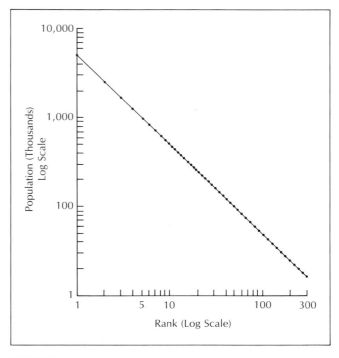

FIGURE 9.27
Rank-size rule: hypothetical size of the population of cities in relation to their ranking.

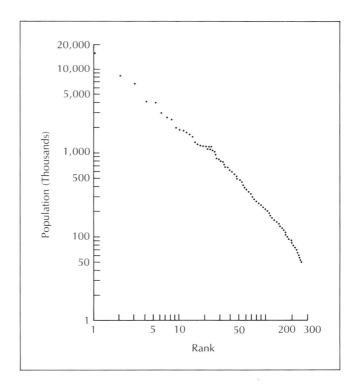

FIGURE 9.28
Rank-size distribution of urbanized areas in the United States, 1980. (Source: U.S. Census.)

274

CITIES AS SERVICE CENTERS

TABLE 9.4
City-size distributions in thirty-seven countries.

Countries with Rank-Size Pattern	Countries with Primate Pattern	Countries with Intermediate Patterns
Belgium	Austria	Australia
Brazil	Sri Lanka	Canada
China	Denmark	Ecuador
El Salvador	Dominican Republic	England and Wales
Finland	Greece	Malaya
India	Guatemala	New Zealand
Italy	Japan	Nicaragua
Korea	Mexico	Norway
Poland	Netherlands	Pakistan
South Africa	Peru	
Switzerland	Portugal	
United States	Spain	
West Germany	Sweden	
	Thailand	
	Uruguay	

SOURCE: Based on Berry, 1961.

into a rank-size distribution, which is the steady state of an urban-growth process.

To what extent is there a correspondence between central-place theory and the rank-size rule? The central-place hierarchy is based on the *functional size* of centers. Functional size is determined by the

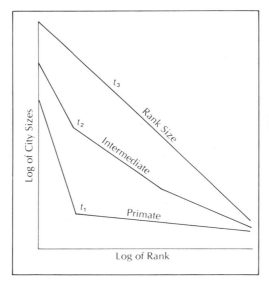

FIGURE 9.29
Idealized evolution of city size: distributions under increasing size through three time periods.

number and order of central functions offered by a place, and is tied to the role of settlement-forming functions. The total population of a place is a function of both settlement-forming and settlement-building functions. Two centers at the same level of the hierarchy; that is, equivalent in functional size, may differ somewhat with respect to population. The rank-size rule is based on the population of centers—not their functional size. Population size is reflected by a smooth rank-size curve; functional size produces a stepped hierarchy. The discrepancy between the stepped and continuous curves may also be a function of scale. Rank-size distributions apply to large economic areas, such as the United States, and the central-place model to their smaller subsystems, such as the Upper Midwest.

Structural Elements of the Central-Place Hierarchy

Much empirical research has focused on structural elements of the central-place hierarchy (Berry 1967). All the elements of central-place theory are structured or tied together logically and proportionately. To illustrate, let us graphically summarize four relationships: (1) the relationship between population size and functional units, (2) the relationship between population size and central functions, (3) the relationship between establishments and population size,

Rank-Size Distribution and Economic Development

Brian Berry (1961) found that rank-size distribution and economic development were not strongly related. Some underdeveloped countries have primate distributions. For example, Dar es Salaam, the largest city in Tanzania, has a population five times larger than the second largest city, Tanga. Some underdeveloped countries have log-normal distributions. India, China, and Nigeria, all with a substantial history of urbanization, are examples.

The kind of primacy of great significance in underdeveloped countries is not necessarily that of population. Political and economic domination and the concentration of communications and transactions are far more important. What is the reason for developmental primacy? Growth is concentrated in the major cities because there is little incentive to decentralize urban activities. The markedly hierarchical, authoritarian nature of political and social organization prevents developmental impulses from filtering down the urban hierarchy and diffusing their effects outward within urban fields.

and (4) the relationship between trade-area size and population density.

Population Size and Functional Units   The term *functional unit* refers to the provision of a central function each time it is offered. A graph of the

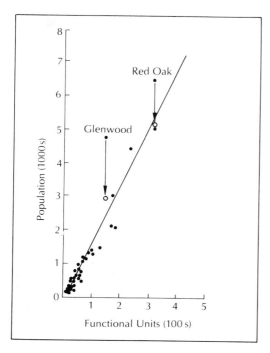

FIGURE 9.30
Relationship between population and functional units in southwestern Iowa. (Source: Based on Berry and Meyer, 1962.)

relationship between population and functional units in southwestern Iowa shows that most centers fall close to the regression line, which is the straight line fitting the data (Figure 9.30). Two centers, Red Oak and Glenwood, however, have larger populations than one would expect, given the number of functional units in each. These discrepancies can be explained by the relatively large settlement-building functions of the centers. When the population of each town that is supported by these noncentral functions is subtracted from the centers' total populations, the number of people supported by settlement-forming functions can be estimated. These estimates fit the regression line quite well.

Population Size and Central Functions   The term *central function* is used to describe a good or service offered by a central place. There is a curvilinear or log-linear relationship between population size and the number of central functions performed by centers (Figure 9.31). This relationship indicates that the population of a central place is a function of the total number of business types offered. Again, there are deviations from the norm. Some settlements that have more central functions than expected may be tourist centers, such as Las Vegas or Reno, Nevada, where excess central functions are supported by transient populations. Other settlements have larger populations than expected, which is usually indicative of settlement-building functions of the centers.

Establishments and Population Size   The term *establishment* connotes ownership and control. In-

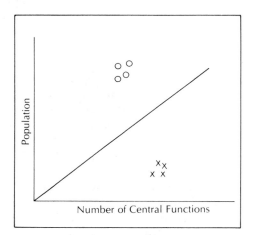

FIGURE 9.31
Anomalies and the relationship between central functions and population.

creases in the number of establishments are proportional to increases in center sizes (Figure 9.32). By contrast, the population/functional-unit and population/central-function relationships are not proportional—an observation that raises the question of how centers meet increases in demand brought about by population changes. Existing establishments may expand, new establishments of the same functional type may be added, or some combination of the two responses may occur. Empirical evidence as revealed in the graph indicates that increasing the number of establishments tends to occur more often—particularly in the case of lower order functions and centers.

Trade-Area Size and Population Density There is a strong tendency for trade-area size to adjust to variations in population density (Berry and Meyer 1962) (Figure 9.33). The forty-five degree line in the figure indicates constant population density. Each level of center is arrayed along a line with a slope greater than forty-five degrees. Thus, variations in trade-area size are greater than variations in total population influenced by central places, suggesting density adjustment.

The central-place hierarchy is sensitive to local variations in population density, but even more to regional variations. If we examine the relationship between trade-area sizes and total population serviced by central places along a traverse from the densely settled area of Chicago, through the corn and dairylands of Illinois, Wisconsin, Iowa, and Minnesota, on to the wheatlands of the Dakotas, and into the rangelands of Montana, we discover remarkable regularities. Instead of what appears as a random scatter of settlements on the map, we find a highly regular set of relationships (Figure 9.34). In the urban areas near Chicago, population densities are high, trade areas are small, and numbers of people served, large. As we move through the suburban areas and across the Corn Belt to the wheatlands and rangelands, popula-

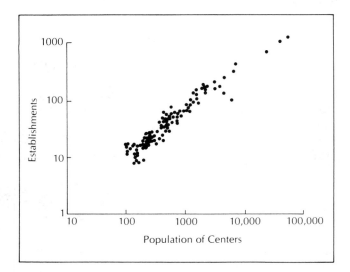

FIGURE 9.32
Relationship between establishments and population of centers.

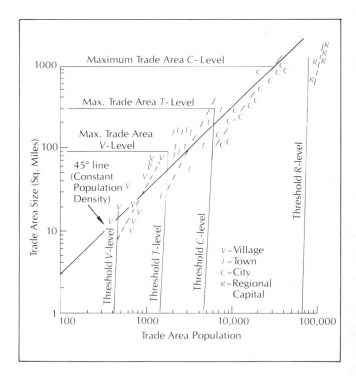

FIGURE 9.33
Density adjustment (southwestern Iowa). (Source: Based on Berry and Meyer, 1962.)

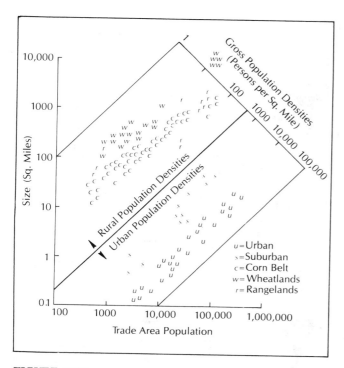

FIGURE 9.34
Density adjustment: large regional variations in population density. (Source: Berry and Meyer, 1962.)

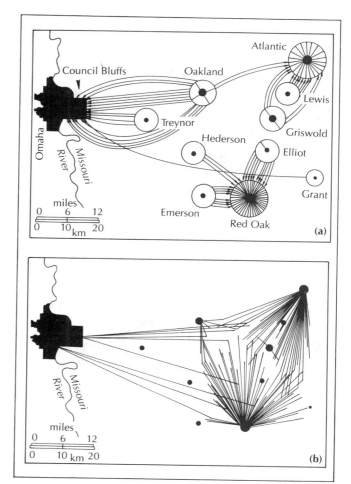

FIGURE 9.35
Purchase movements of (a) urban and (b) rural consumers for clothing in southwestern Iowa. (Source: Berry and Meyer, 1962.)

tion densities decline, but the regular relationship between the trade area and population served is maintained.

Consumer Travel as a Mirror of the Hierarchy

A central-place system depends on consistent consumer behavior. Christaller's theory of central places postulates that consumers behave predictably in that they always will obtain goods and services from the nearest possible center. In reality, however, this may not be the case.

Figures 9.35 through 9.37 show the primary purchase movements of both rural and urban consumers for three different goods in southwestern Iowa. Clothing is the highest level good (city-level) followed by dry cleaning (town-level). Groceries are the lowest level function (village-level). Consumers must consider the order of a good because it limits the number of possible purchase points. Within the framework of where goods are actually offered, however, consumers have some flexibility as to where they make their purchases. They will generally go to the nearest place to obtain *convenience goods*. For *shopping goods*, however, they will often travel to higher

level centers, even if these goods can be obtained locally.

The maps of travel patterns in southwestern Iowa do not replicate the geometrical precision of the central-place model. This is because the normative constraints of the model do not actually exist. Central-place theory can help us better understand and predict spatial patterns of consumer behavior. But we must bear in mind that people are not economic optimizers, although they do adhere to the principle of distance minimization to a limited extent.

CROSS-CULTURAL PATTERNS

So far our discussion has focused on cities as service centers in specialized societies; however, we have not yet considered how cultural differences affect local

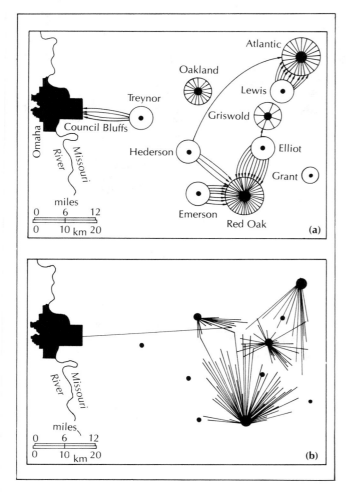

FIGURE 9.36
Purchase movements of (a) urban and (b) rural consumers for dry cleaning in southwestern Iowa. (Source: Berry and Meyer, 1962.)

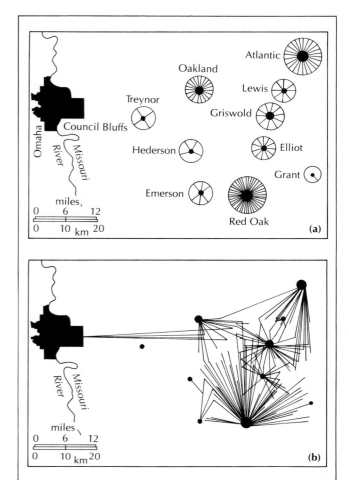

FIGURE 9.37
Purchase movements of (a) urban and (b) rural consumers for foodstuffs in southwestern Iowa. (Source: Berry and Meyer 1962.)

trade. And what of the situation in societies where specialization is less advanced? How do peasant societies organize their market activities? In seeking answers to these questions, we come to appreciate the rich variety of marketing and distribution systems throughout the world.

Cultural Differences in Consumer Travel

A study by Robert Murdie (1965) of an area in Ontario inhabited by both Old Order Mennonites and "modern" Candians provides an example of how cultural factors affect the geography of retailing and services in a dominantly specialized society. Mennonites use modern methods to manage their farms' businesses. But in dress, domestic consumption, and travel, they cling to a lifestyle that existed two hundred years ago.

Homemade clothes and the horse and buggy for transportation prevail. Few goods are demanded.

When Mennonites behave like "modern" Canadians, both groups use the set of central places in the area in much the same way; for example, Mennonites and "modern" Canadians exhibit similar consumer behavior in their banking transactions (Figure 9.38). However, when the traditional beliefs of the Mennonites come into play, two distinct types of behavior with regard to central places become evident. Take for example clothing purchased by "modern" Canadians and yard goods purchased by Mennonites (Figure 9.39). The difference in mode of transportation is one factor crucial to the two types of consumer behavior. "Modern" Canadians demand variety and go for it; hence, the maximum distance they travel to purchase clothing is related to center size. On the other hand,

FIGURE 9.38
Banks used by (a) "modern" Canadians and (b) Old Order Mennonites in an area of Ontario. (Source: Based on Murdie, 1965.)

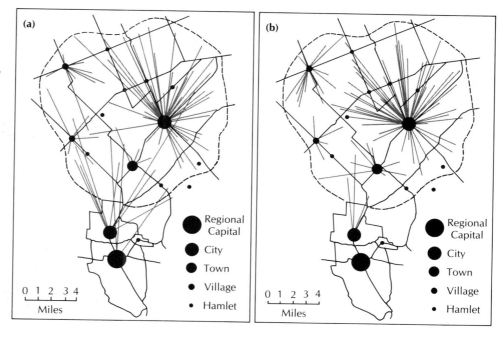

the Mennonites purchase only a limited variety of yard goods and are restricted by the use of the horse and buggy; hence, the maximum distance they travel does not vary with center size.

Periodic Markets

The majority of people in underdeveloped countries do not participate fully in the network of enterprises enjoined in the modern urban hierarchy. Rather than being involved in the production of goods for world markets, for the most part they subsist on what they can grow—and trade. Their local transactions often take place at small rural markets, which often operate on a periodic rather than a permanent basis. The market is likely to be open only every few days on a regular basis because its size is limited by the level of transport technology and the aggregate demand for goods is insufficient to support permanent shops. In this system, several places in a region profit from a

FIGURE 9.39
Towns visited for purchase of (a) clothing and (b) yard goods by "modern" Canadians and Mennonites. (Source: Based on Murdie, 1965.)

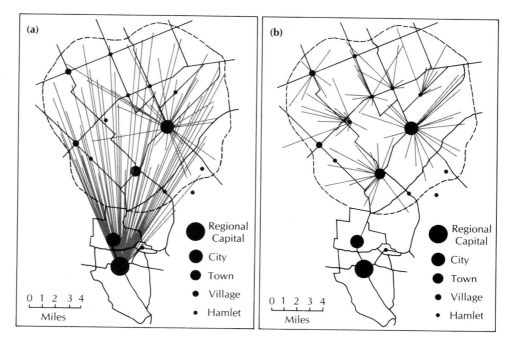

day's trade and each benefits from its participation in the wider network of interaction. People come to these periodic markets on foot, on bicycles, on the backs of their animals, or by whatever other means are available. Periodic markets are a feature of Southeast Asia, China, India, Middle and South America, and across large parts of Africa.

G. William Skinner, in a 1964 study, described periodic marketing systems of traditional rural China. In one system based on the lunar month (*hsün*), merchants moved between the central market and a pair of standard markets in a ten-day cycle divided into units of three: the central market (day 1), first standard (2), second standard (3), central (4), first standard (5), second standard (6), central (7), first standard (8), second standard (9), and central on day 10, when no business was transacted (Figure 9.40). The three-per-*hsün* cycle illustrates the periodicities of a large number of market centers of different levels, and it resembles a Christaller-type *K*-equals-four hierarchy.

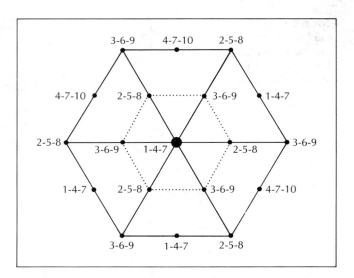

FIGURE 9.40

Periodicity of markets in a traditional Chinese three-per-*hsün* cycle. (Source: Based on Skinner, 1964.)

At Po in southern Burkina Faso, the periodic market occurs on a four-day cycle. (Source: James Pickerell for IDA.)

Elsewhere in the world other cycles predominate: two-per-*hsün* cycles are common in Korea. Seven-day cycles occur in Andean Columbia (Symanski 1971). In Africa, the market week varies from a three-day to a seven-day week. The three-day, four-day, five-day, and six-day weeks stem from ethnic differences, and the seven-day week is a consequence of calendar changes introduced by Islam into Africa.

Periodic markets, then, form an interlocking network of exchange places. As each market in the network gets its turn, it will be close enough to one part of the area so that people in the vicinity can walk to it, carrying what they wish to sell or trade. The staggered pattern of local markets permits a small volume of produce to move through the market chain to larger, regional wholesaling markets where shipments are collected for interregional or perhaps even international trade. What is traded depends on the market's location. For example, in West Africa's savanna zone, sorghum, millet, and shea-butter predominate. Further south, in the forest zone, yams, cassava, corn, and palm oil change hands. And in the south, too, there are some imported manufactured goods, especially in markets near the relatively prosperous cocoa, coffee, rubber, and palm oil areas. But wherever the market, the quantities traded are small—a bowl of rice, a bundle of firewood—and their value is low.

The total amount of goods traded through the periodic marketplace, however, is tremendous; but nobody has any idea of the volume or the value of goods that are actually distributed (Bohannan and

Curtin 1971, p. 162). The task of examining indigenous marketing systems has been largely neglected, primarily in the belief that marketing systems to serve cultivators, distributors, and consumers are economically inefficient and exploitative. According to *The Marketing Challenge* (USDA 1970) this belief is erroneous, an opinion shared by Earl Scott (1972), whose research in Nigeria indicated that indigenous marketing systems can promote development. By contrast, Linda Greenow and Vicky Muñiz (1988) argued that stimulating market trade as it is currently organized is unlikely to encourage development. In their Peruvian study, they showed that market selling for most traders is a means of survival. "Traders, most of whom are women, rarely develop stable or growing businesses that support them and their families over a long run" (p. 416).

In general, periodic markets mainly serve people who live near the subsistence level. Market cycles are determined either by "natural" events, using the motions of the heavenly bodies, or they are "artificial," without reference to natural cycles. "Artificial" cycles dominate today, with the periodicity of the markets influenced by population density. The more people in an area, the greater the aggregate demand, and the greater the frequency with which a market can operate. Eventually, the demand may be sufficient for a market to become continuous and permanent. Periodic markets are, therefore, logically related to the patterns of market centers observed in complex economies.

Just as the periodicity and types of commodity traded vary culturally, so do the locations of indigenous markets. In West Africa, rural populations live away from market sites, and the hierarchy of rural settlements is unrelated to the hierarchy of markets. In other regions, settlements and periodic markets may coincide. An understanding of periodic market sites requires an appreciation of local culture.

PLANNING USES OF CENTRAL-PLACE THEORY

Central-place concepts, confirmed by the empirical evidence, have been used for planning purposes. They were used to establish a hierarchy of market centers on the Dutch polders and to design a new system of settlements on the Lakhish plain in Israel. They were also used to guide the development of the planned suburban community of Park Forest, Illinois. Residential areas were organized into neighborhoods, each served by a local business center, and one large shopping center was established for the whole community with adjacent land set aside for a village hall,

police and fire departments. Analysis of the distribution of shopping centers and their service areas was an important component of the administrative reorganization of Greater London. These examples, cited by Berry (1967) are "symbolic of the practical uses of the central-place idea by regional and city planners for locating retail business, business centers, and market towns, or regionalizing an area" (p. 132).

Since the widespread adoption of the spatial organization theme in the 1960s, geographers have devoted a great deal of attention to the practical uses of the central-place concept. Making use of the complex variable, accessibility, they have analyzed and planned public and private service facilities. Geographers have also been called upon to give advice on questions of planning spatial patterns and structures in developed and underdeveloped countries.

The Importance of Accessibility

Under the title "Being Close to Things and People," Peter Gould (1985, pp. 77–88) emphasized that in a great deal of geographical planning and consulting, questions of accessibility are very close to the surface. He illustrated the idea of accessibility with the practical application of where to locate a new service facility. Suppose you are on a team of geographical consultants working in a poor country where there are only enough resources to build a new school to serve a rather large rural area. (You can substitute a clinic, family-planning center, or any other service, since the nature of the problem remains the same.) Obviously, you need to know where the villages are and how many school children (or people to be served) are in each village. Villages *A* to *D* are close to one another, but *E*, with fifty-two school-age children, is more remote. Where will you build the school? What is the most accessible location for the new school?

To find out, you can build a simple analog computer, the Varignon frame (Figure 9.41). Take a map of the area and glue it to a sheet of plywood. Then at each village drill a hole and thread a smooth string through it. Next, tie the strings together on top of the map, and underneath attach weights proportional to the number of children in each village. If the knot represents the school, then we can think of each village tugging the school toward it with a force equal to the number of children it will serve. Where the knot ends up is the best location; that is, the one that minimizes the aggregate distance children have to travel to school and back. If children are to travel to school by bus, this location could save the school district a good deal of money in fuel costs.

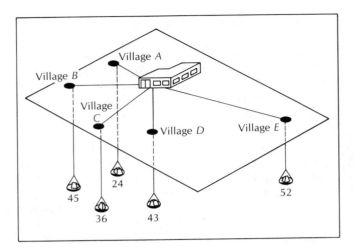

FIGURE 9.41
The best location for a school. (Source: Based on Gould, 1985, p. 80.)

The most efficient location for a new facility, however, is unlikely to be the most fair location from the standpoint of social justice. In our school example, the children in villages A to D would have nothing to complain about. But what about those living at E—they would have a long journey to school. Should we sacrifice efficiency for equity and build the school a bit closer to E? The question of equity, which arises whenever we deal with solutions to problems involving people, derives from the ideas of social justice (Harvey 1973). Viewed in its geographical context, social justice is equated with territorial justice, which expresses a concern for a fair allocation of resources.

The simple analog computer can solve the problem of the best location for a single facility, but in searching for and evaluating all the possibilities in locating multiple facilities, high-speed computers are necessary. Geographers have used computers to find, for example, the best location for hospitals in Sweden (Godlund 1961) and administrative systems in southern Ontario (Goodchild and Massam 1969).

Accessibility is a key to measuring the welfare function of a consumer service. If there are variations in the degree to which a service is available to consumers, then the welfare function of the service is not being fully utilized. In this view, the quality of life for consumers is affected to a degree by access to a "basket" of social goods—a doctor, a dentist, a public library (Smith 1977).

No matter how hard geographers try, exact territorial equality in the provision of services can never be realized. For one thing, there will always be a lag between demand and supply. There is considerable geographical and historical inertia in the loca-

tional distribution of services that leads to overprovision in some places and underprovision in other places.

Streamlining Central-Place Systems in Underdeveloped Countries

In many underdeveloped countries, investment is concentrated in large cities with good transport links and other infrastructural facilities. Is this concentration fair? Should policies be introduced to bring about a Christaller-type pattern of central places to ensure a more equitable distribution of economic development?

Most conservative geographers argue that no intervention is required in the process of spatial organization. Policies intended to reduce the spatial concentration of investment would lead to a less efficient location pattern for economic activities. Many activities must locate in the big city in order to compete with foreign producers. Decentralization policies might scare off foreign investments and result in a loss of jobs. Moreover, decentralization for the sake of interregional equity is costly. The building of roads and railroads, as well as the provision and maintenance of other infrastructural facilities, would cost more than the majority of underdeveloped countries could afford. First and foremost in the development process, conservatives advocate attracting firms and jobs. At least in the early stages, the disadvantage of regional disparities is of secondary importance.

Liberals disagree with this view. They believe that urban and regional planning must ensure development that is more even. They cite increasing regional and rural-urban disparities to emphasize that change must be fostered through the role of urban centers as focal points in the diffusion of innovations. Identification of an urban hierarchy makes possible the evaluation of the system within which change is to take place. The development of a proper hierarchy of centers enables rational planning of facilities to proceed, without waste, and at the correct scales. Liberals believe that upgrading old centers or establishing new ones in peripheral areas can be a powerful stimulus to the development of surrounding areas, setting the pace for their progress.

Radicals have a different spatial image of development patterns in underdeveloped countries. Considering the position of underdeveloped countries in the international economic system, they question conservative and liberal arguments about the nature of economic and social change. Central-place systems in underdeveloped countries form part of the world network of cities. As such, villages, towns, and cities are centers of domination. In the service of international capitalism, regional and national hinterlands are subjected to economic "satellitization" and exploitation. Given that the structure of the capitalist urban system is conditioned by international influence and manipulation, radicals call for revolutionary institutional reform as a prerequisite to regional planning. Otherwise, we are faced with "a very real and present danger of our theories of spatial organization becoming tools for the frustration of social change" (Harvey 1972, p. 2).

WORLD CITIES

To this point, we have considered cities as service centers at the national and regional levels. Now let us shift our attention to the international level, where cities function as centers of international business. The new international division of labor is forging cities of the world into a composite system.

Industrial Restructuring and the Urban Hierarchy

The *industrial restructuring* that started to take place in the 1960s is changing the global urban hierarchy. The process of restructuring involves the movement of industrial plants from developed to underdeveloped areas within or between countries; the closure of plants in older, industrialized centers, as in the American Rust Belt; and the technological improvement of industry to increase productivity. Forces behind restructuring include the need for multinationals to develop strategies to locate new markets and to organize world-scale production more profitably, the national policies of developed countries to improve their future international competitive position, and the national policies of underdeveloped countries to attract subsidiaries of multinationals. These multinational strategies and governmental policies have contributed to major shifts in employment and trade. The greatest impacts have been felt in the urban centers of developed countries and in the larger cities of underdeveloped countries.

The U.S. Urban Hierarchy

Before industrial restructuring affected the organization of the labor process and the location of industry, the "metropolis-and-region" pattern of the United States was a fairly accurate reflection of the urban hierarchy. Each regional center—a Minneapolis-St. Paul, a Miami, or a Cleveland—was an important center of corporate services. For example, there were

a large number of corporate law firms in Cleveland to complement that city's corporations. Major accounting firms were based in New York and Chicago. Important regional banks were a feature of nearly all centers of corporate head offices.

By the 1970s, the "metropolis-and-region" network of corporate head offices and corporate services had expanded, but international business activity had become much more important. International decision making by major firms was concentrated in two cities, New York and San Francisco (Cohen 1981, p. 305). Cities that were important in the earlier, national-oriented phase of the economy began to lose ground to these *global cities*. Jobs connected with international operations did not develop as extensively in places like St. Louis and Boston as they did in New York and San Francisco.

In conjunction with the growth of international operations, advanced corporate services—banks, law firms, accounting firms, and management firms—expanded their international presence in the 1970s. Similarly, these service activities developed strongly only in a handful of centers. Few banks with international expertise could be found in places other than New York, San Francisco, and Chicago. Firms with international legal expertise were mostly confined to New York, Los Angeles, and Washington D.C. (Cohen 1981, p. 301).

In the 1980s, international activities remained concentrated. Los Angeles and Chicago joined New York and San Francisco as top-level international business and banking centers. International activities of firms headquartered outside these cities became increasingly tied to financial institutions and corporate services located within them. In the 1990s, it is expected that only a few additional cities will achieve international status, and that New York and Los Angeles will remain the predominant American global cities.

The rise of Los Angeles from a regional metropolis in the 1960s to a global center of corporate headquarters, financial management, and trade in the 1980s has been remarkable. The Pacific Rim city has become an epicenter of global capital. The transformation of Los Angeles was accompanied by selective deindustrialization and reindustrialization. A growing cluster of technologically skilled and specialized occupations has been complemented by a rapid expansion of low-skill workers fed from the recycling of labor out of declining heavy industry and by a massive influence of Third World immigrants and part-time workers (Soja, Morales, and Wolff 1987, pp. 170–71). Sprawling, low-density Los Angeles symbolizes the process of urban restructuring: it combines elements of Sunbelt expansion, Detroit-like decline,

At the southern tip of Manhattan soar the skyscrapers of the financial district, symbolic of New York City's role as a global city. New York is the nation's preeminent international center for business decision making and corporate services. Firms headquartered in New York account for about 40 percent of foreign sales of Fortune 500 companies. Over 50 percent of foreign bank deposits in the United States are in New York banks. (Source: N.Y. Convention and Visitors Bureau.)

and free-trade zone exploitation. In sharp contrast to Los Angeles, arguably one of the world's most successful cities of reconstituted capitalism, Cleveland, which lost many blue-collar jobs because of plant closures, layoffs, and capital mobility, has been unable to attract many international business operations to cushion its economic decline. Although Cleveland will never become a global city, it may boom like Buffalo and evidence economic revival in the 1990s because of the 1988 free-trade agreement between the United States and Canada.

The International Urban Hierarchy

The new hierarchy of world cities has elements in common with the changing hierarchy of U.S. cities. In the 1950s and 1960s we could use the cities identified by British geographer Peter Hall (1971) to examine the world hierarchy. Hall's world cities included the traditional large national and political centers—London, Paris, Randstad Holland, Rhine-Ruhr, Tokyo, and New York. These places were centers of finance and corporate services.

Starting in the 1970s, multinational business and international finance began to play a more important role in the world economy. This trend was accompanied by a decline of traditional national and regional centers where a high proportion of jobs were tied to old basic industries (e.g., coal mining, iron and steel, and shipbuilding) and where concentrations of international corporations were lacking. Examples include the British cities of Glasgow, Manchester, and Liverpool. Meanwhile, cities predominant as world centers of corporations and finance became still more important. They include some of the centers identified by Hall—London, Tokyo, and New York—but also others, such as Los Angeles, San Francisco, Chicago, Osaka, Frankfurt, and Zurich.

The new world hierarchy of international business and banking reflects a new division of labor between centers of corporate control and more nationally oriented cities. In Europe, such cities as Paris, Randstad Holland, and Rhine-Ruhr, which are more nationally oriented than London or Frankfurt, consequently play a less significant role in the international network of corporate and financial activities.

Beyond the developed world there are no world centers of corporate decision making and control. Singapore and Hong Kong are major international financial centers, but they are more involved in moving and mobilizing financial resources than in decision-making activities.

As previously mentioned, the new international urban hierarchy has had its strongest impact on the national and regional centers of developed countries and on the larger cities of underdeveloped countries. In the developed world, the concentration of corporate decision making in the global cities has been draining decision-making activities from the traditional national and regional centers—a trend that is fostering uneven urban and regional development. For example, in Britain there is a widening gulf between the prosperous "Sunbelt," a swath southeast of a line between Bristol and Cambridge—the outer-outer London metropolitan area—and the "rest." In the underdeveloped world, multinationals, aided by international banks, are establishing more and more subsidiaries in the large cities. Rapid industrialization of parts of the Third World has resulted in a massive flow of migrants to the main cities where, at best, they find menial jobs in low-wage industries. Will cities in developed and underdeveloped countries become centers of social and political turmoil in response to industrial restructuring efforts? Or will they recover from the current capitalist crisis? We will see the outcome in the 1990s, and it will depend on decisions that are made in the office towers of the predominant world cities—London, Tokyo, New York, Los Angeles.

SUMMARY

In this chapter we examined the assumptions, content, limitations, and extentions of classical central-place theory, concentrating first on cities as service centers at the national or regional level and ending with examples of urban hierarchies at the international level.

Classical central-place theory relies on three concepts to explain spatial equilibrium: *threshold, range,* and *hierarchy.* Central-place activities are arranged in a hierarchy according to the functions they

perform. High-order places bind together regions of a national market-exchange economy. Within each metropolitan trade region we find a chain of low-order centers—smaller cities, towns, villages, and hamlets. These centers function as markets for the distribution of goods and services.

The assumptions on which classical central-place theory is based are unrealistic. Nowhere do we find people spread evenly across space. Resources are never the same everywhere. And landscapes are always in a state of disequilibrium. We discussed how actual conditions distort and transform theoretical networks of central places. Nonetheless, one of the strengths of a good scientific theory is that it can be modified to more closely fit reality by relaxing its assumptions. For example, we pointed to several empirical studies conducted by geographers in different areas that reveal systematic relationships between the size of towns, their distance from one another, the trade areas they serve, and densities of their surrounding populations. These empirical regularities make the central-place concept valuable for planning purposes. It has proven useful in deciding where to locate educational and medical facilities, as well as shopping centers. It has been used to recommend change in the spatial pattern of settlements.

To some geographers, however, the application of central-place theory, as well as other theories of spatial organization, is troublesome. British geographer David Harvey (1972) feared that our theories of spatial organization may well be tools for the frustration of social change. Edward Relph (1976) pointed out that much physical and social planning is divorced from places as we know and experience them in our daily lives. He argued that when we reduce places to points or areas, with their most important quality being (profitable) development potential, we are taking an approach that rationalizes draining wetlands for the construction of new regional shopping centers or displacing single-family residences with high-rise office buildings.

A major attribute of central-place theory is that it helps us understand the emergence of an *integrated hierarchy of cities* of different functions and sizes. A weakness is that it fails to explain the underlying forces that control the development of such hierarchies. The urban hierarchy is an important concept that geographers are trying to better understand, particularly because it is instrumental in the development of international capitalism. The consequences of the emergence of a few *global cities*—London, Tokyo, New York, Los Angeles—for decision making and corporate strategy formulation are far-reaching for people in both developed and underdeveloped countries.

KEY TERMS

administrative principle

breakpoint model

central function

central place

convenience good

establishment

functional size

functional unit

global city

hierarchy

law of retail gravitation

linear market

marketing principle

mercantile model

periodic market

range

rank-size rule

settlement-building function

settlement-forming function

settlement-serving function

shopping good

threshold

trade area

traffic principle

SUGGESTED READINGS

Berry, B. J. L. 1967. *Geography of Market Centers and Retail Distribution.* Englewood Cliffs, NJ: Prentice-Hall.

Christaller, W. 1966. *The Central Places of Southern Germany.* Translated by C. W. Baskin. Englewood Cliffs, NJ: Prentice-Hall.

Daniels, P. W. 1985. *Service Industries: A Geographical Appraisal.* New York: Methuen.

Dickinson, R. E. 1964. *City and Region.* London: Routledge and Kegan Paul.

Gore, C. 1984. *Regions in Question: Space, Development Theory and Regional Policy.* New York: Methuen.

Isard, W. 1956. *Location and Space-Economy.* New York: John Wiley.

Johnson, E. A. J. 1970. *The Organization of Space in Developing Countries.* Cambridge, MA: Harvard University Press.

Lösch, A. 1954. *The Economics of Location.* Translated by W. W. Woglom and W. F. Stolper. New Haven, CT: Yale University Press.

Vance, J. E. 1970. *The Merchant's World: The Geography of Wholesaling.* Englewood Cliffs, NJ: Prentice-Hall.

Zipf, G. K. 1949. *Human Behavior and the Principle of Least Effort.* Reading, MA: Addison-Wesley.

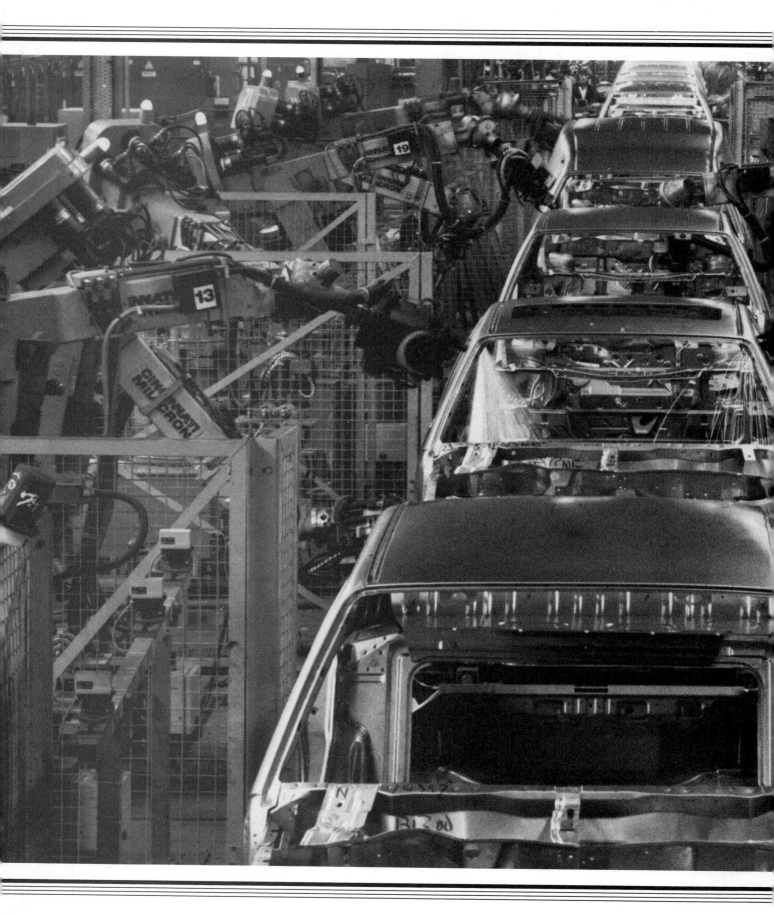

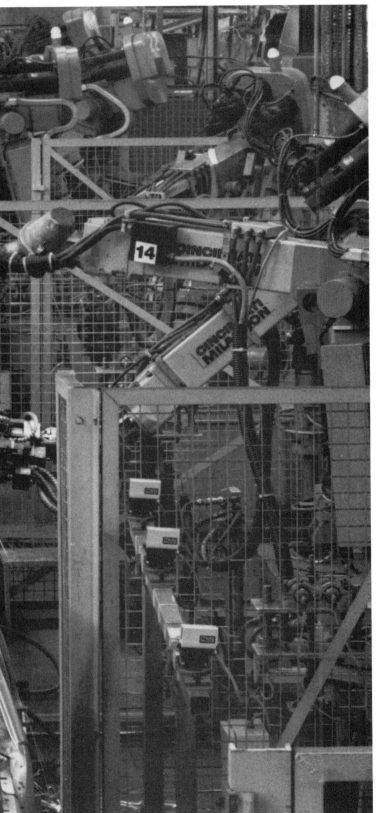

10
INDUSTRIAL LOCATION: FIRMS

OBJECTIVES

- ☐ To consider industrial location in terms of business and management decision making
- ☐ To present the basic elements of industrial location theory
- ☐ To recognize the limitations of industrial location theory
- ☐ To trace the rise of large corporations
- ☐ To show the relationship between large and small firms
- ☐ To explain why and how firms grow
- ☐ To examine the internal geography of corporate systems
- ☐ To describe the industry life-cycle and Kondratieff long-wave models of industrial evolution

A General Motors' robotic welding line. (Source: General Motors Corporation.)

This chapter and the next deal with a crucial activity—manufacturing. To manufacture is to make things—to transform raw materials, under humanly created conditions and in controlled environments, into goods that satisfy our needs and wants. Why is manufacturing so important? Not only does it produce goods that sustain human life, it also improves our standard of living, provides employment, and generates economic growth. It has continued to play this developmental role at least since the industrial revolution that began in England in the late eighteenth century.

Geographers approach the study of manufacturing from a viewpoint that emphasizes either firms or places. When firms are of primary significance, interest centers on the locational choices that firms make. And when areas are emphasized, attention focuses on the nature of industries in a city, region, or country. In this chapter we will concentrate on firms; in Chapter 11 we will examine the changing geography of industrial areas.

Whether they are considering firms or areas, geographers can adopt a variety of theoretical frameworks for interpreting industrial location. These frameworks include normative industrial location theory, the behavioral approach, and the Marxist or structural perspective. Normative industrial location theory derives from classical economics and shares its conservative ideology. It uses abstract models to search for best or optimal locations. The behavioral approach focuses on the decision-making process. Rather than considering how decisions should be made, it examines how decisions are actually made. This liberal and more practical approach recognizes the possibility of suboptimal behavior. The Marxist or structural perspective is an all-encompassing radical approach that "permits industrial location to be analyzed as an integral part of the totality of economic, social, and political processes" (Smith 1981, p. 142). It challenges the ideology of normative and behavioral industrial geography which approaches the question of location from a managerial perspective. The structural approach calls for "a greater awareness of the social implications of shifts in industrial activity . . . and [of] how inequalities are perpetuated by the functioning of the labor market and managerial hiring practices" (Marshall 1982, pp. 675–76).

The various frameworks not only reflect the views of the geographers who use them, they also reflect changes in the nature of manufacturing, itself. Normative industrial location theory, which prevailed until the 1960s, was formulated in the early part of the twentieth century when most manufacturing businesses were single-plant firms and when basic heavy industry was in the vanguard of industrial progress. The behavioral approach came to the fore in the 1960s when rapid economic growth in developed countries provoked an increase of academic and political interest in the practice of decision making. At first, attention centered on the decision-making behavior of single-plant firms; however, this focus became too narrow with the rise of large enterprises. The late 1960s and 1970s witnessed an upsurge of interest in the geography of large corporations, which geographer Robert McNee (1960) had earlier called the "geography of enterprise." Meanwhile, the world economic crisis, affecting the location of industry, could no longer be ignored. Geographers devoted attention to the role of manufacturing in regional development theory and planning (Pred 1977) and to radical interpretations of industrial location change (Massey and Meegan 1978; Massey 1984). By the late 1980s, few geographers were involved in the development of normative industrial location theory, but many were involved in Marxist analyses of industrial restructuring—selective deindustrialization and reindustrialization in developed countries and industrial revolution in parts of the Third World.

This chapter, which emphasizes normative and behavioral approaches, begins with an extended discussion of the general circumstances that influence industrial locations of single-plant firms. Although most location factors apply whether or not a firm is a single plant, individual plants are increasingly part of larger enterprises. In fact, one of the fundamental revolutions in the global structure of manufacturing is the role played by multiproduct, multiplant, multinational operations. Accordingly, a section of the chapter is devoted to the spatial behavior of large industrial enterprises. Just as companies evolve, so do industries. Thus, the final section considers the evolution of industries.

THE NATURE OF MANUFACTURING

Manufacturing involves three distinct phases: gathering together the raw materials at a plant, reworking and combining of the raw materials to produce a finished product, and marketing the finished product. These phases are called *assembly*, *production*, and *distribution*, respectively. The assembly phase and the distribution phase both require movement. Normative industrial location theory attempts to identify those plant locations that will minimize the transport costs of raw material gathering and finished-product distribution. Changing the form of a raw material involves land, labor, capital, and management—production factors that vary widely in cost from place to place. All three steps of the manufacturing process, then, have a spatial or locational dimension.

Changing the form of a raw material increases its utility or value. Flour milled from wheat is more valuable than raw grain. Bread, in turn, is worth more than flour. This increase in labor power is termed *value added by manufacturing*. Value added by manufacturing as a percentage of total value of shipments is quite low in an industry engaged in the initial processing of a raw material. For example, turning sugar beets into sugar yields a value added of about 30 percent. By contrast, changing a few ounces of steel and glass into a watch yields a high value added— over 60 percent. The cost of labor, or the availability of skills, plays an important role in high-value-added manufacturing; the cost of raw materials is the key variable in others. The relative importance of factors of production is called *orientation*. Terms such as "raw-material-oriented" and "market-oriented" are used frequently by geographers to specify the key variable for a given industry. The production orientation of industries affects geographical patterns of industrial locations and concentrations.

UNEVEN DISTRIBUTION OF RAW MATERIALS

Von Thünen's model of agricultural production assumed an even distribution of resources. Points of manufacturing (cities) would develop even if all resources were ubiquitous. Manufacturing would operate at selected points and incur only two kinds of costs: production costs, involving interrelationships among other factors of production and demand, and distribution costs in getting the finished product to dispersed markets.

But in reality resources are not evenly distributed across space—especially those raw materials required for basic heavy manufacturing. Even those industries that utilize manufactured goods as their raw material face an uneven distribution of inputs. Therefore, manufacturing involves a third kind of cost: *assembly costs*—the price that must be paid to bring raw materials together from diverse locations to a plant. Assembly costs are the main concern of classical industrial location theory.

THE SIMPLE WEBERIAN MODEL: ASSEMBLY COSTS

Classical industrial location theory is founded on the work of Alfred Weber (1909), a German economist. Weber was, of course, influenced by the period in which he wrote. His model must therefore be evaluated taking account of the considerable changes in manufacturing industry since the early twentieth century. Nonetheless, it was Weber who taught geographers to think about the distinction between material- and market-oriented industries.

Weber attempted to determine the patterns of manufacturing that would develop in a world of numerous, competitive, single-plant firms given a certain set of normative constraints. He began by assuming that transport costs are a linear function of distance. He required that producers, who face neither risk nor uncertainty, choose optimal locations. He also implied that the demand for a product is infinite at a given price. Producers could sell as many units as they produced at a fixed price. They could sell none at a higher price, and charging a lower price would not affect the total demand for the product. The producer's strategy was therefore to assemble the product at the lowest possible cost, thus maximizing revenue. Weber's system is often called a "least-cost" approach, because he assumed that such locations are optimal.

Weber's theory is also a "general theory"; it can be applied to all types of industries. He was concerned with identifying "those forces which operate as economic causes of location," represented in each case by savings in cost as a result of producing in one place rather than in another place (Weber 1929, pp. 17–18). The forces Weber sought to identify are called *location factors*. Weber also distinguished between "general" factors, which apply to all industries (transport costs, labor, and rent), and "special" factors, which operate only in a specific industry. General and special factors are further subdivided into "regional" and "local" forces. *Regional forces*, which determine the general locational framework of manufacturing, include transport and labor costs. According to Weber, regional forces result from spatial variations of raw material and labor costs. *Local forces*, on the other hand, cause the pattern of manufacturing to deviate from the optimal patterns produced by regional forces alone. They tend to be "economic" in origin; for example, economies of scale and the high rent brought about by competition.

Transportation sets the general regional pattern of manufacturing. This pattern is in turn distorted by

Location Factors

L ocation factors are forces that influence industrial location. They may be separated into two general types: those relating to the friction of distance and those relating to the characteristics of areas. Friction-of-distance variables measure the costs of moving materials or products across space. These costs may be measured in terms of kilometers, money, or time— or, psychologically, by ease or convenience. The second category is concerned with such variables as labor, agglomeration, power, water, and the quality of life.

Normative industrial location theory has traditionally emphasized friction-of-distance variables. Indeed, transport is regarded as the all-important "general" location factor. Without improved means of communications, industries could not produce for export from their own districts. On the other hand, transport developments tend to weaken some of the factors conducive to localization.

Because of transport improvements, the attributes-of-area variables are of increasing importance for most plant locations—especially for firms dealing in high-technology products. These firms produce high-value-added components for which transport costs per unit of value are low. Their inputs come from a variety of sources and locations, and their markets tend to be scattered.

The many factors that influence the location of a firm vary in relative importance as situations vary. They must be considered within the context of individual firms. Nonetheless, as indicated in the table below, a survey of 104 plants identified labor as the most important industrial location factor, not only for high-technology firms, but for most other types of firms as well.

Location Factors Influencing New Manufacturing Plants

Rank	High-Technology Plants	Other Plants
1	Labor	Labor
2	Transportation availability	Market access
3	Quality of life	Transportation availability
4	Market access	Materials access
5	Utilities	Utilities
6	Site characteristics	Regulatory practice
7	Community characteristics	Quality of life
8	Business climate	Business climate
9	Taxes	Site characteristics
10	Development organizations	Taxes

SOURCE: Based on Rees and Stafford, 1986, p. 43.

spatial variations in the cost of labor. The final determination considers the effects of local factors. In Weber's approach, each set of forces is considered in sequence, increasing the complexity of analysis.

Raw Material Classes

The first cost faced in the manufacturing process is the cost of assembling raw materials. In Weber's simple classification system (Table 10.1), raw materials

TABLE 10.1
Solutions to Weber's locational problems.

Material Classes	Location
Ubiquities Only	Market
Localized and Pure	
One Pure	Anywhere between Source of Raw Material and Market
One Pure and Ubiquities	Market
More Than One Pure	Market
More Than One Pure and Ubiquities	Market
Localized and Weight-Losing (Gross)	
One Weight-Losing	Source
One Weight-Losing and Ubiquities	Source or Market Depending on Relative Size of Input
More Than One Weight-Losing	Indeterminate (Mathematical Solution)
More than One Weight-Losing and Ubiquities	Indeterminate (Mathematical Solution)

first are classified by their frequency of occurrence. *Ubiquitous raw materials,* such as air, are universally distributed; they always have a transport cost of zero. *Localized raw materials,* such as coal, are found only at specific locations; their transport costs are a function of the distance they must be moved. Second, Weber classified raw materials on the basis of how much weight they lose during processing. *Pure raw materials,* such as an automobile transmission, lose no weight in processing, whereas *gross raw materials,* such as fuels, do lose weight in processing. A weight-losing raw material is assigned a *material index,* which indicates the ratio of raw material to finished-product weight. The index is obtained by dividing the weight of the raw material by its processed (finished) weight. Pure raw materials have a material index of one. Weight-losing raw materials have a material index of greater than one. Fuels have the highest material index because none of their weight affects the weight of the finished product.

We are now ready to discuss transport costs as they relate to a number of different kinds of raw materials. For each case we must consider (1) the cost of assembling raw materials *(RM),* (2) the cost of distributing the finished product *(FP),* and (3) the total transportation costs *(TTC).* In all cases, we are assuming the existence of a single market point. The best location for a manufacturing plant is the point at which total transport costs are minimized.

Ubiquities Only

Only localized raw materials attract production. Ubiquities merely add to the pull of the market. Ubiquitous raw materials occur everywhere, so the cost of their assembly is always zero. Only finished-product costs are important, and they are reduced to zero with a location at the market point as illustrated by the graph in Figure 10.1. Raw material costs *(RM)* are the line $0-0'$. Finished-product costs rise steadily with increasing distance from the market. The cost line *FP* also marks total transport costs that are minimized at the market.

One Localized Pure Raw Material Given one localized pure raw material and a single market, costs are indicated in Figure 10.2. The material is localized at *RM* and the market is at *M*. The line *RM* represents the assembly costs, which increase as a function of distance from the source of the localized raw material. Similarly, the line *FP* represents the distribution costs for the finished products. Total transport cost *(TTC)* is the sum of *RM* and *FP*. At *RM*, *TTC* equals $7.00 (*RM* = $0, *FP* = $7.00, *TTC* = $7.00). At 0, RM = $3.50 and *FP* = $3.50, so that *TTC* = $7.00. Since total transport costs are exactly $7.00 everywhere along a straight line between mine and market, a manufacturing plant located anywhere along this line can minimize costs.

One Localized Pure Raw Material Plus Ubiquities This case is graphed in Figure 10.3. The assembly costs for the localized raw material *(RM)* are minimized at *RM*. Ubiquitous assembly costs are zero everywhere, and finished-product distribution costs are minimized at *M*. Ubiquitous raw materials, once processed, add to the weight of the finished product, so that total transport costs *(TTC)* are minimized at the market *(M)*. In other words, the market location eliminates the need to move the ubiquitous material in its processed form.

The Hull Rust iron-ore pit near
Hibbing, Minnesota, in 1941.
From the late nineteenth century to shortly after World War
II, high-grade ore from Minnesota's iron ranges was shipped
via the Great Lakes to iron and
steel plants. When much of the
accessible high-grade ore was
exhausted, attention shifted to
the exploitation of low-grade
ore, known as taconite. Before
shipment, taconite is benefici-
ated and pelletized in plants
near the mines. Thus, it falls
into the category of a localized
weight-losing raw material.
(Source: Library of Congress.)

Bottled and canned soft-drink manufacturing exemplifies the use of one pure raw material (syrup concentrate) and water (in Weberian analysis, a ubiquitous raw material). There is a strong association between soft-drink manufacturing and population, indicating that the industry is market-oriented. By locating at the market, the ubiquitous raw material (water), which makes the largest contribution to the

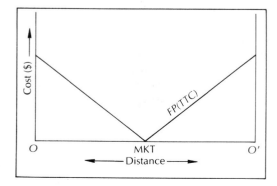

FIGURE 10.1
Weber's model: ubiquities only.

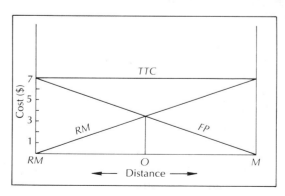

FIGURE 10.2
Weber's model: one localized pure raw material.

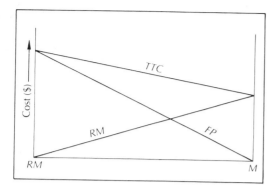

FIGURE 10.3
Weber's model: one localized pure raw material plus ubiquities.

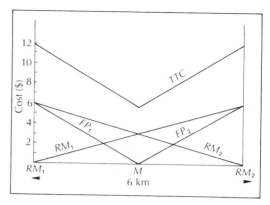

FIGURE 10.4
Weber's model: two localized pure raw materials.

weight of the finished product, does not need to be moved.

Several Localized Pure Raw Materials Figure 10.4 indicates costs for two localized pure raw materials, but the outcome would be the same for more than two. Once again, the single market is at M; one pure raw material is localized at RM_1 and the other is localized at RM_2. The transportation costs for each raw material are given by the lines RM_1 and RM_2. We are assuming that the raw materials are used in equal amounts and that transport costs are \$1 per ton-kilometer. At RM_1, the cost of RM_1 is zero and the cost of RM_2 is \$6, for a total of \$6. But the finished product

weighs two tons; hence, an additional \$6 in transport costs is required to ship the finished product back to M (two tons shipped three kilometers at \$1 per ton-kilometer equals \$6). Total transport costs (*TTC*) at RM_1 are therefore \$12, and they are the same at RM_2. At M, however, total transport costs equal only \$6. Locating at the market eliminates the need to "backhaul" a raw material, so that total transport costs are minimized.

Several Localized Pure Raw Materials Plus Ubiquities Remember that ubiquities always add to the pull of the market. In the graph in Figure 10.5, we are assuming that one ton each of RM_1, RM_2, and the ubiquitous raw material are used; thus, the finished product weighs three tons. Finished-product distribu-

Bottled soft drinks are a weight-gaining commodity. The industry uses one pure raw material (syrup) and one ubiquitous raw material (water). Water is the major raw material by weight. Moreover, the finished product has a low value for its weight. According to the classic Weberian principle, market orientation is the rule for industries processing one pure and one ubiquitous raw material. (Source: Photograph courtesy of The Coca-Cola Company.)

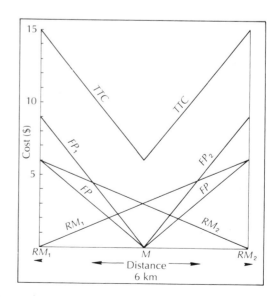

FIGURE 10.5
Weber's model: several localized pure raw materials plus ubiquities.

tion costs at RM_1 and RM_2 are now $9. Localized raw material costs, RM_2, equal $6 and finished-product distribution costs, FP_2, equal $9. Total transport costs equal $15 at RM_1 and RM_2, but equal only $6 at M. The pull of the market is considerably strengthened by the addition of ubiquitous raw materials.

Ready-mixed concrete production is a good example of an industry that uses more than one pure raw material plus ubiquities. The industry uses port-land cement (pure), aggregate (pure and often ubiqui-tous), and water (considered to be ubiquitous). Webe-rian theory indicates that costs are minimized at the market. In the United States, there is a high correlation between industry distribution and population, indi-cating a market orientation.

Weight-Losing Raw Materials

One Localized Weight-Losing Raw Material   Figure 10.6 illustrates this particular situation. Assume that the raw material, which is localized at RM, loses half of its weight in processing. The material index is there-fore two. The transport cost for each point between mine and market is indicated by the line RM. Each unit of the raw material shipped to the market at M costs $10. Each unit of the finished product shipped from the mine, however, costs only $5. Total transport costs *(TTC)* are minimized at the raw material source.

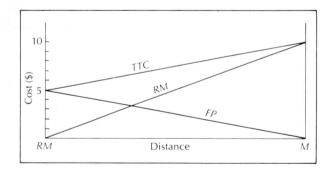

FIGURE 10.6
Weber's model: one localized weight-losing raw material.

The distribution of the copper industry illustrates this situation. Cooper ore has a high material index (99), and manufacturing is concentrated near copper mines. A raw material orientation eliminates transport costs to move waste.

One Localized Weight-Losing Raw Material Plus Ubiquities   Of importance in this situation is the ratio of the weight lost through processing to the weight of the ubiquitous material. Two extreme cases are illustrated in Figure 10.7. In the first case (Figure 10.7a), the weight-losing raw material is a fuel, and all of its weight is lost in the manufacturing process. Assume that one ton of fuel is localized at RM, and that 1,000 kilograms of the ubiquitous pure raw material are required to produce 1,000 kilograms of the finished product. Total transport costs are mini-mized at the source of the weight-losing raw material.

In the second case (Figure 10.7b), a weight-losing raw material has a material index of two. Half of the weight of the localized raw material is lost in process-ing. In this case, however, we are assuming a three-to-one ratio of the ubiquitous raw material to the localized raw material. Two tons of the localized raw material plus three tons of the ubiquitous raw mate-rial are processed into a finished product weighing four tons. At RM, total transport costs are $4, but at M, total transport costs are only $2, which is the trans-port cost for the amount of the localized weight-losing raw material required for one unit of the finished product. Total transport costs are minimized at the market *(M)*. This case typifies commercial brewing. Barley and hops are the localized raw materials that lose weight in processing, but the major ingredient by weight—water—is ubiquitous in Weberian analysis. Brewers tend to be market- rather than raw-material-oriented.

Several Localized Weight-Losing Raw Materials
The situation becomes more complex when several weight-losing raw materials are considered. The Vari-gnon frame, previously mentioned in Chapter 9,

FIGURE 10.7
Weber's model: one localized weight-losing raw material plus ubiquities. (a) Best location at raw material source and (b) best location at market.

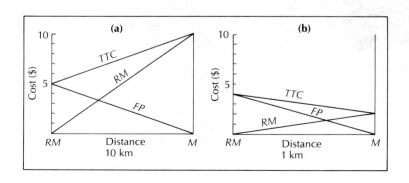

FIGURE 10.8
The Varignon frame to find the best location for a plant using several localized weight-losing materials.

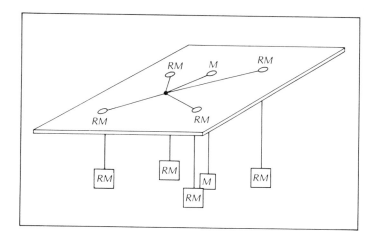

simplifies the problem. The localized raw material sites are located on a map mounted on a board (Figure 10.8). Holes have been drilled in the board at each site. A pulley, which reduces friction, is located at each hole. A raw material is simulated by a weight proportional to the total weight required to produce one unit of the finished product. Cords are run from the weights through the pulleys and tied together into a single knot. When the weights are released, the final location of the knot indicates the optimal location. Finished-product distribution costs are simulated by a weight equal to finished-product weight running through a hole and pulley at the market point *(M)*. Ubiquitous raw materials can be simulated by adding to this weight. This type of analysis has been applied to the steel industry in which several weight-losing materials are processed (Kennelly 1954, 1955).

EXTENSIONS OF WEBER'S MODEL

Space-Cost Curves

Weber's basic system can be extended using the space-cost curves developed by British geographer David Smith (1966). Assume the equal amounts of two localized weight-losing raw materials are required to produce one unit of the finished product. The material index of each is two, so that one ton of RM_1 and one ton of RM_2 yield a one-ton finished product. In Figure 10.9a a series of concentric circles have been drawn around each raw material source and the market point. These isocost lines for each point were called *isotims* by Weber.

Total transport costs are the sum of all costs to all three points. At point X (Figure 10.9b), for example, it costs $3 for XRM_1, $2 for RM_2, and $2 for transporting the finished product. We can find total transport costs for as many points as we want and connect points of

equal value to produce total-cost isopleths, which Weber called *isodapanes*. If we visualize Figure 10.9c in three dimensions, we have mapped a depression. Smith then assumed that the market price for the

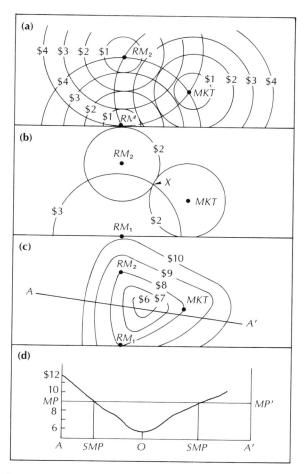

FIGURE 10.9
The development of a space-cost curve: (a) isotims; (b) total cost to a point; (c) isodapanes; (d) space cost along the line $A–A'$.

Case Study: The Iron and Steel Industry

The theoretical principles of industrial location theory can be applied to any industry to help us understand its locational pattern. To apply these principles, we have to determine the relative importance of the inputs used by the industry and the structure of transportation costs for inputs and outputs. We also must know something of the historical development of the spatial pattern of the industry. For example, if a single localized input accounts for 90 percent of the total input costs of Industry *X*, a very simple Weberian model can be used. For more complex patterns, we may have to examine the relative importance of localized and ubiquitous inputs, the cost of labor, and other factors.

To illustrate the classical principles, let us consider the iron and steel industry. The industry requires three primary material inputs—iron ore, fuel (coal or electricity), and limestone. In recent years, the availability of scrap iron as an input has also become important.

The steel industry is a crucial one because it supplies the primary raw material for many other types of manufacturing. The industry outputs very few products directly to consumers. Most of its output flows to other manufacturing industries, which, in turn, fabricate the steel into finished products, such as automobiles. Steel production, then, is the foundation on which a modern industrial complex is built. Changes in steel prices are closely observed by economists as a barometer of price changes in other sections of the manufacturing economy and, ultimately, consumer prices.

The industrial revolution depended on the low-cost production of steel; steel was required for the steam and internal-combustion engines, railroads, and other machinery. The efficient production of steel, however, requires huge capital investments and large-scale operations. Investments are usually so large that the pattern of steel manufacturing remains stable for very long periods of time. Most of the large industrial complexes in the world today reflect the development of the steel industry in the nineteenth century. The mass production of steel required coal as a fuel, and was especially attracted to high-quality coking coal. This led to the localization of the industry in the Pittsburgh area of the United States, the Midlands of England, central Scotland and South Wales, the Ruhr region of Germany, and the Nord-Sambre-Meuse region of France, Belgium, and Luxembourg.

In the twentieth century, the pull of coal lessened because of blast-furnace economies and heat transfers in integrated steel mills. Whereas the coal-to-iron ratio of the nineteenth-century steel industry was 8:1, the coal-to-steel ratio of the modern industry is 1.3:1. With the decline in the pull of coal, ore sources and markets became more important locational determinants. In the United States, steel complexes developed along the Great Lakes to take advantage of the vast iron-ore deposits near Lake Superior, and at tidewater sites, such as Sparrow's Point, Maryland and Morrisville, Pennsylvania, which utilize foreign ores and cheap ocean transport. The Japanese steel industry, dependent on foreign suppliers of coal and ore since the 1920s, is concentrated along the shores of Tokyo Bay and Osaka Bay and on the drained marshes that border the Inland Sea. In Britain, there has also been a tendency to locate new steel works in coastal districts; an example is Llanwern (Newport).

In the post-World War II period, traditional producers in Europe and North America began to flounder and new centers of production began to

The classical principals of industrial location theory are evidenced in the river valley and railroad site of Bethlehem Steel Corporation's plant at Bethlehem, Pennsylvania. This huge plant, which extends for nearly eight kilometers along the south bank of the Lehigh River converts raw materials—Appalachian coking coal and Minnesota iron ore—into structural shapes, large open-die and closed-die forgings, forged steel rolls, cast steel and iron rolls, ingot moulds, and steel, iron, and brass castings. The main market for the steel products is the American Manufacturing Belt with its abundance of metal-using industries. (Source: Bethlehem Steel Corporation.)

Bethlehem Steel Corporation's sprawling plant at Sparrows Point, Maryland, illustrates a modern locational pattern. The works has deepwater access for ore from international sources. (Source: Bethlehem Steel Corporation.)

emerge in Brazil, South Korea, and Taiwan. The migration of steel production to the Third World reflected the growing importance of labor costs, government subsidies, and taxes to the delivered cost of steel. By 1980, the British steel industry was the epitome of all that was wrong with many European and American producers: too many employees, recalcitrant unions, demoralized management, inefficiency, and losses. Eight years later, however, there was a turnaround in the British industry. In fact, the industry went from one of the highest cost steel producers in the world in 1980 to one of the lowest in 1988. The transformation is a multifaceted story, with several forces, including a strong worldwide market for steel, working to bring about the change. It began, however, with the political will of the Thatcher government to force the industry to become internationally competitive or perish.

The steel industry illustrates several locational principles. The initial location of the industry could be simulated using the Varignon frame with fuel

finished product is a spatial constant, the line $MP-MP'$ in Figure 10.9d. The intersections of the space-cost curve and the market-price line delimit the *spatial margins to profitability*. The best location (O) is at the lowest point on the space-cost curve.

Smith's extension of Weber's ideas brings us a step closer to reality. It acknowledges that a least-cost location is not essential for economic survival. Profits can be realized by entrepreneurs who locate farther away from the optimal location at point O.

Distortions of the Isotropic Surface

Weber's assumption of a completely isotropic surface is modified when we account for the effects of localized resources. Thus, we begin a transition from a normative to a descriptive model. The regular patterns implied by central-place theory are distorted to minimize the pull of nonubiquitous resources. The role of the natural environment (localized resources) distorts the ideal patterns of an isotropic surface.

It becomes apparent, then, that the forces controlling the location of manufacturing may be quite different from those that control the location of central places. The tertiary sector is market-oriented, but the orientation of the secondary sector varies from industry to industry. Some types of manufacturing, as we have seen in the Weberian model, are market-oriented. If all industries were of this type, the pattern of manufacturing would match the pattern of central places. Some industries, however, have a cost structure so dominated by localized input costs that they are material-oriented, thereby distorting the pattern.

This distortion is illustrated in Figure 10.10. Point *I* is the ideal location for a given order of central place. The shaded area is a major resource deposit. City *A* was established to exploit that resource and

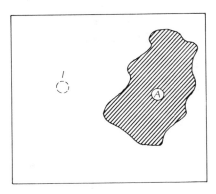

FIGURE 10.10
Distortion produced by localized resources.

has become a center of manufacturing. City *A* also supplies central functions to the surrounding area. Because of its initial establishment and growth, it has superceded the establishment of service functions as the theoretical ideal location (*I*). The purely spatial pattern has been distorted by the uneven distribution of resources.

Real-world patterns are evolutionary; they are not the result of decisions made by optimizers. Most real-world decisions do not result in best (most profitable) locations. As we discussed in Chapter 5 on decision making, locational decisions, once made, lead to inertia. This tendency to keep investing in the nonoptimal site may be great enough to perpetuate the distorted pattern even if more optimal locations are discovered in the future. For example, we now have the analytical skills to locate state capitals at the centroids of state or national populations, but the investment we have in most state or national capitals precludes us from doing so. Tension develops between ideal spatial patterns and the patterns produced by localized resources. As technology (espe-

(coal) showing the greatest amount of "pull" because of its high weight-loss ratio and contribution to total costs. Cheap water transportation can reduce the pull of any of the raw materials used to make steel. Once in place, the high fixed costs of plants hold the pattern stable for long periods of time. Competition, however, can make the industry highly mobile. In the past, competition was national, but now it is global. Thus, one of the classic industries of the industrial revolution has been moving to the Third World. Meanwhile, back in Europe and North America, some producers are facing the competition by investing heavily in equipment to modernize their plants, shifting most of their production to computer-controlled continuous casting, in which lengths of steel are produced without interruption, ready for molding and rolling into various sizes and products.

cially transportation) improves, ideal spatial patterns (from the point of view of the entrepreneur) become more feasible, but the inertia resulting from past actions exerts a constant brake on actualizing them.

We have inherited one aspect of inertia from the nineteenth century. Locational patterns were then dominated by coal, which was used as a source of carbon in the iron and steel industry, as a source of fuel for steam engines, and as a source of heating for homes and businesses. As a result, business and population gravitated to the coalfields in the mid- and late nineteenth century. Although other forms of energy have gradually replaced coal, population distribution has changed even more slowly. Many of the depressed industrial regions in developed countries are found on coalfields.

Let us conclude this discussion of Weber's basic system and its extensions with a brief appraisal. His model distinguishes between material- and market-oriented industries. Gross localized materials encourage material orientation, and this tendency remains to this day. Bulk-reducing industries—mineral processing, metal smelting, timber processing, fruit and vegetable packing—are frequently found near material sources. But manufacturing is more complex than it was in the early twentieth century. Many plants begin with semifinished items and components rather than with raw materials. For producers' goods, there is seldom any large weight reduction and therefore not much tendency toward material orientation.

Ubiquities encourage material orientation, a tendency that remains to this day. However, few materials can be classified as ubiquities without qualification. For example, water is in short supply in many areas. Water may be ubiquitous for firms that use a little (e.g., a bakery), but not for firms that use a lot (e.g., a steel mill).

Weber's model has been criticized for its unrealistic view of transport costs as a linear function of distance. Due to fixed costs, especially terminal costs, long hauls cost less per unit weight than short hauls. Plants tend to locate at material or market points rather than at intermediate points, unless there is an enforced change in the transport mode, such as at a port (Hoyle and Pinder 1981, pp. 4–6). However, with the expansion of the modern trucking industry and its flexibility in short hauls, the disadvantages of intermediate locations have been reduced.

Two other transport developments have a bearing on industrial location in the late twentieth century. First, freight rates have risen more sharply on finished items than on raw materials. As a result, there is a tendency to ship raw materials farther and nearer to the market and to reduce shipments of finished goods. Second, transport costs have been declining, increasing the importance of other location factors. Labor now stands out as the most important of the industrial location determinants (Rees and Stafford 1986, p. 42). This is most obvious in firms producing high-value and high-technology products. For these firms, transport costs are relatively unimportant (Norcliffe 1975, pp. 21–24). Yet, for firms that distribute consumer goods (e.g., soft drinks) to dispersed markets, transport costs remain a significant factor (Osleeb and Cromley 1978).

PRODUCTION COSTS

So far we have not considered the costs of the actual manufacturing process. After materials have been assembled at a point, they must be reworked and combined to produce a finished product. Production costs include labor, capital, and technical and mana-

TABLE 10.2
Variations in labor productivity.

Plant	Total Hourly Wages and Fringe Benefits (per Worker)	Output per Hour in Units (per Worker)	True Labor Cost per Unit Productivity
A	$5.50	100	5.5¢
B	$7.80	200	3.9¢
C	$4.20	76	5.5¢

gerial skills. All of these are necessary for production, and all exhibit spatial variations in both quantity and quality.

The Cost of Labor

Labor inputs are required for all forms of economic production, but the relative contribution of labor to value added by manufacturing varies considerably among industries. For example, the contribution of labor costs is high in the automobile industry, but low in the petroleum-products industry. Both the supply and demand for labor vary across space, but those industries in which labor costs play a major role are much more sensitive to local variations in the cost of this input. Under capitalism, the real cost of labor is determined by the relative productivity of labor rather than the dollar cost of wages and fringe benefits. The hypothetical data in Table 10.2 illustrate this point. The labor cost per unit produced is lowest in Plant *B* even though the hourly total of wages and fringe benefits is highest.

Weber considered the cost of labor to be a "regional" factor controlling patterns of manufacturing. The initial pattern of manufacturing is set by transport costs and then distorted by variations in the cost of labor. Weber's model assumed an infinite amount of available labor at different points, but variation in the cost of labor actually varies from point to point.

Weber's analysis of this problem is illustrated in Figure 10.11. The product involves two localized raw materials distributed to a single market at *M*. Isodapanes, which are isopleths of total transport costs, are indicated in the diagram. Total transport costs are minimized at Point *T*, where the cost is $4. As we move away from *T*, total transport costs increase. At Point *L*, labor costs are $2 per unit less than at *T*. This unit labor savings is used to determine the value of a *critical isodapane*. No savings in total unit cost will result if the increased transport costs encountered at another point are greater than the labor savings at that point. The move, in other words, must not exceed $2 per unit. Transport costs at *T* ($4) plus labor savings at *L* ($2) determine the amount that cannot be exceeded

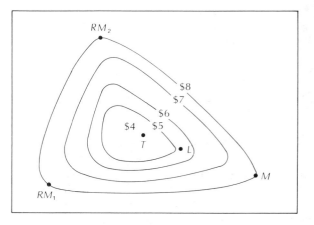

FIGURE 10.11
Critical isodapane for labor.

($6). Point *L* lies inside this critical isodapane and is clearly an economic move. A point on the critical isodapane would result in zero savings; points outside the line would result in higher total costs. It is in this way, within the limits established by critical isodapanes, that variations in labor costs distort the pattern established by general transport costs.

In theory, equilibrium conditions should balance regional differences in the supply and demand for labor, which is a mobile factor of production. A high demand for labor in one place and excess supply in another should be brought into equilibrium through labor migration. Such migration has certainly occurred. Examples are the nineteenth-century migration of people from countryside to city in such countries as Britain and the twentieth-century movement of labor from the Third World and other peripheral countries to the core of industrial Europe, from the Caribbean and South Asia to Britain, from North Africa to France, and from Turkey to West Germany.

As is the case for all factors of production, the response of labor is not instantaneous. Skilled labor, in particular, has a relatively high degree of inertia, especially in the short run. People are reluctant to pull up stakes and leave familiar places even if jobs are plentiful in other areas. They tend to sit out short periods of unemployment or to accept a smaller net income than could be earned elsewhere. Liberal welfare policies, such as unemployment payments and worker's compensation, have reduced the plight of the unemployed and underemployed in advanced industrial countries this century.

The lack of instantaneous adjustment in labor demand and supply has resulted in variations in the cost of labor within and between countries. In the United States, wages tend to be higher in the more industrial states, in densely settled areas, and in highly urbanized environments. At the world scale, developed countries have higher wage rates than newly industrializing countries (Table 10.3). One factor responsible for differential wage rates is the level of

TABLE 10.3

Labor conditions in world manufacturing, 1974–1983.

	Average Hourly Earnings in Manufacturing (U.S.$)			Industrial Disputes Average Annual Working Days Lost per 1,000 Nonagricultural Workers	
	1974	1983		1974–83	
North America					
United States	4.42	8.83		312	
Canada	4.46	8.61		836	
Latin America					
Venezuela	1.41	3.63	(1981)	45	
Mexico	1.10	1.59	(1982)	n.a.	
Columbia	0.41	1.00	(1980)	n.a.	
Western Europe					
Belgium	3.22	5.29		182	(1974–80)
France	2.17	4.41		167	
Germany, Federal Republic of	3.45	5.94		26	
Ireland	1.94	4.40		798	(1974–82)
Sweden	4.57	6.29		134	
United Kingdom	2.61	5.25		470	(1974–82)
Southern Europe					
Italy	1.86	4.95		1,088	
Spain	2.04	3.63		917	(1974–82)
Turkey	0.60	1.15		1,127	(1974–80)
Africa					
Kenya	0.57	0.70		n.a.	
Zambia	0.77	1.32	(1980)	317	
Zimbabwe	n.a.	2.20	(1982)	66	(1977–83)
South Asia					
Bangladesh	0.23	0.15		460	
India	0.18	0.40	(1981)	1,696	
Pakistan	0.17	0.33	(1980)	47	
Sri Lanka	0.19	0.17		383	
East and Southeast Asia					
Hong Kong	0.51	1.26		10	
Korea, Republic of	0.38	1.35		2	
Malaysia	n.a.	n.a.		26	(1975–79)
Philippines	n.a.	n.a.		53	
Singapore	0.52	1.43		2	(1974–82)
Taiwan	0.47	1.67		n.a	
Thailand	n.a.	n.a.		48	(1974–81)
Japan	2.95	6.91		59	
Oceania					
Australia	4.95	8.58		577	

SOURCE: Peet, 1987a, p. 17.

worker organization. Higher rates of unionization are associated with higher wages. Unionization is generally more prevalent in the older, established industrial countries than in the newly industrializing countries. Thus, considerable advantages can be gained by companies relocating to, or purchasing from, newly industrializing countries, especially if those countries are characterized by low levels of capital-labor conflict (Table 10.3). Capital-labor conflict, manifested in industrial disputes, is a powerful force propelling the drift of industrial production outward from the center to the periphery of the world system.

The Cost of Capital

Capital, another necessary factor of production, takes two forms: *fixed capital* and *liquid* or *variable capital*. Fixed capital includes equipment and plant buildings. Liquid capital is used to pay wages and meet other operating costs. Liquid capital is theoretically the most mobile of all factors of production. Its transportation costs are almost zero and it can be transmitted almost instantaneously in our "wired world." About $9 trillion in electronic funds transfer is completed annually over international communication facilities, an amount equal to two-thirds of the global gross national product. Fixed capital is much less mobile than liquid capital. Capital invested in buildings and equipment is obviously immobile and is a primary reason for industrial inertia.

Any type of manufacturing that is profitable has an assured supply of liquid capital stemming from revenues or borrowing. Most types of manufacturing, however, initially require large amounts of fixed capital to establish the operation—or, periodically, to expand, retool, or replace outdated equipment or to branch out into new products. The cost of this capital, which is interest, must be paid from future revenues. Investment capital is not uniformly distributed and does not display great mobility.

Investment capital comes from a variety of sources: personal funds; family and friends; lending institutions, such as banks and savings and loan associations; and the sale of stocks and bonds. Most capital in advanced industrial countries is raised from the last two sources. The total supply of investment capital is a function of total national wealth and the proportion of total income that is saved. Savings become the investment capital for future expansion.

Whether or not a particular type of manufacturing, or a given entrepreneur, can secure an adequate amount of capital depends on several factors. It depends on the supply of and demand for capital, which varies from place to place and from time to

time. Of course, capital can always be obtained if users are willing to pay high enough interest rates. Beyond supply-and-demand considerations, investor confidence is the prime determinant of whether or not capital can be obtained at an acceptable rate. Investor confidence in a particular industry may exist in one area but be lacking in another. Henry Ford, of Ford Motor Company, for example, failed to raise investment capital in one area of the United States, but was able to secure it in his home town of Detroit.

Entrepreneurship and Technical Skills

Management and technical skills are also required for any type of production operation. Corporations are the primary agents responsible for specific industrial patterns. The general pattern is, of course, determined by the localization of other factors of production, subsequent transport costs, and spatial margins to profitability. Ford Motor Company may again be used as an example. The company was established in Detroit, primarily because Henry Ford was able to obtain risk capital there—but any town in the Midwest accessible to raw materials, especially steel, could have supported automobile manufacturing. On the other hand, had Ford attempted to manufacture automobiles on a large scale in Butte, Montana, he would have surely failed. A study by H. Hunker and A. J. Wright (1963) found that the majority of the manufacturing plants in Ohio were in the home towns of their founders. Historically, the Midwest, and the rest of the American Manufacturing Belt, established the regional pattern of successful locations for most types of manufacturing—but the specific locations chosen within these margins were determined by the individual decisions of capitalists.

Theoretically, management should be much more mobile than labor because fewer people are involved, and the higher income of managers should make moving less of a financial burden. But management skills, like labor skills, tend to be highly concentrated. Where are the organizational headquarters of the five hundred largest American corporations? Most of them are in the largest urbanized areas of the country (Figure 10.12). The top ten headquarter metropolitan areas are New York (157 head offices), Chicago (41), Los Angeles (28), San Francisco (25), Philadelphia (18), Minneapolis-St. Paul (15), Detroit (13), Boston (12), Pittsburgh (12), and Houston (Rand McNally 1988).

Technical skills are those skills necessary for continued innovation in terms of new products and processes. These skills are generally categorized as research and development (R&D). In the early phases

FIGURE 10.12
Corporate headquarters: five hundred largest corporations. (Source: Rand McNally, 1988.)

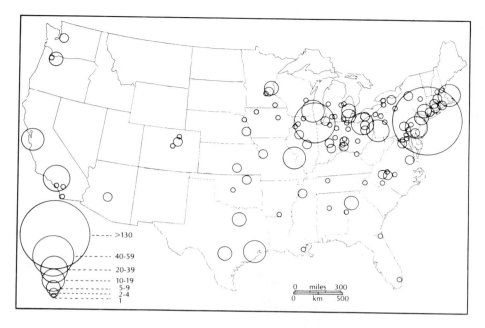

of industrialization in developed countries, product development was usually carried out in tandem with production by small firms, many of which, together with their innovations, failed to survive. Today, the R&D required for new products has become a large and expensive process, involving long "lead" times between invention and production; therefore it is beyond the scope of small firms. The cutting edge of advanced industrial economies, R&D tends to be concentrated in a small number of major research-university clusters and established areas of innovation (Malecki 1979, 1980) (Figure 10.13). Three of these in

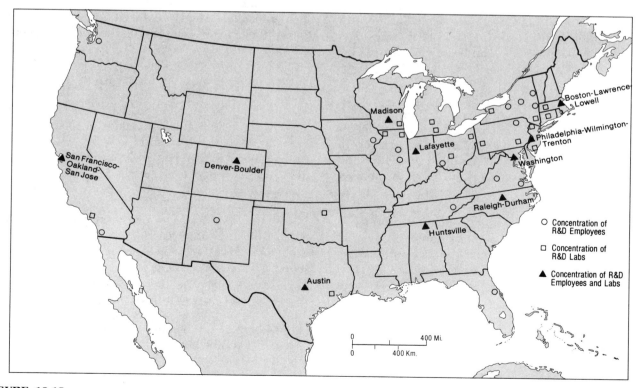

FIGURE 10.13
Major concentrations of research development activity. (Source: Based on Malecki, 1979.)

the United States are Silicon Valley, the region south of San Francisco Bay in the vicinity of Stanford University; Boston and Route 128; and the Research Triangle of North Carolina, so called because of three universities located there—the University of North Carolina at Chapel Hill, Duke University in Durham, and North Carolina State University in Raleigh. Roughly equidistant from the three main cities, Research Triangle Park is home to the labs of IBM, Burroughs Wellcome, Northern Telecom, and other major companies conducting R&D.

For most of the twentieth century, the United States has been the world's leader in technological innovation. In the 1970s, however, the number of new inventions and patents granted declined. Factors that retarded U.S. innovation included a decline in federal support for basic research, an increase in government red tape, an increased managerial interest in improving existing products to yield quick returns, and difficulties in obtaining risk capital. Basically, the United States was not spending enough on R&D. Although outlays for R&D began to rise in the 1980s as foreign competition forced firms to automate in order to reduce costs and increase productivity, U.S. expenditures for R&D represented only 2.7 percent of the gross national product (United Nations 1985). This figure compares favorably, however, with other developed countries—Japan (2.6 percent), West Germany (2.5 percent), Britain (2.4 percent)—which as a group dominates the world in the number of R&D scientists and engineers and R&D expenditures (Figure 10.14).

LOCATIONAL COSTS

Now that we have discussed the various production costs, we can examine their influence on location in greater detail. Smith (1966) pointed out that the establishment of any manufacturing plant in a market economy involves three interdependent decision-making criteria: (1) scale—the size of the operation that will determine the volume of total output; (2) technique—the particular combination of inputs that are used to produce an output; and (3) location. Here, we will concern ourselves with location as a function of input costs and consider technique and scale in subsequent sections.

Let us assume that technique and scale are constant, and that variations in demand, if they exist, are solely a function of price. These assumptions allow us to portray three general industrial location cases (Figure 10.15). In Case (a), market price (revenue) is a spatial constant and costs vary across space. The

optimum location is then the lowest point on the space-cost curve, and the spatial margins are where costs equal revenue. Total revenue (demand) exhibits spatial change in Case (b), and costs are a spatial constant. The optimum location is the highest point on the revenue curve, and the spatial margins to profitability are, again, where costs equal revenue. Variations in both cost and revenue across space are shown in Case (c). The optimum location (O) will be the place where revenue exceeds costs by the greatest amount. For all three cases we can show that both curves determine the spatial margins to profitability, the variable with the steepest gradient determines the best location, and the slope of the curve indicates the relative importance of locational costs.

The concept of spatial margins to profitability is noteworthy because it incorporates suboptimal behavior. Profits are possible anywhere within the defined limits. The graphs in Figure 10.15 represent the most general statement that can be made about locational viability. Defining these margins in reality and determining specific locations to be occupied within them, however, is a much more difficult problem. We can still make one generalization about real-world patterns within spatial margins to profitability—industries that are clustered must face limited spatial margins to profitability and high location costs. This situation is illustrated in Figure 10.16. Remember that any kind of cost and/or revenue may be a critical factor determining the spatial margins to profitability.

Weber's theory is preoccupied with both transportation costs and finding least-cost locations. A more general theory should consider total cost and the possibility of suboptimal decisions. Walter Isard (1956) suggested that locational factors can be divided into three general classes on the basis of their geographical occurrence: (1) transfer charges—costs that can be portrayed as a regular function of distance; (2) spatially variable costs—costs that vary across space (labor, power, capital, management skills) but which do not vary systematically with distance; and (3) aspatial costs—factors that can influence costs but which are independent of location, such as scale changes.

Smith (1966) extended Weber's analysis to all types of cost. He assumed that each input has a least-cost point. Least-cost points for materials may be mines or the factories of parts producers. There is a least-cost point for the particular kind of labor required and there is a point at which finished-product distribution costs are minimized. Each of these points exerts a certain "pull" on location (recall

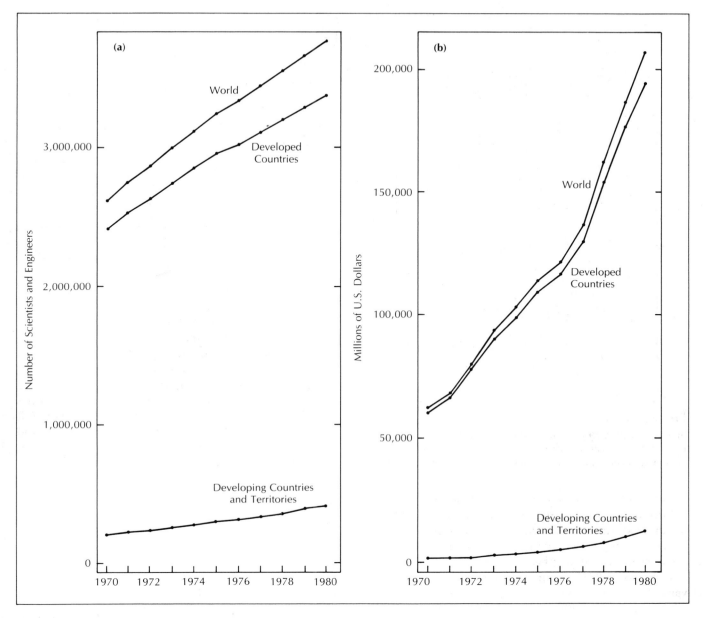

FIGURE 10.14
World trends in (a) R&D scientists and engineers and (b) R&D expenditures, 1970–1980.
(Source: United Nations, 1985, V–10.)

the Varignon frame). The relative weight of all these pulls determines the least-cost location.

Smith also acknowledged the distinction between *basic* and *locational costs*. Basic costs are the minimum that must be paid regardless of location; they represent the lowest point on the cost surface of a particular input. The basic cost of labor, for example, would be the minimum wage. Locational costs are all costs above basic cost. They vary with location and may rise as a function of the distance from the

least-cost location. Figure 10.17 illustrates the two kinds of cost. We assume that some workers will accept the minimum wage. Their location represents the lowest point on the labor cost surface and basic cost. Away from that point, workers demand more than the minimum wage, but the additional amount takes the form of locational costs.

We see then that the total cost of any input is the sum of locational and basic cost. The relative "pull" of a given input therefore depends on the slope of the

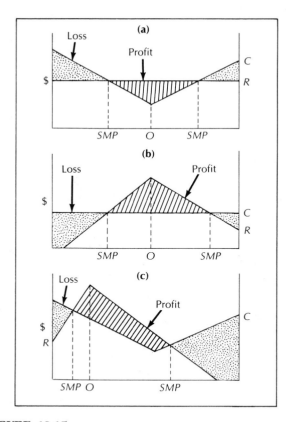

FIGURE 10.15
Spatial margins to profitability: (a) cost variable, revenue constant; (b) revenue variable, cost constant; (c) revenue and cost variable. (Source: Based on Smith, 1981, p. 113.)

(locational) space-cost curve and the percentage contribution of an input to the total cost of output. An input accounting for a large proportion of total basic cost or varying widely in location cost should have the greatest influence on plant location.

Smith (1981) examined this proposition with variable-cost models. He demonstrated that locational costs can occur either because transport costs per unit of a particular input are high, or because a large

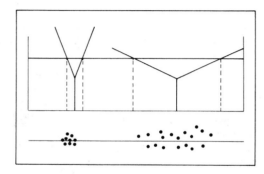

FIGURE 10.16
Spatial margins to profitability and clustering.

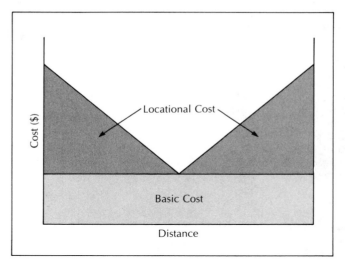

FIGURE 10.17
Basic and locational costs.

quantity (basic cost) of the input is required, even though the per unit costs may be low. The latter point is illustrated nicely by coal, which had a profound effect on past industrial locational patterns for heavy industry. Coal can be moved relatively cheaply on a per ton basis, but the large quantity required in some types of manufacturing has resulted in high locational costs and a pull on industries to locate near coal deposits. This example illustrates the difference between transport costs per unit and locational costs.

THE LOCATIONAL EFFECTS OF TECHNIQUE

Technique, or the particular combination of inputs used to produce a given finished product, can have an important effect on a firm's locational decision. A certain amount of land (resources), labor, and capital is needed to produce any finished product, but, within limits, labor may be substituted for capital, as labor for resources, or similar combinations.

The most evident trend in modern manufacturing has been substitution of capital in the form of machinery and robotics for labor (Sanderson and Berry 1986). More and more autonomous manufacturing systems, which apply sophisticated technology to improve the quality and efficiency of production, are being used to replace certain kinds of labor. Whether or not substitution between factors of production occurs depends on the relative cost of the two inputs and the scale and locational decisions already made by the firm. If, for example, labor costs rise at a given location, the firm may choose to substitute capital for labor at that location, or it may opt to change locations to take advantage of lower labor costs and thus maintain the same labor-to-capital ratio.

The limits set on substitution vary considerably from industry to industry. Petroleum refining, for example, can be readily automated, whereas the manufacture of garments cannot. The textile industry, therefore, is much more sensitive to changes in labor costs than refining. In the late nineteenth and early twentieth centuries, the U.S. textile industry shifted from old multistoried New England mills to new mills in the Southern Piedmont, as labor costs rose in the Northeast. This is an example of the influence options in technique exert to determine the locational decision. Increased labor costs outweighed the costs of moving the industry. Of course, the wage advantage of the South did not persist; as new industry moved south, it raised wages there. This has forced textiles to move into other areas of the United States where there are pools of cheap female labor (e.g., the depressed coalmining towns of eastern Pennsylvania), or to migrate farther afield—to Mexico, Brazil, South Korea, and Singapore. Had capital substitution been a viable option, the textile industry might have remained in place. Many times a firm may wish to change its scale to increase output and earn extra profits. A change in scale may require a change in location and/or technique.

SCALE CONSIDERATIONS IN INDUSTRIAL LOCATION

Scale is important, not only because it is one of the three interdependent production criteria that drive decision making, but also because producers are concerned with the unit cost of production—and adjustments in scale can produce considerable variations in unit cost. Scale is the means by which production is "tuned" to meet demand. In some economies, this "tuning" may be done by the state; in others, by private entrepreneurs.

Principles of Scale Economies

Division of Land and Capital Along with standardization of parts, *division of labor* is a primary component of mass production. Workers who perform one simple operation in the production process are much more efficient than those who are responsible for all phases. Division of labor not only speeds up production, it also facilitates the use of relatively unskilled labor. A worker can learn one simple task in a short time, while the skills required to master the entire operation may take years to learn. Division of labor,

however, requires a relatively large scale because a large pool of workers is generally necessary. A common way to measure the size of a firm is by the number of employees. Capital, once invested in machinery and buildings, becomes fixed capital, and produces income only when in operation. A three-shift firm makes a much more efficient use of its fixed capital than a single-shift firm. The three-shift firm is three times larger in scale measured by employment, yet its fixed capital investment may be no more than that of the single-shift firm.

Massing of Reserves Large operations can maintain proportionally smaller inventories than smaller firms, thereby reducing unit costs. This principle is called the *massing of reserves*. Assume that a particular type of production requires a large, expensive, and complicated piece of machinery. The entire production line is forced to stop if the machine is down. A plant shutdown, even for an hour, is an expensive proposition in that idle workers must be paid while waiting and other operational costs continue to accrue. A firm in this industry must maintain a reserve or inventory of spare machine parts to prevent long shutdowns. Firm *A* has only one machine, but must maintain an inventory of almost one whole machine in equivalent spare parts. Firm *B* has ten machines in operation, but because it is highly unlikely that the same part will fail in all ten machines at the same time, its reserve of parts needs to be only slightly larger than Firm *A*'s.

Imperfectly Divisible Multiples Scale economies also operate when inputs do not allow one-to-one increases in scale. Let's say we are manufacturing hammers. The machine that produces the hammerheads can output 300 per hour, while the hourly output of the handle machine is 400. If we run both machines for an hour, we will end up with 300 complete hammers and 100 extra handles. The production of hammers involves *imperfectly divisible multiples*. The scale of operation can be increased, however, until we hit some unitary combination of head and handle machines. Suppose we increase the number of head machines to four, and the number of handle machines to three. Now we produce 1,200 complete hammers per hour. It is easy to envision to kinds of savings that result from this principle in an industry such as automobile manufacturing, in which perfectly divisible multiples may be reached only in very large operations.

Volume Purchases Large firms generally pay much less for material inputs than small firms. For example, Ford Motor Company can obtain tires for a much lower unit price than an individual dealing with the same tire company, since Ford buys millions of tires a year. Increasing scale, in other words, generally lowers the unit cost of inputs.

Possible Scale Economies

Economists portray scale economies as a curve of long-run average costs, which graphs these costs per unit as a function of scale. Several possible long-run average cost curves are indicated in Figure 10.18. Notice that unit costs fall, reach an optimum point, and then began to rise. The rise in the curve is termed *diseconomies of scale* (diminishing marginal returns to scale) and occurs when a firm becomes too large to manage and operate efficiently. The optimum scale of operation is very small in Industry A, very large in Industry C, and fairly wide-ranging in Industry B. Firms in Industry A should be small; they should be

large in Industry C; and they could range from small to large in Industry B.

Possible scale economies also give some indication of how firms in an industry may expand production. A firm in Industry A, for example, would do well to build a branch plant; increasing the size of operations on the original site would produce diseconomies of scale. Firms in Industry B, however, could increase production either by expanding existing plants or building new ones.

Implications of Economies of Scale

To explore the implications of scale economies, let us consider a company that operates two small breweries, each in a different town. The entire output of the firm is sold in two towns. The long-run average costs (per barrel) for the firms are illustrated in Figure 10.19a. The firm operates the breweries at scale S_1, and costs are $5 per barrel. The firm could reduce its cost per barrel by consolidating its operations into a single plant at scale S_2 ($2.50 per barrel). One plant could be closed and the remaining plant doubled in size, or both plants closed and a new, larger brewery built. However, the firm minimizes its finished-

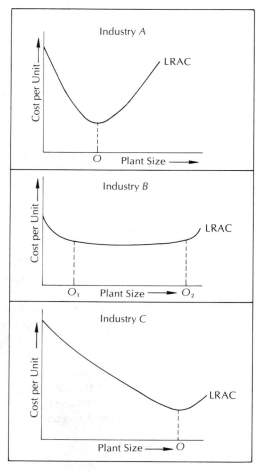

FIGURE 10.18
Variations in long-run average cost (LRAC).

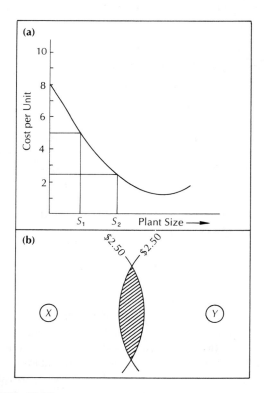

FIGURE 10.19
Spatial implications of scale economies: (a) long-run average costs and (b) transport cost isolines for break-even total cost with plant size of S_2.

product distribution costs by manufacturing beer in each town. Additional distribution costs will have to be paid if a single brewery is used. The question is whether or not the savings from scale economies would outweigh the increased transport costs. These two items balance at a transport cost of $2.50 per barrel. In Figure 10.19b the isocost line of $2.50 per barrel from each town has been drawn. Notice that the two lines intersect, indicating that the scale savings outweigh the increased transport costs. The larger plant could operate in either city or at an intermediate point with a lower cost per barrel than would be possible with the two small-scale plants.

Integration and Diversification

Scale refers to anything that changes the volume of a firm's total output. Besides simply increasing plant size, there are two other means that are commonly employed for effecting scale changes. Some firms may purchase raw material sources or distribution facilities. This is called *vertical integration* (or vertical merger) in that the firm is controlling more "up and down" in the total production process. Some large automobile manufacturing firms, for example, own iron and coal mines and produce their own steel ("down" in the process). They also may own dealerships and do their own transporting and marketing ("up" in the process). Large oil companies also tend to be vertically integrated; they control exploration, drilling, refining, and retailing. By contrast, *horizontal integration* (or horizontal merger), occurs when a firm gains increasing market share of a given niche of particular industry.

Vertical and horizontal integration generally refer to a single finished product. The vertical integration of Ford Motor Company, for example, is focused on controlling the inputs and marketing required for automobile production. However, the trend among corporations in the United States, Japan, and Western

The Ford Motor Company steel mill and auto assembly plants at River Rouge near Detroit, Michigan, is a vertically integrated system. Basic raw materials are used to produce steel, which is incorporated into the engines, frames, bodies, and parts of finished automobiles. (Source: Ford Motor Company.)

Europe has been a strategy of *diversification.* Many large corporations, through *conglomerate merger,* control the production and marketing of diverse products. A company may produce many unrelated products, each with elements of horizontal and vertical integration. Diversification spreads risk and increases profits. Diminishing demand for the products of one division may be offset by rising sales in another.

Most industrial location theory is based on the firm, which implies small, single-plant operations producing a single product. Large corporations are much more complex, but in terms of individual plants, they deal with all the variables of location theory. They still make locational decisions. Although large enterprises may seem to be more concerned with technique and scale decisions, each of their locational decisions has an impact on scale and technique. We should consider two points: First, large firms may be able to operate in less than optimal locations and still make a significant impact on the market through the control they exert over government policies and the prices and sources of raw materials. Conversely, large firms may be able to make optimal locational choices through their employment of the scientists and technical personnel who help top management make more profitable decisions.

Interfirm Scale Economies: Agglomeration

To this point, we have been concerned with intrafirm scale economies. Scale economies also apply to clusters of firms in the same or related industries— the computer firms localized in California's Silicon Valley, the metal trades concentrated in the West Midlands of England. By clustering together and increasing the spatial scale, costs per unit can be lowered for all firms. These economies, often called *externalities, agglomeration economies,* or *linkages,* take several forms. *Production linkages* accrue to firms locating near other producers that manufacture their basic raw materials. By clustering together, distribution and assembly costs are reduced. Close physical links between related businesses were more common a century ago than they are now (Wise 1949; Muller and Groves 1979). Today, component supplies are often far apart. The new Boeing 767 is a case in point. Boeing manufactures its air frame in Seattle with parts from Japan and Italy. The engine is assembled in Ohio with parts from Sweden, France, West Germany, and Italy. Advances in technology, communications, and transportation have given momentum to the economies of globalization.

Service linkages occur when enough small firms are located in an area to support specialized services. The garment industry in New York provides an example of service linkages. Firms in the Garment District are small, but they require specialized service and maintenance activities, such as the repair of sewing and cutting machines. The clustering of the garment industry in Manhattan has also provided the impetus for increased numbers of investment specialists who deal almost exclusively with loans to the garment industry. They understand the special needs of the industry and are much more likely to advance risk capital than other investors.

In addition to production and service linkages there are also *marketing linkages,* for which the garment industry again serves as an example. These linkages occur when a cluster is large enough to attract specialized distribution services. The small firms of the garment industry in New York have collectively attracted advertising agencies, showrooms, buyer listings, and other aspects of finished-product distribution that deal exclusively with the garment trade. Firms located within the cluster have a cost advantage over isolated firms that must provide these specialized services for themselves, or deal with New York firms at a considerable distance and cost.

Some economies are not the result of interfirm linkages, per se, but occur from locating in large cities or industrial complexes. Firms in these locations have an advantage, within limits, over similar firms in more rural areas. Cities provide markets, specialized labor forces and services, utilities, and transportation connections required by manufacturing. *Urbanization* or *industrial-complex economies,* therefore, are a combination of production, service, and market linkages concentrated at a particular location.

DEMAND AND INDUSTRIAL LOCATION

Our discussion thus far has focused almost exclusively on the supply side of the industrial problem, in that we were examining ways in which firms could reduce unit costs. The other side of the problem is demand. Demand determines the scale of output and, in turn, the technique and location of the firm. Concentrations of high demand certainly attract market-oriented industries and, therefore, influence locational patterns. Demand is essentially a function of income and tastes, both of which change over time. Different industries must deal with different kinds of demand. The locational problems of firms producing goods sold to the general public are different from the

Handcarts, delivery trucks, and agile pedestrians mingle on the teeming streets of New York City's garment district. This is Seventh Avenue where out-of-town buyers come to place their bets on tomorrow's fashions. (Source: *Women's Wear Daily.*)

problems of firms producing a specialized product sold only to other manufacturers or to a very select group of consumers. For example, the pattern of demand in the United States a producer of root beer must deal with is considerably different from that for a manufacturer of snowmobile parts.

A Demand-Potential Surface

Geographers have explored the demand aspect of the industrial problem by employing the concept of a *potential surface* (Harris 1954). Market-potential models can show the accessibility of a place to a given population, measured by such data as numbers of people, income, or retail sales. The basic formula is

$$D_i = \sum_{j=1}^{n} \frac{P_j}{d_{ij}}$$

where

D_i = demand potential at i

P_j = population of j (may be income-weighted)

d_{ij} = distance between i and j

The symbol $\sum_{j=1}^{n}$ means we take the sum of demand for all points j from the first point ($j = 1$) to the last point (*n*).

Demand potential is computed for a large number of points. Isolines are then drawn to connect points of equal value. Figure 10.20a illustrates the potential surface of the United States resulting from weighting population by retail sales per county. The actual numbers obtained by this calculation have only relative meaning, so the contours are expressed as a percentage below the highest point. Demand poten-

FIGURE 10.20
(a) Market potential; (b) cross section from New York City to Los Angeles. (Source: Harris, 1954.)

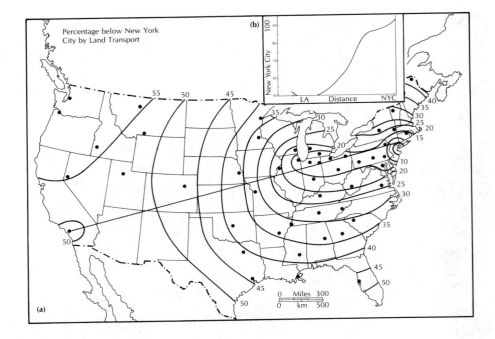

tial is highest at New York City and declines away from the city. This is logical because of the population and purchasing power concentrated in the Northeast. The inset (Figure 10.20b) is a cross section through the demand-potential surface, running from New York to Los Angeles. We might assume that demand is maximized at the highest point of the surface—and potential sales would be highest there.

The problem of demand can also be viewed in another way. If all demand is concentrated at a single point, as in Weber's model, access to the market is maximized and transport costs are minimized at that point. If, however, demand is spread among a number of places, then moving to one point increases transport costs to other points. This is illustrated in Figure 10.21. Moving from Point *B* to Point *C* raises transport costs to other points. A New York location maximizes the distance to a large part of the country.

A Transport-Cost Surface

We can conceptualize a transport-cost surface in much the same way as we did the demand-potential surface:

$$TC_i = P_j d_{ij}$$

where

$$TC_i = \text{total transport costs at } i$$
$$P_j = \text{population of } j \text{ (weighted)}$$
$$d_{ij} = \text{distance between } i \text{ and } j$$

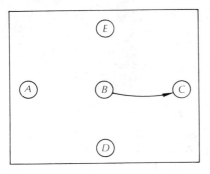

FIGURE 10.21
Changes in aggregate transport costs.

This formula increases the importance of distant points rather than diminishing their importance, as in the potential model. Figure 10.22a shows a transport-cost surface based on the same sample of points used for the potential model. The isolines indicate the percentage above Fort Wayne, Indiana, by land transport. The uneven distribution of population minimizes total cost at Fort Wayne, and total cost rises in all directions as shown in the New York-Los Angeles cross section in the inset (Figure 10.22b). The problem then is to determine the most profitable location: Is it the highest point on the demand-potential surface or the lowest point on the transport-cost surface. Chauncy Harris (1954) summed up the problem neatly with an example. The West Coast comprised 11 percent of the U.S. population in 1950, but accounted

FIGURE 10.22
(a) Transport cost to the national market; (b) cross section from New York City to Los Angeles. (Source: Harris, 1954.)

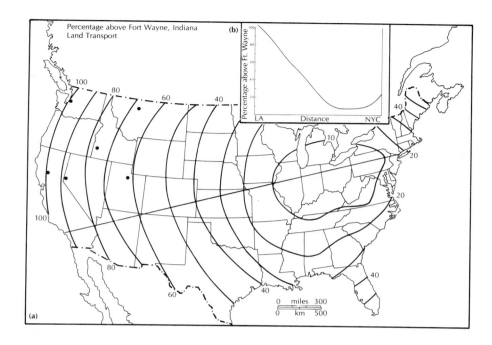

for only 5 percent of the sales from Chicago firms; yet the West Coast accounted for 22 percent of the total transport costs incurred by Chicago firms. The potential model is useful because it allows us to visualize variations in demand. The more localized the market, the more nearly the optimum points on both surfaces coincide, but only for the distribution of the finished product.

LOCATIONAL INTERDEPENDENCE

We turn now to the concept of *locational interdependence*, a concept which implies that competition from rival producers can lower potential revenues at a given point in space. So far, we have assumed that each producer is a *spatial monopolist*—the sole producer of the particular product within the market area. Under this assumption, profit maximization is realized at the level of output at which marginal cost equals marginal revenue. However, nonmonopoly conditions dictate a different strategy for maximizing profits.

In the nonmonopoly situation implied by locational interdependence, economic competition occurs, but not as in the classical model of perfect competition. The kind of market faced by spatial rivals is called an *oligopoly*; that is, a market in which there is more than one producer, but a small enough number of producers so that the actions of one may have a considerable effect on another. Economic

(price) competition is lacking in an oligopoly, but intense nonprice competition occurs.

An oligopoly takes on meaning when producers are considered in a spatial context. A small manufacturing plant is concerned only with the actions of other firms within the same market area. Producers of ready-mixed concrete in Chicago, for example, are not interested in the actions of similar firms in Los Angeles. Even if the Los Angeles firms lowered their plant price to zero, they could not capture the Chicago market because of the transport costs involved. The individual Chicago producer is, however, very interested in the actions of other ready-mixed firms in the Chicago area. Their actions could exert a considerable effect on profits. Locational interdependence, therefore, is a term that applies to spatial oligopolies.

The Ice-Cream Vendor Analogy

Let us consider a simple oligopoly model first developed by H. Hotelling (1929). Imagine a stretch of beach over which people are evenly distributed. On this beach are two ice-cream vendors, each of whom sells an identical product at the same price. People on the beach, therefore, minimize the cost of their ice-cream purchases by buying from the closer vendor. Initially the two vendors are located at the quartile points of the beach (Figure 10.23a). Each person buys from the closer vendor, so that the total market area is equally divided between the two. Vendor *A* could temporarily

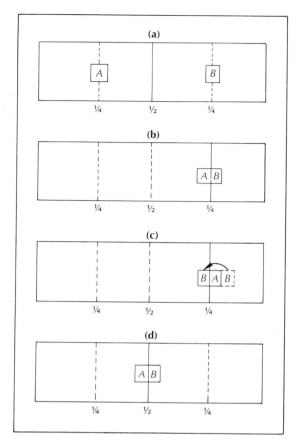

FIGURE 10.23
The ice-cream vendor analogy. (Source: Based on
Hotelling, 1929.)

increase market share by shifting the stand to a site
immediately adjacent to Vendor *B* (Figure 10.23b).
Vendor *B* would then countermove as shown in
Figure 10.23c. In the Hotelling solution, the final
location of the stands once again splits the market
evenly between the two vendors (Figure 10.23d). Since
neither vendor can gain an advantage by moving, each
must turn to other forms of competition, such as
advertising or product differentiation.

The Hotelling solution determines the equilibrium quantity sold by each producer and the equilibrium prices, but we must assume that demand is
completely inelastic at any price. If both producers
charge the same price (plus the same transport costs),
total demand will be shared equally in the equilibrium
situation. In other words, Hotelling assumed that the
demand of consumers at the edge of the market (who
must pay a higher price) is the same as those nearby
the common selling point. Both producers share the
same production costs, so that the common market

price is that at which marginal costs equal zero. The
distance to the most distant consumer is the same
from both producers and neither can affect transportation costs. A producer who raises the market price
will immediately lose the entire market, and neither
producer can lower prices to a point where costs
exceed the price per unit; thus, the equilibrium is
uniquely determined. The Hotelling solution is an
optimum one for each producer. Not for consumers,
however, since a location at the quartile points
minimizes aggregate transport costs.

The most important form of competition in the
initial phase of a spatial oligopoly (before equilibrium)
is price competition based on transport costs. Producers are able to capture parts of market areas in which
their delivered prices are lowest. This outcome holds
only if we assume that transport costs are charged to
each consumer as a function of distance and until
equilibrium conditions are reached.

Price differentials are the only form of competition allowed in technical economic analysis, but we
popularly recognize several other types. Advertising,
which adds to the cost of products, is the most
important type of nonprice competition. A second
strategy is to create perceived quality differentials in
products; for example, in the wide range of automobile types (and prices) that all bear a given producer's
name. Quality differentiation divides a broad market
into a group of submarkets, thus meeting the demand
for a wide range of consumers. A third technique of
nonprice competition is to introduce design differences into the product line. Tennis racket companies,
for example, continually introduce new models that
are purported to be "superior" to last year's design
and to all competition.

Nonprice competition should be the prevailing
form if locational equilibrium prevails. The fact that
this form of competition is the most common in the
United States may imply some sort of short-run
equilibrium, at least in certain industries.

Both long- and short-run locational equilibrium
assume that producers can adjust instantaneously to
changes in competitors' locations and to other marginal changes in costs and revenues. Locational
inertia, however, prevents instantaneous adjustments
from taking place, and transport costs prevent all
factors of production from being as mobile as assumed in the classical models. Equilibrium adjustment also assumes economic rationality and perfect
knowledge, which are not real-world conditions.
Producers are reluctant to make major moves—even
those of potential economic advantage—because of
risk and uncertainty. Spatial equilibrium, if it exists in

the short run, is the result of a trial-and-error process that has often resulted in great social costs.

EVALUATION OF INDUSTRIAL LOCATION THEORY

Industrial location theory helps us gain insight into how individual manufacturing establishments are located with reference to the factors of production and the distribution of customers, suppliers, and competitors. It also helps us to appreciate plant-location decisions. Are industrial location patterns rational? Do firms search for optimal locations? American economist A. Alchian (1950) explored these questions in detail, as we saw in Chapter 5. He distinguished between two types of decision making leading to locational patterns: *adoptive* and *adaptive behavior.*

During the nineteenth and early twentieth centuries, when capitalism came into its own in Europe and North America, decision making was of the adoptive kind. Decisions were made arbitrarily leaving behind a pattern of survivors lucky enough to have selected good locations for their plants—potteries, textile factories, and iron and steel works. In the competitive economic environment, location mattered. Weber's theory therefore helps us understand economic history's success stories. It is a framework for understanding *what is.*

By contrast, adaptive behavior focuses on rational decision making. It involves a systematic analysis of alternative locations, leading to the development of rational industrial landscapes. This type of decision making is expected of multinationals in the emerging one-world economy of the late twentieth century. Location theory can guide these enterprises in selecting optimal locations for their manufacturing plants, development centers, and research laboratories. It is a normative framework suggesting *what should be.*

From the perspective of the behavioral geographer, the main defect of normative industrial location theory, based on recognition of spatial limits to profitability, is that it fails to say what decision-makers actually do (Greenhut 1956; Pred 1967). How do enterprises go about the task of selecting profitable sites for branch plants? John Rees (1972, 1974), a British geographer, provided an answer to this question. In his studies of the investment location decisions of large British and American firms, he reported interviews with executives confirming the validity of a framework of locational search, learning, and choice evaluation, illustrated in Figure 10.24. The first phase

of the decision-making process is the recognition that a growth problem exists ("stress threshold") with respect to the satisfaction of demand. (Rees pointed out that the question of demand—whether or not there exists a potential market area of sufficient size to consume the output of a plant—is the prime variable in the locational choice of a large, modern manufacturing firm.) The alternative responses to in-situ expansion may be relocation, acquisition, or a new plant. A new plant involves a three-stage search procedure, the outcome of which leads to a decision and, finally, to the allocation of resources. It also generates "feedback" into learning behavior and into the decision-making environment. A major virtue of Rees's model is the distinction between short- and long-term responses of the organization. Classical industrial location theory tends to ignore the time frame within which profit maximization is sought. The behavioral approach is much more realistic in recognizing that the environment within which the enterprise operates is in a constant state of flux.

Industrial location theory has been criticized by radicals, primarily because it focuses on firms as abstract entities, without effective structural relationships to the rest of the economy. In the radical view, analysis of location must begin from the top, with the world's capitalist system, not from the bottom, with individual firms (Massey 1973, 1979) (Figure 10.25). The actual behavior of the individual firm takes on its meaning in the broader economic context that the structural approach seeks to reveal. Working up from the bottom can explain neither the individual elements nor the system as a whole. According to radicals, then, industrial location theory is idealistic because it abstracts elements that form only a small part of reality. This charge extends to the new approaches in which the simple conception of the single-plant firm has been replaced with a model of the firm as a complex organizational structure.

THE LARGE INDUSTRIAL ENTERPRISE

Although small, single-plant operations remain the most common type of firm, we live in an era in which giant corporations with transnational bases control a large share of the world economy. In 1988, the six hundred biggest companies in the world—the "billion dollar club" because their annual sales exceed $1 billion—created 20 percent of the world's total value added in manufacturing and agriculture (*The Economist* 1988a, p. 73). And the impact of big companies on the global economy, which is out of all proportion to their numerical significance, is steadily increasing.

FIGURE 10.24
An empirical model of the
decision-making process for
establishing a branch of a large
corporation. (Source: Based on
Rees, 1972, p. 203; 1974, p. 191.)

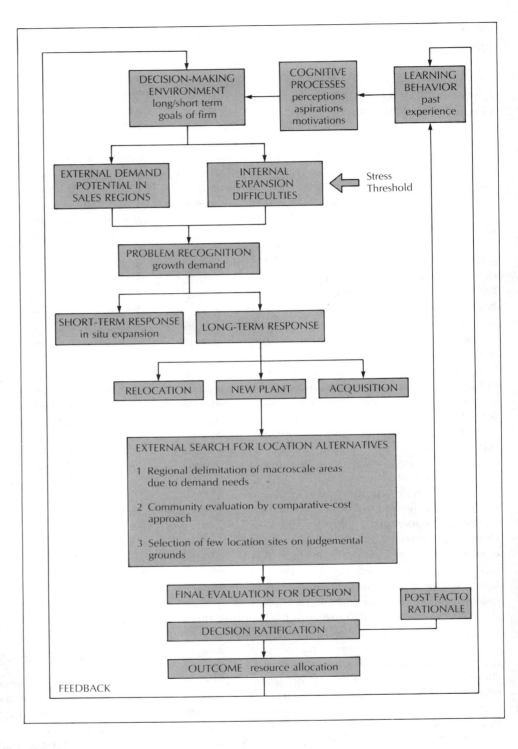

What are the trends in industrial organization? What
is the relationship of large enterprises to small firms?
Why do firms grow? How do they grow? How are
corporate systems geographically organized? Answers
to these questions will help us to appreciate the role
played by multiplant, multiproduct, multinational
enterprises in the world economy.

Trends in Industrial Organization

One accessible measure of business size is annual
sales. Table 10.4 lists the rank order of twenty of the
largest five hundred U.S. industrial corporations in
terms of this measure. The majority of these enterprises would also appear in the combined top-twenty

FIGURE 10.25
The economic context of individual firms from the structural perspective. (Source: Based on Massey, 1977, p. 29.)

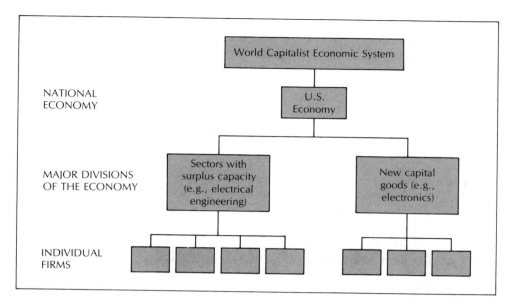

ranking of the largest U.S. and non-U.S. corporations. These huge companies have annual sales that exceed the gross national products of many countries.

Industry concentration and *aggregate concentration ratios* are frequently used to measure the eco-

nomic power of large companies. The industry concentration ratio indicates the percentage of total sales accounted for by the largest enterprises (typically between three and eight) in that market. However, a business may exert little influence in a sector but great

TABLE 10.4
The largest U.S. industrial corporations, 1987.

Rank	Company	Headquarters	Sales ($000)
1	General Motors	Detroit	102,813,700
2	Exxon	New York	69,888,000
3	Ford Motor	Dearborn, MI	62,715,800
4	International Business Machines	Armonk, NY	51,250,000
5	Mobil	New York	44,866,000
6	General Electric	Fairfield, CT	35,211,000
7	American Tel. & Tel.	New York	34,087,000
8	Texaco	White Plains, NY	31,613,000
9	E. I. du Pont de Nemours	Wilmington, DE	27,148,000
10	Chevron	San Francisco	24,351,000
11	Chrysler	Highland Park, MI	22,513,500
12	Philip Morris	New York	20,681,000
13	Amoco	Chicago	18,281,000
14	RJR Nabisco	Winston-Salem, NC	16,998,000
15	Shell Oil	Houston	16,833,000
16	Boeing	Seattle	16,341,000
17	United Technologies	Hartford	15,669,157
18	Procter & Gamble	Cincinnati	15,439,000
19	Occidental Petroleum	Los Angeles	15,344,100
20	Atlantic Richfield	Los Angeles	14,585,802

SOURCE: Rand McNally, 1988.

influence in the economy as a whole. This situation can be represented by calculating an aggregate concentration ratio, which indicates the percentage share of national manufacturing sales accounted for by the largest (typically the top hundred) companies.

Table 10.5 illustrates industry concentration ratios for the United States. The ratios differ markedly from industry to industry, reflecting the ease or difficulty with which a new firm may enter a particular industry. This, in turn, is related to the technology of the industry. For example, the amount of capital required to establish a modern low-cost iron and steel mill is enormous compared to that required to establish a sawmill. What Table 10.5 fails to reveal, however, are changes in industry concentration. In advanced industrial countries, industry concentration increased in the 1950s and 1960s but stabilized in the 1970s and 1980s.

Most large corporations owe their growth and size to diversification. An example of a *multiproduct diversified enterprise* is Tenneco (Figure 10.26). For multiproduct enterprises, aggregate concentration is a better measure of corporate power than industry concentration. Figure 10.27 plots the contribution of the hundred largest enterprises to manufacturing net output in the United Kingdom and United States since 1910. As with industry concentration, aggregate concentration in manufacturing increased in the 1950s and 1960s and stabilized or even declined in the 1970s. Does the reversal signify a change in the scale of economic organization? No, it does not. Many of the largest manufacturing companies have expanded into nonmanufacturing activities (Hughes and Kumar 1984).

Large multiproduct companies are usually *multiplant enterprises.* Their geographical bases are as broad as their product ranges. With factories and offices in other countries, these area-organizing institutions are also *multinational enterprises.* For example, International Business Machines (IBM), a company of 390,000 people doing a $54 billion business in 132 countries by supplying some 5 million customers with some 10,000 hardware, software, and service offerings, has manufacturing plants in more than a dozen countries and major distribution centers in nearly thirty (Figure 10.28). Imperial Chemical Industries (ICI) has factories in more than forty countries and selling organizations in more than sixty. The global dimension of the activities of firms, exemplified by IBM and ICI, is the most obvious element of the economic power of large enterprises.

The emergence of a global system of production, having at its heart the multinational corporation, is a recent phenomenon. As late as 1950 most large corporations were barely multinational. But by 1970 the situation had changed dramatically (Table 10.6). Large corporations, which for years had entered foreign markets via exports, had set up foreign subsidiaries in numerous countries.

In the 1960s and 1970s, public perception of multinational corporations was generally negative. They were widely labelled as exploitative giants — and they still are by radical scholars who view their actions as socially disruptive and likely to promote a general tendency toward world economic stagnation. By contrast, traditional scholars and policymakers in the market-conscious 1980s and 1990s view multinationals as sources of employment and revenue rather than as inherent exploiters.

Multinationals increase employment in their host countries. It is estimated that direct employment of multinationals is 65 million or 3 percent of the

TABLE 10.5
Concentration by industry in the United States, 1977.

Industry	Percentage Value of Total Shipments	
	Four Largest Enterprises	Eight Largest Enterprises
Motor vehicles	93	99
Iron and steel	45	65
Bread, biscuits, cake	33	40
Oil refining	30	53
Agricultural machinery	46	61
Soft drinks	15	22
Pharmaceuticals	24	43
Printing and publishing	14	19
Sawmilling and planing of wood	17	23

SOURCE: U.S. Bureau of the Census, 1984.

FIGURE 10.26
Companies and products controlled by Tenneco.

Division	Products
Tenneco Oil	Crude oil, natural gas, refining, service stations
Tennessee Gas Transmission	Natural gas pipelines
J.I. Case	Two and four-wheel drive agricultural tractors and implements, loader/backhoes, crawler and wheel loaders, excavators, trenchers, industrial and materials handling cranes, skid steer loaders, forklift and compaction equipment.
Tenneco Automotive	Automotive exhaust systems, shock absorbers and ride control products, jacks and lifting equipment, filters, wheel oil seals, fans, pulleys, manifolds.
Tenneco Chemicals	Fine, intermediate, and hydrocarbon chemicals; plastic resins, stabilizers, plasticizers; paint colorants and dispersions. Chemical foam products and fabricated plastic materials. Synthetic and organic chemicals, paper and specialty chemicals.
Newport News Shipbuilding	Naval and merchant ship construction and repair, nuclear vessel refueling, components and services for the nuclear power industry, heavy castings and sheet metal products for industrial use.
Packaging Corporation of America	Corrugated containers, paperboard, folding cartons, molded pulp products.
Tenneco West	Agricultural products (fresh fruits, vegetables, almonds, pistachios, dates, raisins), commercial recreational, and residential real estate.

FIGURE 10.27
Share of the one hundred largest enterprises in manufacturing net output in the United Kingdom and United States. (Source: Chapman and Walker, 1987, p. 76.)

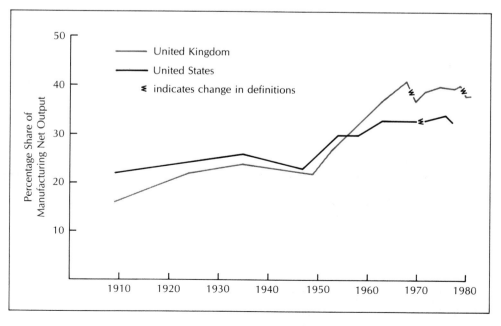

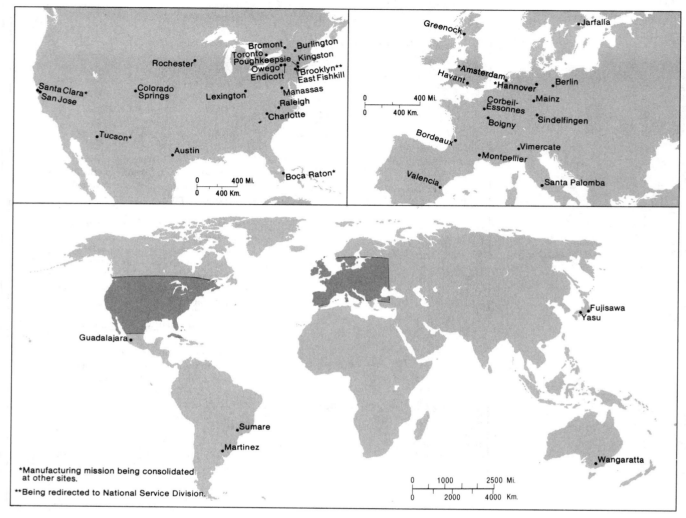

FIGURE 10.28
The worldwide distribution of IBM's manufacturing plants.

world's labor force. Add indirect employment, and such companies may generate 6 percent of the world's employment. In 1984, American multinationals employed about 6.5 million people abroad, 32 percent of these in underdeveloped countries, 42 percent in Europe, 5 percent in Japan, and 14 percent in Canada.

Multinationals also increase a host country's output and exports. This is especially important for Third World countries in need of fast growth and

TABLE 10.6
The foreign manufacturing subsidiary networks of 315 large multinational corporations in 1950 and 1970.

Number of Enterprises with Subsidiary Networks Including:	180 U.S.-based Multinationals		135 European-based Multinationals	
	1950	1970	1950	1970
6 countries	138	9	116	31
6–20 countries	43	128	16	75
20 countries	0	44	3	29

SOURCE: Vernon, 1979, p. 258.

foreign exchange to service bank debt. Foreign-owned companies accounted for 55 percent of Singapore's employment in the manufacturing industry in 1982, 63 percent of its manufacturing output, and 90 percent of its exports of manufactured goods. They produced 70 percent of Zimbabwe's industrial output. In 1983, nearly 30 percent of Argentina's manufacturing output and exports came from multinationals.

American, West European, and Japanese enterprises own most of the world's multinational assets, but new sources of capital are emerging. Some Third World countries—Argentina, Brazil, Hong Kong, India, Mexico, Singapore, and Taiwan—have firms that have been establishing foreign direct investment (Kumar and Kim 1984, p. 45).

As multinationals have spread themselves over the world, there has been an increasing interpenetration of capital. For example, much Japanese private foreign investment ($33.4 billion at the end of 1987) goes to the United States. Japanese direct U.S. investment, however, lags far behind the Europeans (McConnell 1980). At the end of 1987, the Dutch invested $47 billion and the British $74.9 billion. Most of the new capital from abroad favors the traditional Manufacturing Belt of the Northeast and Great Lakes and the newer Sunbelt areas of the West and South (McConnell 1983). The interpenetration of flexible multinational capital means that countries virtually everywhere are facing increased competition from foreign suppliers. It is estimated, for example, that some 74 percent of all U.S. goods produced by domestic corporations face stiff competition inside the United States from foreign suppliers. This level of competition has had a significant impact on the dynamics of U.S. manufacturing, and has registered dramatically as a loss of jobs in Rust Belt industries.

In addition to foreign direct investment, which increased fivefold between the mid-1970s and 1990, there are other forms of international business open to multinationals. For example, international industrial firms engage in *turnkey projects*, arrangements in which the contractor not only plans and builds the project, but also trains the buyer's personnel and initiates operation of the project before "turning the key" over to the buyer. Corporations also engage in *licensing ventures* such as *franchising*. For example, Pepsi-Cola licenses the use of its name and the right to manufacture and sell its drink abroad. Part of the contract, however, requires that the foreign licensee buy the syrup from Pepsi; thus, the company enjoys both royalty and export advantages.

Another form of international business engaged in by multinationals is the *joint venture*. In this situation, a subsidiary is owned jointly by two or more parties. The joint-venture partners may be either from the private sector of the investing company's home country, from a third country, or from the host country. Corporations also engage in *international subcontracting*, sometimes called "offshore assembly" or "foreign sourcing." An important form of international subcontracting, especially in textiles, is an arrangement whereby firms based in the advanced industrial countries provide design specifications to producers in underdeveloped countries, purchase the finished products, then sell them at home and abroad.

The Dual Economy

The dominant position of large enterprises in the modern world economy owes much to their relationships with smaller firms. Robert Averitt's (1968) notion of a *dual economy* captures the essence of these relationships and puts them in perspective. According to Averitt, there are two distinct types of business enterprise. On the one hand, there are a few *core* or *center firms*—large, complex organizations that represent the nucleus of the economy and account for a high proportion of its production and profit-making potential. On the other hand, there are numerous *satellite* or *periphery firms*—small, straightforward organizations that manage to survive in the market through minimizing labor costs and by maximizing labor exploitation. There is no precise boundary between center and periphery firms, but the leading two hundred or so industrial corporations form the heart of the U.S. center economy. And at the world level, the "international center economy" consists of around five hundred to seven hundred firms.

For Averitt, small is not so beautiful from the perspective of industrial relations. The relationship between center and periphery firms is one of dominance and dependence, as reflected in purchasing policies, franchising agreements, and advisory and management contracts. The terms of these arrangements are dictated by the core firms. For example, IBM purchases components for its computers from a large number of smaller firms. However, IBM is able, through its purchasing policies, to "make or break" its business partners and to dictate their location within a specified distance of IBM's own manufacturing facilities (Susman and Schutz 1983). This relationship emphasizes that the power of core enterprises is often much greater than that implied by industry and aggregate concentration ratios, which fail to take account of unequal relationships between business organizations.

What are the prospects for the survival of small firms in the advanced economies? This question is the subject of considerable debate (Curran and Stanworth 1986; Storey 1986). One argument is that small firms will continue to flourish because of their competitiveness, flexibility, dynamism, and innovativeness. The counterargument is that small firms can play only a restricted role in a world in which the terms of production and competition are set by large firms. Indeed, the survival of the small firm is not related to internal advantages so much as to protection from market forces arising from ties with large firms. Moreover, the characteristics of competitiveness, flexibility, dynamism, and innovativeness may be just as applicable to large firms as to small ones.

Why Firms Grow

The notion of the dual economy conflicts with traditional economic thinking about absolute limits on firm size imposed by diseconomies of scale. Most large companies operate at a scale far beyond the initial point on the long-run average cost curve. In fact, evidence of increasing returns to scale has led to a reappraisal of the theory of the firm.

To explain why firms increase their scales of operation, economists make two distinctions. First, they separate *economies of size* (scale) from *economies of growth*. Edith Penrose (1959) emphasized this distinction when she argued that economies of growth may exist independently of economies of size. For the "enterprising firm," she pointed to unused productive services as "a challenge to innovate, an incentive to expand, and a source of competitive advantage. They facilitate the introduction of new combinations of resources—innovation—within the firm" (p. 85). Second, economists separate *actual* from *perceived* scale economies. As W. H. Starbuck (1965) noted, the actual relationship between cost per unit and size is irrelevant. The relationship that is relevant is that which executives believe holds true (p. 457).

The tendency toward increasing scales of operation is therefore based on the motivating force of growth (Cyert and March 1963). This point was elaborated by John Kenneth Galbraith (1967), who said firms expand for two reasons: survival and growth. Both goals are promoted by horizontal and vertical expansion and by diversification.

The view that corporate growth is part of a natural progression is deterministic, however. It flies in the face of reality. The majority of firms in an economy remain small and peripheral. As Michael Taylor and Nigel Thrift (1982) emphasized, only some firms, especially those that manufacture capital goods, have the potential to develop into large corporations. Financial barriers prevent most firms from making successive transitions from a small regional base to larger national organizations and then to multinational operations. Access to finance—banking capital, venture capital, and international bond and currency markets—has become increasingly uneven, favoring some firms and not others. Because these "finance gaps" have become wider, there is much less chance of a small firm evolving into a corporate giant today than there was a hundred years ago.

How Firms Grow

How a firm grows depends on the *strategy* it follows and the *methods* it selects to implement its strategy (Figure 10.29). As we discussed earlier in the chap-

FIGURE 10.29
Strategies and methods of corporate growth. (Source: Chapman and Walker, 1987, p. 86.)

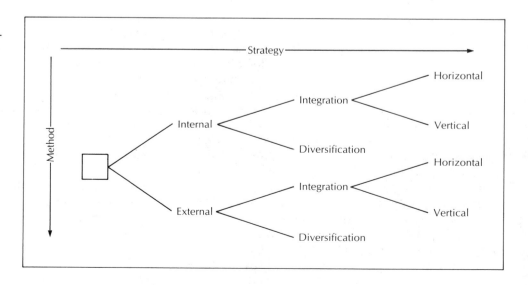

ter, strategies of growth may be *integration* or *diversification*. In the United States, horizontal integration predominated from the 1890s to the early 1900s, vertical integration came to the fore in the 1920s, and diversification has been the principal goal since the 1950s. This three-stage sequence provides a framework for understanding the interrelationship of the various strategies (Bannock 1971). The early growth of large enterprises involves the removal of competition by absorption leading to oligopoly. This is followed by a period in which the oligopoly protects its sources of supply and markets by vertical integration. Once a dominant position is achieved, rapid corporate growth can proceed only via diversification.

Means for achieving growth may be *internal* or *external* to the firm. Growth may be financed internally by the retention of funds or new share issues. Or it may be generated externally by acquiring the assets of other firms through mergers. Most large firms employ both means, but external growth is particularly important for the largest and fastest growing enterprises.

Whatever strategy and method is adopted, corporate growth typically involves the addition of new factories and, thus, a change in geography. Initially, much of the employment and productive capacity of a firm concentrates in the area in which it was founded. An example is Ford Motor Company, which for a long time had most of its operating plants in the Midwest. As enterprises grow, they become more widely dispersed multiplant operations, which is sometimes accompanied by decreasing dominance of the home region. Exceptions tend to be companies confined to one broad product-area, and based in a region where there is a historical specialization within that product-area. Thus in Britain, the huge glass company of Pilkington Bros. remains concentrated in St. Helens. The importance of a home region at the national scale is paralleled by the importance of a home country at the international scale, although the extent of this dominance may also diminish over time.

The choice of growth strategy affects corporate geography. Horizontal integration frequently involves setting up plants over a wider and wider area. The geographical consequences of vertical integration vary according to whether the move is backward ("down in the production process") or forward ("up in the production process"). *Backward integration,* in which a firm takes over operations previously the responsibility of its suppliers, may lead a firm into resource-frontier areas. An example is the development of iron ore deposits by American and Japanese companies in Venezuela and Australia. Conversely, *forward integration,* in which a firm begins to control the outlets for its products, may lead a resource-based organization to set up plants in market locations. Diversification does not have such predictable consequences for the geography of large enterprises.

The method of growth also affects the geography of multiplant firms. When growth is achieved internally, enterprises can carefully plan the location of new branch plants. When growth is achieved externally, enterprises inherit facilities from acquired firms; hence, there is less control over their locations. Moreover, the attractiveness of new facilities often lies in their economic, financial, and technical characteristics. Nonetheless, geography does play a role in the decision process. Firms typically confront the uncertainty and risk of expansion by investing first in geographically adjacent or culturally similar environments. For example, geographer M. David Ray (1971) identified a distance-decay relationship between the location of U.S.-owned manufacturing plants in Canada and the head offices to which they report. Most plants were close to the U.S. border, and the proportion of headquarters in Chicago, Detroit, and New York was much larger than for more distant centers of internationalized American capital such as Los Angeles.

Geographers have developed models of how firms grow. Most of these models postulate a single development path beginning with a small, single-plant operation and culminating with the multinational enterprise (McNee 1974; Taylor 1975; Håkanson 1979). L. Håkanson, for example, proposed a five-stage model that incorporates the transition from "home country" to overseas operations. The top, left diagram of Figure 10.30 illustrates the firm's action space, divided into a "core area" where it was first founded, the remainder of the "home country," and an outer circle representing the rest of the world. In Stage 1, there exists a single-plant firm tied to the immediate environment. In Stage 2, the firm penetrates the home market via sales offices, the expansion of central management, and new production capacity away from the original plant. Stage 3 sees the first incursions into foreign markets via a network of sales agents; at home, production capacity may be expanded outside the original core area. In Stage 4, sales offices replace some of the overseas agents. Finally, production plants appear in foreign markets as acquisitions or subsidiaries. Stage 5, then, marks the fully fledged multinational.

This kind of evolution along a path from a local to a national and then to an international company is exceptional. Unequal access to finance makes it difficult, if not impossible, for many firms to expand beyond the subnational scale. In the late twentieth

FIGURE 10.30
A model of the stages of growth
and geographical expansion of
an industrial corporation.
(Source: Based on Håkanson,
1979, pp. 131–35.)

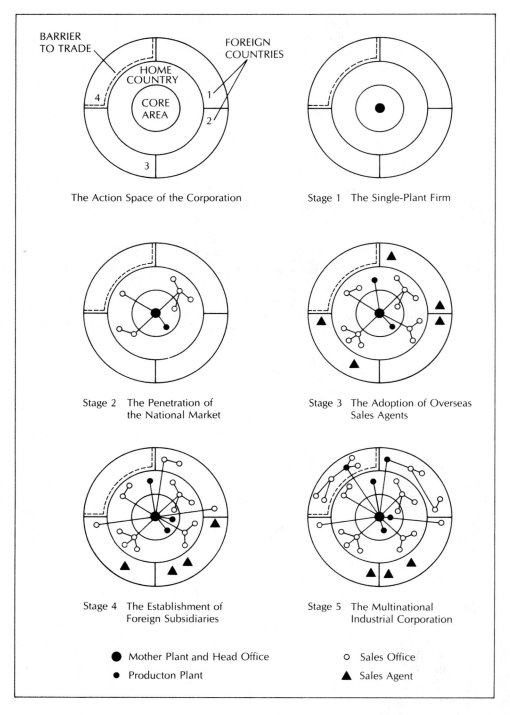

The Action Space of the Corporation

Stage 1   The Single-Plant Firm

Stage 2   The Penetration of
the National Market

Stage 3   The Adoption of Overseas
Sales Agents

Stage 4   The Establishment of
Foreign Subsidiaries

Stage 5   The Multinational
Industrial Corporation

● Mother Plant and Head Office   ○ Sales Office

● Producton Plant   ▲ Sales Agent

century, the size-distribution of firms resembles a
broad-based pyramid in which fewer and fewer firms
can move from one level to another. Rather than the
single development sequence that may have existed in
the nineteenth century, today there are a series of
discrete development sequences through which multinationals follow a distinctive path.

Geographical Organization of Corporate Systems

Multifacility corporate systems, which include manufacturing plants, research laboratories, education centers, offices, warehouses, and distribution terminals,
have their own distinctive geographies. To appreciate

the internal geography of these systems, four issues must be considered: (1) the ways in which corporations are organized to maximize efficiency, (2) the influence of hierarchical management structures on the location of employment, (3) the impact of technology-based hierarchies on corporate spatial organization, and (4) the implications of locational shifts in the productive base of large companies.

Organizational Structure Companies organize themselves hierarchically in a variety of ways to administer and coordinate their activities. The basic formats are (1) functional orientation, (2) product orientation, (3) geographical orientation, and (4) customer orientation. A fifth format, which is a combination of at least two of the basic formats, is called a matrix structure. Different companies may select different formats, but all formats are always subject to review and modification.

The organizational format that is based on various corporate functions—manufacturing, marketing, finance, and research and development—is illus-

trated in Figure 10.31a. With this framework all the company's functional operations are concentrated in one sector of the enterprise. An example of a company with this type of organizational structure is Ford Motor Company. This form of organization works well for companies with relatively confined product bases.

Figure 10.31b illustrates the product-orientation organizational structure. Product groups could be cars, trucks, buses, and farm equipment for a major motor vehicle manufacturer. Although a corporate central staff is needed to provide companywide expertise and to provide some degree of assistance to each product group, each group also has its own functional staff. Thus, a fairly high degree of managerial decentralization is required. The product-orientation format works well for companies with diverse product lines. Pan American Airways and Westinghouse are examples of companies organized in accordance with this format.

A third organizational format is based on geographical orientation—either the geographical location of customers or of the company's productive

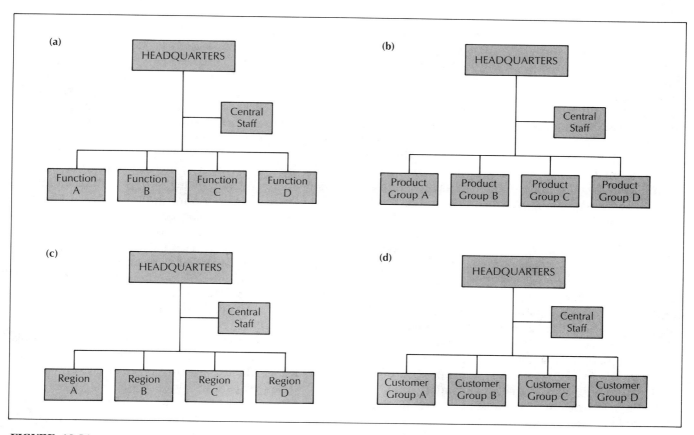

FIGURE 10.31

Organizational structures: (a) functional orientation; (b) product orientation; (c) geographical orientation; (d) customer orientation.

facilities. As shown in Figure 10.31c, the company is organized around regions rather than functions or products. Under this form of organization, most or all of the corporation's activities relating to any good or service that is bought, sold, or produced within a region, are under the control of the regional group head. Each of the geographical regions is under a separate profit center. This organizational format is best suited for companies with a narrow range of products, markets, and distribution channels. It is popular among oil companies and major money-center banks.

Some companies organize according to the types of customers they wish to serve rather than the locations of customers (Figure 10.31d). For example, commercial banks are commonly organized around groups such as the personal, corporate, mortgage, and trust departments. Alternatively, manufacturing corporations might be structured around industrial, commercial, and governmental divisions according to prevalent type of customer for each group.

The various organizational structures all have advantages, but none is ideal for all companies. Indeed, it is safe to say that these formats have drawbacks for most or all the companies that have adopted them. Nonetheless, most companies settle on one basic format as the most satisfactory structure for the company's needs at a particular time in its evolution—or they create a combination of two or more types.

H. A. Simon's (1960) analysis of these forms of business organizational structure identifies three tiers of activities. At the bottom are manufacturing and routine administrative activities. In the middle are coordinating functions that bind together the various elements of the enterprise. And at the top are strategic decision-making functions, which control the relationships of economic ownership (i.e., control the overall investment and accumulation process) and the relations of possession (i.e., the means of production and labor power).

Simon's conceptualization has geographical implications. For the small, single-plant firm, strategy and production functions are not geographically separated; hence, there is no need for an intermediate tier of coordinating activities. As firms grow to become multilocational companies, more complex functional and spatial divisions of labor develop. One of the best-known forms of spatial organization draws on the characteristics of large electronics companies. Strategy functions are performed at the headquarters location. Coordinating functions are dispersed to regional offices that control a number of interdependent production facilities. For simplicity, say there are

two production facilities: one branch plant manufacturing complex components, the other assembling finished products. This organizational structure represents different degrees of removal of job control. It also represents a clear-cut distinction between the functions of conception on the one hand and execution on the other hand, with the parallel distinction between nonproduction and production employment.

Administrative Hierarchies   A major proportion of the employees of large corporations, even those primarily involved in manufacturing, is in nonproduction activities. And the proportion is increasing because of the substitution of capital for labor and because of the growth of R&D activities. The ratio of nonproduction to production employment is less important from a geographical perspective than is the relative location of these activities.

Strategic head-office functions tend to cluster in a relatively few large metropolitan areas, especially in the case of huge manufacturing firms with a financial rather than a production orientation. The concentration of corporate white-collar jobs in or around major metropolitan centers is further reinforced by the distribution of a company's R&D facilities. Corporate R&D establishments often locate close to headquarters. To be sure, there are exceptions. The labor factor has pulled R&D establishments to other locations—in France to the Côte d'Azur on the strength of its glorious climate, and in the United States to Lincoln, Nebraska, and to Austin, Texas, on the strength of their university research environments.

The contribution of head-office and R&D establishments to nonproduction employment within corporations has greater strategic than numerical significance. Important administrative jobs are concentrated at the corporate core. But the majority of nonproduction jobs are dispersed among regional offices, branch plants, and depots. Similarly, a high proportion of R&D staff are not involved in basic research, but in the development of existing products and processes. These jobs are often dispersed to industrial manufacturing sites.

Technological Hierarchies   In addition to administrative hierarchies, there are technology-based hierarchies. Product cycles and production systems help us to appreciate the importance of technological considerations in corporate spatial organization. The *product-life cycle*, which begins with a product's development and ends when it is replaced with something better, is important geographically because products at different stages of production tend to be

IBM designed the Yamato Laboratory with the aim of making it the focal point of development of high-technology products for IBM Japan. The laboratory integrates all development groups at a single location and uses IBM's systems to create products suited to local customer needs. The Yamato Laboratory is one of more than thirty IBM basic research institutes and product development laboratories around the world. (Source: IBM.)

manufactured at different places within corporate systems. Moreover, at any given stage of the cycle, the various operations involved in the manufacture of a product such as a camera are not necessarily concentrated at a single factory. The production of the camera's complex components is at a different place from where the final product is assembled.

Economist Simon Kuznets (1930) developed the concept of the three-stage product cycle (Figure 10.32). In Stage 1, innovators discover, develop, and commercially launch a product. They also benefit from a temporary monopoly and all the special privileges—high profits—that result from it. In Stage 2, competitors buy or steal the new idea, which forces

FIGURE 10.32
A typical product life cycle. (Source: Chapman and Walker, 1987, p. 112.)

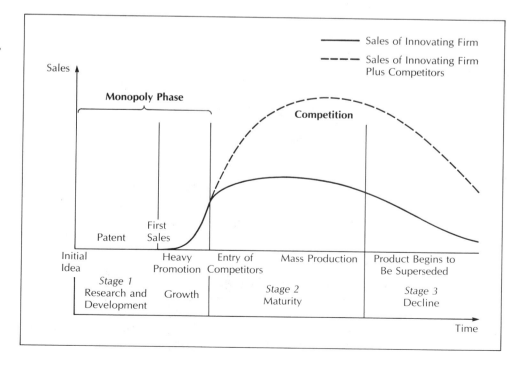

an emphasis on low-cost, standardized, mass-production technologies. Sales of the product increase for a while but the initial high returns diminish. By Stage 3, the product begins to be superseded. Markets are lost to new products and manufacturing capacity is reduced.

The implications of the product-cycle model for industrial location at the international scale were recognized by Raymond Vernon (1966) and a group of associates at the Harvard Business School. Innovation begins in an advanced industrial country. These countries have the science, the technology, and the internal market to justify research and development. As a result, they also have an international advantage, and they export their product around the world. But as the technology becomes routinized, other producers appear on the scene, first in the other advanced countries, then on the periphery. Meanwhile, back in the rich country, investment in the newest generation of sophisticated technology is the cutting edge of the economy.

There is no doubt that developed countries are the innovators of the world economy, and that Third World countries increasingly specialize in the laborious task of transforming raw materials into commodities. But developed countries are also engaged in activities associated with the second and third stages of the product cycle. Indeed, concern has been expressed in Britain and Canada about their recipient status. This concern has also been voiced in the United States. Consider, for example, who makes what for Mazda. the Japanese multinational manufactures the compact MX-6 in Flat Rock, Michigan, as well as the mechanically and structurally identical Ford Probe. The costly high-tech subassemblies—engine, transaxle, suspension, brakes—are Japanese-made, and the less expensive, lower tech subassemblies— carpets, glass, tires—tend to be U.S. made. The upshot of this trend is that American autoparts companies are often excluded from critical R&D programs associated with the design and engineering of new Japanese cars.

The product life cycle is not the only way the technology of production affects corporate spatial organization. Corporations frequently establish fragmented production systems or *part-process structures* in which the division-of-labor principle is taken a step further. As described by Chapman and Walker (1987), "the various tasks are geographically separated so that the motorway networks and shipping routes which link them effectively become integral parts of the assembly line" (p. 114). This type of system, established for a long time on a regional scale, now operates on a world scale. Take the Mercury Tracer,

an automobile designed by Mazda, which is 25 percent owned by Ford. The auto's engine is built in Japan. Its glass, trim, and seats are Mexican-made. With other parts from the United States, the Tracer is assembled in Mexico for U.S. sale under the Mercury insignia.

Not all manufacturing operations are fragmented. Corporate branch plants are often *clones*, supplying identical products to their market areas. Examples abound. Medium-size firms in the clothing industry often have this structure, as do many multiplant companies manufacturing final consumer products. Part-process structures tend to be associated with certain industrial sectors, such as electronics and motor vehicles, characterized by complex finished products made up of many individual components.

Labor is an important variable in the location of facilities making components. Manufacturers seek locations where the level of worker organization, the degree of conflict, and the power of labor to affect the actions of capital are more limited than in long-established centers of production such as Detroit, Coventry, and Turin. Starting in the early 1970s, Fiat began to decentralize part of the company's production away from its traditional base in Turin to the south of Italy. Compared to the workers of Turin, who were relatively strong and well organized, the workers of the south were new to modern industry and had little experience of union organization. At the international level, Ford adopted a similar tactic when it invested in Spain and Portugal in the 1970s. Ford management perceived it could operate trouble-free plants in a region of low labor costs. The labor factor is further emphasized by the practice of *dual sourcing*. To avoid total dependence on a single workforce that could disrupt an interdependent production system, companies such as Ford and Fiat are willing to sacrifice economies of scale for the security afforded by duplicate facilities in different locations.

Locational Adjustment   Corporate production systems undergo continuous locational adjustment. Shifts may be inspired by technical and organizational developments internal to an industry or by changes in the external environment in which they operate, such as the oil price hikes of 1973. Particularly significant from a geographical point of view are adjustments in response to major shocks or stresses placed on an enterprise. For example, when faced with the challenge of competition from lower cost regions and with a falling rate of expansion of global markets, an enterprise could adopt a number of strategies— rationalization, capital substitution, outright closure, reorganization of productive capacity associated with the closure of older plants—which all in one way or another result in losses of employment. The recent industrial experience of Britain provides many illustrations of painful corporate restructuring programs. The ten largest manufacturing employers in the West Midlands reduced their British employment by 25 percent between 1978 and 1981 while at the same time increasing their overseas workforce by 9 percent (Gaffikin and Nickson 1984). This shift in the productive base of these companies abroad undermined the economic well-being of this area. Such employment withdrawals are an aspect of the growing international integration of production and mobility of capital.

One of capital's crucial advantages over labor is geographical mobility; it can make positive use of distance and differentiation in a way labor cannot. Corporations take advantage of such flexibility by shifting production to low-wage regions, setting up plants in areas with low levels of worker organization, or establishing plants in areas that offer incentive policies. Many Third World countries offer tax relief and capital subsidies for new industries. These policies have been subject to much debate in the United States and Britain where "enterprise zones" have been suggested as a way to compete with Third World incentives.

INDUSTRIAL EVOLUTION

Just as firms evolve, so do industries—groupings of firms that have common elements. Industries evolve according to a sequence of developmental stages analogous to youth, maturity, and old age. Models that capture this evolutionary process are industry and Kondratieff cycles.

The Industry Life-Cycle Model

The *industry life-cycle model*, based on a study of historical trends in various U.S. industries between 1885 and 1930 (Burns 1934), is similar to the product-cycle model (Kuznets 1930). Industries tend to experience "a period of experimentation, a period of rapid growth, a period of diminished growth, and a period of stability or decline" (Alderfer and Michl 1942, p. 14). Each of these periods may be related to the technology of an industry. Raymond Vernon (1966) argued that, because of the link between the technology of an industry and its locational requirements, these similarities find geographical expression in characteristic

distributions associated with industries in their youth, maturity, and old age.

Youth During this stage of development, an industry is preoccupied with the design and commercialization of a new product. The industry consists of a number of firms, mainly new startups, which pursue the adaption of an innovation. The preoccupation with product design and commercialization leads to the geographical concentration of the industry in relatively limited areas. For example, the electronics and computer-related industry began to concentrate in an area to the south of San Francisco in the 1950s. Many of the most significant advances in the electronics industry resulted from the work of scientist-entrepreneurs operating in converted garages and workshops in the area (Saxenian 1985).

Maturity During this phase, growth rates in output rise and then slacken as the industry shifts towards mass production and market penetration. Firm size increases and the number of firms decreases. Geographically, this phase is associated with the decentralization of production at interregional and international levels. Cheaper labor costs, better business climates, and proximity to markets pull the more routinized parts of the production process away from the innovating centers of the industry.

Old Age The final stage of the industry life cycle is characterized by market saturation and rationalization. A good example of market saturation is the iron and steel industry in developed countries. Major steel-using industries are relatively less important in developed countries now than they were in the nineteenth century. Consequently, their steel output has stabilized or even declined. In the United States and United Kingdom, iron and steel plants have closed down—a process called "rationalization." And the industry has tended to reconcentrate production in a few places, especially at coastal lower cost production sites.

Kondratieff Cycles

A common criticism of the life-cycle model, which treats industrial history as a natural rather than a social process, is that it neglects relationships between industries. These relationships, of significance to scholars, are interpreted in terms of innovation cycles in the process of economic growth. The cycles are called *Kondratieff cycles*, after the Soviet economist Nikolai Kondratieff (1935) who first identified them in the 1920s.

Kondratieff hypothesized that industrial countries of the world have experienced successive waves of growth and decline since the beginning of the industrial revolution with a periodicity of some fifty to sixty years duration. But it was left to Joseph Schumpeter (1939), a German economist, to explain Kondratieff's observation in terms of technical and organizational innovation. Schumpeter suggested that long waves of economic development are based on the diffusion of major technologies, such as railways and electric power. More recently, another German economist, Gerhard Mensch (1979), argued that throughout capitalist history, innovations have significantly bunched at certain points in time—around 1764, 1825, 1881, and 1935—just when the model of long waves would demand. According to Mensch, innovations come in clusters in response to social needs; they coincide with periods of depression that accompany world economic crises.

Kuznets (1954) described the Kondratieff cycles in terms of successive periods of recovery, prosperity, recession, and depression (Table 10.7). The upswing of the first cycle was inspired by the technologies of water transportation and the use of wind and captive water power; the second by the use of coal for steam power in water and railroad transportation, and in factory industry; the third by the development of the internal combustion engine, the application of electricity, and advances in organic chemistry; and the fourth by the rise of chemical, plastic, and electronics industries. In the present period of crisis in the world economy, with higher energy costs, lower profit margins, and growth of the old basic industries exhausted, scholars are asking whether a fifth wave is emerging. A new technoeconomic paradigm does seem to be emerging based on the extraordinarily low costs of storing, processing, and communicating information. In this perspective, the structural crisis of the 1980s and 1990s is a prolonged period of social adaptation to the growth of this new technological system, which is affecting virtually every part of the economy, both in terms of its present and future employment and skill requirements and its future market prospects.

SUMMARY

In this chapter we discussed manufacturing from the standpoint of firms rather than areas, with emphasis on normative and behavioral approaches to industrial location theory. Classical location theory stresses that patterns of manufacturing are caused by geographical characteristics—*location factors*—rather than by underlying social relations. According to least-cost location theory, assembly costs are incurred because the raw materials required for a particular kind of manu-

TABLE 10.7
Long waves of economic growth.

Phase of Growth[a]	Kondratieff Long Wave:				
	I	II	III	IV	V
Recovery	1770–1786	1828–1842	1886–1897	1940–1954	?
Prosperity	1787–1800	1843–1857	1898–1911	1955–1969	
Recession	1801–1813	1858–1869	1912–1924	1970–1980	
Depression (and new innovation)	1814–1827	1870–1885	1925–1939	1981-	

[a]Macroeconomic characteristics of long-wave phases are as follows:

Characteristic	Recovery	Prosperity	Recession	Depression
Gross national product	Increasing growth rates	Strong growth	Decreasing growth rates	Little or no growth
Investment demand	Increase in replacement investment	Strong expansion of capital stock	Scale-increasing investment	Excess capacity rationalization
Consumer demand	Purchasing power seeks new outlets	Expansion of demand in all sectors	Continued growth of new sectors	For a while continued growth at the expense of savings

SOURCE: Berry, Conkling, and Ray, 1987, p. 280.

facturing are not evenly distributed. Production costs vary because of the areal differences in the cost of labor, capital, and technical skills. Finished-product distribution costs are incurred when producers must sell to dispersed or widely scattered markets. All of these costs are collectively called "locational costs." Classical location theory provides a rationale to help find those points of production at which location costs are minimized.

Once a point of minimum locational costs is determined, however, other determinations must be made. These pertain to the *scale* at which the firm will operate and the particular combination of inputs *(technique)* that will be utilized. A producer must also be concerned with the actions of competitors. We see, then, that the location problem is very complex, but by applying the concept of *spatial margins to profitability* the complexity can be reduced. Locational costs, scale, technique, and locational interdependence together determine spatial margins to profitability. All viable manufacturing, by definition, must take place within these margins. How these limits are empirically determined and how locations within them are chosen, however, are usually discussed by geographers in a behavioral or decision-making context.

Classical location theory provides many important conceptualizations, but it came under attack in the 1960s and 1970s. Behavioral geographers criticized industrial location theory for its failure to examine what managerial decision-makers actually do. Radical geographers argued that dramatic changes in the geography of manufacturing activity were not due to area characteristics (location factors) but to social processes and capital-labor conflict. From this standpoint, the analysis of production, and thus of location, must be set in the context of broad social processes, both inside and outside the firm itself.

Most geographers now question the empirical usefulness of industrial location theory in light of the revolutionary role played by *multiproduct, multiplant, multinational operations* in the global structure of manufacturing. Accordingly, we devoted a major portion of the chapter to the spatial behavior of large industrial enterprises. Attention was given to trends in industrial organization, the relationship of large firms to small ones, the reasons for corporate growth, and the internal geography of corporate systems. In the last section, we looked briefly at models of *industrial evolution*—the industry life-cycle model and the Kondratieff long-wave model. The Kondratieff model reminds us that the present period of crisis in the world economy may be the beginning of a fifth upswing, this one based on a cluster of microelectronics and information technologies.

KEY TERMS

assembly costs
basic cost
cloning spatial structure
conglomerate
distribution costs
diversification
dual economy
dual sourcing
economies of growth
economies of scale
industry life cycle
integration
isodapane
joint venture
Kondratieff cycles
licensing venture
locational costs
localized raw material
market linkage
massing of reserves

material index
multinational corporation
orientation
part-process spatial structure
potential surface
product life cycle
production linkages
pure raw material
service linkages
space-cost curve
spatial margins to profitability
spatial monopoly
spatial oligopoly
technique
transport-cost surface
turnkey project
ubiquitous raw material
value added by manufacturing
Varignon frame
weight-losing raw material

SUGGESTED READINGS   Chapman, K., and Walker, D. 1987. *Industrial Location.* New York: Basil Blackwell.

Greenhut, M. L. 1956. *Plant Location in Theory and Practice.* Chapel Hill, NC: University of North Carolina Press.

Grunwald, J., and Flamm, K. 1985. *The Global Factory.* Washington, DC: Brookings Institution.

Hamilton, F. E. I., ed. 1974. *Spatial Perspectives on Industrial Organization and Decision Making.* New York: John Wiley.

Isard, W. 1956. *Location and Space Economy.* Cambridge, MA: The MIT Press.

Massey, D. 1984. *Spatial Divisions of Labor: Social Structures and the Geography of Production.* New York: Methuen.

Pacione, M., ed. 1985. *Progress in Industrial Geography.* London: Croom Helm.

Rees, J., ed. 1986. *Technology, Regions, and Policy.* Totowa, NJ: Rowman and Littlefield.

Schmenner, R. 1982. *Making Business Location Decisions.* Englewood Cliffs, NJ: Prentice-Hall.

Smith, D. M. 1981. *Industrial Location: An Economic Geographical Analysis.* 2d ed. New York: John Wiley.

Watts, H. D. 1980. *The Large Industrial Enterprise.* London: Croom Helm.

Weber, A. 1929. *Alfred Weber's Theory of the Location of Industries.* Translated by C. J. Friedrich. Chicago: University of Chicago Press.

11
INDUSTRIAL LOCATION: AREAS

OBJECTIVES

☐ To explore the impact of the internationalization of production on regions

☐ To help you appreciate the relationship between social relations and the geography of production

☐ To describe recent changes in the geography of world manufacturing

☐ To acquaint you with the industrial devolution of Britain

☐ To examine the relocation of American manufacturing industry

☐ To explain how Japan became a tower of industrial strength

☐ To present the advantages and disadvantages of export-led industrialization in the Third World

Factories and mill in Waterbury, Connecticut. (Source: Library of Congress.)

Having examined the locational choices of firms, let us now consider the effects of those choices on areas. This chapter explores the implications of industrial location for communities, regions, and countries. It seeks answers to the following questions: How do industrial areas develop and change? Why should there be industrial growth in some areas, while others exhibit industrial decline? What are the major trends of manufacturing in world regions? What is the recent history of the geography of manufacturing in advanced industrial countries and in newly industrializing countries? Geographers are intensely interested in these questions in this period of economic crisis. It is a period marked by the internationalization of production. Rationalization of this program of industrial restructuring has involved closures, openings, and new production technology; the fragmentation of the labor process; and the increasing penetration and control of markets by giant corporations.

The focus of this chapter is on recent changes in the industrial geography of regions. Over the years manufacturing has been a successful activity because it provides the means for its own advancement—it furnishes the tools, machines, and computers that improve productivity. Aided by mechanization and automation, the average rate of manufacturing output in the last two centuries has increased by 2.8 percent per year—"not a terribly impressive figure until one realizes that it has multiplied more than seventeen hundred fold during that period" (Heilbronner 1989, p. 100). Moreover, machines and computers have released people from labor drudgery. On the other hand, new technologies have been applied in ways that have displaced millions of workers. Release from drudgery has to some extent resulted in the collapse of work.

What are the forces that drive this situation? From the traditional viewpoint, technology develops according to its own imperative, with techniques applied to achieve greater productivity with fewer employees. The radical view sees technologies and techniques as social products, the development of which is based on social relations. According to the radical perspective, the framework for analysis is society, not the technologies it produces. The investigative problem lies not with technology, which has the potential for doing social good; rather, it lies with society, which has the power to misuse that potential.

A similar argument applies to the changing geography of industry and employment. Industrial restructuring can also improve human welfare. What can be wrong with the selective deindustrialization and reindustrialization of the polluted environments of the old manufacturing areas? What can be wrong with industrial revolution in the Third World? Nothing is wrong with industrial restructuring, as long as it does not result in social inefficiency.

Unfortunately, however, industrial restructuring has been a painful process. The movement of British capital to the Third World has had serious effects at home—high levels of unemployment, the destruction of communities, and the loss of valuable skills, plants, and equipment. And in Third World countries, the new manufacturing regions have attracted only selected industries or parts of industries, making them vulnerable to outside control by multinationals. In addition, the new industries rarely meet the urgent consumption needs of poor people; yet, they may pollute environments, destroy local cultures, and exploit labor—especially female labor. What drives such corporate behavior? Corporations relocate their operations in order to survive in a highly competitive world. In their never-ending quest for profits, they must seek out new production frontiers.

To appreciate how the industrial geography of a region changes, we must first learn about the economic structure of society. Thus, the opening section of this chapter provides an introduction to a theory of society, its economy, and the relations that influence locational decision making. Following this section, we look briefly at changes in the geography of world manufacturing, and then take a detailed look at industrial decline and growth in advanced industrial countries and at export-oriented industrialization in parts of the Third World.

The central message of this chapter is that industrial change in a region does not proceed along an evolutionary path involving youth, maturity, and old age. Evolutionary history is largely irrelevant to an understanding of regional economic history (Peet 1985). Industrial change in a region is a social, not a physical process. Old industrial landscapes need not die; they can be rebuilt to fit new technologies. Whether or not rebuilding takes place does not depend on the physical age of the industrial region, "[it depends] on its social conditions, especially those relevant to profit making, and in particular the social relations between capital and labor (Peet 1987c, p. 36). Social conditions exert a powerful influence on the geography of manufacturing.

THE ECONOMIC STRUCTURE OF SOCIETY

A dynamic approach helps geographers understand the changing geography of industrial production and employment. Such an approach has its origin in *materialist science* originally developed by Karl Marx and Friedrich Engels in the nineteenth century. In materialist science, all things are perceived to be in a state of continuous change. Thus, traditional social science, which takes "snapshots" of society with a focus on equilibrium and harmony, is not considered a useful approach to understanding real life forces. The analysis of society is rooted in the material basis of life, not in the idealistic theories of conventional social science. Materialist analysis offers a fruitful avenue of study in this period of rapid change.

Forces of Production and Social Relations

Materialist science starts with the premise that people must live to make history. People must produce objects to satisfy their physical needs. The production of material life is, therefore, central to an analysis of society. According to this viewpoint, the basic elements of society are the *forces of production* and the *social relations of production*. Together these elements are known as the *mode of production* and they constitute the *economic structure of society*.

Forces of production include (1) living labor power, (2) appropriated natural resources, and (3) capital equipment inherited from past generations of workers. In the early stages of economic development, labor is the chief productive force. The ability to transform nature is limited, and the lives of people revolve around natural forces beyond their control. As the number of workers increases, and as the legacy of capital equipment grows, more and more of nature is harnessed. With more control over nature, people are able to raise their living standards.

The crucial social relation of production is between owners of the means of production and the workers employed to operate these means. Under capitalism, the means of production are privately owned. Owners of capital control the labor process and control the course of economic and social development. There are two dimensions to private ownership: on the one hand, there are competitive relations between owners; on the other, there are cooperative and antagonistic relations between owners and workers.

Relations between Owners

Capitalists make independent production decisions under competitive conditions. A raw competitive struggle for survival is fundamental to an appreciation of capitalist development. Competition in the market focuses on price, price depends on cost, and cost hinges on the productive forces used. Competition requires producers to apply a minimum of resources to achieve the highest output. It forces companies to minimize labor costs, which means extreme specialization of labor and subordination of workers to the dictates of machines. It demands large-scale production to lower costs and, if possible, to control a segment of the market. It also entails the acquisition of linked or competing companies and the investment of capital in new technology and in research and development.

Competition is the source of capitalism's immense success as a mode of production. And through coercion, capitalist productivity is enhanced. "Progress in the economy is shaped by competitive relations experienced by each producer as an external, coercive force, whereas historical change takes the form of the development of inherent contradictions and reactions to crises. Thus, although the productive development enabled by competition erodes the power of nature to determine the course of existence, equally uncontrollable powers, contradiction and competition, have been substituted in their place" (Peet 1987a, pp. 13–14). "Contradiction" means tension between opposing elements that cannot be solved without fundamental change. Take for example environmental crises generated by the contradiction between capitalism and the natural environment. For productive forces to continue to expand without a reduction in standards of living, new values must be built into the production system. These values are already evidenced by the use of renewable energy sources and the imposition of pollution controls.

Relations between Capital and Labor

Capital-labor relations are both cooperative and confrontational. Without a cooperative workforce, production would be impossible. However, cooperative relations tend to be subordinate to antagonistic relations.

Because producers make decisions based on their desire to make profits, they try in every way possible to pay workers only part of the value produced by their labor. Value produced by workers in excess of their wages—called "surplus value"—is the basis for profit. On the other hand, workers try to increase their wages in order to enjoy a higher standard of living. They may organize into unions and, if necessary, strike to demand higher wages. If management agrees to meet labor demands, cooperative relations may exist for a time before antagonistic relations resume. Cooperation turns into coercion by competitive necessity (Peet 1987a, p. 15).

Production development occurs under conflictual relations. Struggle between employers and employees diverts surplus product into the hands of management. Competition forces management to invest as much as possible in technology and research to increase productivity. Production increases. Struggle between employers and employees puts higher wages into the hands of workers. Increasing purchasing power means expanding markets to absorb a growing supply of commodities. Production development continues in a process of cumulative causation.

The upward thrust of capitalist development, however, causes us to harbor doubts about future events. The future depends on solutions to struggles between capital and labor. These "solutions" have flaws. Machines and/or low-wage labor can replace high-wage labor. Low-wage peripheral regions can sell products to high-wage center regions. Industrial migration to the periphery removes jobs in the center, which disciplines organized labor. Pressures to increase wages slacken, and mass demand decreases. A crisis of underconsumption develops. In capitalism, the solution to one crisis may prove to be the breeding ground for the development of new problems.

Competition and Struggle in Space

Relations between owners and between capital and labor are sources of change in the geography of production. Competition between owners may drive a company to relocate all or parts of its operation to a place where it can secure low-wage labor. From the company's perspective, this strategy is mandatory for survival; if other companies lower their costs and it does not, it will inevitably lose out in the competitive struggle. Capitalists must expand to survive, and the struggle for existence leads to the survival of the biggest. In their search for profits, giant corporations have extended their reach so that few places in the world remain untouched.

The incessant struggle of companies to compete successfully is especially evident in the entrepreneurial response to differential levels of capital-labor conflict. Old industrial regions of the capitalist core— Europe-North America—have high levels of conflict. By contrast, peripheral regions have various combinations of lower conflict and/or lower wages. Organized labor in the old industrial areas induced capital to switch production and investment to countries that were not yet industrialized or to newly industrializing countries. What allowed mobile capital to avoid the demands of organized labor was the development of productive forces—an increased ability to traverse

space and conquer the technical problems of production—and the emergence of a huge alternative labor force in the Third World following the colonial revolution in Africa, Asia, and the Caribbean.

These dramatic changes in the 1960s and 1970s put an end to the original international division of labor that was formalized in the nineteenth century. Under the old imperial system, the advanced powers were the industrialists, and the colonies were the agriculturalists and producers of raw materials. After decolonization, light industry and even some heavy industry began to emerge in the former colonies. The advanced economies assisted this process. The increasing internationalization of production was accompanied by a new international division of labor. The world became a "global factory" (Barnet and Müller 1975), in which the developed countries garnered the sophisticated technology and the underdeveloped countries were left with the boring manufacturing jobs (Froebel, Heinrich, and Kreye 1977). The emergence of this new international division of labor, thanks in large measure to the activities of the footloose multinational corporations, resulted in deindustrialization in the old industrial regions of advanced economies and a precarious export-led industrial revolution in parts of the Third World.

TRENDS IN THE GEOGRAPHY OF WORLD MANUFACTURING

As the new international division of labor asserted itself, the rate of world economic growth declined. Lower growth rates coincided with the end of the "long boom" of the quarter-century period after World War II and the beginning of a prolonged period of economic crisis. The world economic crisis started with a deep recession in 1974–1975 following the first oil shock in 1973. One of its most visible effects in the advanced economies was deindustrialization—reflected in the loss of jobs in manufacturing. As firms restructured or went out of business in a climate of intense competition, so workers were laid off.

Change in the geography of manufacturing began in the postwar period of rapid growth, but accelerated in the crisis of the 1970s and 1980s. Although the advanced countries maintained a huge share in world manufacturing output, their output of manufactures grew less quickly than that of the underdeveloped countries (Tables 11.1 and 11.2). Nonetheless, manufacturing output in the advanced countries increased in the 1960s, with most economies coasting along with annual growth rates of

TABLE 11.1

Share in manufacturing production by country group.

Country Group	Share in Production		
	1965	1973	1985
Industrial market economies	85.4	83.9	81.6
Underdeveloped countries	14.5	16.0	18.1
Low-income	7.5	7.0	6.9
Middle-income	7.0	9.0	11.2
High-income oil exporters	0.1	0.1	0.3

SOURCE: World Bank, 1987, p. 47.

between 5 and 8 percent (Table 11.3). Only Britain, with a growth rate of 3.3 percent, hinted at trouble to come. Manufacturing output of the advanced economies slowed dramatically in the 1970s, and production actually declined in Britain. The number of workers in manufacturing in the advanced countries, which grew in the early 1970s, stabilized in the middle 1970s, and fell in the late 1970s and 1980s. Job losses were greatest in Britain and Belgium; each country lost 28 percent of its manufacturing workers between 1974 and 1983. During the same period, West Germany recorded a loss of 16 percent, France 14 percent, and the United States 8 percent. The highest rate of manufacturing job loss in the United States was in the Midwest—over 11 percent between 1975 and 1982. However, manufacturing employment increased in new industrial areas—parts of the Southwest, the Mountain States, the Dakotas, and Florida. It also increased in areas successful in restructuring their industrial bases, such as southern New England. With few exceptions, U.S. regions that registered a rapid growth in manufacturing output in the late 1970s and 1980s were low-conflict and/or low-wage states.

Since 1960, manufacturing output has increased sharply in lower wage industrializing countries of the periphery. The output of manufactures in southern Europe and Latin America grew at annual rates of between 5 and 11 percent in the 1960s (except for Argentina). Although this performance was achieved during a period of unprecedented real growth in world output, these regions sustained their progress in the 1970s and 1980s. Their high rates of production were usually sufficient to secure increases in industrial employment.

The most rapid growth of manufacturing output took place in East and South Asia. Japan, with quite high wages but relatively low labor militancy, recorded spectacular annual increases in manufacturing output in the 1960s. Its manufacturing output also expanded impressively in the 1970s, but with a smaller labor force. Several newly industrializing countries equaled or exceeded Japan's annual growth rate in manufacturing output in the period from 1960 to 1982. They also registered prodigious increases in manufacturing employment: 27 percent in South Korea between 1974 and 1983, 53 percent in Taiwan, 43 percent in Hong Kong, and 75 percent in Malaysia.

In Africa and South Asia, the growth of manufacturing has been slower. One or two countries, such as Bangladesh and the Ivory Coast, have achieved vigor-

TABLE 11.2

Growth in manufacturing production by country group.

Country Group	Growth in Production		
	1965–73	1973–85	1965–85
Industrial market economies	5.3	3.0	3.8
Underdeveloped countries	9.0	6.0	7.2
Low-income	8.9	7.9	7.5
Middle-income	9.1	5.0	6.6
High-income oil exporters	10.6	7.5	8.4

SOURCE: World Bank, 1987, p. 47.

TABLE 11.3
Manufacturing in world regions, 1960–1983.

Region and Country	Average Annual Growth Rate in Manufacturing Production		Employment in Manufacturing (Millions)	
	1960–70	1970–82	1974	1983
North America				
United States	5.3	2.4	20.08	18.50
Canada	6.8	2.5	1.94	1.86
Latin America				
Brazil	n.a.	7.8	6.27 (1976)	7.79 (1982)
Venezuela	6.4	4.9	0.29 (1975)	0.41 (1981)
Mexico	10.1	6.8	0.40	0.53
Argentina	5.6	−0.2	n.a.	n.a.
Columbia	5.7	5.2	n.a.	n.a.
Western Europe				
Austria	5.2	3.2	0.94	0.85
Belgium	6.2	2.3	1.10	0.79 (1984)
France	7.8	2.9	5.56	4.78
Germany, Federal Republic of	5.4	2.0	9.00	7.60
Netherlands	6.6	1.9	1.07	0.83
Sweden	5.9	0.5	0.67	0.53
United Kingdom	3.3	−0.8	7.87	5.64
Southern Europe				
Italy	n.a.	n.a.	5.19	4.44
Portugal	8.9	4.5	0.86	0.92 (1982)
Spain	n.a.	4.1	2.96	2.25 (1982)
Turkey	10.9	5.2	0.78	1.03 (1982)
Africa				
Egypt	4.8	9.3	1.35	1.58 (1981)
Kenya	n.a.	9.0	0.10	0.15
Ivory Coast	11.6	5.4	n.a.	n.a.
Zimbabwe	n.a.	−4.1	0.15	0.17
South Asia				
Bangladesh	6.6	10.4	0.30 (1975)	0.44 (1981)
India	4.7	4.5	5.13	6.19
Pakistan	9.4	5.0	0.54	n.a.
Sri Lanka	6.3	2.4	0.21	0.18 (1980)
East and Southeast Asia				
Hong Kong	n.a.	n.a.	0.60	0.86
Korea, Republic of	17.6	14.5	1.54	2.71
Malaysia	n.a.	10.6	0.28	0.48 (1982)
Philippines	6.7	6.6	0.51	0.94 (1981)
Singapore	13.0	9.3	0.21	0.30
Thailand	11.4	9.9	1.69	2.01 (1982)
Taiwan	15.5	11.5	1.48	2.27
Japan	13.6	6.6	12.00	11.75
Oceania				
Australia	5.5	1.5	n.a.	n.a.

SOURCE: Peet, 1987a, pp. 22–23.

England, the first country to industrialize and the first country to deindustrialize, has industrial landscapes that are both heroic and tragic. One of the heroic symbols of England's industrial revolution is the cast-iron bridge over the River Severn in Shropshire. The bridge was completed in 1779 due largely to the energy and determination of Abraham Darby III, grandson of the inventor of the coke-smelting process. By the time Iron Bridge opened for traffic, the essentials of the landscape of the industrial revolution had appeared: the coke-using blast furnace, the cotton mill, the canal, the steam engine house, the primitive iron railway, and the turnpike road. (Source: British Tourist Authority.)

ous growth rates on small manufacturing bases. On the other hand, several countries, such as Tanzania and Zaire, have registered reductions in their manufacturing output.

What conclusions can be drawn from this review of changes in the distribution of manufacturing output and employment? Much depends on your perspective. The traditional view is that deindustrialization in some places and industrialization in others are mirror images of each other. Industrial growth and

decline are offsetting tendencies, representing a zero-sum, or even positive, global game. The shift of production processes from the industrial heartland to the underdeveloped periphery releases a skilled labor force for more sophisticated forms of production in developed countries and allows labor in the Third World to move from relatively unproductive employment to more highly productive employment in industry. The shift may lead to some transitional unemployment, but job losses in the industrial heartland are of little significance compared to the enormous rewards attached to a global reallocation of production.

The radical argument is that the process of global deindustrialization and industrialization, orchestrated by giant corporations, constitutes a negative-sum game. Nomadic capital, rather than leading to a socially efficient allocation of the world's resources, instead leads in the opposite direction. For example, between 1974 and 1983 the advanced industrial countries lost eight million jobs while the newly industrializing countries gained six million jobs. Jobs lost in the advanced industrial countries paid from $4 to $9 an hour, but those gained in the newly industrializing countries paid only $1.50 or less. The gains from expansion in the newly industrializing countries were more than offset by the losses in the advanced industrial countries. Indeed, the shift led to lower global wage shares that could contribute to stagnationist tendencies. For radicals, nomadic capital, although it may well serve individual company interests, is socially inefficient because it is motivated by the concerns of control and distribution. Those who hire labor control the work process, and distribution is always in favor of those who control the location of production. The allocation of production and investment by a corporation is guided primarily by profitability concerns, where profitability is determined by the price of labor and the amount of work that can be extracted at that price. Nomadic capital is also socially inefficient because giant corporations are rarely faced with the full social costs of their locational decisions. Shifting production from country to country not only means that communities built up to serve capital in advanced industrial countries are abandoned, with all the social costs absorbed by those countries, but also that the costs of social infrastructure required by newly industrializing countries are borne by those countries. Radicals view locational change as socially inefficient in a world dominated by giant firms with the power to set the terms under which they operate.

THE DEINDUSTRIALIZATION OF BRITAIN

Deindustrialization, an expression of the growing integration of national economies, hit Britain earlier and harder than elsewhere. It began with a decline of a range of male-employing basic industries and continued with a loss of employment in virtually all industries. Manufacturing employment began to decline in terms of the total number of jobs it provided in the 1960s. It has since continued to decline, with

only occasional stirrings of growth. Moreover, the distribution of job losses has not been even throughout the country. Between 1981 and 1987 northern areas lost 20 percent of their manufacturing employment, whereas the south lost only 10 percent (Watts 1988, p.2).

What these numbers illustrate is the existence of a north-south divide. It separates the prosperous south, especially the Home Counties around London, from the rest of the country. The south—"Britain's Sunbelt"—is part of Europe's "Golden Triangle," the corners of which are Birmingham (England), Dortmund (West Germany), and Milan (Italy). The "Rest"— much of northern England, most of Wales, and all of Scotland and Northern Ireland—is a major problem area on Western Europe's periphery. This economic border, despite a boom rippling north in the late 1980s, is expected to persist through the 1990s (Gribben 1989, p. 2).

Why did deindustrialization hit Britain so hard? How has the employment that remains been restructured geographically? Will the main regional contrast in the future be between control and conception functions in the south and production and clerical functions in the north? To answer these questions, we need to examine changes in the British economy as a whole, and the changing role of Britain in the international system. Fundamental to an appreciation of the deindustrialization of Britain is the international orientation of British capital (Gamble 1981).

The International Orientation of British Capital

Britain's deindustrialization problem owes much to the international posture of its banking and industrial capital. To a particularly large extent, British capital was shaped by the growth of Empire and of a wider world role. These historical opportunities encouraged British capital to invest overseas rather than at home, retarding the development of a strong domestic industrial base. The impact of relatively low levels of domestic investment was that domestic productivity fell relative to other advanced economies without such strong international connections, which in turn led to lower levels of investment in new technologies and products, and therefore to a relative decline in internal and external demand for the output of British goods. From the late nineteenth century onward, this led into a process of downward cumulative causation.

After the mid-1960s, the long-term weakness of the British economy became clear. A telling legacy of the high degree of internationalization of British capital was the collapse of the weak, small-sized firm sector. Many small-sized firms with their outdated technologies and old physical plants were unable to compete against the multinationals that dominated their product markets.

Meanwhile, Britain experienced a net manufacturing foreign direct investment deficit. In the period from 1965 to 1981, the gap between outward and inward manufacturing investment increased (Figure 11.1). According to Ash Amin and Ian Smith (1986), the gap has a lot to do with the high level of industrial concentration in the economy acting as a disincentive for inward investment and as an incentive for outward investment. The gap also has a lot to do with the fact that Britain is increasingly a low-buying-power market, which discourages market-oriented inward investment and fosters the need for British-based multinationals to reorganize capacity internationally in the search for new economies. This has been reflected in the rationalization of capacity by the largest British-based multinationals (Stopford and Dunning 1983; Gaffikin and Nickson 1984). The growing gap between outward and inward manufacturing investment has contributed to Britain's deindustrialization problem.

The problem of deindustrialization has been aggravated by the unwillingness of the state to deal with Britain's weak domestic industrial base. For much of this century, the state was more interested in preserving Empire and class rule than in intervening directly to modernize British industry. Even had the

FIGURE 11.1
British inward and outward foreign direct investment in manufacturing, 1965–1981. (Source: Amin and Smith, 1986, p. 59.)

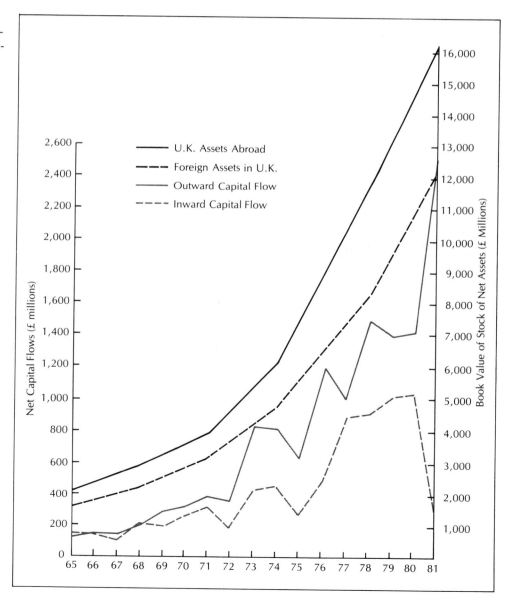

state intervened to secure a breakout from the vicious circle of relative decline, success would have been difficult to achieve given the resistance to change of the well-organized working class.

The Geographical Inheritance

From the nineteenth century up to the 1930s, Britain's internal geography reflected its dominant role in the world economy. British dominance contributed to the concentration of governmental, financial, and commercial activities in London. It contributed to the growth of a small group of exporting industries—coal-mining, iron and steel, shipbuilding, textiles—and eventually to the development of a regional problem.

The traditional industries concentrated all stages of production in a single geographical area. In establishing this pattern of production, producers sought access to ports, coal, and a plentiful supply of labor. These requirements were not available everywhere, so each major industry centered its production in one, or a small number, of regions. Ships were built on Clydeside (Scotland) and Typeside (England); coal was mined in South Wales, central Scotland, and northeast England; the production of steel focused on Sheffield and Birmingham; cotton textiles were made in the Manchester area, and woolens in Leeds and Bradford; and pottery was produced in Stoke-on-Trent. When Britain faded from an eminent world power to a lesser world power, production in the traditional industries fell drastically, and the previ-

The Etruria pottery factory, built for Josiah Wedgwood by Joseph Pickford, began operations in 1769. The waterway in the foreground is the Trent and Mersey Canal. All major British pottery factories concentrated in the Stoke-on-Trent area, forming a most dramatic industrial landscape. (Source: Josiah Wedgwood & Sons, Ltd.)

ously dominant spatial structures produced a regional problem.

The Geography of Decline

Britain's descent from Everest status is most frequently associated with the Great Depression, accumulated debts of two world wars, and the loss of Empire. Undoubtedly, the collapse of traditional industries was to blame for Britain's diminishing share of world gross national product. By the mid-1930s, Japan had replaced Britain as the major supplier of cottons, coal exporters faced stiff competition from Germany and Poland, and iron and steel imports had outstripped exports. Meanwhile, new light manufacturing and consumer goods industries grew up in the Midlands and southeast England where they flourished on the edge of such cities as London, Luton, Oxford, and Coventry. Leaders of right-wing unions and some members of the Labour Party accepted the decline of the traditional industries as the start of a "second industrial revolution" and facilitated the sectoral and geographical refocusing of the economy. The demise of the traditional industries produced appalling poverty and signaled the emergence of the north-south divide.

The classic yardstick of the north-south division of Britain is unemployment. In 1931, 12.4 percent of the males over fourteen and 8.6 percent of the females who might otherwise have been gainfully employed were out of work. Because the Great Depression had a greater impact on manufacturing industries than on service industries, some regions were hit especially hard. Northern Ireland, central Scotland, South Wales, and northern England suffered the most. Within regions, places that depended on one or two basic industries recorded very high rates of unemployment.

In County Durham, the male unemployment rate climbed to 56.3 percent. By contrast, in the southeast, Hertfordshire maintained a rate of only 6.2 percent, and reached a low of 2.7 percent in affluent Harpenden.

The main characteristics of Britain's industrial structure in the 1930s were reinforced in the 1950s. The long postwar boom allowed British industries to "muddle along" without major reorganization. During these complacent and wasted years, when the British deluded themselves that they "never had it so good," industrial decline continued. The nature of the decline was competitive and technological. Britain's share of world trade in manufactures—an index of competitiveness—fell from over 20 percent of the total to less than 9 percent between 1939 and 1985. Investment in manufacturing also declined at a time when manufacturing was becoming increasingly capital intensive and technologically sophisticated. Expansion of consumer goods industries and services, however, proceeded apace and held unemployment at about 2 percent—fewer than 500,000 people—from 1946 to 1965. The expansion drew on domestic supplies of labor, with immigrants from the West Indies, Africa, and Asia providing additional workers until the tighter controls of the 1960s cut this supply.

The failure to put the economy on a sound footing during the postwar boom became apparent in the mid-1960s. National employment in manufacturing declined in 1966. Britain was the first country to industrialize and the first to deindustrialize. Large cities and inner cities, with their preponderance of old and small plants, suffered the most from the decline in manufacturing employment (Figures 11.2 and 11.3). London lost 51 percent of its manufacturing employment between 1960 and 1981. Inner cities lost manufacturing jobs faster than outer cities in the

FIGURE 11.2

Percentage change in manufacturing employment for Britain's metropolitan and nonmetropolitan areas, 1960–1981. (Source: Watts, 1988, p. 3.)

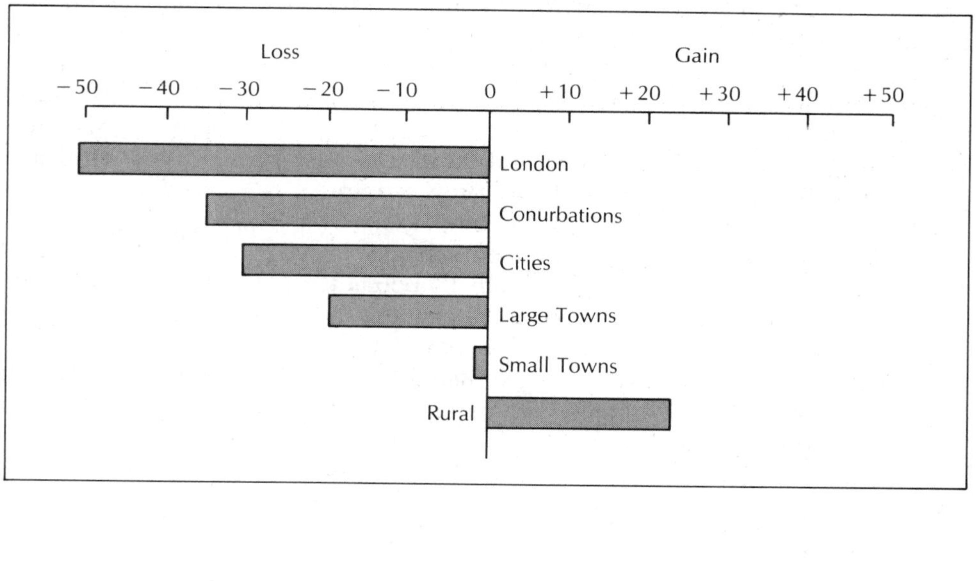

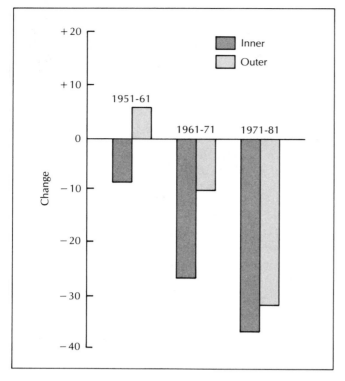

FIGURE 11.3
Percentage change in manufacturing employment in Britain's inner and outer cities, 1951–1981. (Source: Watts, 1988, p. 3.)

1960s, but the rate of job loss became more even in the 1970s because fewer and fewer inner-city firms remained. Unlike the collapse of traditional industries in the 1930s, this newer loss of employment in manufacturing was widely dispersed throughout the country. Even the southeast could not withstand the onslaught; there, manufacturing employment increased by 16.6 percent between 1952 and 1966 but decreased by almost 20 percent between 1966 and 1975. The decline in manufacturing employment continued in the late 1970s and 1980s (Figure 11.4). Thus, after 1966 many of the industries associated with the postwar boom also began to employ fewer people—food, drink, and tobacco; mechanical engineering and construction; gas, electricity and water; and the distributive trades. By the end of the 1970s only tertiary activities registered a net increase in employment. Unemployment soared with the reduced capacity of the economy to provide jobs. It rose from 1.5 percent in 1965 to 10.4 percent in 1980, and to 13.5 percent in 1985, a year that saw three million people out of work (U.K. Department of Employment 1985). Reminiscent of the 1930s, the north suffered higher unemployment rates than did the south (Figure 11.5).

Although much less smoky, the north of today looks much the same as it did during the Great Depression. True, there are new shopping centers, high-rise office and apartment buildings, greenfield industrial estates, and large tracts of inner-city derelict land awaiting redevelopment. But many of the grimy old factories, warehouses, and row houses remain. In the heart of working-class Britain, factories stand idle, high cranes hang useless over closed shipyards, and people are on welfare, losing their self-respect. For too many people, life has become too hard. Since 1979 their hardship has been exacerbated by cuts in social services, health care, and housing, which have lowered living standards especially for low-paid workers, single parents, the elderly, and the infirm. These cuts reflect the policies of a ruling Conservative party that believes in the free-enterprise capitalism and self-reliance popular with Britain's new, rising, hard-working, low-middle-class majority. With this rising lower middle class in mind, the government has accepted high unemployment and the transfer of capital abroad to keep real wages going up and to enable Britain to play a major role in international oil, business, and finance. Unlike the United States, real wages in Britain are going up, rising by 3.4 percent in 1986; as a result, domestic industries are finding they can no longer compete and are closing down. The burden of this policy has been borne by the unemployed, concentrated in the north and its cities. Consett, Durham, became one of the poorest cities in Britain in the 1980s when a steelmaking plant closed and helped push the unemployment rate to 25 percent. Wrenched agonizingly out of its dependence on one major industry, the city has attracted new branch-plant industry which, unfortunately, produces virtually no employment growth. In Manchester, most inner-city wards exceed 40 percent unemployment, and throughout the whole city more than one-half of the children receive free school meals. Central cities of the industrial north as well as those in the south are becoming home to an underclass who have begun to express themselves through increased crime, terror, and violence especially in minority "ghetto" areas.

The Shape of the New Britain

For some of the people who live there, modern Britain seems like a rich and booming society. But in this Britain, it is better to be highly trained than untrained, white than black, male than female, and young than old. It is also better to live in the south than in the north.

FIGURE 11.4
Percentage change in Britain's
manufacturing employment,
1981–1987. (Source: Watts, 1988,
p. 1.)

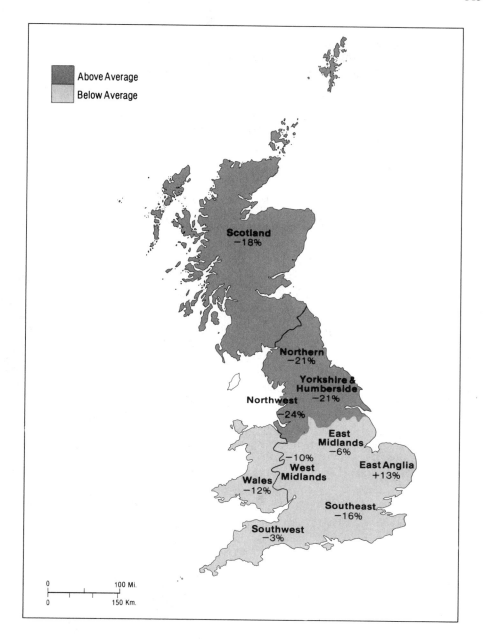

The South   Southern England is booming, with few of the benefits spreading over into the north. Its rapid economic growth in recent years has been built around control and conception functions. The City of London has a thriving banking and business sector, which is absorbing many of Britain's most able people. After the oil price rise in the 1970s, the famous Square Mile—Britain's Wall Street—became the center of the Eurodollar market and the world headquarters for the oil companies. Spreading out over the poor lands of the East End and onto the old docklands, once the heart of British imperial sea trade, it is the core of a new empire, now based on invisible transactions, electronic impulses, video display terminals, and fax machines. The city is now the world capital of foreign investment with the most foreign banks, a tradition of free entry, plus markets in shipping, insurance, commodities, and banking all located closely together.

The south is the location of choice for multinational corporations and company head offices. Over 75 percent of the head offices of the largest manufacturing companies are located in the south (Watts 1988, p. 3). The statistic is even more revealing in light of the fact that Britain is also home to most of Europe's giant

FIGURE 11.5
Percentage unemployed, December 1986. (Source: *The Economist*, 1987a, 21 February, p. 8.)

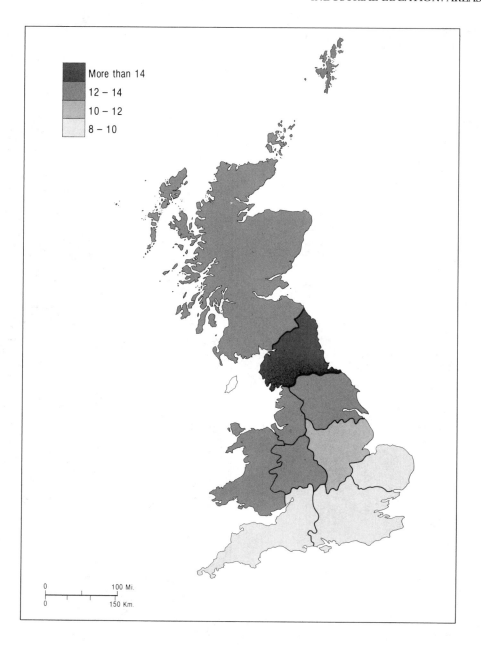

More than 14

12 – 14

10 – 12

8 – 10

0   100 Mi.

0   150 Km.

firms. A survey published by the *Financial Times* noted that no fewer than twenty-five of the top fifty corporations in Europe are based in Britain (Rapor-port 1982).

The concentration of head offices in the south serves to attract research and business services. In fact, 80 percent of the entire British employment in business services is in the south, rendering it fertile ground for the formation of new companies specializing in such activities as electronics and biotechnology. Outside London, the biggest concentration of microelectronics industries in England is along the M4 motorway (freeway) from Slough to Swindon and

the M11 to Cambridge. Small, high-technology companies are scattered throughout the region, however, especially in such areas of considerable environmental advantage as Plymouth and Bournemouth.

The south also benefits from its location close to the international core of Europe. Since joining the European Economic Community (EEC) in 1973, trade with its new partners has increased. The EEC now accounts for nearly one-half of the country's exports and imports. Britain's largest container port, Felixstowe, and its two largest airports, London Heathrow and Gatwick, are in this region. Investment in the third London airport at Stansted to the north of

London and the Channel Tunnel, scheduled to open in 1993, will further strengthen the European and international accessibility of the region.

The booming south, however, acts as a drag on the rest of the country. Imports are escalating at an enormous rate to satisfy middle-class consumer demand. Increasing subsidies are being poured into the region to finance new infrastructure to cope with transport congestion and mounting mortgage tax relief as housing prices soar. Housing prices are more than twice as high in the south as they are in the north (Table 11.4). The high cost of houses in the south is a major obstacle to job recruitment.

The North The area north of the Trent and west of the Bristol Avon is not all in decline. Britain's Rust Belt is being restructured. In contrast to the south's control and conception functions, the north is increasingly home to new production functions. It is becoming a "branch-plant" economy.

South Wales provides a good example of industrial restructuring in the north. In the early nineteenth century, South Wales was moorland, trees, and green valleys. Its crystal clear streams flowing south from the Black Mountains teemed with speckled trout. By 1900, the valleys were all pits. From the Black Mountains in the north to the Vale of Glamorgan in the south, the valleys—Rhondda, Taff, Rhymney, Ebbw—were home to miners who lived in coherent and closed communities such as Pontypridd, Treorchy, and Aberfan. Coal, especially anthracite from the

western part of the coalfield, generated valuable export revenues and attracted industry; notably, iron and steel and heavy engineering. After World War I, the decline of Britain's imperial position and the coal-exporting industry resulted in the economic collapse of South Wales.

In under 150 years South Wales went full circle. The population of the Rhondda Valley, for example, was 4,000 in 1821, 180,000 in 1901, but only 81,000 in 1981. Unemployment in the coal valley now ranks as one of the highest in Britain. Only 61 percent of Rhondda's 1,200 school-leavers found jobs in 1983. And the last of its sixty-six pits closed down in 1986. In the 1970s and 1980s, the pit closures in the coal valleys reflected the decline of Britain's steel production, but also coal imports from lower cost producers such as the United States, Poland, Australia, and South Africa. Today, new food stores as in Tonypandy and Treorchy appear to be the only sign of prosperity in the mining valleys, with their bleak terraced houses, shut-down chapels and railway tracks, and their grassed-over slag heaps and capped mines.

Since World War II the depressed status of the Welsh economy has come about largely through decisions made outside the country. For years, coal and steel production were subject to the control of nationalized industries based in London. In reaction to the transformation of the world economy, the government in London was forced to dismantle the traditional industries of Wales. Between 1966 and 1982, employment in mining and quarrying declined by 57 percent, and metal manufacture by 56 percent. Closing of the Shotton steelworks in North Wales meant the loss of 7,000 jobs. Employment in the giant steel plants of Llanwern and Port Talbot in South Wales was cut drastically.

The grimmer days of the post-World War II period are retracting as South Wales, like the other old British coalfield industrial areas, is experiencing growth through decentralization. New footloose industries are coming in that are not only employing redundant miners and steel workers, but also taking advantage of another labor reserve—women. The locational pattern of the new industries is very different from the old. Large factories housing modern flowline manufacturing equipment lie on greenfield sites outside towns. And smaller factories cluster together around the shared infrastructure of trading estates.

For many companies, the greenfield sites and trading estates present an opportunity to escape the stranglehold of labor-oriented trade unions which protect workers in the face of mechanization, automa-

TABLE 11.4
The house price divide.

Region	Average Price (U.S. $)
Greater London	175,328
Southeast	159,240
East Anglia	146,190
Southwest	129,738
East Midlands	97,462
West Midlands	105,607
Yorkshire and Humberside	73,082
Northwest	74,832
Northern	63,541
Scotland	77,012
Wales	77,884
Northern Ireland	60,518

SOURCE: *Financial Times*, 1989, p. 35.

tion, and computerization. A nonunionized workforce can be found in the small towns and resorts of central Wales—Aberystwyth, Brecon, Cardigan, Lampeter, and Rhayader. Even in South Wales, companies can avoid a unionized male labor force in such cities as Llanelli, Port Talbot, Ebbw Vale, and Llanwern by pricing new jobs to attract female workers who are willing to work for less.

In South Wales the most favored location of the incoming branch plants is close to the M4 motorway that runs from near Chepstow to the west of Swansea. Contact with the "outside world" is more desirable than intraregional links. The major markets for Welsh manufactures are in the Midlands and southeast England. Inputs and components for the new branch plants often come from outside Wales too. "Transport demands of the new industrial economy could hardly be more different from those the inherited transport network grew up to serve" (Humphrys 1972, p. 66). The completion of the Severn Bridge linking England and Wales by motorway in 1966—the modern alternative to the Severn rail tunnel—symbolized the restructing of spatial relations.

The state, both local and central, played a key role in restructuring the Welsh economy. The motorway, new towns, and industrial estates are nearly all state organized and financed. The most conspicuous result of reorganization has been the movement of economic activity from the valleys to valley mouths and to the narrow coastal plain dominated by the cities of Newport, Cardiff, and Swansea.

For some people, the industrial restructuring of South Wales has meant either residential change or longer journeys to work. Many old settlements in the valleys are now dormitories. For many people, however, the new factories have not adequately compensated for hundreds of jobs lost through the dismantling of the old industries. Although the new factories have produced about 10,000 jobs, over 100,000 jobs have been lost as a result of the decline of the coal and steel industries.

The Shape of Things to Come

Figures for gross domestic product (GDP), which serve as an index of the level of economic activity in an area because they reflect both incomes and output, indicate that the geographical division of wealth between north and south Britain widened in the decade from 1977 to 1987 (Table 11.5). In order to take account of the large population differences among regions, the GDP figures are calculated per head. In 1987 Greater London ranked top at 29.4 percent above average. Next highest was the rest of the southeast. Other regions were all below average, giving some impression of the tilt towards the south. GDP figures magnify the division of wealth due to the effect of house prices, but there are other measures that reflect general wealth and confidence about economic prospects. One snapshot indicator of the quality of life is ownership of consumer durables, such as video recorders. In 1984–1985, video recorder ownership varied from 22 percent in Northern Ireland to 32 percent in the southeast. Another indicator is the result of a 1988 survey of business leaders' opinions by

TABLE 11.5
The widening geographical division of wealth, 1977–1988.

Region	Percentage Gross Domestic Product Per Head (U.K. = 100)		
	1977	1981	1987
Greater London	123.8	128.0	129.4
Southeast	112.2	117.3	118.5
East Anglia	97.4	96.3	99.8
Southwest	92.1	93.2	94.0
East Midlands	97.2	97.1	95.1
West Midlands	97.4	90.5	91.6
Yorkshire and Humberside	95.1	91.7	92.7
Northwest	96.6	94.3	92.8
Northern	94.9	93.7	88.9
Scotland	97.1	96.3	94.5
Wales	86.9	83.3	82.4
Northern Ireland	79.9	78.2	77.4

SOURCE: Based on *Financial Times*, 1989, p. 34.

the Manchester Business School. Reported findings show that a majority of chief executives and finance directors in southern England regard a significant part of the north as a cultural desert set in attractive countryside, but with a unionized, disruptive workforce.

Although the gulf between the north and south is wide and may be becoming wider, an economic recovery in the late 1980s slowed the deepening of Britain's center-periphery structure. Unemployment, which in 1988 stood at 8.8 percent, declined in all regions (Figure 11.6). Regions adjacent to the southeast did particularly well.

Is economic revival in parts of the north in the late 1980s an inevitable result of Britain's booming economy? Will the selective reindustrialization of the north continue to disperse industry from the old and dying industrial cities to smaller towns and rural areas where conditions are presently more favorable for profit making? Is the north destined to be a dependent branch-plant economy where tedious assembly and clerical jobs are the main sources of employment? And will the south maintain its dominance as a center of corporate head offices, research

and development laboratories, and new high-tech industries? The 1990s may be the decade that reveals whether the striking contrast between the British "Sunbelt" and the "Rest" constitutes a "permanent" regional problem (Figure 11.7).

The 1990s may also be the decade that reveals whether Britain is on its way to becoming a semiperipheral economy within the international capitalist hierarchy. Already, Britain is dependent on imported technology and on imported manufactured goods. Whereas in 1979 Britain was a net exporter of manufactured goods, by 1988 it was a net importer of manufactured goods.

THE RELOCATION OF AMERICAN MANUFACTURING INDUSTRY

The United States also experienced industrial devolution in the 1970s and 1980s, a period during which its share of world manufacturing output fell. This points to a more rapid growth of manufacturing output in other countries, especially Japan. Can the relative decline of the American manufacturing economy be attributed to Japanese expansionism? Certainly, Japan has increased its share of world industrial production and exports, but a different picture emerges if changes in world sales are classified by the nationality of the parent company. Although Japanese industrial capital made gains at the expense of U.S. capital in the 1960s, almost no further advances were achieved in the 1970s and 1980s. Thus, deindustrialization within the United States was occurring at a time when American capital was either increasing or maintaining its share of the world economy—at a time when American corporations were reacting to the prolonged period of economic crisis. Inside the United States, corporate profit rates were declining. The advantages that promoted rapid capital accumulation in the old manufacturing areas were giving way to contradictions to high profits—rising real wages and obsolete infrastructure. As profit rates declined, corporations switched capital in space. The impact of locational change has been most severe in the American Manufacturing Belt.

The American Manufacturing Belt

North America has numerous manufacturing regions (Figure 11.8). By far the largest is the so-called Anglo-American manufacturing region, which accounts for about 53 percent of the manufacturing capacity of the United States and Canada. The U.S. portion of this region is called the *American Manufacturing Belt*, the

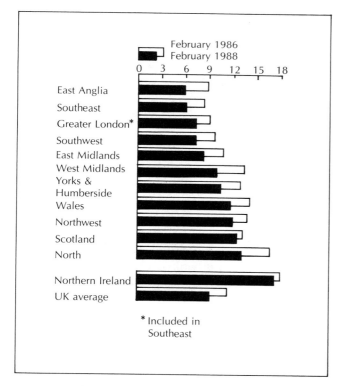

FIGURE 11.6
Regional unemployment as a percentage of working population in February 1986 and February 1988. (Source: *The Economist*, 1988b, p. 45.)

FIGURE 11.7
The shape of things to come?
(Source: Based on Massey, 1987,
p. 115.)

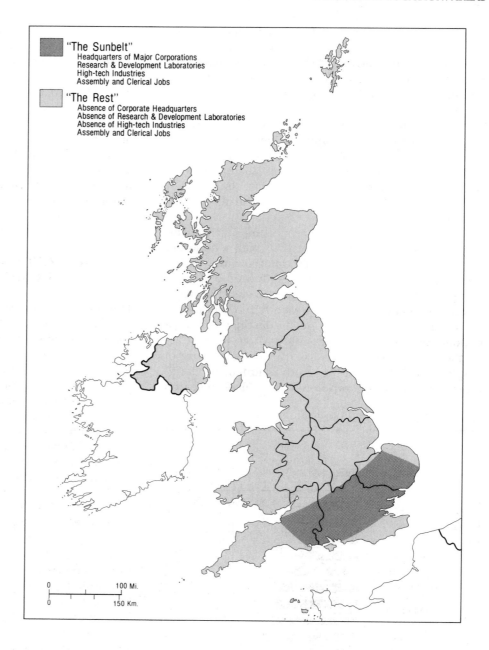

"The Sunbelt"
Headquarters of Major Corporations
Research & Development Laboratories
High-tech Industries
Assembly and Clerical Jobs

"The Rest"
Absence of Corporate Headquarters
Absence of Research & Development Laboratories
Absence of High-tech Industries
Assembly and Clerical Jobs

historic "heartland" of the nation. The Belt extends from Boston westward through upstate New York, southern Michigan, and southeastern Wisconsin. At Milwaukee it turns south to St. Louis, then extends eastward along the Ohio River Valley to Washington D.C. This great rectangle encompasses some ten districts, each with its own specialities that reflect the influences of markets, materials, labor, power, and historical forces.

The first major factories in the Belt—the textile mills of the 1830s and 1940s—clustered along the rivers of southern New England. When coal replaced water as a source of power between 1850 and 1870,

and when railroads integrated the Belt, factories were freed from the riverbanks. Industrialists began to pursue their profits in towns and cities.

Between 1850 and 1870, many urban areas of all sizes enjoyed rapidly expanding industrial production. But after 1870, manufacturing came to be concentrated in a few large cities. Manufacturing employment in New York, Philadelphia, and Chicago soared by over 200 percent between 1870 and 1900. The ten largest industrial cities increased their share of national value added in manufacturing from under 25 percent to almost 40 percent between 1860 and 1900 (Pred 1966, p. 20). Why did metropolitan complexes

FIGURE 11.8
Manufacturing regions and districts of the United States and Canada. (Source: Fisher, 1989, p. 155.)

draw such a great proportion of manufacturing activity?

The orthodox view is that factories concentrated in cities such as Baltimore, Chicago, Cleveland, Cincinnati, Philadelphia, and Pittsburgh for some combination of the following reasons: (1) they could be near large pools of workers; (2) they could secure easy rail and water access to major resource deposits, such as the Appalachian coalfields and the Lake Superior-area

iron mines; (3) they could be near industrial suppliers of machines and other intermediate products; and (4) they could be near major markets for finished goods. In other words, *agglomeration economies* accounted for the concentration of industrial activity in the Belt.

In the radical view, these important factors are insufficient to explain industrial concentration. According to David Gordon (1977), huge cities became loci for factories because of the nature of the relation between factory owners and their employees. Problems of labor discipline plagued owners after they adopted the factory form of production. Artisans resisted the degradation of work and laborers struggled against insecure wages and dangerous working conditions. When the period of prosperity after the Civil War gave way to the depression of the 1870s, workers fought to resist layoffs and wage cuts throughout the Belt. In the smaller cities, employers had a terrible time trying to overcome periodic outbursts of worker resistance. Middle-class residents, used to earlier preindustrial capital-labor relationships, disliked the factory system. When workers went out on strike, the middle classes often supported them. By contrast, in the larger cities, the middle classes had much less sympathy for the plight of workers, and often failed to support them in their strikes. Employers in large cities, therefore, had a tremendous advantage. With a disciplined labor force, they experienced fewer and shorter strikes and extracted more surplus value from their workers than could their competitors in small cities.

The highly concentrated pattern of industrial production in the Belt served the nation well for almost 100 years—roughly the century between 1870 and 1970. Of course, *inertia*, the immobility of the investment forces and social relations, assured considerable locational stability. Inertia was particularly pronounced in the capital-intensive steel industry.

New England became the first and foremost textile manufacturing region in the United States in the late eighteenth century. The mills pictured here are in Lawrence, Massachusetts. By the 1940s, the textile region of southern New England had been in decline for more than twenty years. Firms left the region in search of more profitable operating conditions and workers were forced to seek other employment. Recently, the region has experienced a revival as new industries, notably electrical engineering, have replaced the older, declining ones. (Source: Library of Congress.)

However, cracks in the regime of accumulation appeared as early as the late nineteenth century. Contradictions erupted. Labor unrest intensified. After 1885, the number of workers involved in strikes increased rapidly with many of the most bitter strikes occurring in the largest manufacturing complexes. Gradually, owners lost power to labor—a power that enabled labor to negotiate higher wages than were paid previously or elsewhere, to organize high levels of unionization and extract good working conditions, and to command progressive welfare policies. By the early twentieth century, the dense centralization of industrial workers in inner-city areas backfired on factory owners.

As labor control subsided, manufacturing started to move out of central cities to the suburbs. Between 1899 and 1909, central-city manufacturing employment increased by 40 percent, whereas outer-city manufacturing employment increased by nearly 100 percent. After the late 1920s, the use of the truck for freight transport accelerated the movement of manufacturing to the suburbs. But as transport costs equalized across the nation, even the suburbs of the older cities of the Manufacturing Belt were unable to compete with more agreeable labor environments in the South and West. The decade of the 1960s marked the start of the steady gain of manufacturing employment in the South, parts of the Southwest, the Mountain States, and the Dakotas. Since the recession of the early 1980s, however, there has been evidence that these areas where class conflict is low are being bypassed in favor of even cheaper labor regions in Mexico and East Asia.

The Domestic Movement of Manufacturing

The locational change of manufacturing in the United States was particularly strong in the 1970s and 1980s. Virtually all states in the American Manufacturing Belt experienced manufacturing job loss and virtually all states in the South and West registered manufacturing job gains (Figure 11.9). With the exception of the West, states having low class conflict gained significant manufacturing employment whereas states having high class conflict lost manufacturing employment (Figure 11.10). The migration of employment from areas of high class struggle to areas where the struggle was less developed saved U.S.-controlled companies billions of dollars. Roughly 1.7 million jobs shifted from states with high class conflict to states with low class conflict in the period from 1960 to 1980, yielding an annual wage saving of over $5 billion in 1980 (Peet 1987b, p. 63).

The expansion of manufacturing in the West is not immediately explained by class struggle. California is characterized as a state of high class struggle, yet it has registered substantial increases in manufacturing employment. In California, class struggle loses its primary determining effect to physical and environment factors, the role of the state (defense spending), and the dimension of consciousness (the "California image").

The West Coast manufacturing district does, however, represent an outstanding example of industrial restructuring in response to economic crisis and labor unrest. The Los Angeles-San Diego district has been extremely successful. Since the 1960s, the district has shed much of its traditional, highly unionized heavy industry, such as steel and rubber. At the same time, it has attracted a cluster of high-tech industries and associated services, centered around electronics and aerospace and tied strongly to defense and military contracts from the U.S. government. These industries are expanding rapidly and now make up more than a quarter of the region's manufacturing employment. Added to the combination of Frostbelt-like deindustrialization and Sunbelt industrialization has been the vigorous growth of "peripheralized" manufacturing, which resembles the industrialization of Hong Kong and Singapore, based on a highly controllable supply of cheap, typically immigrant and/or female labor.

Meanwhile, industrial restructuring continues to be a painful process throughout much of the American Manufacturing Belt. The region contends with problems of obsolescence and reduced productivity, especially in such leading industries as steel, automaking, and shipbuilding. It contends with inner-city areas littered with closed factories, bankrupt businesses, and struggling blue-collar neighborhoods. The impact of disinvestment on workers and their communities has been devastating.

Victims of plant closing sometimes lose not only their current incomes but their total accumulated assets as well. And when savings run out, people lose their ability to respond to life crises. Although job loss respects neither educational attainment nor occupational status, some groups are more vulnerable than others. Because blacks are concentrated in areas where plant closings have been most pronounced, this group has been especially hard hit.

Plant closings can be extremely costly to a community. J. Wiss & Son was a large cutlery manufacturer in Newark, New Jersey for seventy-five years. In 1978 it was acquired by a Texas conglomerate and relocated to North Carolina. This shutdown resulted in a direct loss of 760 manufacturing jobs and an

FIGURE 11.9
Manufacturing employment
shifts from 1967 to 1982.
(Source: Fisher, 1989, p. 158.)

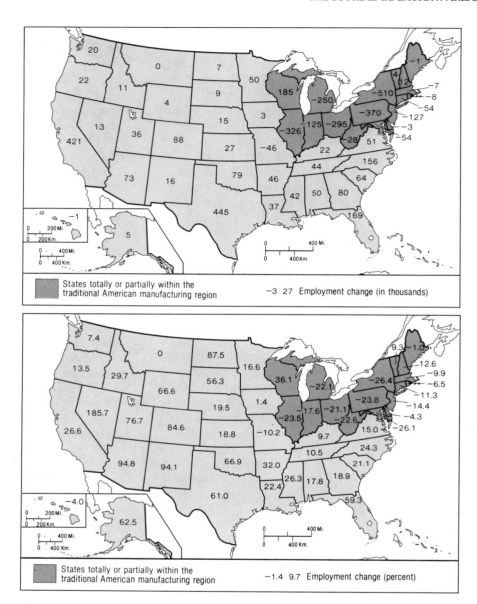

additional 468 jobs in stores, banks, and other local businesses. "More than $14 million in purchasing power was removed from the local economy, half of which had resided in local bank deposits used for loans to finance mortgages, home improvements, purchases of automobiles, televisions, refrigerators, and other major appliances" (Bluestone and Harrison 1987, p. 88). Literally hundreds of communities have experienced the agony of unregulated deindustrialization. And these communities are not restricted to the Manufacturing Belt. Perhaps the most dramatic example is the case of Anaconda, Montana, a classic "company town." In 1978 Anaconda Copper & Mining Co. was acquired by the Los Angeles-based Atlantic Richfield Co. (ARCO). Two years later ARCO closed the

town's copper smelter, eliminating 80 percent of the payroll in the community of 12,000 people.

Although widespread manufacturing decline has produced a lasting impact on people and communities in the Manufacturing Belt, all is not doom and gloom in the region. There are already attempts to respond to the economic crisis. Old industrial cities such as Pittsburgh are building new bases for employment, and so too are the major urban complexes of Megalopolis. Southern New England stands out as a bright spot. The region, which suffered higher than average unemployment rates throughout much of the post-World War II period, now has the lowest unemployment rate in the Belt. A new round of industrial expansion is taking place based on a disciplined pool

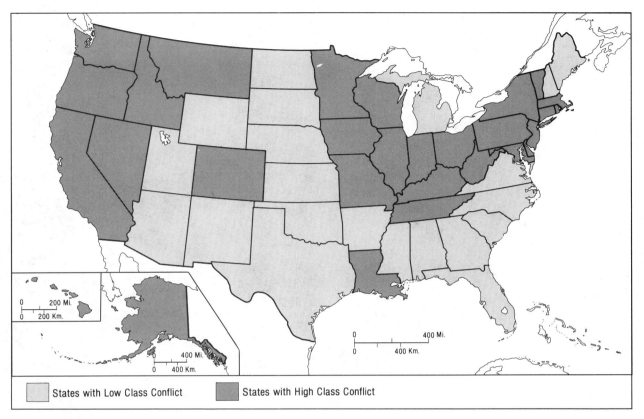

FIGURE 11.10
States of high class conflict and low class conflict in the 1970s. (Source: Based on Peet, 1987b, p. 52.)

of highly skilled and unskilled workers. The industrial revival of southern New England emphasizes high-value products—electronic equipment, electrical machinery, firearms, and tools. A current worry, however, is the permanence of the revival. In the late 1980s, high-technology firms in "Silicon Valley East" were affected by the sluggish national economy and were forced to lay off workers, casting doubt on the Massachusetts miracle.

The International Movement of Manufacturing

The relocation of manufacturing within the United States is only one aspect of a wider dispersal of American manufacturing capital. Foreign direct investment by American enterprises was established as early as the end of the nineteenth century. But only since World War II have American enterprises become major foreign investors. The 1940s saw heavy investment in Canada and Latin America; the 1950s in Western Europe; and the 1960s and 1970s in Western Europe, Japan, the Middle East, and South and East

Asia. "[By 1977] some 1,841 United States manufacturing companies had 15,316 foreign affiliates, the result of an accumulated direct foreign investment of $62,019 million, over $40,000 million of which had been made since 1966" (Peet 1987c, p. 59). Most of this investment took place in advanced industrial countries rather than in Third World countries (Figure 11.11).

Between 1945 and 1960 most U.S.-based companies were content to produce in the old industrial districts. But by 1960, the European Common Market and Japan had turned into competitors. Mounting international competition and falling rates of profit at home coerced American companies to decentralize not only within the United States, but also abroad. By 1980 the five hundred largest U.S.-based corporations employed an international labor force almost equivalent to the size of its national labor force. In the period from 1960 to 1980, manufacturing employment outside the United States directly controlled by U.S. corporations increased from 8.7 percent to 17.5 percent of the total, a 169 percent increase compared with a 20 percent increase within the United States.

In the foreground are the steelmill workers' houses in Midland, Pennsylvania, in 1941. The decline of smokestack industry within the Manufacturing Belt led to high unemployment rates in the 1970s and 1980s. Will this old industrial region continue to decline in the 1990s, or will it be rebuilt to fit new technologies? (Source: Library of Congress.)

The dispersal of manufacturing investment to foreign lands has resulted in a more competitive base and in enormous savings in wages for American firms. In 1980 the annual wage savings from 1.6 million jobs opened by U.S.-based corporations in developed countries between 1960 and 1980 was $8.4 billion, and the annual savings from 1.1 million jobs opened in underdeveloped countries between 1960 and 1980 was $14.5 billion (Peet 1987c, p. 64). Even greater savings were achieved in the 1980s as U.S.-based companies increasingly established manufacturing operations in low-wage regions of the Third World.

THE INDUSTRIALIZATION OF JAPAN

Japan's record of economic achievement has no equal among advanced industrial countries in the post-World War II period. Between 1970 and 1984, when industrial production declined by 4 percent in Britain and increased by 48 percent in the United States, Japan's industrial output soared by 162 percent (World Bank 1987, p. 215). Unemployment in 1985, which registered 13.5 percent in Britain and 7.2 percent in the United States, was a modest 2.5 percent in Japan (International Monetary Fund 1985, p. 24). And when, in the 1980s, the U.S. trade deficit mushroomed, Japan's trade surplus mounted. In that decade, Japan took America's place as chief creditor, buying stocks, bonds, and real estate all over the world. Although the U.S. economy is still clearly the world's biggest—producing 26 percent of total global output in 1987 compared to Japan's 9 percent (Samuelson 1989, p. 43)—the economic pendulum is swinging slowly toward Japan. Given Japan's increas-

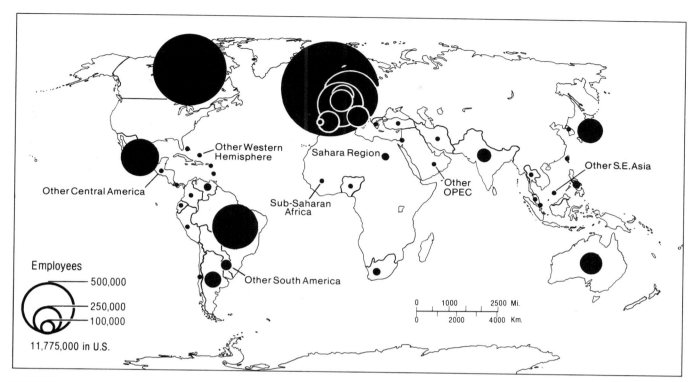

FIGURE 11.11
World employment in manufacturing by U.S.-based multinational corporations in 1981.
(Source: Peet, 1987b, p. 60.)

ingly powerful economy, which seems certain to become more dominant towards the twenty-first century, it is timely to answer the following questions: What is the basis for Japan's astonishing industrial record? What price is Japan paying in its bid to become the world's foremost industrial nation? Is Japan the working model for industrial success?

Physical Resources

What gave Japan, an island nation that is slightly smaller than California, the opportunity to become an industrial juggernaut? What part of the answer lies in its raw material base? Compared with the United States and Britain—countries with the physical resources to sustain an industrial revolution—Japan is much less well-off. Except for coal deposits in Kyushu and Hokkaido, which provided a stimulus for nineteenth-century industrial development, Japan is practically devoid of significant raw materials for major industry. It has depended in large measure on imported raw materials for its recent industrial growth (Table 11.6).

Human Resources

Japan may be short in physical resources, but it does not lack the human resources for industrial development. There are more than 120 million Japanese, mostly crammed into an urban-industrial core that extends from Tokyo on the east to Shimonoseki at the western end of Honshu (Figure 11.12). The homogeneity that characterizes this population is regarded by the Japanese, themselves, as a major contributor to their nation's industrial success. Within that homogeneity, Confucianism and Buddhism, acquired from China and in place for more than a thousand years, have instilled such traits as self-denial, devotion to one's superiors, and the prevalence of group over individual interests. These social attributes lend Japan a high degree of *national concensus*. And when a strong work ethic combines with a high level of collective commitment, it produces a work culture in which everyone, from the top to the bottom, knows his or her place, and can pull in the same direction. A chilling degree of national consensus was apparent after World War II when the Japanese set about the task of rebuilding their shattered economy.

An Emerging Postindustrial Economy?

The economic restructuring of the United States since 1970 is regarded by sociologist Daniel Bell (1973) as evidence of the emergence of a postindustrial society. The term *postindustrial* refers to a fundamental change in the character of technology use—from fabricating to processing—in which telecommunications and computers are vital for the exchange of knowledge. Information becomes the basic product, the key to wealth and power, and is generated and manipulated by an intellectual rather than a machine technology. Yet, postindustrial society does not displace industrial society, just as manufacturing did not cast aside agriculture. Instead, the new developments simply overlie the previous layers.

Economic activities involving the collection, processing, and manipulation of information are called *quaternary economic activities*. These activities are increasingly dominating the workforce: they employed 30 percent of U.S. workers in 1950, 46 percent by 1980, 60 percent in the late 1980s, and are expected to employ more than 70 percent by the mid-1990s. There is a fear that the new service economy will eliminate more jobs than it creates. With growing automation, high-tech companies will increasingly employ more highly trained scientists and fewer less-skilled workers. As a result thousands of production and clerical workers may soon lose their jobs. Is education the key to solving this problem? Will the U.S. educational system create a broad, educated workforce, with flexible, high-technology skills in order to better match people with jobs? Or will postindustrial society remain a long way off for millions of Americans?

SOURCE: Based on de Blij and Muller, 1985, p. 214.

TABLE 11.6

Natural resources: Import dependency and world trade share for selected countries, 1985.

Resource	Degree of Import Dependency (Percentage)					Share of World Trade (Percentage)				
	Japan	United States	West Germany	France	United Kingdom	Japan	United States	West Germany	France	United Kingdom
Energy	83.1	11.9	50.1	59.5	−12.4	14.2	13.6	7.3	6.6	2.9
Coal	81.4	−11.5	−0.8	49.0	−1.6	28.5	0.5	3.7	7.0	1.7
Oil	99.8	33.3	95.1	96.8	−44.4	17.3	20.4	8.8	7.4	3.2
Natural gas	94.2	4.3	65.5	77.4	26.1	12.4	13.2	19.3	11.3	6.2
Iron Ore	99.7	16.0	97.8	61.0	97.4	40.1	12.9	13.0	4.3	4.8
Copper	96.5	18.1	99.8	99.4	99.8	25.0	8.9	14.0	7.2	6.5
Lead	78.1	25.1	85.9	97.2	97.5	8.1	20.1	13.9	5.9	5.6
Zinc	55.6	73.9	70.4	84.1	97.6	4.1	39.0	9.5	4.1	8.3
Tin	98.3	99.6	100.0	100.0	0	25.3	30.3	15.5	5.9	3.5
Aluminum	100.0	82.3	100.0	−100.0	100.0	28.0	13.0	10.3	6.9	2.9
Nickel	100.0	95.7	100.0	0	100.0	15.1	24.7	14.0	8.4	7.5
Wood and lumber	64.3	1.2	20.7	68.6	12.2	18.7	16.9	7.0	4.6	6.3

SOURCE: Williams, 1989a, p. 338.

A high degree of national consensus, however, in no way implies a passive society. The Japanese undoubtedly prefer to conform, but they are also fiercely competitive and assertive. After World War II that assertiveness was channeled not only into trade and industry, but into capital-labor conflict as well. Labor unrest certainly unmasks the image of the docile Japanese worker, unwilling to oppose the wishes of his or her boss. In concert with workers in Western Europe and North America, the Japanese worker greeted the postwar period with an outburst of dissatisfaction. In 1946 General McArthur, Supreme Commander of the Allied Powers, warned that mass violence would severely damage Japan's development prospects. Widespread demonstrations and strikes were not contained until the mid-1950s however, when enterprise unions, lifetime employment, and other measures were introduced to integrate workers into the fabric of Japanese industry. These measures have effectively reduced strikes in Japanese industry to a rare occurrence. In 1987, Japan lost only 256,000 worker-days to disputes compared to the U.S. total of 4,481,000.

Although permanent workers in large firms are well paid, especially when viewed in relation to part-time workers in small and medium-sized firms, the relative share of the product going to labor is lower in Japan than in any other advanced industrial country. Savings and profits are directed by the state toward whatever goals are set forth by a unique collaborative partnership between MITI—Japan's Ministry of International Trade and Industry—and private enterprise. This marriage between government and private enterprise, helping to make Japan the envy of the West, is sometimes called "Japan Incorporated." The days of the successful relationship between MITI and industry, however, may be numbered. MITI has less controlling power than it once had. Japanese firms no longer need the watchful eye of MITI or much of its money. For example, Hitachi spent about $2.2 billion on R&D in 1988, or about 50 percent more than MITI's total R&D budget.

Substantial change also may be looming on Japan's labor front. The wealth generated by the Japanese system in the 1960s and 1970s has produced a workforce that is gingerly experimenting with traditions and customs. Japan's young people still adhere to the ideal of consensus, but they are unwilling to sacrifice their individuality. They are not satisfied with simply working hard. They prefer to work less and take all the vacations their bosses offer. In the 1990s there are bound to be more and more clashes between the young and old over the commitment of the individual to the ideals that propelled postwar rebuilding.

Domestic Foundations

Feudal traditions and customs, now contested by young Japanese, were preserved in Japan because of the extremely rapid transition from feudalism to capitalism. Japan entered the modern world suddenly, following the overthrow of the old feudal rulers in 1868. The rebellion is known as the Meiji Restoration—the return of enlightened rule.

In the 1860s, Japan had a small industrial base consisting of widespread cottage industries producing textiles, porcelain, wood products, and metal goods from domestic raw materials. Planners who took charge of the country in 1868 realized that an antiquated network of small enterprises provided an inadequate base for industrial modernization. To achieve rapid growth, resources had to be concentrated. With no model of socialist development to follow, the concentration of resources fell into private hands. "Hence, the *zaibatsu*, or financial cliques, emerged out of the close relationship between government and business. By the 1920s the *zaibatsu*—particularly the big three of Mitsui, Mitsubishi, and Sumitomo—controlled a large part of the nation's economic power" (Williams 1989b, pp. 350–51).

The *zaibatsu* using primarily internal self-generating capital, developed a strong domestic industrial base from which they exploited foreign markets. The strategy was effective. Before World War II Japanese industry blossomed, as inexpensive light-industrial and consumer goods competed with Western products in the world market. Without doubt, the Japanese war machine of the 1940s provided convincing proof of just how far Japan's industrial modernization had gone: airplanes, tanks, warships, and ammunition were all manufactured by Japanese industries.

A Change in Relative Position

Japan lost World War II, but it is winning the peace. The war improved Japan's world position. At the time of the Meiji Restoration, Britain was preeminent in the world, and the United States was a developing country. The imperial wars of the twentieth century saw Japan defeat Britain and France in East Asia, and the United States and its allies defeat Germany and Italy. Although Japan was also a defeated country in 1945, the global balance of power shifted. The United States, Japan's trans-Pacific neighbor, became the hegemonic world power, and Britain became a lesser world power with its Empire on the verge of collapse.

FIGURE 11.12
Japan's core region and
selected cities. (Source:
Williams, 1989a, p. 331.)

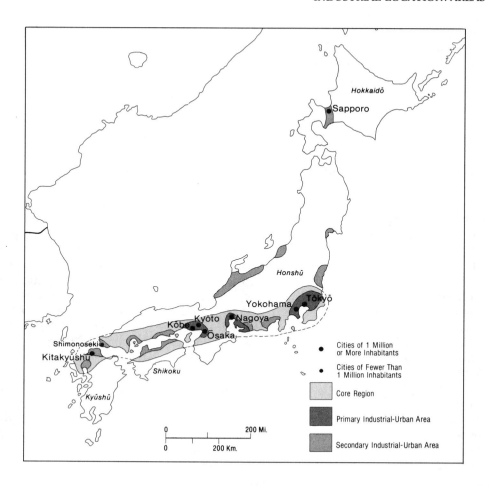

Japan's *relative position*—its location relative to the world's dominant power—had changed, and this change gave Japan much of its postwar opportunity. A few decades after Emperor Hirohito's surrender, Japan rose from the ashes of two atomic bombs and is now about to become a superpower, supplanting America as the colossus of the Pacific, and perhaps even the world's number one economic force.

Postwar Reconstruction and Development

After the U.S. occupation, the *zaibatsu* reemerged to lead the industrial revival of Japan. Initially, the revival was based on large, labor-intensive industries such as steel manufacturing and shipbuilding. Because the need to export to improve the nation's balance of payments was a crucial factor of the early stages of Japan's reindustrialization, the government restricted the influx of imported foreign goods and services. This made it difficult for overseas companies to invest directly in Japan and, at the same time, promoted Japanese export trade. In addition to these initiatives, the Japanese saved, deposited money in the banks, and the banks lent to industry.

The United States also played a major role in the reconstruction of Japanese capitalism. It provided financial aid and an open-door policy for Japanese exports. It also sold technology to Japan at bargain prices. By 1960 Japan was giving the United States a run for its money. It had the "advantage" of losing much of its own plant during World War II; therefore, it was starting from a very modern scratch.

Japan's gross domestic product (GDP) grew at an average of 10.5 percent between 1950 and 1973, compared with a worldwide growth rate of 4.7 percent in the same period. Even after two major oil shocks in the 1970s, raising prices and threatening to shut off the nation's energy supply, Japan fared much better than most of its industrial rivals. Although some of its small firms were forced to the wall, Japan's GDP advanced by an average of 4.7 percent in the following years, whereas its rivals grew at half that rate.

In the 1980s, Japan became a victim of its economic miracle. Western Europe and North America erected trade barriers to shield their declining industries from Japanese competition in key areas such as motor vehicles, computers, and steel. The protectionist tendencies of the West combined with a slowdown in Japan's demand for consumer goods, resulting in a more modest economic growth. In the late 1980s, Japan expanded at a rate nearer to 3 percent compared with over 10 percent during the miracle years.

As early as the late 1960s, the Japanese government realized the need to diversify its industrial base. Emphasis switched from smokestack, mass-production industries to shirt-sleeved brain industries such as pocket calculators, color televisions, and hi-fi equipment. Then, in the 1980s, Japan emphasized microchips, computers, and robots. In addition to the burgeoning electronics industry that will be the powerhouse for the country's continued growth and development in the 1990s, Japan is also seeking to establish significant manufacturing facilities in such areas as biotechnology, aerospace, pharmaceuticals, and new raw materials to replace metals, nuclear power, and lasers.

The transition from the mass-produced, labor-intensive industries of the past is still far from complete, and even when it is, there still will be a role for "old" industries such as automobile manufacturing. But the shift in emphasis from industries demanding more brain than brawn is pronounced, and it has been achieved more easily in Japan than in the United States or Britain. Japan championed industrial restructuring, whereas countries like Britain chose to protect struggling industries.

Long-term planning, allied to the national characteristics of consensus and a strong work ethic, has played a vital role in determining Japan's industrial restructuring efforts. Although private enterprise dictates industrial policy, it is MITI that has shaped new industrial patterns. MITI's major role has been that of nursing new industries and technological developments, while at the same time coordinating the orderly run-down of decaying industries. These tasks of "midwife" and "undertaker" involve a series of workshops in which all aspects of a particular industry, whether birth or death, are discussed.

There are signs, however, that MITI, which masterminded Japan's rise, may now be losing its grip. These days, companies even signal to MITI what key technologies should be on its annual list of urgent projects. Nonetheless, MITI remains a think tank—a strategic organization that still has a tremendous ability to guide capital.

The Problems of Japan Incorporated

In the postwar period, Japan set about the task of becoming a potent economic force. All other considerations were subordinated to that one overriding good. The drive for economic growth was at the expense of social welfare, the environment, and international relations. Japan is beginning to pay the price for its industrial achievement.

International Relations In the 1980s, the gap between Japan's imports and exports created tensions with its trading partners (Figure 11.13). As a result, Japan found its markets in key exports restricted. Protectionist tendencies have been side-stepped to some extent by foreign direct investment. Japan has invested heavily in big projects in the advanced industrial countries. It has also established numerous joint ventures that reduce the capital and political risks for Japanese companies. Examples include the link between American steel giant USX and Japan's Kobe Steel to manufacture tubular steel for automakers producing vehicles in the United States and the link between Boeing and Fuji Heavy Industries, Kawasaki, and Mitsubishi to build commercial aircraft. For critics who espouse the notion of economic nationalism, Japan's foreign investment policies are subject to as much "Japan bashing" as its trading policies.

The Dual Economy The most pressing Japanese problem is its dual economy. At the top, are a handful of great international corporations that thrive and change. Under MITI's guidance, Japan has relocated industries such as steelmaking and shipbuilding "offshore" in the newly industrializing countries (NICs) where labor costs are lower. Now, countries such as South Korea are developing their own higher technologies (e.g., consumer electronics). Meanwhile, Japan is challenging the United States in the newest generation of sophisticated technology. Even if they succeed, the Japanese worry about the transition to postindustrialism with less manufacturing and more stress on services. Manufacturing industry's share of both output and employment is predicted to decline by the turn of the century.

At the low end of the Japanese economy are thousands of tiny workshops. The large corporations job out parts of their production to the small firms with their underpaid and exploited workers. About 70 percent of Japan's labor force still works in these tiny firms. It is this "mom-and pop" structure that prevents Japan from playing its superpower role as the world's buyer of last resort, soaking up foreign goods to maintain international economic order and growth.

Environmental Pollution The pursuit of economic efficiency was the be-all and end-all of Japanese endeavor until the late 1960s, when the consequences

FIGURE 11.13
Japan's balance of trade, 1970–
1986. (Source: Williams, 1989b,
p. 359.)

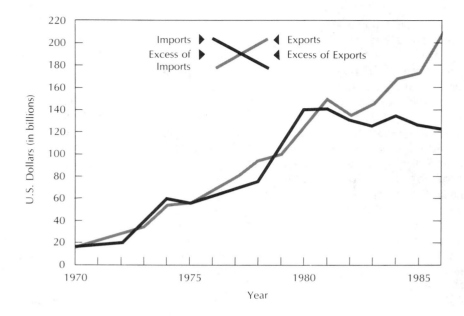

of environmental pollution demanded immediate attention. The most serious aspects were air and water pollution, which killed hundreds of people who lived around the factories (Junkerman 1987). In the 1970s, the government introduced pollution-control measures and tried to shift polluting industries out of congested areas. Still, Japan remains the most environmentally polluted country in the developed world.

Regional Imbalance and Urban Ills Japan's uncontrolled and rapid industrial development created an unusually sharp economic divide between the core region and the rest of the country. In the late 1970s and 1980s, as efforts to overcome environmental pollution by relocating industry to less developed parts of the country started to take effect, the gap between the rich core region and the poor periphery began to narrow. Yet, the regional contrast will persist throughout the 1990s.

Another by-product of rapid economic growth are the problems of Japan's large cities. These problems include traffic congestion, noise, parking, accidents, air pollution and, of course, land madness. When the Japanese government put sixty-six new apartments on the market in Tokyo in 1987, more than 18,000 people rushed to apply for what was considered a bargain: $200,000 for a small two-bedroom apartment. In one of the world's richest countries, most people cannot afford to buy their own home. Housing is a great social problem, with young couples forced into two-hour commutes into Tokyo just for the luxury of owning their own "rabbit hutches," as Japan's cramped quarters have come to be known.

The Japanese Model

Japan's postwar industrialization has been remarkable. It has created a rich country, but a poor people. Is Japan really the working model for industrial success? Would Americans embrace a system in which the majority of the workforce is controlled in a fuedal-like serfdom? Would a "job-for-life" policy be realistic in contemporary Britain? Even if it were desirable, the Japanese model could not be readily adopted by other countries; it is the product of a unique culture and of a unique regional historical experience.

THIRD WORLD INDUSTRIALIZATION

Deindustrialization in the West in the 1970s and 1980s did not induce widespread industrialization in the Third World. In 1985, forty-three countries accounted for 66 percent of manufacturing exports from developing countries; the top fifteen alone accounted for about 60 percent (World Bank 1987, p. 49). Even more striking is that about one-third of all exports from the Third World came from three Southeast Asian countries—Hong Kong, South Korea, and Singapore. Industrialization occurred, therefore, only in selected parts of the Third World.

Manufacturing was slowest to take hold in the poorest countries of the periphery, most of which are in Africa. It grew fastest in the newly industrializing countries (NICs). These countries made a transition from an industrial strategy based on import substitution to one based on exports. The exporters may be divided into two groups. First, there are such countries as Mexico, Brazil, Argentina, and India that have a relatively large domestic industrial base and established infrastructure. All four of these countries are primarily exporters of traditional manufactured goods—furniture, textiles, and leather and footwear—exports favored by natural-resource conditions. Second, there are such countries as Hong Kong, Taiwan, South Korea, and Singapore that have few natural resources, small domestic markets, and little infrastructure. But by tailoring their industrial bases to the needs of the world economy, they have become successful exporters to developed countries. These countries emphasize exports in clothing, engineering and metal products, and light manufactures. The success of South Korea, for example, has encouraged other Third World countries to adopt a similar program of export-led industrialization.

Why did import-substitution industrialization fail? What are the characteristics of export-led industrialization? What are the consequences of this strategy on economies and people? Can this form of industrialization in the periphery be sustained if the tendency toward slower economic growth in the center of the world economy continues? In the following sections, we will attempt to answer these questions.

Import-Substitution Industrialization

In the post-World War II period, newly independent Third World countries sought to break out of their domination by, and dependence on, developed countries. Their goal was to initiate self-expanding capitalist development through a strategy of *import-substitution industrialization*. This development strategy involved the production of domestic manufactured goods to replace imports. Only the middle classes could support a domestic market; thus, industrialization focused on luxuries and consumer durables. The small plants concentrated in existing cities, increasing regional inequalities. The "infant industries" developed behind tariff walls in order to reduce imports from developed countries, but local entrepreneurs had neither the capital nor the technology to begin their domestic industrialization. Foreign multinational corporations came to the rescue. Although projects were often joint ventures involving local capital, "independent" development soon became *dependent industrialization* under the control of foreign capital. Many countries experienced an initial burst in the growth of manufacturing and a reduction in imports. But after awhile, the need to purchase raw materials and capital goods and the heavy repatriation of profits to home countries of the multinationals dissipated foreign-exchange savings.

Export-Led Industrialization

By the 1960s, it was apparent to Third World leaders that the strategy of import-substitution had failed. Only countries that had made an early transition to *export-led industrialization* were able to sustain their rates of industrial growth. Once again, Third World

In this textile factory in Fortaleza, Brazil, women constitute the largest part of the workforce. Brazil is a major exporter of textiles to advanced industrial countries. (Source: World Bank.)

The city-state of Singapore, which lacks space, minerals, materials, food, and energy, depends on global demand conditions and trade for its economic growth. Its major trading partners are Japan, the United States, and the European Economic Community. Since the mid-1980s the dampened international economic environment adversely affected Singapore's manufacturing sector and trade. For the 1990s and beyond, the Singaporean government is depending on the growth of "brain industries"—on the ability of its 2.7 million people to sell their skills and services to the rest of their region and the world. (Source: Singapore Tourist Promotion Board.)

development became strongly linked to the external market. In the past, export-oriented development had been tied to the export of primary commodities to developed countries. Now, export-oriented development was to be based on the production and export of manufactures.

The growth of export-led industrialization coincided with the international economic crisis of the 1970s and 1980s. It took place at a time when the demand for imports in the advanced industrial countries was growing despite the onset of a decline in their industrial bases. It was a response to the new international division of labor.

Export-oriented industrialization tends to concentrate in *export-processing zones* where four conditions are usually met. "First, import provisions are made for goods used in the production of items for duty-free export and export duties are waived. There is no foreign exchange control and there is generally freedom to repatriate profits. Second, infrastructure, utilities, factory space and warehousing are usually provided at subsidized rates. Third, tax holidays, usually of five years, are offered. Finally, abundant, disciplined labor is provided at low wage rates" (Thrift 1986, p. 52).

The first export-processing zone was not established in the Third World; it was established in 1958 in Shannon, Ireland, with the local international airport at its core. In the late 1960s, a number of countries in East Asia began to develop export-processing zones, the first being Taiwan's Kaohsuing Export Processing Zone, set up in 1965. By 1975 there were thirty-one zones in eighteen countries. By the early 1980s at least sixty-eight zones were established in forty, principally Third World, countries. Most of them are located in the Caribbean, Central and Latin America, and in Asia (Figure 11.14).

Central to the growth of Third World manufacturing exports to the developed countries are multinational corporations, which establish operating systems between locally owned companies and foreign-owned companies. The arrangement is known as *international subcontracting*, or offshore assembly and sourcing. Although there are numerous legal relationships between the multinational and the subcontractor, from wholly owned subsidiary to independent producer, the key point is that Third World exports to developed countries are part of a unified production process controlled by firms in the advanced industrial countries. For example, Sears might contract with an independent firm in Hong Kong or Taiwan to produce shirts; yet, it will retain control over design specifications, advertising, and marketing. This is similar to the putting-out system in textiles that was developed in preindustrial England. "With modern transport and communications, it is probably no more difficult for today's merchants to organize a putting-out system between New York and Hong Kong, or between Tokyo and Seoul, than it was for the early English merchants to organize their putting-out system between London and the surrounding villages" (World Bank 1987, p. 46).

Consequences of Export-Led Industrialization

Export-led industrialization moves work to the workers instead of workers to the work, which was the case

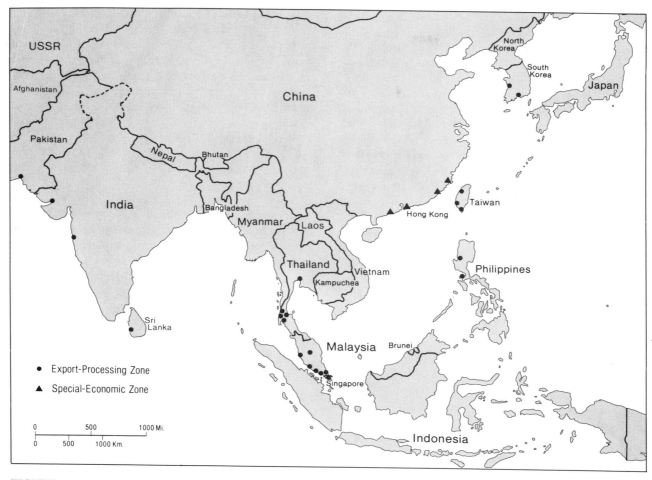

FIGURE 11.14
Export-processing zones in Asia. (Source: Wong and Chu, 1984, p. 4.)

during the long postwar boom. In some countries this form of industrialization has generated substantial employment. For example, since their establishment, export-processing zones have accounted for at least 60 percent of manufacturing employment expansion in Malaysia and Singapore. But, in general, the numbers of workers employed in the export-processing zones' labor forces are modest. It is unlikely that they employ more than a million workers worldwide.

Much of the employment in export-processing zones is in electronics and electrical assembly or in textiles. Young, unmarried women make up the largest part of the workforce in these industries—88 percent of zone employment in Sri Lanka, 85 percent in Malaysia and Taiwan, and 75 percent in the Philippines (Morello 1983). Explanations for this dominance of women in the workforce vary; it is often attributed to sexual stereotyping, in which the docility, patience, manual dexterity, and visual acuity of female labor are presupposed. Of much greater significance is the fact that women are often paid much less than men for the same job. Cheap labor is essential in the labor-intensive industries of the global assembly line.

According to A. Sivanadan (1987), export-led industrialization gives rise to *disorganic development*—an imposed economic system at odds with the cultural and political institutions of the people it exploits. People produce things of no use to them. How they produce has no relation to how they used to produce. Workers are often flung into an alien labor process that violates their customs and codes. For example, female factory workers often pay a high price for their escape from family and home production, especially in Asia where women's family roles have been traditionally emphasized. "Because of their relative independence, westernized dress and changed lifestyles, women may be rejected by their families and find it hard to reassimilate when they can no longer find employment on the assembly line" (Fuentes and Ehrenreich 1987, p. 209).

Although export-oriented industrialization leads to growth in production and employment, as well as to increases in foreign exchange, Martin Landsberg (1987) argued that "it will not lead to the creation of an indigenous, self-expanding capitalist economy" (p. 235). The linkages between "export platforms" and local economies are minimal. Scholars who oppose Landsberg's view point to South Korea as a shining example of a country that has completed a successful transition to industrial capitalism. But so far Korean industrial expansion has not taken place because of domestic demand. It is exports and international competitiveness that the Koreans have been seeking. This may be changing, partly because of the general global tendency to stagnation.

Economic stagnation in developed countries is a major concern of countries that have enjoyed great success with the strategy of export-led industrialization. For developed countries where production and investment is moving out, purchasing power will be lost. The resultant spiraling down of general economic activity would choke off dependent industrialization and increase poverty and suffering for Third World workers and peasants.

SUMMARY

In this chapter we explored the social relations that lead to industrial change, described worldwide manufacturing trends, and examined the recent history of industrial devolution and industrial revolution in

Pusan, South Korea, is a purpose-built city for shipbuilding and the export-import trade. Other towns in South Korea dedicated to specialized industrial functions include Changwan for machine tools and heavy plant, Ulsan for automobiles, and Yosu for petrochemicals. (Source: World Bank.)

advanced industrial countries and in the Third World. It was argued that the processes of *deindustrialization* and *industrialization* are not offsetting tendencies within the global system; rather, they constitute a negative-sum global game played by multinational nomadic capital. Multinationals switched production from place to place in the 1970s and 1980s because of varying relations between capital and labor and new technological innovations in transportation and communication. With improved air freight, containerization, and telecommunications, multinational corporations can dispatch products faster, cheaper, and with fewer losses.

Nomadic capital has left a trail of disruption in its wake. Many industrialized countries are facing the serious social consequences of factory closures and job losses. In the United States 900,000 manufacturing jobs per year were lost between 1978 and 1982 just by the closure of plants with over one hundred workers. These losses were hidden to some extent by selective reindustrialization and the migration of manufacturing from the American Manufacturing Belt to the South and West. In Britain, however, losses occurred in virtually all industries and regions. In underdeveloped countries, *export-led industrialization* has produced *disorganic development* and *dependent development*. Workers and peasants have had to bear the deleterious consequences of this form of industrialization. Japan, on the other hand, has been an industrial success story. However, its economic miracle has been achieved at the expense of social welfare, the environment, and international relations. And in the future, its economic miracle may be stymied by its aging population. The median age of Japanese workers is already about forty-one, and it is predicted to rise to nearly forty-four by 2020.

KEY TERMS

American Manufacturing Belt	industrial restructuring
Britain's north-south divide	industrialization
capital-labor relations	international subcontracting
deindustrialization	Japan Incorporated
dependent industrialization	materialist science
disorganic development	MITI
economic structure of society	mode of production
export-led industrialization	postindustrial society
export-processing zones	quaternary economic activities
forces of production	social relations of production
import-substitution industrialization	zaibatsu

SUGGESTED READINGS

Belassa, B. 1981. *The Newly Industrializing Countries in the World Economy.* New York: Pergamon Press.

Blackaby, F., ed. 1979. *De-industrialization.* London: Heinemann.

Bluestone, B., and Harrison, B. 1982. *The Deindustrialization of America.* New York: Basic Books.

Dicken, P. 1986. *Global Shift: Industrial Change in a Turbulent World.* London: Harper and Row.

Hoare, A. G. 1983. *The Location of Industry in Britain.* Cambridge: Cambridge University Press.

Kirkpatrick, C. H., and Nixson, F. I., eds. 1983. *Trade and Employment in Developing Countries.* Chicago: University of Chicago Press.

Markusen, A; Hall, P.; and Glasmeier A. 1986. *High Tech America.* Winchester, MA: Allen and Unwin.

Massey, D. 1984. *Spatial Divisions of Labor: Social Structures and the Geography of Production.* New York: Methuen.

Morishima, M. 1982. *Why Has Japan Succeeded?* Cambridge: Cambridge University Press.

Nash, J., and Fernandez-Kelly, M. P. 1983. *Women, Men, and the International Division of Labor.* Albany: State University of New York Press.

Peet, R., ed. 1987. *International Capitalism and Industrial Restructuring.* Winchester, MA: Allen and Unwin.

UNIDO. 1983. *Industry in a Changing World.* New York: United Nations.

12
INTERNATIONAL BUSINESS

OBJECTIVES

☐ To consider the nature of international business

☐ To explain the bases of international trade and factor flows

☐ To examine the effects of natural and artificial barriers on international business

☐ To acquaint you with the major international institutions that deal with problems of trade, investment, and development

☐ To describe the evolving pattern of international commerce

☐ To assess the impact of East Asia as an economic powerhouse on the industrial democracies of North America and Western Europe

Multinational corporate advertising, Piccadilly Circus, London, England. (Source: Photo by A. R. de Souza.)

Since World War II, economies of the world have become more integrated than ever before. *International integration* refers to the concept of international specialization or division of labor. Contributing to this greater integration have been great technological breakthroughs in transportation and communication and massive transformations in business behavior. These innovations and developments have greatly enhanced the role of *international business*, which is any form of business activity that crosses a national border. International business includes the international transmission of merchandise, capital, and services. International trade is expanding and its composition and patterns are changing. But in many respects, it is now less significant in the global business structure than the international movement of capital and services. More and more companies are investing in foreign countries to acquire raw materials, to penetrate markets, and to exploit cheap labor. The expansion of production overseas has been matched by a parallel, symbiotic expansion of service enterprises, which now account for an increasing share of foreign direct investments.

As we saw in Chapter 5, the actors in the international business arena have become more numerous and relationships among them more complex in the postwar years (Robinson 1981). The immediate postwar decade was primarily a *two-actor era*, the firm and its foreign commercial constituents—customers, suppliers, joint-venture partners, licensees. During these years the United States spent billions on the reconstruction of Japan and West European countries. The economic revival of these countries represented huge markets for U.S. capital equipment and consumer goods, and few political barriers impeded their flow.

By the mid-1950s, with postwar reconstruction virtually complete, the economic dominance of the United States was challenged by Japan and several West European countries. The high value of the dollar in relation to other currencies dampened demand for U.S. goods and services and encouraged other countries to aggressively seek export markets. Between 1955 and 1970, the years of the long postwar boom, an increasing volume of trade was associated with multinationals domiciled in the United States, Western Europe, and Japan. These giant companies intensified the sensitivities of host governments, which then came to represent a *third actor* in international decision making. Corporate strategists had to contend not only with host-country policies in developed countries, but with policies in the new, self-conscious underdeveloped countries as well.

The early 1970s marked another watershed as the world economy entered a prolonged period of disorder. This time of crisis stemmed from four structural changes. First, the industrialized countries experienced a marked slowdown in their rates of economic growth. Second, competitive rivalry between industrialized countries increased significantly. This was stimulated by their slower and more unstable growth rates and, in turn, contributed to them. It gave rise to an increase in restrictive policies as each country sought to overcome its national crisis at the expense of other countries. Third, the collapse of the Bretton Woods monetary arrangements in 1973, involving the replacement of fixed-exchange rates and the convertibility of the dollar into gold by a system of more or less freely fluctuating exchange rates, permitted the United States to devalue its currency in an effort to retrieve lost competitiveness with its trading rivals. The new world monetary system, in which exchange rates shift almost daily, fueled inflation and destabilized commodity markets. The fourth structural change, that of massive increases in oil prices by 400 percent in 1973–74 and 165 percent between 1979 and 1981, reduced real income in the advanced countries and dealt a particularly harsh blow to the oil-importing Third World countries. The oil crisis induced worldwide recession in the mid-1970s and again in the early 1980s. Recovery from the recessions has been weak in all countries except the western Pacific nations. In fact, Japan and other East Asian nations emerged from the recessions stronger than ever, their industrial growth fed by a rising market in the West.

While these events were unfolding, there was a substantial growth in the activities of multinational corporations. In pursuit of larger profits than could be obtained domestically, multinationals built up industrial capacity in "offshore" production centers. Parent governments recognized that the ability of multinationals to transfer capital, production, and labor across national boundaries was a major cause of instability in the global economy. So began the *four-actor era* as parent governments sought to regulate their activities.

In the late 1970s international business became more and more politicized at home and abroad. An increase in government regulations at both ends was in response to mounting public concerns about pollution, natural resource allocation, income and wealth distribution, consumer protection, energy, and the governance of corporations. These concerns were expressed by a variety of special interest groups—ethnic, religious, occupational, and political.

We now live in a world in which special interest

groups are developing international linkages and loyalties as they strive to create international orders in their own image. It is the world of the *multiactor era*, where a variety of actors are relevant to corporate decision making. In the new environment, multinational corporations find it difficult to react swiftly enough to changing opportunities and constraints. As a result, new forms of business entities such as trading companies, financial groups, and service companies are developing, and they will probably become preeminent features in the international business climate of the 1990s.

The increasingly complex international business environment warrants the attention of geographers. Knowledge of the international sphere of business helps us to understand what is going on in the world as well as within our own countries. The purpose of this chapter is to examine the concepts and patterns that underlie the expanding world of international business. It seeks answers to the following questions: What theories shed light on the processes of international interaction? What are the dynamics of world trade and investment? What are the patterns of international commerce?

INTERNATIONAL TRADE

Why International Trade Occurs

Why are so many countries, large and small, rich and poor, deeply involved in international trade? One answer lies in the unequal distribution of productive resources among countries. Trade offsets disparity with regard to the availability of productive resources. But whether a country can export successfully depends not only on its resources, but also on the conditions of the economic environment; the opportunity, ability, and effort of producers to trade; and the capacity of local producers abroad to compete.

Natural and Human-Made Resources   The *factors of production*—land containing raw materials, labor, capital, technology, entrepreneurship—vary from country to country. One country is rich in iron ore and another has tremendous oil deposits. Some countries have populations large enough to support industrial complexes, whereas others do not. People are not only a natural resource, they are also a precious human-made resource with differential skills. One country is home to an enormous pool of workers adept at running modern machinery; another abounds with scientists and engineers specializing in research-laden products. In some countries, entrepreneurs are more able and knowledgeable than in

others. The imbalance in natural and human-made resources accounts for much of the international interchange of the factors of production and/or the products and services that the factors can be used to produce.

Conditions of the Economic Environment   A country that is well endowed in natural and human-made resources has an edge over countries that lack these assets. But the assets, in and of themselves, are insufficient to guarantee success in the export market. American producers, for example, tend to be less successful exporters than their Japanese or European counterparts. Numerous economic environmental factors may reduce the ability of countries to fully utilize their resources and productive advantages. These factors include inflation, exchange rates, labor conditions, governmental attitudes, and laws.

Inflation, which is a rise in the general level of prices of goods and services, can be detrimental to a country's ability to compete domestically or internationally. Exchange rates, the prices of currencies in foreign-exchange markets, can influence competitiveness. For example, if a currency is overvalued in relation to other currencies, local producers may find it difficult to compete with foreign imports and difficult to export successfully. Recurring labor disputes that interrupt production may create serious obstacles for exporters. Governments can encourage or discourage their export sectors. And the competitiveness of exporters may also be affected by laws—labor laws, tax laws, and patent laws.

Opportunity, Ability, and Effort of the Producer to Trade   Success in the international trade arena hinges on demand for the good or service produced, an awareness of the demand by suppliers, the availability of appropriate foreign distribution channels, and a minimum of governmental controls. But even if all these conditions are met, many producers fail to respond. Some may lack the desire to try, while others may have the desire but never make the effort. The importance of desire and effort in determining success in international trade is exemplified by Japan. Although this island nation is poor in raw materials, it has successfully imported materials and components for use in the manufacture of goods for domestic and foreign markets.

Competitiveness of Local Producers Abroad   The ability of a country to export is affected by the capacity of foreign producers to compete. A crucial element in the ability of domestic producers to compete is the relative cost of production. Countries with high labor, capital, and energy costs can expect strong competition from abroad. The existence of strong competitors may also act as a disincentive to successful and profitable exporting.

Trade by Barter and Money

At one time, trade was very simple and was conducted on a barter basis. *Barter* or *countertrade* is the direct exchange of goods or services for other goods or services. It still occurs in some traditional markets in underdeveloped countries and is of increasing importance in the modern world economy. Roughly 30 percent of world commerce is now countertrade. The Soviet Union and East European countries use barter to trade among themselves and with underdeveloped countries. Major oil-exporting countries such as Iran and Nigeria barter oil and gas for manufactured goods.

Despite its widespread use, particularly by governments that have turned toward national economic protectionism, barter is a cumbersome way of conducting international exchange. Even within a country, consumers would find it difficult to take the goods or services their families produce and barter for their daily needs. In fact, more time would be devoted to the exchange aspect than to the production aspect. Money represents a means by which to simplify the domestic exchange procedure. This also holds true, of course, for trade between countries. Then again, money does present problems, such as those associated with exchange rates. But introducing the factor of money as an exchange medium does not alter the theoretical bases for international trade.

Classical Trade Theory

Absolute and Comparative Advantage The flow of trade arises from an economic advantage that one country has over another in the output of a good or service. It may occur because of the *absolute advantage* of one of the countries in the production of a good. For example, Country *A* produces cloth twice as efficiently as Country *B*, whereas Country *B* is 50 percent more productive than Country *A* in the output of wheat; thus, there is a tendency for Country *A* to exchange its cloth for Country *B*'s wheat.

Countries need not have an absolute advantage for trade to take place. Indeed, countries can successfully export goods in which they have absolute cost disadvantages. This phenomenon is called the *theory of comparative advantage* or the *theory of comparative cost*. Developed by eighteenth- and nineteenth-cen-

tury English economists, notably David Ricardo (1912), the theory states that all countries have comparative advantages, and that countries will export the goods they can produce at the lowest relative cost. For example, Country *A* specializes in the export of raisins because it can produce them more cheaply compared to other goods than can Country *B*, and Country *B* exports paper because it can produce paper more cheaply than other goods. Raisins may be cheaper than paper in both countries, but the cost differential is wider in Country *A* than in Country *B*. To explain the structure of foreign trade of a particular country, we must identify its comparative advantage, which involves a study of its productive resources.

A Simple Model To show how a difference in productive resources can lead to international trade, consider a simple labor-cost model, such as the one used by David Ricardo in the nineteenth century. The model excludes economies of scale; neglects transport costs; and assumes free trade, full employment of productive resources, and the same technological conditions and tastes everywhere. To make things even more simple, assume that there are only two countries, *A* and *B*, and that these two countries produce only two commodities, coal and corn.

Countries *A* and *B* are the same in every respect except one. Both countries have 120 person-days of labor at their disposal. Both countries require two person-days of labor to produce a ton of corn, and they have enough arable land to employ all their workers in corn farming. In Country *A*, however, coal deposits are much nearer the surface than in Country *B*. As a result, Country *A* requires only one person-day of labor to mine a ton of coal, whereas Country *B* needs four person-days.

Table 12.1, which is a production-possibilities schedule, illustrates that if Country *A* decided to grow only corn or mine only coal, it could produce either 60 tons of corn or 120 tons of coal. It also shows that Country *A* could produce both corn and coal by choosing from various production opportunities.

TABLE 12.1
Production-possibilities schedule for Country *A*.

Opportunity Points	Corn	Coal
A	60	0
B	45	30
C	30	60
D	15	90
E	0	120

FIGURE 12.1
Production-possibilities curve
for Country A.

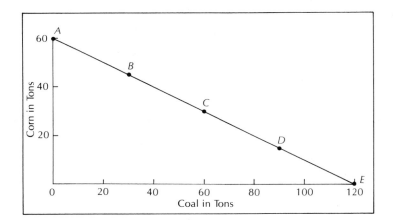

Each opportunity point represents a mutually exclusive combination of corn and coal. Thus, if Country A selects any one combination, it must reject all other combinations. The opportunity points in Table 12.1 are graphed in Figure 12.1. The output of coal is plotted on the horizontal axis and the output of corn is plotted on the vertical axis. The sloping line, AE, connecting the various points on the graph, is called the *production-possibilities curve*. Without international trade, Country A would have to select one combination of corn and coal.

Table 12.2 and Figure 12.2 illustrate the production-possibilities schedule and curve for Country B. The maximum output of corn is the same as in Country A, because both countries have the same amount of labor and are equally efficient in growing corn. But maximum coal output in Country B is smaller than in Country A because its mines are deeper and therefore more expensive to operate. In the absence of international trade, Country B would have to select some combination of coal and corn along its production-possibilities curve.

Suppose now that Country A and Country B are no longer isolated, and that trade between them is possible. An opportunity for trade creates a single market, and a common price for coal is established. Let's say this new price for coal is lower than the previous price in Country B, but higher than the

previous price in Country A. Country B can now obtain a ton of coal without giving up so much corn as in the past, when it had to mine coal domestically. It can now specialize in growing corn and use some of its corn to buy coal from Country A. Similarly, Country A can now obtain more corn for its coal. It can now specialize in mining coal and use some of its coal to buy corn from Country B.

Figure 12.3 illustrates one possible rearrangement of production where the common price for coal is set at one ton of corn for one ton of coal. The left-hand triangle is the production-possibilities curve for Country A, and the upside-down triangle is the production-possibilities curve for Country B. In the absence of trade, when each country was confined to its own production-possibilities curve, Country A produced 60 tons of coal and 30 tons of corn, while Country B produced 22.5 tons of coal and 15 tons of corn. The opportunity for trade enables both countries to rearrange production and consumption to

TABLE 12.2
Production-possibilities schedule for Country B.

Opportunity Points	Corn	Coal
A_1	60	0
B_1	45	7.5
C_1	30	15
D_1	15	22.5
E_1	0	30

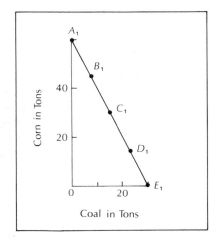

FIGURE 12.2
Production-possibilities curve for Country B.

FIGURE 12.3
Trade between Country *A* and
Country *B*.

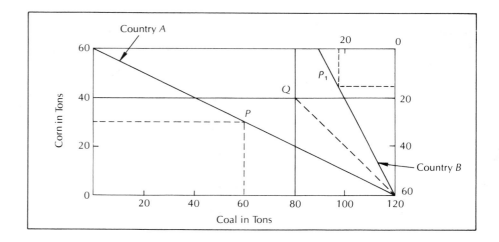

mutual advantage. Country *A* can specialize in coal production and mine 120 tons, and Country *B* can specialize in corn production and grow 60 tons. Reading from the graph, Country *A* now consumes 80 tons of coal and exports 40 tons to buy corn, and Country *B* consumes 20 tons of corn and exports 40 tons to buy coal. Country *A*'s consumption shifts from *P* to *Q*, and Country *B*'s consumption shifts from *P₁* to *Q*.

Our simple Ricardian model shows that both countries enjoy a higher level of consumption with trade than without. Moreover, trade enlarges world output of coal and corn by allowing both countries to specialize. Before trade, coal output was 82.5 tons (60 tons for Country *A* plus 22.5 tons for Country *B*). With trade, coal output increases to 120 tons. Before trade, corn output was 45 tons (30 tons for Country *A* plus 15 tons for Country *B*). With trade, corn output increases to 60 tons. This increase in output points to a fundamental principle in orthodox trade theory: Free trade is best, because it allocates economic tasks so as to maximize world output and income.

Modern Trade Theory

Although David Ricardo's two-country, two-product, labor-cost model is very simple, it provides the basis for modern trade theory. The Ricardian model may be expanded by taking into account several countries and commodities and by allowing several factors of production. The multifactor approach to trade theory derives from work by two Swedish economists, Eli Heckscher (1919) and Bertil Ohlin (1933). In brief, the Heckscher-Ohlin theory takes the view that a country should specialize in the production of those goods that demand the least from its scarce factors of production, and that it should export its specialties in order to obtain the goods it is ill-equipped to make

(Olsen 1971, pp. 3–14). Thus, if Countries *A* and *B* have different endowments of labor and machinery, both of them can gain from trade. Country *A* with abundant labor and few machines can concentrate on, say, corn production and export its specialty in order to import cloth. Similarly, Country *B* with little labor and abundant machinery can specialize in cloth and export some of it to import corn. Again, free trade is best from a global standpoint. By fostering specialization, it maximizes world output.

Not only does the Heckscher-Ohlin theory argue that there will be gains from trade, but also that there will be a tendency toward equalization of wage rates as the trade pattern develops. The reasoning behind this "factor-price equalization," as it came to be called, is as follows: As Country *A* specializes in the production of corn, thus diverting production from cloth, its pattern of production becomes more labor intensive. As a result, Country *A*'s abundance of labor is diminished, the marginal productivity of labor rises, and wages also increase. Conversely, in Country *B*, as cloth production replaces corn production, labor becomes less scarce, the marginal productivity of labor falls, and wages also fall.

Some economists find the notion that foreign trade evens out the relative scarcely of factors of production too simplistic. But others cling to the Heckscher-Ohlin theory with considerable tenacity. The theory has ideological importance, and in 1919, when Heckscher first put it forward, it was particularly opportune. After World War I, the United States introduced restrictions on immigration, and there was also a growing interest in protectionism. With the interests of free-traders under threat, a strong case for free trade needed to be made. The Heckscher-Ohlin theory not only showed that free trade was desirable, but that it also could compensate for restrictions on labor migration.

Inadequacies of Trade Theories

Trade theories are based on restrictive assumptions that limit their validity. They generally ignore considerations such as scale economies and transport costs. Scale economies improve the ability of a country to compete even in the face of higher factor costs. The cost of moving a product greatly affects its "tradeability." Brick, which has a high transport cost relative to value, and therefore is not extensively traded internationally, is a good example.

Trade theories assume perfect knowledge of international trading opportunities, an active interest in trading, and a rapid response by managers when opportunities arise. However, executives are often ignorant of their trading opportunities. And even if they are aware, they may fear the complexities of international trade.

Other inadequacies of trade theories include the assumptions of homogeneous products, perfect competition, the immobility of factors of production, and freedom from governmental interference. Products are not homogeneous. Oligopolies exist in many industries. Such factors of production as capital, technology, management, and labor are mobile. Governments interfere with trade; they can raise formidable barriers to the movement of goods and services.

The most important shortcoming of trade theories, however, is their failure to incorporate the role of firms, especially multinational corporations. Trading decisions are usually made on the microeconomic level by managers, not by governments in Country *A* or *B*. Multinational corporations also operate from a multinational rather than from a national perspective. When international trade occurs between different affiliates of the same company, it is referred to as *intra-multinational trade*. Special considerations, such as tax incentives or no competition from other affiliates of the same company, can often play a pivotal role in a company's international decisions.

Despite their limitations, trade theories provide an essential basis for our understanding of international business. They still underlie the thinking of many scholars, managers, labor leaders, and government officials. They offer a background for understanding the barriers to international business. They also explain much commodity trade, such as the international movement of wheat.

Is Free Trade Fair?

Free trade is best from the standpoint of efficiency, but is it fair given the relationship of *unequal exchange* between developed and underdeveloped countries?

This question is raised by radical theorists for whom imperialism is associated with relatively free trade (Baran 1957; Frank 1969; Emmanuel 1972; Sunkel 1972; Wallerstein 1974: Amin 1976). Their argument is that an artificial division of labor has made it difficult for most Third World countries to earn a good income from free trade.

An Artificial Division of Labor The British were instrumental in creating an unfair division of labor. Implicit in the early nineteenth-century argument for free trade was the notion that what was good for Britain was good for the world. But free trade was established within a framework of inequality among countries. Britain found free trade and competition agreeable only after becoming established as the world's most technically advanced industrial nation. Having gained an initial advantage over other manufacturers, Britain then threw open its markets to the rest of the world in 1849. Other countries were instructed or lured to do the same. The pattern of specialization that resulted was obvious. Britain concentrated on producing manufactured goods, such as vehicles, engines, machine-tools, paper, and textile yarns and fabrics, and exporting them in exchange for a variety of primary products. Imports included specialized cargoes such as Persian carpets, furs, wines, silks, and bulk imports such as timber, grains, fruit, and meat. Although many countries gained from the application of this artificial division of labor, none gained more than Britain.

The only way other countries could break out of this artificial division of labor was by interfering with free trade. The United States and Germany did so in the 1870s by adopting protectionist policies. France and a few other European countries with embryonic industries did the same. Underdeveloped countries, however, failed to escape, either because of colonialism, or because it was not in the interest of their ruling groups to do so.

The original division of labor changed little until after World War II, when a new structure began to evolve. Some underdeveloped countries were given a limited license to industrialize. As we saw in Chapter 11, the basic trend was export-led industrialization, concentrated in a few countries. For the best-off poor countries, industrial growth is geared to the needs of the old imperial powers. Thus, the growth of manufacture in the Third World, under multinational corporate auspices, is not a portent of its emancipation from an artificial division of labor.

The Worsening Terms of Trade A deterioration in the *terms of trade*—the prices received for exports relative to prices paid for imports—exemplifies the problem of unequal exchange for Third World countries. By and large, underdeveloped countries export raw and semiprocessed primary goods—agricultural commodities (cocoa, tea, coffee, palm oil, rubber, sisal, sugar, jute, and cotton) and minerals (tin, iron ore, bauxite, oil, copper, and uranium). In 1985 primary commodities accounted for 72 and 51 percent of the total exports of low- and middle-income countries (excluding China and India), respectively. The proceeds from these exports are needed to pay for imports of manufactures, which are vital for continuing industrialization and technological progress. Shifts in the relative prices of commodities and manufactures can therefore change the purchasing power of the exports of underdeveloped countries dramatically (World Bank 1988, p. 24).

Between 1970 and 1986 Third World countries experienced a worsening in their terms of trade. This was caused by a decline in the prices of primary commodities and an increase in the prices of manufactures. In some years the adverse shift was offset by an increased volume of Third World exports. For the period as a whole, however, import volume growth exceeded export volume growth and, given the overall deterioration in the terms of trade, the result was large current account deficits. Maintenance of these deficits was possible only because the Third World had access to external sources of finance.

Economist Keith Griffin (1969, pp. 110–16) provided an account of the theoretical causes for the decline in the Third World terms of trade for export commodities, especially food crops. According to Griffin, the cause of a decline in the terms of trade for

A tea-buying center in Kenya. Sixteen percent of Kenya's export earnings come from tea and 34 percent from coffee. Thus, Kenya depends largely on two commodities for export income. (Source: World Bank.)

any country depends on (1) the nature of the product exported, (2) the degree of structural rigidity in the economy, and (3) the bias of technical progress. Let us now look at each of these factors in turn.

We can use a statistical finding known as *Engel's law* to account for a deterioration in the terms of trade. Nineteenth-century German statistician Ernst Engel, who examined the income and spending patterns of wage-earning families in several European countries, arrived at the following conclusion: As incomes rise beyond a certain point, the proportion of disposable income spent on food declines. In the United States, for example, the percentage of disposable income spent filling supermarket carts is greater for families earning \$10,000 a year than it is for families earning \$30,000 a year. If we extended the concept of Engel's law to international trade, we could argue that as consumption of manufactured goods increased, agriculture would form a decreasing proportion of total trade, and income elasticity of demand would be greater for manufactured goods. Thus, we would have a built-in structural disequilibrium, which would result in worsening terms of trade for exporters of largely agricultural produce.

Economies of many underdeveloped countries are characterized by structural rigidity. They cannot alter the composition of exports rapidly in response to changing relative prices. Thus, if their commodity export prices fall, they have no alternative but to accept declines in their terms of trade. This argument is illustrated in Figure 12.4. Assume, for example, that the price of coffee is initially P_0, as determined by the intersection of the supply and demand curves—S_0S and D_0, respectively. Assume further, that there is an increase in demand to D_1 caused, say, by the outbreak

of war. The price of coffee will at first rise very sharply due to the fixed capacity of the existing coffee plantations. These extraordinary high prices will encourage people to invest in this sector; output will eventually increase substantially, and the price will settle at P_1. Increased prices may encourage expansion of output among established producers and may encourage new competitors to enter the market. If, now, demand falls, say to its original level, it will move along a new supply curve—S_1S. Price will not return to its initial level; on the contrary, it will fall considerably below that level, to P_2. Once capacity has been installed in new, stable plantations, variable costs of production may be very low, and, hence, supply may be quite insensitive to price reductions. Once resources have become fixed in specific and long-lived capital—in this case, coffee trees—the economy becomes inflexible and is unable to transform resources from declining-price to rising-price sectors.

A third factor that may lead to worsening terms of trade is technological advances in developed countries. Advanced technology (1) enables the industrial economies to reduce the primary content of final products, (2) enables the wealthy nations to produce high-quality finished products from less valuable or lower quality primary products, and (3) enables the advanced economies to produce entirely new manufactured products, which are substitutes for existing primary products. These three technological developments are irreversible. The demand for many primary products may be inelastic for price decreases, but in the long run it may be very elastic for price increases. A rise in the price of a raw material provides an incentive for industrial research geared to economizing on the commodity, or substituting something else for it, or producing it in the importing country. For example, a fall in the world price of copper may result in only a very small increase in the quantity demanded, but a rise in the price of copper may result in the use of aluminum and silicon as permanent substitutes. Such an event has dealt a severe blow to Zambia and Zaire, the economies of which are overwhelmingly dependent on exports of copper ore to developed countries.

Griffin concluded that slow technical development is one of the major factors accounting for the inflexibility of economies in underdeveloped countries. Terms-of-trade difficulties of underdeveloped countries are based upon their inability to shift resources from declining to expanding sectors. Until underdeveloped countries reduce structural rigidities by transforming their economic, social, and institutional frameworks, they will continue to experience trade difficulties.

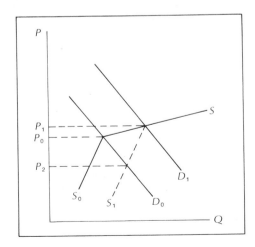

FIGURE 12.4
Structural rigidity and commodity price changes. (Source: Griffin, 1969, p. 113.)

INTERNATIONAL FACTOR MOVEMENTS

Why Factor Flows Occur

Besides trade, international factor movements are the other way to overcome differences between countries in the availability of resources. Profit and economic efficiency are the basic forces underlying the demand and supply incentives for international factor flows. From the supply side, the search for more profitable employment of factors of production is the primary motive for most factor flows. For example, capital commonly goes to places where interest, profits, and capital gains promise to be greater. Labor—unskilled, technical, or managerial—often flows to where opportunity and potential returns are greater. And the incentive in international technology transfer results from a desire to tap additional markets. From the demand side, international factor flows are frequently initiated in a similar way: the company that needs capital, labor, and technology starts the search in response to its need to lower costs, improve its productive efficiency, and to introduce new products.

Let us look at capital flows in detail, and then look briefly at labor and technology flows. The market for capital flows is far more efficient and integrated than the markets for labor and technology. Labor and technology markets generally suffer from poor information flows. And the labor market is the most politically and socially sensitive of the international markets and the most heavily regulated.

Forms of Capital Flow

Capital movement takes two major forms. The first type involves the lending and borrowing of money. Lenders and borrowers may be in either the private or the public sector. The public sector includes governments or international institutions such as the World Bank and agencies of the United Nations.

The second type of capital movement involves investments in the equity of a company. If a long-term investment does not involve managerial control of a foreign company, it is called *portfolio investment*. If the investment is sufficient to obtain managerial control, it is called *direct investment*. Multinational corporations are the epitome of direct investors.

Sources of Capital Flow

Monetary capital is the result of historical development. Unlike a "natural" resource like iron ore, it must be accumulated over time as a result of the willingness of a society to defer consumption. Low-income countries have a low capacity to generate investment capital; all of the capital that they do generate is usually employed domestically. Developed countries have a much greater capacity for generating investment capital. They provide most of the world's private sector capital, although a few fast-growing underdeveloped countries, such as South Korea, are also capital exporters.

Optimally, financial markets should produce an efficient distribution of money and capital throughout the world. However, there are many barriers to their optimal distribution. Personal preferences of investors, practices of investment banking houses, and governmental intervention and controls confine money and capital movements to well-worn paths. They flow to some areas and not to others, even though the need in neglected areas may be greater.

International Money and Capital Markets

The global expansion of the financial system has three components: the internationalization of (1) domestic currency, (2) banking, and (3) capital markets. *International currency markets* developed with the establishment of floating exchange rates in 1973 and with the growth in private international liquidity, mostly in the form of Eurocurrencies. The growth of Eurocurrencies was only partly a reflection of the decline of the dollar, because the dollar remains the major trading currency. It was more the result of continued integration of the world economy—with the growing internationalization of productive and financial capital—and of increased competition between financial institutions, especially the commercial banks.

What are Eurocurrencies? *Eurocurrencies* are bank deposits that are not subject to domestic banking legislation. With relatively few exceptions, they are held in outside countries "offshore" from the country in which they serve as legal tender. They have accommodated a large part of the growth of world trade since the late 1960s. The Eurocurrency market is attractive because it provides funds to borrowers with few conditions; it also offers investors higher interest rates than can be found in comparable domestic markets.

At first, Euromarkets involved U.S. dollars deposited in Europe; hence, they were called *Eurodollar* markets. Although the dollar still represents about 80 percent of all Eurocurrencies, other currencies, such as the deutschmark and yen, are also vehicles of international transactions. Therefore, "Eurocurrencies" is preferred to the less accurate term, "Eurodollar." However, even "Eurocurrencies" is a misnomer. Only 50 percent of the market is in Europe, the major

The city of London is a major center of Eurocurrencies, international banking, and capital markets. (Source: British Tourist Authority.)

center of which is London. Other Eurocenters have developed in such offshore banking centers as the Bahamas, Panama, Singapore, and Bahrain.

Eurocurrencies first became significant with the growth in the Eurodollar deposits of the USSR. In the immediate postwar years, the Soviets doubted the safety of holding dollar reserves in the United States (where they could be confiscated) and transferred them to banks in Paris and London. However, three occurrences added real impetus to the market in Eurocurrencies (Figure 12.5). First, during 1963 and 1964 President Kennedy, worried by the increased flow of dollars abroad, announced a program of capital control that lasted until 1973. As a consequence, international borrowers looked to Europe and the Eurocurrencies market. The main borrowers were U.S. multinational corporations raising loans to

continue their expansion abroad. Second, in 1971 the United States began to finance its budget deficit by paying its own currency, flooding the world with dollars that helped to fuel worldwide inflation. Third, the oil crises of the 1970s were a major stimulus to the growth of Euromarkets. *Petrodollars* (OPEC oil surpluses) poured into the major Eurobanks.

The banks had to find outlets for all the money they suddenly found in their coffers. One outlet was to send money to Third World countries. Commercial lending to underdeveloped countries—along with official lending and aid—grew rapidly between 1974 and 1982. As a result, the total debt of underdeveloped countries rose fourfold, from about $140 billion at the end of 1974 to about $560 billion in 1982. Third World countries were happy to take advantage of this unaccustomed access to cheap loans with few strings

FIGURE 12.5
The Eurocurrency take-off.
(Source: Thrift, 1986, p. 29.)

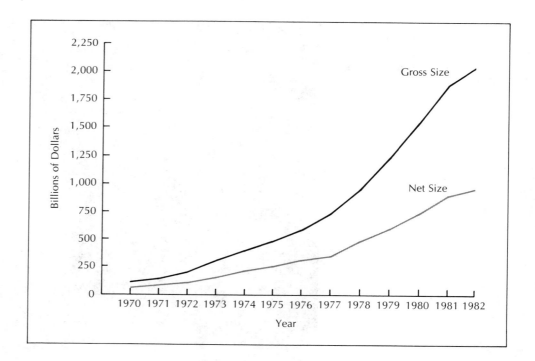

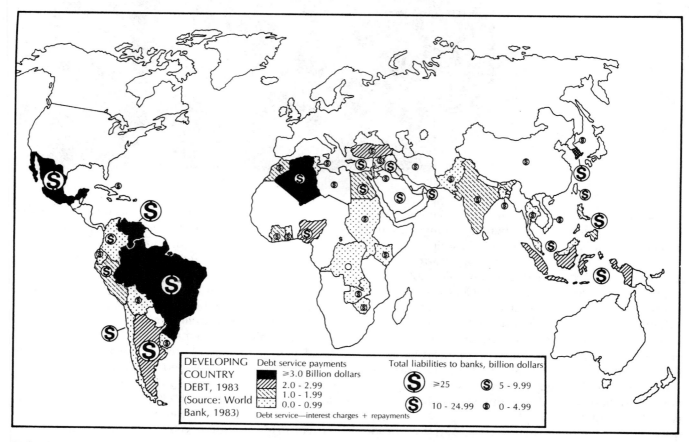

FIGURE 12.6
The debt crisis, 1983. (Source: Thrift, 1986, p. 31.)

attached. The borrowing enabled them to maintain domestic growth. However, these countries could not pay off the debts they incurred, so that now a widespread *debt crisis* exists among them, especially in countries in Central and South America such as Mexico, Brazil, and Argentina (Figure 12.6).

In 1982 concern was expressed by top-level bankers about the stability of the international monetary system. The cause of this instability was the overexpansion of credit, particularly through the Eurocurrency market in the 1960s and 1970s, leading to a crisis that had its roots in the overaccumulation of capital and declining rate of profit. The general crisis of a declining rate of profit was exacerbated by the imbalances caused by the oil-price hikes of the 1970s.

The financial crisis came to a head in 1982. A sharp rise in bankruptcies involving industrial capital put pressure on the banks and other financial institutions. In May 1982, when the American brokerage Drysdale went bankrupt, the heavy losses sustained by Chase Manhattan Bank forced the Federal Reserve Bank to pump some $3 billion into the banking system (*The Economist* 1982, p. 21). Worse followed. In August 1982 Mexico ran into difficulties meeting interest and capital payments on its debts. Brazil and Argentina also appeared ready to default. A collapse of the financial system was forestalled by a series of emergency measures designed to prevent large debtor countries from defaulting on their loans. These measures involved banks, the International Monetary Fund (IMF), the Bank for International Settlements, and the governments of lending countries in massive bail-out exercises that accompanied debt reschedulings. The debt overhang will no doubt persist in the 1990s, because debt-service ratios—annual interest and amortization payments as a percentage of total exports—will remain at dangerously high levels. In 1987, it was estimated that Third World external debt as a proportion of exports was 21 percent and equal to 38 percent of gross national product. (World Bank

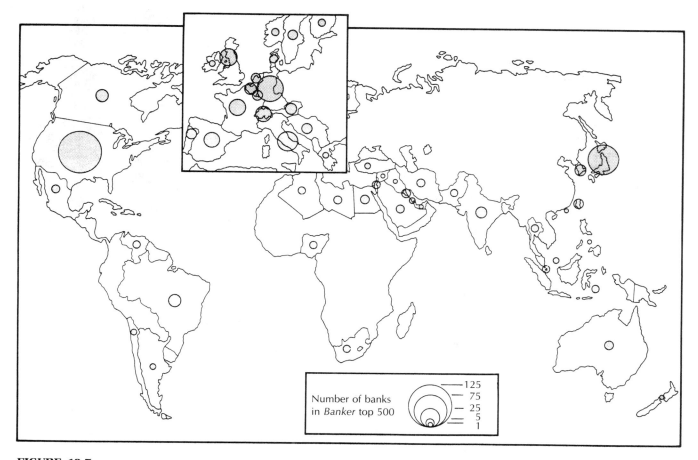

FIGURE 12.7
Number of banks in the top five hundred banks in the world by country, 1985. (Source: Thrift, 1986, p. 33.)

1988, p. 31). Consequently, the Third World is extremely vulnerable to changes in the world economy.

Paralleling the internationalization of domestic currency is the *internationalization of banking*. There have, of course, been international banks for centuries; for example, banking houses such as the Foggers, the Medici, and the Rothschilds helped to finance companies, governments, voyages of discovery, and colonial operations. The banks of the great colonial powers—Britain and France—have long been established overseas. American, Japanese, and other European banks "went international" much later. Major American banks—Bank of America, Citicorp, Chase Manhattan—moved into international banking in the 1960s, and Japanese and their European counterparts in the 1970s. Today, Japanese-based banks, such as Sumitomo Bank, Fuji Bank, and Mitsubishi Bank, are second only to the U.S.-based banks in global banking (Figure 12.7).

Banks were dragged into international banking because of the explosion of foreign investment by industrial corporations in the 1950s and 1960s. The banks of different countries "followed the flag" of their domestic customers abroad. Once established overseas, many of the banks found international banking highly profitable. From their original focus on serving their domestic customers' international activities, banks evolved to service foreign customers as well, including foreign governments.

A major problem for the banks is that their Third World lending decisions were often imprudent, resulting in excessive indebtedness. The lent too much money. For example, in 1981 the ratio of the banks' own capital to total assets was around 4 percent, whereas in the early nineteenth century it was about 40 percent. Loans to Mexico from the Bank of America amounted to more than 70 percent of the bank's capital (*The Economist* 1982, p. 23). Thus, the banks have a collective interest in the debts of countries (Table 12.3). In 1986 Mexico's foreign debt stood at

close to $100 billion. Mexico owed $26 billion to U.S. Banks, and the rest to multilateral lending institutions, Western Europe, and Japan (*Newsweek* 1986, pp. 34–35). If indebted countries such as Mexico were to default, a number of the global banks would fail. This would dim prospects for further internationalization of banking and capital, and for continued growth in the world economy in the 1990s.

Capital markets, or long-term financial markets, form the third component of the international financial system. Stock exchanges, futures exchanges, as well as tax havens, have proliferated. American, European, and Asian multinational corporations take advantage of *tax-haven* countries near their home country where taxes are low or nonexistent on foreign-source income and/or capital gains (Figure 12.8). The internationalization of capital markets has made

Located on Broad Street between Wall Street and Exchange Place, the New York Stock Exchange is a hub of financial activity—not only of the city and nation but of the world as well. The New York Stock Exchange is a domestic financial market open to participation by foreign corporations, governments, and international institutions, as both users and suppliers of funds. Foreign companies also have shares of stock listed on the New York Stock Exchange, just as they do on the London and Tokyo exchanges. (Source: New York Convention and Visitors Bureau.)

TABLE 12.3
Countries ranked by debt to foreign banks.

		1983 in Billions U.S. $			
1.	Mexico	85.0	6.	Phillipines	14.7
2.	Brazil	73.7	7.	Yugoslavia	14.5
3.	Argentina	24.1	8.	Indonesia	13.3
4.	South Korea	23.4	9.	Egypt	12.0
5.	Venezuela	21.2	10.	Chile	11.9

SOURCE: Watson, Keller, and Mathieson, 1984, p. 89.

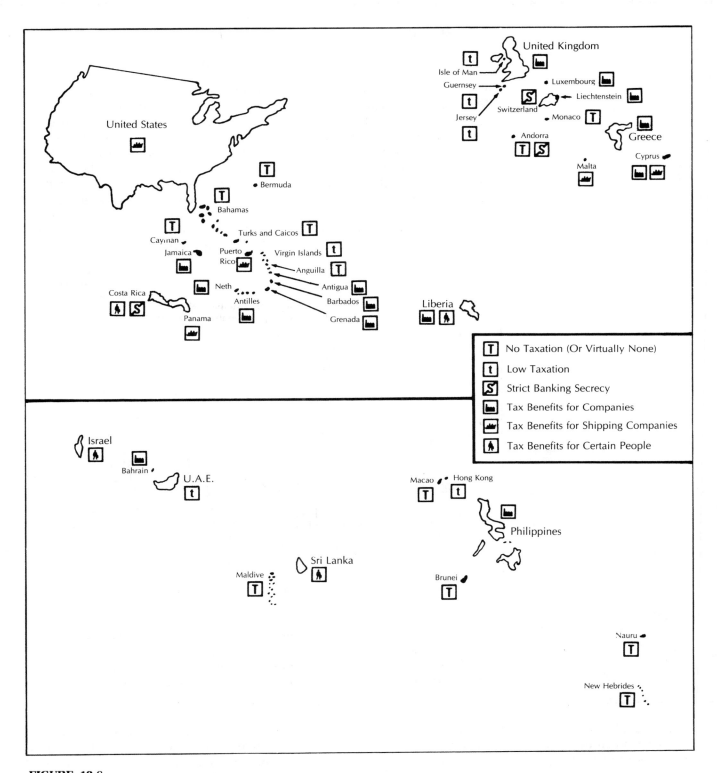

FIGURE 12.8
Tax havens as islands. (Source: Swenson, 1986, p. 110.)

Third World Debt

Since the late 1960s, Third World countries have been experiencing increasing economic difficulties. In the early 1980s, these problems came to a head when the newly industrializing countries, along with other underdeveloped countries, found themselves faced with a worldwide increase in interest rates. This caused an enormous increase in their debt-service payments and a decline in the markets for their manufactured goods as a result of economic recession in the developed countries. By 1984 the cost of servicing external debt reached 22 percent of the export earnings of all underdeveloped countries, with the largest borrowing countries having much higher debt-service rates. In 1982, Brazil would have needed 89 percent of the value of its exports to make its debt-service payments!

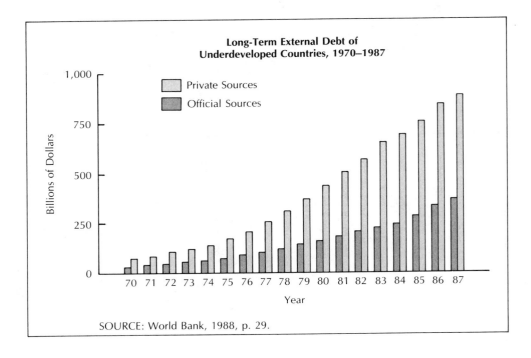

SOURCE: World Bank, 1988, p. 29.

In 1982, rising-debt service and a cut in lending led to a reversal of net resource transfers to underdeveloped countries. Between 1977 and 1982 underdeveloped countries received positive net resource transfers of $147 billion. Since 1982 resource transfers have become negative, totalling $85

international finance a "round-the-clock" business, with trade in currencies, stocks, and bonds transversing the world with the passage of the sun.

Classical Capital Theory

In the nineteenth century, foreign portfolio investment overshadowed foreign direct investment. Theorists concentrated therefore on foreign portfolio investment, which was directed toward raw material extraction, agricultural plantations, and trade facilities. The theory of foreign direct investment received relatively little attention and remained underdeveloped. Given the massive scale of foreign direct investment today, however, an understanding of the rationale for such investment is important. About the only help classical capital theory gives us is that under free-market conditions capital will flow from where it

billion. More money now flows from the Third World to the First World in debt payments than from the First World to the Third World in new loans, investment, and aid.

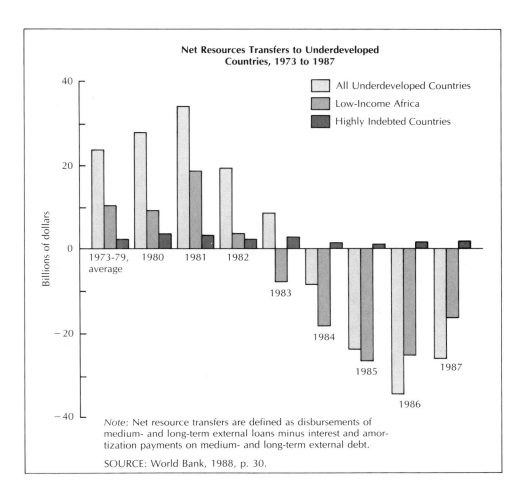

Net Resources Transfers to Underdeveloped Countries, 1973 to 1987

Legend:
- All Underdeveloped Countries
- Low-Income Africa
- Highly Indebted Countries

Y-axis: Billions of dollars (40, 20, 0, −20, −40)

X-axis: 1973-79, average; 1980; 1981; 1982; 1983; 1984; 1985; 1986; 1987

Note: Net resource transfers are defined as disbursements of medium- and long-term external loans minus interest and amortization payments on medium- and long-term external debt.

SOURCE: World Bank, 1988, p. 30.

The drain on resources forced many underdeveloped countries into debt restructuring under the supervision of the International Monetary Fund. Debtor countries made efforts to curtail imports by slowing the economy through such means as reducing government spending, reducing the growth of the money supply, and imposing wage restraints. These efforts have resulted in increased unemployment, higher prices and, in some cases, violent demonstrations and food riots.

is abundant to where it is in short supply or, to put it in another way, from where the rates of return are low to where they are high.

As with classical trade theory, classical capital theory is macroeconomic. However, in reality international money and capital flows are dependent on managerial decisions. Therefore, it is necessary to examine international capital movements from a microeconomic perspective. Even a brief examination reveals that although foreign investment is a simple process conceptually, a complex of motivations is involved.

Motivation for Foreign Direct Investment

The primary reason for a firm to "go international" is the profit criterion. And there are three strategic profit motives that drive a firm's decision to operate abroad (Mason, Miller, and Weigel 1975, pp. 204–210; Behrman 1984, pp. 82–83). One motive for many direct investments is to obtain natural or human resources. *Resource-seekers* are looking for raw materials and/or low-cost labor that is also sufficiently productive. A second motive is to penetrate markets, especially when *market-seekers* have been stopped from exporting to a particular country. The third goal is to increase operating efficiency. *Efficiency-seekers* are looking for the most economic sources of production to serve a worldwide, standardized market. These three motives are not mutually exclusive. Some segments of a corporation's operation may be aimed at obtaining raw materials, whereas other segments may be aimed at penetrating markets for the products made from the raw materials. These operations may also result in some productive and market efficiencies.

There may be a strong motivation for a firm to internationalize, but there also may be compelling constraints. Prominent among these are the uncertainties of investing or operating in a foreign environment. Consumers' incomes, tastes, and preferences vary from country to country. Japanese consumers, for example, are wary of foreign products, at least those that are not name brands. Cultural differences in business ethics and protocol, attitudes regarding time, and even "body language" in interpersonal relationships complicate the task of conducting business in two or more languages (McConnell and Erickson 1986, pp. 99–100). Added to these barriers are problems relating to currencies, laws, taxation, and governmental restrictions.

Bias in Foreign Direct Investment

Although managers may have the initiative and capability to implement rational investment scenarios, they often take a path of least resistance, which results in a less than ideal allocation of the world's investment capital and of the investors' capital. For example, the patterns of direct investment of American companies overseas exhibit considerable bias. In the 1980s, 45 percent of foreign direct investment by American companies was in Europe, 20 percent in Canada, and 13 percent in Britain, but only 3 percent was in Japan and under 2 percent in Africa (excluding South Africa). These patterns indicate a geographical bias (investing close to home), a cultural bias (investing in countries with similar cultures, especially the same language), and a historical bias (investing in

countries to which they are tied historically). Historical bias is often encouraged by the government of the investor. This bias maintains a strong national presence in these countries.

Origin and Destination of Foreign Direct Investment

The period since World War II has been characterized by a massive flow of foreign direct investment associated with the growth of multinational corporations. Capital export was five times greater in 1986 than it was in 1970 (United Nations 1988). The postwar years have seen the development of the international car (Figure 12.9), television set, cassette recorder, and home computer, with different components produced in different countries under the same corporate control. In addition to manufacturing multinationals, the growth of international banks and of service multinationals has also been strong. Service multinationals sell services related to business and professional activities, medical, publishing, agro-technology, warehousing, distribution, computer science, laboratory testing, hotel management, education, entertainment, and personal and social activities. Services' share of America's outward investment rose from 24 percent in 1975 to 34 percent in 1985; from 29 percent to 35 percent of Britain's; and from 36 percent to 52 percent of Japan's. In the 1990s, a still greater share of outward investment will be devoted to exportable services, particularly those related to improving international markets, such as information. In fact, "the firm may simply be the supplier of information to those essentially national firms responsible for physically moving the goods and services and for investment in fixed industrial assets" (Robinson 1981, p. 17).

American firms lead the world in foreign direct investment, but their share of the total is slipping. Until the early 1970s, U.S.-based multinationals accounted for nearly two-thirds of the world's corporate investment abroad. This figure dropped to 45 percent in 1977, and it continued to fall throughout the 1980s as corporations headquartered in other countries stepped up their rate of foreign direct investment. The rate of increase has been most rapid for companies domiciled in Western Europe and Japan; however, there has also been an increase in the outflow of foreign direct investment from a small group of underdeveloped countries (Figure 12.10). Major bases are Hong Kong, Brazil, Singapore, South Korea, Taiwan, Argentina, Mexico, and Venezuela.

Foreign direct investment. (Top) Ford Motor Company's headquarters in Britain. (Bottom) Ford Motor Company's assembly plant in South Africa. (Source: Ford Motor Company.)

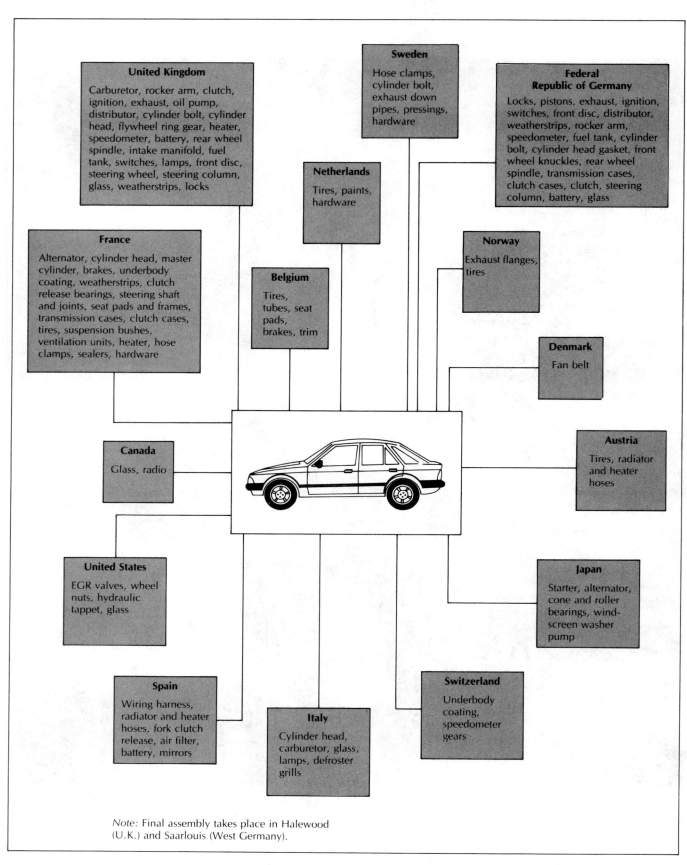

United Kingdom

Carburetor, rocker arm, clutch, ignition, exhaust, oil pump, distributor, cylinder bolt, cylinder head, flywheel ring gear, heater, speedometer, battery, rear wheel spindle, intake manifold, fuel tank, switches, lamps, front disc, steering wheel, steering column, glass, weatherstrips, locks

Sweden

Hose clamps, cylinder bolt, exhaust down pipes, pressings, hardware

Federal Republic of Germany

Locks, pistons, exhaust, ignition, switches, front disc, distributor, weatherstrips, rocker arm, speedometer, fuel tank, cylinder bolt, cylinder head gasket, front wheel knuckles, rear wheel spindle, transmission cases, clutch cases, clutch, steering column, battery, glass

France

Alternator, cylinder head, master cylinder, brakes, underbody coating, weatherstrips, clutch release bearings, steering shaft and joints, seat pads and frames, transmission cases, clutch cases, tires, suspension bushes, ventilation units, heater, hose clamps, sealers, hardware

Netherlands

Tires, paints, hardware

Norway

Exhaust flanges, tires

Belgium

Tires, tubes, seat pads, brakes, trim

Denmark

Fan belt

Canada

Glass, radio

Austria

Tires, radiator and heater hoses

United States

EGR valves, wheel nuts, hydraulic tappet, glass

Japan

Starter, alternator, cone and roller bearings, windscreen washer pump

Spain

Wiring harness, radiator and heater hoses, fork clutch release, air filter, battery, mirrors

Italy

Cylinder head, carburetor, glass, lamps, defroster grills

Switzerland

Underbody coating, speedometer gears

Note: Final assembly takes place in Halewood (U.K.) and Saarlouis (West Germany).

FIGURE 12.9

The international car: the component network for the Ford Escort (Europe). (Source: Dicken, 1986, p. 304.)

Significant changes in the destination of foreign direct investment are the increased flow to the United States and to the Third World (Figure 12.10). In 1975 the United States accounted for only a small proportion of the stocks held by foreign companies; ten years later the United States emerged as a major host country. Investment in the Third World has focused mainly on eight countries—Brazil, Mexico, Singapore, Indonesia, Malaysia, Argentina, Venezuela, and Hong Kong—which accounted for more than one-half the stock for foreign investment in underdeveloped countries in the early 1980s (Figure 12.11). Availability of natural resources, recent strong growth, and political and economic stability were among the factors that attracted foreign investment to these countries.

The Impact of Foreign Direct Investment

Are the effects of widespread foreign direct investment desirable? Should the operations of multinationals be controlled? There is no unanimity of opinion, particularly when Third World development is the issue.

There are two polar attitudes among scholars regarding the presence of multinationals in the underdeveloped world. Those on the right of the political spectrum argue that the multinational firm has a high potential to aid the process of economic development. According to Herman Kahn (1973),

> the transnational corporation (TNC) is probably the most efficient social, economic and political institu-

FIGURE 12.10
Multinationals' foreign direct investment, 1975 and 1985. (Source: *The Economist*, 1988a, p. 73.)

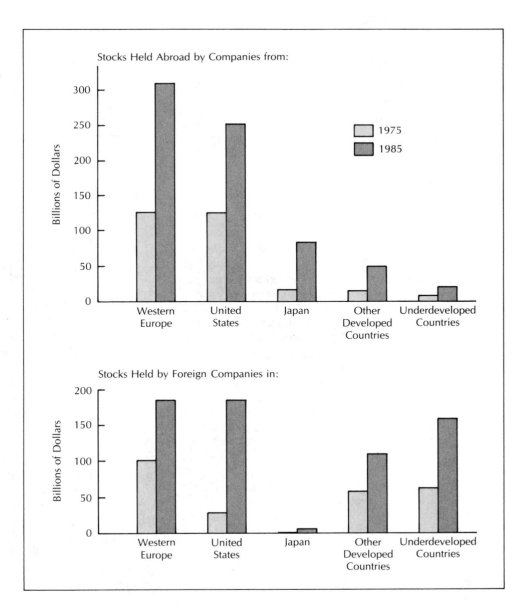

FIGURE 12.11

The stock of foreign investment in underdeveloped countries in percent: (a) where it is (1983); (b) where it came from (1982). (Source: World Bank, 1987, p. 117.)

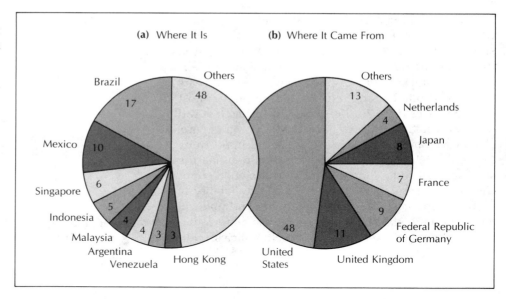

tion ever devised to accomplish the following tasks for the less developed nations:

(1) Raising, investing, and reallocating capital.

(2) Creating and managing organizations.

(3) Innovating, adopting, perfecting and transferring technology.

(4) Distribution, maintenance, marketing, and sales (including trained personnel and providing financing).

(5) Furnishing local elites with suitable—perhaps ideal—career choices.

(6) Educating and upgrading both blue collar and white collar labour (and elites).

(7) In many areas, and in the not-so-distant future, serving as a major source of local savings and taxes and in furnishing skilled cadres (i.e., graduates) of all kinds to the local economy (including the future local competition of the TNC).

(8) Facilitating the creation of vertical organizations or vertical arrangements which allow for the smooth, reliable, and effective progression of goods from one stage of production to another. In many cases, while such organization is a partial negation of the classical free market, it is still often a very efficient and useful method of stable and growing production and distribution.

(9) Finally, and almost by themselves, providing both a market and a mechanism for satellite services and industries that can stimulate local development much more effectively than most (official) aid programmes.

Of course, the transnational corporation is not doing any of this for altruistic or public interest rea-

sons (though sometimes elements of such motivations are important), nor do TNCs always operate in the best interest of the host country. I am simply saying that under proper conditions the above nine points should, and in fact often do, hold at least to an important degree. (p. 2)

This view is in marked contrast to that of scholars who argue that the multinational corporation is counterproductive to development. In the view of dependency theorists, modern capital-intensive industry does not result in rapidly increasing employment. "Its development as an enclave with limited links with the surrounding economy reduces its effectiveness in propagating change. . ." (Livingstone 1971, p. 244). Further, multinationals engender balance-of-payments problems because of heavy profit repatriations. Although the balance-of-payments problem could be avoided, in part, if multinational firms reinvested more of their profits in the host country, it is uncertain that the national interest would be served. Reinvestment causes "growing foreign control of the economy and the denationalization of local industry" (Griffin 1969, p. 148). The multinational firm is an assault on political sovereignty. Moreover, "[the] transnational system internationalizes the tendency to unequal development and to unequal income" (Galbraith 1973, p. 174).

The contentions of dependency theorists, however, do not always stand up to empirical verification. To illustrate, this author (de Souza 1985, p. 94) tested the relationship between multinational corporation penetration and average annual percentage growth in per capita gross national product. Growth rates in per capita GNP from 1962 to 1982 were regressed on the logarithm of 1967 multinational corporation penetration scores. Data on growth rates were from the World Bank (1984) and information on the extent to which countries are penetrated by multinationals was from Thanh-Huyen Ballmer-Cao and Jürg Scheidegger (1979). Ballmer-Cao and Scheidegger defined MNC penetration as the ratio of capital controlled by multinationals to the geometric mean of domestic capital and population. The 1967 figures were taken by the author to represent the initial level of penetration. The correlation between MNC penetration and subsequent economic growth was weak ($r = -0.208$). A separate correlation for First World countries was also weak ($r = -0.317$). A scattergram revealed no systematic relationship between MNC penetration and subsequent economic growth in Third World countries, and for that matter in First World countries (Figure 12.12). The results of this bivariate test tempt one to conclude that the dependency paradigm is insufficient to explain differential patterns of economic growth among countries. It seems that endogenous factors, particularly the autonomous role of the state, may have more to do with economic growth than such exogenous influences as the role of the multinational.

To be sure, multinationals are imperfect organs of Third World development, and their potential for the exploitation of poor countries is great. There is,

therefore, an inherent tension between the multinational's desire to integrate its activities on a global basis and the host country's desire to integrate an affiliate with its national economy. Maximizing corporate profits does not necessarily maximize national economic objectives. Stephen Krasner (1985) pointed to a host of issues over which conflict could develop:

> Host-country governments generally prefer that vertical links be established among operations within their national boundaries; MNCs may prefer to locate upstream and downstream facilities in other countries. The technology possessed by multinationals has usually been developed in industrialized countries. Less developed countries may prefer technology more suited to the local environment. Multinationals have been accused of introducing inappropriate products to developing countries, products that may be tolerable in wealthier countries but involve a misallocation of resources in poorer ones. Similarly, multinationals have been accused of generating tastes and preferences that reflect standards in rich countries but are inappropriate for poor ones. Fundamental decisions about corporate activity are taken by executives in advanced countries whose behavior cannot be directly controlled by host-country officials. Because they can affect economic performance, tastes, and the direction of development, MNCs pose a threat to

FIGURE 12.12

Relationship between MNC penetration, 1967 and average annual percentage growth in per capita GNP, 1960–1982. (Source: Compiled from Ballmer-Cao and Scheidegger, 1979, and World Bank, 1984.)

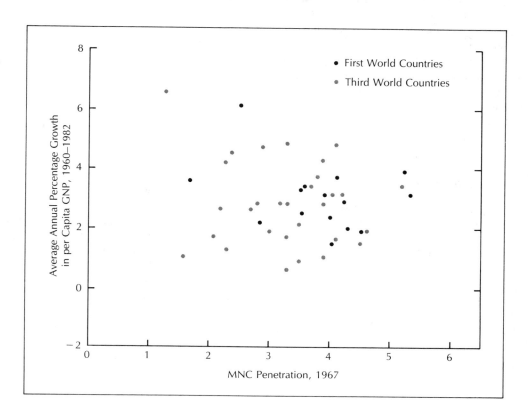

the functional control a state can exercise within its own territorial boundaries. (pp. 179–80)

Conflicts with host countries are a feature of multinational corporate activity. To deal with multinationals, governments have introduced rules and regulations regarding the establishment of branches, repatriation of profits, debt refinancing, employment of nationals, and tax rates. Formal rules and regulations, however, are one thing, effective control another. Aside from nationalization, no government action guarantees total and effective control.

In general, the relative bargaining power of host countries has increased over time because the number of multinationals has grown, giving host countries a wider range of choice. Larger and wealthier Third World countries have greater bargaining leverage. A consumer-products manufacturing corporation will accept more controls to gain access to a country with a large market. Finally, the degree of host-country control varies across industries. Manufacturing industries with advanced and dynamic technologies are more difficult to control than firms in the raw materials area.

Third World countries have changed the rules of the game for foreign direct investment. The new rules, however, have made corporations hesitant to put large amounts of capital at risk in the raw materials area and in smaller and poorer Third World countries. Corporations prefer to invest in countries that follow an outward-oriented development strategy, impose few controls, offer incentives, and therefore, appreciate the employment, skills, exports, and import-substitutes that foreign investment can bring. The newly industrializing countries exemplify this posture, and they do not align themselves with Third World countries that wish to see multinational activity regulated.

Labor and Technology Flows

Labor and technology constitute the other readily movable factors of production. International labor flows fall into two categories: unskilled and highly skilled (technological and managerial). Unskilled labor flows occur on large scales in various parts of the world as we saw in Chapter 3. Aside from political and religious motivations, workers migrate for income reasons and also for learning purposes. A smaller number of migrants may be motivated by a desire to travel or to get away from family or locale. Technological and managerial labor flows occur on a much smaller scale. These flows involve the permanent emigration of highly skilled professionals, managers,

and technicians—the so called brain drain. They may also be due to the temporary assignment of managers and technicians abroad. Increasing immigration and even guestworker controls are being imposed by countries to limit the impact of foreigners. These controls are tighter for the unskilled than for the highly skilled. They are partly responsible for the movement of capital to labor-abundant areas.

Technology is internationally mobile, but it has fragmented and inefficient markets. It may be subject to control by a firm's parent government. On the other hand, it may be encouraged by a host country, which can help to introduce a company's products into a new market. Technology transfer may be the only way a company can penetrate restricted markets.

BARRIERS TO INTERNATIONAL BUSINESS

International flows of the factors of production help to reduce imbalances in the distribution of natural resources, just as trade can. Whereas trade *offsets* differences in factor endowments, factor movements *reduce* such differences. International trade and factor flow would be much greater if it were not for the existence of barriers. The main barriers relate to management, distance, and government.

Management Barriers

A number of managerial characteristics reduce trade and investment expansion. These include limited ambition, unawareness of opportunity, lack of skills, fear, and inertia.

Limited Ambition Firms may have the potential to expand but fail to do so because they are *satisficers*— settling for less than the optimal. Until the economic crisis of the 1970s, many U.S. firms gave little attention to foreign markets. They were satisfied with the large domestic market.

Unrecognized Opportunity Firms may have the will to "go international" but may lack knowledge of potential markets. "Even the largest multinational firms cannot possibly access, much less interpret, all of the potential information about other countries that may be available. Managers' mental maps and images of world order, including such aspects as size, shape, proximity, intensity of activities, or geopolitical affiliations, are relative and reflect considerable amounts of distortion from reality" (McConnell and Erickson 1986, p. 101). The burden of recognizing export opportunities rarely falls on the managers of individual companies, however. Most national and local governments are actively involved in increasing international awareness and in promoting exports.

Lack of Skills Firms may have the potential and will to "go international," and an awareness of the opportunities, but they may be thwarted by the complexity of international business and ignorance of foreign cultures. Governments and universities can come to the assistance of companies and provide help in the form of educational efforts. Knowledge of intermodal rate structures, freight forwarders, shipping conferences, and customs-house brokers (firms that contract to bring other companies' imported goods through local customs) is vital for the conduct of international business. Just as necessary is a knowledge of foreign cultures. "More than a few international business 'blunders' can be attributed to a lack of information or misinterpretation of basic cultural patterns" (McConnell and Erickson 1986, p. 101). In the past, for example, U.S. firms were unable to crack the Japanese market partly because of a failure to appreciate the local culture. That is changing. American entrepreneurs are no longer likely to lose deals by "botching" respectful bows at the beginning of a meeting.

Fear and Inertia Firms may shy away from international business activities because of a fear of the unknown or what is foreign—different currencies, laws, documentation requirements, taxation, political systems, languages, and customs. They may also fail to capitalize on opportunities because of a failure to act.

Distance as a Barrier

Companies that "go international" confront the geographical barrier of distance. Obviously, distance affects international business in that all movement costs. But the international movement of goods is not restricted to line-haul costs. Shipments of goods to foreign destinations incur bank collection charges, freight forwarders' and custom-house brokers' fees, consular charges, and cartage expenses. These costs entail extra clerical costs for the preparation of bills of lading (receipts given by carriers to exporters), customs declarations, and other shipping documents. Adding these terminal costs to line-haul costs yields a total outlay called *transfer costs*, which makes goods more expensive to importers and less valuable to exporters. As we saw in Chapter 6, total transportation costs vary from commodity to commodity. They are higher on finished goods than on bulk shipments of raw materials requiring less care and less special handling. Small firms must pay what the market will bear. However, multinationals, through intrafirm trade, do have the opportunity to practice "transfer pricing"—fixing prices for the movements of goods between affiliates.

Distance also influences trade in ways other than cost. Commercial relations are often smoother and less complicated between neighboring countries, if only because managers are more aware of export opportunities. Propinquity brings with it the possibility of frequent contact. A high level of interaction between neighboring countries enables each to better understand the other's economic and political system and culture.

Government Barriers to Trade

No country permits a free flow of trade across its borders. Governments have erected barriers to achieve objectives regarding trade relationships and indigenous economic development. Trade barriers include *tariffs*—schedules of taxes or duties levied on products as they cross national borders—and *nontariff barriers*—quotas, subsidies, licenses, and other restrictions on imports and exports. These kinds of obstacles (apart from *political bloc prohibitions*) are the most pervasive barriers to trade.

Costs of Protection Free-marketeers advocate free trade because it promotes greater economic efficiency and higher productivity via international specialization. They argue that trade, a substitute for factor movements, benefits each participating nation, and that deviation from free trade is bound to inhibit production. It follows, then, that *protectionism* will adversely affect the welfare of the majority. For example, it is estimated that in 1983 every dollar spent to preserve employment in the U.S. steel industry cost consumers $35 and amounted to a net loss of $25 for the economy (World Bank 1988, p. 36).

What are some of the major arguments for protectionism? One of the most common is the "cheap-foreign-labor" argument, which suggests that a country such as the United States with its high union wages must protect itself against a country such as Taiwan with its low-paid workers. This argument contradicts the principle of comparative advantage. Others, more compelling, appeal to national gain. One argument asserts that a country with market power can improve its terms of trade with a tax that forces down the price at which other countries sell to it. Another argument is that tariffs may be used to divert demand from foreign to domestic goods so as to shift a country's employment problem onto foreign nations. Still another argument is that tariffs may be used to protect an "infant industry" that is less efficient than a well-established industry in another country. The *infant-industry argument* was invoked to justify protectionist policies in eighteenth-century American and nineteenth-century Germany. It was also used to justify the protection that developed in the Third World in the 1960s. Although these arguments do have some merit, free-marketeers recommend other approaches to attain desired goals. For example, they suggest that if there are grounds for protecting an infant industry until it has grown large enough to take advantage of economies of scale, protection could be given through a subsidy rather than through a protective tariff.

Marxists are also skeptical about protectionist policies. They argue that protectionism in a capitalist state is likely to benefit capital at the expense of labor, because within such a state it is generally capital that makes and breaks the rules. They believe that protectionist policies are acceptable only if they lead to increased control of production by workers, which is unlikely in a state driven by capitalist interests.

Tariff and Nontariff Barriers   Tariffs are the most visible of all trade barriers, and they may be levied on a product when it is exported, imported, or in transit through a country. The tariff structure established by the developed countries in the post-World War II period works to the detriment of underdeveloped countries. The underdeveloped countries encounter low tariffs on traditional primary commodities, higher tariffs on semimanufactured products, and still higher tariffs on manufactures. These higher rates are, of course, intended to encourage firms in industrial countries to import raw materials and process them at home. They also discourage the development of processing industries in the Third World.

In recent years, the relative importance of tariff barriers has decreased, whereas nontariff barriers have gained significance. The simplest form of non-tariff barrier is the *quota*—a quantitative limit in the volume of trade permitted. A prominent example of a range of products hit by import quotas into developed countries is textiles and clothing. Since the early 1970s, textiles and clothing have been subject to quotas under successive Multifibre Arrangements (MFAs). These arrangements have created a world-wide system of managed trade in textiles and clothing in which the quotas severely curtail underdeveloped-country exports. Another common nontariff barrier is the *export-restraint agreement*. Governments increasingly coerce other governments to accept "voluntary"

export-restraint agreements, through which the government of an exporting country is induced to limit the volume or value of exports to the importing country. The United States has employed this special type of quota—an export quota—extensively. It has concluded "bilateral export agreements with . . . the Republic of China with respect to footwear and color television sets, Hong Kong with respect to textiles, Korea with respect to footwear, textiles and color television sets and with Japan as regards color television sets" (International Monetary Fund 1978, pp. 6–7). Other nontariff barriers include discretionary licensing standards; labeling and "certificate-of-origin" regulations; health and safety regulations, especially on foodstuffs; calandriers, which allow foodstuffs to be imported only at certain seasons to avoid competing with the peak production of the importers; and packaging requirements. Increasingly, loose or "break-bulk" cargo is unacceptable to developed-country mechanized transport handlers. Dockers and longshoremen often demand bonuses for handling such items as unpacked skins and hides. Consumers, too, demand agricultural products in packing that requires more investment on the part of the exporting country. These represent only a few of the hundreds of nontariff barriers devised by governments. The evidence indicates that these barriers in developed countries are higher for exports from underdeveloped countries than they are for exports from rich, developed countries (Edwards 1985, p. 219).

Stimulants to Trade   Governments not only attempt to control trade, they also attempt to stimulate trade. Free-marketeers consider government intervention to promote trade as yet another type of obstacle to free trade. In their view, gains from trade should result from economic efficiencies, not from government support. Examples of governmental assistance to promote exports include market research; provision of information about export opportunities to exporters; international trade shows; trade-promotion offices in foreign countries; and free-trade zones, areas where imported goods can be processed for re-export without payment of duties.

The Reduction of Trade Barriers   The most notable effort to reduce trade barriers has been a multilateral effort known as the *General Agreement on Tariffs and Trade* (GATT). GATT was put into operation in 1947. When twenty-three developed and underdeveloped countries signed the agreement, they thought they were putting in place one part of a future International Trade Organization (ITO). The organization would have wide powers to police its trading charter and regulate international competition in such areas as restrictive business practices, investments, commodities, and employment. It was to be the third in the triad of Bretton Woods institutions charged with overseeing the postwar economic order—along with the International Monetary Fund and World Bank. But the draft charter of the ITO ran into trouble in the United States Congress and was never ratified. Only GATT remained—a treaty without an organization.

GATT is now administered on behalf of ninety-five member countries, which make decisions by a process of negotiation and consensus. That process has resulted in a substantial reduction of tariffs. However, GATT's rules have proved inadequate to cope with new forms of nontariff barriers such as export restraint agreements. Such areas as services, which now account for about 30 percent of world trade, are not covered by GATT at all. GATT has also been of little help to underdeveloped countries with limited trading muscle. True, underdeveloped countries did gain acceptance of the General System of Preferences (GSP). Under GSP, which was adopted by developed countries in 1971, tariffs charged on imports of manufactured and semimanufactured products are granted preferential treatment. However, one of the more striking features of GSP schemes is the low proportion of manufactured goods that are eligible for preferential treatment. Because most GSP schemes are restrictive, few underdeveloped countries have benefitted.

Since the mid-1970s, and especially since 1980, there has been a steady erosion of the liberal trading order that GATT helped to uphold. The resurgence of protectionism, especially in the guise of nontariff barriers, is a reflection of the world economic crisis. Between 1981 and 1986, the proportion of imports to North America and the European Economic Community (EEC) affected by nontariff barriers increased by more than 20 percent. Trade between developed and underdeveloped countries is increasingly affected by nontariff barriers; roughly 20 percent of underdeveloped-country exports were covered by such measures in 1986 (World Bank 1988, p. 16). And in the coming years, pressure on governments in developed countries to "protect" domestic jobs through trade barriers is likely to mount.

Government Barriers to Factor Movement

Although not as complex as trade barriers, obstacles to the free flow of capital, people, and technology constrain international managerial freedom. Exchange and capital controls represent the main types of control that interfere with the movement of money and capital across national borders. *Exchange controls*, which restrict free dealings in foreign exchange, include multiple exchange rates and rationing. In multiple-exchange-rate systems, rates vary for different kinds of transactions. For example, a particular commodity may be granted an unfavorable rate. Foreign exchange may also be rationed on a priority basis or on a first-come, first-served basis. Thus, exchange rates are political tools, bearing little relation to economic reality. *Capital controls* are restrictions on the movement of money or capital across national borders. They are typically designed to discourage the outflow of funds.

All countries regulate migration, but the movement of workers from poorer to richer countries was the dominant pattern during the long postwar boom. When the boom ended, jobs moved to the workers. One of the reasons for the switch was the tightening of immigration laws in the advanced industrial countries, which strengthened the position of labor. The consequence was a growth in managed trade, and a decline in managed migration.

Technology, which is highly mobile, can be transferred in many ways: export of equipment, provision of scientific and managerial training, provision of books and journals, personal visits, and the licensing of patents. However, political and military controls do regulate the export of technology. Although controls over the transfer of technology are not yet terribly onerous, demands for more stringent controls are on the increase. One source of demand for control comes from labor unions in advanced industrial countries. These unions attribute domestic job loss to the export of high technology.

MULTINATIONAL ECONOMIC ORGANIZATIONS

In the world today, as nations turn inward to concentrate on problems of economic growth and stability, we are witnessing a resurgence of protectionism. But also in evidence is a strong, simultaneous countermovement toward international interdependence. This movement is exemplified by scores of multinational organizations, which for the most part are loosely connected leagues entailing little or no surrender of sovereignty on the part of member nations.

Some of these international organizations are global in scale. The most inclusive is the United Nations (UN) with 159 member nations, accounting for more than 98 percent of humankind. Much of the work of the UN is accomplished through approximately two dozen specialized agencies such as the

World Health Organization (WHO) and the International Labor Organization (ILO). Other international organizations have a regional character; for example, the Association of Southeast Asian Nations (ASEAN) and the Asian Development Bank (ADB). Many international organizations are relatively narrow in focus—mostly military, such as the North Atlantic Treaty Organization (NATO), or economic, such as the Organization of Petroleum Exporting Countries (OPEC). Some international organizations are discussion forums with little authority to operate either independently or on behalf of member states; for example, the General Agreement on Tariffs and Trade (GATT) and the Organization of Economic Cooperation and Development (OECD). Others have independent, multinational authority and power, performing functions that individual states cannot or will not perform on their own; for example, the International Monetary Fund (IMF) and the World Bank. There are also international organizations that integrate some portion of the economic or political activities of member countries; for example, the European Economic Community (EEC) and the European Free Trade Area (EFTA). International organizations to promote regional integration are the most ambitious of all. Some observers believe that regional federations are necessary to the process of weakening nationalism and developing wider communities of interest. However, if a rigid, inward-looking regionalism is substituted for nationalism, the ultimate form of international integration—world federation—will be difficult to achieve (Schwartzberg 1987, pp. 246–52).

This section examines international economic organizations that affect the environment within which firms operate, thus influencing the development of underdeveloped countries. We will look at international financial institutions, groups that foster regional economic integration, and groups such as commodity cartels, which deliberately manipulate international commodity markets. We will also assess the attempt of the United Nations Conference on Trade and Development (UNCTAD), the so-called trade union of the Third World, to establish a New International Economic Order (NIEO).

International Financial Institutions

International Financial institutions are a phenomenon of the post-World War II period. The International Monetary Fund (IMF) and the International Bank for Reconstruction and Development (IBRD), or World Bank, were established in 1945. Regional development banks—the Inter-American Development Bank (IADB), Asian Development Bank (ADB), and African Development Bank (AFDB)—were established in the 1960s. Various other multilateral facilities, of which the United Nations Development Program (UNDP) is the most important, were also established after 1960. These institutions are significant sources of multilateral capital, especially aid (i.e., capital provided on concessional terms) for underdeveloped countries. Multilateral capital is particularly important for the poorer underdeveloped countries that do not have access to private capital markets.

The IMF is an international central bank that provides short- to medium-term loans to member countries, and the IBRD is an international development bank that provides longer term loans for particular projects. Both institutions are clusters of governments, each government paying a subscription or quota determined by the size of its economy. Since quotas determine a member's voting power, the banks are dominated by the most powerful economies—particularly, by the United States.

The IMF and the World Bank were established to prevent a recurrence of the crisis of the 1930s. They embody Keynesian principles, which offer a rationale for state intervention in the market. The right of the state to act in the economy is a principle of great importance to many Third World countries, which prefer an authoritative to a market allocation of resources. Despite weighted voting, both institutions give Third World members a degree of formal power in excess of their share of actual financial contributions. Over time, underdeveloped countries have obtained more resources on better terms, especially as a result of the creation of two subsidiary World Bank organizations: the International Finance Corporation (IFC), founded in 1956, and the International Development Association (IDA), founded in 1960. These organizations provide loans with stipulations less stringent than those of the IBRD. For example, the IDA may provide loans with no interest charges, ten-year "periods of grace" (no repayment of principal for the first ten years), or up to fifty years for repayment for poorer underdeveloped countries. Because the IDA is much less creditworthy than the IBRD, all of its resources must come from member-government contributions.

Although the IMF and World Bank have become more solicitous of Third World opinions and preferences, these institutions remain firmly wedded to liberal, as opposed to dependency, interpretations of development. The market-oriented position is consistent with the basic orientation of the industrialized world, especially that of the United States. Loans from the IMF and World Bank, therefore, tend to uphold the basis of U.S. economic and foreign policy.

The atrium of the International Monetary Fund headquarters in Washington, D.C.
(Source: International Monetary Fund.)

The Third World has never been satisfied with the IMF and World Bank, particularly with regard to the level of available resources and the conditions imposed on their use. One counter has been the regional development banks—the IADB, ADB, and AFDB. These banks reflect the desire of underdeveloped countries to enhance their control. Of the three banks, the ADB is the one most under the control of developed countries, in particular Japan. The AFDB has been the most independent, but it is also the smallest.

Another counter was the creation of the UNDP in 1965. In terms of formal voting structure, the UNDP provides the Third World with dominant influence, even though approximately 90 percent of the contributions come from advanced industrial countries. The UNDP provides assistance to a wider variety of countries than does the World Bank. It also supports the demands embodied in the call for a New International Economic Order (NIEO). For example, the program has offered assistance to commodity-producer associations, has encouraged regional cooperation among underdeveloped countries, and has made efforts to increase the bargaining power of underdeveloped countries vis-à-vis multinational corporations.

International financial institutions are important for international business. The IMF, World Bank, and regional development banks annually finance billions of dollars of the import portion of development projects. This can be valuable business for foreign companies involved in the projects, either occasionally as part owners or, more commonly, as contractors or suppliers.

Although international financial institutions facilitate international business, their project aid may not promote development. Both conservative and radical critics agree that development must be primarily an indigenous process. Foreign aid has served many underdeveloped countries as an easy substitute for devising means to generate domestic development. It is also apparent that aid from institutions heavily influenced by developed countries is a palliative designed to ensure the continuity of unequal exchange in the world economy.

Regional Economic Integration

Regional integration is the international grouping of sovereign nations to form a single economic region. It is a form of selective discrimination in which both free trade and protectionist policies are operative: free trade among members and restrictions on trade with nonmembers. According to economist Bela Balassa (1961), five degrees of economic integration are possible. At progressively higher levels, members must make more concessions and surrender more sovereignty. The lowest level of economic integration is the *free-trade area*, in which members agree to remove trade barriers among themselves but continue to retain their own trade practices with nonmembers. A *customs union* is the next higher degree of integration. Members agree not only to eliminate trade barriers among themselves, but also to impose a common set of trade barriers on nonmembers. The third type is the *common market*, which, like the customs union, eliminates internal trade barriers and imposes common external trade barriers; this regional grouping, however, permits free factor mobility. At a still higher level, an *economic union* has the common-market characteristics plus a common currency and a common international economic policy. The highest form of regional grouping is full *economic integration*, which requires the surrender of most of the international sovereignty of its members.

Table 12.4a lists the different levels of integration of a variety of economic groups. In part b, the main provisions of the groups are described. These groups range from loosely integrated free-trade areas such as the Latin America Free Trade Association (LAFTA) to common markets such as the European Economic Community (EEC). There are also links between members of regional blocs. Thus, there are East-West ties between EEC countries and the Eastern countries'

Committee for Mutual Economic Assistance (COMECON); there are North-South ties between the EEC and LAFTA; there are South-South ties between LAFTA and ASEAN; and there are some East-South ties between COMECON and various underdeveloped countries. Most of these links are bilateral; that is, agreements between nations within different regions. Fully fledged interregional integration has yet to be achieved. Indeed, regional groups are more concerned with closer economic integration *within* regions than *among* regions.

Barriers to successful regional integration are greater in underdeveloped countries than in developed countries. The most significant barriers are political—an unwillingness to make concessions. Without concessions to the weaker partners of a regional group, the benefits from cooperation pile up in the economically more prosperous and powerful countries. This problem causes great strain and may lead to the dissolution of a regional integration scheme. The breakup of the East African Community (EAC) in 1978 was caused partly by the inability of Kenya to make concessions with its two weaker partners, Uganda and Tanzania. Another difficulty is that underdeveloped countries have not historically traded extensively among themselves. Still another obstacle to integration is the issue of integrating transport and power networks. Nonetheless, the potential for integration is very great in underdeveloped countries, particularly because many of them are too small and too underdeveloped to grow rapidly as individual units.

Many underdeveloped countries turned to regional integration schemes in the 1960s and 1970s. Reasons for integration included a need to gain access to larger markets, to obtain more bargaining power with the developed countries than they could if they adopted a "go-it-alone" policy, to create an identity for themselves, to strengthen their base for controlling multinational corporations, and to promote cohesion solidarity. It was for the last reason that the Southern African Development Coordination Conference (SADCC) was formalized in 1979. The main provision of SADCC is sectoral integration to build regional self-reliance for the front-line countries of Angola, Botswana, Lesotho, Malawi, Mozambique, Swaziland, Tanzania, Zambia, and Zimbabwe. These countries are adjacent to a dominant South Africa.

Regional groupings are rejected by conservatives but viewed with sympathy by most liberals and radicals. For free-marketeers, regional integration is unnecessary (Viner 1950). The "open economies" of Singapore, Hong Kong, Taiwan, and South Korea are a vindication of comparative advantage. By contrast,

TABLE 12.4
Levels and examples of regional integration.

	A. Levels of Regional Integration	
Level	*Characteristics*	*Examples*
Free-trade area	Common internal tariffs, but differing external tariffs	EFTA, LAFTA
Customs union	Common internal and external tariffs	UDEAC, CEAO
Common market	Common tariffs and few restrictions on factor mobility	EEC, COMECON

	B. Examples of Regional Integration	
Year	*Grouping*	*Main Provisions*
1949	Council for Mutual Economic Assistance (COMECON): USSR, Bulgaria, Czechoslovakia, GDR, Hungary, Poland, Romania, Mongolia, and Cuba	Trade and development agreements and contracts
1957 (1973: plus U.K., Ireland, Denmark) (1981: plus Greece) (1986: plus Spain and Portugal)	European Economic Community (EEC): France, West Germany, Italy, Belgium, the Netherlands, and Luxemburg	Common market (common internal and external tariffs and common agricultural and industrial policies)
1960 (1961: plus Finland as an associate member) (1970: plus Iceland) (1973: minus U.K. and Denmark)	European Free Trade Association (EFTA): U.K., Switzerland, Austria, Denmark, Norway, and Sweden	Common internal tariffs but not common external tariffs
1960	Latin American Free Trade Association (LAFTA): includes Mexico and all of South America, except the Guyanas	Free-trade area (no common external tariff) and sectoral agreements
1966	Union Douanière et Economique de l'Afrique Centrale (UDEAC): Cameroon, Central African Republic, Congo, Gabon	Customs union with common central bank
1967	Association of South-East Asian Nations (ASEAN): Indonesia, Malaysia, Philippines, Singapore, and Thailand	Some regional trade preferences and sectoral agreements
1969 (1973: plus Venezuela) (1976: minus Chile)	Andean Common Market (ACM): Bolivia, Chile, Colombia, Ecuador, and Peru	Common market envisaged, common policy on foreign investment
1979	Southern Africa Development Co-ordination Conference (SADCC): Angola, Botswana, Lesotho, Malawi, Mozambique, Swaziland, Tanzania, Zambia, Zimbabwe	Sectoral integration

dependency theorists are pessimistic about the benefits from "open-economy" policies. They claim that workers in the "open economies" are "superexploited" (Frank 1981), and that access to the markets of the developed world will not lead to authentic indigenous development (Landsberg 1987).

The impact of regional groupings differs from one company to another. Companies that enjoy a secure and highly profitable position behind national tariff walls are unlikely to favor removal of these barriers. Conversely, companies that see the removal of trade barriers as an opportunity to expand their markets see integration as a favorable development. Similarly, companies that traditionally exported to markets absorbed by a regional grouping have a strong interest in integration. They perceive these enlarged markets to be more attractive than they were in the past. But as outsiders, the shipments of these companies will be subject to trade controls, whereas barriers for internal competitors will decrease. Thus, foreign companies may face the prospect of losing their traditional markets because they are outside the integrated group of countries. As a result, there is an incentive to invest inside the regional grouping. This is why many U.S. firms invested directly in the EEC countries in the late 1950s and early 1960s, and again in the late 1980s.

Trade Restriction Agreements

As a group, Third World countries find the existing market-oriented regime unsatisfactory. The regime exposes underdeveloped countries, which rely very heavily on foreign-exchange receipts from a very limited range of commodity exports, to shocks from the international environment. Underdeveloped countries find access to markets of the developed countries restricted by a revival of protectionism, experience fluctuating prices for their exports, and suffer unfavorable terms of trade. As mentioned previously, these problems have compelled Third World countries to alter the rules of the game so as to lessen their vulnerability. Through cartels and commodity price agreements, they have attempted to replace the existing regime governed by market-oriented principles with new regimes governed by authoritative principles.

A *cartel* is an agreement among producers that seeks to artificially increase prices by arbitrarily raising them, by reducing supplies, or by allocating markets. The most successful Third World commodity cartel is the Organization of Petroleum Exporting Countries (OPEC). Founded in 1960, OPEC consists of thirteen countries—Saudi Arabia, Iran, Venezuela, Kuwait, Libya, Nigeria, Iraq, Indonesia, Algeria, Gabon, Qatar, Ecuador, and the United Arab Emirates. In the 1970s it forced acceptance of authoritative, rather than market-oriented, principles. The success of OPEC at raising oil prices encouraged other underdeveloped countries to create new regimes.

Since 1974, the United Nations Conference on Trade and Development (UNCTAD) has been trying to obtain an international agreement for an integrated commodity program through a Common Fund in order to combat price instability and price deterioration. The cornerstone of this multicommodity approach was the proposal to establish international commodity stocks for a number of commodities. Eighteen commodities of special interest to underdeveloped countries were considered suitable for such stocks. In successive meetings, the original eighteen commodities became seventeen, representing about 75 percent of the Third World's total nonpetroleum mineral and agricultural exports, but priority was afforded to ten commodities—cocoa, coffee, cotton, copper, jute, rubber, sisal, sugar, tea, and tin. These ten commodities were alleged to have characteristics suitable for price stabilization through buffer-stock schemes. To date, not much progress has been made. The Common Fund was accepted by the North in 1980, but it was funded at a meager level. Some existing commodity agreements, such as the International Coffee Agreement and the International Tin Agreement, continued. A few new arrangements have been concluded, the most important of which dealt with rubber.

Resistance to commodity control of developed countries, especially the United States, remains intense. American private and public actors view commodity agreements as unfortunate departures from the liberal, market-oriented principles governing the movement of most traded goods. Thus, except for oil, which is a special case, commodity cartels are unlikely to be successful. Oil has a high-income elasticity of demand; that is, as individuals get richer, so their expenditures on oil increase proportionately. Oil is concentrated in a few countries. And it has no close substitutes.

The most comprehensive and important commodity agreement between the North and South is the *Lomé Convention* signed in 1975 by the EEC and states in Africa, the Caribbean, and the Pacific (ACP states). This North-South agreement gives Third World countries who are associate members of the EEC preferential access for their exports of primary products. Thus, the Ivory Coast, an associate member of the EEC, receives preferential access for its coffee exports, whereas Brazil, a nonmember, does not. The Lomé Agreement, therefore, provides a framework for continuing a colonial-type relation and for discriminating against non-ACP states. As does all trade restriction agreements, it obstructs market forces.

A New International Economic Order

In the late 1960s and early 1970s, there was a growing demand among underdeveloped countries to change the rules and principles that govern most kinds of international transactions, especially in the areas of trade, private capital flows, and direct foreign investment. As we discussed in Chapter 1, demands for authoritative resource allocation in the interests of equity and justice were consolidated in 1974 at the Sixth Special Session of the United Nations General Assembly in a call for the establishment of a New International Economic Order (NIEO). The call for a NIEO, which took developed countries by surprise, was made at a time when many underdeveloped countries perceived a golden opportunity to tip the balance of international power in their favor. Commodity producers thought that they might be able to emulate OPEC in bidding up prices for their primary products. However, it soon became clear in the crisis of the 1970s and 1980s that they had less bargaining power than they thought.

The NIEO was not an exercise in empty rhetoric among underdeveloped countries. The kinds of demands embodied in the call for a NIEO, which included such areas of concern as trade, primary commodities, aid, debt, multinational corporations, and shipping, will not go away. The structural conditions that prompted them are defining and enduring characteristics of the international system.

The intensity of the North-South conflict could be reduced by three developments, however. First, some underdeveloped countries may generate the national power capabilities needed to cope with the existing international system. Second, developed countries could pay less attention to existing international organizations. If developed countries ceased to concern themselves with UN happenings or ceased to fund its activities, the underdeveloped countries would have a program without an audience. Third and less likely, North-South conflict could be reduced if there were more collective self-reliance in the South and consequent widespread delinking from the North.

EVOLVING PATTERNS OF WORLD COMMERCE

Thus far in this chapter we have considered the nature of international business—the forces that foster international commerce and the forces that interfere with it, or modify it. In this section, we turn to an historical and geographical account of actual flows. What factors influence the strength of trade flows? What major changes have occurred in the volume and structure of international commerce? What are the consequences of the global crisis on world trade and foreign investment? And to what extent has the rise of Asia altered patterns of international commerce?

Modeling Commodity Flows

Several scholars have attempted to predict commodity flows between pairs of countries by using interaction or gravity models. According to the gravity model, the intensity of trade flows between two countries is directly proportional to their trading capacities and inversely proportional to the barriers separating them. A significant study by Dutch economist Hans Linneman (1966) provides a generalized explanation for the existence of trade flows. According to Linneman, three groups of influences determine the size of trade flows: potential total demand of the importing country, potential total supply of the exporting country, and the physical and artificial barriers impeding the flow of goods between pairs of countries. Based on these influences, Linneman developed a model using the following variables for each of eighty countries: (1) gross domestic product, (2) population size, (3) distance, (4) preferential trading relations, and (5) commodity composition of flows. All five variables proved to be important bases for trade. The most influential were gross national product—a measure of potential demand—and distance. Also significant was preferential trading relations, particularly between colonial powers and their dependencies.

A cartogram of trade power supports Linneman's findings (Figure 12.13). World trade is dominated by rich, densely populated industrial countries. In particular, it is dominated by the member countries of the European Economic Community (EEC). These countries are so busy trading with one another that they account for over one-third of all world commerce. Some observers would argue, however, that trade between EEC neighbors is domestic in character rather than international, similar to U.S. interstate commerce. But the EEC is still only a qualified

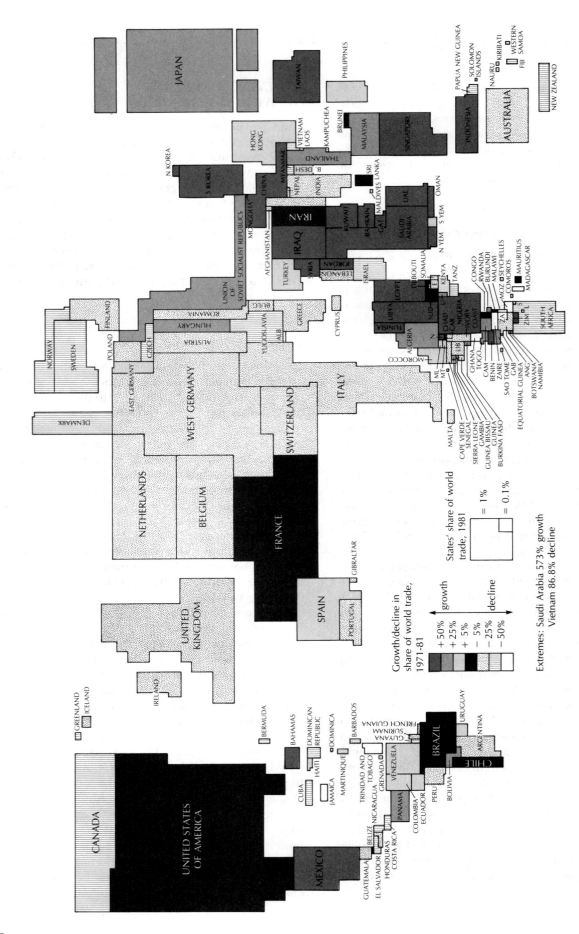

FIGURE 12.13

Trade power. (Source: Kidron and Segal, 1984, Map 18.)

States' share of world trade, 1981

$= 1\%$

$= 0.1\%$

Growth/decline in share of world trade, 1971–81

growth

+50%
+25%
+5%

decline

−5%
−25%
−50%

Extremes: Saudi Arabia 573% growth
Vietnam 86.8% decline

international association. In any event, the immense trading power of the members of the EEC owes much to their physical proximity and the absence of internal trade barriers, as well as to such factors as high demand and supply potential.

The cartogram also reveals major changes in the relative share of world trade enjoyed by particular countries. Between 1971 and 1981, declines were registered in Europe, North America, and in parts of the Third World. At the same time, sharp increases took place in oil-exporting countries, Japan, and in the "little dragons" of Singapore, Hong Kong, Taiwan, and South Korea. Clearly, the world economy is in transition.

The World Economy in Transition

International commerce has evolved far beyond the original pattern in which industrial countries ex-

ported manufactured goods to underdeveloped countries in exchange for primary commodities. Today, a few underdeveloped countries are among the world's most successful exporters of manufactures. In advanced industrial countries, intraindustry trade has reached a high level of specialization. Production of a single good now spans several countries, with each country on the global assembly line performing tasks in which it has a cost advantage. Immense changes have taken place in international specialization and trade over the last two hundred years.

The first major change occurred with the advances in technology spawned by the industrial revolution. Innovations in cotton textiles, the steam engine, iron and steel, railways, and steamships took place in a relatively free-enterprise environment, increasing output and international trade, particularly between 1820 and 1870 (Figure 12.14). Between 1870 and 1913 some of the further advances in technology

FIGURE 12.14
Historical trends in the growth of gross domestic product (GDP) and exports in selected countries, 1720–1985. (Source: World Bank, 1987, p. 40.)

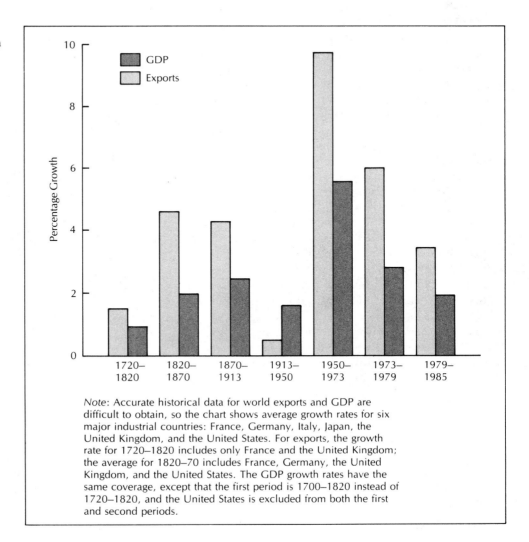

Note: Accurate historical data for world exports and GDP are difficult to obtain, so the chart shows average growth rates for six major industrial countries: France, Germany, Italy, Japan, the United Kingdom, and the United States. For exports, the growth rate for 1720–1820 includes only France and the United Kingdom; the average for 1820–70 includes France, Germany, the United Kingdom, and the United States. The GDP growth rates have the same coverage, except that the first period is 1700–1820 instead of 1720–1820, and the United States is excluded from both the first and second periods.

reinforced the trend toward greater international integration. For example, refrigeration made it possible to ship frozen meat from Australia to Britain by the 1880s. Despite advances in technology and greater international integration, output in the major industrial countries was not much greater than it was between 1820 and 1870, and the growth rate of exports fell (Figure 12.14). A major reason for this was the onset of protectionism in the 1870s.

Economic liberalism, which waned between 1870 and 1913, collapsed with either stagnation or depression on the world market between 1913 and 1950. Although the period inherited past technological innovations and contributed many of its own, their spread was impeded by political and economic turmoil. Growth of output plummeted, and there was a still greater fall in the growth of trade (Figure 12.14).

Between 1950 and 1973 the world enjoyed unprecedented prosperity. GATT agreements liberalized trade. Decolonization swept Africa, Asia, and the Caribbean. Multinational corporations rose to prominence. World output and trade expanded (Figure 12.14), with manufacturing leading the way in both output and export growth (Figure 12.15). The growing trade in manufactures reflected the ever-increasing integration of world markets. This integration was fostered by transport innovations that cut travel time, telecommunications that made it easier for multinationals to coordinate the activities of their subsidiaries, and electronics media that helped to shape a world market with increasingly similar consumer tastes.

The era of unprecedented growth came to an abrupt end in the early 1970s when a series of crises hit the world economy. The first crisis was the collapse of the Bretton Woods agreement. A second development was a dramatic rise in the prices of industrial raw materials that ended the commodity price stability of the postwar period. This increase occurred at a time of high demand from developed countries and of rising nationalism among underdeveloped countries supplying these commodities. These conditions ignited world inflation, which soared after the 1973 oil-price increases. The oil shock brought on a deep worldwide recession reminiscent of the 1930s. After a weak recovery, another economic downturn followed in the early 1980s.

The recessions, which led to immediate cutbacks in import demand by the industrialized world, hit Third World countries particularly hard. Many of them have yet to recover. Recovery has also been slow in the older industrial countries. Only the western Pacific nations, whose cheaply produced goods

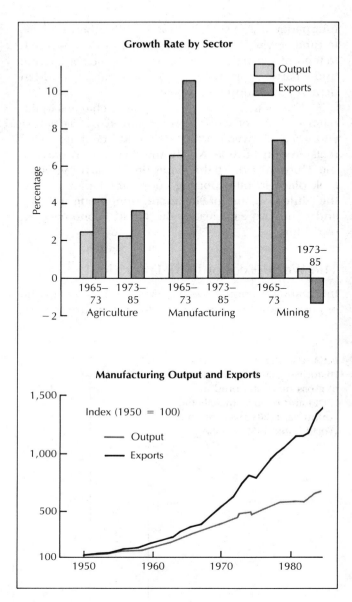

FIGURE 12.15
Postwar growth in world ouput and exports. (Source: World Bank, 1987, p. 43.)

swamped world markets, emerged from the recessions stronger than ever.

Underlying the crises of the 1970s and 1980s, and contributing independently to global instability, has been a fundamental reordering of world economic relationships. The original international capitalist division of labor gave way in the face of increased rivalry and competition among advanced industrial countries to a new international division of labor based on the internationalization of production. As we saw in

Chapter 11, this development resulted in deindustrialization in Western Europe and North America, where countries are now competing with each other in developing still more sophisticated technology and attaining a leadership position in supplying the world with capital and services.

The turbulent decades of the 1970s and 1980s saw major changes in the volume and composition of trade. World trade grew throughout the period, reaching about $2 trillion in 1986. Rates of trade growth, however, declined after 1973 (Figure 12.14). Manufacturing exports, with the exception of a dip in the mid-1970s, continued their rapid growth (Figure 12.15). They now account for about 60 percent of world exports by value. Fuel exports doubled their value share in the 1970s from under 10 percent to over 20 percent, but they retreated with oversupply of oil, and weakening demand, in the 1980s. The export value share of other primary commodities—food, beverages, and crude materials—fell from nearly 30 percent in the mid-1960s to under 15 percent in the mid-1980s.

The changing structure of trade has affected different types of countries differently. OPEC countries recorded a meteoric rise in the value of their exports in the 1970s and a precipitous decline after 1980. The industrial countries of North America, Western Europe, and East Asia experienced a drop in their export earnings after the oil crisis. But as a group they recovered nicely and now account for 80 percent of the value of world trade. With the exception of the major oil exporters, Third World countries that depend heavily on the export of a few primary commodities fared badly. For them, the growth in volume of primary commodity exports has been negative since 1980.

Increased diversification of trade ties represents one of the most significant developments in the contemporary world economy. Advanced industrial countries still trade primarily among themselves, but the proportion has declined from over 75 percent in 1970 to around 66 percent today. They have increased their share of exports to underdeveloped countries and, despite a resurgence of protectionism, their imports from underdeveloped countries have increased by a still greater amount. Another major development has been the growth of manufacturing exports from Third World countries to developed countries, and to a lesser extent to other Third World countries (Figure 12.16). Manufacturing exports now account for about 40 percent of total nonfuel exports of these countries compared with 20 percent in 1963, and Third World countries now supply 13 percent of

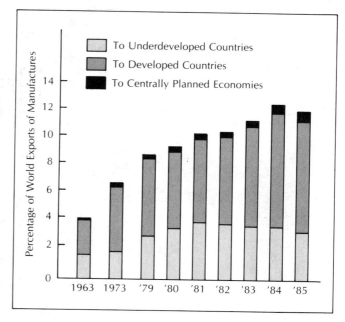

FIGURE 12.16
Underdeveloped countries' exports of manufactures by destination, 1963–1985. (Source: World Bank, 1987, p. 135.)

the imports of manufactures by developed countries compared with only 7 percent in 1973. Yet, only a handful of Asian and Western Hemisphere countries are involved in this development.

A New Focus of International Economic Activity

Undoubtedly, the most significant structural development in the world economy in recent years is the shift in focus of international economic activity. At least from the age of colonization to around 1960, the North Atlantic basin dominated world commerce. As a result of the rise of East Asia, this is no longer true (Figure 12.17).

Since 1960, the East Asian economies have grown at around 6 percent a year. Over the same period the United States and the EEC countries have experienced only a 3 percent growth rate. East Asia's share of gross world product more than doubled during 1967–1987. Its share of manufactured exports increased from 8 percent to 17 percent. Equally remarkable has been the growth of East Asia's financial power. Of the world's ten biggest banks by asset value, seven are Japanese. Since the yen began rising in 1985, Japan's net capital outflows have amounted to a staggering $400 billion, and it provided nearly 15

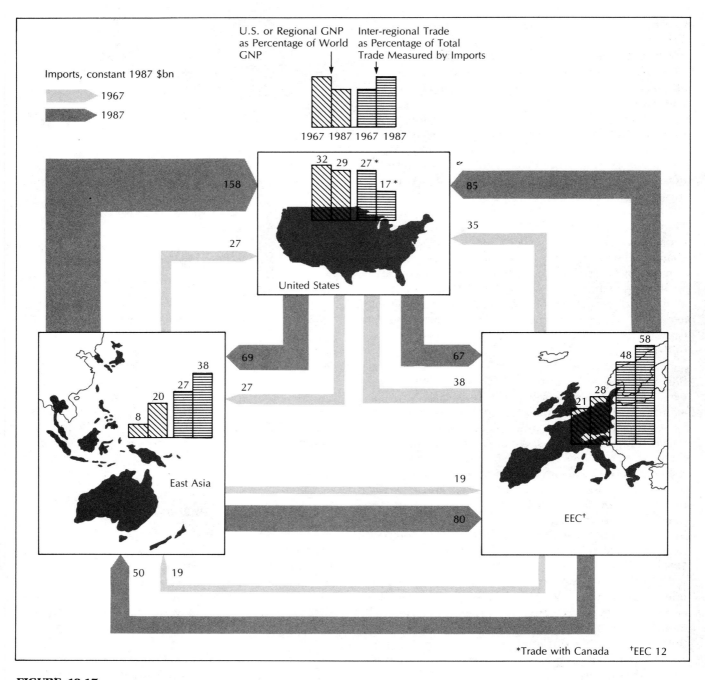

FIGURE 12.17
Trade flows and gross national products for the United States, EEC, and Asia. (Source:
The Economist, 1988c, p. 41.)

percent of the foreign capital imported into the United
States in 1987 (Table 12.5).

What do these figures mean? East Asia's rise has
made for a sharp increase in the dependence of U.S.
and East Asian economies on one another. However,
America's trade with Canada is still greater than its
trade with Japan—by $129 billion with Canada to

$116 billion with Japan in 1987. The EEC still imports
almost as much from the United States as all the
countries of East Asia do—$61 billion for Europe, $62
billion for Asia in 1987. The EEC is also America's
biggest foreign direct investor; Japan is a distant
second (Table 12.5).

The rough parity in the sphere of international

The South Korea World Trade Center is symbolic of the rise of East Asia as a locus of international economic activity. A combination of trade tower, exhibition complex, and other supportive facilities, the center provides all services required for the transaction of international business. (Source: Korean Information Service.)

business between the blocs of the Atlantic and Pacific basins (Figure 12.18) will change if East Asia's economic growth and trade growth rates continue to outstep those of the United States and Europe. But how will the picture change? Surely the United States' trade with East Asia will grow faster than its trade with Europe, but then again Europe's trade with East Asia will likewise grow faster than its trade with the United

TABLE 12.5
Sources of foreign direct investment in the United States.

From	Stock at the End of 1987		Inflow 1987	
	$billion	Percentage	$billion	Percentage
EEC	157.7	60.2	31.4	74.7
Other Europe	20.3	7.8	3.6	8.6
Japan	33.4	12.8	6.2	14.8
Canada	21.7	8.3	1.0	2.4
Latin America	15.3	5.8	−1.5	−3.6
Other	13.6	5.1	1.3	3.1
Total	216.9	100.0	42.0	100.0

SOURCE: *The Economist*, 1988d, p. 42.

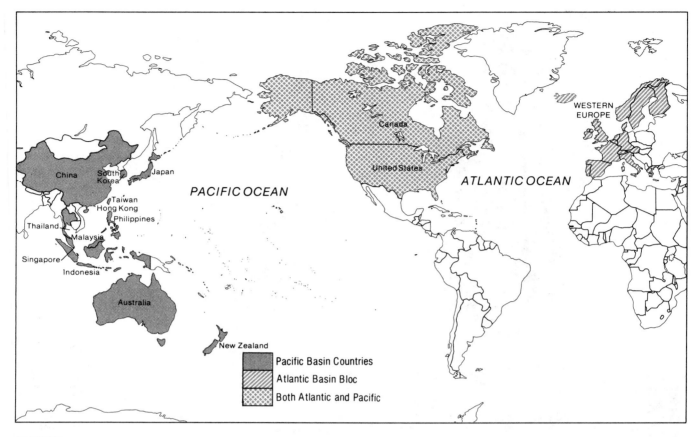

FIGURE 12.18
Countries/blocks of the Atlantic and Pacific basins. (Source: Conkling and McConnell, 1985, p. 3.)

States. Since 1967 trade between the EEC and East Asia increased by 240 percent; trade between the EEC and the United States increased only by 108 percent. Another likely change will be increased economic ties between Japan and the newly industrializing countries of East Asia. Already Japan is superseding the United States as their main source of foreign direct investment; and the biggest increases in manufactured exports to Japan since 1985 have come from Taiwan, Thailand, and South Korea—not from the United States or the EEC.

There is much talk that the economic rise of East Asia will prompt the United States to turn away from Europe. However, despite growing U.S.-East Asia economic links, the attachments and interests of the United States still lie more with Europe than with Asia, at least for now. Project 1992 has the potential to change America's world view, however. By passing the Single European Act, all EEC members committed themselves to creating a frontier-free internal market by 31 December 1992. If that means putting in place a

protectionist Fortress Europe, America's allegiance to Europe could be diverted.

The way the United States views the world may also hinge on events taking place in California, the nation's most populous state. By 2010, Hispanic, black, and Asian Californians will outnumber Europeans. Asian money is also pouring into the state. After Canada, Japan has the biggest single stake of foreign capital in California; Japanese companies represent the largest foreign source of employment. The de-Europeanization of California, of its population and of its sources of wealth, is likely to carry over to the rest of the country. As a result of this impending change, will the United States be forced to choose between the Pacific and the Atlantic in the next century?

SUMMARY

This chapter examined aspects of the international sphere of business. *International business* is any form of business activity that crosses a national border. It includes the international movement of almost any type of economic resource—merchandise, capital, or services.

Our discussion of traditional trade theory pointed to *comparative* rather than *absolute advantage* as the underlying explanation for much of the trade that occurs. Beyond predicting that everyone gains something from trade, classical trade theory neglects to consider the distribution of benefits. Free trade was established in the nineteenth century within a framework of inequality between countries. An artificial division of labor was established between developed and underdeveloped countries. Third World countries as primary producers became dependent on foreign demand and, therefore, vulnerable to the business cycle of expansion and contraction in developed countries.

The theoretical basis for international business was extended in a consideration of the basis of *factor flows*. Factors that are most readily movable are capital, technology, and labor. We focused primarily on *capital movements*, enhancing understanding of foreign direct investment by utilizing a managerial perspective. In many respects, the international movement of capital, technology, and managerial know-how is now more important than is international trade. In fact, the preeminent international business organizations of the future will be those "devoted to improving international markets in terms of special inputs—services, skills, knowledge, capital. . . . The guts of such firms will be information network and data banks" (Robinson 1981, pp. 18–19).

Theories of international trade and factor movements emphasize the benefits of a liberal, market-oriented business environment. However, a number of obstacles significantly impede the flow of merchandise, capital, technology, and people. These include distance barriers, managerial barriers, and governmental barriers. Much progress was made in reducing governmental barriers—*tariffs* and *nontariff barriers*—during the long postwar boom. But the 1970s and 1980s saw a steady erosion in the liberal trading order as governments started to erect new barriers to international business.

Despite the chillier economic climate since the mid-1970s, countries continue to participate in a myriad of multinational operations. Major organizations that can be very important to international business are *international financial institutions* and groups that promote *regional integration*. Groups that obstruct market forces include *commodity cartels*. Leaders in developed countries view commodity cartels as an unfortunate departure from market-oriented principles. By contrast, most Third World leaders view commodity cartels as a means to reduce their vulnerability in a world of unequal exchange.

We ended the chapter with a review of patterns of international commerce. During the last two hundred years, the intensity, structure, and direction of flows have changed considerably. Undoubtedly, the most significant development in recent years has been the rise of Pacific Rim countries. The great triangle of the capitalist democracies—with its three points in North America, Western Europe, and East Asia—now accounts for 75 percent of gross world product and 80 percent of the value of world trade, even though it contains only a fifth of the world's people. The dominance of North America, Western Europe, and East Asia emphasizes that capitalist development is uneven. In the next chapter, the argument that capitalist development has never been a smooth process is explored with special reference to the underdeveloped countries.

KEY TERMS

absolute advantage	economic union
aid	Engel's law
cartel	Eurocurrency
common market	Euromarket
comparative advantage	factors of production
countertrade	free trade
customs union	free-trade area
development bank	General Agreement on Tariffs and Trade (GATT)
direct investment	infant industry
economic integration	

International Monetary Fund (IMF)

intramultinational trade

Lomé Convention

multinational corporation

New International Economic Order (NIEO)

nontariff barrier

Organization of Petroleum Exporting Countries (OPEC)

production-possibilities curve

protectionism

specialization

tariff

tax-haven country

terms of trade

unequal exchange

United Nations Conference on Trade and Development (UNCTAD)

World Bank

SUGGESTED READINGS

Behrman, J. N. 1984. *International Policies: International Restructuring and Transnationals.* Lexington, MA: D. C. Heath.

Cline, W. R. 1983. *International Debt and the Stability of the World Economy.* Washington, DC: Institute for International Economics.

Daniels, J. D.; Ogram, Jr., E. W.; and Radebaugh, L. H. 1982. *International Business: Environment and Operations.* 3d ed. Reading, MA: Addison-Wesley.

Edwards, C. 1985. *The Fragmented World: Competing Perspectives on Trade, Money and Crisis.* New York: Methuen.

Helleiner, G. K. 1981. *Intra-Firm Trade and the Developing Countries.* London: Macmillan.

Krause, L., and Sekiguchi, S., eds. 1980. *Economic Interaction in the Pacific Basin.* Washington, DC: The Brookings Institution.

Korth, C. M. 1985. *International Business: Environment and Management.* 2d ed. Englewood Cliffs, NJ: Prentice-Hall.

Murray, R., ed. 1981. *Multinationals Beyond the Market.* Brighton, England: Harvester Press.

Robock, S. H., and Simmonds, K. 1983. *International Business and Multinational Enterprises.* 3d ed. Homewood, IL: Richard D. Irwin.

Terpstra, V., and David, K. 1985. *The Cultural Environment of International Business.* 2d ed. Pelham, NY: Southwestern Publishing.

United Nations. 1983. *Transnational Corporations in World Development, Third Survey.* New York: United Nations.

———. 1988 *Transnational Corporations in World Development: Trends and Prospects.* New York: United Nations.

13

DEVELOPMENT AND UNDERDEVELOPMENT

OBJECTIVES

☐ To outline the goals of development

☐ To clarify the distinction between underdevelopment as an initial condition or state and as an active process

☐ To acquaint you with the attributes of underdevelopment

☐ To examine major perspectives on development

☐ To trace the evolution of the world economy

☐ To recognize the limitations of the standard Western regional development model

☐ To describe the proto-proletariat as an example of a marginal social formation

☐ To consider the basic-needs crisis

Collecting water from a well in Ethiopia. (Source: World Bank.)

The modern world has its origin in the European societies of the late fifteenth and early sixteenth centuries. One of its most striking characteristics is the division between rich and poor countries. Early on, this division was achieved through an international system in which the wealthy minority industrialized using primary products produced by the impoverished majority. More recently, as we have seen in Chapters 11 and 12, this original division of labor gave way to a new division of labor. Now, the wealthy minority are increasingly engaged in office work and the masses in hands-on manufacturing jobs on the global assembly line as well as in agriculture and raw material production. The creation of today's world with a rich core and a poor periphery was not the result of conspiracy among developed countries, but of an "invisible hand." It was the outcome of a systemic process—that process by which the world's political economy functions.

This chapter deals with how this world of unequal development came about; how present structures are the result of the past. It also outlines a positive, idealistic proposal for enhancing Third World development. We begin with a discussion of the characteristics of underdevelopment and of some frequently propounded views on the nature of development and underdevelopment. Goals for development are introduced, and development objectives that most people would subscribe to are listed. This list provides a basis of comparison for arguments developed later in the chapter

WHAT'S IN A WORD? "DEVELOPING"

From Primitive to Underdeveloped

If America, with its high level of material consumption, is described as a developed country, then what adjective should we use to describe Third World countries? Certainly, there are many to choose from. In the past half-century, each of the following terms has flourished in succession: primitive, backward, undeveloped, underdeveloped, less developed, emerging, developing, and rapidly developing. Today, Western social scientists use the word *developing* and, increasingly, the phrase "less-developed countries," but social scientists in the Marxist tradition favor the term *underdeveloped*.

"Underdeveloped" was formerly used by Western social scientists to describe situations in which resources were not yet developed. People and resources were seen as existing, respectively, in a traditional and natural state. Scholars in the Marxist tradition are now using "underdeveloped" to describe

not an initial state, but rather a condition arrived at through the agency of imperialism, which set up the inequality of political and economic dependence of poor countries on rich countries. Thus, instead of viewing underdevelopment as an initial or *passive state*, it is viewed by Marxists as an *active process* (Rodney 1972).

Figure 13.1 illustrates the important distinction between underdevelopment as an initial state and as an active process. In the popular view of underdevelopment as a state, a developed and an underdeveloped country exist side by side, independently. The developed nation is modern and the underdeveloped nation is backward. According to the conventional view, the backward state of an underdeveloped nation can be corrected through the diffusion of modernization from the developed nation. In the Marxist view of underdevelopment as a process, the developed country and the underdeveloped country are on opposite sides of the fence, with no possibility for such "corrective" diffusion. The developed country grows richer and the underdeveloped country grows poorer as a consequence of the operation of international capitalist relations.

THE GOALS OF DEVELOPMENT

In his plea for a definition of development based on human well-being, Dudley Seers (1972) asked, "Why do we confuse development with economic growth? . . . Development means the condition for the realization of the human personality. Its evaluation must therefore take into account three linked economic criteria: Whether there has been a reduction in (i) poverty; (ii) unemployment; (iii) inequality" (p. 21). He pointed out that some countries have experienced not only rapid growth of income per capita, but also increases in poverty, unemployment, and inequality. He urged for measures of development at the family level based on nutrition, health, infant mortality, access to education, and political participation.

Seers cited works indicating that during the United Nations Development Decade of the 1960s "the growth of economic inequality and unemployment may actually have accelerated" (p. 34). For example, in India, the much heralded Green Revolution, which depends on high fertilizer and water inputs, has benefited mainly the farmers in the Punjab who were already wealthy and who owned large tracts of land (Wharton 1969). Seers also urged the use of measures that indicate degree of national independence. Among them, "the proportion of capital inflows in exchange receipts, the proportion of the supply of

FIGURE 13.1
Underdevelopment as a state
and as a process.

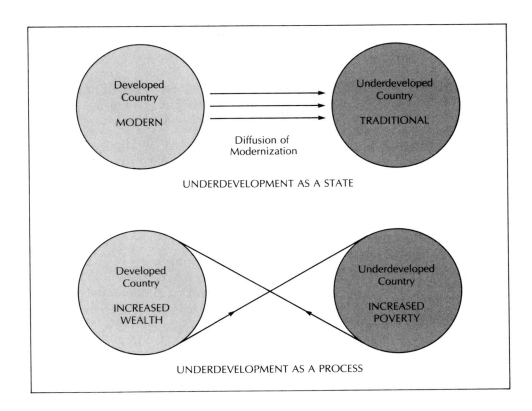

capital goods (or intermediates) which is imported, the proportion of assets, especially subsoil assets owned by foreigners, and the extent to which one trading partner dominates the pattern of aid and trade" (Seers 1972, p. 30).

A related view of development goals was expressed by Denis Goulet (1971), who echoed Seer's concern: "There may be considerable merit . . . in asking whether higher living standards, self-sustained growth and modern institutions are good in themselves or necessarily constitute the highest priorities" (p. 85). Goulet argued for three general goals of development: (1) life-sustenance, (2) esteem, and (3) freedom (p. 87).

Life-Sustenance   There can be no dispute that food, health, adequate shelter, and protection are essential to human well-being. When they are sufficient to meet human needs, a state of development exists; when they are insufficient, a degree of underdevelopment prevails.

Esteem   All people value respect. The feeling that "one is being treated as an individual who has worth, rather than as a tool for the satisfaction of other individuals' purposes, is . . . the basic source of human contentment" (Hagen 1968, pp. 411–12). Es-

teem or recognition is closely associated with material prosperity. Consequently, it is often difficult for those who are materially deprived or "underdeveloped" to experience a sense of pride or self-worth. Mass poverty cuts people and societies off from due recognition or esteem. Development may also be rejected. For example, if people are humiliated or disillusioned through their contacts with the "progress" introduced by foreigners, they may return to their traditional ways in order to regain a sense of self-respect.

Freedom   Freedom may be defined as "the capacity, the opportunity, and the incentive to develop and express one's potentialities" (Warwick 1968, p. 498). As with life-sustenance and esteem, the degree which freedom exists in a society may be used to assess development.

Donald Warwick asked students of development to "devote explicit attention to the values used in gauging progress [of individuals or societies]" (1968, p. 498). Moreover, he remarked that it is not useful to define development in terms of urbanization, commercialization, industrialization, or modernization. Instead, he advised that development be viewed as a coordinated series of changes from a phase of life perceived by a population as being less human to a phase perceived as being more human.

World Variation in Human Welfare

Geographers' Robert Tata and Ronald Schultz (1988) constructed an index of development status as defined by the goals of life-sustenance, esteem, and freedom. They utilized the following variables:

Physical
1   total value of primary industry output per capita, and
2   persons per square kilometer of arable land.

Economic
1   gross national product per capita, and
2   manufacturing value-added per capita.

Social
1   infant deaths per thousand live births,
2   percentage of age group in higher education, and
3   percentage of rural population.

Political
1   government expenditures per capita,
2   political rights index, and
3   number of radios per thousand population.

By means of a factor analysis, Tata and Schultz obtained four main factors corresponding with the physical, economic, social, and political systems. Using factor scores, they then ranked and mapped countries for overall human welfare.

As the map indicates, underdeveloped countries concentrate in Africa, East Asia, and the Middle East. Middle America leads the world in the number of moderately developed nations, followed by the Middle East, East Europe, and South America. Most of the Middle American countries are small island nations that rank high in social and political welfare, but are only average with regard to physical and economic welfare. Several Middle Eastern nations

Freedom of expression and achievement of a humane lifestyle are ultimate, essentially unresolvable, issues. More down-to-earth goals of development include the following: (1) a balanced, healthful diet; (2) adequate medical care; (3) environmental sanitation and disease control; (4) labor opportunities commensurate with individual talents; (5) sufficient educational opportunities; (6) individual freedom of conscience and freedom from fear; (7) decent housing; (8) economic activities in harmony with the natural environment; and (9) a social and political milieu promoting equality.

In conventional usage, "development" is treated as a synonym for economic growth. But growth is not development, except insofar as it enables a country to achieve the nine goals. If these goals are not the objectives of development, if modernization is merely a process of technological diffusion, and if spatial integration of world power and world economy is devoid of human referents, then "development" should be redefined. The realities of the contemporary world, however, do not offer much hope for achieving these human objectives any time soon.

THE ATTRIBUTES OF UNDERDEVELOPMENT

The attributes of underdevelopment have been summarized by H. Leibenstein (1957) as follows:

I. *Economic*

A. General
1. A high proportion of the population in agriculture, usually 70 to 90 percent.
2. "Absolute over-population" in agriculture; that is, it would be possible to reduce the number of workers in agriculture and still obtain the same total output.

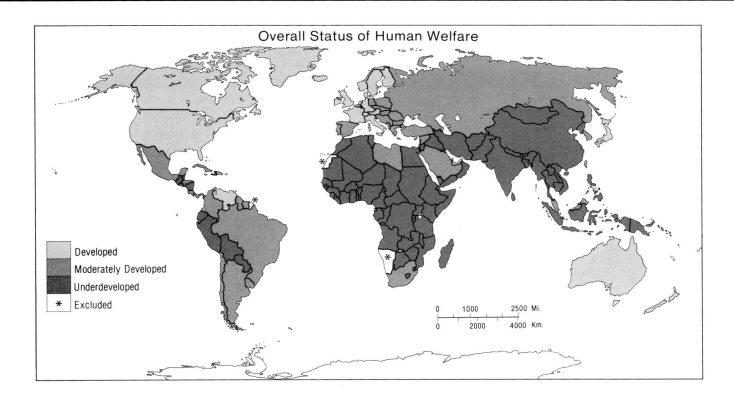

Overall Status of Human Welfare

Developed

Moderately Developed

Underdeveloped

* Excluded

0 1000 2500 Mi.

0 2000 4000 Km.

(Kuwait, Qatar, United Arab Emirates, Bahrain, and Saudi Arabia) rank very high because petroleum wealth greatly raises their physical- and, to a lesser extent, economic-welfare ranking, compensating for their low political-welfare ranking. Brunei and Libya follow this pattern also. Low political welfare depresses Eastern European countries and detracts from strong social and economic welfare.

SOURCE: Based on Tata and Schultz, 1988, pp. 580, 585–89.

3. Evidence of considerable "disguised unemployment" and lack of employment opportunities outside agriculture.

4. Very little capital per head.

5. Low income per head and, as a consequence, existence near the "subsistence" level.

6. Practically zero savings for the large mass of the people.

7. Whatever savings do exist are usually achieved by a landholding class whose values are not conducive to investment in industry or commerce.

8. The primary industries, that is, agriculture, forestry, and mining, are usually the residual employment categories.

9. The output in agriculture is made up mostly of cereals and primary raw materials, with relatively low output of protein foods. The reason for this is the conversion ratio between cereals and meat products; that is, if one acre of cereals produces a certain number of calories, it would take between five to seven acres to produce the same number of calories if meat products were produced.

10. Major proportion of expenditure on food and necessities.

11. Export of foodstuffs and raw materials.

12. Low volume of trade per capita.

13. Poor credit facilities and poor marketing facilities.

14. Poor housing.

B. Basic characteristics in agriculture

   1. Although there is low capitalization on the land, there is simultaneously an uneconomic use of whatever capital exists due to the small size of holdings and the existence of exceedingly small plots.

2. The level of agrarian techniques is exceedingly low, and tools and equipment are limited and primitive in nature.

3. Even where there are big landowners as, for instance, in certain parts of India, the openings for modernized agricultural production for sale are limited by difficulties of transport and the absence of an efficient demand in the local market. It is significant that in many backward countries a modernized type of agriculture is confined to production for sale in foreign markets.

4. There is an inability of the small landholders and peasants to weather even a short-term crisis, and, as a consequence, attempts are made to get the highest possible yields from the soil, which leads to soil depletion.

5. There is a widespread prevalence of high indebtedness relative to assets and income.

6. The methods of production for the domestic market are generally old-fashioned and inefficient, leaving little surplus for marketing. This is usually true whether or not the cultivator owns the land, has tenancy rights, or is a sharecropper.

7. A most pervasive aspect is a feeling of land hunger because of the exceedingly small size of holdings and small diversified plots. The reason for this is that holdings are continually sub-divided as the population on the land increases.

II. *Demographic*

A. High fertility rates, usually above 40 per thousand.

B. High mortality rates and low expectation of life at birth.

C. Inadequate nutrition and dietary deficiencies.

D. Rudimentary hygiene, public health, and sanitation.

E. Rural overcrowding.

III. *Cultural and Political*

A. Rudimentary education and usually a high degree of illiteracy among most of the people.

B. Extensive prevalence of child labor.

C. General weakness or absence of the middle class.

D. Inferiority of women's status and position.

E. Traditionally determined behavior for the bulk of the populace.

IV. *Technological and Miscellaneous*

A. Low yields per acre.

B. No training facilities or inadequate facilities for the training of technicians, engineers, etc.

C. Inadequate and crude communication and transportation facilities, especially in the rural areas.

D. Crude technology (pp. 40–41).

The list, of course, could be expanded, and some might take issue with certain of the stated facts and observations, but social scientists would generally agree that Leibenstein has cited many of the attributes of underdeveloped countries. A crucial question, however, is whether inhibiting internal factors, either separately or in their aggregate, provide a logical and acceptable explanation of underdevelopment. We will consider population, climate and resources, capital and labor, and the circle of poverty into which the poor countries are said to be locked.

Rapid Population Growth

Can we ascribe underdevelopment to rapid population growth? After all, the present rapid increase of population is most apparent in underdeveloped countries, many of which have an average annual population growth rate of at least 2.5 percent. It seems there are just too many millions of people in underdeveloped countries who must be fed, housed, clothed, educated, employed, cared for in illness, and, finally looked after in old age. Many would argue that their populations should be controlled if development is to take place.

Assuredly, a rapid increase in population—especially the number and proportion of young dependents—creates serious problems in terms of food supply, public education, and health and social services; it also intensifies the employment problem. However, a high rate of population growth was once a characteristic of the present-day developed countries, and it did not prevent their development. This observation makes it difficult to argue that population growth necessarily leads to underdevelopment or that population control necessarily aids development.

Climate and Resources

Can underdevelopment be traced to adverse climate, insufficient rainfall, poor soils, and a lack of mineral resources? Obviously the uneven allocation of the gifts of nature makes development more difficult in some areas than in others. East Africa is a case in point.

Large areas of East Africa have poor soils and low, unpredictable rainfall. The dry wooded steppe in the rain shadow of Mount Meru, Tanzania, is on the arid margins of agriculture, and supports Masai pastoralists at low population densities. By contrast, large numbers of East African farmers live in better watered areas—along the coast, near the lakes, and in the highlands. For example, in the Kigezi district of southwest Uganda, fertile volcanic soils and ample rainfall makes agriculture highly productive on carefully terraced hillsides. In many densely populated areas of East Africa, the main problems are not environmental but economic and political.

It is untenable to attribute underdevelopment solely to a lack of resources or a poor climate. Vagaries of weather, exposure to natural disasters such as flood or drought, and danger of soil erosion are not exclusive to the underdeveloped world. Despite technical advances, climate still poses recurring problems for farmers in North America, Europe, and the Soviet Union. Furthermore, some developed countries have unfavorable natural resource endowments, and yet they developed. Cases in point are Japan and the Netherlands. For centuries, the Netherlands has been able to obtain necessary resources through various long-distance trading connections.

Years of subnormal rainfall brought severe drought to the Sahelian region of Africa in the 1970s and 1980s. The effects of hunger are evident on the faces and bodies of these destitute nomads from Mali. In 1973 they journeyed to northern Burkina Faso in search of food and water for themselves and their cattle, but all that awaited them was wasteland. Is human tragedy the inevitable consequence of such environmental circumstance? Is hardship exacerbated by national elites and international organizations, including multinational corporations? (Source: FAO photo by F. Botts.)

The North-South Scientific Divide

It is common to define underdevelopment on the basis of statistical indices based on income, industry, agricultural productivity, commerce, trade, housing, health, nutrition, urbanization, and education. Such data are often used to illustrate development differences or to support various explanations for underdevelopment.

One of the most vivid contrasts between the rich, developed North and the poor, underdeveloped South is in quantity of scientific research. The scientific divide is so enormous that it is tempting to argue that countries must have vigorous and productive scientific communities if they are to develop.

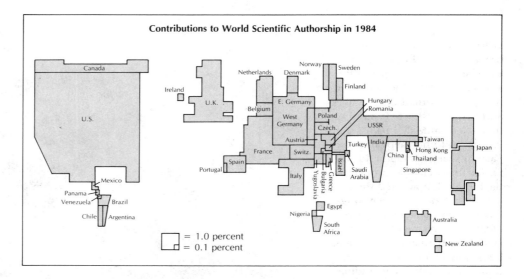

One indicator of the development potential of a country is the size of its pool of publishing scientists. This measure is crude because it does not take into account country-by-country variations in the quality of work published, yet it is an easier base from which to make comparisons than one which is dependent on budget data, such as the proportion of gross national product a country spends on science.

Data on the number of publishing scientists in 164 countries in 1984, compiled by the Institute for Scientific Information in Philadelphia, show a remarkable imbalance: forty-seven countries accounted for 99 percent of scientific authorship. Within this framework, the United States alone accounts for 36 percent, and ten countries produce 80 percent.

Industrial market economies and East European nonmarket economies are home to nearly 95 percent of all publishing scientists. India, which has a venerable history of technical and scientific education, and which is one of the biggest contributors of scientists in the world, is home to nearly 50 percent of all the publishing scientists of the South. China and a handful of newly industrializing and oil-exporting countries such as Singapore, Nigeria, and Mexico account for much of the remainder.

The information that is so vital to the conduct of scientific research is most abundant in major metropolitan areas and specialized science centers.

And, although it can be communicated to scientists elsewhere by various methods, there are inherent advantages in personal exchanges. However, the geographical concentration of scientists may often operate against such exchanges, since it varies considerably both within the North and between the North and South.

In the United States, patterns of communication and cooperation among scientists are informal, and no single city or region has a monopoly of talented scientists. New York is the leading U.S. scientific city with its universities, medical centers, industrial laboratories, zoological and botanical parks, and museums. Yet it is home to only 3 percent of American publishing scientists.

Outside the United States, scientific effort tends to be more concentrated geographically, Moscow, the world's largest scientific city, supports 38 percent of the USSR's publishing scientists. Moscow, Leningrad, and Kiev together account for 55 percent of the country's scientific capacity.

City	Number of Publishing Scientists	Percentage Share of National Scientific Effort
Largest Scientific Cities of the South in 1984		
Beijing	2,334	38.0
Buenos Aires	2,109	59.1
Bombay	1,539	8.0
Santiago	1,496	71.1
New Delhi	1,292	6.7
Cairo	1,266	60.0
Calcutta	1,221	6.3
Mexico City	1,211	70.2
Shanghai	1,143	18.6
São Paulo	1,079	23.2
Largest Scientific Cities in 1984		
Moscow	25,511	37.8
London	14,784	23.7
Tokyo	10,875	18.9
Paris	10,707	23.3
New York	8,994	3.1
Boston	7,300	2.5
Washington	6,982	2.4
Philadelphia	6,275	2.1
Los Angeles	6,183	2.1
Leningrad	6,120	9.1
Chicago	5,777	2.0
Bethesda, Maryland	5,443	1.9
Kiev	5,431	8.1
Houston	5,106	1.7
Toronto	4,143	13.4

The concentration of scientists in most West European countries and Japan falls somewhere between that of the United States and East Europe. London has 24 percent of Britain's publishing scientists; Paris 23 percent of France's; and Tokyo, 19 percent of Japan's. London has more than five times the number of scientists of Britain's second- and third-ranked scientific cities—Cambridge and Oxford.

In the South, scientific research is concentrated in a few institutions in capital cities. For example, Mexico City boasts 70 percent of Mexico's scientific community. India is among the few countries of the poor South where scientific effort is dispersed among a number of regional centers. Only 21 percent of India's publishing scientists live in Bombay, New Delhi, and Calcutta.

Countries with a large pool of publishing scientists have a high technological potential. If countries are classified by technological levels, high-technology countries with industries such as aeronautics and aerospace, telecommunications and telematics, nuclear energy, computers and bio-industry account for 80 percent of all scientific authorship. The United

Capital and Labor

Is underdevelopment attributable to capital shortage and low labor productivity? It is true that a day's toil in an underdeveloped country produces very little compared with a day's work in a developed country. This is particularly evident in agriculture. American farmers spread their labor over thirty to sixty hectares; African or Asian farmers pour their energies into a hectare or so. As a consequence, human productivity in an underdeveloped country may be as little as one-fiftieth of that in a developed country.

Why is agricultural labor in the underdeveloped world so unproductive? According to some economists, the answer lies in the small scale of operations, the unskilled working population, and, in particular, the absence or shortage of capital. Most underdeveloped countries lack the machines, engines, power lines, and factories that enable people and resources to produce more than is possible with bare hands and simple tools. Although it must be acknowledged that a shortage of capital and low labor productivity are universal attributes of underdevelopment, they are not *causative* factors. The important question to consider is, What factors prevented capital from accumulating and labor productivity from improving in underdeveloped countries?

Vicious Circles of Poverty

Is underdevelopment the consequence of a catalogue of causally related internal factors? The idea of causal links between attributes of underdevelopment is summarized in the often-used expression "vicious circles of poverty." Vicious-circle explanations emphasize the multicausality of underdevelopment. These explanations suggest that it is not "just" a lack of ambition, or "just" an absence of specialization, or "just" a low output per capita, or "just" a population problem, or even "just" a political problem that holds back underdeveloped countries. Rather, a combination of interwoven limiting factors thwarts development. An example of a vicious circle is: low output→low real incomes→low demand levels→low investment→capital deficiency→low output (Figure 13.2). According to Hungarian economist Tamás Szentes (1971), "the main weakness of the vicious cycle theories is that they reveal neither the historical

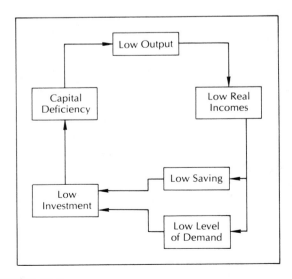

FIGURE 13.2
Closed circle of poverty.

428

States, Canada, Japan, Sweden, Denmark, Italy, Switzerland, West Germany, the Netherlands, Belgium, the United Kingdom, Australia, the USSR, and East Germany fall into this category. In only two of these countries, the USSR and East Germany, is science highly regulated by government. The countries with a classic technology; that is, all the remaining countries in the study except for Panama, Nigeria, and Saudi Arabia, account for 19 percent of scientific authorship. The vast majority of the third group of technologically dependent countries do not register statistically because they have too few publishing scientists.

It appears that countries must "publish" if they are to develop. But this conclusion is ethnocentric. All societies have people versed in science. Traditional farmers and herders in the poor South are scientists. They know a great deal about their environments, and they apply that knowledge to solve practical problems. Their science, or systematic knowledge, is as important to their livelihoods as our science is to ours. Moreover, it is becoming increasingly clear that our technology is inappropriate for most people in technologically dependent countries.

circumstances out of which the assumed "magic" circle originated, nor the underlying socio-economic relations and the fundamental, determinant causes (p. 54).

The specification of *limiting factors* serves as a illustration of the gravity of the problem of underdevelopment. But some scholars go further and use limiting factors as a starting point for certain theories of underdevelopment. For example, internal factors hindering development often serve the view that underdevelopment is an original state or a lagging behind in the development of productive forces.

MAJOR PERSPECTIVES ON DEVELOPMENT

Development is usually equated with economic growth (Partant 1982). The following definition of Eugene Havens and William Flinn is characteristic:

> Development . . . involves three interrelated societal activities: (1) the establishment of increased wealth and income as a perceived, attainable goal for the broader masses of society; (2) the creation and/or selection of adequate means to attain this goal; and (3) the restructuring of society so that there is persistent economic growth. (1975, p. 469)

"Theories" of development have existed for many years. The earliest of them can be traced to the classical economists. But discussion of the term *development* in the social sciences is fairly recent. It was not required before the collapse of the colonial system or before the onset of the cold war between the United States and the USSR for power and

influence in the world. Since the late 1940s, however, the problem of how to push the pace of development in roughly one hundred ex-colonial countries has generated intense interest among planners and in the academic world.

Three groups of perspectives on development can be identified in terms of the scale upon which they concentrate (national, global) and whether or not development is defined exclusively in terms of economic growth. The first and most widely accepted theories of development are *modernization theories*. These concentrate on the national scale and define development in terms of economic growth and Westernization. Their underlying assumption is that modernization influences are projected to peripheral regions from Western Europe and North America; hence, the path to progress from traditional to modern is unidirectional. In this view, rich industrial countries, without rival in social, economic, and political development, are modern, whereas poor countries must undergo the modernization process to acquire these traits (Tipps 1973; Pletsch 1982).

The second group of theories are *world political economy theories*. They focus on the structure of political and economic relationships between dominant and dominated countries. They pay special attention to the global history of economic growth that brought poor countries to their present position (Agnew 1982). Their underlying assumption is that the poverty of the Third World is the outcome of a worldwide network of intrusion by the rich countries into the poor.

Theories that make up a third group come from scholars who wonder whether certain kinds of development are desirable, and if, indeed, development will ever materialize for people in underdeveloped countries. These *ecopolitical economy theories* concentrate on the ecological and cultural consequences of economic growth. Their proponents are disenchanted with research that neglects the diverse value systems and world views of societies engaged in the process of development, that equates development with economic growth, that advocates the "trickling down" of benefits to the poor instead of the channeling of resources directly into basic human needs, and that ascribes no merit whatsoever to the contributions of indigenous systems to the process of development (Yapa 1980).

Modernization Theories

The best known modernization theories are *growth-stage theories*, and the one most often cited was advanced by economic historian Walt W. Rostow (1960). He identified in European history five stages of growth: (1) the traditional society, (2) the transition or preconditioning stage, (3) take-off, (4) drive to maturity, and (5) the stage of high mass consumption (Figure 13.3). According to Rostow, this sequence can be used as a framework for the national development of underdeveloped countries. The problem is to get poor countries, which must pass through these stages in order to develop, into that crucial third stage after which sufficient surplus is generated to sustain economic growth. It is necessary in the take-off stage to reallocate a punishing amount of annual production for reinvestment—the equivalent of 10 percent of national income each year. The underdeveloped

country is treated as a self-contained unit that generates its own transformation. Agriculture is the most important sector in the transformation from "traditional" to "modern" society, and technology plays a decisive role in development by transforming subsistence agriculture into commercial agriculture. According to some modernization theorists, the commercialization of agriculture is the central feature of development (Mellor 1962; Wharton 1963).

The most widely accepted economic theory of underdevelopment is that of the *dual economy*—one sector modern and tied through export, organization, capital support, and use of technology to the developed countries of Europe and North America; the other sector traditional and engaged in subsistence activities (Lewis 1954; Higgins 1956). These sectors, according to the theory, exist independently, yet side by side, in the underdeveloped country. An additional assumption of the theory is that the traditional sector is at one end of a continuum of development. The concern of dual-economy theorists is to generate interaction between the two sectors. For example, Arthur Lewis (1954) observed that productivity increases in agriculture are central to the modernization process because they permit the movement of surplus labor from the traditional agricultural sector to the modern industrial sector.

Modernization and *institutional reform theories* are the domain of sociologists, psychologists, and political scientists (McClelland 1961; Hagen 1962; Cochran 1966; Tipps 1973; Said 1981). Development is viewed as dependent on transforming a stagnant, traditional society that lacks the qualities, propensities, motivations, and incentives of advanced capitalist

FIGURE 13.3
Rostow's five stages of economic growth.

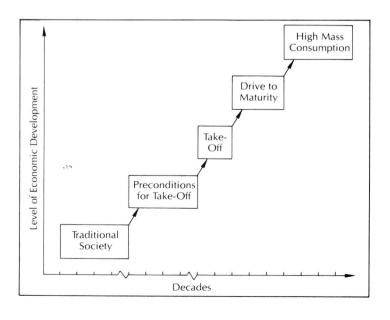

This market near Toussiana in Burkina Faso exemplifies the so-called traditional sector of a Third World country. (Source: UNESCO/Labordiére.)

society. It requires the spread of a strong achievement orientation, a profit incentive, a willingness to take entrepreneurial risks, and the institutionalization of efficiency and productivity.

Geographical studies of modernization have drawn on the ideas of economists, sociologists, historians, and political scientists, and have relied strongly on two concepts to explain how the nation and its space economy develop. These concepts are (1) unilineal evolution of societies, epitomized by Rostow's stages of economic growth, and (2) growth of and diffusion within a world hierarchy of urban centers.

Peter Gould (1964) spearheaded the study of modernization as a spatial diffusion process. The modernization theme exemplified by geographers who followed the lead of Gould dealt explicitly at the macroscale with the evolving structure of urban

places, the interconnections of these places through transport and communication, and the penetration of indigenous social systems by Western elements of modernization (Soja 1968; Gould 1970; Riddell 1970). Gould (1970) argued that the diffusion of Western elements of modernization would promote the downfall of traditional societies. In his study of the spatial impress of the modernization process in Tanzania, he interpreted modernization, as defined by a host of infrastructural variables such as roads, railways, telephones, postal stations, hospitals, schools, and administrative offices, as diffusion outward from foreign enclaves. His modernization surface maps (Figure 13.4) and accompanying descriptions indicate that beyond towns, and in some cases their rich agricultural hinterlands, levels of modernization decrease sharply. Peripheral areas are illustrated in the sequence of maps as shrinking areas of "no moderniza-

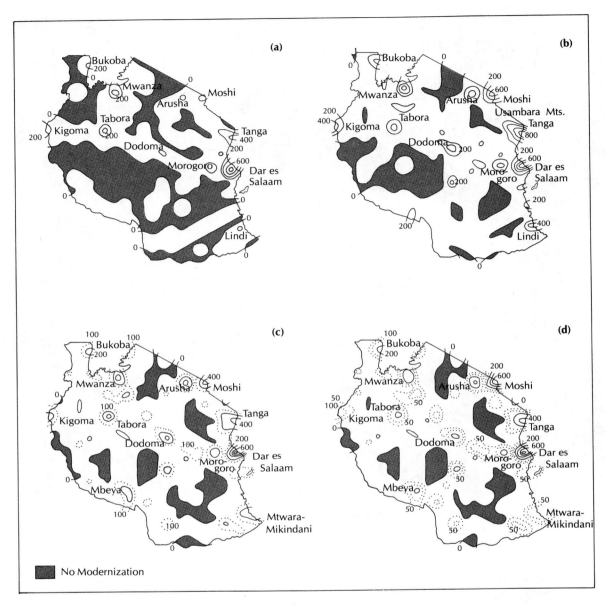

FIGURE 13.4
The diffusion of modernization in Tanzania: (a) early 1920s; (b) late 1920s and early
1930s; (c) late 1940s and early 1950s; (d) late 1950s and early 1960s. (Source: Gould,
1970.)

tion." Gould noted that in the 1920s there were a few
islands of development focused on Dar es Salaam and
the lower order centers of Tanga, Mwanza, and
Tabora that "float in the still mill-pond of traditional-
ism" (p. 156). By the 1960s, the spatial pattern of
modernization was more widespread and intense, but
the larger towns remained the major centers of
change.

The final modernization theory comes from the
classic Marxist writing on development. Like Rostow's
stage theory, it provides a deterministic model for the
evolution of society. Unlike Rostow's theory, however,
it stresses the institution of private property, the
transition from feudalism to capitalism, the growth of
different classes, and the spread of capitalism from
Europe (Agnew 1987, p. 277). Central to the *Marxist
theory* is the dictum, "The country that is more
developed industrially only shows to the less developed the image of its own future" (Marx 1967, pp.
8–9). The inference is clear enough: The experience of
the presently rich countries is the working model for
the present and future of poor countries.

World Political Economy Theories

These theories concern imperialistic relations and owe much to the ideas of V. I. Lenin. According to Lenin, imperialism represents the geographical extension of capitalism from its historical center to the rest of the world. To increase the rate of capital accumulation, capitalists expanded their operations to collect the surplus product of peripheral regions. Capitalism became a global economic system, controlling all aspects of life in the periphery. Lenin's theory of imperialism was popularized in the writings of Paul Sweezy (1942) and Paul Baran (1957), which led to the elaboration of world system theory and the theory of the development of underdevelopment.

World-system theory provides a framework for understanding the development of the capitalist system and its three component parts—the core, semi-periphery, and periphery—from the start of the sixteenth century (Wallerstein 1974). The *development-of-underdevelopment theory* owes much to the work of André Gunder Frank (1969). He drew on the Latin American experience to argue that the development of the West depended upon the impoverishment of the periphery. The development-of-underdevelopment theory pays special attention to a complement of the theory of imperialism, a theory of dependence that relates the effects of imperialism on underdeveloped countries.

An attractive theory for geographers is Johan Galtung's (1971) *structural theory of imperialism* based on *center-periphery relations* (Figure 13.5). The Center is represented by wealthy industrial nations, the Periphery by underdeveloped nations. Both the Center and the Periphery have centers of their own,

The periphery in the Center is illustrated by these shacks occupied by North African migrant workers in Paris. (Source: ILO, I-France-Migration: 26.)

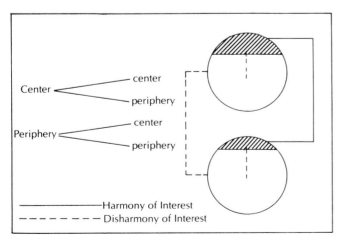

FIGURE 13.5
The structure of imperialism. (Source: Galtung, 1971, p. 84.)

mainly urban elites and some rural elites, and peripheries, essentially the rural poor and also the urban powerless. The dominant economic and political power lies with the center in the Center (i.e., the elites in the industrialized countries); the dominant strength in numbers lies with the periphery in the Periphery (i.e., the majority of Third World people). For Galtung, the center-periphery theory of imperialism provides a fruitful basis for empirical research within liberal and radical schools of thought.

Another way to examine imperialistic relations is to focus on the *role of the multinational corporation* as a source of political and economic control (Barnet and Muller 1974). The buildup of crises in the capitalist core, frequently expressed as conflicts between capital and labor, has forced firms to emphasize multinational production and channel capital in the direction of peripheral regions where hourly wage rates and fringe benefits are low (Table 13.1). The theory empha-

TABLE 13.1
Hourly wage and fringe benefits in the apparel industry.

Country or City	U.S. $
Sweden	7.22
Netherlands	5.68
Belgium	5.49
New York (legal)[1]	4.58
United States	4.35
Puerto Rico	2.57
New York (sweatshops)[1]	1.75
Singapore [1]	1.10
Hong Kong	0.96
Brazil	0.86
Taiwan	0.56
South Korea	0.41

NOTE 1: No fringe benefits.
SOURCE: Ross and Trachte, 1983, p. 417.

sizes that the global corporation is the linchpin of a precarious dependent development. Despite the economic benefits derived from the transfer of capital, the foreign enclaves of multinationals, their "export platforms," create very few jobs relative to the size of the massive industrial reserve army now encamped in the Third World. Moreover, the relocation of industry to the periphery is a prime cause of the crisis now afflicting the major metropolitan areas, and which threatens the social harmony that has prevailed in the core.

Ecopolitical Economy Theories

Ecopolitical economy theories stem from concern over the meaning of development and the costs and benefits of economic growth and cultural change. These theories ae reflected in the work of anthropologists on the cultural ecology of development (Geertz 1963) and in the work of economists who question why we make a fetish of growth (Mishan 1969; Schumacher 1973).

Geographer Lakshman Yapa (1980), who coined the term *ecopolitical economy*, pointed to insights derived from world political economy theory in criticizing the conventional wisdom of striving for higher and higher rates of economic growth in underdeveloped countries in the hope that benefits will diffuse to the poor. The benefits of economic growth fail to reach the poor because the economic surplus is diverted to national and foreign elites, in effect preempting the basic-goods fund. The only way economic development can improve the living condi-

tions of the poor is by using resources directly in the production and distribution of basic goods.

Bring Culture Back In

With the possible exception of the ecopolitical approach, all major perspectives on development emphasize the economic and downplay the cultural dimension. To promote a fuller understanding of the process, John Agnew (1987) entreated geographers to bring culture back into their development studies. Agnew stressed that every part of the world has had its own particular and peculiar relationship to the evolution of the world economy. The success of Japan in the world economy, the dependence of South African economic growth upon apartheid, the religiously inspired backlash against American-style development in Iran, and even the rise of the modern world economy in Europe cannot be explained solely in economic terms. In Europe, it was the *cultural system* of exchange and value dating back to medieval times that paved the way for the modern world economy.

COLONIALISM AND CORE-PERIPHERY RELATIONS

Thus far we have dealt with attributes of underdevelopment and ideas about development that find expression in the social sciences. The balance of the chapter examines the themes of inequality and unequal development in greater detail. We begin with the development of the capitalist world economy viewed in terms of waves of colonialism and core-periphery relations.

Cycles of Colonialism

Colonialism existed from the beginning of the world system and, for a period, embraced nearly every part of the globe. In 1500, Europeans controlled 9 percent of the world's land surface. By 1800, they ruled about 35 percent; by 1878, 67 percent; and by 1914, 85 percent. Expansion continued until the 1930s, when parts of Arabia, Afghanistan, Mongolia, Tibet, China, Siam, and Japan were the only significant areas that had never been under formal colonial government. After World War II, formal colonies quickly disappeared, and by the early 1970s practically none were left.

Periods of colonial expansion and contraction can be examined from what is known as a world-system perspective. In this view, colonialism is part of the world system: it is a cyclical phenomenon and a structural linkage between the core and the periphery. Changes in the rate of colonial activity reflect changes in the political and economic configuration at the center of the world system.

In modern history, there have been two waves of colonialism (Figure 13.6). The first wave began in 1415, when the Portuguese seized control of the commercial naval base of Ceuta on the Strait of Gibraltar, and ended soon after 1800. The second wave began in the late nineteenth century and ended shortly after 1945. During the first wave, European power centered on the Americas; during the second wave, the focus switched to Africa, Asia, and the Pacific (Figure 13.7). Colonies of the first wave were mainly settlement colonies where quasi-European societies were created by immigrants. The second wave involved colonies of occupation, in which a small number of Europeans exercised political control. Exceptions to the latter included nineteenth-century settler colonies in Australasia and in southern and eastern Africa.

In each wave, a few colonial powers overshadowed the rest (Figure 13.8). During the first wave,

Spain and Portugal stood apart from the Netherlands, Britain, and France. In the second wave, when the number of major colonial powers increased from five to ten, Britain and France were far ahead of their contemporaries. At its peak in 1933, the British Empire covered over 24 percent of the world's land surface and included nearly one-quarter of the world's population (502 million people) (Fieldhouse 1967, p. 271).

The first wave of colonialism involved conquest, plunder, slavery, and the annihilation of indigenous people. The Spaniards, for example, virtually exterminated the Carib population of Hispaniola; in 1492, the Caribs numbered 300,000, but by 1548 the figure was down to 500 (Griffin 1969, p. 45). The arrival of the Spaniards in Mexico led to the destruction of Aztec civilization and a population decline from thirteen to two million (Griffin 1969, p. 46). In Africa, the slave trade greatly reduced the population in large parts of the Congo basin and in the West Africa forest.

During the second wave, there was less destruction and disruption of local societies. Conditions varied from colony to colony, however. For example, the impact of colonialism was generally greater in

FIGURE 13.6

Waves of colonialism. (Source: de Souza, 1986, p. 15. Based on data in Henige, 1970.)

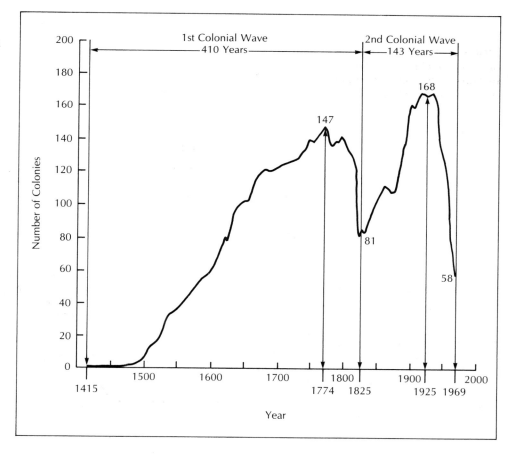

FIGURE 13.7
The colonized periphery.
(Source: de Souza, 1986, p. 16.
Based on data in Henige, 1970.)

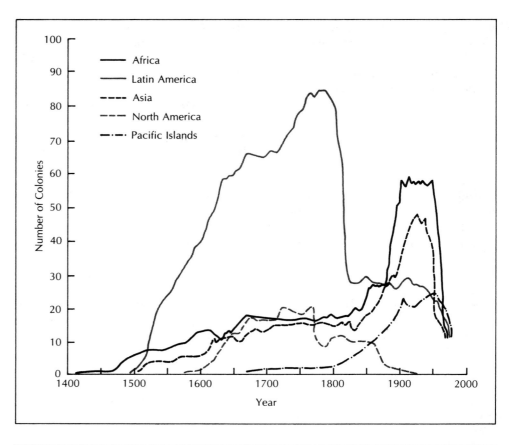

FIGURE 13.8
Major colonial powers. (Source:
de Souza, 1986, p. 16. Based on
data in Henige, 1970.)

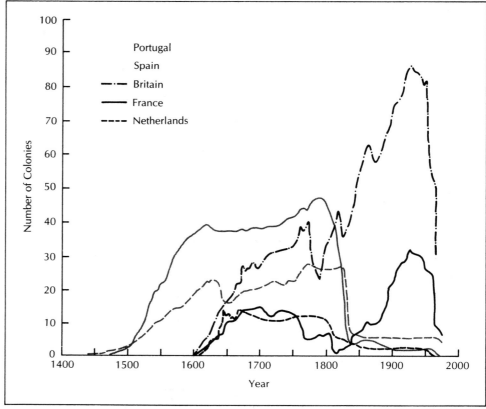

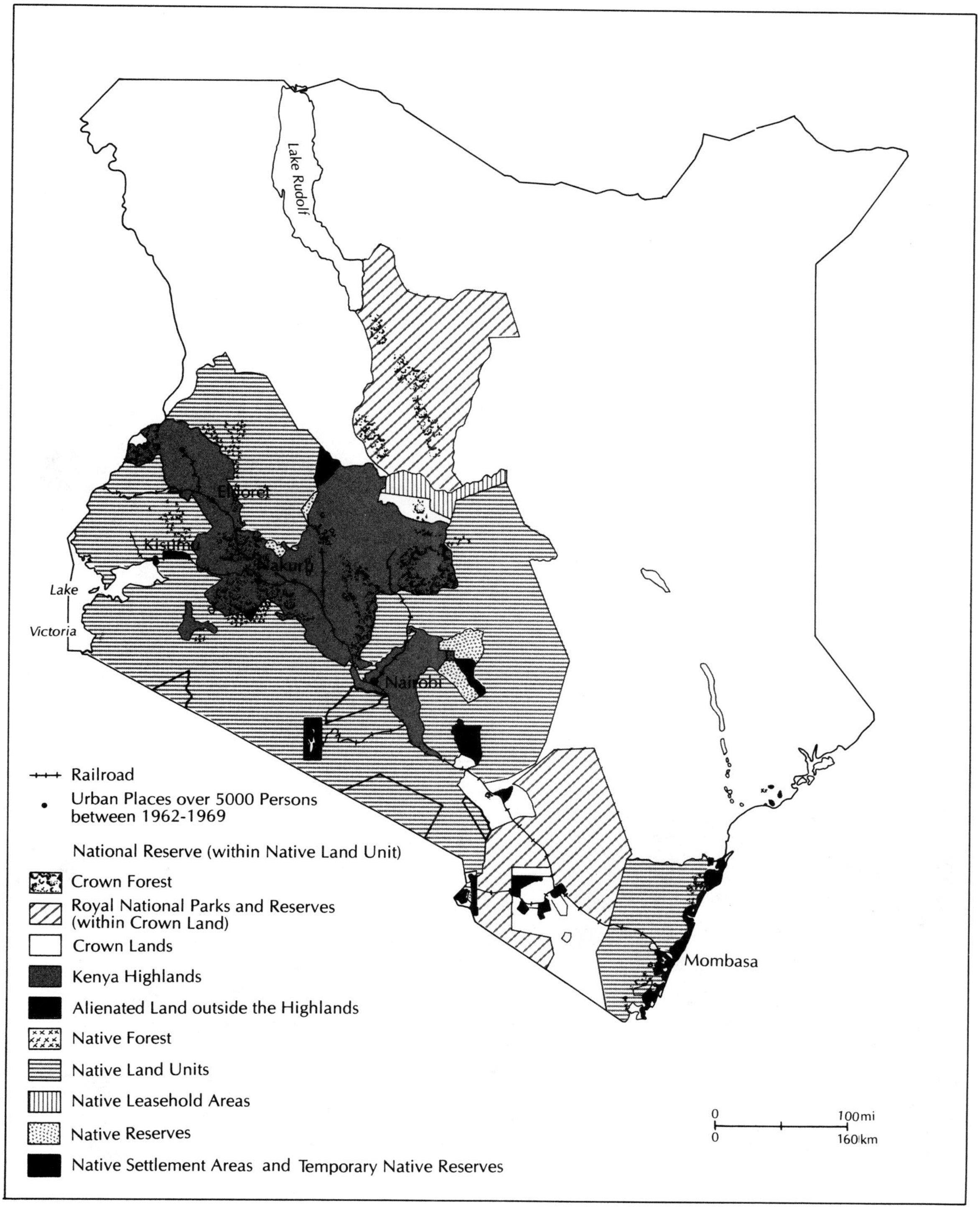
Lake Rudolf
Eldoret
Kisumu
Nakuru
Lake
Victoria
Nairobi
Mombasa
Railroad
Urban Places over 5000 Persons between 1962-1969
National Reserve (within Native Land Unit)
Crown Forest
Royal National Parks and Reserves (within Crown Land)
Crown Lands
Kenya Highlands
Alienated Land outside the Highlands
Native Forest
Native Land Units
Native Leasehold Areas
Native Reserves
Native Settlement Areas and Temporary Native Reserves
0
100mi
0
160km

FIGURE 13.9
Land allocations in Kenya, 1957. (Source: de Souza and Porter, 1974, p. 42.)

southern Africa and East Africa than in West Africa. In southern Africa and East Africa, the British alienated land to build an export-oriented economy. The British in Kenya created a complex classification of land use that governed who could use a given piece of land and for what purpose. *The Kenya Political and General Map* of 1957 summarizes the long process of land allocation that evolved over a period of about sixty years (Figure 13.9). The four main land types were Native Land Units for Africans; Kenya Highlands for Europeans; Alienated Land Outside the Highlands for Asians, Europeans, and Coastal Arabs; and Crown Land, reserved for the Crown to use at will (Morgan 1963). Crown Land was not developed, and neither was a

large part of the immense acreage of land allocated to European settlers. By denying Africans control over land and the principal means of production, the European settler population forced a change in the social organization of indigenous society and obliged its members to participate in the development of a new mode of production in which the settlers and international companies were the principal beneficiaries.

In British West Africa, no land was alienated for European settlement, and there were few plantations and estates. British policy was geared to economic exploitation rather than political control. Instead of acquiring the means of production as they did in

Nairobi, capital of Kenya, is a city created by Europeans out of the African "wilderness." Home to more than 2 million people, Nairobi originated in 1899 as a railway camp during the building of the Mombasa-Lake Victoria railway line. To the north and west of the city, the fertile "White Highlands" were alienated to European farmers who specialized in wheat, corn, pyrethrum, sheep, and cattle. Land was also alienated along the coast for European use—often as a vacation spot on the Indian Ocean. Since independence, colonial land ownership and use has been modified. Land in the "White Highlands," for example, has been acquired by Africans and divided into small holdings. (Source: World Bank.)

Kenya and Zimbabwe, the British purchased the output of existing producers. To a far greater degree than in East Africa, small landholders in West Africa were drawn into export agriculture, requiring them to make considerable adjustments in their farming practices, land tenure arrangements, settlement, and trading patterns.

During the second wave of colonialism, the imperialist countries saw the underdeveloped regions as immense supply depots for the cheap production of raw materials from which their economies could profit. The economies of underdeveloped countries were often deformed into subsidiaries of the colonial powers: Jamaica became a sugar plantation, Sri Lanka a tea plantation, Zambia a copper mine, and Arabia an oil field.

Tanzania provides an example of how the colonial mind organized space to serve its own imperatives. Between 1905 and 1967, the colonial space economy rooted itself ever more firmly in Tanzania, as early locational decisions that shaped the system were subsequently reinforced. The result was a concentrated and polarized pattern of development. Throughout the period, the primate city of Dar es Salaam increased its dominance. As the capital and hub of regional trade routes, Dar es Salaam was linked to a network of provincial towns. Regional towns that functioned as administrative headquarters, transport nodes, or centers surrounded by zones of export

agriculture grew steadily: Tanga benefited from the sisal industry, Mwanza from the cotton-growing area to the south of Lake Victoria, and Moshi from the nearby coffee farms on the well-watered slopes of Mount Kilimanjaro. Growth also occurred along transport corridors linking extractive regions to port cities. Beyond the towns, major transport routes, and export enclaves, levels of infrastructural development decreased sharply. Overall, development was greater in northern than in southern Tanzania because the British neglected the southern part of the country and its productive potential. In fact, parts of the south were isolated from Dar es Salaam and the rest of the country by a lack of roads or by high water during the rainy season.

Core Structure and Center-Periphery Relations

Why did colonialism expand at a particular time and contract at another? World-system theory suggests that the key to understanding waves of colonialism is the changing structure of the core: periods of instability and stability in the core coincide with periods of colonial expansion and contraction in the periphery (Figure 13.10). During periods of instability, when there is competition among rival core countries, colonialism expands. In the presence of a single, hegemonic core country, colonialism contracts. A

FIGURE 13.10
The relationship between colonialism and center stability.

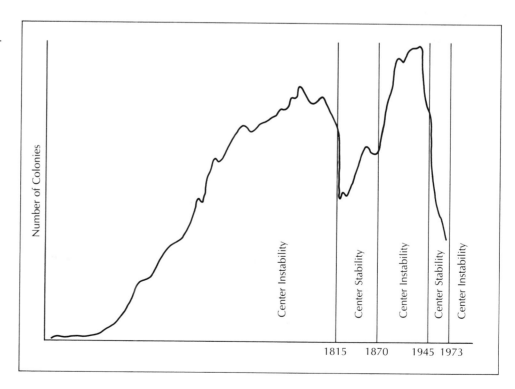

FIGURE 13.11
The relationship between colonialism and trade regulation.

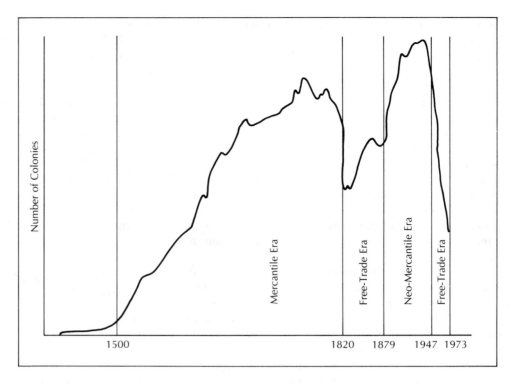

hegemonic power can control the world without the expensive encumbrances that colonies represent.

Hegemony exists when one core power enjoys supremacy in production, commerce, and finance and occupies a position of political leadership. The hegemonic power owns and controls the largest share of the world's production apparatus. It is the leading trading and investment country, its currency is the universal medium of exchange, and its primate city is the financial center of the world. Because of political and military superiority, the dominant core country maintains order in the world system and imposes solutions to international conflicts that serve its self-interests. Consequently, hegemonic situations are characterized by periods of peace as well as by universal ideologies such as freedom to trade and freedom to invest.

During a core power's rise to hegemony, core-periphery relations become more informal. Economic linkages between center and periphery increasingly focus on the hegemonic power. This reorientation results in decolonization. The hegemonic power relies on economic mechanisms to extract the surplus value of the periphery. Lopsided development between the core and the periphery flourishes, and terms of trade deteriorate for the colonized periphery. During a power's fall from hegemony, rival core states, which can focus on capital accumulation without the burden of maintaining the political and military appara-

tus of supremacy, catch up and challenge the hegemonic power.

Competition exists when power in the center of the world system is dispersed among several countries. With pluralization, competing centers control and own a larger part of the world's production apparatus. They increase their share of world trade, enclose national economic areas behind tariff and nontariff barriers, and use their national currencies in a growing volume of transactions. Without a hegemonic power dominating the world system, political tensions increase and may develop into armed conflicts.

Competition forces increasingly more formal core-periphery relationships. Competing core countries rely on the mechanism of colonialism to extract the surplus of the periphery. Economic linkages between the colonized and the colonizers become multilateral to a greater extent, and economic transactions with core countries become more frequent.

World-system theory maintains that periodic fluctuations from a single, hegemonic power to a group of competing countries are essential to the survival of the world system. The system would break into separate empires if competition at the center were to persist, or mutate into world empire if hegemony were to last. Moreover, this cyclic realignment of core-periphery relations is not limited to colonialism; it is manifested in all the ways the world system binds itself together. Trade, for example, is more formally structured during periods of core instability (Figure 13.11).

The History of Center-Periphery Relations

During the five-hundred-year history of the world system, there have been three periods of formal core-periphery relations (1415–1815, 1871–1945, and 1973–present) and two of informal relations (1816–1870 and 1946–1972). Western Europe began the first formal period with a slight edge on the rest of the "civilized" world. Its open social structure facilitated the transition from feudalism to capitalism and the growth of centralized monarchies. Because there were several competing countries, the core of the world system was unstable. This was a time of almost constant conflict. There were nineteen major wars during the period, beginning with the Italian Wars (1495–1504) and ending with the Napoleonic Wars (1805–1815). There were religious wars, commercial rivalries, balance-of-power conflicts, and revolutionary wars.

It was also an age of exploration and colonization. The territorial empires of the Spanish, Portuguese, Dutch, British, and French were unevenly developed. The colonial powers occupied the Americas and remained on the perimeters of Africa and Asia. This was due in part to European motives and in part to European resources. The Americas were defenseless against the Europeans. Although Africa was as defenseless as the Americas, it was not as attractive to Europeans. In general, Europeans were content with slaves, gold, and ivory that required only the maintenance of coastal bases there. Asia was not technically feasible for Europeans to acquire: it had powerful political organizations, professional armies, and guns.

Colonial trade in this era was politically controlled. The mercantile regulation of trade began with the Spanish and Portuguese empires, but eventually became common to all core countries with colonial possessions. Regulations included the exclusion of foreign ships from colonial ports, the routing of colonial imports and exports through the ports of the core country, and limitations on the manufacture of certain products in the colonies.

After the Napoleonic Wars, Britain emerged as the hegemonic power, thereby creating a stable core. Competition and conflicts among core powers declined and colonialism receded. The mercantile regulation of trade gave way to an era of free trade in the 1820s. For a short while (1850–1870) Britain controlled the world economy almost single-handedly. As the predominant power, Britain established monopoly relations with most of the periphery and prevented other core countries from interfering with its operations.

British hegemony, however, was short-lived, eroding with the onset of world economic crisis in the 1870s. Germany, Japan, and the United States emerged as major powers. The resulting instability that returned to the core was reflected in the "Second Thirty Years War" (1914–1945) and in a new wave of colonialism in Africa, Asia, and the Pacific. Imperial expansion was especially rapid in Africa after 1880. The mad scramble for colonies forced 96 percent of Africa's territory and perhaps 92 percent of its people into colonial status by 1914 (Figure 13.12). From the last quarter of the nineteenth century onward, trade between the core and the periphery was again more formally regulated. Tariffs rose and economic blocs based on preferences proliferated. Multinational corporations emerged to eventually become dominant actors in the conduct of world business.

By the end of World War II, Western Europe, Japan, and the USSR lay in ruins. The United States alone emerged from the war as a tower of economic and political strength, and when it moved into the vacuum left behind by its competitors, core stability once again became apparent. Colonial holdings disappeared and, in 1947, the General Agreement on Tariffs and Trade set out to liberalize trade along lines more favorable to the United States.

Between 1945 and 1973, the United States was dominant in the Western camp, but the nature and extent of its dominance differed strikingly from Britain's nineteenth-century hegemony. Whereas British dominance involved formal and informal imperialism, American dominance involved foreign direct investment and manipulation of the world monetary system. Moreover, U.S. hegemony was constantly contested by the USSR in the cold war. The British never faced a challenge from a state representing a different image of world order. "Finally, and most importantly, American hegemony [was] achieved through a globalization of the world economy to an extent unknown in previous times. Large American-based multinational corporations [were] major instruments of principles and values" (Agnew 1987, p. 279).

In the 1970s, and 1980s American hegemony was challenged by the recovery or emergence of other capitalist countries; notably, members of the European Economic Community (EEC) and Japan. As before, American military hegemony was challenged by the USSR. Even Third World countries, which had gained access to the international organizations that were created after World War II to reflect American

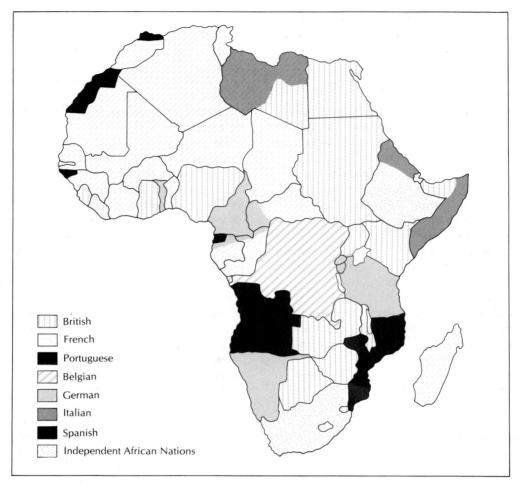

FIGURE 13.12
The mad scramble for colonies in Africa.

interests, began to attack the United States and realize some of their policy objectives.

The core of the world system is moving once again from domination by a hegemonic power to intense competition and rivalry among several states. The Third World is being divided into spheres of influence—arms dependence, political influence, and client states—instead of colonies. The reversal to protectionist policies also signals more formal core-periphery relationships.

REGIONAL DISPARITIES WITHIN UNDERDEVELOPED COUNTRIES

Inherited colonial structures inhibit Third World development efforts in the postindependence era. Major cities of underdeveloped countries are still "export platforms." They link the rich industrial countries and their sources of raw materials. And under the new industrial division of labor they also supply a small core of developed countries with manufactures: engineering and metal products, clothing, and miscellaneous light manufacturing. As a result, modern large-scale enterprise remains concentrated in capital and port cities. Injections of capital into urban economics attract new migrants from rural areas and provincial towns to principal cities. Urban primacy increases. Migrants, absorbed by the system, are maintained at minimal levels. There is little incentive to decentralize urban economic activities. The markedly hierarchical, authoritarian nature of political and social organization retards the diffusion of ideas throughout the urban hierarchy.

The relationships between the different parts of the capitalist system accentuate inequality. Polarizing effects within former colonies concentrate services and innovations at the center, promoting the imbalance between center and periphery. Capital movements, trade flows, internal migration, and institutional controls all tend to have an absolute negative effect on the rate of growth and development of the periphery. In this section, we will survey the persistence of disequilibrium within underdeveloped countries.

The Center-Periphery Concept

The center-periphery concept is one of the most geographical ideas presented by regional analysts. It echoes the Marxist argument that the center appropriates to itself the surplus of the periphery for its own development. The center-periphery phenomenon may be regarded as a multiple system of nested centers and peripheries, like a Chinese puzzle box. At the world level, the global center (rich industrial countries) drains the global periphery (most of the underdeveloped countries). But within any part of the international system, within any national unit, there are other centers and peripheries. Centers at this level, although considerably less powerful, still have sufficient strength to appropriate to themselves a smaller, yet sizeable, fraction of remaining surplus value. A center may be a single urban area, or a region encompassing several towns that stand in an advantageous relation to the hinterland. Even in remote peripheral areas there are likely to be local, regional imbalances, with some areas growing, and others stagnating or declining.

There are reverse flows from the various centers to the peripheries—to peripheral nations, to peripheral rural areas. Yet these flows, themselves, may further accentuate center-periphery differences. In a study of foreign aid to Tanzania for 1971, Giovanni Arrighi and John Saul (1973, p. 278) observed that agreements were concluded for projects that tended to reflect and buttress its dependence upon and integration into the center. World Bank, USAID, and IDA loans generally support major infrastructural projects such as roads and power stations, which are proven money earners, and which reinforce the centrality and drawing power of the cities and the modern export sector of agriculture. AID strongly supports projects dealing with agriculture (so long as they do not upset U.S. farm interests), health and family planning, school construction, and road building; industrialization projects are seldom financed.

For the most part, the infrastructural projects supported by Western and international development agencies aid underdeveloped countries in ways that allow for international capitalism to function. Such

aid generally serves to improve harbors, construct roads and dams, increase levels of health and education, improve urban housing, and train administrators, doctors, and scientists. Factories established by international companies are often built for the assembly and re-export of manufactures at low labor cost. These developments tend to reinforce the status quo of the world economy. The principal beneficiaries are the bourgeoisie of developed and underdeveloped countries. Poor people in their billions are not a problem, but a solution.

Yet many Western social scientists see core regions in underdeveloped countries as " 'beachheads' . . . the centres from which the benefits of modernization flow outwards to revitalize the stagnating agricultural sector" (McGee 1971, p. 13). Such a vision could cast social scientists in the role of augmenting national, regional, and individual inequalities in underdeveloped countries. Let us see why by describing and analyzing some of the major center-dominant models of regional development.

Center-Dominant Models of Regional Development

One view of regional development stems from the studies of neoclassical theorists. They hypothesize that differences between center and periphery are only temporary within a free-market system. Regional development inequalities that occur at first will be corrected by the mobility of factors under pure competition. For example, if wages are higher in Region *A* than in Region *B*, labor will move from the lower paid area to the higher, thereby leading to an adjustment in relative wage rates. Since the mechanism in a free-market economy is self-regulating, no government intervention is necessary: regional differences in wage rates and income will occur automatically. Unfortunately, there is little evidence to support such a view—especially in underdeveloped countries, where perfectly mobile factors of production are hardly characteristic features.

Two models offering an alternative explanation of regional differentials emerged in the late 1950s. Both models suggest that, over time, interaction *increases* rather than *decreases* inequalities between rich and poor regions. The models of Swedish economist Gunnar Myrdal (1957) and American economist Albert Hirschman (1958) indicated that in an underdeveloped country operating under a capitalist system, *deviation-amplifying forces*, rather than *deviation-counteracting forces*, increase and rigidify the differences between center and periphery. "Deviation-amplification" (as opposed to "deviation-reduction") refers to any process that amplifies an initial "kick," and increases divergence from an initial condition.

Myrdal argued that during early stages of development, economic inequalities are increased through the operation of *circular and cumulative causation* (Figure 13.13). He reasoned that "change does not call forth contradicting forces [as equalization models suggest] but, instead, supporting changes, which move the system in the same direction as the first change but much further" (1957, p. 13). According to Myrdal, once growth has been initiated in favored locations in a free economy, inflows of labor, skills, capital, and commodities develop spontaneously to support those locations. The flows, however, induce *backwash effects*, amplifying inequalities between expanding and other regions. Myrdal argued that if events follow an uncontrolled course, backwash effects perpetuate growth in expanding regions and retard growth elsewhere. For development to occur throughout a country, *spread effects* must, on the average, be stronger than backwash effects.

In underdeveloped countries, spread effects very often refer to the benefits that trickle down from a major city to surrounding areas. These may include increased demand for primary commodities, increased investment, and the diffusion of modern

technology. Conversely, backwash effects are the demands by the city on surrounding areas. These may include an inward flow of commodities, capital, and skilled workers. Even a new transport route may initiate backwash. It may permit industrial plants in the growing city to supply stagnating areas with goods formerly supplied by the poor region's own craft industries.

Hirschman advanced a similar model of polarized development. His model shows that once an initial decision is made to locate a particular industry at a specific point, it has an initial multiplier effect, as shown in Figure 13.14. New local demands are generated by the factory and by the purchasing power of its labor force. The labor force creates a demand for housing and for a set of services. The new factory attracts additional industries, producing complementary goods. Linked industries either provide needed inputs or purchase semifinished products from the initial factory. The entire process has a cumulative self-generating momentum; after the first cycle of growth is completed, a new spiral of growth is initiated at a higher threshold. The diagram of circular and accelerative growth illustrates that cycles of growth can be carried through *any* number of times — at least until the process is arrested by diseconomies

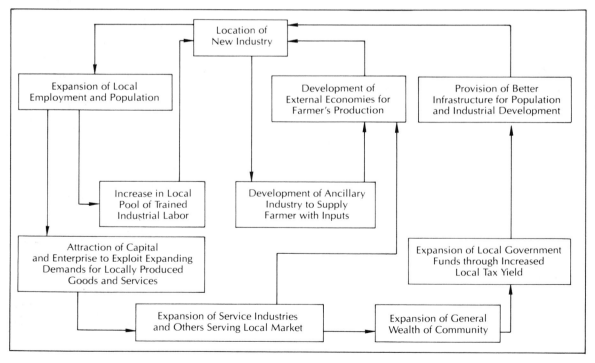

FIGURE 13.13

Myrdal's model of circular or cumulative upward causation. (Source: Keeble, 1967, p. 258.)

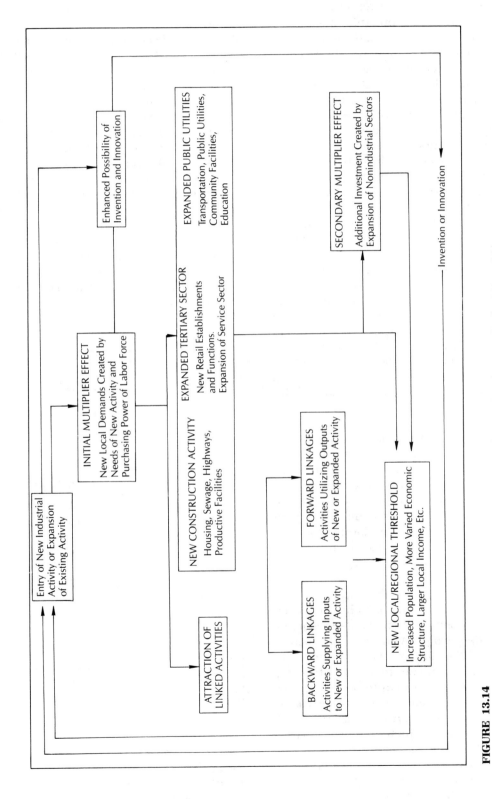

FIGURE 13.14

Initial multiplier effect and the process of cumulative upward causation. (Source: Pred, 1966, p. 25.)

or interrupted by the competitive advantages of other growth points. The diagram also shows that the initial multiplier stimulates expansion of nonindustrial activities; they, in turn, trigger a second multiplier which induces further growth and still higher thresholds.

Thus, through the operation of unrestrained market forces, the center grows, feeding on more and more resources from the hinterland. The result is unbalanced or polarized growth. According to Hirschman, *polarization effects* are offset eventually by *trickling-down effects*—the equivalent of Myrdal's spread effects. However, Hirschman thought that only governments can provide enough incentives for positive trickling-down effects to outweigh negative polarization effects and ensure sustained peripheral growth.

Both Myrdal and Hirschman agreed that a free-enterprise economy encourages center growth at the expense of the periphery, especially in the early stages of development. They differed, however on the role of governments in ameliorating differences between center and periphery. Hirschman believed that governments could reduce inequalities by providing aid to backward regions, or by applying progressive taxation programs. Myrdal, on the other hand, pointed out that governments do not always act in the best interest of lagging regions, and that their activities often tend to accentuate regional differences in income and welfare.

The models of Hirschman and Myrdal help us to understand the process of regional-income divergence, but they do not relate the problem to the interaction between cities and their hinterlands. To some extent this gap has been filled in Western social science by John Friedmann (1966). His descriptive four-stage model relates the process leading to regional inequality to the stage of development and to the city-system typical of that stage (Figure 13.15). Friedmann recognized the following stages of spatial evolution:

1   A *preindustrial phase*, characterized by a number of small independent urban centers spread throughout a large region. With no urban hierarchy, the possibilities for growth are soon exhausted and the economy tends to stagnate. Friedmann assumed the system to be in balance, each center by and large serving only its local area.
2   A period of *incipient-industrialization*, characterized by a primate city (C) which dominates a large region and exploits the natural resources of its periphery (P). Local economies in the periphery are undermined in consequence of a mass movement of would-be entrepreneurs, intellectuals, and

labor to the primate city. Friedmann viewed the primacy-dominated organization of space as unstable, since the system is generated by exogenous forces.

3   A *transitional stage* toward industrial maturation in which the primate city (C) still dominates the large region, but not to the extent that it did previously. The construction of strategically located urban centers or growth centers (SC_1 and SC_2) reduces the influence of the large city. Friedmann regarded the third stage as still unstable due to the persistence of "backwardness" in peripheral areas (P_1, P_2, P_3, and P_4).
4   A final stage consisting of a *fully-fledged spatial organization* based on the hierarchy principle and encompassing the entire national territory. According to Friedmann, this functionally interdependent system of cities will fulfill essential goals of internal spatial organization such as national integration, efficiency of location, maximum growth potential, and a high degree of interregional balance.

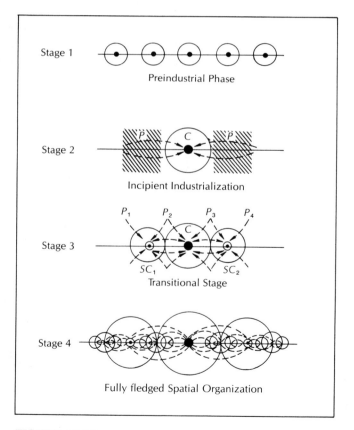

FIGURE 13.15
Friedmann's stages of spatial evolution. (Source: Friedmann, 1966, p. 36.)

Friedmann's evolutionary model posits ultimate convergence between center and periphery. He emphasized the prolonged nature of the process, convergence occurring only when a society has reached an advanced stage of industrial maturation. Friedmann suggested, however, that continued urban-industrial expansion in major metropolitan areas should lead to catalytic impacts on surrounding regions. He offered a number of propositions which reflect the ongoing urban-regional development process in the United States. The propositions, which have an explicit link with central-place theory and innovation-diffusion theory, are as follows:

> Economic growth takes place in a matrix of urban regions through which the space economy is organized. . . . Cities organize the space economy. They are centers of activity and of innovation, focal points of the transport network, locations of superior accessibility at which firms can most easily reap scale economies and at which industrial complexes can obtain the economies of localization and urbanization. Agricultural enterprise is more efficient in the vicinity of cities. The more prosperous commercialized agricultures encircle the major cities. . . . There are two major elements in this organization of economic activities in space:
>
> (a) A system of cities, organized in a hierarchy according to the functions performed by each;
> (b) Corresponding areas of urban influence or urban fields surrounding each of the cities in the system.
>
> Generally we can argue the following about this system of spatial organization:
>
> (a) The size and function of a central city and the size of the urban field are proportional.
> (b) The spatial incidence of economic growth is a function of distance from the central city. Troughs of economic backwardness lie in the most inaccessible areas along the intermetropolitan peripheries.
> (c) Impulses of economic change are transmitted in order from higher to lower centers in the urban hierarchy, in a "size-rachet" sequence, so that continued innovation in large cities remains critical for extension of growth over the complete economic system.
> (d) The growth potential of an area situated along an axis between two cities is a function of the intensity of interaction between them. (Cited in Berry, 1969a, p. 288)

Brian Berry concurred with Friedmann that Western growth theory suggests that cities are gateways for development, transmitting economic change to smaller centers. Berry noted, however, that growth impulses do not always "trickle down" from town to country. "As a consequence, growth and stagnation polarize; the economic system remains unarticulated" (Berry 1969b, p. 207). Here, Western regional science recommends that planners provide a hierarchy of growth centers to link central cities with interstitial areas. In this hierarchy, "growth impulses and economic advancement should 'trickle down' to smaller places and ultimately infuse dynamism into even the most tradition-bound peripheries (Berry 1969a, p. 288). Cities, as centers of influence over regional and national hinterlands, are catalysts to development.

Those who favor the center-dominant thesis argue that "the history of the West from the nineteenth century onward is being reiterated in the underdeveloped countries today" (Reissman 1964, p. 158). However, according to André Gunder Frank (1969) or to Lin Piao (1965), both of whom acidly see cities as capitalist structures, this article of faith is nothing more than colonialism thinly disguised. According to Frank, cities in underdeveloped countries are centers of colonial domination. In the service of international capitalism, they subject regional and national hinterlands to economic "satellitization" and exploitation. Certain forms of international influence and manipulation condition the structure of urban systems in underdeveloped countries; thus, mercantile cities are dependent on overseas metropolitan centers, and they in turn dominate domestic fields of influence. This view calls into question Friedmann's assumption that urbanization is necessarily coupled with development. On the contrary, it asserts that unless external dependency is eliminated, the urbanization process stimulates the underdevelopment of hinterlands.

THE PROTO-PROLETARIAT

Many political and economic theorists in underdeveloped countries argue that center-periphery relationships are features of the world economy that contribute strongly to the poverty of peasants in the rural areas and their urban counterparts, the *proto-proletariat*, who often inhabit squatter settlements. In a world viewed as a set of von Thünen rings, the peasants and proto-proletariat exist at its outer fringe—poor and discriminated against with respect to use and control of the world's resources (Figure 13.16). Their access to credit, insurance, manufactured goods, technical knowledge, and infrastructure is virtually nil.

FIGURE 13.16
The world's stratified society.
(Source: de Souza and Porter,
1974, p. 81.)

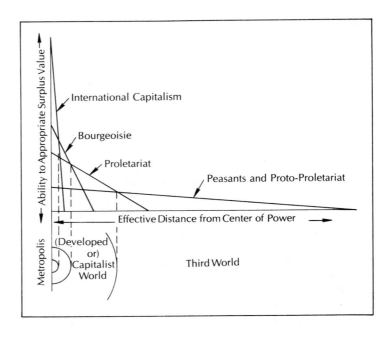

Let us have a closer look at the proto-proletariat as an example of a marginal social formation, the rapid growth of which is tied to the metropolitan intrusion into underdeveloped countries. Members of the proto-proletariat are engaged primarily in the economic activity of the "traditional" as opposed to the "modern" sector—therefore, they are not regular wage earners. In underdeveloped countries, urban and rural areas have a dual economy: one sector "traditional" and the other an intrusive "modern" sector. These two sectors do not exist independently side by side; they are interlaced and unequal.

Urban Growth with Dependent Industrialization

Fundamental to the development of the United States was its emphasis on the domestic requirements of the national economy. The first need to be met was food, followed by the establishment of producer-goods and mass-consumption-goods industries. By contrast, the allocation of economic resources in most underdeveloped countries is topsy-turvy. Urban-industrial growth takes priority over rural development. Industrial growth is increasingly based on the production and export of manufactures. The chief beneficiaries of this kind of dependent industrialization are the already wealthy people of developed and underdeveloped countries. Except for a few privileged industrial workers, the broad mass of population is more or less excluded from the export-oriented economy.

Although urban areas have achieved remarkable industrialization since 1945, industrial employment has not kept pace with population growth. The employment situation has been aggravated by the introduction of advanced technology that permits high worker-output ratios. As a consequence, the proto-proletariat is absorbed by small-scale family enterprises, personal services, and unemployment. Its members are victims of urban growth with dependent industrialization, which itself is a consequence of the internationalization of direct production capital.

A Neglected Occupational Element

Today alarm is voiced about an impoverished and jobless class in Third World cities. But until the late 1960s, most social scientists failed to examine the proto-proletariat for at least three reasons. First, there was lack of data. Most systems of data collection recorded activities of the wage-earning population only. Second, most development models tended to concentrate on the economic growth features of the *modern* sector, to the exclusion of the *traditional* sector. Third, the modern-traditional dichotomy—a major evolutionary theory of social and economic change—encouraged social scientists to view development as the intrusion of traditional systems by Western elements of modernization.

By the late 1960s there was a growing awareness of the size and activities of the proto-proletariat. Again, three main factors may be suggested. First, a group of writings drew attention to the emergence of the proto-proletariat as a major element in the class structure of urban areas. Frantz Fanon's (1963) *The Wretched of the Earth* and André Gunder Frank's (1969) *Capitalism and Underdevelopment in Latin America* are examples. Second, members of international organizations such as the United Nations drew attention to the grave employment problem in most cities of the underdeveloped world. Finally, some scholars began to examine their own recommendations for development. More specifically, these scholars were questioning the validity of equating development with Western economic growth. Some of their disillusionment traced to the ecological and energy crises in developed countries. They began to exhibit less interest in capital-intensive systems of production and more interest in labor-intensive systems of production that minimize waste and pollution and that do not rely on high-energy consumption of fossil fuels.

Those who now study the proto-proletariat in the urban economies of underdeveloped countries may be divided into two main groups. One group sees the process of occupational formation as *evolutionary*. In this view, problems posed by the proto-proletariat are temporary. With continued economic growth, the proto-proletariat will be absorbed into the bourgeoisie, just as in nineteenth-century Europe. The other group sees the process of occupational formation as *involutionary*. Comparison of the accelerated curve of technological evolution on the one hand, and of population explosion on the other, leads this group to fear the permanent establishment of an impoverished and jobless class. High rates of population growth in town and country, together with a large volume of urban migration, pose a constraint on labor absorption in capital-intensive enterprises. The result is mass unemployment and a proliferation of mainly service activities.

Despite the rapid growth of modern-sector activity in the 1970s and 1980s, it seems unlikely that most Third World cities will be able to provide labor-absorptive environments in the 1990s. With slower growth at the center of the world economy, the export-oriented route to industrialization in the periphery may be cut off. Moreover, demographic projections also support the view that the process of occupational formation is involutionary. Trends indicate that cities in the underdeveloped world will absorb more than a billion people between 1980 and the year 2000. Population growth of this magnitude— from 972 million city dwellers in 1980 to 2,115 million in 2000—will ensure that unemployment and under-

employment will remain acute problems for years, especially in population giants such as India.

Defining the Proto-Proletariat

Thus far, we have noted that the proto-proletariat is a persistent and expanding class of people, but we have not delineated precisely who these people are. We can define the proto-proletariat in terms of structural, institutional, and income dimensions.

First, members of the the proto-proletariat conduct their activities within one sector of the dualistic structure of a Third World city (Figure 13.17). American anthropologist Clifford Geertz (1963) divided the structure of a Third World city into two economies: (1) a *firm-centered economy* (modern and capital-intensive), where trade and industry occur through a set of impersonally defined social institutions with a variety of specialized occupations organized with respect to some particular or distributive ends, and (2) a *bazaar economy* (traditional and labor-intensive), based on the independent activities of a set of highly competitive commodity traders who do business mainly by means of an incredible volume of ad hoc acts of exchange.

This model was refined by Milton Santos (1971; 1977) and G. Missen and M. Logan (1977). Santos emphasized the interlocking nature of the firm-centered economy and the bazaar economy. He viewed these as circuits, each with its own internal flow. The firm-centered economy, the *upper circuit*, and the bazaar sector, the *lower circuit*, have the following characteristics, respectively: capital-intensive versus labor-intensive technology; bureaucratic versus family organization; abundant versus scarce capital; fixed versus negotiable prices; regulated versus unregulated hours of work; bank versus noninstitutionalized credit; indirect versus direct client relations; significant versus insignificant government; and strong versus weak dependence on foreign countries. Members of the proto-proletariat operate in the lower circuit of the urban economy.

Missen and Logan noted that the upper circuit is a network of enterprises enjoined in the urban hierarchy, whereas the lower circuit is a swelling "globule" of small-scale enterprises functioning within each town, but not directly related with other towns (Figure 13.18). They also pointed out that

> at the national scale, the upper circuit reaches into the rural areas to link with the estates, loggers, and mines of the capitalist enterprises and with the more productive of the small farming regions. While the urban field of the modern distribution

FIGURE 13.17
The economic setting of the
Third World primate city.
(Source: McGee, 1971, p. 70.)

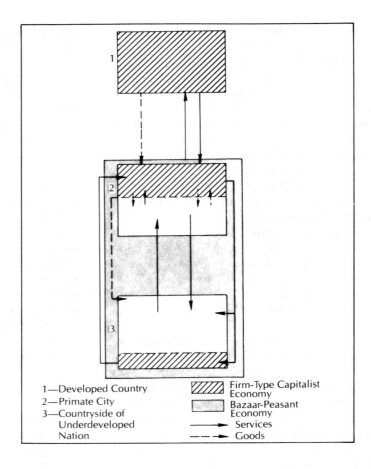

1—Developed Country
2—Primate City
3—Countryside of
   Underdeveloped
   Nation

Firm-Type Capitalist
Economy
Bazaar-Peasant
Economy
Services
Goods

FIGURE 13.18
The Third World urban system.
(Source: Missen and Logan,
1977, p. 61.)

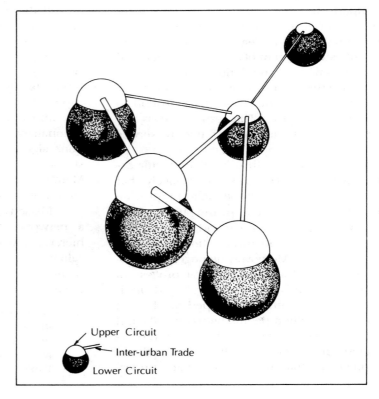

Upper Circuit
Inter-urban Trade
Lower Circuit

FIGURE 13.19
Third World national and regional trade. (Source: Missen and Logan, 1977, p. 62.)

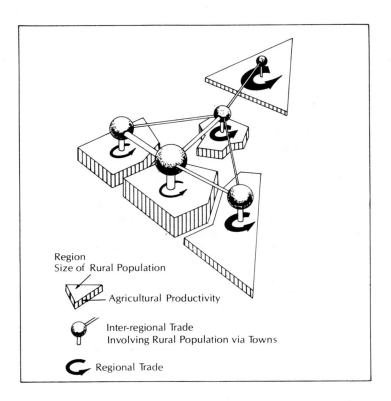

Region
Size of Rural Population

— Agricultural Productivity

Inter-regional Trade
Involving Rural Population via Towns

Regional Trade

system is greatest around the main cities, the significant feature of this circuit is that it is selective in its spatial links: thus, in the main field there may be pockets of local farmers isolated from the national circuit, while in the poor peripheral areas the modern sector may tap isolated mines and logging camps. Beneath this circuit lies the lower circuit localized by regions. The energy which drives the local circuit is partly derived from its connections with the upper circuit . . . and is partly fed by local commodity production and abundant local labor. (1977, pp. 60–61) (Figure 13.19)

Second, the proto-proletariat may be defined institutionally. There are three systems of production: capitalist, socialist, and peasant. Like small farmers in the countryside, the proto-proletariat are engaged in a peasant system, but within the urban environment.

Third, the proto-proletariat may be defined in terms of income opportunities (Table 13.2). *Formal* income opportunities are associated with the legal activities of the upper circuit. *Informal* income opportunities, both legal and illegal, are associated with activities of the lower circuit. The proto-proletariat gain income mainly from informal opportunities.

On the basis of structural, institutional, and income dimensions, it is possible to define the proto-proletariat as a substantial group engaged in a peasant system of production in the lower circuit and deriving income mainly from informal opportunities.

Economic, Ecological, and Political Features

Economic   Some economists, Arthur Lewis (1954) for one, have suggested that the economic activities of the proto-proletariat are unproductive. Moreover, these economists believe that the number of occupations can be reduced without decreasing output. In other words, there is "hidden unemployment" or "disguised unemployment" in the traditional sector. Various estimates have been made of the percentage of adult male population that can be withdrawn from a local economy without impairing productivity. The Firestone Plantation Company used a figure of 30 percent of Liberia's healthy adult male population in the 1950s.

Although nobody has any idea how much the economic activities of the proto-proletariat contribute to total income generated in the Third World city, it is clear that this group is engaged in an immense range of activities:

1   trade and transportation activities—taxi and truck operators, wholesalers, market vendors, and street traders;
2   services—self-employed mechanics, car washers, shoe cleaners, and bicycle-tire pumpers;
3   industrial activities—food preparers, furniture makers, carvers, and potters; and
4   financial activities—money lenders.

TABLE 13.2
Income opportunities in a Third World city.

Formal Income Opportunities
  (a) Public sector wages.
  (b) Private sector wages.
  (c) Transfer payments—pensions, unemployment benefits.

Informal Income Opportunities: Legal
  (a) Primary and secondary activities—farming, market gardening, building contractors and associated activities, self-employed artisans, shoemakers, tailors, manufacturers of beers and spirits.
  (b) Tertiary enterprises with relatively large capital inputs—housing, transport, utilities, commodity speculation, rentier activities.
  (c) Small-scale distribution—market operatives, petty traders, street hawkers, caterers in food and drink, bar attendants, carriers, commission agents, and dealers.
  (d) Other services—musicians, launderers, shoeshiners, barbers, night-soil removers, photographers, vehicle repair and other maintenance workers; brokerage; ritual services, magic, and medicine.
  (e) Private transfer payments—gifts and similar flows of money and goods between persons; borrowing; begging.

Informal Income Opportunities: Illegal
  (a) Services—hustlers and spivs, receivers of stolen goods; usury, and pawnbroking (at illegal interest rates); drug-pushing, prostitution, poncing, smuggling, bribery, political corruption Tammany Hall-style, protection rackets.
  (b) Transfers—petty theft (e.g., pickpockets), larceny (e.g., burglary and armed robbery), embezzlement, confidence tricksters (e.g., money doublers), gambling.

SOURCE: McGee, 1974.

The relative importance of lower circuit economic activities compared to the upper circuit varies inversely with city size (Figure 13.20). In absolute terms, however, the volume and degree of specialization of activities varies directly with the importance of cities. Whereas in the small city, the economic activities of the proto-proletariat sometimes replace nonexistent modern services, in the large city the activities of this class serve growing populations that do not have regular access to upper circuit activities, and also may function as external economies for upper circuit activities (Santos 1977, pp. 53–4).

Ecological Members of the proto-proletariat inhabit three main ecological milieu: they live on streets, rivers, canals, or waterfronts; in overcrowded inner-city slums; and in squatter settlements on the outskirts of cities. Squatter homes are built of makeshift materials, and sanitation and water facilities are often inadequate. Squatter settlements are far from ideal, but they do form an integral part of the informal sector, and they embody a number of features that favor the activities of the proto-proletariat.

Consider some of the advantages of squatter settlements. They contribute to capital formation in the housing sector and add to social overhead in the form of schools, churches, and halls. They offer the proto-proletariat work, both full-time and part-time. They support economic pursuits—bars, restaurants, repair shops, grocers, and fruit stores. They stimulate

the growth of markets. Their strong social organization lends support to the proto-proletariat in times of crises. Squatter settlements enable residents to live close to work, to carry out activities such as food preparation that are subject to legal restriction in the modern sector, to employ labor of all ages, and to conceal illegal activities, such as the preparation of drugs. Since they are often illegal, squatter settlements also enable residents, at least in theory, to live tax- and rent-free.

Although most politicians and planners believe that cities offer the best hope for the future of underdeveloped countries, they tend to condemn squatter settlements. Two solutions to the "squatter problem" are generally advocated. One is to replace "uncontrolled" settlements with housing projects. The other is to tear down the settlements and send the squatters back to the countryside. Now, however, a third solution is being considered: government help for projects undertaken by residents. Through the provision of suitable sites, of water and sanitation services, and of technical assistance for building, governments can accelerate housing improvements.

Political Some observers (Fanon 1963) liken the proto-proletariat to a revolutionary force. They argue that the unequal distribution of power and wealth within cities of the underdeveloped world frustrates, angers, and alienates the urban poor. But Terry McGee (1971, pp. 64–94), in one of the most interest-

A greengrocer in Kathmandu, Nepal. The informal sector helps city dwellers in the Third World to cope with the employment problem. In fact, it is often the only means of survival for the large underclass of urban poor who have little hope of gaining employment in the formal sector. (Source: UNESCO/Cart.)

FIGURE 13.20
Relative importance of the two circuits in the systems of Third World cities. (Source: Santos, 1977, p. 54.)

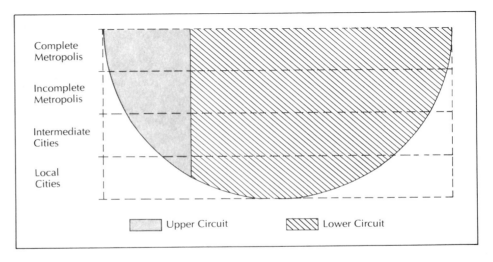

Complete Metropolis

Incomplete Metropolis

Intermediate Cities

Local Cities

Upper Circuit   Lower Circuit

ing applications of Clifford Geertz's (1963) involutionary construct, argued that "the dualist economic structure of the Third World city and its relationship with the rural hinterland will prevent the emergence of . . . a revolutionary demand among the urban poor in the short term" (p. 28). He illustrated how available income is spread through a system of reciprocity, which facilitates the absorption of an ever-larger proto-proletariat population.

According to McGee, the traditional sector acts as a safety valve and maintains the social and political status quo; but the traditional sector in a Third World city is heavily dependent upon the existence of a traditional agricultural resource base, and the activities and policies of the modern sector. He argued that "under conditions of penetration of the traditional structure—whether in the city or in the countryside—by capitalist modes of production and/or appropriation, traditional labour absorptive capacity would fall and the polarization between the modern capital-intensive sector [and the unemployed proto-proletariat] would come out into the open" (p. 85) (Figure 13.21).

It "came out into the open" in Cuba during the late 1950s. Western imperialism penetrated to such an extent that indigenous urban-rural involution was unable to develop further, creating a revolutionary situation. Such a situation was averted in Jamaica and Puerto Rico where an additional safety valve, external migration to Britain and the United States, was operative. Of course, other "Cubas" are not inevitable. Underdeveloped countries are at various stages of capitalist penetration. Much will depend on the degree of penetration by Western capital, the ability of political leaders to set the terms under which the capital penetrates, and the ability of political leaders to solve internal problems of development within their own societies.

Policy Issues

The proto-proletariat is a direct result of the export-led economic model pursued in many underdeveloped countries. This model prescribes that the mass of people of the underdeveloped world work for others, not for themselves. It ensures a continuing

FIGURE 13.21
The economic setting of the Third World primate city (dynamic model). (Source: McGee, 1971, p. 87.)

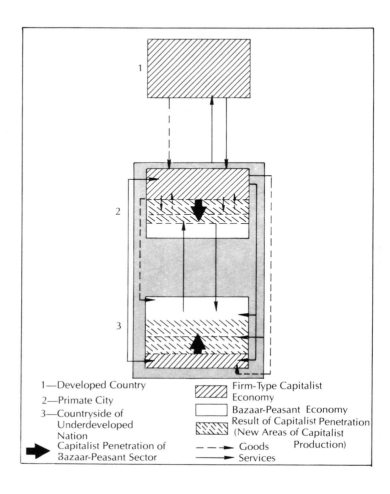

1—Developed Country
2—Primate City
3—Countryside of Underdeveloped Nation

Capitalist Penetration of Bazaar-Peasant Sector

Firm-Type Capitalist Economy
Bazaar-Peasant Economy
Result of Capitalist Penetration (New Areas of Capitalist Production)
- - -► Goods
——— Services

process of underdevelopment that will encourage the growth of population in most Third World cities. Planning strategies will be necessary to cope with exacerbating unemployment and poverty. If the traditional pejorative view of the proto-proletariat prevails, policies will be devised to eliminate their activities. Conversely, if more positive views prevail, policies may be designed to increase income and growth of the traditional sector. Policies should be directed toward improving rural life and reversing, or at least slowing, the trend toward urban development at the expense of the rural areas. They should also be directed toward solving the unprecedented crisis in basic-needs satisfaction.

THE BASIC-NEEDS CRISIS

The United Nations Development Decades of the 1960s, 1970s, and 1980s held out promise of freeing the people of the Third World from poverty, ignorance, and disease. Hundreds of development plans were generated by experts in the interest of achieving this ambitious goal. Despite all the years of effort, however, the Third World still faces a basic-needs crisis in the 1990s.

In *Stranglehold on Africa*, René Dumont, a French expert on agricultural economics, and Marie-France Mottin (1983) demonstrated that the basic-needs crisis is far more acute now than it was during colonial times. They placed much of the blame for the worsening crisis on Third World leaders who took the Western model as their starting point for development. This model, based on the philosophy of Walt Rostow (1960), indicates that poor countries have only to replay the industrial revolution essentially as it happened in the West to arrive at a position where all their people will enjoy wealth—the wealth of a mass-consumer society.

The model emphasizes economic growth in the hope that benefits will trickle down to the poor. But in the incoherent economies of the Third World, growth in gross national product (GNP) does not filter down to the masses. Moreover, it is the composition and distribution of GNP—not its absolute size or rate of growth—that is critical for the social welfare of poor people. A graph of the relationship between GNP per capita and the Physical Quality of Life Index (PQLI) shows that a large increase in income per capita is neither a necessary nor a sufficient condition for improving the social welfare of poor people (Figure 13.22). The case of Sri Lanka illustrates that some of the more pressing needs can be met even at quite low levels of income per head. The PQLI was developed by

M. D. Morris (1979) to measure the condition of the world's poor. On the basis of three indicators—life expectancy at age one, infant mortality, and adult literacy—each country can score from 0 to 100.

Faced by failure of the income-oriented approach to development, some scholars began to hammer out a basic-needs approach in the late 1970s (Streeten 1981). The approach is based on the assumption that the essential needs of all—food, clothing, shelter, water, and sanitation—should be satisfied before the less essential needs of a few are met. Although there is almost universal agreement on this objective, there is little agreement on the most effective way of achieving it.

One method of implementation—the count, cost, and deliver approach—consists of counting the number of the deprived, figuring out the cost of the goods and services needed to eradicate deprivation, and delivering them to target groups. Another approach focuses on providing economic opportunities for the poor, raising their productivity, and improving their access to both inputs and markets. A third approach involves seeking out processes by which the system that perpetuates poverty can be destroyed or reformed.

American geographer Lakshman Yapa (1980) favors the last approach. He argues that the allocation of resources to basic needs cannot be divorced from the circumstances of the means of production. Therefore, the direct eradication of poverty must proceed from a study of the institutions that tend to maintain poverty.

The Development of Underdevelopment

Contrary to what is commonly believed, underdevelopment is not a state caused by physical and cultural factors, subject to the corrective influence of modernization. What is critical to underdevelopment is a world economic structure that perpetuates backwardness. To illustrate, let us trace the development of underdevelopment in Kenya.

For the last hundred years, Kenya's dominant groups have not placed a high priority on the production of goods for mass consumption. Consistently, the surplus has been diverted elsewhere resulting in the preemption of the basic-goods fund. During the colonial era, a portion of the surplus went to enrich Britain and the European elite of Kenya.

In the late nineteenth century, European settlers established the Scheduled Areas—three million hectares of mainly moist, high-potential land alienated for the use of Europeans. A major objective of establishing the Scheduled Areas was to transform part of the

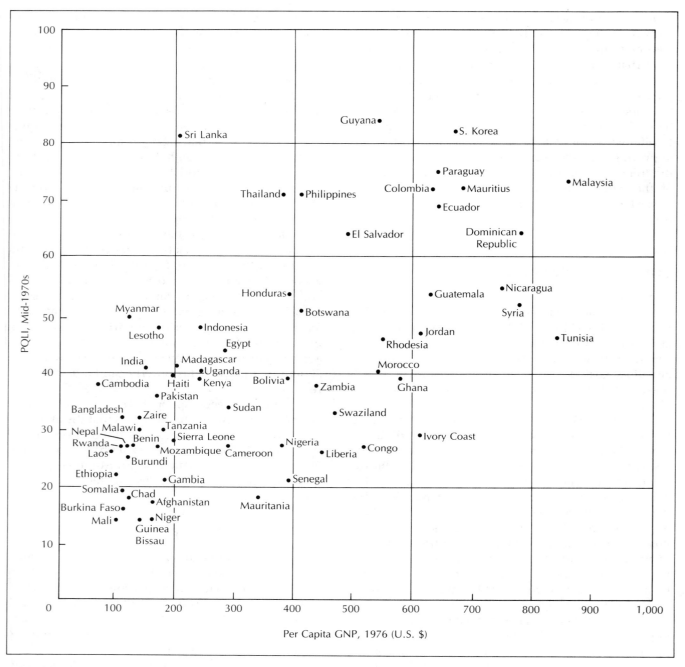

FIGURE 13.22

The relationship between the Physical Quality of Life Index, mid-1970s, and gross national product per capita, 1976. (Source: Compiled from data in Morris, 1979, and World Bank, 1978.)

African population into a proletarian labor force to serve the needs of the capitalist sector. Africans were needed to work on the farms, ranches, plantations, and other enterprises owned and run by the European settlers. Because simple commodity production of indigenous agriculture enabled Africans to be more or less self-sufficient, it became necessary to upset that self-sufficiency and mandate that they supply their labor. A labor force came into being through various actions on the part of the British.

An early device (1902) was the hut tax, which was replaced a year later by a pole tax payable by all adults when it was discovered that people were crowding into fewer houses. Other means included the regulation and confiscation of African livestock and the control of wages. Europeans encouraged Africans to live on their farms and estates as squatters rather than to work as contract laborers. Africans were prohibited from growing coffee, tea, sisal, and pyrethrum, and from selling livestock and dairy products on the European export market. They were paid a lower market price for corn than were European farmers. They could not open shops without a government license, and they had no access to credit. Europeans, on the other hand, were assisted at every turn. The road and rail network that focused on Nairobi and Mombasa served the alienated land—a built-in locational advantage that helped Europeans market their produce. European settlers could acquire land cheaply. They received agricultural research and extension services. They were given tax breaks on imported equipment and exported crops. The government helped Europeans recruit labor and obtain credit.

This arsenal of devices, from inequitable taxes to dual pricing systems, illustrates the manner in which the European capitalist sector served its own ends. The capitalist sector forced Africans to buy more goods and services from Europeans, substituted market uncertainty for ecological uncertainly for the African people, and, because of high rates of African population growth, the result was overcrowding and tremendous land fragmentation, as well as landlessness on the reserves.

At the peak of the *colonial division of labor* in 1960, the European highlands had 3,600 Europeans in agriculture, overseeing an African labor force of 268,000, about seventy-five workers per farm. Europeans received a per capita income of $29,450 for commercial agriculture, whereas Africans received, $3.50. "The rate of profit in 1960, taking into account replacement of capital investment, loan repayments, and the wage bill, was over 130 percent" (Porter 1979, p. 49).

The end result of the colonial organization of space and division of labor was Mau-Mau, the Swynnerton Plan, and independence for Kenya in 1963. Mau-Mau was a land rebellion, a violent uprising of Africans, mainly Kikuyu, against European colonial authority. The war began in 1951 and ebbed in 1957. Eventually it led to independence, but immediately to major social changes, particularly concerning land rights. Reform began in 1954 when a Royal Commission investigating the land grievances behind Mau-Mau recommended sweeping changes. The Commission's work led to the 1955 Swynnerton Plan, which called for consolidating small parcels of land, giving Africans access to credit, to farmer training, to research findings, to technical assistance, and to improved water supplies. It also called for lifting the ban on Africans from growing coffee and other cash crops. The objective of the Plan was to encourage the development of an agrarian middle class.

The policies of the colonial period were carried on into the postcolonial period, despite the fact that Africans rather than Europeans were making decisions. International trade played an ideological function by representing the various needs of the elite as coincident with the interests of the nation at large, legitimatizing the continued preemption of the basic-goods fund. Within Kenya, many of the larger farms were left intact and in the hands of individuals. Moreover, there was an extension of the Swynnerton European Highlands model to the high-potential former reserves. Consequently, the whole highlands became "a developing core following a market-oriented private entrepreneurial path of development. The semi-arid areas . . . continued to play the role of periphery—the location of landless migrants who try to farm areas drier than they are experienced with, the source areas of male migrants who work for farmers in the highlands." (Porter 1979, p. 53).

The postindependence period witnessed the continued functioning of three processes which result from modernization and which exert great influence on the basic-needs crisis. They are proletarianization, marginalization, and commodification. *Proletarianization* is the process that separates people from the means of production (land) so that they begin to sell their labor power. *Marginalization* is the process that forces people to sell land in order to survive. And *commodification* is the process whereby a good or service, normally considered free, comes to be exchanged for a price on the market. For example, with the privatization of land ownership, conventional rights to water and vegetation entered the marketplace.

Fuelwood and Basic-Needs Satisfaction

The process of underdevelopment has made it impossible for all Kenyans to live full lives. It has created and sustained a crisis in basic-needs satisfaction. To illustrate this crisis, let us take as our example the case of fuelwood. Fuelwood relates to other basic-needs goods and services in three ways. First, it can satisfy other basic needs through its sale. Second, it can complement the satisfaction of other basic needs—house construction (shelter need), fruits (nutrition need). Third, it can compete with the satisfaction of other basic needs (Table 11.3). The conflict between a need for fuelwood and other basic needs may be in terms of the allocation of land, labor, and money.

Fuelwood/Nutrition Conflict Allocation of land for the growth of cash crops for commodified basic-needs satisfaction produces a conflict between nutrition and fuel needs. The cash crop displaces food production, intensifying land-use competition for the remaining decreased area available for food production. As fallow periods decrease or disappear, fuelwood/food

competition intensifies. Fuelwood from secondary regrowth on fallow land becomes less abundant. Its acquisition shifts from the fallow zone to the public domain. This increases the distance that must be covered to collect the volume of wood required for basic survival purposes. When fallow land reaches zero, fertilizer must be purchased, leading to a fuelwood/nutrition conflict over scarce income.

Many small farmers are locked into a cost-price squeeze whereby the prices they are paid for small quantities of cash crops fail to keep pace with the cost of essentials they must purchase. One response is to

A woman gathering wood kindling in Sub-Saharan Africa. (Source: World Bank.)

TABLE 13.3
Conflict between fuelwood need
and other basic needs.

Basic Need with Which Fuelwood Need Is in Conflict	Area of Competition		
	Labor-Time	Money	Land
Nutrition	X	X	X
Housing		X	X
Clothing		X	X
Education	X	X	
Health	X	X	
Water	X		
Transportation	X	X	

grow more cash crops, displacing more food acreage and putting additional pressure on fuelwood/food-crop competition.

As more and more food must come off less land, the labor of women, who are generally responsible for food production, increases. The use of crop-improvement packages requires more labor to plant, weed, and to dust crops with insecticides. The hardship for women is intensified by the need to travel farther and farther for wood. The time devoted to food production and wood collection reduces the amount of time that can be spent on food preparation. As a result, many Kenyan households have switched from more nutritious mixed grain/legume meals to prepackaged refined maize meals. They have also switched from eating two meals a day to one meal a day.

Other Conflicts Fuelwood need is also in conflict with other basic needs. There is competition over shelter and fuel needs. Wood may be used for house construction or for fuel. Money may be spent on charcoal or on an aluminum sheet roof. There is a clothing/fuelwood conflict. Here the competition is monetary; for example, school uniforms must be purchased for children. There is an education/fuelwood conflict. Families spend hundred of shillings to pay primary and secondary school fees. In addition, school attendance draws child labor away from fuelwood collection and haulage. There is a health/fuelwood conflict. A visit to a clinic involves the cost of treatment and transport as well as travel time. About 85 percent of rural families are more than two kilometers from a health center and 51 percent of them are more than six kilometers away. There is a water/fuelwood conflict. One to two liters of water daily is a physiological necessity; without it, people cannot survive. For a reasonable minimum standard of living, people need a daily twenty-five to forty liters of water for drinking, food preparation, and personal

hygiene. In semiarid areas in the dry season, water is not readily available. The time-consuming task of fetching it from sources that may be three to six kilometers away diverts women from fuelwood collection. There is also a transport/fuelwood conflict. Here competition is in the area of cash expenditures and labor time. In many parts of Kenya, people are a long way from public transport facilities. Easy access to public transport would give women more time to meet fuelwood and other basic needs.

In a country where at least 40 percent of the farming population have incomes scarcely sufficient to provide them with the necessities of life, the whole interrelated system of basic needs is in crisis. The crisis is primarily a social one, and with regard to some needs—water and fuelwood—an increasingly environmental crisis. For most other Third World countries, a similar story of people unable to earn or obtain the necessities for full life could be told.

Policy Issues

Given the existing world system and the impossibility of providing each family with a Western-style middle-class basket of goods, it seems that the only way for economic development to improve the living conditions of the Third World poor is to use resources directly in the production and distribution of basic goods. Issues that are central to implementing that goal include questions related to overpopulation and population growth, questions of productive forces, questions of the social relations of production, and questions related to the role of the international community.

A direct attack to reduce population growth is often regarded as a way to increase available resources to satisfy basic needs. However, overpopulation is the result of the exclusion of people from their means of livelihood. "Irrational as it may seem, high

This Ghanian woman is collecting water from a well dug into the bed of a dried-up pond. Easy access to an adequate supply of safe water would spare women from the time-consuming task of fetching it and free them to better attend to other basic needs. (Source: World Bank.)

fertility rates are a rational response to this externally induced condition" (Yapa 1985, p. 246). Government-sponsored fertility control programs will be unsuccessful unless they are accompanied by concomitant programs for providing jobs and changing conditions of employment.

Some observers wonder whether the productive resources are available to employ the millions of urban and rural poor. Much depends on the social relations of production and the choice of technology. Limited employment in the export-processing zones is one of the main causes of urban poverty. And unequal access to land is one the prime determinants of rural poverty. In many countries, under 10 percent of landowners control anywhere from 80 to 90 percent of the land (World Bank 1974). The large farms concentrate on the cultivation of crops for export. Removed from the land, the rural poor cannot produce food themselves; neither can they purchase their basic needs in the marketplace. Export-oriented agriculture and export-led industrialization block the development of an indigenous, self-expanding economy in most Third World countries.

Most of the technology used in the Third World also arrests autonomous development. Capital-intensive technology, which comes from and is designed to reproduce the social and consumption systems of the advanced industrial countries, keeps poor countries dependent. This imported technology is also inappropriate in countries with large supplies of labor. Studies have shown that a considerable range of technology is available, and the least-cost choice often lies closer to the labor-intensive than the capital-intensive end of the spectrum (Pickett 1977).

The international community can do much to eradicate poverty. If the New International Economic Order (NIEO) were adopted, it could generate more resources for underdeveloped countries, and those resources could be channeled directly into providing basic human needs. Acceptance of the NIEO, however, appears to be highly unlikely in the face of opposition not only from developed countries, but from underdeveloped countries as well. The elites of center countries have vested interests to protect. And so do elites of the periphery who prefer to remain an appendage of, and dependent upon, the advanced industrial countries.

The basic-needs approach to development is one positive way to help the poor emerge from their poverty. But this approach is still viewed with suspicion by those who hold to the premise that history can repeat itself, so that the wealth of a mass-consumer society eventually will be enjoyed by all. The wretched of the earth cannot wait for the benefits of growth to spread from the top downward. They need a basic-needs approach—an approach that emphasizes the fundamental concern of development, which is human beings and their needs. This approach, viewed by many as laudable but idealistic, was promised when John F. Kennedy launched the first Development Decade in the United Nations in 1960. Without a direct attack on the basic-needs crisis, there will be more than half a billion absolutely poor people in the underdeveloped countries at the end of this century (World Bank 1979).

SUMMARY

In this chapter, we considered problems of Third World development. We began by discussing goals for development and by listing objectives that are by and large universally endorsed. We then explored typical characteristics of underdevelopment—overpopulation, lack of resources, capital shortage—considering the question of whether or not these attributes can be properly construed as causative factors.

In discussing major perspectives on development we saw how modernization theories, which stress economic growth and Westernization, have obscured important aspects of underdevelopment. World political economy theories explain why the Third World does not develop. They touch on a fundamental concept: Underdevelopment is a world economic structure that perpetuates backwardness. Ecopolitical economy theories question the desirability of the income-oriented approach, instead emphasizing the feasibility of the basic-needs approach to development.

Some scholars believe that the economic dimension of the development process has been overemphasized by development theorists. Culture plays an important role in the process, too. For example, the rise of Japan as a tower of economic strength can be understood only in terms of the country's unique isomorphism of state-oriented values and policy efforts. Japan's success challenges the American and West European approach to capital accumulation.

As the world system expanded, it became differentiated into a core of rich countries and a periphery of poor countries. One distinctive linkage between the core and the periphery was colonialism. Our discussion of waves of colonialism demonstrated that underdevelopment is not a state but a process.

When colonial holdings disappeared after World War II, experts drew up plans to push the pace of development in underdeveloped countries. Regional scientists emphasized the center-dominant model. Although this approach tends to concentrate income and wealth, especially in the early stages, conservatives contend that eventual convergence between rich and poor regions is the norm. Liberals believe that only progressive taxation, social services, and other government actions can spread the benefits of growth. By contrast, radicals argue that because underdeveloped countries are dependent on core regions, and spread from center to periphery is limited, institutional reform must precede planning.

To illustrate the unequal distribution of wealth generated by capitalism in underdeveloped countries, the proto-proletariat served as our example. Like the peasants in the countryside, these people are poor and discriminated against with respect to the use and control of resources. We followed with a discussion of the basic-needs crisis and ended with a proposal to alleviate Third World poverty by means of a basic-needs approach.

Although there is a little disagreement about the priority for meeting basic needs, there is much disagreement over the feasibility of implementation. There is conflict concerning appropriate economic policies which, in some instances, is exacerbated by organized interest groups. For example, the ruling classes in many underdeveloped countries, who are the beneficiaries of concentrated and uneven growth, are often unwilling to share the fruits of economic growth with the poor of their own countries.

Is there a human right to basic needs? Should the basic needs of the vast majority be satisfied before the less essential needs of a few are met? Would a commitment to provide everyone with a decent existence prove too expensive? And would it blunt incentives to work and save? Your answers to these questions depend on your world view. They may also depend on whether you think the "poverty bomb" holds equal threat for global destruction as a nuclear bomb.

KEY TERMS

backwash effects	land alienation
basic needs	limiting factors
bazaar economy	lower circuit
center-periphery	modernization
colonial division of labor	multiplier
colonial organization of space	polarization effects
dependency	proto-proletariat
development	spread effects
deviation-amplification	squatter settlements
deviation-counteraction	trickling-down effects
dual economy	underdevelopment
ecopolitical economy	upper circuit
firm-centered economy	vicious circle
involution	world system

SUGGESTED READINGS   Armstrong, W., and McGee, T. G. 1985. *Theatres of Accumulation: Studies in Asian and Latin American Urbanization.* New York: Methuen.

Brookfield, H. 1975. *Interdependent Development.* New York: Methuen.

Chisholm, M. 1982. *Modern World Development: A Geographical Perspective.* London: Hutchinson.

Corbridge, S. 1986. *Capitalist World Development: A Critique of Radical Development Geography.* Totowa, NJ: Rowman and Littlefield.

Frank, A. G. 1981. *Crisis in the Third World.* London: Heinemann.

Gilbert, A., and Gugler, J. 1981. *Cities, Poverty, and Development: Urbanization in the Third World.* Oxford: Oxford University Press.

Gore, C. 1984. *Regions in Question: Space, Development Theory, and Regional Policy.* New York: Methuen.

Griffin, K. 1969. *Underdevelopment in Spanish America.* London: Allen and Unwin.

Lipton, M. 1977. *Why Poor People Stay Poor: A Study of Urban Bias in World Development.* Cambridge, MA: Harvard University Press.

Mabogunje, A. O. 1980. *The Development Process: A Spatial Perspective.* London: Hutchinson.

Peet, R., ed. 1980. *An Introduction to Marxist Theories of Underdevelopment.* Research School of Pacific Studies. Department of Human Geography. Canberra: The Australian National University.

EPILOGUE

The world economy is becoming ever more integrated. It is therefore essential that we come to understand the interconnected, international, and global character of our lives. And this is a matter of scale. In an essay on the Midwest, American geographer Cotton Mather (1986) acknowledged the role scale has played in changing the way we live and think:

> A century ago our capital in the Midwest was the county seat. It was the center through which our lives were regulated. The county seat was the authority and the administrator of our roads and our communication system. The county superintendent reigned supreme over our education. The county sheriff enforced the law. The county home took care of our aged. And we had the county fair and the county pole tax.
>
> Then came the role of the state capital as our central seat of authority and regulation. We had state roads and state communication systems. We had state boards of education and state universities. We had state police, state laws pertaining to our old folk, state fairs, and the state tax.
>
> The national capital reached ever more into our lives. Eventually, we had national regulation of our waterways, railways, education, and even our drinking water. Then we had national regulation of air transportation, but that came after the Wright brothers.
>
> Today we have international agreements on Antarctica, and the Law of the Sea is an evolving international instrument. There are international agreements on communication, on health, and the exchange of scholars. Additionally, we have international currency exchanges, international trade centers, international bridges, and real World Fairs. And we have the International Geographical Union that some of us are yet to join. (pp. 193–94)

Mather was suggesting, just as this book has, that we can no longer afford an insular view of the world. We must link our local geographies with a complex, internationalized, and rapidly shifting political economy. To address problems of population growth, of planetary pollution and resource depletion, of food and famine, of patterns of production and land use, of social and economic development, and of multinationals and international trade, we must think and act globally. Moreover, we must appreciate different ways of explaining world events. We must be aware of how different attitudes and views influence approaches to solving global problems of interest to the economic geographer.

GLOSSARY

absolute advantage The ability of one country to produce a product at a lower cost than another country.

absolute location Fixed position in relation to a standard grid system.

abstract space A geographical space, homogeneous in all respects. Movement over this space is equally easy in all directions.

accessibility A measure of aggregate nearness. It refers to the nearness of a given point to other points.

accessibility index A measure of the shortest path between one vertex and another.

administrative principle The spatial organization of central places in which a higher order administrative place is surrounded by six lower order administrative places.

African Development Bank An international financial institution that extends loans to African countries for purposes of development.

agglomeration economies The savings in cost that result from the clustering of firms.

agglomeration A measure of aggregate nearness. It refers to total aggregate nearness among a number of points.

agribusiness Food production by commercial farms, input industries, and marketing and processing firms that contribute to the total food sector.

agricultural involution The ability of the agricultural system in densely populated areas of Asia to absorb increasing numbers of people and still maintain minimal subsistence levels for all in rural communities.

areal differentiation The study of geographical areas for purposes of comparing their similarities and differences.

Asian Development Bank An international financial institution that extends loans to Asian countries for development projects.

assembly costs The costs of bringing new materials together at a factory.

average product The total output divided by the number of units of input used to produce it.

average total costs Total costs divided by the quantity of output.

backhaul A carrier's return trip.

balance-oriented lifestyle A mindset that insists that because resources are finite, they must be recycled, and input rates slowed down to prevent ecological overload.

basic cost The cost of an input for a firm at its least-cost location.

bazaar economy The traditional and labor-intensive sector of a Third World city.

behavioral matrix A device used for analyzing nonoptimal decision making. It shows the location of decision-makers with respect to information and their ability to use information.

beta index A measure of linkage intensity.

birth rate Annual number of births per thousand population.

break of bulk   The stage at which a shipment is divided into parts. This typically occurs at a port where the shipment is transferred from water to land transport.

Bretton Woods   The New Hampshire location of a 1944 international meeting of treasury and bank officials of the Allied countries. The meeting designed the International Monetary Fund and the International Bank for Reconstruction and Development. It also led indirectly to the creation of the General Agreement on Tariffs and Trade.

capital accumulation   The engine that drives economic growth under the capitalist system.

capital goods   Manufactured items that can be used to create wealth or other goods. For example, a home washing machine is a consumer good, but the machines used to make that washing machine are capital goods.

capital-intensive   A term that applies to an industry in which a high proportion of capital is used relative to the amount of labor employed.

capitalism   The political-economic system based on private property and profit.

carrying capacity   The maximum population an ecosystem can support.

cartel   An organization of buyers and sellers, capable of manipulating price and/or supply.

ceiling rent   Maximum rental that a particular user pays for a site.

central business district   The downtown area of a city.

central function   A good or service offered by a central place.

central-place theory   A theory that attempts to explain the size and spacing of settlements and the arrangement of their market areas.

cloning spatial structure   A headquarters/branch plant structure allowing for the complete production process to take place at each site.

colonial division of labor   An artificial form of labor specialization imposed on underdeveloped countries by colonial powers.

colonial organization of space   The European organization and zoning of land at all scales—urban, regional, national—to serve Europe's own interests during the colonial period.

commercial geography   The study of products and exports of the main regions of the world.

common market   A form of regional economic integration among member countries that disallows internal trade barriers, provides for common external trade barriers, and permits free factor mobility.

comparative advantage   The theory that stresses relative advantage, rather than absolute advantage, as the true basis for trade. Comparative advantage is gained when countries focus on exporting the goods they can produce at the lowest relative cost.

competitive-bidding process   The aspect of classical location theory in which those people willing and able to pay the highest price for a particular site win the competition and put the site to the highest and best use.

complementarity   A concept in which two places interact based on a demand in one place and a supply in the other, the demand and the supply being specifically complementary.

concrete space   The actual surface of the earth in all its geographical complexity.

conglomerate   A widely diversified corporation that controls the production and marketing of dissimilar products.

connectivity   A measure of the relation between places.

conurbation   A continuously urban area formed by the expansion and consequent coalescence of previously separate urban areas.

convenience goods   Central functions that are low in price, uniform in quality and style, and purchased frequently. They include goods and services needed on a day-to-day basis, such as groceries, gasoline, and drugstore items.

cost-insurance freight pricing   A policy whereby each consumer is charged production costs plus a flat markup to cover transportation charges.

cost-space convergence   The reduction of travel costs between places as a result of transport improvements.

countertrade   The direct exchange of goods or services for other goods and services

cumulative causation   The process by which economic activity leading to increasing economic development tends to concentrate in an area with an initial advantage, draining investment capital and skilled labor from the peripheral area.

customs union   A form of regional economic integration among countries that disallows internal trade barriers and provides for common external trade barriers.

death rate   Annual number of deaths per thousand population.

demand and supply   Demand is the quantity of a good buyers would like to purchase during a given period at a given price in a competitive market economy. Supply is the quantity of a good sellers would like to sell during a given period at a given price.

demographic transition   The historical shift of birth and death rates from high to low levels in a population.

dependence   A conditioning situation in which the economies of one group of countries are underdeveloped by the development and expansion of other groups.

depletion curves   Graphs used to project lifetimes of resources.

development   A historical process that encompasses the entire economic and social life of a nation, resulting in change for the better. Development is related to, but not synonymous with, economic growth.

development bank   An investment and/or loan fund that aids the development of underdeveloped countries.

direct investment   The purchase of enough of the equity shares of a company to gain some degree of managerial control.

direction The orientation of places toward each other.

disguised unemployment A term used by some economists to describe the surplus of labor that is thought to exist in the traditional sector of underdeveloped countries.

disorganic development A form of "development" at odds with local cultural and political institutions.

distance A measure of the cost to overcome the space between two places.

distance-decay effect With increase in distance, the decline in the level of interaction between two places.

division of labor The specialization of workers in particular operations of a production process. Labor specialization is a source of scale economies, a necessary ingredient in the evolution of a market-exchange economy.

dual economy In the study of industrial location, a term used to refer to two types of business enterprises, fundamentally different from one another: large, organically complex center firms and small, simply structured periphery firms. In the study of development, the term is used to refer to two types of social and economic systems existing simultaneously within the same territory: one system modern, the other traditional.

dual-sourcing A strategy of cloning used by multilocational companies to guarantee continuity of production, usually by undermining the potential monopoly control of a workforce in one place over a particular production process.

economic integration The ultimate form of regional integration. It involves removing all barriers to interbloc movement of merchandise and factors of production and unifying the social and economic policies of member nations. All members are subject to the binding decisions of a supranational authority consisting of executive, judicial, and legislative branches.

economic liberalism Sometimes used as a synonym for capitalism.

economic rent The monetary return from the use of land after the costs of production and marketing have been deducted.

economic union A form of regional economic integration having all the features of a common market, as well as a common central bank, unified monetary and tax systems, and a common foreign economic policy.

edge A link; a route in a topological diagram.

egalitarian society A society that has as many positions of prestige in any given age-sex sector as there are persons capable of filling them. It is forged through cooperative behavior.

elasticity The responsiveness of prices to changes in supply and/or demand for a good.

Engel's Law The principle according to which, with given tastes or preferences, the proportion of income spent on food decreases as income increases.

environmental determinism The notion that human behavior is environmentally prescribed.

environmental perception The ways in which people form images of other places, and how these images influence decision making.

Eurocurrency A currency deposited in a commercial bank outside the country of origin.

Eurodollar The major form of Eurocurrency.

Euromarkets The international financial markets that usually exist outside of the country whose currency is utilized.

European Economic Community A group of European countries established in 1958 on the basis of a treaty signed in Rome in 1957. The community consists of twelve members—France, West Germany, Italy, Belgium, the Netherlands, Luxemburg, Britain, Ireland, Denmark, Greece, Spain, and Portugal—whose aim is to establish a United States of Europe.

European free-trade area A group of European countries established in 1960 for the purposes of trade, aiming to abolish tariffs on imports of goods originating in the group. The original members were Britain, Norway, Sweden, Denmark, Portugal, Austria, and Switzerland. Finland joined as an associate member in 1961. Iceland joined in 1970. Britain and Denmark left the free-trade area in 1973 upon joining the European Economic Community.

exchange value The value at which a commodity can be exchanged for another commodity.

export-led industrialization A development strategy emphasizing the production and export of manufactures. Its success depends on a rising world economy.

factor of production One of the economic inputs—land, labor, capital, entrepreneurship, technology—essential to a production effort.

fertility The actual reproductive performance of an individual, a couple, a group, or a population.

filtering process The relocation of people within a city under free-market conditions. Filtering may be upward or downward. Upward filtering refers to the movement of people into higher quality housing. Downward filtering refers to the movement of people into lower quality housing.

firm-centered economy The modern and capital-intensive sector of a Third World city.

fixed cost The cost of the investment in land, plant, and equipment that must be paid, even if nothing is subsequently produced.

forces of production In materialist science, forces including living labor power, appropriated natural resources, and capital equipment provided by past generations of workers.

Fordism A mode of capital accumulation based on integrated production and assembly.

free-trade area A form of regional economic integration in which member countries agree to eliminate trade barriers among themselves, but continue to pursue their independent trade policies with respect to nonmember countries.

free-trade zones Areas where imported goods can be

processed for reexport without paying duties, since the goods will not be used locally.

freight rates   Payment to a carrier for the loading, transporting, and unloading of goods.

freight-on-board pricing   A policy whereby a consumer pays the plant price plus the cost of transportation.

functional region   An area differentiated by the activity within it; that is, by the interdependence and organization of its features.

game theory   Developed primarily by John von Neumann, a mathematical approach to decision making in the face of uncertainty.

General Agreement on Tariffs and Trade   An international agency, headquartered in Geneva, Switzerland, supportive of efforts to reduce barriers to international trade.

general systems theory   A theory that applies the principles of organization, interaction, hierarchy, and growth to any system.

geographical inertia   The tendency of a place with established infrastructure to maintain its importance as a focus of activity after the original conditions influencing its development have altered, ceased to be relevant, or no longer exist.

graph theory   The branch of mathematics concerned with the properties of graphs; that is, with the vertices and edges. Graph theory is used to describe and evaluate networks.

Green Revolution   A popular term for the greatly increased yield per hectare that followed the introduction of new, scientifically bred and selected varieties of such food crops as wheat, maize, and rice.

growth-oriented lifestyle   A mindset that insists on maximum production and consumption. It assumes an environment of unlimited waste and pollution reservoirs and indestructible ecosystems.

hierarchy   In central-place theory, the arrangement of settlements in a series of discrete classes, the rank of each determined by the level of specialization of functions.

hierarchical marginal good   The highest order good offered by a center at a given level of the central-place hierarchy.

highest and best use   The notion that land is allocated to the use that earns the highest location rent.

horizontal integration   A business strategy to increase a firm's scale by buying, building, or merging with another firm at the same stage of production of a product.

import-substitution industrialization   A development strategy to replace imports of final manufactures through domestic production. Subsidies, loans, and protective tariff regulations are often the means of assuring local production.

industrial restructuring   A term used to refer to the alternating phases of growth and decline in industrial activity. It emphasizes changes in employment between regions, and links these with change in the world economy.

industry life cycle   The typical sequence of developmental stages in the evolution of an industry.

infant industry   A young industry which, it is argued, requires tariff protection until it matures to the point where it is efficient enough to compete successfully with imports.

infrastructure   The services and supporting activities necessary for an economy to function; for example, transportation, banking, education, health care, and government.

innovation   A new idea applicable to something useful for humankind.

Inter-American Development Bank   An international financial institution that extends loans for development to countries in Latin America and the Caribbean.

intermediate technology   Low-cost, small-scale technologies "intermediate" between "primitive" stick-farming methods and complex Western agri-industrial technical packages.

International Bank for Reconstruction and Development   An international financial institution that extends loans to underdeveloped countries at commercial rates of interest; also called the World Bank.

International Development Association   An adjunct of the International Bank for Reconstruction and Development. It extends loans with generous interest and repayment terms to the poorer underdeveloped countries.

International Finance Corporation   An adjunct of the International Bank for Reconstruction and Development. It provides either loans or equity investments to private-sector companies in underdeveloped countries.

International Monetary Fund   An international financial agency that attempts to promote international monetary cooperation, facilitate international trade, promote exchange stability, assist in the establishment of a multilateral system of payments without restrictions on foreign currency exchange, make loans to help countries adjust to temporary international payment problems, and lessen the severity of international payments disequilibrium.

international subcontracting   The arrangement by multinational corporations to use Third World firms to produce entire products, components, or services in order to cover markets in an advanced industrial country.

intervening opportunity   An alteration in the complementarity of places.

involution   The ability of the peasantry or the protoproletariat in the Third World to absorb an unusual number of people. The process of involution is characterized by a tenacity of basic pattern, internal elaboration and ornateness, technical hair-splitting, and unending virtuosity.

isodapane   The locus of points of equal transport cost from a factory.

isotropic surface   A plain that is homogeneous in all respects, with equal ease of movement in all directions from every point.

Japan Incorporated   Sometimes used by Japan's competitors, an appellation acknowledging the successful marriage between Japanese businesses and government.

joint venture   An enterprise undertaken by two or more parties. It may be a jointly owned subsidiary, a consortium, or a syndicate.

Kondratieff cycles   Successive cycles of growth and decline in industrial economies, occurring with a periodicity of some fifty to sixty years duration.

labor-intensive   A term that applies to an industry in which a high proportion of labor is used relative to the amount of capital employed.

labor process   The nature and degree of the division of labor.

labor force   The economically active population consisting of productively employed and temporarily unemployed people.

land alienation   A term referring to the land taken away from indigenous people by Europeans for their own use.

law of diminishing returns   The law according to which, when factors of production (land, labor, and capital) are doubled, output doubles; but if one factor of production or only some factors are doubled, output increases, but fails to double. The law assumes given levels of technological knowledge.

least-cost-to-build network   A transport system designed to keep the cost to the builder as low as possible.

least-cost-to-use network   A transport system designed to keep the cost to the user as low as possible.

licensing venture   The rental of patents, trademarks, or technology by a company in exchange for royalty payments.

line-haul costs   Costs involved in moving commodities along a route.

linear market   The spatial organization of central places into a $K = 2$ hierarchy.

location   See **absolute location**; **relative location**.

location theory   A compilation of ideas and methods dealing with questions of accessibility.

locational costs   Costs over and above the basic cost of an input; any costs over and above the least-cost price.

locational inertia   The stabilizing effect of invested capital in a region.

localized raw material   A material that is not available everywhere; thus, it exerts a specific influence on industrial location.

Lomé Convention   A 1974 trade agreement signed by the European Economic Community and forty-six countries in Africa, the Caribbean, and the Pacific.

lower circuit   The traditional and labor-intensive sector of a Third World city.

malnutrition   A state of poor health in which an individual does not obtain enough essential vitamins and nutrients, especially proteins.

marginal product   The addition to total output attributable to the last unit of the variable input employed.

market area   The territory surrounding any central point of exchange. It includes all potential customers for whom market price plus transport cost will still be sufficiently low to justify their purchases at that price in the central place.

market exchange   An economic system that establishes market prices. The prices are the mechanism for connecting economic activity among a large number of individuals and for controlling a large number of decentralized decisions.

market linkage   The connection resulting from the sale of a firm's output to nearby firms.

marketing principle   The spatial organization of central places when a central place of any order is at the midpoint of each set of three neighboring places of the next higher order.

massing of reserves   The principle that states that large firms can maintain smaller inventories of spare machines or machine parts than can small firms.

material index   In Weberian analysis, a measure of the weight a raw material loses in processing; the weight of raw materials divided by the weight of the finished product.

maximum sustainable yield   Maximum production consistent with maintaining future productivity of a renewable resource.

mean information field   A model indicating the probability of a given individual receiving information from a given point in all directions.

megalopolis   A giant, sprawling urban region encompassing many cities, towns, and villages. The term was coined by geographer Jean Gottman to describe the Atlantic Urban Region that extends from Boston to Washington, D.C.

mercantile model   A model that attempts to explain the wholesale trade relationships that link regions.

mercantilism   A theory popular among European nations in the early modern period stating that the economic and political strength of a country lay in its acquiring gold and silver, to be achieved by restricting imports, developing production for exports, and prohibiting the export of gold and silver.

migration   Movement of a population, resulting in a change of permanent residence.

minicity   A multifunctional urban node that is the focal point of the outer city, especially in North America. Suburban minicities include a variety of land uses— retailing, wholesaling, manufacturing, and entertainment and medical functions.

modernization   A word full of hope, enthusiasm, and the idea of progress; in common usage, suggesting that

Western culture invented or perfected most things associated with development and that in due course people in underdeveloped countries will enjoy them too.

Monte Carlo simulation A probabilistic model that accounts for sheer chance and reproduces a particular process by discovering the major rules of the game.

multinational A company with established operations in several host countries, usually headquartered in one parent country.

multiplier An "injection" into the spending stream in the belief that total output will increase as a result. The opening of a new factory in a region is an example of an injection. New funds flow into the region from the outside, thereby raising the level of regional income.

net energy The amount of energy available minus the quantity used to find, concentrate, and deliver energy to the consumer.

net migration The net effect of immigration and emigration on an area's population in a given period, expressed as an increase or decrease.

network Any set of interlinking routes that cross or meet one another at nodes, junctions, or terminals.

New International Economic Order A 1974 United Nations resolution originating with the underdeveloped countries, and calling for a more equal distribution of the world's income.

nontariff barriers Obstacles to trade other than tariffs.

nonrenewable resources Resources that are fixed in amount—that cannot regenerate—such as fossil fuels and metals.

normative model A model that attempts to describe how people should behave and make decisions if they wish to achieve certain well-defined objectives.

optimizers Economic persons who organize themselves and their activities in space so as to optimize utility.

Organization of Petroleum Exporting Countries The international cartel of oil-producing countries.

organizational structure of capital A term that is often applied to the size and associated characteristics of firms.

overpopulation A level of population in excess of the "optimum" level relative to the food supply or rate of consumption of energy and resources.

part-process spatial structure A headquarters/branch plant structure in which the production process is geographically fragmented or differentiated.

plantation A large landholding or estate devoted to the production of export crops, such as coffee, tea, sugar cane, sisal, and hemp. Plantations are usually located in underdeveloped countries and depend on foreign capital for their operation.

polarization effects The negative influences prosperous regions exert on less prosperous regions.

population pyramid A special type of bar chart indicating the distribution of a population by age and sex.

population density The number of people per unit of land, normally a square kilometer or square mile.

population growth rate The difference between the birth rate and death rate; generally expressed as so many persons per hundred.

postindustrial society The stage of an evolving society in which traditional manufacturing activity has given way to the growth of high-technology industry and an employment emphasis on services, government, and management-information activities.

primary economic activity An economic pursuit mainly involving natural or culturally improved resources, such as agriculture, livestock raising, forestry, fishing, and mining.

product life cycle The typical sequence through which a product passes, from its introduction into the market to when it is replaced by a new product.

production function The technological and organizational characteristics of a firm that transform inputs into outputs. In the short run, at least one input is fixed in amount. In the long run, all the inputs are variable.

production linkages Economies that accrue to firms that locate near other producers manufacturing their basic raw materials.

protectionism An effort to protect domestic producers by means of controls on imports.

proto-proletariat An urban class engaged within a peasant system of production. Most of its income is gained from informal income opportunities.

pure competition model A market structure of industry made up of many small firms that produce homogeneous products and that have no real influence on the market price of their products.

pure raw material A material that does not lose weight in processing.

pyschic income Nonmonetary rewards gained from operating at a particular point.

quaternary economic activity An information-oriented economic activity, as pursued, for example, in research units, think tanks, and management-information services.

range The average minimum distance consumers are willing and able to travel to purchase a good (or service) at a particular price in a central place.

rank-size rule An empirical rule describing the distribution of city sizes in an area. It states that the population of any given city tends to be equal to the population of the largest city in the set divided by the rank of the given city. For example, if the population of the largest city numbers 10,000, the population of the fifth largest city will be 2,000—that is, 10,000 divided by 5.

rank society A society in which positions of valued status are circumscribed, so that not all with sufficient talent to hold such positions actually achieve them.

reciprocity A mutually beneficial form of economic exchange, common in egalitarian societies.

redistribution A form of economic exchange in which equity is maintained by a central authority that redistributes production.

relative location Position with respect to other locations.

renewable resources Resources capable of yielding output indefinitely if used wisely, such as water and biomass.

rent gradient A sloping net-profit line. The intersection of the line and the point of zero profit indicates the limit of commercial crop production.

reserve A known and identified deposit of earth materials that can be tapped profitably with existing technology under prevailing economic and legal conditions.

resource A naturally occurring substance of potential profit that can be extracted under prevailing conditions.

saddle point The minimum-maximum point in game theory.

satisficers Decision-makers who make choices that are satisfactory rather than optimal.

scale economies The cost-reducing changes that lower the average costs of firms as they grow in size. These changes may be internal or external to firms.

second law of thermodynamics The law according to which any voluntary process has as a consequence a net increase in disorder or entropy. It can also be expressed as the degradation of energy into a less useful form, such as low-grade heat.

secondary economic activity The processing of materials to render them more directly useful to people; manufacturing.

service linkages Economies that occur when a cluster of firms becomes large enough to support specialized services.

settlement-building function Sales of goods and services beyond the local retail and service hinterland of a central place.

settlement-forming function Sales of goods and services that occur totally within the hinterland of a central place.

settlement-serving function Sales of goods and services to residents of a central place.

Shimble index A graph-theoretic measure of the compactness of a network; sometimes called the dispersion index.

shopping goods Central functions that are normally higher in price than convenience goods. They vary in quality and style, and are purchased infrequently.

social relations of production Class relations between owners of the means of production and the workers employed to operate these means.

social surplus The portion of annual production of any society that is neither consumed by the direct producer nor used for the reproduction of the stock of means of production available at the start of the year. In a class-divided society, the social surplus is always appropriated by the ruling class.

spatial diffusion The spread of information, goods, or people over space.

spatial fetishism Attributing the cause of an event to locational factors.

spatial interaction The movement, contact, and linkage between points in space; for example, the movement of people, goods, traffic, information, and capital between one place and another.

spatial margins to profitability The intersection of a space-cost curve and the market price of a finished product.

spatial monopoly A situation in which a single firm controls a given area of the market by virtue of its location.

spatial oligopoly A situation in which a few firms compete for a given segment of the total market space.

spatial organization A theme in geography emphasizing how space is organized by individuals and societies to suit their own designs. It provides a framework for analyzing and interpreting location decisions and spatial structures in a mobile and interconnected world.

spatial process A movement or location strategy.

spatial structure The internal organization of a distribution that limits, channels, or controls a spatial process.

spread city A term that usually refers to the contemporary suburban or multifunctional American metropolis. The spread city encompasses more territory and has less "centrality" than the compact nineteenth-century industrial city.

spread effects The beneficial influences prosperous regions exert on less prosperous regions.

squatter settlements Residential areas that are home to the urban poor in underdeveloped countries. The various terms used to identify squatter settlements include the following: calampas, tugurios, favelas, mocambos, ranchos, and barriadas in Latin America; bidonvilles and gourbivilles in North Africa; bustees, jhoupris, jhuggis, kampongs, and barung barong in South Asia and Southeast Asia.

stages of production According to the law of diminishing returns, the three stages that total product passes through as successive units of variable input are applied to a fixed input. In Stage 1, the average product curve rises to its peak; in Stage 2 it declines; and in Stage 3 the total product curve declines.

stratified society A society in which members of the same sex and equivalent age status do not have equal access to the basic resources that sustain life.

stationary state The dynamic state of a system in which input and output are balanced at a point below the maximum limits of the system and its surroundings.

stochastic model A model that assumes bounded rationality; it recognizes the major role of chance in the decision-making process.

suburb An outlying residential district of a city.

surplus value The difference between the value produced by a worker (value of units of labor produced) and the worker's wage (value of labor power).

tariff   A schedule of duties placed on products. A tariff may be levied on an *ad valorum* basis (i.e., as a percentage of value) or on a specific basis (i.e., as an amount per unit). Tariffs are used to serve many functions—to make imports expensive relative to domestic substitutes; to retaliate against restrictive trade policies of other countries; to protect infant industries; and to protect strategic industries, such as agriculture, in times of war.

Taylorism   The application of scientific management principles to production.

technique   The method of procedure by which inputs are combined to produce a finished product.

technostructure   Corporate technical personnel, including scientists and technicians.

terms of trade   The relative price levels of exports to imports for a country.

terminal costs   Costs incurred in loading, packing, and unloading shipments, and preparing shipping documents.

tertiary economic activity   An economic pursuit in which a service is performed, such as retailing, wholesaling, servicing, teaching, goverment, medicine, and recreation.

threshold   The minimum level of demand needed to support an economic activity.

time-space covergence   The reduction in travel time between places that results from transport improvements.

trade area   The area dominated by a central place; sometimes called a hinterland or tributary area.

traffic principle   The spatial organization of central places when as many central places as possible lie on a traffic route between two important cities.

transferability   The condition that costs be acceptable in order for exchange of goods to occur between a supply area and a demand area.

transport costs   The alternative output given up when inputs are committed to the movement of people, goods, information, and ideas over geographical space.

trickling-down effects   The beneficial impact of prosperous regions on less prosperous regions.

turnkey project   A technique of competitive duplication of Western industrial facilities employed by multinationals. The contractor not only plans and builds the project, but also trains the buyer's personnel and initiates operation of the project.

ubiquitous raw material   A material that is available everywhere; thus, it does not exert a specific influence on industrial location.

undernutrition   A state of poor health in which an individual does not obtain enough calories.

United Nations Conference on Trade and Development   A UN organization that includes most underdeveloped countries. Although it has little statutory authority, it serves as a forum for discussion of common problems of its members.

upper circuit   The modern and capital-intensive sector of a Third World city.

urbanization   The process through which the proportion of population living in urban areas increases.

use value   The usefulness of a commodity to the person who possesses it.

value added   The difference between the revenue of a firm obtained from a given volume of output and the cost of the inputs (the materials, components, services) used in producing that output.

variable costs   Expenditures firms incur as output changes. As output rises, variable costs rise; as output falls, variable costs fall.

vertex   A point; a node in a topological diagram.

vertical integration   A business strategy to increase a firm's scale by buying, building, or merging with another firm in a different stage of production of the same product; may be forward or backward.

vicious circle   A concept emphasizing the multicausality of underdevelopment; that is, a combination of interwoven limiting factors, rather than "just" a single factor, thwarts development.

weight-losing raw material   A raw material that undergoes a loss of weight in the process of manufacture.

World Bank   A group of international financial agencies including the International Bank for Reconstruction and Development, the International Finance Corporation, and the International Development Association.

world economy   A multistate economic system created in the late fifteenth and early sixteenth centuries by European capitalism and, later, its overseas progeny.

zaibatsu   A large Japanese financial enterprise, similar to a conglomerate in the West.

zero-sum game   A game in which the "payoff" to one player is exactly the value "lost" by the opponent.

REFERENCES

Abler, R., J.S. Adams, and P. Gould. 1971. *Spatial Organization*. Englewood Cliffs, NJ: Prentice-Hall.

Abu-Lughod, J. 1987–88. The shape of the world system in the thirteenth century. *Studies in Comparative International Development* 22 (No. 4): 3–25.

Aglietta, M. 1979. *A Theory of Capitalist Regulation: The U.S. Experience*. London: New Left Books.

Agnew, J.A. 1982. Sociologizing the geographical imaginaion: Spatial concepts in the world-system perspective. *Political Geography Quarterly* 1:159–66.

———. 1987. Bringing culture back in: Overcoming the economic-cultural split in development studies. *Journal of Geography* 86:276–81.

Alchian, A.A. 1950. Uncertainty, evolution, and economic theory. *Journal of Political Economy* 58:211–21.

Alderfer, E.B., and H.E. Michl. 1942. *Economics of American Industry*. New York: McGraw-Hill.

Allen, B.J. 1985. Dynamics of fallow successions and introduction of Robusta coffee in shifting cultivation areas of the lowlands of Papua New Guinea. *Agroforestry Systems* 3:227–38.

Amin, A., and I. Smith. 1986. The internationalization of production and its implications for the UK. In *Technological Change, Industrial Restructuring, and Regional Development*, edited by A. Amin and J.B. Goddard, pp. 41–76. Boston: Allen and Unwin.

Amin, S. 1976. *Unequal Development*. New York: Monthly Review Press.

Arrighi, G., and J.S. Saul. 1973. *Essays on the Political Economy of Africa*. New York: Monthly Review Press.

Asimov, I. 1978. *The Naked Sun*. London: Granada.

Augelli, J.P. 1985. Food, population, and dislocation in Latin America. *Journal of Geography* 84:274–81.

Averitt, R.T. 1968. *The Dual Economy: The Dynamics of American Industry Structure*. New York: W.W. Norton.

Balassa, B. 1961. *The Theory of Economic Integration*. Homewood, IL: Richard D. Irwin.

Ballmer-Cao, T., and J. Scheidegger. 1979. *Compendium of Data for World System Analysis*. Zürick: Sociologisches Institut der Universität.

Bannock, G. 1971. *The Juggernauts: The Age of the Big Corporation*. Harmondsworth, England: Penguin Books.

Baran, P. 1957. *The Political Economy of Growth*. New York: Monthly Review Press.

Barnet, R., and R. Müller. 1975. *Global Reach*. New York: Simon and Schuster.

Batty, M., and E. Saether. 1972. A note on the design of shopping models. *Journal of the Royal Town Planning Institute* 58:303–6.

Behrman, J.N. 1984. *Industrial Policies: International Restructuring and Transnationals*. Lexington, MA: D.C. Heath.

Bell, D. 1973. *The Coming of Postindustrial Society*. New York: Basic Books.

Berry, B.J.L. 1961. City size distributions and economic development. *Economic Development and Cultural Change* 9:573–88.

———. 1967. *Geography of Market Centers and Retail Distribution.* Englewood Cliffs, NJ: Prentice-Hall.

———. 1968. Interdependency of spatial structure and spatial behavior: General field theory formulation. *Papers and Proceedings of the Regional Science Association* 21:205–27.

———. 1969a. Relationships between regional economic development and the urban system—The case of Chile. *Tijdschrift voor Economische en Sociale Geografie* 60:283–307.

———. 1969b. Policy implications of an urban location model for the Kanpur region. In *Regional Perspective of Industrial and Urban Growth—The Case of Kanpur,* edited by P.B. Desai et al., pp. 203–19. Bombay: Macmillan.

Berry B.J.L., E.C. Conkling, and D.M. Ray. 1987. *Economic Geography.* Englewood Cliffs, NJ: Prentice-Hall.

Berry, B.J.L., and H.M. Meyer. 1962. *Comparative Studies of Central Place Systems.* Final Report NONR 2121-18 and NR 389-126. Washington, DC: Geography Branch, U.S. Office of Naval Research.

Blaikie, P.M. 1971. Spatial organization of agriculture in some north Indian villages: Part 1. *Transactions,* Institute of British Geographers 52:1–40.

Blaikie, P.M., and H. Brookfield. 1987. *Land Degradation and Society.* New York: Methuen.

Bluestone, B., and B. Harrison. 1987. The impact of private disinvestment on workers and their communities. In *International Capitalism and Industrial Restructuring,* edited by R. Peet, pp. 72–104. Boston: Allen and Unwin.

Bohannan, P., and P. Curtin. 1971. *Africa and Africans.* Garden City, NY: Natural History Press.

Borchert, J.R. 1961. The Twin Cities urbanized area: Past, present, and future. *Geographical Review* 51:47–70.

———. 1963. *The Urbanization of the Upper Midwest: 1930–1960.* Upper Midwest Economic Study, Urban Report No. 2. Minneapolis: University of Minnesota.

———. 1967. American metropolitan evolution. *Geographical Review* 57:301–31.

———. 1987. *America's Northern Heartland: An Economic and Historical Geography of the Upper Midwest.* Minneapolis: University of Minnesota Press.

Borchert, J.R., and D.D. Carroll. 1971. *Minnesota Settlement and Land Use 1985.* Center for Urban and Regional Affairs. Minneapolis: University of Minnesota.

Boserup, E. 1965. *The Conditions of Agricultural Growth: The Economics of Agrarian Change under Population Pressure.* Chicago: Aldine.

———. 1970. Present and potential food production in developing countries. In *Geography and a Crowding World,* edited by W. Zelinsky, L.A. Kosiński, and R.M. Prothero, pp. 100–110. New York: Oxford University Press.

———. 1981. *Population and Technology.* New York: Blackwell.

Brown, L.R. 1981. Eroding the base of civilization. *Journal of Soil and Water Conservation* 36:255–60.

Bunge, W. 1966. *Theoretical Geography.* Lund Studies in Geography, Series C1. Lund: Gleerup.

———. 1971. *Fitzgerald: The Geography of a Revolution.* Cambridge, MA: Schenkman Publishing Company.

Burgess, E.W. 1925. Growth of the city. In *The City,* edited by R.E. Park, E.W. Burgess, and R.D. McKenzie, pp. 47–62. Chicago: University of Chicago Press.

Burns, A.F. 1934. *Production Trends in the United States.* New York: National Bureau of Economic Research.

Cassen, R.W. 1976. Population and development: A survey. *World Development* 4:785–830.

Chapman, K., and D. Walker. 1987. *Industrial Location.* New York: Basil Blackwell.

Chisholm, G.G. 1899. *Handbook of Commercial Geography.* London: Longmans, Green.

Chisholm, M. 1979. *Rural Settlement and Land Use: An Essay in Location.* 3d ed. London: Hutchinson.

———. 1982. *Modern World Development.* Totowa, NJ: Barnes & Noble.

Christaller, W. 1966. *The Central Places of Southern Germany.* Translated by C.W. Baskin. Englewood Cliffs, NJ: Prentice-Hall.

Clarke, B., and L. Bolwell. 1968. Attractiveness as part of retail potential models. *Journal of the Royal Town Planning Institute* 54:477–78.

Clarke, W.C. 1977. The structure of permanence: The relevance of self-subsistence communities for world ecosystem management. In *Subsistence and Survival: Rural Ecology in the Pacific,* edited by T.P. Bayliss-Smith and R. Feachem, pp. 363–84. London: Academic Press.

Coale, A.J., and E.M. Hoover. 1958. *Population Growth and Economic Development in Low-Income Countries.* Princeton, NJ: Princeton University Press.

Cochran, T.C. 1966. The entrepreneur in social change. *Explorations in Entrepreneurial History,* 2d series, 4:25–38.

Cohen, R.B. 1981. The new international division of labor, multinational corporations and urban hierarchy. In *Urbanization and Urban Planning in Capitalist Society,* edited by M. Dear and A.J. Scott, pp. 287–315. New York: Methuen.

Cole, J. 1987. *Development and Underdevelopment.* London: Methuen.

Commoner, B. 1975. How poverty breeds overpopulation (and not the other way around). *Ramparts,* August-September, pp. 21–25, 58–59.

Conkling, E., and J. McConnell. 1985. The world's new economic powerhouse. *Focus,* January, pp. 2–7.

Curran, J., and J. Stanworth. 1986. Trends in small firm industrial relations and their implications for the role of the small firm in economic restructuring. In *Technological Change, Industrial Restructuring, and*

Regional Development, edited by A. Amin and J.B. Goddard, pp. 233–57. Winchester, MA: Allen and Unwin.

Cyert, R.M., and J.G. March. 1963. *A Behavioral Theory of the Firm*. Englewood Cliffs, NJ: Prentice-Hall.

Daniels, P.W. 1985. *Service Industries: A Geographical Appraisal*. New York: Methuen.

Darst, G. 1987. Energy worries fading: Conservation drive wanes in Washington. *Minneapolis Star and Tribune*, 15 March, pp. 1 and 3.

Datoo, B.A. 1976. Toward a reformulation of Boserup's theory of agricultural change. Dar es Salaam: Department of Geography, University of Dar es Salaam. Mimeographed.

de Blij, H.J., and P.O. Muller. 1985. *Geography: Regions and Concepts*. 4th ed. New York: John Wiley.

de Souza, A.R. 1985. Dependency and economic growth. *Journal of Geography* 85:94.

———. 1986. To have and have not: Colonialism and core-periphery relations. *Focus* 36 (No. 3):14–19.

de Souza, A.R., and J.B. Foust. 1979. *World Space Economy*. Columbus OH: Merrill.

de Souza, A.R., and P.W. Porter. 1974. *The Underdevelopment and Modernization of the Third World*. Resource Paper No. 28. Washington DC: Association of American Geographers.

Demko, G.J., and W.B. Wood. 1987. International refugees: A geographical perspective. *Journal of Geography* 86:225–28.

Dicken, P. 1986. *Global Shift: Industrial Change in a Turbulent World*. London: Harper and Row.

Dickinson, R.E. 1964. *City and Region*. London: Routledge and Kegan Paul.

Doxiadis, C.A. 1970. Man's movements and his settlements. *Ekistics* 29:318.

Dumont, R., and M-F. Mottin. 1983. *Stranglehold on Africa*. London: André Deutsch.

Edwards, C. 1985. *The Fragmented World*. New York: Methuen.

Emmanuel, A. 1972. *Unequal Exchange: A Study of the Imperialism of Trade*. London: New Left Books.

Encyclopaedia Britannica. 1987. *1987 Britannica Book of the Year*. Chicago: Encylopaedia Britannica.

Engels, F. 1958. *The Condition of the Working Class in England*. Stanford, CA: Stanford University Press.

Ewart, W.D. and W. Fullard. 1973. *World Atlas of Shipping*. London: Philip and Son.

Food and Agriculture Organization. 1983. *Per Capita Dietary Energy Supplies in Relation to Nutritional Requirements*. World Food Report, Series 211. Rome: FAO.

———. 1985. *The State of Food and Agriculture 1984*. Rome: FAO.

Fanon, F. 1963. *The Wretched of the Earth*. New York: Grove Press.

Fieldhouse, D.K. 1967. *The Colonial Empires*. New York: Delacorte Press.

Financial Times. 1989. Britain's regions: A test for Thatcherism, 27 January, pp. 33–40.

Fisher, J.S. 1989. Anglo-America: Economic growth and transformation. In *Geography and Development*, edited by J.S. Fisher, pp. 146–66. Columbus, OH: Merrill.

Frank, A.G. 1969. *Capitalism and Underdevelopment in Latin America*. New York: Monthly Review Press.

———. 1981. *Crisis in the Third World*. London: Heineman.

Franklin, S.H. 1965. Systems of production: Systems of appropriation. *Pacific Viewpoint* 6:145–66.

Freeman, M. 1986. Transport. In *Atlas of Industrializing Britain, 1780–1914*, edited by J. Langton and R.J. Morris, pp. 80–93. New York: Methuen.

Fried, M. 1967. *The Evolution of Political Society*. New York: Random House.

Friedmann, J. 1966. *Regional Development Policy: A Case Study of Venezuela*. Cambridge, MA: The MIT Press.

Froebel, F., J. Heinrich, and O. Kreye. 1977. The tendency towards a new international division of labor. *Review* 1 (No. 1):77–88.

Fuentes, A., and B. Ehrenreich. 1987. Women in the global factory. In *International Capitalism and Industrial Restructuring*, edited by R. Peet, pp. 201–15. Boston: Allen and Unwin.

Fusfeld, D.R. 1986. *The Age of the Economist*. 5th ed. Glenview, IL: Scott, Foresman.

Gaffikin, F., and A. Nickson. 1984. *Job Crisis and the Multinationals: Deindustrialization in the West Midlands*. Birmingham: Third World Books.

Galbraith, J.K. 1967. *The New Industrial State*. Boston: Houghton Mifflin.

———. 1969. *The Affluent Society*. Boston: Houghton Mifflin.

———. 1973. *Economics and the Public Purpose*. Boston: Houghton Mifflin.

Galtung, J. 1971. A structural theory of imperialism. *Journal of Peace Research* (No. 2):81–107, 110–16.

Gamble, A. 1981. *Britain in Decline: Economic Policy, Political Strategy, and the British State*. London: Macmillan.

Geertz, C. 1963. *Agricultural Involution: The Processes of Ecological Changes in Indonesia*. Berkeley: University of California Press.

George, S. 1977. *How the Other Half Dies—The Real Reasons for World Hunger*. Montclair, NJ: Allanheld, Osmun.

Ginsburg, N.S. 1961. *Atlas of Economic Development*. Chicago: University of Chicago Press.

Globe and Mail (Toronto), 1986, 6 May.

Godlund, S. 1961. *Population, Regional Hospitals, Transport Facilities and Regions: Planning the Location of Regional Hospitals in Sweden*. Lund: Gleerup.

Goliber, T.J. 1985. *Sub-Saharan Africa: Population Pressures on Development.* Population Bulletin, Vol. 40, No.1. Washington, DC: Population Reference Bureau.

Goodchild, M.F., and B. Massam. 1969. Some least-cost models of spatial administrative systems in southern Ontario. *Geografiska Annaler* 52, B-2:86–94.

Gordon, D.M. 1977. Class struggle and the stages of American urban development. In *The Rise of the Sunbelt Cities,* edited by D.C. Perry and A.J. Watkins, pp. 55–82. Beverly Hills, CA: Sage Publications.

Gottman, J. 1964. *Megalopolis.* Cambridge, MA: The MIT Press.

Gould, P.R. 1960. *The Development of the Transportation Pattern in Ghana.* Department of Geography, Studies in Geography, No. 5. Evanston, IL: Northwestern University Press.

————. 1964. A note on research into the diffusion of development. *Journal of Modern African Studies* 2:123–25.

————. 1970. Tanzania 1920–63: The spatial impress of the modernization process. *World Politics* 22:149–70.

————. 1975. *Spatial Diffusion: The Spread of Ideas and Innovations in Geographic Space.* Learning Package Series No. 11. Columbus, OH: The Ohio State University.

————. 1983. Getting involved in information and ignorance. *Journal of Geography* 82:158–62.

————. 1985. *The Geographer at Work.* London: Routledge and Kegan Paul.

Goulet, D. 1971. *The Cruel Choice.* New York: Atheneum.

Grandstaff, T. 1978. The development of swidden agriculture (shifting cultivation). *Development and Change* 9:547–79.

Greenhut, M.L. 1956. *Plant Location in Theory and Practice.* Chapel Hill, NC: University of North Carolina Press.

Greenow, L., and V. Muñiz. 1988. Market trade in decentralized development: The case of Cajamarca, Peru. *The Professional Geographer* 40:416–27.

Gribben, R. 1989. Economic divide will stay but shift northward. *The Daily Telegraph,* 3 January, p. 4.

Griffin, E., and L. Ford. 1980. A model of Latin American city structure. *Geographical Review* 70:397–422.

Griffin, K. 1969. *Underdevelopment in Spanish America.* London: Allen and Unwin.

Hagen, E.E. 1962. *On the Theory of Social Change.* Homewood, IL: The Dorsey Press.

————. 1968. Are some things valued by all men? *Cross Currents* 18:406–14.

Hägerstrand, T. 1965. A Monte Carlo approach to diffusion. *European Journal of Sociology* 6:43–67.

Haggett, P. 1965. *Locational Analysis in Human Geography.* London: Edward Arnold.

Haggett, P., and R.J. Chorley. 1969. *Network Analysis in Human Geography.* London: Edward Arnold.

Håkanson, L. 1979. Towards a theory of location and corporate growth. In *Spatial Analysis, Industry and the Industrial Environment. Volume 1: Industrial Systems,* edited by F.E.I. Hamilton and G.J.R. Linge, pp. 115–38. New York: John Wiley.

Hall, P., ed. 1966. *Von Thünen's Isolated State.* Translated by C.M. Wartenberg. Oxford, England: Pergamon.

————. 1971. *The World Cities.* New York: McGraw-Hill.

————. 1982. *Urban and Regional Planning.* London: Allen and Unwin.

Hardin, G. 1974. Living on a lifeboat. *Bioscience* 24:561–8.

————. 1968. The tragedy of the commons. *Science* 162:1243–48.

Harrington, M. 1977. *The Vast Majority: A Journey to the World's Poor.* New York: Touchstone.

Harris, C. 1954. The market as a factor in the localization of industry in the *U.S. Annals,* Association of American Geographers 44:315–48.

Harris, C., and E. Ullman. 1945. The nature of cities. *Annals of the American Academy of Political and Social Science* 242:7–17.

Harris, M. 1966. The cultural ecology of India's sacred cattle. *Current Anthropology* 7:51–59.

Harvey, D. 1972. *Society, the City, and the Space-Economy of Urbanism.* Resource Paper No. 18. Washington DC: Association of American Geographers.

————. 1973. *Social Justice and the City.* London: Edward Arnold.

————. 1974. Population, resources, and the ideology of science. *Economic Geography* 50:256–77.

————. 1985. *The Urbanization of Capital.* Baltimore, MD: Johns Hopkins University Press.

Havens, A.E., and W.F. Flinn. 1975. Green revolution technology and community developement: The limits of Action programs. *Economic Development and Cultural Change* 23:468–81.

Heckscher, E. 1919. The effect of foreign trade on the distribution of income. *Economisk Tidskrift* 21. Reprinted in *Readings in the Theory of International Trade,* edited by H. Ellis and L. Metzler, pp. 272–300. Homewood, IL: Richard D. Irwin, 1950.

Heilbronner, R. 1989. Reflections: The triumph of capitalism. *The New Yorker,* 25 January, pp. 98–109.

Henige, D. 1970. *Colonial Governors.* Madison, WI: University of Wisconsin Press.

Herbert, D.T. 1982. The changing face of the city. In *The Changing Geography of the United Kingdom,* edited by R.J. Johnston and J.C. Doornkamp, pp. 227–55. London: Methuen.

Higgins, B. 1956. The dualistic theory of underdeveloped areas. *Economic Development and Cultural Change* 4:99–115.

Hirschman, A.O. 1958. *The Strategy of Economic Development.* New Haven, CT: Yale University Press.

Horvath, R.J. 1969. Von Thünen's Isolated State and the area around Addis Ababa, Ethiopia. *Annals*, Association of American Geographers 59:308–23.

Hotelling, H. 1929. Stability in competition. *Economic Journal* 39:41–57.

Howard, E. 1946. *Garden Cities of Tomorrow*. London: Faber.

Hoyle, B.S., and D.A. Pinder. 1981. Seaports, cities and transport systems. In *Cityport Industrialization and Regional Development*, edited by B.S. Hoyle and D.A. Pinder, pp. 1–10. Oxford: Pergamon.

Hoyt, H. 1939. *The Structure and Growth of Residential Neighborhoods in American Cities*. Washington, DC: Federal Housing Administration.

Hubbert, M.K. 1962. *Energy Resources: A Report to the Committee on Natural Resources*. Washington, DC: National Academy of Sciences.

Huff, D.L. 1963. A probability analysis of shopping center trade areas. *Land Economics* 53:81–89.

Hughes, A., and M.S. Kumar. 1984. Recent trends in aggregate concentration in the United Kingdom economy. *Cambridge Journal of Economics* 8:235–50.

Huke, R.E. 1985. The Green Revolution. *Journal of Geography* 84:248–54.

Humphrys, G. 1972. *South Wales*. Newton Abbott, England: David and Charles.

Hunker, H., and A.J. Wright. 1963. *Factors of Industrial Location in Ohio*. Columbus, OH: The Ohio State University Press.

Huntington, E. 1924. *Civilization and Climate*. New Haven: Yale University Press.

Hurni, H. 1983. Soil erosion and soil formation in agricultural systems, Ethiopia and northern Thailand. *Mountain Research and Development* 3:131–42.

International Institute for Environment and Development and World Resources Institute. 1987. *World Resources 1987*. New York: Basic Books.

International Monetary Fund. 1978. *29th Annual Report on Exchange Restrictions*. Washington, DC: IMF.

———. 1985. *IMF Survey*, 21 January. Washington, DC: IMF.

Isard, W. 1956. *Location and Space Economy*. Cambridge, MA: The MIT Press.

———. 1960. *Methods of Regional Analysis: An Introduction to Regional Science*. Englewood Cliffs, NJ: Prentice-Hall.

Jackson, W.A.D. 1962. The Virgin and Idle Lands Program reappraised. *Annals*, Association of American Geographers 52:69–79.

Janelle, D.G. 1968. Central place development in a time-space framework. *The Professional Geographer* 20:5–10.

Jefferson, M. 1921. *Recent Colonization in Chile*. Research Series No. 6. New York: American Geographical Society.

Junkerman, J. 1987. Blue-sky management: the Kawasaki story. In *International Capitalism and Industrial Re-*

structuring, edited by R. Peet, pp. 131–44. Boston: Allen and Unwin.

Kahn, H. 1973. If the rich stop aiding the poor . . . *Development Forum* 1 (No. 2):1–3.

Kansky, K.J. 1963. *Structure of Transportation*. University of Chicago, Department of Geography, Research Papers, 84.

Keeble, D.E. 1967. Models of economic development. In *Models in Geography*, edited by R.J. Chorley and P. Haggett, pp. 243–302. London: Methuen.

Kennelly, R.A. 1954. The location of the Mexican steel industry. *Revista Geografica* 15:109–29.

———. 1955. The location of the Mexican steel industry. *Revista Geografica* 16:60–77.

Keynes, J.M. 1936. *The General Theory of Employment Interest and Money*. New York: Harcourt, Brace.

Kidron, M. and R. Segal. 1984. *The New State of the World Atlas*. New York: Simon and Schuster.

Knight, C.G., and J.L. Newman, eds. 1976. *Contemporary Africa: Geography and Change*. Englewood Cliffs, NJ: Prentice-Hall.

Knight, C.G., and R.P. Wilcox. 1976. *Triumph or Triage: The Third World Food Problem in Geographical Perspective*. Resource Paper No. 75-3. Washington, DC: Association of American Geographers.

Kolars, J.F., and J.D. Nystuen. 1974. *Human Geography: Spatial Design in World Society*. New York: McGraw-Hill.

Komorov B. 1981. *The Destruction of Nature in the Soviet Union*. London, Pluto Press.

Kondratieff, N.D. 1935. The long waves in economic life. *Review of Economic Statistics* 17:105–15.

Krasner, S.D. 1985. *Structural Conflict*. Berkeley and Los Angeles, CA: University of California Press.

Kumar, K., and K.Y. Kim. 1984. The Korean manufacturing multinationals. *Journal of International Business Studies* 1:45–61.

Kuznets, S. 1930. *Secular Movements in Production and Prices*. Boston: Houghton Mifflin.

———. 1954. *Economic Change*. New York: W.W. Norton.

Landsberg, M. 1987. Export-led industrialization in the Third World: Manufacturing imperialism. In *International Capitalism and Industrial Restructuring*, edited by R. Peet, pp. 216–39. Boston: Allen and Unwin.

Lappé, F.M., and J. Collins. 1976. More food means more hunger. *Development Forum* 4 (No.8):1–2.

———. 1977. *Food First*. Boston: Houghton Mifflin.

Lecomber, R. 1975. *Economic Growth versus Environment*. New York: John Wiley.

Leibenstein, H. 1957. *Economic Backwardness and Economic Growth*. New York: John Wiley.

Leontief, W. et al. 1977. *The Future of the World Economy. A United Nations Study*. New York: Oxford University Press.

Lewis, P. 1983. The galactic metropolis. In *Beyond the Urban Fringe: Land-Use Issues of Nonmetropolitan America*, edited by R. Platt and G. Macinko, pp. 23–49. Minneapolis: University of Minnesota Press.

Lewis, W.A. 1954. Economic development with unlimited supplies of labour. *Manchester School of Economic and Social Studies* 22:139–91.

Lin Piao, 1965. Long live the victory of the People's War. *Peking Review* 3:9–30.

Linneman, H. 1966. *An Econometric Study of International Trade Flows.* Amsterdam: North-Holland Publishing.

Livingstone, I. 1971. Agriculture versus industry in economic development. In *Economic Policy for Development*, edited by I. Livingstone, pp. 235–49. Harmondsworth, England: Penguin Books.

Lloyd, P.E., and P. Dicken. 1972. *Location in Space: A Theoretical Approach to Economic Geography.* New York: Harper and Row.

Lord Ritchie-Calder. 1973/4. UNICEF's grandchildren. *UNICEF News* 78, December/ January.

Lösch, A. 1954. *The Economics of Location.* Translated by W.H. Woglom and W.F. Stolper. New Haven, CT: Yale University Press.

Mabogunje, A.L. 1980. *The Development Process: A Spatial Perspective.* London: Hutchinson.

Mackay, J.R. 1958. The interactance hypothesis and boundaries in Canada. *Canadian Geographer* 11:1–8.

Magirier, G. 1983. The eighties: a second phase of crisis? *Capital and Class* 21:61–86.

Malecki, E.J. 1979. Locational trends in R&D by large U.S. corporations. *Economic Geography* 55:309–23.

———. 1980. Dimensions of R&D locations in the U.S. *Research Policy* 9:2–22.

Malthus, T.R. 1970. *An Essay on the Principle of Population and a Summary View of Principle of Population.* Harmondsworth, England: Penguin Books.

Manners, G. 1971. *The Changing World Market for Iron Ore 1950–1980.* Baltimore, MD: Johns Hopkins University Press.

Mantoux, P. 1961. *The Industrial Revolution in the Eighteenth Century.* New York: Macmillan.

Marshall, J.N. 1979. Organization theory and industrial location. *Environment and Planning* A 14:1667–83.

Marx, K. 1967. *Capital*, 1st ed. Volume 1. New York: International Publishers.

Mason, R.H., R.R. Miller, and D.R. Weigel. 1975. *The Economics of International Business.* New York: John Wiley.

Massey, D. 1973. Towards a critique of industrial location theory. *Antipode* 5 (No.3):33–9.

———. 1977. *Industrial Location Theory Reconsidered.* Unit 26, Course D204. Milton Keynes, England: The Open University.

———. 1984. *Spatial Divisions of Labor: Social Structures and the Geography of Production.* New York: Methuen.

———. 1987. The shape of things to come. In *International Capitalism and Industrial Restructuring*, edited by R. Peet, pp. 105–22. Boston: Allen and Unwin.

Massey, D., and R.A. Meegan. 1978. Industrial restructuring versus the cities. *Urban Studies* 15:273–88.

———. 1979. The geography of industrial reorganization: The spatial effects of restructuring the electronical engineering sector under the Industrial Reorganization Corporation. *Progress in Planning* 10:155–237.

Mather, C. 1986. The Midwest: Image and reality. *Journal of Geography* 85:190–94.

McCall, M.K. 1977. Political economy and rural transport: An appraisal of Western misconceptions. *Antipode* 53:503–29.

McCarty, H.H., and J.B. Lindberg. 1966. *A Preface to Economic Geography.* Englewood Cliffs, NJ: Prentice-Hall.

McClelland, D. 1961. *The Achieving Society.* New York: Van Nostrand.

McConnell, J.E. 1980. Foreign direct investment in the United States. *Annals*, Association of American Geographers. 70:259–70.

———. 1983. The international location of manufacturing investments: Recent behavior of foreign-owned corporations in the United States. In *Spatial Analysis, Industry and the Industrial Environment: Volume 3: Regional Economics and Industrial Systems*, edited by F.E.I. Hamilton and G.J.R. Linge, pp. 337–58. New York: John Wiley.

McConnell, J.E., and R.A. Erickson. 1986. Geobusiness: An international perspective for geographers. *Journal of Geography* 85:98–105.

McGee, T.G. 1967. *The Southeast Asian City.* London: Bell.

———. 1971. *The Urbanization Process in the Third World.* London: Bell.

———. 1974. The persistence of the proto-proletariat: Occupational structures and planning for the future of Third World cities. Monash, Victoria: Department of Geography, Monash University.

McNee, R.B. 1960. Towards a more humanistic geography: The geography of enterprise. *Tijdscrift voor Economische en Sociale Geografie* 51:201–6.

———. 1974. A systems approach to understanding the geographic behavior of organizations, especially large corporations. In *Spatial Perspectives on Industrial Organization and Decision Making*, edited by F.E.I. Hamilton, pp. 47–76. New York: John Wiley.

Meadows, D. et al. 1972. *The Limits to Growth.* New York: Universe Books.

Meinig, D. 1962. *On the Margins of the Good Earth: The South Australian Wheat Frontier 1869–1884.* Association of American Geographers, Monograph Series No. 2. Chicago: Rand McNally.

Mellor, J.W. 1962. Increasing agricultural production in early stages of economic development. *Indian Journal of Agricultural Economics* 17:29–46.

Mensch, G. 1979. *Stalemate in Technology: Innovations Overcome the Depression.* Cambridge, MA: Ballinger.

Merrick, T.W. 1986. *World Population in Transition.* Population Bulletin, Vol. 41, No. 1. Washington, DC: Population Reference Bureau.

Mikesell, M.W. 1969. Patterns and imprints of mankind. In *The International Atlas.* Chicago: Rand McNally.

Miller, G.T., Jr. 1975. *Living in the Environment: Concepts, Problems, and Alternatives.* Belmont, CA: Wadsworth.

Mishan, E.J. 1977. *The Economic Growth Debate: An Assessment.* London: Allen and Unwin.

Missen, G.I., and M.I. Logan. 1977. National and local distribution systems and regional development: The case of Kelantan in West Malaysia. *Antipode* 9:60–74.

Morello, T. 1983. Sweatshops in the sun? *Far Eastern Economic Review,* 15 September, pp. 88–89.

Morgan, W.T. 1963. The "White Highlands" of Kenya. *Geographical Journal* 129:140–55.

Morrill, R.L. 1963. The development and spatial distribution of towns in Sweden. *Annals,* Association of American Geographers 53:1–14.

———. 1970. *The Spatial Organization of Society.* Belmont, CA: Wadsworth.

Morris, M.D. 1979. *Measuring the Condition of the World's Poor: The Physical Quality of Life Index.* New York: Pergamon.

Muller, E.K., and P.A. Groves. 1979. The emergence of industrial districts in nineteenth century Baltimore. *Geographical Review* 69:159–78.

Muller, P.O. 1976. *The Outer City: Geographical Consequences of the Urbanization of the Suburbs.* Resource Paper 75-2. Washington, DC: Association of American Geographers.

Murdie, R.A. 1965. Cultural differences in consumer travel. *Economic Geography* 41:211–33.

Murphy, R. 1978. *Patterns on the Earth.* Chicago: Rand McNally.

Myrdal, G. 1957. *Economic Theory and Underdeveloped Regions.* London: Duckworth.

National Research Council. 1986. *Population Growth and Economic Development: Policy Questions.* Washington, DC: National Academy Press.

Nations, J.D., and D.I. Komer. 1983. Central America's tropical rainforests: Positive steps for survival. *Ambio* 12:232–38.

Newsweek. 1986. Mexico slips into reverse, 17 March, pp. 34–35.

Norcliffe, G.B. 1975. A theory of manufacturing places. In *Locational Dynamics of Manufacturing Industry,* edited by L. Collins and D.F. Walker, pp. 19-59. New York: John Wiley.

Notestein, F.W. 1970. Zero population growth: What is it? *Family Planning Perspectives* 2:20–24.

Ohlin, B. 1933. *Interregional and International Trade.* Cambridge, MA: Harvard University Press.

O'Loughlin, J. 1988. Review of *Production, Work, Territory,* edited by A.J. Scott and M. Storper, 1986. *Geographical Review* 78:83–85.

Ogden, P. 1984. *Migration and Geographical Change.* Cambridge, England: Cambridge University Press.

Olsen, E. 1971. *International Trade Theory and Regional Income Differences.* Amsterdam: North-Holland.

Osleeb, J., and R.G. Cromley. 1978. The location of plants of the uniform delivered price manufacturer: A case study of Coca Cola, Ltd. *Economic Geography* 54:40–52.

Paddock, W., and P. Paddock. 1976. *Time of Famines— America and the World Food Crisis.* Boston: Little, Brown.

Park, R.E., and C. Newcomb. 1933. Newspaper circulation and metropolitan regions. In *The Metropolitan Community,* edited by R.D. McKenzie, pp. 98–110. New York: McGraw-Hill.

Partant, F. 1982. *La fin du développement: Naissance d'une alternative?* Paris: La Découverte.

Peet, R. 1985. The social origins of environmental determinism. *Annals,* Association of American Geographers 75:309–33.

———. 1987a. Industrial restructuring and the crisis of international capitalism. In *International Capitalism and Industrial Restructuring,* edited by R. Peet, pp. 9–32. Boston: Allen and Unwin.

———. 1987b. The geography of class struggle and the relocation of United States manufacturing industry. In *International Capitalism and Industrial Restructuring,* edited by R. Peet, pp. 40–71. Boston: Allen and Unwin.

———, ed. 1987c. *International Capitalism and Industrial Restructuring.* Boston: Allen and Unwin.

Pelzer, K.J. 1945. *Pioneer Settlement in the Asiatic Tropics.* Special Publication No. 219. New York: American Geographical Society.

Penrose, E. 1959. *The Theory of the Growth of the Firm.* Oxford: Basil Blackwell.

Perrons, D. 1981. The role of Ireland in the new industrial division of labor: A proposed framework for analysis. *Regional Studies* 15:81–100.

Pickard, J.P. 1972. U.S. metropolitan growth and expansion, 1970–2000, with population projections." In *Population Growth and the American Future.* Washington, DC: U.S. Government Printing Office.

Pickett, J., ed. 1977. The choice of technology in developing countries. *World Development Special Issue* 5 (Nos. 9/10):773–879.

Pletsch, C.E. 1981. The three worlds or the division of social scientific labor, circa 1950–1975. *Comparative Studies in Society and History* 23:565–90.

Polanyi, K. 1971. *Primitive, Archaic, and Modern Economics:*

Essays of Karl Polanyi, edited by G. Dalton. Boston: Beacon Press.

Population Crisis Committee. 1987. *The International Human Suffering Index.* Washington, DC.

Population Reference Bureau. 1986a. *The United States Population Data Sheet.* Washington, DC.

————. 1986b. A potpourri of population puzzles. *Population Education Interchange* 15, No. 2.

————. 1987. *World Population Data Sheet.* Washington, DC.

Porter, P.W. 1965. Environmental potentials and economic opportunities: A background for cultural adaption. *American Anthropologist* 67:409–20.

————. 1979. *Food and Development in the Semi-Arid Zone of East Africa.* Syracuse, NY: Maxwell School of Citizenship and Public Affairs, Syracuse University.

Pred, A.R.. 1966. *The Spatial Dynamics of U.S. Urban-Industrial Growth, 1800–1914.* Cambridge, MA: The MIT Press.

————. 1967. Behavior and location: Foundations for a geographic and dynamic location theory, Part 1. *Lund Studies in Geography, Series B.* 27.

————. 1977. *City-Systems in Advanced Economies.* London: Hutchinson.

Price, A.G. 1939. *White Settlers in the Tropics.* Special Publication No. 23. New York: American Geographical Society.

Rae, J.B. 1965. *The American Automobile: A Brief History.* Chicago: University of Chicago Press.

Rand McNally. 1988. *Rand McNally Commercial Atlas and Marketing Guide.* Chicago.

Raporport, C. 1982. The FT European 500: Financial Times survey. *Financial Times,* 21 October.

Ravenstein, E.G. 1885. The laws of migration. *Journal of the Royal Statistical Society* 48:167–227.

————. 1889. The laws of migration. *Journal of the Royal Statistical Society* 52:241–301.

Ray, D.M. 1971. The location of United States' manufacturing subsidiaries in Canada. *Economic Geography* 47:389–400.

Rees, J. 1972. The industrial corporation and location decision analysis. *Area* 4:199–205.

————. 1974. Decision-making, the growth of the firm and the business environment. In *Spatial Perspectives on Industrial Organization and Decision-making,* edited by F.E.I. Hamilton, pp. 189–212. New York: John Wiley.

Rees, J., and H.A. Stafford. 1986. Theories of regional growth and industrial location: Their relevance for understanding high-technology complexes. In *Technology, Regions, and Policy,* edited by J. Rees, pp. 23–50. Totowa, NJ: Rowman and Littlefield.

Reilly, W.J. 1931. *The Law of Retail Gravitation.* New York: The Knickerbocker Press.

Reissman, L. 1964. *The Urban Process: Cities in Industrial Societies.* New York: Free Press.

Relph, E. 1976. *Place and Placelessness.* London: Ron.

Replogle, M.A. 1988. *Bicycles and Public Transportation: New Links to Suburban Transit Markets.* 2d ed. Washington, DC: The Bicycle Federation.

Ricardo, D. 1912. *The Principles of Political Economy and Taxation.* New York: E.P. Dutton.

Riddell, J.B. 1970. *The Spatial Dynamics of Modernization in Sierra Leone: Structure, Diffusion, and Response.* Evanston, IL: Northwestern University Press.

Robinson, R.D. 1981. Background concepts and philosophy of international business from World War II to the present. *Journal of International Business Studies* Spring/Summer:13–21.

Rodney, W. 1972. *How Europe Underdeveloped Africa.* Dar es Salaam: Tanzania Publishing House and Bogle-L'Overture Publications.

Roepke, H.G. 1959. Changes in corn production on the northern margin of the Corn Belt. *Agricultural History* 33:126–32.

Ross, R., and K. Trachte. 1983. Global cities, global classes: The peripheralization of labor in New York City. *Review* 6:393–431.

Rostow, W.W. 1960. *The Stages of Economic Growth: A Non-Communist Manifesto.* Cambridge, MA: Cambridge University Press.

Ryan, W. 1972. *Blaming the Victim.* New York: Vintage Books.

Saarinen, T.F. 1969. *Perception of Environment.* Resource Paper No.5. Washington DC: Association of American Geographers.

Sack, R.D. 1974. The spatial separatist theme in geography. *Economic Geography* 50:1–19.

Said, E.W. 1981. *Covering Islam: How the Media and the Experts Determine How We Shall See the Rest of the World.* New York: Pantheon.

Samuelson, R.J. 1989. Superpower sweepstakes. *Newsweek,* 20 February, p. 43.

Sanderson, S.W., and B.J.L. Berry. 1986. Robotics and regional development. In *Technology, Regions, and Policy,* edited by J. Rees, pp. 171-86. Totowa, NJ: Rowman and Littlefield.

Santos, M. 1971. *Les Villes du Tiers Monde.* Paris: Editions M-Th. Génin.

————. 1977. Spatial dialectics: The two circuits of urban economy in underdeveloped countries. *Antipode* 9:49–60.

Saxenian, A. 1985. The genesis of Silicon Valley. In *Silicon Landscapes,* edited by P. Hall and A. Markusen, pp. 20–34. Boston: Allen and Unwin.

Schaefer, F. 1953. Exceptionalism in geography: A methodological examination. *Annals,* Association of American Geographers 43:226–49.

Schlebecker, J.T. 1960. The world metropolis and the history of American agriculture. *Journal of Economic History* 20:147–208.

Schumacher, E.F. 1973. *Small Is Beautiful*. London: Blond and Briggs.

Schumpeter, J.A. 1939. *Business Cycles: A Theoretical, Historical, and Statistical Account of the Capitalist Process*. 2 vols. New York: McGraw-Hill.

Schwartzberg, J.E. 1987. The US Constitution, a model for global government. *Journal of Geography* 86:246–52.

Scobie, J.R. 1964. *Argentina: A City and a Nation*. New York: Oxford University Press.

Scott, A.J., and M. Storper, eds. 1986. *Production, Work, Territory: The Geographical Anatomy of Industrial Capitalism*. Boston: Allen and Unwin.

Scott, E. 1972. The spatial structure of rural northern Nigeria: Farmers, periodic markets, and villages. *Economic Geography* 48:316–32.

Seers, D. 1972. What are we trying to measure? *The Journal of Development Studies* 8:21–36.

Shabecoff, P. 1987. Peering into the energy future and sighting gas shortages. *New York Times*, 25 September, p. 26.

Shipler, D. 1987. Reagan is preparing to sail into uncharted policy waters. *New York Times*, 31 May, Section 4, p.1.

Simon, H.A. 1957. *Models of Man*. New York: John Wiley.

————. 1960. *The New Science of Management Decision*. New York: Harper and Row.

Simon, J.L. 1980. Resources, population, environment: An oversupply of false bad news. *Science* 208:1431–37.

————. 1986. *Theory of Population and Economic Growth*. Oxford, England: Basil Blackwell.

Simoons, F.J. 1961. *Eat Not This Flesh*. Madison, WI: University of Wisconsin Press.

Sivanandan, A. 1987. Imperialism and disorganic development in the silicon age. In *International Capitalism and Industrial Restructuring*, edited by R. Peet, pp. 185–200. Boston: Allen and Unwin.

Skinner, G.W. 1964. Marketing and social structure in rural China. *Journal of Asian Studies* 24:3–43.

Smith, D.M. 1966. A theoretical framework for geographical studies of industrial location. *Economic Geography* 42:95–113.

————. 1977. *Human Geography: A Welfare Approach*. London: Edward Arnold.

————. 1981. *Industrial Location: An Economic Geographical Analysis*. 2d ed. New York: John Wiley.

Soja, E.W. 1968. *The Geography of Modernization in Kenya*. Syracuse, NY: Syracuse University Press.

Soja, E., R. Morales, and G. Wolff. 1987. Industrial restructuring: An analysis of social and spatial change in Los Angeles. In *International Capitalism and Industrial Restructuring*, edited by R. Peet, pp. 145–76. Boston: Allen and Unwin.

Starbuck, W.H. 1965. Organizational growth and development. In *Handbook of Organizations*, edited by J.G. March, pp. 451–522. Skokie, IL: Rand McNally.

Stebelsky, I. 1983. Wheat yields and weather hazards in the Soviet Union. In *Interpretations of Calamity from the Viewpoint of Human Ecology*, edited by K. Hewitt, pp. 202–18. Boston: Allen and Unwin.

Stopford, I.M., and J.H. Dunning. 1983. *Multinationals: Company Performances and Global Trends*. London: Macmillan.

Storey, D.J. 1986. The economics of smaller businesses: Some implications for regional economic development. In *Technological Change, Industrial Restructuring, and Regional Development*, edited by A. Amin and J.B. Goddard, pp. 215–32. Winchester, MA: Allen and Unwin.

Streeten, P. 1981. *First Things First: Meeting Basic Human Needs in Developing Countries*. New York: Oxford University Press.

Sunkel, O. 1982. Big business and dependency. *Foreign Affairs* 24:517–31.

Susman, P., and E. Schutz. 1983. Monopoly and competitive firm relations and regional development in global capitalism. *Economic Geography* 59:161–77.

Sweezy, P. 1942. *The Theory of Capitalist Development*. London: Dobson.

Symanski, R. 1971. *Market Cycles in Andean Columbia*. Ph.D. dissertation. Syracuse, NY: Syracuse University.

Szentes, T. 1971. *The Political Economy of Underdevelopment*. Budapest: Adademiai Kiadó.

E.J. Taaffe, R.L. Morrill, and P.R. Gould. 1963. Transport expansion in underdeveloped countries. *Geographical Review* 53:503–29.

Tata, R.J., and R.R. Schultz. 1988. World variation in human welfare: A new index of development status. *Annals, Association of American Geographers* 78:580–93.

Taylor, M.J. 1975. Organizational growth, spatial interaction and location decision making. *Regional Studies* 9:313–23.

Taylor, M.J., and N. Thrift, eds. 1982. *The Geography of Multinationals*. New York: St. Martin's Press.

Teitelbaum, M.S. 1975. Relevance of demographic transition theory for developing countries. *Science* 188:420–25.

The Economist. 1982. Money and finance, 16 October.

————. 1987a. Britain: the best of times, the worst of times, 21 February, pp. 1–26.

————. 1987b. Japanese property: A glittering sprawl, 3 October, pp. 25–28.

————. 1988a. Come back multinationals, 28 November, p. 73.

————. 1988b. The regions revive, 2 April, pp. 45–46.

————. 1988c. The pleasures of three-part harmony, 24 December, p. 41.

————. 1988d. Why it's still a triangle, 24 December, pp. 41–44.

Thrift, N. 1986. Geography of international economic disorder. In *A World in Crisis*, edited by R.J. Johnston and P.J. Taylor, pp. 12–67. New York: Blackwell.

Tipps, D. 1973. Modernization theory and the comparative study of societies: A critical perspective. *Comparative Studies in Society and History* 155: 199–226.

Toffler, A. 1981. *The Third Wave.* New York: Bantam.

Troughton, M.J. 1985. Industrialization of U.S. and Canadian agriculture. *Journal of Geography* 84:255–63.

U.K. Department of Employment 1985. *Employment Gazette.* London: HMSO.

Ullman, E.L. 1940–1941. A theory of location for cities. *American Journal of Sociology* 46:853–64.

———. 1943. *Mobile: Industrial Seaport and Trade Center.* Chicago: University of Chicago Press.

United Nations. 1975. *Women in Africa.* New York: United Nations.

———. 1982. *Estimates and Projections of Urban, Rural and City Populations, 1950–2025: The 1980 Assessment.* New York: United Nations.

———. 1985. *Statistical Yearbook.* New York. United Nations.

———. 1987. *Yearbook of World Energy Statistics.* New York: United Nations.

———. 1988. *Transnational Corporations in World Development: Trends and Prospects.* New York: United Nations.

U.S. Bureau of the Census. 1984. *Statistical Abstract of the United States.* Washington, DC: GPO.

U.S. Bureau of Mines. 1985. *Minerals Yearbook.* Washington, DC: GPO.

———. 1986. *Mineral Commodity Summaries: An Up-to-Date Summary of 87 Nonfuel Mineral Commodities.* Washington, DC: GPO.

U.S. Department of Agriculture. 1970. *The Marketing Challenge.* Foreign Economic Development Report No. 7. Washington, DC: USDA.

———. 1985. *Yearbook of Agriculture.* Washington, DC: USDA.

Vale, T.R. 1985. What kind of conservationist? *Journal of Geography* 84:239–41.

Van Valkenburg, S., and C.C. Held. 1952. *Europe.* New York: John Wiley.

Vance, J.E. 1970. *The Merchant's World: The Geography of Wholesaling.* Englewood Cliffs, NJ: Prentice-Hall.

———. 1977. *This Scene of Man: The Role and Structure of the City in the Geography of Western Civilization.* New York: Harper & Row.

———. 1986. *Capturing the Horizon: The Historical Geography of Transportation.* New York: Harper & Row.

Vernon, R. 1966. International investment and international trade in the product cycle. *Quarterly Journal of Economics* 80:190–207.

———. 1979. The product cycle hypothesis is a new international environment. *Oxford Bulletin of Economics and Statistics* 41:255–68.

Viner, J. 1950. *The Customs Union Issue.* New York: Carnegie Endowment for International Peace.

Vogeler, I. 1981. *The Myth of the Family Farm: Agribusiness Dominance of U.S. Agriculture.* Boulder, CO: Westview.

Vogeler, I., and A.R. de Souza, eds. 1980. *Dialectics of Third World Development.* Totowa, NJ: Rowman and Allanheld.

Von Thünen, J.H. 1826. *The Isolated State.* Hamburg: Perthes.

Wallerstein, I. 1974. *The Modern World-System: Capitalist Agriculture and the Origins of the European World-Economy in the Sixteenth Century.* New York: Academic Press.

Watson, M., P. Keller, and D. Mathieson. 1984. *International Capital Markets: Development and Prospects.* Washington, DC: IMF.

Watts, D. 1988. Thatcher's Britain—A manufacturing economy in decline? *Focus,* Fall, pp. 1–5.

Webb, W.P. 1931. *The Great Plains.* New York: Grosset and Dunlap.

Weber, A. 1929. *Alfred Weber's Theory of the Location of Industries.* Translated by C. J. Friedrich. Chicago: University of Chicago Press.

Weber, M. 1930. *The Protestant Ethic and the Spirit of Capitalism.* New York: Scribners.

Wharton, C.R., Jr. 1963. Research on agricultural development in Southeast Asia. *Journal of Farm Economics* 45:1161–74.

———. 1969. The green revolution: Cornucopia or Pandora's box? *Foreign Affairs* 47:464–76.

Wheeler, J.O., and P.O. Muller. 1981. *Economic Geography.* New York: John Wiley.

Williams, J.F. 1989a. Japan: Physical and human resources. In *Geography and Development,* edited by J.S. Fisher, pp. 330–43. Columbus, OH: Merrill.

———. 1989b. Japan: The economic giant. In *Geography and Development,* edited by J.S. Fisher, pp. 346–65. Columbus, OH: Merrill.

Williams, M. 1979. The perception of the hazard of soil degradation in South Australia: A review. In *Natural hazards in Australia,* edited by R.L. Heathcote and B.L. Thom, pp. 275–89. Canberra: Australian Academy of Science.

Wise, M.J. 1949. On the evolution of the jewellery and gun quarters in Birmingham. *Transactions,* Institute of British Geographers 15:59–72.

Wolpert, J. 1964. The decision process in a spatial context. *Annals,* Association of American Geographers 54:537–58.

Wong, K., and D.K.Y. Chu. 1984. Export processing zones and special economic zones as generators of economic development: The Asian experience. *Geografiska Annaler,* Series B, 66:1–16.

World Bank, 1971. *World Tables 1971.* Washington, DC: World Bank.

———. 1974. *Land Reform.* Washington, DC: World Bank.

———. 1978. *World Development Report.* Washington, DC: World Bank.

———. 1979. *World Development Report.* Washington, DC: World Bank.

———. 1984. *World Development Report.* New York: Oxford University Press.

———. 1985. *World Development Report.* New York: Oxford University Press.

———. 1987. *World Development Report.* New York: Oxford University Press.

———. 1988. *World Development Report.* New York: Oxford University Press.

Yapa, L.S. 1980. Diffusion, development and ecopolitical economy. In *Innovation Research and Public Policy,* edited by J.A. Agnew, Geographical Series No. 5, pp. 101–41. Syracuse, NY: Syracuse University Press.

———. 1985. The population problem as economic disarticulation. *Journal of Geography* 84:242–47.

Yeates, M. 1975. *Main Street: Windsor to Quebec City.* Toronto: Macmillan.

———. 1984. The Windsor-Quebec City axis: Basic characteristics. *Journal of Geography* 83:240–49.

Zipf, G.K. 1949. *Human Behavior and the Principle of Least Effort.* Reading, MA: Addison-Wesley.

INDEX

DATE DUE